JOURNAL FOR THE STUDY OF THE NEW TESTAMENT
SUPPLEMENT SERIES
23

Executive Editor, Supplement Series
David Hill

Publishing Editor
David E Orton

JSOT Press
Sheffield

Paul the
Letter–Writer
and the
Second Letter to Timothy

Michael Prior, C.M.

Journal for the Study of the New Testament
Supplement Series 23

Copyright © 1989 Sheffield Academic Press

Published by JSOT Press
JSOT Press is an imprint of
Sheffield Academic Press Ltd
The University of Sheffield
343 Fulwood Road
Sheffield S10 3BP
England

Printed in Great Britain
by Billing & Sons Ltd
Worcester

British Library Cataloguing in Publication Data available

ISSN 0143-5108
ISBN 1-85075-147-1

CONTENTS

PREFACE

It was while I studied the Pastoral Epistles under the direction of Dr Aidan McGing, C.M., in 1966, that I first met the problems of these letters. I was introduced to the different solutions proposed: (a) that the Pastoral Epistles are genuinely Pauline; (b) that they contain only fragments of genuine Pauline letters, and (c) that they are totally Pseudepigrapha.

While in *University College, Dublin,* I studied under the direction of Professor Dermot Ryan, afterwards Archbishop of Dublin. He ensured that students of the Bible would be at home in Greek, Aramaic, Hebrew, Syriac, and modern European languages. Archbishop Ryan died in 1985. I am very grateful for the direction he gave me in my studies.

While studying at the *Pontifical Biblical Institute, Rome,* my interest in the Pastoral Epistles was further stimulated by the very thorough and original scholarship of Mons. Jerome D. Quinn. He has encouraged me in my research since that time, and I owe him a great debt. He will not be in the least disappointed that a pupil of his has reached conclusions so different from his own!

Over many years I examined the list of qualifications of the overseer (*episkopos*) in 1 Tim 3.1-7. While I was able to live for some time in a state of indecision concerning the authorship of the Pastoral Epistles, I subsequently considered it necessary to opt for a definite position on that question. None of the proposed solutions seemed adequate to me. Those who supported Pauline Authenticity were compelled to seek refuge in the unknown quantity of the last years of Paul's life. I could never view the Fragments Theory as anything other than a recourse of desperation on the part of those wishing to maintain Pauline authority in the letters. The Theories of Pseudepigraphy proposed seemed to me to require a movement from the theoretically possible to the historically probable. Such movement was lacking in truly rigorous support: even the vaguest of historical reconstructions was regarded as adequate. It was necessary to make a new start.

Canon C.J.A. Hickling of *King's College, London*, oversaw my first reflections on the question of Pauline authorship. While I was revelling somewhat in the experience of sailing in uncharted waters Professor Jerome Murphy-O'Connor, O.P. of the *École Biblique, Jerusalem* impressed upon me the necessity of raising what was theoretically possible into an historical probability. The subsequent appearance of the notion of co-authorship in some authoritative commentaries on the Pauline letters has convinced me that my insistence on regarding the majority of Pauline compositions as the fruit of co-authorship was not altogether an eccentricity. My suggestions concerning 2 Timothy are altogether novel. I take refuge in the counsel of Descartes. Advising those who doubted his conclusions, he recommended they peruse the works of others, to see how weak in probability are the reasons they adduce to explain the same problems he attempted to solve.

The scholastic community of Dominicans and others in the *École Biblique, Jerusalem*, where I spent a sabbatical year, 1983-84, provided an excellent climate of dedicated scholarship, and I am grateful in particular to Jerome Murphy-O'Connor, O.P., and Justin Taylor, S.M. Throughout the period of my research Canon Hickling, Professor G.N. Stanton and Dr Francis Watson of *King's College, London* were very helpful to me.

My celibate state has spared me the necessity of imposing upon a wife the unreasonable sacrifices which a work such as this would normally demand. Nevertheless, there are many to whom I am indebted. I wish to acknowledge the constant encouragement of my confrère and former teacher Brian M. Nolan, C.M., and of the Principal, the Vincentian Community, members of staff, and a great number of students of Religious Studies of St Mary's College, Strawberry Hill. Miss Sheila Kent and the Library Staff of my college have helped me enormously over the years, as have Mrs Eileen Walker, the Head of the Secretarial Services, and Mrs Carol Lourdas, the Secretary of the Religious Studies Department. I am grateful to Professor Stanton, Dr G. Beasley-Murray, and Professor J.D. Quinn for making many valuable suggestions. While recovering from an illness in September 1987 Mons. Quinn stayed in this college, and offered many excellent comments on the manuscript of this book. I owe a great debt to Dr David Hill, Editor of the

Supplement Series, for his encouragement and practical assistance. I am grateful to Dr David E. Orton, Publishing Editor, Ms Pauline Climpson, Production Manager, Ms Pauline Bates, typesetter and the staff of Sheffield Academic Press for their careful production of the book.

My mother Eileen, brothers John and Jim, sister Nuala, and their families, and many friends have been very supportive and tolerant of me during the difficult period of writing this work. My older brother, John, and my mother died during the final stages of its preparation, and I wish to dedicate it to their memory and to that of my father who died in 1968.

Michael P. Prior, C.M.
St. Mary's College
Strawberry Hill
Twickenham
September 27, 1987

ABBREVIATIONS

Bib	*Biblica*
BJRL	*Bulletin of the John Rylands University Library of Manchester*
BTB	*Biblical Theology Bulletin*
BZ	*Biblische Zeitschrift*
CBQ	*Catholic Biblical Quarterly*
EvQ	*Evangelical Quarterly*
ExpTim	*Expository Times*
HTR	*Harvard Theological Review*
Int	*Interpretation*
JBL	*Journal of Biblical Literature*
JNES	*Journal of Near Eastern Studies*
JSNT	*Journal for the Study of the New Testament*
JTS	*Journal of Theological Studies*
Loeb	The Loeb Classical Library, ed. T.E. Page, E. Capps, W.H.D. Rouse, L.A. Post and E.H. Warmington. Cambridge/Mass.-London
Migne *PL*	Migne, J.P., *Patrologiae cursus completus, series latina (Patrologia Latina)*. 221 Vols. Paris 1844–1855
Migne *PG*	Migne, J.P., *Patrologiae cursus completus, series graeca (Patrologia Graeca)*. 161 Vols. Paris 1857–1866
NovT	*Novum Testamentum*
n.s.	New Series
NTS	*New Testament Studies*
OBO	*Orbis Biblicus et Orientalis*
RB	*Revue Biblique*
RevExp	*Review and Expositor*
RHPR	*Revue d'Histoire et de Philosophie Religieuses*
RivB	*Rivista Biblica*

RSPT	*Revue des Sciences Philosophiques et Théologiques*
RSR	*Revue de Science Religieuse*
SBL	Society of Biblical Literature
ScrB	*Scripture Bulletin*
Sem	*Semitica*
SEv	*Studia Evangelica*
SNTS	Society for New Testament Studies
ST	*Studia Theologica*
Supp.	Supplement
TDNT	*Theological Dictionary of the New Testament* (see Kittel and Friedrich 1933-73)
TRu	*Theologische Rundschau*
TLZ	*Theologische Literaturzeitung*
VC	*Vigiliae Christianae*
WMANT	Wissenschaftliche Monographien zum Alten und Neuen Testament
WUNT	Wissenschaftliche Untersuchungen zum Neuen Testament
ZNW	*Zeitschrift für die neutestamentliche Wissenschaft*
ZTK	*Zeitschrift für Theologie und Kirche*

Chapter 1

THE PROBLEM OF THE PASTORAL EPISTLES

The problem of the Pastoral Epistles is, undoubtedly, that of their
authorship (Dibelius 1966: 1). It is the key issue in assessing their
value and authority.

If the Pastorals are genuine Pauline compositions, written towards
the end of his life, they witness to a considerable change in Paul
himself, and in the church communities. One might say that he had
learnt much from his experiences, and now that he was coming to the
end of his days he was anxious that his charism would not disappear
from the Church on his death. The sound teaching of the faith, and
the good conduct of the communities would be best guarded by the
structured organization of the communities, which is a feature of the
Pastorals. However one might evaluate this kind of ecclesial model,
one would have to recognize it as having the authority of Paul who,
on earlier occasions, proposed quite different expressions of
community life.

If, on the other hand, the letters are pseudepigrapha, coming as
late as two generations after the death of the Apostle, they could
easily be adjudged to be inferior to the writings of Paul, if not indeed
a downright corruption of his message, accommodating it to a period
which was characterized by a systematization of doctrine, a
deadening of faith, and an encasement of the Spirit who blows where
he wills. In this interpretation the Pastorals must be placed alongside
the documents of 'early Catholicism', which in the judgment of many
Lutheran theologians are 'a sad declension from the apostolic—
especially the Pauline—gospel', and are judged to be 'not only post-
apostolic in date but sub-apostolic in standard'.[1]

1. *The Pastoral Epistles in the History of Criticism*

Every commentator draws attention to the factors which mark the
Pastorals off from the other Paulines, and the question of authorship

has been hotly debated for over a century. The questioning of the authenticity of the Pastorals is a relatively modern phenomenon. Except for some doubts in the early second century, the authenticity of the letters to Timothy and Titus was unquestioned until the beginning of the nineteenth century.[2]

Friedrich Schleiermacher was the first scholar to seriously question the authenticity of one of the Pastoral Epistles (1807). His work was the point of departure for all subsequent comparisons of style and vocabulary in the letters of Paul (Spicq 1969: 22). Arguments from style and vocabulary, coupled with the difficulty of fitting into the known life of Paul the personal circumstances of the letter, and the nature of the opposition presupposed in it, convinced Schleiermacher that 1 Timothy was not written by Paul. It was written by a clever forger after Paul's death.

Although his published contribution did not appear in print until later, J.G. Eichhorn claimed to have anticipated Schleiermacher's conclusions and he went further in arguing that Titus and 2 Timothy also were non-Pauline. In addition to arguing from considerations of vocabulary, language, and the implied historical situation, he judged that such instructions as are contained in the three letters were not necessary, since Paul knew Timothy and Titus so well, and looked forward to an early meeting with them. He rejected the hypothesis of a second Roman imprisonment.[3]

Nevertheless, even though Leonhard Usteri was well aware of the views of his teacher Schleiermacher, and of Eichhorn, he included all the letters of Paul in his study of the development of Paul's doctrine (1824).[4]

By the time he wrote his major work on the Pastorals (1835), Ferdinand Christian Baur's Pauline studies had already channelled his thoughts into a particular interpretation of developments in the early Church.[5] He argued that Paul developed his theology in complete opposition to that of the primitive community. In his view, the later NT writings show how the two factions within earliest Christianity gradually approached each other, until, under the threat of a Gnosticism equally inimical to each, they were resolved into the single, united Church.[6] The heretics implied in the Pastorals, Baur claimed, could not possibly be situated in the apostolic period, and had to be placed within the Gnosticism of the second century. The Pastorals, he claimed, were the work of second century Paulinists (living perhaps in Rome where Paul was being misused by Gnostics and attacked by Judaizers) who wished to give the impression that the well-established second-century Gnosticism was no more than a revival of what Paul had encountered during his lifetime.[7]

H.J. Holtzmann's work was the most serious assault on the authenticity of the Pastorals, and quickly established itself as the classic statement of the case against Pauline authorship. His attack was launched on several fronts: the letters could not be fitted into the known life of Paul; the testimony of Eusebius concerning a second Roman imprisonment, and that of Clement suggesting a mission to Spain had to be dismissed; the implied situation of the addressees was contrary to the historical reality; the opponents were not the Judaizers of Paul's lifetime, but the Gnostics of the second century. But it was above all the vocabulary and literary style of the Pastorals that told against their Pauline authorship (Holtzmann 1880: 15ff., 21-25, 37-45, 54ff.).

In his view, the author of the Pastorals was a *pedisequus* of Paul, who, with the authentic letters of Paul before him, addressed himself to the problems of his own day, thus giving the impression that Paul in his lifetime had encountered something similar, and had successfully dealt with it. He did not hesitate to call Paul from his grave to come to the aid of the second-century Church in its need. The intention of the author was to derive Pauline authority for the closed presbyteral government within the Church, which was transmitted by ordination, and his method was to create the fictitious correspondence from Paul to Timothy and Titus (pp. 109f., 157f., 159, 276). The reader of these letters, then, would recognize in them the Pauline authentication of the church government with which he was already familiar, and for which, as is clear, Holtzmann had little sympathy.[8]

If Holtzmann's 'definitive argument' against the authenticity of the Pastorals was not enough to bring Anglo-American scholarship with him,[9] P.N. Harrison (1921) shifted the balance very much against the traditional view. Although Harrison confessed that the linguistic argument was only one of several arguments that forced him to place the composition of the Pastorals in the second century, it was for him the decisive one.[10] He claimed that a comparison of the language of the Pastorals with that of Paul's other letters on the one hand, and with that of the Apostolic Fathers and the early Apologists on the other, left one with evidence that 'is fatal to the traditional opinion' (p. 6). The language alone, he claimed, puts the author of

the Pastorals much later than Paul's period, and right into the second
century.

Harrison affirmed that even though the Pastorals were composed
in the second century they contain a 'notable quantity of definitely
Pauline matter bearing the unmistakable stamp of the Apostle'
(1921: 87). Passages such as 2 Tim 4.6-22 and Tit 3.12 are 'so vivid,
so concrete, so entirely in the vein of the references to be found in
every letter that Paul ever wrote, that . . . no one would ever have
dreamed of doubting their authenticity, had it not been for the
context in which they occur' (p. 93). When separated from their
context they fit into the regular Pauline pattern of *hapax legomena*.

Like Holtzmann, he disregarded the testimony of Eusebius
concerning a second Roman captivity (p. 103), and he gave a novel
interpretation of Clement's text which implies a Pauline mission
west of Rome (p. 107).[11] His hypothesis rendered that of a second
Roman imprisonment redundant. His genuine fragments, consisting
of several brief personal notes addressed by the Apostle at various
times to Timothy and Titus, preserved by them, and still in existence
some fifty years after the death of Paul, were put together by a
Paulinist, and form part of our present texts of 2 Timothy and
Titus.

2. *Contemporary Solutions to the Problem of the Pastoral Epistles*

The arguments for and against the authenticity of the Pastorals focus
on whether the differences between the Pastorals and the Paulines in
the matter of language and literary style, theological perspective,
church organization, and the nature of the opponents, are such as to
demand for the Pastorals a date of composition considerably later
than the lifetime of Paul. In addition there is the difficulty of fitting
the Pastorals into the otherwise known life of Paul.

In broad terms, scholars' views fall into three categories: A. The
Pastorals are genuinely Pauline; B. they contain genuine Pauline
fragments; C. they are pseudepigrapha.

A. *The Pastoral Epistles are authentically Pauline*
The supporters of this view maintain that the differences between
the Pastorals and the Paulines are not of such substance as to render
the assumption of common authorship untenable, and can be
accounted for without having recourse to theories of fragments or
pseudepigrapha.

Harrison affirmed that 'the whole modern case for the authenticity of the Pastorals depends upon the second imprisonment' (1921: 109). The difficulties in accommodating the biographical information of the Pastorals into the life of Paul are removed by postulating Paul's release from prison in Rome, and his subsequent missionary activity.[12]

Among the other factors appealed to to explain the differences between the Pastorals and the other Paulines is the suggestion that the Pastorals are the latest of Paul's letters, written towards the end of a life that had worn him out. Recourse is also had to the fact that only the Pastorals are private letters.

Many scholars who are not disposed to reject the Pauline authorship of the Pastorals but who, nevertheless, discern quite un-Pauline elements in them, account for the evidence by suggesting that in these epistles Paul allowed his amanuensis greater freedom. Roller stressed the difficulties involved in assuming that Paul wrote 2 Timothy while in chains, with the same liberty with which he wrote his other letters. He suggested that the secretary drafted the letters from notes made while Paul dictated. Paul approved the rough copy, and then gave his approval to the finished letter (Roller 1933: 20f.). Several scholars have taken up Roller's suggestion, and some have even named the secretary.[13]

B. *The Pastoral Epistles contain genuinely Pauline Fragments*
In 1921 Harrison argued that the Pastorals contain five genuine Pauline fragments:

(i)   Tit 3.12-15;
(ii) 2 Tim 4:13ff., 20, 21a;
(iii) 2 Tim 4.16-18a (? 18b);
(iv) 2 Tim 4.9-12, 22b;
(v)   2 Tim 1.16ff.; 3.10f.; 4.1, 2a, 5b; 4.6ff., 4.18b, 19, 21b, 22a.

He situated each of the five fragments in a known period of Paul's life (pp. 115-35).

In his later modification of the proposal Harrison left the first fragment intact, and then effectively joined fragments (iv) and (ii), to make fragment 2, and (v) and (iii) to make fragment 3, thus giving a more simplified picture:

(1)   Tit 3.12-15;
(2)   2 Tim 4.9-15, 20, 21a, 22b; and,

(3)   2 Tim 1.16ff.; 3.10f.; 4.1, 2a, 5b, 6ff., 16-19, 21b, 22a (1955/
       56: 80f.; and 1964: ch. XII).

In his earlier commentary Hanson adopted the fragment theory as
'that of most modern English commentators' (1966: 6; see also
1968: 3).

C. *The Pastoral Epistles are Pseudepigrapha*

Perhaps the majority view among recent scholars is that the
Pastorals are wholly pseudonymous works, written after Paul's
lifetime by someone claiming Pauline authority for them.[14] The view
is so widespread that two recent popular works do not even mention
alternative positions.[15]

The most impressive recent statement of the case is that of
Norbert Brox in his 1969 commentary on the Pastorals. As well as
giving an overall framework to the letters he has advanced a number
of novel interpretations of the text. The personal elements in the
letters, he claims, function as paraenesis.[16] They present Paul as the
tupos, or archetype of Christian behaviour: 2 Tim 1.15-18 presents
him as the abandoned prisoner who serves as a model for 'Timothy'
who is encouraged to bear his own suffering (2 Tim 1.8; 2.3). The
exhortation is not without a certain warning of the danger of
abandoning Paul.

Luke (2 Tim 4.11) and Onesiphorus (2 Tim 1.16-18) also are types,
and Demas and Alexander are anti-types (2 Tim 4.10, 14), and so the
reader is presented with two possible responses. 2 Tim 1.5 presents
Timothy himself as a model for the readers, and 1 Tim 4.14 and
2 Tim 1.6 function as a paraenesis for the leaders of the community.
Titus is presented as a model for the young, post-Pauline office-
holders in the Church (Brox 1969b).

According to this view the pseudepigraphic writer had before his
mind the requirements of the church in his own day, with its need to
resist false teaching and to stabilize its structure and hierarchical
organization. Around 100 AD this church official put on paper, in the
literary form of three fictitious letters giving Paul's advice and
direction to his two aides, what was important for the church of his
own day. What Paul 'had dictated' in his lifetime should obtain for
the church of the author's day.

The author used several devices to create the impression that it
was Paul who was writing: the normal Pauline style of letter-writing,

with the address, greeting, and personal details (1 Tim 1.1f.; 6.21; 2 Tim 1.1-3; 4.9-22; Tit 1.1-4; 3.12-15). He created such texts as 2 Tim 4.13; 1.3; 1.4, with their appeal to Paul's everyday needs, to strengthen the fiction. He rooted the church offices of his own day in the personal bond between Paul and Timothy (2 Tim 1.6; 1 Tim 4.14), and he invested freedom from ascetic practices with Paul's authority (1 Tim 5.23; 4.3-9). Finally, Timothy is presented as the model church officer (2 Tim 3.10; 2.22; 1.7f.; 2.3-13; 1 Tim 4.12; 2 Tim 2.22).

Stenger speaks of a 'double pseudonymity', with the pseudonymous Paul writing to his pseudonymous aides, with the author making available to the community of his own day the 'apostolic *parousia*' (1974).

Trummer follows Brox's overall view, and taking his cue from Funk (1967: 249), sees the Pastorals as having the function of the quasi-presence of Paul in the community (1978: 99). After the death of Paul, these letters, which during his lifetime had only a local and restricted function, now assumed a wider horizon. The Pauline Corpus was being assembled, and this served as the first stage in the interpretation of Paul for the period after his death, and served as the connecting link between the historical letters of Paul and the pseudepigraphical ones composed after his death (Trummer 1978: 99ff.).

Similarly, Zmijewski views the Pastorals as a prolongation of vital Pauline insights into the present and the future. He stresses that they are eminently consistent with the Pauline tradition. For him, the question of historical authenticity is less important than the author's aim, and the content of his work. The author did Paul the service of not only conserving his message, but of making it relevant to the church of the writer's own day (1979: 118).

Hoffmann argues that the author of the Pastorals was a member of an Ephesian circle. Polycarp, he adds, is the most likely author (1984: 283ff.).[17] The heresy envisaged in the Pastorals, he concludes, is Marcionism, and the insertion of the pseudepigraphical letters was to reclaim Paul for orthodoxy over against Marcion's form of Paulinism (pp. 281-305).

D. *Evaluation*
It is clear that considerable problems have to be overcome before one can regard the Pastorals as coming from the hand of Paul. It is no less

true that the alternative hypotheses have their weaknesses.

The variety of fragments proposed by supporters of a fragments theory, and the rather arbitrary dissection of them to become part of our present text, does not inspire confidence in the theory.[18] As well as making a number of very dubious assumptions, proponents of the theory do not take seriously the many difficulties of the hypothesis.[19]

There is little to commend this theory. We sympathize with Moule in his amazement that it ever gained such wide currency (1965: 448). Hanson, once such a staunch supporter of the theory, has changed his mind: 'I now believe that such a view cannot be effectively defended' (1981: 402; and 1982: 10f.). Cook's recent investigation of the language of the fragments leads him to the conclusion that the problem of the authorship of the Pastorals rests between those who support their authenticity, and those who deny it: 'the intermediate ground occupied by the defenders of the fragment hypothesis proves to be rather a no man's land not suited for habitation' (Cook 1984: 131).

The great weakness of the theories of pseudepigraphy is that they rest on a number of assumptions that are questionable. It is all the more important, then, that these assumptions be brought to the surface and be evaluated.[20] The first concerns the question of whether the early Christians engaged in the practice of pseudepigraphy, and the second questions if the practice was ethically acceptable. We shall examine these in turn.

The practice of pseudepigraphy was common among both Greeks and Jews. However, although epistolary pseudepigraphy was common among the Greeks,[21] only two Jewish works have an epistolary form, and neither the *Epistle of Jeremiah* nor the *Letter of Aristeas* is in the strict sense a letter. Moreover, we do not know of any spurious or pseudepigraphical Aramaic letters (Fitzmyer 1979: 185).

The assumption that pseudepigraphical letters were perfectly acceptable in the early Christian community is by no means secure. In the early centuries of the Common Era, the practice of composing pious and legendary gospels, heretical books, infancy and passion gospels, acts and apocalypses was widespread.[22] The evidence for pseudepigraphical letters, however, is comparatively small,[23] perhaps because the letter-type did not lend itself to the purpose of the apocryphal literature (Schneemelcher 1964: 90). James suggests that the reluctance to use the letter-form arose from the fact that the epistle was 'too serious an effort for the forger, more liable to detection, perhaps, as a fraud, and not so likely to gain the desired popularity as a narrative or an Apocalypse'.[24]

Nevertheless, the view that the NT itself contains pseudepigraphical letters is very widely held. With respect to the Pauline letters many scholars hold that in addition to the Pastorals, 2 Thessalonians, Colossians, and Ephesians are pseudepigrapha, although in each case there is no shortage of supporters of Pauline authenticity. If any one of these letters is a pseudepigraphon the case for regarding the Pastorals also as pseudepigrapha is strengthened.

If the Pastorals belong to an acceptable literary genre of pseudepigraphical letters, one might expect them to have much in common with other examples of the genre. But even Hanson acknowledges that among the pseudepigrapha of the NT the Pastorals are *sui generis* (1982: 27). Outside the NT there are only three letters that offer the remotest points of contact with the Pastorals.

The *Letter to the Laodiceans* is a patching together of Pauline passages and phrases, mainly from the Epistle to the Philippians, and has been described as 'a cento of Pauline phrases strung together without any definite connection or any clear object'.[25] This pseudepigraphical letter is totally lacking in any personalia, which are such a feature of the Pastorals. It will be remembered that Holtzmann suggested that the forger supplied these to add verisimilitude to the letters. Moreover, almost nothing in the letter reflects the Pastorals.[26] If this letter is anything to go by, a Pauline pseudepigraphical letter would be written to a church rather than to an individual, and would be a slavish copy of verses from Paul's letters. In addition, it would not contain any personalia. The reality, however, is that the contrast between the Pastorals and the *Letter to the Laodiceans* could hardly be more striking.

The differences between the Pastorals and *3 Cor* are no less obvious. In *3 Cor* there is no customary thanksgiving, no salutation from anyone with Paul, nor to anyone, and no farewell. It is purely a doctrinal statement, making a most obvious frontal attack on gnostic deviations in the author's time, and has no paraenesis. Moreover, although it has a rough letter form, it is imbedded in a pious legend. It contains no personalia, and has no interest in either time or place. As for the view that personalia are added to give verisimilitude, one notes that the fifty-six names mentioned in the legend bear no resemblance to NT figures, and that there are several historical inaccuracies. Indeed the personalia take away from, rather than add to the letter's verisimilitude.

The so-called *Letter of the Apostles* is really a dialogue between Jesus and the disciples. Clearly it was directed against (second-century) gnostics. Its form and content rule it out of discussion here.

There is, therefore, little support to be found in Christian sources that pseudepigraphical letters were common, and the examples we have are not at all like the Pastorals.

A feature of (almost) all theories of pseudepigraphy is the insistence that the conduct of the author is above moral reproach. In his version of the theory, wherein the author used genuine Pauline fragments, Harrison insisted that the author was not conscious of misrepresenting the Apostle in any way. Indeed, he claims, it is not necessary to suppose that he did deceive anybody (1921: 112). The author was a devout and earnest Paulinist, who thought the greatest service he could render the Church would be to issue Paul's farewell letter, etc. to the Timothys, and the Church of his own day, 'such as he believed the Apostle would have delivered, had he been still alive' (p. 85). Since the Pastorals were ascribed to a person of such pious and pastoral motives the way was open for the theory to gain much wider acceptance in Church circles than it would had there been any suggestion that the author was a forger.

Zmijewski (1979), too, insists that the Pastorals are neither a fraud, nor a holy cheat. The pious end of making Paul's views relevant to the church of the writer's own day, it would appear, is sufficient to justify any means!

However, the evidence to suppport the view that the practice of pseudepigraphic letter-writing was eminently acceptable to the early Church is by no means convincing. The early Christians were aware of the existence of both authentic and pseudepigraphical letters and other works, and they adjudged the inauthentic ones to be forgeries.[27] Thus, the widespread assumption among supporters of the theory that Christian pseudepigraphical letters were both common, and eminently acceptable is not based on a solid foundation.[28]

With regard to the question of whether 2 Timothy is a pseudepigraphon several questions remain unanswered. Why would a pseudepigrapher break the Pauline practice of writing to communities rather than to individuals? Why would a pseudepigrapher compose both 1 Timothy and Titus, since they cover so much of the same ground? Since 2 Timothy contains the names of no less than twenty-one persons, surely some of them, or their relatives, would be on hand to cast a critical eye over what purports to have happened: would a pseudepigrapher risk composing such extensive personalia? One would expect of a clever pseudepigrapher a much higher level of exactitude particularly in the matter of the personalia. If he had the Pauline corpus available to him, and the text of Acts, one would expect him to square the details of the Pastorals with the life of Paul known from these sources. That scholars have found it well-nigh impossible to fit the Pastorals into the known framework of Paul's life suggests authenticity, rather than pseudepigraphy. The suggestion that such details as mentioned in 2 Tim 4.13 and 20 were created to give the appearance of genuineness is not very convincing, since these verses themselves, as we shall see in Chapter 7 create problems.

Up to very recently no supporter of the theory regarded the author as a deceitful and deceiving forger, and today all see him as a faithful disciple of Paul who by engaging in a perfectly acceptable literary practice preserved and reinterpreted Pauline tradition.[29] This assumption has become a safe theological sanctuary, preserving at one and the same time the moral integrity of the author and the theological authority of the work.[30] However, that an unscrupulous church official set out to deceive his readers is no less likely. To say that he deceived nobody in his own generation is an unwarranted assumption. What is certain is that he managed to deceive all subsequent generations up to very recent times!

Against this general benign attitude to the motives of a pseudepigrapher Penny (1979: ch. 1) sees in the pseudonymous Pastorals, 2 Thessalonians, and Ephesians the device being used as a polemical tool to secure their authors' own understanding of Paul over against competing claims to the Apostle's authority. With regard to the Pastorals he suggests that the pseudepigrapher placed his own non-Pauline 'early Catholic' type of Christianity under the very high and exclusive authority of Paul (ch. 3). Penny insists, quite rightly, that one cannot assume that the pseudo-Pauline letters are 'innocent' devices; one must determine the nature of their pseudonymity from the evidence of the text (ch. 2).

In the nature of things, of course, it is impossible to disprove a theory of pseudepigraphy. All that needs to be done is to propose that some unknown person, on some unknown occasion, and for some supposed reason produced his own theological viewpoint under the guise of Pauline letters.[31] The question that scholars must face is whether the solution to the problem of the Pastorals demands such a series of assumptions as are demanded in any theory of pseudepigraphy.[32] One wonders, with Guthrie, 'if New Testament criticism in attempting to solve one type of problem has created another which it has never satisfactorily solved'.[33]

3. *Conclusion*

In this chapter we have surveyed the history of the critical scholarship of the Pastoral Epistles. We have shown how opinion has shifted from the general acceptance of Pauline authenticity to the most widely held view today, namely that the Pastorals are pseudepigrapha. Several factors have contributed to that shift, but the arguments from language, and particularly vocabulary have played the dominant part in the discussion.

We have exposed the weakness of the fragments theories, and since theories of pseudepigraphy in general require a considerable number of assumptions, and since such a theory has its own difficulties when applied to 2 Timothy, we consider that recourse should be had to it only when the authenticity of the letter has to be altogether abandoned.

Methodologically, it is preferable to accept the Pauline authorship of the Pastorals unless the arguments against it are of such strength as to render the traditional position untenable. In the following chapter we examine one of the major obstacles to accepting the traditional view, namely that which deals with the comparison of the language and literary style of the Pastorals and the Paulines.

Chapter 2

STATISTICAL METHODS AND THE PASTORAL EPISTLES

1. *The Contribution of P.N. Harrison*

The wealth of statistics and graphs which Harrison presented in 1921 was sufficient to win widespread support for his view that the Pastorals were not authentically Pauline, but were, rather, the arrangement by an admirer of Paul of fragments of his letters which he adapted to the needs of the Church of his own time. The figures, and their arrangement in graphs were detailed, and at first sight very impressive. Because Harrison's conclusions have had such influence it is instructive to subject his evidence and arguments to close scrutiny. More generally, since so much weight has been placed on the application of statistical methods to the investigation of the Pastorals it is necessary to examine the evidence carefully, and to assess the value of the technique.

Since Harrison's major argument is from statistics, and since it has had the most weight, and appears to give his case a measure of 'mathematical certainty',[1] a summary of his claims is called for.

For Harrison it is the high number of *hapax legomena* that marks off the vocabulary of the Pastorals from that of Paul. No less than 306 of the 848 words of the Pastorals' vocabulary (omitting the 54 proper names) do not occur in Paul, and 175 of them do not occur either in the NT. On the basis of the number of Pauline and NT *hapax legomena* in the thirteen letters Harrison concluded that the Pastorals stand right outside the other ten Paulines to such an extent as to create very serious doubts regarding their common authorship with the rest.[2] The large number of words shared by the Pastorals and the Paulines are 'universal Christian terms, indispensable to any Christian writer and distinctive of none' (p. 26).

Moreover, the absence in the Pastorals of 103 proper names, and some 1635 other words which occur in Paul, constitutes a very serious objection to accepting the Pauline authorship of the

Pastorals. Such omissions would require nothing less than 'a change of perspective, a shifting of horizons, a profound modification of the whole mental and spiritual outlook for which two or three, or even five years would hardly be sufficient in any man' (p. 34).

The second major argument Harrison advances against the Pauline authorship of the Pastorals is the absence in the Pastorals of 112 Pauline particles, prepositions, pronouns, etc. Not only are the stones (nouns/verbs) used by the builder of the Pastorals of a different shape and substance from those used by Paul, but the very clamps and mortar that hold them together (particles, etc.) are different too, a fact which is, according to Harrison, still more striking and significant, if possible, than the omission of the main Pauline words (p. 34). He adds that the 77 particles that do occur appear also in practically every book of the NT. He claims that the divergence in the use of particles between the Pastorals and the Pauline letters cannot be explained away by appealing to changed circumstances, or a different subject matter. One is dealing with 'nothing less than a radical peculiarity of style', and he adds that *le style, c'est l'homme* (p. 58).

Harrison then contrasts the styles of the two blocks of writing: Paul is vivid, dynamic, even volcanic, while the author of the Pastorals is sober, didactic, static, conscientious and domesticated.

Harrison is at his weakest when he examines whether the differences in style and vocabulary between the Paulines and the Pastorals can be explained other than by predicating a different author. This is particularly true of his treatment of the question of Paul's use of a secretary (his fourth argument). Not only does he spend no more than two pages on this question, but he immediately reduces the possibilities of a secretary to the suggestion that Luke was the amanuensis, and then he simply states that the 175 NT *hapax legomena*, and the Pauline words Luke used, and Luke's use of some of the 112 particles are sufficient proof that while the authors of Luke–Acts and the Pastorals display clear and indisputable affinity, 'their identity would be quite incredible on linguistic grounds alone' (p. 53). But even within the very narrow boundaries within which Harrison deals with the possibility of Luke as the secretary, his use of the statistical evidence is misleading.[3]

His first three arguments, dealing with the writer, the circumstances, and the subject matter are subjective, and depend on unverifiable judgments and assumptions (pp. 45-52). The fifth argument, dealing with the recipients, comes back to the question of the *hapax legomena* and the missing Pauline particles.

The sixth argument deals with the possibility of the Pastorals being forgeries. Harrison excuses himself from the task of enquiring carefully into the procedure, the motives, the ethics and the psychology of the process of pseudepigraphy, but vehemently rejects the charge that the author could be called a 'forger', since that would suggest moral depravity and a will to deceive.

The argument from literary analogies does little more than show that Workman's views about the relationship of *hapax legomena* to authenticity are not valid. Harrison glides over the final three arguments that might account for differences in vocabulary: he is not impressed by the fact that some of the Pastoral *hapax legomena* are derivatives of Pauline words, or are to be found in the LXX (pp. 65f.), nor is he shaken by the fact that although some of the words are not in the NT, they do occur in classical literature (p. 66). But even within the narrow boundaries of his own statistical arguments his conclusions are not warranted, as we shall indicate.

Since circumstances alone may be sufficient to account for differences of vocabulary, it might appear that Harrison's argument from the absence of the 112 'Pauline' particles, prepositions, pronouns, etc. is conclusive. But even here the argument is not as substantial as one might be led to believe. For example, in examining Harrison's own figures (pp. 36f.), it can be seen that no less than 35 of the 112 'Pauline' particles occur in only one Pauline letter, 23 in only two, 12 in only three, 18 in only four, 7 in five, 6 in six, 6 in seven, 4 in eight, and 1 in nine epistles. Therefore, no less than 70 of the 112 'Pauline particles, etc.' are absent from at least seven other epistles in addition to the Pastorals, and only 17 of them are present in six epistles or more. Harrison point out that Romans has 58, 1 Corinthians 69, 2 Corinthians 53, Galatians 43, Ephesians 22, Philippians 29, Colossians 18, 1 Thessalonians 27, 2 Thessalonians 12, and Philemon 12 (p. 35). However, by subtracting those figures from 112, one sees that 54 of the 'Pauline . . . clamps and mortar' are missing from the edifice of Romans, 43 from 1 Corinthians, 59 from 2 Corinthians, 69 from Galatians, 90 from Ephesians, 83 from Philippians, 94 from Colossians, 85 from 1 Thessalonians, 100 from 2 Thessalonians, and 100 from Philemon. When one remembers that some 77 other (Pauline) particles, etc., do appear in the Pastorals one is left with a certain unease about the validity of the statistics of particles, etc. as a criterion for authorship.

Clearly, this criterion rests on the assumption that the repeated use of commonplace prepositions and connectives reveals a writer's personal habits. Even leaving aside for the moment the possibilities of co-authorship and the use of a secretary for the Pauline letters one must look with care at this criterion. For example, one gets some impression of the fluctuation in the use of particles when one sees from Harrison's own tables that ἕκαστος, the only one which occurs in as many as nine letters, appears 22 times in 1 Corinthians, and only 5 times in Romans; σύν, which occurs in eight letters, appears twice as often in Colossians (7 times) as it does in Romans (4 times), although Romans is four times as long as Colossians; τέ occurs in five epistles, 18 times in Romans, but only 7 times in the other letters; ναί occurs 6 times in 2 Corinthians, and only 3 times elsewhere in the letters; ἄρτι occurs 7 times in 1 Corinthians, 3 times in Galatians, once each in 1 and 2 Thessalonians, and nowhere else in Paul. These examples show that even the evidence offered by Harrison is suspect, and the conclusion he draws from it is misleading.

Having argued that the vocabulary of the Pastorals is not consistent with the traditional view of Pauline authorship, Harrison presents his arguments for placing the author in the second century. He point out, for example, that 93 of the Pastoral *hapax legomena* occur in either the Fathers or Apologists, 'proving that they did in fact belong to the current speech of the Church and the working vocabulary of Christian writers and thinkers in this period (second century)' (1921: 68). Guthrie points out that out of the 92 *hapax legomena* found in the Apostolic Fathers and Apologists no fewer than 32 occur in the whole range of the writings only once, and that no more than 17 of the 175 *hapax legomena* are used in more than one writer of the Apostolic Fathers (Guthrie 1956: 10).

Moreover, it can easily be verified that no less than 95 of the 175 *hapax legomena* occur, some with great frequency, in the writings of Philo, who died some twenty years earlier than Paul.[4] Indeed as early as 1929 Hitchcock showed that at least 153 of the 175 *hapax legomena* can be quoted before 50 AD, and 125 of the 131 of the Pastorals' vocabulary found elsewhere in the NT but not in Paul also occur before 50 AD. Altogether, then, of the 306 Pastorals' words which do not occur in the Paulines, 278, i.e. 90%, occur before 50 AD.

Hitchcock also exposed the fallacy of Harrison's conclusions concerning the proximity of the language of the Pastorals to that of the Apostolic Fathers and Apologists (1929: 278f.).

Harrison's other arguments do little to support his conclusion that the vocabulary and literary style of the Pastorals belong in the period of the Apostolic Fathers and the early Apologists, rather than in the Pauline period.

Although the weakness of his arguments from language had long been exposed by several scholars,[5] Harrison, returning to the question later, appears to have been unaware of these criticisms, or to have ignored them. Indeed, he claims to have been strengthened in his conviction, giving as a reason, 'the inability even of those who reject (my) hypothesis to deny the facts on which it rests' (1955/6: 77). Instead of recognizing that the appearance in Philo of so many of the Pastoral *hapax legomena* weakens his second-century date, he concluded only that the author must have read Philo!

Writing some three years later, Metzger rightly castigated Harrison for not having dealt with the devastating criticism of his method that had appeared since his earlier work (1958/9: 92). But even still, Harrison continued to ignore the critique of his basis for postulating a pseudonymous second-century writer, namely, the alleged second-century vocabulary of the Pastorals. He did modify much of the structure of the 1921 edifice, but he seems to have ignored the assaults on its foundation (Harrison 1964). In our view Harrison's primary argument for placing the Pastorals in the second century, namely the second-century nature of the vocabulary, has no validity whatsoever, and should have been withdrawn from the discussion long ago.

2. *Recent Application of Statistical Methods*

The criticisms of Harrison's method gave an impetus to the application of somewhat more sophisticated techniques to the question of the authorship of the Pauline Letters. In 1966 Morton and McLeman applied statistical analysis as an 'objective method' of determining the authorship of the Greek prose found in the Pauline Epistles. The two linguistic criteria used were sentence length, and the occurrence of some common words, such as καί, δέ, ἐν, εἶναι, and αὐτός. The authors contend that these elements define the style of an author, and they applied their method to both classical Greek texts, and to the NT. They acknowledge that the argument from sentence-length is an exclusive one in that it 'can never prove that two works were written by one author but only that two works cannot have been written by one author' (p. 63). The use of the common words, they claim, is as characteristic of an author as are his habits of walking, speaking, breathing, and writing (p. 88). Their statistical analysis led them to the conclusion that one author wrote Galatians, Romans, and the Corinthian Letters, and that Ephesians, Philippians and Colossians were written by men with contrasting habits in their grouping of sentences (p. 96).

In the same year Levison, Morton and Wake examined the statistical homogeneity of the individual letters, and they reached the conclusion that the Pauline letters can be grouped thus: Group 1, containing Romans, 1 Corinthians, two samples of 2 Corinthians, and Galatians; Group 2, embracing Philippians, Colossians, 1 and 2 Thessalonians, and a sample of 2 Corinthians. In addition, they concluded that Hebrews and the Pastorals were statistically distinguishable from the Paulines and from each other, even if the degree of difference between them and Group 2 is less than that between them and Group 1 (Levison, Morton and Wake 1966). They do issue a *caveat* on the use of a statistical method for the Pastorals: 'None of the Pastorals are long, and Titus is certainly too short at 36 sentences to be used reasonably for tests of significance' (p. 96).

Michaelson and Morton have examined Greek writings, including the Pauline Letters, on the basis of their placing different classes of words as the last word in a sentence (1971-2), but their method has been rightly criticized by P.F. Johnson (1974).

The major contribution of Grayston and Herdan was to apply a more precise statistical procedure to the Pauline letters than Harrison had done (Grayston and Herdan 1959). Instead of operating with *hapax legomena*, they introduced a relationship which they designate 'C', where

$$\text{`C'} = \frac{\text{Words peculiar to a chosen part}}{\text{Vocabulary of the chosen part}} + \frac{\text{Words common to all parts}}{\text{Vocabulary of the chosen part}}$$

Their calculations show a sensible stability of 'C' for the Pastorals, whereas the 'C' values for James, 1 Peter, 2 Peter, John and Jude show a lack of stability, which points to a difference in style, if not necessarily of authorship among the Catholic Letters.

In order to reduce the fluctuation that would occur due to different text-length, they group the Pastorals together, and also the Thessalonian Letters, and show their calculations of 'C' for all the letters attributed to Paul (except Philemon). 'C' for each of the letters falls between 32-34%, except for the Pastorals (46%) and the Thessalonian Letters (29%). They conclude that the magnitude of 'C' for the Pastorals strongly supports the hypothesis of a non-Pauline authorship, and thus their 'improved statistical method' gives a result which agrees with Harrison's conclusion (p. 10).

They then display the most striking evidence for the singular position of the Pastorals among the Paulines, by introducing the bilogarithmic type/token ratio. Theoretical considerations show that this should be constant for samples of a given text.[6] It is, in fact, constant for all the Paulines, except for the Pastorals, which are cumulatively and individually the only exception to the rule.

They sum up their findings by claiming that 'the linguistic evidence is strong enough to justify the conclusion of a very different style in the Pastorals. Whether this implies a difference in authorship depends upon one's conception of what style means. Statistics can do no more than establish such difference' (p. 15). They end on a flurry which begs several questions: 'If ever a writer was in the grip of his own words, it was Paul, and that makes it highly improbable that he should change his style at will, and according to circumstances' (p. 15).

Kenny is the most recent scholar to apply statistical analysis to the NT writings (1986). His is a study of stylometry, i.e., of the quantifiable features of style of a written or spoken text (p. 1). He uses stylometry as an indication of NT authors. While the earlier part of the book deals with the whole of the NT, the later part examines whether the stylometric evidence he assembles supports or conflicts with the hypothesis that Luke and Acts are the work of the same author, that John and the Apocalypse are by the same author, and that the thirteen epistles of the Pauline Corpus are by the same author.

He uses no less than ninety-nine features in comparing the major sections of the NT, and all but three of these for comparisons within the Pauline Corpus, which he deals with in chapter 14. He tabulates the distribution in the Pauline writings of conjuctions, verbs compounded with prepositions, articles by case, articles by gender and number, nouns by case, nouns by gender and number, pronouns by case, pronouns by gender and number, kinds of adjectives, distribution of adjectives by case, adverbs, verbs, moods of verbs distribution by tense and by voice. Significantly, he excludes sentence-length since he regards it as of very ambiguous value (chapter 15).

In moving towards his conclusions he adopts the method of asking if any one letter of the traditional corpus is marked out as different from the whole. He combines the ninety-six features, and concludes that there is a great deal of diversity between the epistles, suggesting a great deal of versatility in respect of the quantifiable features under investigation. Secondly, he finds that the Epistle to Titus stands at a great distance from the others. The order in which the epistles conform to the whole is Romans, Philippians, 2 Timothy, 2 Corinthians, Galatians, 2 Thessalonians, 1 Thessalonians, Colossians, Ephesians, 1 Timothy, Philemon, 1 Corinthians, and Titus.

His results give no support to the view that the single letters of a group of epistles (e.g., the Tübingen four) are closer to each other, or that a single group (e.g., the Pastorals) is diverse from its surrounding context. '2 Timothy, one of the commonly rejected Pastoral Epistles, is as near the centre of the constellation as 2 Corinthians, which belongs to the group most widely accepted as authentic. It is only Titus which is shown as deserving the suspicion cast on the Pastorals' (p. 100). On the basis of stylometry, then, he concludes that there is no reason to reject a hypothesis that twelve of the Pauline Epistles are the work of a single, unusually versatile author (p. 100).

3. *Evaluation*

The presentation of results in a mathematical or statistical form gives the appearance of exactness. If our generation has moved away from the concept of 'Gospel-truth', it still holds on to that of 'mathematical certainty'.[7] Unlike other judgments, those made on the basis of mathematics appear to be uninfluenced by personal opinions and ideological stance.

But the desired 'objectivity of knowledge' is arrived at only if the mathematical tool is applied within a system of thought that respects the complexity of the subject matter, and in this respect the results of Grayston and Herdan are no real advance on those of Harrison since they both suffer from having applied seriously defective models of style and authorship. It is clear that the major constitutive element of their 'C' is 'the vocabulary of the chosen part', and that the other elements of the ratio also deal exclusively with vocabulary.[8] Even if their investigation had demonstrated gross fluctuations in vocabulary, no firm conclusion could be drawn on the question of authorship, any more than one could conclude, on the basis of his 'scientifiction' and children's books, that C.S. Lewis did not also write his scholarly and critical works on English literature, and his popular, apologetic works on Christianity.

Furthermore, the diverse results of Morton/McLeman and Grayston/Herdan demonstrate the fragility of tests of authorship carried out on the basis of independent criteria.[9] Moreover, the altogether different findings of Kenny further weaken one's confidence in the fruitful application of simple mathematical techniques to the complex question of literary authorship.

Nowhere in the discussion does Kenny consider the alleged co-authors named in the first verse of several Pauline letters. Nor does he deal with the possibilities offered by Paul's undoubted use of secretarial help for some of the letters at least. Nor does he deal with the epistolary context, either at the level of sender or receiver—rhetorical style does not enter in. The model of authorship on which Kenny proceeds is simplistic, and therefore his results are of dubious value as far as the Pauline letters are concerned.

In his conclusion he mentions that he has made some experiments in the use of more advanced methods such as cluster analysis, but has not published them. The results, he assures us, are no different from those given in the book (p. 122).

4. *The Task Ahead*

Scholars will have to show much more sensititity to the complexity of authorship. Already there are signs that that is beginning to take place.

Although Radday's investigation into the authorship of Isaiah was based on one criterion, namely word-length,[10] he recognizes that one would need to construct a model of authorship that consists of a specified number of criteria in order to arrive at author-identity.[11] But even that alone would not be sufficient, if the criteria were examined independently of each other.

Drake recognizes the complexity of 'the style of an author'. He does not agree with Radday, who separates style and language. He asks how the style of an author is likely to vary with, (a) a different subject-matter, (b) a different audience, (c) a different literary form, (d) a different intent (e.g. informing, rebuking, or consoling), and (e) factors such as family problems, that may cause an author's feelings to change. He calls for a scientifically acceptable definition of authorship, which demands the recognition of the multiplicity of parameters that must be borne in mind *simultaneously* (Drake 1972). The relevance of these remarks to the whole question of Pauline authorship will be discussed in more detail in Chapter 3.

5. *Conclusion*

We have seen that much of the statistical work carried out so far has enquired into the question of authorship on the basis of only one criterion, and where more than one criterion has been used they have been examined independently of each other.[12] A more promising line of enquiry is becoming possible by the application of the technique of 'automatic pattern recognition', which uses a large number of parameters simultaneously in an attempt to define all of the characteristics of the object under study. The object can, with the use of computers, be represented in multi-dimensional-, or hyper-space. Patterns of similarity appear as clusters.[13]

In order to apply the method to the question of authorship one must first decide upon the maximum number of parameters that is required to describe literary style. Each element is considered in association with the others. But even this more sophisticated method of describing the characteristic style of an author leaves one with the more fundamental question of deciding what level of multiple, simultaneous similarity of style is necessary to decide on identity of authorship. Indeed, one wonders if criteria of style alone can ever identify authorship.

It is clear, however, that the method of statistical analysis employed so far has been crude in the extreme. Even when one is considering the unaided work of a single author the whole matrix of variety of subject-matter, circumstances of composition, genre, readers, intention, and of content must be examined simultaneously before one can begin to draw conclusions about authorship.

But before deciding on the question of the authenticity of the Pastorals one must consider several other factors that have a bearing on the question. In the case of the Pauline Letters we are dealing with the additional complexity of both single authorship and different kinds of co-authorship, and of different secretaries or perhaps none, as well as with both public and private correspondence.

Chapter 3

THE PAULINE EPISTLES AND THE PASTORAL EPISTLES

All commentators on the Pastorals operate with a very inadequate model of Pauline authorship. In particular, in drawing attention to the differences between the Pauline letters and the Pastorals they pay no attention to the fact that several of the former purport to be written by an apostolic team, and at least six of them to have been written with the use of a secretary. In addition, the Paulines were written to communities, rather than to individuals. On the other hand the Pastorals are presented as the composition of one person, with or without the use of a secretary, and directed in each case to one person. Rather than rehearse once more the many arguments and counter-arguments for the Pauline authorship of the Pastorals we consider it more fruitful to examine more closely those features of the Pastorals which separate them from the Paulines.

1. Co-Authorship and the Pauline Epistles

Among the many points of difference between the Pauline Corpus and the other letters of the NT is the fact that Paul is the only one of the NT letter writers who names other people with himself in the opening of some of his letters. Every other NT writer, and Ignatius of Antioch too, writes in his own name only. The fact that Paul writes several of his letters in co-authorship with others distinguishes them from the vast bulk of epistolary literature, and deserves more attention. Yet the presence of names in the place of co-senders is almost totally ignored in the literature.[1]

In his 'comprehensive' and 'inclusive' study of late Hellenistic and early Christian epistolary literature Doty does not deal with the question of co-authorship (Doty 1973). He does not appear to distinguish between the two kinds of Pauline co-workers, those mentioned at the end who send greetings, or in the course of the letters, and those whose names appear more solemnly at the beginning of the letter where the authors are named, although he does allow that these co-workers may have contributed substantial parts of the letters' contents (p. 41). He says that Paul mentions those co-workers 'for a two-fold reason: first he wanted to establish that what he wrote derived not from his own fantasy, but from the developing Christian communities; second the persons mentioned by name were often the trusted persons who were transmitting the letters and whose authority the addressees were to acknowledge' (p. 30). These claims carry no conviction.[2]

Similarly, in his overview of NT epistolary literature White does not even mention the presence of co-senders, and seems to confuse them with a secretary (1984: 1741).

Paul writes in his own name only in Romans, Ephesians and the Pastorals. Galatians is written not only in Paul's name, but also in that of the unnamed brothers with him (1.1f.). Sosthenes is named with Paul in 1 Cor 1.1, and Timothy figures with him in 2 Cor 1.1, Phil 1.1, Col 1.1 and Phlm 1, while Silvanus and Timothy are named with Paul in 1 and 2 Thess 1.1. The fact that the names occur at the beginning of the letter ought to alert us to the difference between such people and those mentioned at the end of the letters.[3] While it is just possible that some of the people who send greetings contributed something to the writing of the letters in question, Sosthenes, Timothy and Silvanus appear to be co-authors with Paul.

Paul's practice of naming someone with himself at the beginning of a letter is unusual. In fact, one author could find only a solitary reference to the phenomenon of co-authorship in ancient letter writing, Cicero *Ad Att.* XI,v,1 (Bahr 1966: 476). There are, however, several other examples of plural authorship, which deserve attention. Where more than one person is named as author we would expect to find the first person always in the plural, and where the first singular is used we would expect to find some indication as to which member of the group is intended at that point. Let us examine some examples.

The following papyrus letters come from more than one person: *P. Oxy.* 118; 1033; 1672, *P. Haun.* 16, *P. Amh.* 33; 35, *B.G.U.* 1022, *P. Gen.* 16, *P. Thead.* 17, *P. Ryl.* 131; 243; 624; *P. Tebt.* 28, *P. Magd.* 36; *P. Ross.-Georg.* 8. This, of course, is a tiny proportion of all the extant papyrus letters. Letters written in the name of more than one person are very much the exception. Among the royal Hellenistic letters only two were written by more than one person (Welles 1934,

Letters 9 and 35).[4] The *Apocryphal Letter to Paul* was written by Stephanas and four presbyters.

In all of these cases, with the single exception of *P. Ryl.* 131, the first person is always plural.[5] Those letters which name more than one person as author, then, were, in some sense co-authored. We have no way of knowing how the letters were composed, or what part each member of the co-authorship team played. The indications are that the writers are on an equal footing.[6]

In the case of those letters which are written by more than one person we have no way of knowing how the process of co-authorship was effected. One member of the group may have been responsible for the content, form and language of the letter, with the other(s) being more or less consenting partners. Or, both may have from the beginning contributed equally to the composition. And in between these two models there is a wide spectrum of possibilities.

Paul's practice in letter-writing is remarkable in the very high proportion of his letters that include authors other than himself. Scant attention has been paid to this remarkable phenomenon. The commentaries on the Pauline letters virtually never take seriously the possibility that the person named together with Paul had a real share in the authorship of the letters. Moreover, one never reads of the Letter of Paul and Sosthenes to the Corinthians, or of the Letters of Paul and Timothy to the Corinthians, to the Philippians, to the Colossians, and to Philemon (i.e. the Paul-Timothy Corpus), and the two letters of Paul, Silvanus and Timothy to the Thessalonians (i.e. the Paul-Silvanus-Timothy Corpus). We consider this to be due to the powerful influence Paul has had in the history of Christianity.

When seen against the background of the massive amount of ancient epistolary material, and its relatively tiny fraction of letters from more than one hand, we should expect that a letter purporting to be written by Paul and someone else was genuinely co-authored.

Moreover, we should expect that only in letters written by Paul alone would we find the first person singular. This is seen to be true of Romans,[7] Ephesians,[8] and the Pastorals,[9] in which there is no suggestion of co-authorship.[10]

In the letters written by more than Paul, however, one would expect some use of 'we' referring to the co-authors. Indeed, one would wonder to whom 'I' refers in such letters.

The evidence of co-authorship in the two letters of Paul, Silvanus and Timothy is abundant. The first person is always plural in 1

Thessalonians, except at 2.18; 3.5, and 5.27. At 2.18 Paul breaks into a 'we' section with an emphatic ἐγὼ μὲν Παῦλος, as if to inject a stressed personal note into the letter of the trio. In the case of 3.5 it appears that Paul is stating a previous personal position after he had sent Timothy to them on an earlier occasion. The final example, the command to have the letter read to all the brethren is in the singular (5.27); the obvious temptation is to conclude that Paul is the subject, but since the words occur almost at the end of the letter other explanations are possible. The situation in 2 Thessalonians is similar, with only two deviations from the use of the first plural. At 2.15 Paul (?) breaks into a 'we' section, while at 3.17 he gives his signature to authenticate the letter which was written by a scribe.

Another indication of the co-authorship of these two letters is seen in that they emply ἐγώ only once between them (while Philippians and 2 Timothy use it 52 and 33 times respectively), whereas they use ἡμεῖς 71 times. These two letters are remarkable in their almost exclusive use of the plural form. No other letter gives as clear an impression of coming from more than one hand as do these two letters of Paul, Silvanus and Timothy to the Thessalonians.[11]

The situation is quite different in the case of the Letter of Paul and Timothy to Philemon, Apphia, Archippus and Philemon's house-church. Although this letter gives the formal impression of coming from two people to a group, nothing in the letter suggests that it is any different from a letter written by one person, and addressed to one person.[12] Keeping in mind the very different practice in 1 and 2 Thessalonians one wonders what role Timothy played in the composition of this letter. Co-authorship is obvious in the former, while the latter reflects individual authorship. If, then, Timothy had no part in the composition of Philemon, why is he mentioned in a different place from the four who send greetings (v. 24)? One possibility is that Timothy acted as the secretary here (v. 19), while Silvanus was the secretary in 1 and 2 Thessalonians (cf. 1 Pet 5.12).

Despite the fact that Philippians is written in the name of Paul and Timothy the author uses the first singular throughout, except where it clearly means 'you, Philippians, and I', or 'we believers' (1.2; 3.3, 20, 21; 4.20). The intensely personal nature of the correspondence is confirmed by the occurrence of ἐγώ and its parts no less than 52 times, against 6 of ἡμεῖς. The only significant exception to the preponderance of the first singular is at 3.17.[13] It is truly remarkable that in this letter there is no other indication of its coming from the combined authorship suggested by the opening greeting.[14] As in the case of Philemon it is possible that Timothy was Paul's scribe for this letter, and did not function as a real co-author (see Schenk 1984: 76).

In Galatians, the only NT letter which includes unspecified authors (1.1),[15] there is no other indication that it was the work of more than Paul. Galatians is a strongly personal statement, with abundant use of the first singular: ἐγώ occurs no less than 38 times, and only one of the 21 uses of ἡμεῖς could refer to the co-authors, and even there it seems to refer to those who had preached in the Galatian area with Paul, such as Silas and Timothy. The failure to reflect in the body of the letter the fact of co-authorship could possibly be accounted for by the fact that it was Paul's personal authority that was at stake in the letter, and that the challenge might best be met by Paul alone. In any case, nothing in the letter suggests co-authorship.[16]

Paul and Timothy are named as co-authors in Colossians also. The thanksgiving is in the first plural (1.3), as it is also in 1 Thess 1.2 and 2 Thess 1.3, but not in 1 Cor 1.4, Phil 1.3 and Phlm 4 which also have co-authors. There are also indications within the letter that there is more than one author, at 1.4, 9, 28, and perhaps 1.7, but very definitely at 4.3, and probably at 4.8. In 4.3 there is a double use of ἡμεῖς which obviously refers to the writers, while in the same verse Paul refers to his own personal situation of being bound. On the other hand, the first singular is used with great frequency. At 1.23 and 4.18, in particular, Paul speaks in a purely private capacity, and in each case he inserts his own name. The personal note struck in 1.23 is carried on to the end of that chapter, and continues to 2.12. The plural at 2.13f. clearly refers to believers in general. The remainder of chs. 2 and 3 is mainly in the second person, and while 4.3 reverts to the first plural the remainder of the chapter is in the first singular, with the single exception of τὰ περὶ ἡμῶν (4.8). Of this verse Lohse says, 'Despite the plural only the personal situation of the apostle is in view' (1968: 170), but since Paul has already used the phrase τὰ κατ᾽ ἐμέ in 4.7 it seems to us more likely that Timothy is included. In Colossians, then, the letter opens with indications that both Paul and Timothy are co-authors, and this is also reflected in 4.8. Paul himself interjects a very strong personal element into the writing, and in two cases he even gives his own name (1.23; 4.18).

The movement from 'we' to 'I' in this letter is exceptional, and suggests a mixture of co-and single authorship.

Although 1 Corinthians purports to be from two authors, Paul and Sosthenes, much of the letter appears to come from one person. Even the thanksgiving is in the singular (1.4), and the singular occurs extensively throughout the sixteen chapters. Although some uses of 'we' could refer to Paul and Sosthenes alone (1.23; 2.6f., 11.16, all in the present tense), others probably have a wider meaning (4.10; 9.12). However, the use of the first singular is abundant, with 75 occurrences of ἐγώ.[17] Once again we are led to wonder what part Sosthenes, whose name occurs in the place of a co-author, rather than a sender of greetings (cf. 16.19), played in the composition of the letter. Barrett's comment, 'There is no doubt that Paul is the senior partner; or that Sosthenes genuinely is a partner' (1971: 31) does not bring us very far. It is possible that Sosthenes was the secretary (cf. 16.21). Timothy, in any case, is ruled out as secretary here, since he had already left Paul's company (16.10f.).

Although some scholars continue to argue for the unity of 2 Corinthians many are convinced that chs 10–13 must be separated from chs 1–9.[18] In 2 Corinthians, written in the name of Paul and Timothy, the pattern of singular/plural is very mixed.[19] In this letter, then, we have very definite evidence for co-authorship, and also clear evidence of a single author. Perhaps the explanation for this strange mixture is connected with the question of the integrity of the letter, or that Paul and Timothy wrote one letter with many interruptions, sometimes writing together, and at other times with Paul alone dictating the contents to a secretary, who may have been Timothy himself.

The fact that in more than half of his letters Paul wrote with a partner sets his letters apart from the vast bulk of ancient letters. When one examines Paul's letters against the background of the ancient co-authored letters we have uncovered, one should begin by regarding them as genuinely co-authored letters. Although there are relatively few extant ancient co-authored letters every one of them has all the markings of equality of responsibility for the authorship. Unfortunately, we have no way of knowing the contribution of each member of the team.[20]

The persons named in the prescripts of the letters must be understood to have played some part in the composition of the letters. There simply is no precedent for regarding such people as anything other than co-authors. All the examples of ancient letters which have more than one person in the prescript were truly co-authored, and one should begin examining eight of Paul's letters with the assumption that each person named in the prescript was in reality a co-author. The alternative is to insist on withdrawing Paul from the general epistolary practice of antiquity.

It is remarkable that Paul's practice varied so much. Sosthenes appears to have taken a back seat in the composition of 1 Corinthians, as Timothy also appears to have in Philippians and Philemon. We have proposed that the predominance of the first singular in Galatians is due to the fact that it was Paul's personal authority that was at stake. In 2 Corinthians there is definite evidence of co-authorship with Timothy, although several sections of the letter appear to have come from one writer only. Timothy appears to have been a co-author of Colossians also, and in the case of 1 and 2 Thessalonians we are clearly dealing with letters written not by Paul alone, but by the apostolic trio, Paul, Silvanus and Timothy. Several different modes of co-authorship suggest them-selves, ranging from that of a strong participatory role in the Thessalonian correspondence, to a passive, assenting one for Sosthenes in 1 Corinthians.

Scholarship must reckon with the phenomenon of co-authorship in most of Paul's letters. Unfortunately, it would be very difficult to quantify the contribution of each member of the co-authoring team. The phenomenon of co-authorship introduces a great variety of possibilities into the content and form of the finished work. The authors may have premeditated the content individually, and even gone over in their minds the general plan of what they were to compose, and perhaps even suggested the style and expression which they had separately settled upon after correcting their individual drafts, which was how Pliny the Younger operated before he dictated to his secretary (IX,xxxvi). Only then did they pool their individual contributions, and work towards an agreed content and form. The variations in possibilities are considerable, and ought to be investigated for each letter in turn. *A priori*, we ought to expect some difference between those letters written in Paul's name, and those written by some form of co-authorship.[21]

However, particular notice must be taken of the fact that Timothy appears in the prescript of six of the eight. It is to be expected that those letters in which Timothy played no part should betray some differences from those in which he was a co-author.

Secondly, as we have seen, Paul's practice varies enormously, between the two extremes of what looks like single authorship (Philippians, Philemon) to total co-authorship (1 and 2 Thessalonians), with examples of mixture in between (e.g., Colossians, 2 Corinthians).

If the variation in Pauline practice has been noticed, it certainly has not been carefully examined. Lofthouse did deal with the Pauline use of 'I' and 'we' in two short articles, but he did not even consider the question of co-authorship as a possible starting point in the discussion (1946/7; 1952/3). Moreover, he does not differentiate between those named in the prescript and those mentioned elsewhere in the letter. He never suggests co-authorship as an explanation of the occurrence of the first person plural. His proposal is that when Paul uses 'I' he means 'I, Paul' 'as distinct from his companions, his hearers and the Church in general, and of experiences which others could not share'. When, on the other hand, he used 'we', 'he was thinking of himself as one of a number, either the little band of his companions, or his readers, or the whole company of believers always in the background of his mind'. The circle enclosing 'us' 'expands or contracts; but it is always there when the plural is used; never when it is not' (1952/3: 241). Lofthouse's attempts to account for the variations in Paul's practice are as unconvincing as they are inconsistent. Clearly his arguments stand on shifting sands.[22]

Neither does Cranfield take seriously the possibility of co-authorship. The first person plural occurs when Paul joins himself to those being addressed (e.g. Rom 8.12); for this he suggests the designation 'the first person plural of humility'. When he wished to acknowledge his own personal involvement (as in Rom 8.15b, 17) he used the 'confessional first person plural'. In other places he used the plural to indicate Christians generally (e.g., 1 Cor 15.19; Phil 3.3) (1982: 284f.). He does raise the question of whether the fact that the superscriptions of some letters include names alongside that of Paul suggests that such persons were associated with him in the composition of the letters. But he is clearly reluctant to diminish Paul's contribution in any way.[23] He acknowledges that there is scope for a good deal of further, and more careful, investigation of the occurrences of the first person plural in Paul's epistles (p. 287).

In more than half of the Pauline letters, then, a colleague writes in association with Paul. When seen against the background of ancient co-authored letters one would expect a real co-authorship for those letters. Yet, we have seen that the Pauline practice is not consistent. While co-authorship is obvious in 1 and 2 Thessalonians, almost no trace of it appears in Philippians and Philemon, and some elements of it appear in Colossians and 2 Corinthians.

Indeed, Schweizer expounds Colossians neither on the basis that it is simply Pauline nor post-Pauline. Rather, he suggests that one must take seriously the joint authorship of Philemon, Philippians and 2 Corinthians, as well as of Colossians. He suggests that Timothy might have written Colossians in the name of both himself and Paul at a time when Paul could neither write nor dictate it, and he suggests that the occasion of the letter was shortly after the writing of Philemon, when Paul was imprisoned in Ephesus (1976). In his recent commentary on Colossians, Bruce also draws attention to the evidence within the letter that Timothy's name is not attached to Paul's in the prescript merely as a courtesy, but that Timothy was in some degree joint-author, and more so in Colossians than in the other letters. He even suggests that the literary style of Colossians might be that of Timothy (1984: 30). In the same volume he repeats his view that 1 and 2 Thessalonians also were co-authored (pp. 40f.).

Since Timothy is named as co-author with Paul in 2 Corinthians, Philippians, Colossians, Philemon, and with Paul and Silvanus in 1 and 2 Thessalonians, it must be the case that Timothy's role in the composition of the Paulines was quite significant. And since two of the Pastorals are written by Paul alone to Timothy, it could well be the case that some of the differences between the Pastorals and the Paulines can be attributed to the fact that the Pastorals are written by Paul alone, while most of the Paulines were written with some degree of co-authorship, particularly that of Timothy.

Two other factors also separate the Pastorals from the Paulines, and it is to them that we now turn.

2. *Paul's Use of Secretaries*

In chapter 1 we referred to the views of several scholars who suggest that the differences between the Pastorals and the Paulines can be accounted for by proposing that Paul gave greater liberty to the secretary of the Pastorals than he did to those of his other letters. However, rather than speculate about Paul's possible use of a secretary for the Pastorals, it is wiser to draw attention to the implications of the fact that he definitely did use secretarial help for several of his other letters.

Paul certainly used secretarial help for at least six of the thirteen letters, and in one case the secretary actually sends greetings in his own name (Rom 16.22). If we had the originals, the change in handwriting would make it quite clear how much of the letter was written by the secretary, and how much by Paul. The handwriting would also show how many different secretaries Paul used.

In the absence of first-hand information from the original manuscripts of Paul's letters we turn our attention to a review of the role of ancient amanuenses which will help us to speculate on how Paul may have used his secretarial services, and we shall also examine the letters themselves to see if they suggest how much of the letter was written in Paul's hand, and how much by the secretary.

The functions of a Mesopotamian scribe run the gamut from the all-important and efficient secretary who participates in the composition of a letter, to the town scribe who translates the inarticulate complaints of the poor into the stereotyped eloquence of a petition (Oppenheim 1967: 65). In the case of Aramaic letters, it is clear that secretaries were employed, in widely separated regions, and over a long span of time. The secretary appears to have drafted the letter, and a scribe copied it or took dictation for it. However, the letters do not indicate the freedom of composition that was allowed the secretary.[24] With regard to the extra-Biblical Hebrew letters the most we can say is that the use of a secretary is attested in the Bar Kokhba period. Beyond that we learn nothing about the use of a secretary that might illuminate us in our investigations of how Paul operated.[25]

The practice among letter-writers and literary people in Greco-Roman society offers a considerable background against which to view the composition of the Pauline letters. Cicero, one of the most prolific writers of ancient times wrote to, or received letters from no less than 99 different correspondents between the years 68-43 BC.[26] Of particular interest to us is his use of a secretary. Marcus Tullius Tiro functioned as his secretary much of the time, and on one occasion Cicero apologized to Rufus for the inconvenience of having to write without Tullius (*Ad Fam.* V,xxi). Using a secretary imposed some limitations. He was, at times, less complete than he would have been had he written himself (e.g., *Ad Att.* VII,xiiia; VIII,xv,3). More confidential and controversial matters could not be entrusted to a secretary: in those situations he either took over from his secretary (*Ad Att*. XI,xxiv,2), or wrote the whole letter himself (*Ad Att*. IV,xvii,1).[27]

He dictated his letters to the secretary, sometimes while walking, and used the opportunity to exercise his voice (*Ad Att*. II,xxiii,1). In one letter to Atticus he explains why he chose to dictate to Spintharus rather than to Tiro. Spintharus's method, apparently, was to take dictation syllable by syllable, whereas Tiro took down the material in blocks (*Ad Att*. XIII,xxv,3).

With regard to his manner of using a secretary we can say that he allowed Atticus great liberty in writing to anyone in his name. Atticus, apparently, wrote in Cicero's name to anyone to whom he considered Cicero ought to write (*Ad Att*. III,xv,8; XI,iii,3; vii,7; vii,8; viii,5).[28] Should the recipients of those letters notice the absence of Cicero's seal or hand, he was to tell them that Cicero had withheld them on account of the sentries (*Ad Att*. XI,ii,4). We cannot be sure what liberties Atticus took in the composition of those letters written in Cicero's name, but is is clear that Cicero had the fullest confidence in his prudence.

Although Quintilian's *Institutio Oratoria* deals more with the art of rhetoric than with letter-writing, he does deal with the skills of writing, and the use of dictation to a secretary in the first century.[29] Book X,iii is given over completely to writing as an aid to the training of an orator.[30] He is particularly disdainful of the practice of dictation, because an amanuensis hurries the writer on, and imposes a discipline of speed on the composer, who might wish, but would be too embarrassed to pause (19). On the other hand, the amanuensis might be a slow writer, or somebody lacking in intelligence, in which case he becomes a stumbling-block that checks the speed and interrupts the thread of ideas (19f.). Moreover, 'secretum in dictando perit' ('A secret is lost through speaking') (22). He stresses the need to emend what has been written, by addition, excision, and alteration (X,iv,1). He recommends putting the uncorrected work aside for a while before embarking on the correction, lest one indulge it like one does one's newborn child (X,iv,30).

Both the process of dictating to a secretary and the secretary's taking of the dictation allowed of considerable variety.[31] Much depended on the style and preference of the composer of the letter, and on the ability of the amanuensis. The dictation could be either slow, like stammering (cf. Seneca, *Ad Luc*. XL, 10), or in blocks of material as between Cicero and Tiro. Cicero used a different secretary for the two extremes. Two very contrasting modes of dictation are illustrated by Julius Caesar and Pliny the Younger. Julius had such mental vigour that he could write, or read, or dictate and listen all at the same time, and he could dictate four, and as many as seven letters to his secretary at once (Pliny the Elder, *Hist. Nat.* VII,xxv,91f.). At the other end of the scale, Pliny the Younger's practice was to be alone, with the shutters of his room closed to ward off distractions, and to go over in his mind not only the general plan of what he was composing, but even the style and expression itself; only then did he call his secretary for dictation (*Letters* IX,xxxvi).

Since we know that Paul used a secretary for six of his letters at least (Rom 16.22; 2 Thess 3.17; 1 Cor 16.21; Gal 6.11; Col 4.18 and Phlm 19), the question arises as to how he operated, and how much of each letter was written by Paul, and how much by the secretary.

Bahr (1968) argues that Paul takes over from the secretary at Gal 5.5; Col 2.8; Phlm 17; 1 Thess 4.1; 2 Thess 3.1; 1 Cor 16.15 and 2 Cor 10.1.[32] The starting point of his hypothesis is the fact that an abundance of business records in Latin and among the Greek papyri, as well as some examples in the Talmud, show that two parts of the record can be separated: the body of the record written by a scribe, and the 'subscription' written by the subscriber himself, or an agent (Bahr 1966: 467ff.). This subscription can be seen to have been more than a mere signature very often, and in some cases the subscriber summarized the terms of the body of the record. The ancients, he claims, made no sharp distinction in form between records and letters, and he points to an abundance of evidence to two hands both in the papyri and in letters, one of the scribe who wrote the body, and the second of the writer of the material who added not only his signature but sometimes sufficient postscript material to be almost equivalent to another, more personal letter.

A major part of the support for these suggestions is the undoubted similarity between material in the subscription and in the body, so that one recognizes in the subscription a certain summary of what the secretary had written in the body. In addition to the proposals mentioned, Bahr suggests that in Philippians Paul wrote on his own from 3.1 to the end. In Romans Paul began at 12.1, but yielded the pen to Tertius again at 15.14. Paul took over in Ephesians at 4.1. Clearly the implications of his view for our understanding of Paul, and for our concept of Pauline authorship are immense.[33]

Not only does Bahr not take account of the fact of co-authorship, but he seems to imply that Paul handed over to the secretary the composition of the body of the letter, which would appear to be a strange abrogation of his apostolic authority. Furthermore, although there is some little support for such extended subscriptions in ancient literature, the vast bulk of letters give no support to the view that the author distanced himself from the body of the letter in the way Bahr suggests for Paul.

Unfortunately, the available sources do not allow us to be sure of how much liberty a first-century secretary had in the composition of letters.[34] And it is impossible to say how much liberty Paul allowed his amanuenses. However exaggerated Bahr's reconstruction is, there is no reason to insist that Paul's secretary did not exercise some degree of freedom in the composition of those letters for which Paul used a secretary.[35]

When we begin to take seriously the fact of Paul's use of secretarial assistance, we have to face up to a great variety of possibilities. Even if Paul were the sole writer we would have to consider at least the following options available to him in the composition of his letters. He may have premeditated a letter, with or without having written out notes, and, having made corrections, then dictated it to an amanuensis, who took the dictation, perhaps syllable by syllable as Spintharus did to Cicero's dictation, or by the use of some form of shorthand, which would seem to have been necessary for Tiro.

On the other hand, Paul could have given the substance of his thoughts to the secretary, and left the precise formulation of the thoughts and the style of the composition to him, before reading over the letter, and adding his signature to the end. He may, of course, have added much more than his signature. In each of these models Paul would have maintained considerable personal control over what was going out under his name. But as we saw in the case of Cicero's employment of Atticus, Paul could have authorized his amanuensis to write of his concern about particular questions, and could leave the expression of thoughts and their literary execution to the amanuensis, without even having to check it at the end. This would be far less likely if the amanuensis were not thoroughly familiar with the mind and heart of Paul. We know that Timothy was.

In these examples we do not pretend to have exhausted the possibilities of the use of a secretary, nor is it necessary to demand that Paul used only one mode. We ought not to presume that Paul's mode was uniform; much could have depended on the circumstances obtaining at the time of writing, on whether, for example, Paul was free or in prison, or was with or without trusted co-workers, co-writers, or secretaries. In addition, Paul could have used any combination of the models referred to.

Since the Pastorals are private letters in a double sense, that is, they were written by one person, and the recipient is a specific individual, we propose that Paul did not use a secretary for them. There is considerable support in ancient letters for such courtesy. When writing to his friend Atticus, it was Cicero's practice to write in his own hand, so much so that he apologized for using a secretary (*Ad Att.* II,xxiii,1).[36] Atticus, too, usually wrote in his own hand to Cicero, but on occasion he too resorted to secretarial help (*Ad Att.* VI,vi). Cicero presumed that Atticus must have been ill to have had to rely on a secretary, Alexis (*Ad Att.* VII,ii). It was also Seneca's practice to write in his own hand to his friends (*Ad Luc.* XXVI,8), and also Julius Caesar's when writing to Cicero (Suetonius *De Vita Caes, Julius* LVI,6). Finally, Quintilian commended the skill of calligraphy because of its importance in writing to friends (I,28f.).

If, then, as we propose, Paul wrote the personal letters we call the Pastorals Epistles without the use of a secretary, it may well be the case, once again, that some of the differences between the Pastorals and the Paulines can be attributed to the fact that most, if not all, of the ecclesial letters were written with the help of a secretary, whereas the Pastorals, being private letters, were written by Paul himself. Clearly, if Timothy also functioned as a secretary for some of the ecclesial letters the argument is even stronger. We shall now consider a third important quality of the Pastorals that separates them from the Paulines.

3. *The Pastoral Epistles as Private Correspondence*

Another feature of the Pastorals that separates them from the other Paulines is the fact that they are addressed to individuals rather than to communities. And since they, unlike the majority of the Paulines purport to be written by Paul alone, the Pastorals are 'personal letters' in a double sense.

A. *The Pastoral Epistles among the Pauline Epistles*
While it cannot be said of Paul that in his letter-writing he created a
new genre, it is clear that there are even formal features of his letters
that are extremely rare in the vast history of epistolography. An
outstanding feature of much of his correspondence is its ecclesial
nature, both at the level of sender and receiver.[37]

It is only in the case of the Pastorals, Romans and Ephesians that
Paul wrote in his own name alone, while in the case of every letter,
except the Pastorals, he addressed himself to at least one local
community. In particular, Romans, Philippians, Colossians, 1 and 2
Thessalonians and Philemon are addressed by the author(s) to one
localized group of believers.[38] In the case of the letter to the church at
Colossae it is clear that it was the writers' intention that that letter be
read also in Laodicea, and that the Colossians in their turn would
read the letter to the Laodiceans (Col 4.16). The other letters of Paul
and his associates appear to have been intended by the authors to be
read by a public wider than even the local community.[39]

The work of Adolf Deissmann has been critical in preventing
scholars from being sensitive to the difference between the private
and public correspondence of Paul.[40] A reader should clearly
recognize that the Pauline Letters do not fit into either of the only
two categories of letter and epistle into which he divided all
correspondence.[41] The key factor in distinguishing between a letter
and an epistle, according to Deissmann, is the intention of the
author.[42] But in saying that Paul's letters are 'genuine, confidential
letters, not intended for the public or for posterity', and that 'they
were not ever intended for the Christian public of that time', but
were intended 'for the addressees only' (1929: 23f.), he overstated his
case, and somewhat misled scholarship. It is of the very nature of
letter writing that the writer cannot determine the extent of the
readership. It is only the Pastorals that purport to be private letters,
and the others required some form of public dissemination. The
community letters of Paul and his co-writers were intended for some
kind of public dissemination, and so with respect to the intentionality
of the authors they obviously differ from the bulk of the papyrus
letters.[43] It seems to have escaped Deissmann's attention that some
papyrus letters also were intended for publication.[44]

The Royal Correspondence of the Hellenistic period is at the other
end of the scale from the mainly private and intimate communications
of the papyrus letters, and provides a background against which to

measure the public nature of the Pauline correspondence.[45] In 74 of
the 75 letters extant, it is the ambassadors who in the first instance
approached the king. They were granted an audience at which they
presented their petition to the king. They read a decree of the city in
the presence of the king and supplemented its contents with
speeches. The king made a courteous reply, and if he was not able at
that moment to make up his mind he consulted with his experts, and
then directed the office of his *epistolographus* to prepare a draft of a
letter in reply, and then added ἔρρωσθε in his own hand to the final
document. The letter was then carried back to the city by the
embassy, and preserved in the archives as evidence (Welles 1934:
xxxix). The letters that have survived had another level of publication.
They were inscribed in stone, and erected either as *stelae*, or set into
a wall in a prominent place, to be seen by all. The king sometimes
gave specific instructions about the manner of publication.[46] Some of
these letters, then, had three forms of public dissemination, a verbal
form to the ambassadors, a written form for the archives, and, the
most public of all, the inscription of the letter on stone for all to see
'both now and in the future' (Letter 36 in Welles 1934: 158).

We are not suggesting that Paul intended the local communities to
preserve his letters for posterity, and certainly not by the erection of
ecclesial *stelae*. It could well be the case, however, that the
community promulgated the contents of the letter in a place where it
could be read, in addition to having heard it read.[47] Clearly the
letters were considered to be sufficiently important that the
communities preserved them, or copied them, in such a way that
they could at a later time be published as a corpus.

We have considered two types of ancient letter, the mainly
familiar, one to one family or business letter of the papyri, most of
which were written for immediate purposes and with no eye to
posterity, and the formal royal letters which were chiselled in stone.
Which class do Paul's letters most resemble?

Despite the claim of Deissmann, it must be insisted that Paul's
letters show only the most superficial resemblance to any letter
within the papyrus collection.[48] However, neither would one want to
claim royal authority for them. They find their place somewhere
between the two poles of the private and ephemeral messages of the
papyri, and the public, official letters of legislators.

Schubert correctly took exception to Deissmann's insistence on the
private character of the Pauline correspondence but he, too, failed to

recognize the public nature of the Pauline letters as intended by Paul himself.[49] Paul wrote to communities, and was anxious that his message would receive public dissemination (cf. Col 4.16; 1 Thess 5.27).[50] The fact that the letters were subsequently published as a collection merely introduces another aspect of their public character.[51]

Deissmann insisted that even when the recipients of a letter are in the plural, such as in the case of a *Gemeindebrief*, the true letter is always private. Even a term such as 'congregational letter' is not helpful, since a piece of correspondence is either a true letter or an epistle (1903: 18ff.). However, anyone familiar with the practice of writing to groups as well as to individuals will be aware of the peculiar character of each correspondence.

The letters of Paul present us with a most important source for understanding Paul as a person. It would, however, be mistaken to imagine that the Paul of the letters is identical with the historical Paul.[52] It would be unwise even to presume that the characteristics of Paul as reflected in his letters are typical of him. The most one could say is that in the face of such and such a situation in a particular community that is how Paul behaved. Each letter was composed with particular needs in mind, and it would not be immoderate to classify the letters as 'crisis correspondence'.[53]

Each letter ought to be examined in its own right, and the reader must be open to the possibility that very different aspects of Paul's character are revealed as one moves from one letter to another.[54] In particular, one would expect significantly different aspects of Paul's character to appear in his private, as contrasted with his ecclesial correspondence. This fact also could account for some of the difference between the Pastorals and the other Paulines.

A particularly telling example of each of the two modes of correspondence is provided by two letters of Ignatius of Antioch, one to the community at Smyrna (public), and the other to its bishop, Polycarp (private).

B. *The Example of the Ignatian Letters to Smyrna and to Polycarp*
Ignatius was the leader of the Christian community in Antioch, a city of great cultural and religious pluralism,[55] which became the capital of the Christian community after the collapse of Jerusalem, and the centre for the missionary activity by which the Gospel was preached in Asia Minor and Greece. The religious life of the city must have left its mark on Ignatius,[56] and it has recently been argued that Ignatius's

insistence on avoiding disputes and divisions was due to his own experience of things in Antioch, rather than to his knowledge of the different churches to which he wrote.[57] However, in addition to keeping in mind the influence of the various Christian tendencies in Antioch,[58] it is also necessary to consider the peculiar circumstances of each community to which Ignatius addressed himself.[59]

Although we cannot be sure of the precise route followed by Ignatius, we know that he actually spent some time in Philadelphia, and a longer time in Smyrna, during which latter experience at least he was informed, perhaps in a biased way, of the situations obtaining in different churches. Armed with his own theological and pastoral concerns,[60] Ignatius embarked on his journey to martyrdom. Although in general terms we see in his letters the challenge to the local and universal church which was posed by forms of Judaizing, docetism, and community fission, it is clear from the individual letters that the problems in each community were not identical.[61]

It would be fascinating if we had, in addition to the letters to the churches, letters from Ignatius to the bishops of the churches. We would then be able to judge better how Ignatius considered the personality and the capacity of the particular bishop to be responsible for the ills of each community in turn. We are, however, fortunate to have both the letter sent by Ignatius to the church in Smyrna, and also that sent by him around the same time to its bishop, Polycarp.

Clearly, the church in Smyrna was beset with a problem of docetism that was even more serious than that in any other church in the region to which Ignatius wrote. In his letter to the community in Smyrna, Ignatius wastes no time in going into the attack, and his polemic is more virulent than in the other letters.[62] The docetists in Smyrna were indifferent to the needs of the widows, orphans, and the various distressed members of the community (*Smyrn*. VI). The threat of docetic tendencies, then, did not lie merely in some deviant arrangement of theological terms, but struck at the heart of the social gospel. There are also several exhortations to community love throughout the letter (e.g. *Smyrn*. I; V; VII).

In addition to being neglectful of the poor, the docetists within the community abstained from the eucharist and prayer, since they did not confess that it was the flesh of Our Saviour who died for our sins (*Smyrn*. VII). Indeed, it would appear that alternative eucharists were being held, celebrated neither by the bishop himself, nor by someone appointed by him (cf. *Smyrn.* VIII)—Ignatius states that it is not lawful to baptize or hold an ἀγάπη without the bishop (*Smyrn.* VIII). The bishop was to be the focus of the community, as Jesus Christ was that of the catholic church (*Smyrn.* VIII).

The names of the offending members of the community of Smyrna were, of course, well known to the community itself. They were also, apparently, known to Ignatius, but he did not think it right 'to put into writing their unbelieving names' preferring, indeed, to forget the names until such times as their bearers repent concerning the passion which is our resurrection (*Smyrn.* V).

If we did not also have a letter to the bishop of Smyrna, we would be left speculating as to what extent the quality of the bishop's leadership contributed to the evils that beset the church. If we had only the letter to the community at Smyrna we would have concluded that there was in that community a very strong docetic element, which effectively broke away from the community overseen by the bishop, and carried on its sacramental life in independence of him. We would have little sympathy for its deviance, since it led to such neglect for the poor.

But with the letter to the bishop of the community we get a different picture of the problem in Smyrna.[63] The tone of the letter to Polycarp is one of exhortation from beginning to end. The prominence of this theme is clear from I,1 wherein the author wastes no time in indicating the epistolary intent, namely to exhort Polycarp to carry out his ministry with all diligence. This general exhortation is made specific throughout the letter, and deals with both Polycarp's personal piety and the exercise of his ministry (I,3).

Ignatius is not in any doubt about the demands of Polycarp's task. The sheer variety of images, medical and nautical, with which Ignatius colours his exhortation to deal with the troublesome people (II,1-3) reflects his sensitivity to the pressure on Polycarp. That the task of maintaining unity in the community may involve suffering, and even martyrdom is suggested by the martyrological term, 'attain God', and the emphatic 'you too' as Ignatius reflects on his own condition (Schoedel 1985: 264f.). This is further supported by the emphasis on 'standing firm', and 'enduring' in the face of the battering he receives at the hands of the false teachers (III).

It is clear from that letter that Polycarp himself is, in Ignatius's estimation, a major problem within the Christian group in Smyrna.[64] He needed more wisdom (*Pol.* I.). He tended to opt for dealing with the easier members of the community, than with the difficult ones (*Pol.* II). He ought to pray for more gifts (*Pol.* II), which is probably a gentle phrase suggesting Ignatius' reservations about the suitability of Polycarp. Indeed, Ignatius regards Polycarp himself as being in danger of being overcome by false teachings (*Pol.* III). He needs the discipline and determination of an athlete (*Pol.* II; III). In a word, he needed to be more diligent (*Pol.* III).

Ignatius was critical of the relationship between various communities and their bishop, but, unfortunately, we do not have any letters from him to the bishop of those communities.[65] But armed with the personal letter of Ignatius to Polycarp it is difficult to conclude that Polycarp was not, in the estimation of Ignatius, seriously deficient in meeting his responsibilities to the community in Smyrna. The fruits of his ministry are clearly to be seen in the letter to the church at Smyrna. In that letter we have the strongest denunciation of the docetic element within the community, which expressed itself in a deviation in its theology, in its liturgical practice, and in its social implications which led to a neglect of the poor.

It is also significant to note the very specific instructions which Ignatius gave to Polycarp about the exercise of his responsibilities towards the various categories within the community: the care of the widows, which is mentioned only here in Ignatius (*Pol.* IV); the advice for sisters, and brothers, and the regulations concerning marriage and celibacy, as well as directives about behaviour towards slaves (*Pol.* IV; V).[66]

Finally, one notes that nowhere in the letter to the church at Smyrna does it appear that Polycarp's personality, and his capacity to lead the community were suspect. In any case, they were never criticized. Indeed, one would get the impression from the letter to the church that the problem of the church at Smyrna resided with the community itself, rather than with the capacity of the bishop to do his job, at least to the satisfaction of Ignatius. Presumably, more in hope than in confidence, Ignatius, in his letter to the community, tried to bolster up the local leadership by appealing for unity under the bishop and his co-leaders. But he never gave the community the impression that he considered its bishop, Polycarp, to be part of the problem.

The picture of Polycarp which follows from our reading of Ignatius's, Letters to Smyrna and to Polycarp is far less flattering than that given by his pupil Irenaeus, or than that in the account of his martyrdom composed shortly after the event,[67] or in the later tradition.[68] However, in addition to the evidence of Ignatius's letters, there are other indications that Polycarp did not satisfy Ignatius's expectations.[69]

While there is no doubt that Ignatius had great affection for Polycarp (*Eph.* 21; *Magn.* 15) it must be kept in mind that Polycarp's lifetime (c. 70-156) was a period of great turbulence.[70] His task in Smyrna was fraught with problems.

From our investigation of Ignatius's *Letter to Polycarp*, and of Polycarp's own letter, we have seen sufficient indication as to why Ignatius regarded Polycarp as lacking in some of the qualities Ignatius preferred to help Polycarp cope with the difficult task that confronted him. Relying only on Ignatius's *Letter to the Smyrnaeans* nobody would suspect that Ignatius considered Polycarp to be so significantly in need of correction and encouragement.

We shall point out that 2 Timothy, like the *Letter to Polycarp*, is a personal letter, with a very strong paraenetic character, and that Timothy's fidelity and ability as an evangelist is a major concern of Paul as he pens it. The above comparison between Ignatius's public and private letters disposes one to expect some considerable difference between a public letter of a church leader and one he sends to the community's bishop. We propose that some of the differences between the Pastorals and the Paulines can be attributed to the fact that the former are private letters, and the latter are public.

4. *Conclusion*

When we add the implications of the fact that the Pastorals are private, rather than ecclesial letters to the complexity implied by the phenomenon of the various forms of co-authorship, and the equally varied options for Paul's use of secretaries, we have to acknowledge that in the question of the authorship of the Pauline Epistles we are dealing with a veritable maze of interlocking variables. It is, then, only to be expected that there should be some notable differences in expression and content between the Pastorals and the Paulines.

On the basis of the evidence produced in this chapter we wish to make some suggestion about the composition of the Letters of Paul. The key person in our scenario is Timothy who was a very significant aide to Paul in his mission. He was, of course, a key figure in the mission described in Acts 16–20, and his role as co-worker with Paul is portrayed in a prominent fashion. We wish to stress also his role in the co-authorship of the letters. He was a joint author with Paul of 2 Corinthians, Philippians, Colossians and Philemon, and with Silvanus and Paul of 1 and 2 Thessalonians. The other references to Timothy in the letters offer evidence that also must be assessed. Timothy appears as Paul's emissary to the Corinthians (1 Cor 4.17; 16.10f.) and it could well be the case that he is still with Paul as Paul and Sosthenes wrote the letter. Why, then, Timothy does not appear in the prescript is an intriguing question. In Philippians he is mentioned both as co-author in the prescript and also as an emissary in Phil 2.19. He had on a previous occasion been an emissary of Paul to the Thessalonians (1 Thess 3: 1f.), but at the time of writing he is, of course, with Paul and Silvanus as joint-author (1 Thess 3.6; 1.1). Timothy, then, is mentioned in no less than ten Pauline letters (all except Galatians, Ephesians and Titus), and is named as co-author in six.

It is significant that even though Timothy is present with Paul in the composition of Romans (Rom 16.21) he appears neither in the prescript as co-author, nor as secretary (Rom 16.22). Could it be that in the composition of Romans Paul presented himself as the single author of this very extensive and sensitive letter, and that he employed the otherwise unknown Tertius as his secretary? Cicero, it will be remembered, employed the otherwise unknown Spintharus as secretary in his letter to Varro with which he took so much care (*Ad Att*. XIII,xxv,3). Timothy, then, had no part in the composition or writing of Romans, but we propose that in those letters in which his name appears as co-author, he played the part of a co-author. It would require a new and thorough investigation to determine what thoughts and what expressions within 2 Corinthians, Philippians, Colossians, Philemon, 1 and 2 Thessalonians come from Paul alone, or from Paul influenced already by Timothy, and what in those letters emanates from Timothy. Unfortunately, in the nature of the case it is extremely difficult to quantify the extent of Timothy's participation. Our investigation into the degree of co-authorship suggests that the pattern was not consistent: the evidence for co-authorship is almost nil for Philippians and Philemon, while for 1 and 2 Thessalonians it is almost total.

If, then, Timothy contributed some substance to the thought and expression of those letters in which his name occurs as co-author, it is to be expected that there should be differences in thought and expression between them and those Paul wrote on his own. And since in the case of the Pastorals Paul did not use a secretary either, one might claim that they give a unique view of Pauline thought and concerns.

When, then, one takes into account that two of the Pastorals were written to, rather than with Timothy, and that they, unlike many of the Paulines, were written without a secretary, and that they are the only extant letters by Paul to individuals, it must be conceded that the criteria of comparison by which the Pastorals have been excluded from the Pauline Corpus are not as secure as many scholars appear to suppose. We suggest, then, that each of the three features of the Pastorals which distinguish them from the other letters of Paul which we have examined in this chapter helps to account for at least some of the differences between these letters and the other Paulines.

Chapter 4

SECOND TIMOTHY AMONG THE PASTORAL EPISTLES

1. *The Purpose of Each of the Pastoral Epistles*

It is normal in the literature to speak of the Pastoral Epistles in such a way as to give the impression that they constitute a homogeneous block of material. They are said to 'form a unity in their language, theological concepts, and intention' (Koester 1980, II: 297). They 'need to be viewed together. They are in full agreement in their religious and ethical teaching. They deal with the same problems' (Scott 1936: xv). 'On any showing, they all exhibit roughly the same range of concerns' (Houlden 1976: 21), and 'taken together, are all three expressions of one and the same concept' (Dibelius 1966: 8). Commentators have harmonized the Pastorals and have tended to so concentrate on questions of vocabulary and thought that relatively little attention has been given to the real nature of the epistolary communication.

Too often critics begin their discussion of the letters on the assumption that they are unreal letters written pseudonymously. This obviates the task of situating each of them in a specific historical context, and too often the conclusions reached are vague generalizations, which reflect only the information of 1 Timothy and Titus. Although there are undoubtedly similarities between the three letters, and especially between 1 Timothy and Titus, it is not wise to ignore some very substantial differences between them. Since the primary question for the commentator ought to be, 'What does the author hope to achieve in each letter?'[1] let us first consider the individual character of each of the three Pastorals.

A. *The Purpose of Second Timothy*
It is not unexpected that the opening lines of any correspondence introduce the major concerns of the letter writer, and this is certainly true of Paul. Paul Schubert has demonstrated that the Pauline

thanksgivings have an epistolary function, namely that they serve to introduce the main themes of a letter.[2] O'Brien carries Schubert's insights further (1974/5; 1977; 1980). He points out that Paul reveals in his thanksgivings his deep concern for his addressees, his desire to see them, and his personal concern for their spiritual growth, and he concludes that the thanksgivings are integral parts of the letters, that they serve to set their tone, and introduce the themes which are to be the concerns of the letters (1977: 262f.).

Unfortunately, both Schubert and O'Brien exclude the Pastorals from their consideration.[3] Further evidence of neglect is provided by the suggestion that 2 Tim 1.3-5 and 1 Tim 1.12-17 are of the same form.[4] 1 Tim 1.12-17 is, of course, a genuine thanksgiving, but it belongs to the category of interjected thanksgivings which we meet also in Rom 7.25, wherin Paul remembers God's favour to himself, rather than to the addressees.[5] 2 Tim 1.3-5, on the other hand, clearly functions in much the same way as do the other Pauline thanksgivings.

This thanksgiving introduces the major themes of the letter, which we see to be Paul's longing to see Timothy (v. 4), and his concern for Timothy's faith (v. 5). Since, in the circumstances, it is not possible for Paul to visit Timothy he appeals to him to speed towards him (4.9), and to do so before winter if possible (4.21).[6] The desire to see Timothy, then, occurs as the first item of the thanksgiving period (1.4), and is the last item before the final farewell (4.21). The body of the letter, therefore, is framed by the reference to Paul's desire to see Timothy, so that his joy may be complete (1.4). Furthermore, the two urgent appeals to come quickly (4.9, 21) frame that section in which Paul gives details of his condition (4.9-21). The exhortation to Timothy to come is, therefore, a major concern of Paul, and must constitute a primary purpose of the letter.

The other major concern of the letter is also introduced in the thanksgiving period, and it is to Timothy's faith that Paul turns his attention immediately after the thanksgiving period. He appeals to Timothy to fan into a flame the fire of the gift of God which he received at his hands (1.8). This general exhortation, and much else in the letter is related to the fundamental gift of faith which was also in Timothy's mother and grandmother (1.4). So much of the letter can be subsumed under the appeals of Timothy to be faithful to his witness to that faith, both by avoiding bad behaviour and by practising good behaviour.[7] These are a development of the fundamental appeal Paul makes to Timothy's faith in the thanksgiving period (1.5). Timothy is to be loyal to his faith, and not to be ashamed of bearing witness to our Lord, or to Paul (1.8), anymore than Paul himself was ashamed to bear his own witness (1.12; 4.6ff.).

Fidelity to his original vocation demanded also of Timothy that he follow the pattern of the sound words which he had heard from Paul in the faith and love that are in Christ Jesus (1.13), and that he guard the good deposit through the Holy Spirit who dwells within them.[8] Although the term διδασκαλία occurs three times in the letter, the stress on suffering and martyrdom, as well as the emphasis on upright conduct make it clear that the deposit of faith involves more than an intellectual fidelity to a body of truth.

Timothy is very soon exhorted to take his share of the suffering for the Gospel in the power of God (1.8), and this item is placed first after the exhortation not to be ashamed of bearing witness to the Lord (1.8), nor to be ashamed of Paul (1.8), who himself suffers all for the sake of that Gospel (cf. 1.12, 16), and who is fettered like a criminal (2.8-10). In addition, Paul alludes to his sufferings in the past at Antioch, Iconium and Lystra, from which the Lord had delivered him (3.11).[9] Suffering, Paul assures Timothy, is the lot of anyone wishing to live a godly life in Christ Jesus (3.12), and will be that of Timothy also (2.3), if it is not so already. Finally, towards the end of the letter Paul describes his recent trial and his present state of mind as he faces into the future (4.16ff.).

The emphasis throughout this letter, then, is on Timothy's own vocation and ministry, although there is mention of his responsibility to instruct others, who in their turn will become teachers (2.2). He is not to dispute about words, nor to engage in godless chatter (2.14), and stupid controversies (2.23). There follows immediately a description of the Lord's servant, with particular regard to the role of gentleness of manner in teaching, which behaviour may contribute to the conversion of opponents (2.24-26). The apocalyptic language describing the vices of the people in the last days can hardly be taken as a reference to the actual opponents of Timothy at this time (3.1-5), although the admonition to avoid people who have merely the form of religion (3.5) could suggest that Paul considered the end time to have come already by way of anticipation. The reality of the threat is illustrated by Paul's reporting that weak women, burdened by sins, and swayed by various impulses are liable to fall prey to the troublemakers (3.7). These people, being of corrupt mind and counterfeit faith oppose the truth, as Jannes and Jambres opposed Moses (3.8). The most comprehensive way to deal with such opposition to the preaching is to follow the pattern laid down by Paul himself (3.10-17).

We have seen, then, that the opening thanksgiving of 2 Tim 1.3-5 functions in a fashion comparable to the other Pauline thanksgivings. It introduces the themes of the letter, and shows great concern for the addressee: Paul exhorts Timothy to come quickly, and he shows his concern for Timothy's faith. If the first theme frames the whole letter (1.4; 4.21; cf. 4.9), the intervening material is directed towards the second, namely, the exhortation to Timothy personally to remain faithful to his calling. This is done in various ways, by recommending abstinence from inappropriate behaviour, by practising virtue, and by bearing witness both in the manner of his life, and in his teaching, to the Gospel of God, on behalf of which he, like Paul himself, must expect to suffer.

Such is the insistence of Paul on these two matters that we must suspect that behind this double call of Paul to Timothy to come quickly, and to be faithful, lies Paul's real fear that Timothy would, like so many of his erstwhile trusted co-workers, succumb to the temptation to abandon Paul and the faith. It may indeed already be the case that Paul had learned of some of Timothy's difficulties, and was therefore more than anxious to see Timothy as soon as possible in order to deal with him even more forcefully *tête-à-tête*. Behind the allusions to the useless chattering may be Paul's fear that Timothy himself was in danger of falling victim to that particular threat, and the insistence on taking his share of the suffering may reflect Paul's fear that Timothy was in danger of flinching from the persecution that Paul was sure was to be the lot of any real disciple of Jesus.

By way of contrast with the other Pastorals it should be noted that there is no indication within this letter that Timothy is to pay attention to the appointment to various ministries within the community, which is one of the major concerns of both 1 Timothy and Titus. Moreover, there is no element of anti-Jewish polemic in the letter.[10]

B. *The Purpose of First Timothy*

We have already indicated that there is not the customary thanksgiving period in this letter, which would serve as a clue to the preoccupations of the writer of the letter. However, it is clear that the emphasis in 1 Timothy is on the contrast between the sound teaching of the deposit, and the challenge offered to it by the false teaching of others. There is great emphasis on the arrangement of things in Ephesus along the lines of a well-ordered family, with each member of the family knowing exactly his role within the group, and his responsibility towards others (cf. 1 Tim 3.15). There are some details concerning the nature of the false teaching that may suggest a link with some other system known to us from the early history of the Church. That the suppression of false teaching is in the forefront of Paul's mind in this letter is clear from the fact that it is to that topic that he immediately turns his attention after the initial greeting.

However, there is no indication within the letter that Timothy's faith and fidelity to ministry are under any threat. This contrasts very strongly with the situation in 2 Timothy where it is seen that Timothy's own welfare is a major concern of Paul. Moreover, one notes the complete absence of a theme of suffering in this letter, and this aspect makes it stand out as being very different in tone from 2 Timothy. There is no indication that Paul himself is in prison, nor in fact that he ever was in prison. Nor is there any mention of the possibility that either Paul or any believer will have to suffer for the Gospel. The mood of 2 Timothy is utterly different, which letter was written under the shadow of suffering. Although there is reference to the apostates Hymenaeus and Alexander (1.20), there is nothing approaching the 2 Timothy list of people who have abandoned Paul.

Among the elements which distinguish this letter from the other two Pastorals are the following: (a) the false teachers, against whom Paul issues his condemnation in the very opening of the letter, desire to be νομοδιδάσκαλοι (1.7); (b) the section on the purpose of the law (1.8-11) also draws attention to the anti-Judaizing element in the letter; (c) the section on public prayer, and the intercessory prayer for all men, and especially for kings, etc., is unique among the Pastorals; (d) considerable attention is given to the place of women in the assembly, with remarks concerning their dress, behaviour, silence, submission to men, ending with the reference to Adam and Eve, and the woman's salvation through childbearing (2.9-15); (f) the qualities required of deacons (3.8-10, 12f.) and of women (3.11) are given; (g) among Paul's specific exhortations to the direction of different elements of the community is the extended passage about the widows (5.3-16); (h) there is a section on the question of the payment of the elders who teach, and the treatment of those elders who diverge from what is appropriate, ending with the warning not to be hasty in the laying on of hands (5.17-22); (i) towards the end of the letter there is a rather lengthy section on attitudes to money, and on the attitude of those who regard godliness as a means of gain (6.5-10), followed by directions on the treatment of the rich (6.17-19).[11]

C. *The Purpose of Titus*

Since the letter to Titus, like 1 Timothy, has not a thanksgiving period, we do not have a formal opening statement of the themes of the letter. We shall first outline the main contents of the letter, and then suggest the reasons why Paul wrote it.

The letter seems to concern itself almost entirely with the question of Titus being directed by Paul to set up a structure for the community in every town in Crete. It would appear from 1.5 that Paul had left Crete, leaving Titus behind him. Whether or not Paul had already orally requested Titus to set up a group of elders in every town, he does so now in the letter immediately after the greeting. Paul undoubtedly realized that the most effective way of countering the false teaching was by organizing the community.[12] In Titus the appointment of community leaders is the first task, and the list of exhortations to each group in the hierarchy is interspersed with references to false teachers and their teaching (*passim*).

There is a great stress on good behaviour throughout this letter, as if to emphasize that the Christian life is not a matter of mere words or ideas, but one that expresses itself in the living out of life.[13] Such is the concentration on good behaviour that one could well suggest that Paul's main intention in writing this letter was to require of Titus an insistence upon a religion of good behaviour and good deeds. This is abundantly clear in the series of instructions given for the bishop (1.7-11), for older men (2.3), older women (2.3), younger women (2.4f.), younger men (2.6), and slaves (2.9f.). It is clear above all else in the insistence of the appeal to good behaviour that runs through the letter like a chorus.[14]

We propose that Paul's purpose in writing this letter to Titus was threefold: (a) Paul wished Titus to amend what was defective in the church in Crete, and to set up a group of elders in every town;[15] (b) Paul wished Titus to show his authority, and exercise his responsibility in his way of governing the community;[16] and (c) Paul insists on a religion of good behaviour, whose 'missionary' character is accented.

D. *Evaluation*

Our examination of the contents of the Pastoral Letters makes it quite clear that each of them has its own particular purpose. They should not be treated as if they shared the same preoccupations. We have indicated a real epistolary situation for each letter. Our major concern is 2 Timothy, which as we have shown is quite different from the other two in the primary question of purpose. We have argued that Paul had two major concerns as he wrote 2 Timothy, namely, his desire for Timothy to come, and his fears for Timothy's faith and fidelity to his vocation. We shall see that these two items are interrelated, but first we must propose a more precise setting for the letter.

When one attempts to situate 2 Timothy in the life of Paul, two items of information are vital. In the first place, while writing the letter Paul appears to be in prison (2 Tim 1.16; 4.16ff.), and, secondly, he was either in Rome, or had already been there (2 Tim 1.17). The combination of these two factors suggests that the letter was written most likely from a Roman imprisonment, although one cannot rule out the possibility that the imprisonment may have been elsewhere, but after Paul had been to Rome. Rather than speculate about possible but unknown conditions after a Roman imprisonment, it is more appropriate to attempt to make sense of the text in terms of the known movements of Paul's life.

We argue that Paul was in prison in Rome at the time of writing 2 Timothy. We must enquire into his circumstances in the imperial capital, consider the likely outcome of his trial, and examine the evidence for the last years of Paul's life.

2. *The Place of Writing of Second Timothy: Rome*

2 Timothy is the only captivity letter of Paul that appears to give its place of origin. Some attempts have been made to try to avoid the natural meaning of 2 Tim 1.17. The suggestion that ῥώμῃ means 'strength', rather than Rome, would give the meaning, 'May the Lord give mercy to the household of Onesiphorus, for he often refreshed me and was not ashamed of my chains, but when he regained his strength he diligently sought and found me' (2 Tim 1.16f.). But this suggestion has not been taken seriously.[17]

Duncan's suggestion that 'in Rome' should read 'in Priene', and later 'in Laodicea' is no less fanciful (1929: 106; ·1956/7: 218). Badcock, too, emended the text of 2 Tim 1.17, and attempted to show how the original 'in (Pisidian) Antioch' became 'in Rome'. He claimed that his conclusion 'is all but irresistible' (1937: 158). Badcock's arguments, however, appear to have convinced nobody but himself, and rightly so. Lewis Johnson regarded the offending phrase in 1.17 as a highly probable gloss (1956/7: 25). Robinson suggests that Onesiphorus indeed searched out Paul when he got to Rome, but did not find him there, but found him subsequently in Caesarea (1976: 75f.).[18] Wilhelm-Hooijbergh, another supporter of a Caesarean origin for 2 Timothy, leaves 'in Rome' intact, as does Robinson, but her reading, 'But having been in Rome he searched for me hastily (in Caesarea) and found me, etc'. (1980: 436) is based on a fundamental error concerning the tense of a participle. She insists that γενόμενος means 'being (in the past)', and 'having been' (p. 435). This is not so, since the proper and leading function of the Aorist Participle is not to express time, but to mark the fact that the action of the verb is conceived of indefinitely, as a single event.[19]

None of the attempts to interpret 2 Tim 1.16f. which we have discussed, is sufficiently strong to undermine the obvious meaning of the text. Respect for the manuscript tradition should eliminate any interpretation that demands regarding 'in Rome' to be either a gloss, or a corruption of an original reading. The arguments of Reicke and Robinson force the text into an already preconceived framework for the letter, while that of Wilhelm-Hooijbergh, which is based on a basic error concerning the tense of participles, lacks all conviction.[20]

There seems to be no compelling reason to abandon the almost universally agreed reading of the text, namely, that at the time of writing that verse Paul himself was in Rome, or, in the event of 2 Timothy being a pseudepigraphon, the author intended to place Paul there at that time.

3. *Paul's Circumstances in Rome and his Likely Release*

We regard it as very likely, then, that at the time of writing 2 Timothy Paul was in prison in Rome (2 Tim 1.16f.), and that the first part of a hearing against him had already taken place (2 Tim 4.16ff.). The question naturally arises as to what period in Paul's life this Roman imprisonment refers. The most obvious candidate must be the only Roman imprisonment about which we have definite information, namely that which followed his arrival in the city of Rome. We suggest that is mainly the conventional understanding of 2 Tim 4.6ff. that makes this interpretation problematic, and the reading of that critical text which we propose in Chapter 5 goes a long distance in removing the difficulty.

What were Paul's circumstances in Rome? We shall examine the evidence concerning the charges against Paul, and the likely outcome of the Roman trial. The major source of information here is the Acts of the Apostles, but we shall also examine other early Christian documents which suggest the outcome of the Roman legal process.

A. *The Value of the Evidence in Acts*

Because of the importance of Acts as a source for the life of Paul, and in particular for his later years with which we propose to deal in some detail, it is necessary to consider the vexed question of the value of the Acts as a historical source. One would like to know 'What really happened?' The question is a legitimate one, even if there is difficulty in answering it satisfactorily. It is a question of historicity, and no amount of purely literary, or theological investigation can give us the answer to the question.

Clearly the value of the final statement of Acts is dependent upon the reliability of the sources available to the author, and upon his faithfulness in recording the information of his sources. Unfortunately for our purposes there is no one theory of sources which claims the widespread support of scholars.[21] In particular there is a great spread of opinion regarding the authenticity of the 'we-section' of Acts. At one pole stands the opinion that the author of Acts was an eyewitness of the events encompassed by the 'we-sections', or at least that those sections were part of an eye-witness source available to the author. At the other pole one finds the interpretation that the 'we-sections' were merely a literary device of the author designed to make the reader feel that he was actually participating in the events (Dupont 1964: 167; followed by Haenchen 1965). But Dupont's solution is not sufficient to answer the historical question. The most that one can say is that the author could possibly have used such a device, and it is incumbent on the supporters of that view to give reasons why this possibility should be raised to a probability, if not indeed to an historical fact.[22]

Although it is beyond the scope of the present study to engage in an exhaustive examination of the merits of Luke as some blend of historiographer and theologian, it is necessary to record some observations, since the reliability of so much of our knowledge of Paul depends on the validity of Luke's testimony in the Acts.

The *Actaforschung* over the last century and a half warns us against a simplistic interpretation of the text. The value of the documents as a historical work is very much in question. Most exegetes in this century have shown more interest in source and redaction questions, than in ones of historicity.[23] Dibelius, the most influential figure in the *Actaforschung* since Baur, shared with Baur an assessment of the author of Luke–Acts as a creative writer, who invented speeches, who was not primarily interested in communicating what really happened, and whose orientation was fundamentally influenced by his post-apostolic theology.[24]

Haenchen systematically applied Dibelius's general methodology to the interpretation of each part of the Acts. His commentary on Acts (1965) marks a turning-point in the interpretation of the book. He goes further than Dibelius in his scepticism concerning the historical value of the work. He allows great literary scope to the author who embellished at will the elements of tradition passed on to him, so that he could more effectively influence the Church of his own day. Haenchen is not unaware of the arbitrariness of his procedure. He confesses that in his hypothesis the line between tradition and literary embellishment cannot always be clearly drawn. He acknowledges that one is moving within the realm of the possible, at most the probable, but in no sense the rigorously demonstrable (1965: 88). The reader gets the impression that Haenchen's discussion is hampered by his view of the *Tendenz* of the author. The two theological questions of the *author's* day were concerned with the expectation of the imminent end of the world, and the mission to the Gentiles without the law (p. 94).[25]

Such, according to Haenchen, was the author's theological task. Whatever got in the way of a straightforward history of primitive Christianity had to be smoothed out or omitted (pp. 98f.). Luke could not write a history of the dawn of Christianity, because he lacked an adequate historical foundation, and the right readers. His work had to be one of *edification*.[26]

Conzelmann allows an even greater freedom of composition to the author than Haenchen does, and thereby has even less regard for Acts as an historical work.[27] Other scholars, however, including some who are not primarily NT exegetes, have been impressed by Luke's calibre as a historiographer. Both Ramsay[28] and Harnack[29] were converts to the assessment of Acts as a reliable historical work. The ancient historian, Eduard Meyer, put Luke on the same level as the great historians of ancient times, Polybius, Livy, and others (1923).[30] Sherwin-White, too, is very impressed by Acts' detailed knowledge of first century Asia Minor and Greece (1963: 85-93, 120).

There is an increasingly louder chorus of voices calling attention to a more critical view of Luke as historiographer,[31] even though it is sometimes the case that only lip-service is paid to the view that Luke is a historian as well as a theologian.[32] If source and redaction questions have dominated the *Actaforschung* up to very recently, it is clear that the value of Luke as a historian is being considered afresh. The future *Actaforschungen* will take much more account of the historical value of Acts, and this will have to be done in conjunction with the closest attention to matters of form and redaction criticism.

The primary interest here is in the value of Acts as a source of information about the last years of Paul's life. Unfortunately, we do not possess an alternative presentation of that material. In the case of the Synoptic Gospels, we have the 'parallel' gospels of Matthew and Mark to guide us in our assessment of Luke as a historian. One does not get the impression from the third Gospel that the author was disrespectful to his sources, or that he behaved in a way that would have been irresponsible for a historian of his own day. It would be strange, then, if the same author displayed altogether opposite characteristics in that half of his work for which we have no parallel.

We have also the evidence presented by Ramsay showing the familiarity of the author (or his sources) with the geography and the administrative procedures of Asia Minor and Greece. In addition there is the material discussed by Sherwin-White[33] and others such as Hemer, and the sources they quote, which deal with constitutional and other matters. Those authors were very impressed by the author's accuracy in his information. It does not follow, of course, that an author is reliable throughout his whole work simply because he has been shown to be for some parts of it. However, although there is a wide spectrum of opinion as to the historicity of Acts it is the case that scholars in general have more confidence in the reliability of that part of the work which is of interest here.[34]

Our judgment is that whether or not the author depended on his own reminiscences of what happened, or on those of Aristarchus of Thessalonica, or some other companion of Paul, the account is as close to what actually happened, as his accounts of Paul's movements elsewhere in the Acts conform to what really happened. It is only to be expected that the core events should be mediated through the literary skills and theological interests of the author.[35]

Our view is that the scepticism regarding the historical reliability of Acts is strongly influenced, if not altogether determined by decisions taken by scholars regarding the intention of the author. A clear distinction must be made between the conscious intention of an author, and what readers consider it to be from reading the text. Because of the diversity of dispositions among readers there will always be a legitimate diversity of views concerning the significance of a work. It is not acceptable, however, to ascribe one's own understanding of a text to the conscious intentionality of the author.[36]

The position taken here is that Luke–Acts was completed before the death of Paul. The compelling argument for us is the failure of the author to mention Paul's fate, or to allude to situations which occurred after the date implied in the conclusion to the second volume. There is no hint of any persecution under Nero, which is remarkable, since that experience must have made a great impression on the Roman Christians. And, of course, there is no mention of the destruction of Jerusalem, which might well have been alluded to in Acts 6–7 or 21–23. This position has not been reached without a careful examination of the problems which this dating implies.[37] As any broad survey of the history of critical investigation shows, there has always been a great diversity of views concerning the historicity of Acts.[38] None of the problems posed by our dating is incapable of a satisfactory explanation. It is our view that no solution to the dating of Acts which puts it after the death of Paul adequately solves the problem of the abrupt ending, a subject to which we shall return.

Whether the author was Luke, or some other companion of Paul, and an eye-witness of much of what he records we leave to one side.[39] Authorship by a companion of Paul is no guarantee of trustworthiness, and a reliable second-hand witness can excel the first-hand impressions of eye-witnesses (Cadbury 1958: 363). Nor does it follow that accuracy, or inaccuracy in some details guarantees, or vitiates the reliability of the whole work. Where the author's accuracy is susceptible to some degree of testing, e.g., in the Gospel with which we can compare the accounts in Matthew and Mark, and in the Letters wherein we find some corresponding material, and in the archaeological, geographical, political and legal context, we judge him to be generally reliable.

Since the position taken in this work is that 2 Timothy was composed by Paul while he was on trial in Rome it is of particular interest to enquire into the nature of the charges against Paul, and the likely outcome of the legal process. The Acts of the Apostles is our major source of information for these matters. We shall deal with the arrest and trials of Paul in Palestine, and the likely outcome of his case in Rome.

B. *The Arrest and Trials of Paul*

Although there are seven stages in the process which began with the private arrest of Paul in the Temple in Jerusalem, and ended with his departure from Caesarea to Rome,[40] only three of those seven elements describe formal court hearings: that before Lysias, the tribune, in Jerusalem, and those before Felix and Festus in Caesarea. The hearing before Lysias is presented in a rather diffused manner, with the charges being made by the Asian Jews. It was only after the ensuing commotion that the tribune arrived, and then the council sat to act as Lysias's *consilium*. Lysias gave his verdict in his *Libellus* to Felix.

The hearing in the presence of Festus had two sessions, with the second functioning also as a *consilium* to help him compose his *Libellus* for the Roman hearing. The first stage gives important background information. It is clear from it that the community of the Way in Jerusalem is presented as being aware of the criticism which Paul's mission had brought on himself. The complaint of the Jews was that Paul had apostatized from the Mosaic traditions (21.21). This is also one of the 'charges' brought by the Asiatic Jews in the Temple (21.27f.). Furthermore, Paul's protestation before the Sanhedrin that he was a most observant Pharisee (23.6) highlights the Jewish nature of his problem. A charge of seditious behaviour among Jews everywhere is formally made by the High Priest and elders, through their spokesman, Tertullus (24.5). Charges of transgression of the Law were made before Festus (cf. 25.8), and in his defence speech before Agrippa, Paul once more defended his position *vis-à-vis* the Law and the Prophets (26.5-8).

It is clear, then, that central to the legal accusation against Paul was the claim that he behaved in a totally unacceptable way as far as orthodox Jews were concerned. But the actual charge made against Paul is difficult to determine, since Luke merely gives a covering phrase, such as 'against the law of the Jews' (25.8), or 'against the people and the law' (21.28). The only specific element is the reference to Paul's being said to have advocated diaspora Jews not to circumcize, nor observe some Mosaic customs (21.21). These crimes were alleged to have taken place in the course of Paul's journeys, rather than in Jerusalem. The only witnesses to that behaviour were the Jews of the diaspora who are never reported by Luke as formally making any charge in the presence of the appropriate official: in Jerusalem it was only after the commotion following the charges that Lysias arrived on the scene (22.22), while we know that the Asiatic Jews were not present in Caesarea since Paul drew attention to the absence of his accusers (24.17ff.).

The best explanation of the procedure is that the Sanhedrin took over the charges of the diaspora Jews and dealt with them in their submission through Tertullus (24.5f.); they had already dealt with the question at the Sanhedrin 'hearing' described in chapter 23. That the charges involved considerable discussion about the Law is clear from Lysias's *Libellus* to Felix (23.29), and from Festus's summary of the situation for Agrippa (25.18f.), and from the 'hearing' before Agrippa during which Paul dealt at some length with the interpretation of the Prophets and Moses. In the nature of the case it is most unlikely that the civil authority would have considered itself competent to judge on such matters, and, like Gallio in Corinth (Acts 18.12-17), they would have put the ball back into the court of the Jewish authorities.

Considering the public disturbance that accompanied Paul in the course of his missions it is remarkable that such matters were not alluded to in the course of the hearings. The charge that Paul was a λοιμός (a common term of abuse, corresponding to our 'plague', or 'pest') does not necessarily imply a public disturbance. That there was no serious charge of being a public nuisance is suggested by the 'verdicts' of Lysias (23.29), Festus (25.18f.), and Agrippa (26.31f.).

Concerning the charge that Paul had defiled the Temple, we are dealing with the incident in the Temple soon after Paul had arrived in the city. On balance it would appear that Paul did not in fact defile the Temple. In any case Luke points out that the Asiatic Jews had seen Trophimus *in the city*, and *had supposed* that Paul had brought him into the Temple (21.29). And before Felix, the charge was diluted, becoming only an attempt to profane the Temple (24.6). The absence of the Asiatic Jews who were witnesses also suggests that this charge could not be substantiated. However, such a charge appears to have been made again two years after the event, before Festus, since we find Paul denying it (25.8).[41]

In any case it appears that the secular authorities at each point considered Paul to have done nothing worthy of death, or even imprisonment (23.29; 25.18f.; 26.31). That the Jews considered their charge to be unlikely to be upheld in a law court is suggested by the hatching of two plots to assassinate Paul outside the court (23.12-15; 25.3). Moreover, when Paul got to Rome he informed the Roman Jews that the Roman authorities had acquitted him of any crime that was punishable by death, and that indeed he would have been released had he not appealed to Caesar (28.18). Furthermore, he makes it clear to them that he did not intend pressing any charges against his nation—presumably he had in mind those difficulties he could cause the Jews since they had not been able to make good their accusations (Lake and Cadbury 1933a: 346).

In the hearing before Felix, Paul is formally charged with being a ringleader, or even *the* ringleader of the sect of the Nazareans (24.5), which, of course, had not only religious but also civil implications. That there was a strong theological element in the charge against Paul is suggested also by Paul's own insistence that he was on trial 'with respect to the hope and the resurrection of the dead' (23.6; cf. 24.20f.; 25.6ff.; 28.20); see also the many references to his position within the tradition of the Law and the Prophets (24.14; cf. 26.22), and his tactic of bringing the Pharisee party over to his side at the meeting of the council (23.9). Such a charge would also appear to be behind Paul's insistence before Festus that he had done no wrong against Caesar (25.8).

The civil authority at several stages pointed to his innocence of any civil crime, and it appears that whatever trouble would come Paul's way would come from the Jews.[42] Significantly, one of Paul's first acts on reaching Rome was to call together the local leaders of the Jews (28.17). They might have been expected to host the Jewish witnesses from Jerusalem, or to present the Jewish case before the Roman tribunal. Their response to Paul leads one to conclude that the presentation of the Jewish side of the affair was not going to be very powerful, since the Roman Jews had not heard, either by letter or from an ambassador, anything incriminatory of Paul (28.21).

When Paul arrived in Rome he was, according to the Western Text handed over to the *stratopedarchos*, the commander of the camp (Acts 28.16), who is most likely to have been in executive control of prisoners awaiting trial in Rome. With regard to the identity of the person before whom Paul is most likely to have appeared we know only that while Claudius was particularly zealous to hear such cases of appeal, Nero normally delegated the responsibility of hearing the case to someone else, and he responded to the delegate's judgment as he saw fit. If Paul was brought to trial some time after the two years of Acts 28.30, then, somebody other than the Emperor himself most likely heard the case.[43] What was the likely outcome of the hearing?

The assurance of the Roman Jewish leaders that they had received no instructions about the case, or no bad report about Paul (Acts 28.21) might very well suggest that the Jewish authorities did not pursue the charge against Paul, and in particular did not send any authorized witnesses to press their case. But such a conclusion does not follow, since the necessary steps could have been taken after Paul had met the Jews of Rome.

The absence of exact knowledge of the legal procedure prevents us being certain of what is likely to have happened. Lake suggested that the prisoner would have been released if the accusers failed to appear, and he proposed that the two-year time-span mentioned at the end of the Acts marked the end of the waiting period. After that, he suggested, Paul was released. His solution, he claimed, relieves us of the necessity of accounting for what some refer to as Luke's abrupt ending of the Acts, and supplies us with a conclusion favourable to Paul and consistent with the other optimistic hints in the book. But the absence of direct evidence, he confessed, prevents the suggestion from rising above the level of an attractive conjecture (Lake and Cadbury 1933a: 330). Sherwin-White, however, shows convincingly that the Roman tradition in this matter, rather, insisted that the prosecutor prosecute, and that the prisoner be tried: 'The protection of the accused person lay not in any provision for automatic release if the accuser were absent, but in the severity of the sanctions against defaulting prosecutors'.[44]

It is our contention that Paul was actually tried, and that

2 Timothy contains very important hints about the outcome. But at this point we wish only to bring together some reflections on the likely outcome of such a trial, in view of the charges made against Paul.

Our reading of the evidence presented by the Acts suggests that Paul's life was in no danger from the imperial authorities in Rome. This seems the obvious conclusion from the Acts when one takes account not only of the several protestations of Paul's innocence on the Part of the Roman authorities (Lysias, Festus, and Agrippa in turn), but also of the non-appearance of vital witnesses in Caesarea, of the extra-judicial plots to assassinate Paul, and of the ignorance of the Roman Jews concerning the matter. It is confirmed by the relative freedom Paul enjoyed in Caesarea, and on his way to, and while in Rome itself. His ability in the capital to call big numbers to his apartment, and his freedom to preach and teach with all boldness and unhindered make it appear most unlikely that his appeal to Caesar on that occasion would result in his being condemned to death. All the evidence points in the opposite direction.

Since the author consistently reports the favourable judgments of the secular authorities on each occasion, it is very difficult to imagine that he considered that the course of events would now at this final stage take a quite different direction. The account in Acts nowhere suggests that Paul was about to meet his end, at least as long as his fate was in the hands of the secular authority. On the contrary, there is every indication in the text that the case would be resolved in Paul's acquittal, just as it was before in Philippi (16.35), Corinth (18.15) and Ephesus (19.37), and would have done in Caesarea before Festus and Agrippa, had Paul not appealed to Caesar.

It can, or course, be objected that the author of Acts was not interested in presenting the course of the legal proceedings with any precision. His motivation, rather, could have been the desire to assure his readers that the new movement was neither a threat to the Empire, nor a deviation from an authentic interpretation of the Law and the Prophets. Or, perhaps his desire was to show that the Way turned from the Jewish community only because the latter had rejected its message. Or the whole work can be viewed as being aimed at Gentiles, showing that they have nothing to fear from associating with Christianity.[45]

It is our contention that the readers of Acts would have been led, at least from Acts 21.27 on, to the expectation that Paul would be

adjudged innocent of any serious crime. It is a recurring theme of the
later chapters of Acts that Roman law protects a Christian.[46] It is,
then, difficult to believe that at the time of writing, the author, and
also his Roman readers at least, knew that Paul was not in fact
acquitted, but that the Roman authorities had found him guilty and
even executed him. If that had already happened, all of the author's
earlier protestations of Paul's innocence by the secular authorities
would most certainly be hollow, and would scarcely encourage the
reader to take the author seriously. If at the time of writing of the
final chapters of Acts Paul had already been found guilty and
condemned to be (or in fact had already been) executed by the
Roman authorities, the author would have to have had recourse to
exceptional literary ingenuity to defend the innocence of the
Christian religion.

It is true, of course, that the Acts' account of Paul's innocence may
witness only to the author's optimism about the outcome of the legal
process, which is not at all the same thing as saying that Paul was in
fact acquitted. If, however, the author was even close to the historical
circumstances of Paul's process his optimism is a powerful argument
against the likelihood of a gloomy outcome for Paul.

But despite what we consider to be the optimistic picture of Paul's
legal processes which Luke gives in the Acts, there is a considerable
body of opinion which claims that Paul's death came immediately, or
at least soon after the period mentioned at the end of Acts.[47]

C. *The Ending of Acts*

The general optimistic picture of Paul's innocence which impresses
the reader of the Acts 21–28, is reflected also in the final verses of
that work. It is one of the great surprises of the eight-chapter account
of Paul's trial and journey to Rome in the Acts that it is silent about
the outcome of Paul's trial and about the end of his life. Harnack
remarked that that is scarcely more unexpected than if somebody
ended the history of Jesus with his being brought before Pilate (1911:
67). Haenchen, however, offers an altogether different explanation.
He ends his commentary by claiming that Luke implies the
execution of Paul (Acts 20.25, 28), but avoids describing it for fear of
creating a martyr piety (1965: 732). We note in passing that Luke
does not seem to have had any such qualms about describing the fate
of Jesus and Stephen.[48]

Many reasons have been suggested for the abrupt ending.[49] Some of those suggestions seem to be recourses of desperation, and a major factor in tolerating them is the judgment that the Acts was written long after the events described.[50]

Harnack's own view was that at the time the Acts was written the outcome of Paul's trial was not known. There is no point, he claims, in struggling against that conclusion (1911: 68f.). He had proposed a date of composition no later than 78 AD, and changed first to the early sixties, and finally opted for a date of composition immediately after the termination of the two years of Acts 28.30.[51] This also is substantially the view of Bruce, Munck, and others.[52] However, rather than propose that the whole of Luke–Acts was composed before the death of Paul, we would suggest only that the ending of the Acts reflects the situation as known at the time of the composition of that section, since it is advisable to allow for the possibility that the work was composed in several stages.[53]

We propose, then, that Acts 28 reflects the situation known in approx. 62 AD. There is nothing in that chapter or the earlier ones that leads one to expect the imminent or approaching condemnation of Paul in the Roman court. Rather it is in line with the thrust of the Acts that Paul has nothing to fear from the civil Roman authorities, and that the process would result along the optimistic lines indicated in so many places in the course of the lengthy legal process. We agree with Lake that the account in Acts seems 'to point to an issue favourable to Paul, for there is a continuous and surely intentional emphasis throughout the book on the fact that Paul was never found guilty by any Roman court. I find it hard to think that Luke would have written in this way, if he had known that the last and most important trial of all was unfavourable to his argument' (1909: 327).

We see nothing in the Acts to justify the conclusion that Paul's death followed immediately on the course of events described at the end of the Acts. On the contrary, there is considerable support for the conclusion that Paul was likely to have been acquitted in Rome, and was, therefore, free, if he so wished, to bring his message further afield.[54]

D. *Other Supporting Evidence*

In addition to the Acts of the Apostles, other sources support the claim that Paul did not suffer death on the occasion of his first visit to Rome. Some verses in the Captivity Letters reflect Paul's confidence of his release, while several traditions demand a release and a subsequent mission.

Of the four Captivity Letters, only Philippians and Philemon explicitly reflect Paul's confidence about the outcome of his imprisonment. The relevance of these two to the discussion of Paul's legal process is compromised by the fact that there is great uncertaintly about their place(s) of origin, and there does not appear to be any significant movement towards a consensus on the matter, nor has any fresh evidence been advanced to settle the question.[55] A further problem is posed by the uncertainty whether the text of Philippians as we have it is that of one letter, or whether it was composed of material from two or three letters sent at different times.[56]

The nature of the evidence does not permit one to prove conclusively the place of origin of Philippians and Philemon. We are left with a choice between degrees of probability. Most commentators acknowledge the difficulty of deciding the question, and those who do make a choice indicate their preference with timidity.[57] We have argued elsewhere that Philippians is more likely to have been written from a Roman prison, than from either the imprisonment in Caesarea or a hypothetical one in Ephesus. We also concluded that the argument for a Roman origin for Philemon is not as strong, and that the absence of precise information prevents one from deciding with any confidence between Rome and Caesarea (Prior 1985: 105-15). In addition we draw attention to the similarity of the situation reflected in Philippians and in 2 Timothy, which letter contains the clearest indication of its place of origin. We note the similar striking metaphors in Phil 2.17 and 2 Tim 4.6; Phil 2.16; 3.12ff. and 2 Tim 4.7; Phil 1.27, 30; 4.3 and 2 Tim 4.7; and Phil 4.13 and 2 Tim 4.17. Moreover, the situation in both (e.g., Phil 1.7 and 2 Tim 4.16) is consistent with what was likely to have happened after the two-year period with which Acts concludes its account (pp. 109f.).

Writing to Philemon, Apphia, Archippus and the house-church, Paul (with Timothy at his side) asks that a guest room be prepared for him (Phlm 22). Phil 1.25 clearly expresses Paul's confidence for the future, and at 2.23f. he writes of his confidence that he shall be able to visit the Philippian community. If either of these letters was written from a Roman prison we have clear evidence that Paul considered his liberation to be only a matter of time. If either was written from Caesarea the strong confidence would reflect his hopes of release after the hearing of the case against him, or at least of sufficient liberty to spend some time with his friends. If one, or both were written from an imprisonment in Ephesus or Corinth they are irrelevant for our purpose.

Philippians very likely, and Philemon somewhat less so, reflects Paul's optimism about the favourable outcome of his case in Rome, a confidence that echoes Luke's account of Paul's innocence,[58] and one that is consistent with our reading of 2 Timothy. And even if Philippians is from Caesarea rather than Rome, it also reflects Paul's confidence that he would be released, and thus escape death.

Later traditions also point in the same direction. The earliest evidence in support of a supposed ministry of Paul that included a territory west of Rome is that of *1 Clement*. The value of his testimony is enhanced by the fact that the letter was written only some thirty years after the Apostle's death (c. 96 AD),[59] and from the city in which Paul spent at least two years (Acts 28.30f.), and in which he died. Even if Clement did not know Paul personally, it is reasonable to suspect that his knowledge of Paul was reliable.[60] The fact that Clement does not specify the location of Paul's further activity is not important for our discussion at this point. It is sufficient to recognize that Clement appears to refer to Pauline activity beyond Rome, which demands, of course, that Paul was released from his imprisonment in Rome.

1 Clement relates that Paul preached ἔν τῇ ἀνατολῇ καὶ ἐν τῇ δύσει and that he taught righteousness ὅλον τὸν κόσμον; that he reached the furthest limits of the west (καὶ ἐπὶ τὸ τέρμα τῆς δύσεως ἐλθών), and that bearing testimony before the rulers (ἐπὶ τῶν ἡγουμένων) he passed out of this world and was received into the holy place (*1 Clem.* V). It does not seem plausible that a Roman, writing from Rome, could describe Rome by ἐν τῇ δύσει, since almost half of the Empire lay west of the capital.[61] Clement was writing only thirty years after Paul's death, in a church which must have had the fullest information about the last years of Paul's life. Moreover, the time of writing was sufficiently close to the deeds referred to for several members of the community to be able to check the facts. Therefore, it is reasonable to conclude that Clement offers reliable evidence in support of our contention that Paul was not condemned to death on the hearing of his case in Rome, but that he was released from prison.[62]

Paul's visit to Spain is the core of par. 1-3 of *The Acts of Peter*, is referred to in par. 4.2, 6, while in par. 40 Paul is reported to have returned to Rome after Peter's death. The Greek original of this document dates from c. 180-190. As early as 180, then, there was a tradition of Paul having been given permission by Quartus, a prison officer, to go where he wished, as a result of which he went to Spain.

But the historical value of that testimony to a Pauline journey to Spain is questionable, since it can be proposed that the tradition, embellished as it is by many legendary elements, arose not from fact, but from Paul's known intentions as outlined in Rom 15.24, 28.[63] However, the text itself does not mention Paul's apostolic intentions as stated in Romans 15, which one might expect were that text the source of the author's creative imagination, and it must be insisted that there is no reason to identify this Quartus with the brother of the same name in Rom 16.23. The possibility that the document preserves a historical core of a Pauline mission to Spain ought not to be rejected out of hand. That the author attributes such a trip to the freedom Paul enjoyed while under guard opens up the fascinating question of whether it was possible for Paul to move out of Rome while awaiting the hearing of his case there. The document is silent on the death of Paul.

The value of the testimony of *Fragmentum Muratorianum* is dependent upon its date and place of composition. The consensus is that it was written in Rome towards the end of the second century AD, and we shall proceed on that basis.[64] Lines 38f. clearly state that Paul went from the city (Rome) to Spain, and the text, therefore, is further support to our contention that Paul was released from prison in Rome, and embarked on further missionary activity.[65]

In his *His. Eccles.* Bk. II, ch. 22, Eusebius deals with Paul's arrival in Rome. He uses the information in the Acts to relate that Paul had been tried before Festus, and had been taken as a prisoner to Rome. He knows from Acts 27.2 that Aristarchus was with Paul, and he reminds the reader that this man is called a fellow prisoner in one of the epistles (Col 4.10). He then refers to Luke's having finished the Acts with the statement that Paul spent two whole years in Rome in freedom, preaching the word without hindrance (Acts 28.30f.). He goes on to say 'tradition has it', or, 'there is a report' (λόγος ἔχει) that Paul, 'after defending himself', or, 'having been brought to trial' (ἀπολογησάμενον) set out on a ministry of preaching (ἐπὶ τὴν τοῦ κηρύγματος διακονίαν). There is no mention of any place in which this ministry was carried out, but it is clear that it was outside Rome, for he records that Paul came to Rome a second time, and suffered martyrdom under Nero.

He goes on to say that it was during this second imprisonment that Paul wrote 2 Timothy, and he takes 2 Tim 4.16 to refer to a first imprisonment. He considers Paul's delivery from the lion's mouth (which he takes to refer to Nero and his ferocity) to refer to Paul's having some time before been released from the Roman imprisonment. But now the situation was worse, for he regards 4.18 as indicating Paul's impending martyrdom, which, he claims, was foretold even more clearly already in 4.6. During the earlier trial no one was with him, but now Luke was in his company. Nero, he suggests, had gentler dispositions in the earlier situation, but the emperor was now becoming more reckless and was attacking even the Apostles.

Once more we have to acknowledge that the value of Eusebius's testimony depends on his reliability as a historian, which is a highly disputed subject.[66] We consider that 2 Timothy provided Eusebius with a text which he interpreted in a way that was consistent with a tradition that Paul had been released and had embarked on another mission.

E. *Evaluation*

We have examined the evidence offered by Acts, the Captivity Letters Philippians and Philemon, *1 Clement*, the *Acts of Peter*, the *Muratorian Fragment* and Eusebius concerning the (likely) outcome of Paul's process in Rome. The evidence from the Acts of the Apostles points in the direction of a favourable outcome to Paul's trial. It appears to be the author's view that the legal process against Paul,which began in Jerusalem, looked favourable in Caesarea, and which reached its conclusion in Rome, would issue in his acquittal. If Philippians and Philemon were written from a Roman imprisonment they reflect Paul's confidence also that he would be released. If either one was written from Caesarea the strength of the evidence for a future release is somewhat diluted, but not eliminated. The evidence of *1 Clement* demands a release from imprisonment and a mission west of the Capital. Both the *Acts of Peter* and the *Muratorian Fragment* witness to a tradition of a release from Rome and a mission to Spain. There is no evidence to indicate that those traditions are based on a fulfilment of Romans 15. Eusebius testifies to a tradition that Paul was released, that he engaged in subsequent missionary activity, and that he was subsequently re-arrested, tried and condemned.[67]

The combination of evidence from all these sources suggests that Paul was likely to be acquitted, was in fact acquitted and undertook additional missionary activity.[68] Such an interpretation of the evidence will be seen to fit our interpretation of Second Timothy, namely, that it was written by Paul from his Roman prison, after the first difficult hearing of his case (after which he was, nevertheless, confident of his release), and before his acquittal, at a time when his eyes were fixed on another missionary journey for which he was preparing an apostolic team.

But our knowledge of the outcome of the Roman legal process is advanced also by enquiring into the last years of the Apostle's life, and it is to this that we now turn.

4. *The Last Years of Paul's Life*

Our knowledge of the circumstances of the last years of Paul's life is altogether unsatisfactory. 'The historian ... has no option but to ... admit frankly (if not cheerfully) that from the primary sources he can recover practically no hard data, chronological or geographical, about the last days of the apostle'.[69] In particular, we would like to know what amount of time was available to Paul between his acquittal in the Roman court and his subsequent death.

The problem is exacerbated by the uncertainty regarding the chronology of Paul's life.[70] The dates of particular interest here are those of the change-over from Felix to Festus as governor of Judea, and the death of Nero, since the first suggests a date for Paul's arrival in Rome, and the latter is the latest possible date for Paul's death, according to some sources. We do know that Nero committed suicide in 68 AD, but as to the date of the accession of Festus there is still keen debate.

Autumn 52 and Spring 53 are the favoured dates for the accession of Felix as governor of Judea.[71] At the other end we know that Festus's successor was in office in 62 AD. (Josephus *Bell. Jud.* VI,301ff.), and most historians assume that he came to power in that year. We have, then, a ten-year period spanning the time in office of Felix and his successor, Festus. The problem is how to divide the period between the two.

Josephus (*Antiq.* XX,8.9) informs us that after Felix was recalled from Judea his brother, Pallas, saved him from complete disaster. Although the sources are not in agreement, it is likely that Pallas fell from office late in 55 AD, thus placing Felix's recall before the end of 55, and probably in the spring of that year.[72] If, then, one understands the two-year period of Acts 24.27 to refer to Felix's proconsulship, rather than to Paul's imprisonment,[73] we could have Paul leaving Caesarea for Rome in the second half of 55 and arriving in the capital no later than spring 56. The end of the two year period in Acts 28.30f. would, in this scenario, come as early as 58 AD, no less than ten years before the death of Nero.[74].

On the other hand one gets the impression from Josephus (*Bell. Jud.*, II,247-276) that Felix was highly active, while Festus's activities are mentioned only in the most general terms and very briefly, during the period we know to be c. 52-62 AD. Indeed, it has been suggested that no less than seven or eight years would have been necessary for Felix to have accomplished so much.[75] That and the reference to Felix's 'many years' as judge over the nation (Acts 24.10) put Festus's accession later, probably in the summer of 59, or 60 AD.[76] In this scenario, then, Paul arrived in Rome early in 60 AD, bringing the period of the 'house-arrest' to an end in 62, six years before the death of Nero. Although this conclusion has much to commend it, it is not without its critics.[77]

If, then, Paul's death occurred during the reign of Nero it did so between the years 58-68 AD, or the years 62-68 AD.[78] Let us examine what the sources say. The evidence from Christian sources can be categorized as follows: those which describe the death as a martyrdom under Nero; those which specify the manner of death as a beheading; and those which associate Peter and Paul together in their death. The works of Suetonius and Tacitus are the major secular sources.

A. *Sources which describe the Death as a Martyrdom under Nero*
In *The Acts of Peter* the death of Paul is not reported as a fact, but only as a prediction in a message from heaven, which said, 'Paul the servant of God is chosen for (this) service for the time of his life; but at the hands of Nero, that godless and wicked man, he shall be perfected before your eyes' (1, 1). There is no account in the text that the prophecy was fulfilled, although the crucifixion of Peter is described in detail (37). Peter was killed without the knowledge of Nero, who would have preferred a more severe end for him (41). His

death, apparently, occurred while Paul was still away, presumably in Spain (1, 1-3; 40). Peter was to be charged with irreligion and to be crucified, although there is no description of any trial (36).

According to *The Martyrdom of Paul (Acta Pauli, 11)* Paul was rounded up in a general drive against the Christians (2f.). He was tried by Nero, who agreed to have him beheaded (4). The charge against Paul appears to be no more than that he was a Christian, and there is no linking of the persecution with any act such as a fire in Rome. Unfortunately, as in the case of the *Acts of Peter*, there is no way of knowing with confidence how much the author was relying on local Roman tradition.[79]

The later accounts are less detailed. Origen's testimony is referred to by Eusebius (*His. Eccles.* III, 1f.) who begins his third book with a list of the parts of the world in which the apostles preached, and when it comes to Peter we read, 'But Peter seems to have preached to the Jews of the Diaspora in Pontus and Galatia and Bithynia, Cappadocia, and Asia, and at the end he came to Rome and was crucified head downwards, for so he had demanded to suffer' (I). It continues, 'What need be said of Paul, who fulfilled the gospel of Christ from Jerusalem to Illyria and afterward was martyred in Rome under Nero? This is stated exactly by Origen in the third volume of his commentary on Genesis' (I). The next paragraph begins, 'After the martyrdom of Paul and Peter . . . ' (II). There is no mention of any particular cause for the martyrdom, and no reference to any trial or official condemnation, nor is there any suggestion that the two were martyred as part of a general crackdown on Christians.

In his *De Mortibus Persecutorum* Lactantius records that Peter and Paul were put to death by Nero in Rome, and that Peter's death was by crucifixion (5f.).

Eusebius notes that Nero was the first emperor to be the foe of Christianity, and he quotes Tertullian to that effect. He relates that Paul was beheaded in Rome, and that Peter was crucified. He quotes the witness of Caius who could point to the places housing the sacred relics of each. He also gives the testimony of Dionysius of Corinth associating the deaths of Peter and Paul *(His. Eccles.* II,xxv).

All of the above evidence situates the death of Paul in the reign of Nero. None of it, however, records precise historical circumstances. In particular we have no information about a legal process (with the exception of that in the *Acts of Paul*), and there is no indication that the condemnation to death occurred as a result of the legal process begun in Jerusalem. Rather, it appears to be linked with a general clampdown on Christians for religio-political purposes (*Acts of Paul* 11,2). There is no association with such external events as the fire in Rome. We consider the relevant evidence from Suetonius and Tacitus below.

B. *Sources which describe the Manner of Paul's Death*
When the sources mention this, it is always by beheading, and no place is mentioned other than Rome: e.g., *Acts of Paul* 11,4, Tertullian (*De praescriptione haereticorum* 36,3), and Eusebius (*His. Eccles.* II,xxv). Peter, on the other hand, was crucified.

C. *Sources which associate Peter and Paul in their Deaths*
These include Ignatius (*Rom.* IV), Dionysius of Corinth, who said that they were martyred 'at the same time' (Eusebius *His. Eccles.* II,xxv), Origen (Eusebius, *His. Eccles.* III,1f.), Lactantius (*De mort. persec.* 5f.), Eusebius (*His. Eccles.* II,xxv), and, most important of all, Clement of Rome (*1 Clement* 5f.).

Clement provides the earliest information about the death of Peter and Paul, and since he was writing from Rome within a generation of the events one might hope to obtain from him the most reliable and definite information. Unfortunately, this is not the case. Indeed, the evidence might not have even been read as demanding martyrdom if we did not have independent traditions suggesting that kind of death.[80] There is no mention of when it happened, or how. There is no indication of what the charge was, nor is it necessary to insist that the death had any relation to either a more general persecution, or to any specific incident such as the fire in Rome.

In the texts which we have examined there is little that allows us to reconstruct, with any precision, the last days of Paul's life. Although we have no text earlier than towards the end of the second century that speaks of it as a martyrdom during the reign of Nero, the tradition seems to reflect a core of historical fact, namely that Paul was martyred during the reign of Nero, and that the manner of his death was beheading. But one other item of information from Clement suggests that the secular historians, Suetonius and Tacitus, may offer additional evidence.

D. *Secular Sources*

Tacitus (c. 55–c. 117) and Suetonius (c. 70–c. 160) mention Christianity only once each in their surviving works. In his *Life of Nero (De Vita Caes.* Book VI), Suetonius concluded his litany of Nero's brutal actions (X-XXXVI) by saying, 'After this he showed neither discrimination nor moderation in putting to death whomsoever he pleased on any pretext whatever' (XXXVII). But in addition Suetonius mentions some of Nero's achievements, including his generosity, his entertainments, his administration of justice, his building projects, etc. (X-XVI). At XVI he lists some of the abuses which Nero eradicated, and in particular he mentions that he inflicted punishment on the Christians, a class of men given to a new and mischievous superstition ('Afflicti suppliciis Christiani, genus hominum superstitionis novae ac maleficae', XVI,2) This is the only reference to Christians in the course of Suetonius's *Life of Nero*, and the mention of it suggests that it was an act of some public significance. He mentions also Nero's hatred for all cults except that of the Syrian Goddess (LVI). However, although Suetonius describes the fire in Rome in some detail, and Nero's leading hand in it (XXXVIII), he does not make any connection between it and the punishment of the Christians.

Tacitus's account of the fire *(Ann.* Book XV), and in particular Nero's part in it, is very different from that of Suetonius. According to Tacitus Nero was in Antium at the time (XXXIX) and when he got back to the city he diligently mounted rescue operations. Tacitus reports it as only a rumour that Nero mounted his own stage, and sang the destruction of Troy (XXXIX). The popular story of Nero fiddling while Rome burned is not enhanced by the discordance of three accounts, and indeed the charge of arson is universally disbelieved by modern scholars.[81]

What is of particular interest here, however, is the aftermath of the fire, as reported by Tacitus (XLIV). He describes how neither human help, nor the various modes of placating Heaven had managed to stifle the scandal, and dispel the belief that the fire had taken place by order. Therefore, to scotch the rumour Nero substituted as culprits, and punished with the utmost refinements of cruelty, a class of men, loathed for their vices, whom the crowd styled Christians. As a first step the confessed members of the sect were arrested; next, on their disclosures vast numbers were convicted, not so much on the count of arson, but because of their hatred of the human race ('quam odio humani generis'). Tacitus describes the tortures, and ends by recording the pity of the crowd. This scene may be the context of Clement's mention of the vast multitude of the elect who endured many indignities and tortures and 'were gathered unto Peter and Paul' (*1 Clement* 5f.). If, then, Paul's death is to be closely associated with the Neronian pogrom it did not take place until over two years after (what we claim to be) Paul's acquittal in Rome.

It is noteworthy that while subsequent Christian tradition affirms that Nero subjected Christians to punishment (as does Suetonius), nowhere is there any suggestion that it had anything to do with the fire in Rome (which indeed Suetonius records, but without any reference to Christians).[82] This is remarkable, particularly when such a charge of incendiarism, preferred from the basest motives, would easily be seen as affirming the innocence of the martyrs. One must, then, cast doubt on the reliability of Tacitus's report.

But even if Tacitus were correct, it does not follow that Paul's death had anything to do with the incident he records. If there were a connection it is likely that the persecution of the Christians subsequent to the fire in Rome did not take place until some time after July 64, since, as Tacitus implies, some kind of legal processes (involving confessions, disclosures and convictions) took place.[83] Furthermore, since Paul was a Roman citizen it is less than likely that he was put to death without a trial, and the form of his death corresponds with that usual for a condemned Roman citizen. In fact, there is not any evidence whatsoever which demands that Paul was put to death earlier than the last year of Nero's life, which, incidentally, is the date given by Jerome.

5. *Conclusion*

In this chapter we have suggested the major purpose of each of the Pastoral Epistles. We have situated 2 Timothy during Paul's imprisonment in Rome. We have given substantial evidence that argued for the conclusion that Paul was likely to be released from imprisonment in Rome, was in fact released, and engaged in further missionary activity. His release, we suggest, took place in 62 AD.

Having examined the evidence for the last years of Paul's life it appears very likely that Paul was beheaded some time before the death of Nero, which took place in 68 AD. There is no solid evidence that requires the date of his execution to be earlier than 68. It seems likely, however, that it was some time after July 64, the date of the fire. Taking the latest date for the death, and an early date for the accession of Festus, leaves some ten years to account for after the two-year period of Acts. This is reduced to six years if one takes the later date for Festus's accession. And if the death is brought back earlier than 68 (say 65) we still have as many as seven, or perhaps only three years to account for between the date of the end of Acts and the likely date of Paul's death.[84]

In our reading of 2 Timothy Paul is confident of his release from the Roman imprisonment, and is collecting a team for missionary activity which could have gone on for between three and seven years. If that was the case there was more than enough time to visit Spain, Philippi and Colossae (as well as to undertake such activity as is implied in 1 Timothy and Titus).

One of the major obstacles to regarding the Pastoral Letters as authentically Pauline is the difficulty of accommodating them within the framework of Paul's life as known from the Acts and the other letters. The argument that the Pastorals must be excluded from the Pauline Corpus on such a basis is not plausible, and Dibelius and Conzelmann's dismissal of this kind of reconstruction as a taking 'flight into areas about which we know nothing' (1966: 126) is less than convincing. Understandably, historians do not like to deal with unknowns, but the fact is that the circumstances surrounding the last years of the life of Paul constitute one of the great unknowns not only of the New Testament but of all of the early Christian traditions.

The argument we have advanced, and the reconstruction we have suggested help to fill in the gaps in our knowledge of the last years of Paul's life. At first sight, however, 2 Tim 4.6ff. would appear to rule out the possibility that Paul had any confidence that he would be acquitted in Rome. We shall now deal with these critical verses.

Chapter 5

SECOND TIMOTHY: A FAREWELL LETTER?

1. *The Problem*

One of the most universally agreed positions within the interpretation of the whole of the New Testament is that 2 Timothy presents Paul as writing his farewell message. This view is affirmed by the proponents of each of the main schools of interpretation of the letter. Whether Paul wrote the letter 'himself', or wrote it with the use of a secretary who had more freedom than on previous occasions, or whether the letter is a later redaction of genuine Pauline fragments, or whether, finally, the work is entirely pseudepigraphical, all commentators are agreed that Paul is presented in the letter as being (very) close to death, writing his swan song.[1]

Many scholars go further and regard the letter as a final testament, or *discours d'adieu*,[2] without, however, making clear what exactly they mean by such a designation. The literary genre 'testament' has been the object of several studies in recent years,[3] and some studies on the basis of the comparison of a variety of texts proposed a definite literary form for the genre.[4] Nordheim claims that the genre consists of three parts: the *introduction*, (giving the title, the name of the [fictitious] writer, the addressees, the statement of the supposed author's imminent death, his age, his situation, and a formula introducing the discourse), the *discourse* itself (with its review of the past, and instruction regarding appropriate behaviour, and a statement about the future), and, thirdly, the *conclusion* (with the formal ending of the discourse, more advice, and the death of the speaker).[5]

Nordheim does not deal with the New Testament, but several other studies do, focusing particularly on John 13–17 and Acts 20.18–35.[6] It has been argued that the key element in Paul's speech is 'You . . . will see my face no more',[7] while Cortès insists throughout his work that at the heart of all farewell discourses is the imminence of death.

It is quite clear that many elements of a testament are found in 2 Timothy, but one would expect several of those elements to appear in any personal correspondence, and especially in that between a master and his servant, or a senior and his assistant.[8] What encourages scholars to regard this letter as a testament, and in all cases the term is used without defining the genre, is the common interpretation of 2 Tim 4.6-8.[9] Nothing else in the entire letter supports the interpretation that Paul was on the brink of the grave when he wrote it. If these verses were not in the letter no one would ever have suspected that at the time of writing Paul considered that the lamp of his life was on the point of being extinguished. Many commentators, in fact, go further and speak of martyrdom in this connection.

All translations of the key verse 6 reflect the commentators' interpretation.[10] The critical words in the verse are σπένδομαι and ὁ καιρὸς τῆς ἀναλύσεώς μου ἐφέστηκεν. Since so much depends on the translation of those words it is necessary to consider their meaning in some detail. And since σπένδομαι and ἀνάλυσις are used only twice and once respectively in the NT, it is all the more necessary to take account of the wide use of these terms over a long period of time. In addition to considering the antecedent and contemporary use of the words, it is very important to pay due attention to the context in which the terms are used. In particular, it may not be the case that σπένδομαι means exactly the same thing in 2 Tim 4.6 as it does in Phil 2.17, nor should the meaning of the verb ἀναλύω in Phil 1.23 be allowed to determine the meaning of the noun ἀνάλυσις in 2 Tim 4.6. We shall examine the terms in turn, and then enquire into the context of 2 Tim 4.6.

2. σπένδω/σπένδομαι

A. σπένδω *outside the New Testament*

The dictionaries point out that in its religious sense σπένδομαι means 'to make an offering of a liquid', and in a secular sense, 'to make a treaty, to make peace'.[11] Clearly these meanings are very different from that given to the verb in Phil 2.17 and 2 Tim 4.6. There is not even one example from the Greco-Roman period where the verb means 'to pour out blood', not to speak of pouring out one's own blood.[12]

None of the twenty-two occurrences of the verb in the LXX mentions blood as an element of the libation offered. σπένδομαι translates only נסך and its derivatives, a verb which almost always means 'to pour out'.[13] In two cases the liquid is water (2 Sam 23.16; 1 Chron 11.18), in one it is wine (Hos 9.4), in one some strong drink (Num 28.7), while in the other cases the liquid is not specified.[14]

Josephus retains the meaning of the pouring out of a drink-offering for God (*Antiq.* VI, 22), and the context suggests that it was water. The tendency to spiritualize the cult is reflected in Qumran's claim that the prayers of the lips and proper behaviour have the same atoning value as cultic offerings (e.g. 1QS 8.5f.; 9.3-6).

In Philo the verb σπένδω is used five times, once in the sense of making an agreement with (*In Flacc.* 18), and four where it is a question of libation imagery. In *Leg. Alleg.* II, 56, in the course of his allegorical comment on Leviticus 16, Philo uses the verb for the pouring out (as a libation) of the blood of the soul, and the offering of the whole mind to God under the imagery of an incense offering. There is, of course, no question here of the offering of one's life by death, but rather it is a case of the elements of the sacrificial ritual serving as metaphors for the dedication of oneself. In praising Hannah's sobriety (*De Ebr.* 152) Philo declares that her abstinence from wine and strong liquor enabled her to offer her whole mind to God, just as if a libation were given him. In *Quis Rerum* 183 the wine offering is allegorized in terms of two kinds of wisdom, and, finally, in *De Vita Mosis* II, 150 the reference is to the pouring out of blood around the altar. It is clear, then, that Philo also offers no support for associating the verb with the giving of oneself in death. For him the verb functions as a metaphor for the dedication of oneself to God.

Greek literature and the papyri[15] abound in examples of the use of σπένδω for the making of a drink-offering to a god, where the liquid is often wine (as in Homer, *Il.* 11.775; *Od.* 18.151), and sometimes water (as in Homer *Od.* 12.363). Again, there is no support for associating the verb with the offering of one's life through death, which is the meaning given to the verb in Phil 2.17 and 2 Tim 4.6.

Two texts from Tacitus are sometimes advanced as bridging the gap between the general uses outlined above and the very different meaning given in the case of the two NT texts, but Denis has shown convincingly that the libation in *Ann.* 15,64 and 16,35 is made at the moment of death, and does not signify the death itself (Denis 1958: 630f.). Elsewhere the same author shows that the Berlin *Gr. Pap.* 11

517, which in any case is dated some hundred years after the death of Paul, does not support the conventional reading of Phil 2.17 (1957).

Denis concluded his survey of the practices of libations among the Greek peoples by saying, 'Il ne semble pas que le verbe σπένδειν signifie jamais, dans le monde grec, un sacrifice sanglant, une mise à mort dans un but religieux, ni, sans autre précision, verser le sang au sens d'immoler' (1958: 633).

It is clear, then, that there is no support, either among the Semites or Greeks for understanding the verb σπένδομαι to mean the offering of oneself in a bloody oblation. And yet this is manifestly the meaning given to the word in both Phil 2.17 and in 2 Tim 4.6. Since the other uses of the word offer no support for such a meaning it can be justified only if the context in each case demands it. Let us examine the two contexts.

B. σπένδομαι *in Phil 2.17*

Almost all exegetes understand the verb to refer to Paul's death, and several use the phrase 'shedding his life-blood' and speak of martyrdom.[16]

It should be noted that almost all commentators on Phil 2.17 look to 2 Tim 4.6 as a support for that interpretation. Predictably, commentators on 2 Tim 4.6 refer the reader to the use of the verb σπένδομαι in Phil 2.17, and also draw attention to the use of the verb ἀναλύω in Phil 1.23.[17] No commentator appears unduly shaken by the failure to provide even one example of the use of σπένδομαι in either Greek or Semitic sources with the meaning they assign to it in the two NT texts. It is obvious that the argument from context in Phil 2.17 would need to be very powerful to compensate for the absence of the appropriate meaning in the sources we have investigated.

We shall now demonstrate that the context of Phil 2.17 does not at all demand the conventional reading, and indeed it seems to call for a different understanding. It is clear that while writing to the Philippians Paul was in prison, and that he was well aware of the suffering that fidelity to the gospel demanded of him, and demanded also of the Philippians (Phil 1.29f.). He had to come to terms with the prospect of death, and in his difficult choice between his desire to depart and be with Christ, and to respond to the needs of the community he had opted for the latter, confident that he would remain and continue with them, for their progress and joy in the faith (cf. Phil 1.23-26). Indeed, he is sure that he will come to visit them again (v. 26).

It would seem that the discussion which preoccupied Paul in Phil 1.23-26 has been resolved in favour of the demands of his apostolic mission, irrespective of his own personal preferences.[18] In the difficult choice facing him he had decided to opt for life rather than death, as is clear from Phil 1.19-26, and from his determination to visit them, of which he writes (2.24) just after the critical verse (2.17). It is hardly possible, then, that in using the verb in Phil 2.17 he had the shedding of his blood in mind. The life-or-death discussion that took place in Phil 1.23-26 has been resolved in favour of living, and should not force on Phil 2.17 (either by 'attraction', or by some kind of literary osmosis) a meaning of σπένδομαι that finds absolutely no lexicographical support anywhere (apart from the supposed support of 2 Tim 4.6). If, then, in Phil 2.17 Paul is not referring to the shedding of his life-blood, what is the meaning of the verb σπένδομαι in that text?[19]

We regard Phil 1.27–2.28 as a unit of paraenesis within the letter, and several commentators agree in regarding those verses as a unit,[20] although some regard Phil 2.17f. as fitting with 2.19-30.[21] At 1.27 Paul leaves aside his discussion of his life-or-death dilemma (1.19-26) and moves on to exhort the community. He encourages them to conduct themselves in a manner worthy of the Gospel of Christ (1.27), and becomes more specific in his exhortation to unity in faith (1.27; 2.2-4), which theme is clearly a preoccupation of Paul, and must surely have been of particular relevance to the Philippians.[22] The hymn of 2.6-11 is introduced at this point, and commentators rightly point out its connection with what follows,[23] a view which is confirmed by the use of ὥστε in 2.12. Against a background of the humiliation, suffering and exaltation of Jesus, then, Paul exhorts the Philippians to work out their salvation in fear and trembing (2.12), to be blameless and innocent children of God in the midst of a wicked and perverse generation (2.15), holding up the word of life, so that in the day of Christ Paul may be proud that he did not run or labour in vain (2.16; cf. Gal 2.2 and 2 Tim 4.7). It is at this point that Paul introduces the liturgical metaphor (2.17f.).

There are two elements in the metaphor, Paul's libation and the sacrifice and liturgy of the faith of the Philippians (2.17). Since the Philippians are the agents throughout 2.12-16, the interpretation that it is the Philippians themselves, rather than Paul, who offer the faith of the community makes rather more sense.[24] It should not be necessary here to deal with all of the many questions which the commentaries discuss at this point.[25] Suffice it to state that in v. 17 Paul places side by side with the offering of the faith of the Philippians his own accompanying libation.

The question of immediate concern is whether the component offered by Paul refers to his death by the shedding of his blood, or whether it refers to something else. In the case of the Hebrew ritual it is the θυσία, rather than the σπονδή that suggests death/destruction, be it the death of an animal, or the consumption of the elements by fire. In the sacrificial ritual the two elements are separate: the blood of the victim is poured out at the foot of the altar, but this is never called the נֶסֶךְ/σπονδή. Instead, the libation is the pouring out of a drink for God which accompanies the sacrifice, and in late Judaism signalled the completion of the liturgy of the daily sacrifice. It never signifies the pouring out of blood, but rather the accompanying libation (of wine) for the daily sacrifice.[26]

If, then, σπένδομαι refers to the offering of a libation to accompany the offering of the faith of the Philippian community, what kind of offering does Paul have in mind? We suggest that his accompanying offering is not his death, but his apostolic activity insofar as that is related to the Philippian community. Although his present state is in reality a real apostolic self-emptying it is very much a religious and liturgical act, which accompanies and solemnly brings to completion the sacrifice of the Philippians.[27]

Since, then, the death of Paul is not suggested either by the verb σπένδομαι, or by the immediate context of Phil 2.17, an interpretation of the libation in terms of Paul's apostleship is not unlikely. Dupont, in another context, has alluded to the relationship between apostolate and cult in the language of Paul, and he suggests that in preaching the Gospel Paul considered himself to be fulfilling a sacred function, making an agreeable offering of the Gentiles to God (Rom 15.16), and offering himself as a libation for the sacrifice of the Philippians (Phil 2.17). In the apostolic preaching, then, God finds a more agreeable odour than in the fumes of sacrifices.[28]

We consider that Phil 2.17 reflects the exceptional relationship that Paul had with the Philippian community. Not only had the community been established by him (Acts 16), but it had made a special κοινωνία with him in the furtherance of the Gospel, from the first day right down to the present (Phil 1.5). This relationship was particularly warm (1.8), and while Paul had steadfastly refused aid from the Corinthian community (2 Cor 11.9), it is clear that he had no such hesitations with the Philippians, from whom he received aid at least three times (Phil 4.10-20). In fact, the gift and his receiving it constituted a κοινωνία (Phil 4.15). Indeed, Paul used cultic language to describe this gift (Phil 4.18). But the community whose common-wealth was in heaven (Phil 3.20) had not yet reached its goal, and it had to deal with its problems from the circumcision party (cf. Phil 3.2-11), and with the disruption of the community, as reflected in 2.1-11 and 2.12-18.[29]

But the achievement of unity among the Philippians is also a concern of Paul himself (Phil 1.7; 2.2; 4.10). In between the first day (1.5) and the day of Christ (1.6) the process of purification must go on (1.10f.). Meanwhile, the Philippians must live a life worthy of the Gospel (cf. 1.27–2.16). They are not, however, alone, since they have God with them (2.13), and they also have the assurance of Paul's concern and presence, either in person (1.26, 27; 2.24), or through a delegate (1.27; 2.19). Such indeed is the quality of the unity between the two parties (1.8, 19, 30; 3.17, 20; 4.1, 9, 14), and their combined responsibilities for the furtherance of the Gospel (his preaching and their financial support),[30] that it could best be described in the metaphorical terms of the daily worship referred to in Phil 2.17.

We suggest, then, that the liturgical terminology does not function as a metaphor for the death of Paul, but expresses well the combination of the unity of the faith of the Philippians and the apostolic activity of Paul; each complemented the other, and together they constituted an offering to God comparable with that of the daily sacrifice.[31]

Only a small number of scholars seem prepared to shift from the traditional interpretation of Phil 2.17, despite the very careful study of Denis. Ricciotti, however, rules out Paul's imprisonment as an element of the libation since, he insists, Paul is very confident of his release; he suggests instead that Paul had in mind the innumerable dangers of the apostolate (cf. 2 Cor 11.23-26) (1958: 592). Although Murphy-O'Connor acknowledges that the verse could be an allusion to Paul's martyrdom, on the basis of Denis's study he regards 'the humiliating circumstances of Paul's imprisonment' as the more probable interpretation (Murphy-O'Connor 1964: 297, n. 36).

C. σπένδομαι *in 2 Tim 4.6*
Because the verb occurs only twice in the NT, and also because the
two texts are used in virtually every relevant commentary to
interpret each other it was necessary to examine in some detail the
use of the verb in Phil 2.17. We have argued that in using the
liturgical metaphor in that text Paul does not refer to his death, but
rather has in mind, more generally, his apostolic activity, especially
that part of it in which the Philippians had such a stake. If, then, the
use of the verb in Phil 2.17 is to be brought into the discussion of its
meaning in 2 Tim 4.6, it will have nothing to say about Paul's
death.

Nevertheless, it could still be the case that the conventional
understanding of σπένδομαι in 2 Tim 4.6 is valid, despite the fact
that nowhere, either in Greek or Hebrew sources, nor, as we have
now seen, even in Phil 2.17, does it have such a meaning. It can only
be the context, then, which demands that the verb refer to the death
of Paul, and if that were the case we would have to admit that the
verb has a meaning in 2 Tim 4.6 which it has nowhere else. Before
considering the wider context of 2 Tim 4.6 let us first examine the
other word in that verse that has led the commentators to conclude
that Paul is referring to his impending death, the noun ἀνάλυσις.

3. ἀναλύω/ἀνάλυσις

Generally speaking, commentators on 2 Tim 4.6 offer no meaning of
the noun other than 'death'. They do point out that originally the
word meant some kind of 'loosing', or 'moving away from', but that it
later came to be associated with that kind of loosing we call death.
Supporting evidence is offered but, as we shall see, it is neither
abundant nor impressive.

The noun does not occur elsewhere in the NT and is absent from
the LXX. It has only one entry in Goodspeed's *Index Patristicus*
(1 Clem. 44.5), and none in his *Index Apologeticus* (Goodspeed 1907;
1912). We have discovered only one occurrence in the papyri.[32]

A. ἀνάλυσις *in the Dictionaries*
Liddell and Scott (1925-40) give several meanings: loosing, dissolving
(with σώματος, of death), resolution of a problem, reduction of the
imperfect into one, solution of a problem, and (from the passive),
retrogression, retirement, departure, and, finally, death. They refer

to the third class of meaning of the related verb, ἀναλύω with the intransitive meaning, 'loosing from moorings, weighing anchor, depart, go away', and, metaphorically, 'to die'; they also record the meaning 'to return' for the verb in Luke 12.36 and Wis 2.1.

The examples given for the meaning 'death' are few, and they require comment. In his *Sententiae* Secundus of Athens poses the question at 19, what is death? He answers with no less than eleven descriptions, of which two use the noun: ἀνάλυσις σώματος (the example given by Liddell and Scott), and ἀνάλυσις μέλων.[33] Note that in each case ἀνάλυσις is qualified by another noun, which suggests that the noun on its own was not understood by this second-century Greek philosopher to mean death.

In fact the only example given by Liddell and Scott where the noun stands alone and has the meaning 'death' is 2 Tim 4.6. One must enquire further into the lexicographical support for that interpretation.

B. ἀνάλυσις *in Spicq*

While Dibelius in his commentary adduces only three texts in support of the usual reading (Phil 2.17 [and 1.23], *1 Clem.* 44.5, and Philo, *In Flacc.* 187) Ceslaus Spicq offers considerably more supporting evidence, and since his lexicographical work is both so impressive and so influential, it will be of considerable interest to examine in detail his comments on the noun.[34]

His first comment, after he has dealt with σπένδομαι, is that we have in v. 6 another metaphor for death. He claims that ἀνάλυσις is unknown in the papyri, which is not quite correct, since it does occur in the letter of Dionysios to Diogenes in which it refers to financial matters and has nothing to do with death (Wilckens 1957: 219). The noun, which comes from the verb ἀναλύω, has, he says, two meanings, one, the departure from life, and the other, the liberation from the body. For the first meaning he offers only one text, Philo, *In Flacc.* 187. Let us consider Philo on this point and on his other uses of the noun.

There is no doubt that in *In Flacc.* 187 the noun occurs in a context which suggests death. However, it does not stand on its own in this text, but is accompanied by the qualifying adjective 'final', thereby suggesting to the reader that Philo needed to qualify the noun to make it clear that he had no ordinary leave-taking in mind, but rather death itself. He uses the same expression in *In Flacc.* 115

where he speaks of Flaccus's arrest: 'Thus it was from a convivial gathering that he made his final departure (τελευταίαν ταύτην ἀνάλυσιν). The obvious meaning here is Flaccus's arrest and removal from the gathering, although one might argue that it was Flaccus's ultimate death after exile that Philo had in mind already. In both cases, however, Philo qualified the noun by the adjective 'final'.

The next evidence adduced by Spicq in support of the meaning 'death' for the noun are the two texts Luke 2.29 and Tob 3.6. However, not only do these texts not use that noun, but they use a quite different verb, ἀπολύω, and this question shall be dealt with below.

To support the meaning, 'the liberation from the body', Spicq offers two supporting texts, Epictetus I, 9,16, and Plutarch's *Consolatio ad Apollonium* 13. Let us examine the evidence in turn.

Epictetus discusses at I, 11-17 the question of the self being imprisoned in a paltry body, and being desirous of going back to God. The person enquiring of him is anxious to quit the body and return to his God. Epictetus advises him to wait upon God, and ends with the exhortation to 'stay, and be not so irrational as to depart' (17). It must be pointed out, however, that the noun ἀνάλυσις does not occur at all in the discussion, nor does its related verb, ἀναλύω. Instead we have two different verbs, ἀπέρχομαι (11, 14, 17) and ἀπολύω (16).

In Plutarch's 'Letter of Condolence to Apollonius' we encounter the typical Platonic negative assessment of the human body: it is the prison in which the finer human qualities are incarcerated. Death, then, instead of being evil, allows one to live unenslaved by the flesh and the emotions. Death brings good fortune, and can thus be described as a release from the body. However, once again, it must be noted that neither ἀνάλυσις nor ἀναλύω occurs in the text. We have, instead, the verb ἀπολύω, and in the quotation from the unknown poet, 'Let no one fear death, which is release from toils', the noun ἀπόλυσις.

These two texts, then, offer no support to the view that in 2 Tim 4.6 ἀνάλυσις means death (as a release from the body). The tenuous nature of the common interpretation of that text is further illustrated by the fact that two other texts offered by Spicq in support of this meaning, Philo *Leges* I, 106-8 and *De Congressu* 30 use neither ἀνάλυσις nor ἀναλύω.

It is clear, then, that several examples proposed by Spicq in support of the conventional understanding of ἀνάλυσις in 2 Tim 4.6 do not employ either this noun or its associated verb. Instead, in several of the texts we find ἀπόλυσις/ἀπολύω. This word-group also exhibits a wide range of meaning: loosing of a bandage or cord.[35] To use any occurrence of this word group in support of a meaning for a different noun, ἀνάλυσις, is to take a number of hermeneutical steps which need to be justified. Spicq's usually massive lexicographical evidence is in this case misleading—indeed much of the 'supporting evidence' actually points in the opposite direction.[36] If, then, the verb ἀπολύω is to be regarded as having anything to contribute to the interpretation of the noun ἀνάλυσις in 2 Tim 4.6 (which we, unlike Spicq, would not wish to claim), one would, on the basis of the 63 NT uses of the verb, have to be very doubtful whether it could ever mean death, and one might be pardoned for suspecting, on the basis of no less than 28 NT texts, that it refers to 'release from detention'!

C. ἀνάλυσις *and the Papyri*

The papyri present us with pictures of the ordinary events of (mainly Egyptian) life, from 200 BC to the Byzantine period, approximately. Marriage contracts, bills of divorce, census details, domestic and business affairs, etc., give us a vivid picture of the preoccupations of ordinary people. The (almost total) absence of the noun in the papyri argues against the conclusion that in 2 Tim 4.6 the noun means 'death'.

The prospect of death focuses people's attention on matters of property, inheritance, succession, and care for dependants. People cooly provide for the future by writing wills, and settling questions of inheritance. The bereaved write the perfunctory death notices, and consolers write letters of condolence. The papyri abound in examples of wills (e.g. *P. Oxy.* 104-7; 489-495; 968; 990; 1034), death notifications (e.g. *P. Oxy.* 262; 1030; 1198; 1550; 1551), statements of the death of a parent in claims of ownership (e.g. *P. Oxy.* 131; 713), reference to death in marriage contracts (e.g. *P. Oxy.* 265; 496), and other contracts (e.g. *P. Oxy.* 1201; 1208), and in petitions (e.g. *P. Oxy.* 1032), in census returns (e.g. *P. Oxy.* 203) and in lists of properties (e.g. *P. Oxy.* 1269). There are specific letters of condolence (e.g. *P. Oxy.* 115, pagan; *P. Oxy.* 1874, Christian), and allusions to the death of someone in ordinary letters (e.g. *P. Oxy.* 1295). If ἀνάλυσις was understood as a word for death in this long period it is truly remarkable that there is not even one occurrence of it in this connection among the papyri and, as we have seen, in the only place where the word is used it has no relation to death.

The noun θάνατος does occur quite frequently in the papyri, and is the most common word for death in the NT.[37] However, the most common word for death in the papyri is τελευτή, although this is very poorly attested in Christian circles.[38]

D. ἀνάλυσις *and Phil 1.23*

The key text adduced in support of the meaning 'death' for ἀνάλυσις in 2 Tim 4.6 is Phil 1.23, in which we have the verb ἀναλύω. In that text Paul is clearly agonizing over his conflicting desires, to die and be with Christ, on the one hand, and to continue his apostolic service of the faithful, on the other.[39]

There is no doubt that Paul had his own death in mind as he wrote these words. It is noteworthy, however, that even in a context which is so clearly describing the life/death option, each of the two verbs, to depart, ἀναλύω, and to remain on, ἐπιμένω, is modified to make it clear that Paul is referring to death/life, and not simply to any departure/remaining. The question that concerns us is whether the verb without the modifying 'and to be with Christ' would signify Paul's death, any more than ἐπιμένω without 'in the flesh' would mean 'to live'. We submit that it is only the modifying explanatory phrase in each case that makes Paul's meaning clear. But even if one were to conclude from this text that ἀναλύω alone signified death for Paul it would not follow that even the same verb, not to speak of the cognate noun, must have the same meaning in another context.[40]

And yet the movement from the meaning of the verb in Phil 1.23 to that of the noun in 2 Tim 4.6 is unchallenged in scholarship, even when the general context of 2 Timothy, and particularly 4.9-21, seems to make a reference to Paul's death highly unlikely.[41] The uncertain nature of the argument linking the two texts, Phil 1.23 and 2 Tim 4.6, is clearly reflected in Büchsel's treatment of the words. Having noted that the verb literally means 'to undo again' (Homer *Od.* 2, 105), Büchsel adds that it has a richly developed usage, but that in the NT its predominant meaning is 'to leave' (Büchsel 1964). It must be pointed out, however, that the verb occurs only twice in the NT, and in the other occurrence, Lk 12.36, it means 'to return'!

E. *Evaluation*

It is clear that the lexicographical support for reading ἀνάλυσις to refer to Paul's death is singularly weak. Where death is associated with the noun in the examples examined it is generally some other phrase that makes that clear. Had Paul intended to refer to his death in 2 Tim 4.6 there were several terms available to him. One could understand his reluctance to use τελευτή since this common word for death might have suggested a finality that was unacceptable to Christians. He might, however, have used the well-attested euphemism, ὕπνος, although none of its six NT uses has that meaning.[42] Although none of the twenty-two uses of καθεύδω in the NT means more than 'to sleep', no less than fifteen of the eighteen occurrences of κοιμάω mean 'to die'.[43] Indeed this is Paul's way of describing the dead in 1 Thess 4.13, 14, 15 and in 1 Cor 15.18, 20. Paul could well have used this word if he wished to signify his death. The cognate noun, κοίμησις, would also have been a possibility, although its single occurrence in the NT (Jn 11.13) associates it with ordinary sleep (ὕπνος) rather than with θάνατος. θάνατος, of course, would have been an obvious choice, and Paul does use it with reference to the death of Jesus in 2 Tim 1.10.

We submit, then, that the case has not been convincingly argued that ἀνάλυσις in 2 Tim 4.6 must refer to Paul's impending death. The overall context of 2 Timothy and the immediate context of the relevant verse argue against the conventional interpretation, and it is to these matters that we now turn.

4. *The Context of 2 Tim 4.6*

It is indeed strange that a letter which is generally regarded as a farewell letter does not employ the normal terminology for death. Neither the much attested LXX and papyri word τελευτάω/τελευτή, nor θανατόω/θάνατος/ἀποθνῄσκω occurs with reference to Paul's thoughts about the future. It has been argued above that Paul's use of σπένδομαι in 2 Tim 4.6 does not likely refer to his death, and sufficient reason has not been found for concluding that the noun ἀνάλυσις in the same verse must refer to it. This conclusion will now be supported by an examination of both the wider and more immediate context of this verse.

A. *The Context of 2 Timothy*

In our view it is only 2 Tim 4.6-8 which suggests that at the time of writing the letter Paul considered himself to be close to death. If these verses were not in the letter no one would ever have suspected that that was the position. Indeed, much of the rest of the letter suggests an altoghether different Pauline *Sitz im Leben*.

As soon as one leaves v. 8 one enters a different world. In 4.9-21 Paul gives the impression of a man who has his eyes fixed determinedly on the future. He wants Timothy to speed himself and come quickly (4.9; cf. 1.4), and to do so before winter (4.21), and this desire is surely one of the major reasons for the writing of the letter. Because of the distance involved it is likely that some considerable time would have elapsed before Timothy, who was as far away as Troas, at least (2 Tim 4.13), would have received the letter and have come to Paul, who was probably in Rome (2 Tim 1.17). Paul's desire that Timothy should bring Mark ('who is useful to me for service', 2 Tim 4.11) along with him, suggests that he required them for some purpose other than his own confort in a Roman prison. In Chapter 7 we argue that these requests, together with that for the cloak and the parchments (2 Tim 4.13), are related to Paul's future plans. Finally, the mood of 2 Tim 4.16ff. suggests that Paul had set his eyes on further missionary activity.

Let us consider how the commentators deal with what appears to be the stark contrast between the conventional meaning of 2 Tim 4.6-8 and the clear meaning of 4.9-21.

(i) Those who support the Pauline authorship of the letter tend to play down the sharp contrast. Whatever difficulty Spicq had with the text, his curiosity is satisfied by Paul's desire to have a copy of the Scriptures (1969: 810, 816). Jeremias does not appear to see any contradiction between Paul writing 'im festen Blick auf den Tod', and his requesting a visit that would take a long time to realize (1968: 56). While Kelly suggests that there could have been a delay of three or four months between the *prima* and the *secunda actio* of the Roman court, which would have been sufficient time for Timothy to arrive (1963: 212, 218), Guthrie allows that even if Timothy did not arrive in time he would have 'this last precious document' from his beloved master (1957: 22f.).

(ii) One group of those who do not accept Pauline authorship view the situation very differently, and regard as impossible the co-existence within the same letter of the two moods of 4.6-8 and 4.9-21.

Harrison says flatly: 'Paul could perfectly well have written both—Farewell (2 Tim 4.5ff.) and twofold Summons (4.9, 21)—but not at the same time, nor as parts of the same letter. Not even with the help of a second imprisonment, then ... do we get rid of the inner contradiction between one personal detail and another in 2 Timothy'. He goes on: 'If we are to take that noble and impressive farewell seriously, he must have known that it was a physical impossibility for Timothy to carry out these commissions until too late. And if we are to take the commissions seriously, they compel us to suppose that in that farewell Paul exercised a mental reservation which would rob it of half its impressiveness and pathos' (1921: 115). Harrison deals with the problem by proposing his Fragments Theory, and all adherents of such a theory embrace it precisely because of the difficulty of reconciling the existence of two apparently opposite moods in the same letter.[44]

(iii) Understandably, those who propose that the Pastorals are pseudepigrapha are less embarrassed by historical unlikelihoods. For them the supposed paraenetic end justifies the means. The placing side by side of two such strange bed-fellows as 4.6-8 and 4.9-21 poses less of a problem once one accepts that the intention of the author was to give paraenesis, rather than history. The otherwise difficult reference to cloak, papyrus rolls and parchments is explained by proposing that they function as indications of the *apostolische Selbstgenügsamkeit* of the model apostle, and of his attachment to the Holy Scriptures right up to the very end.[45] Once the author is presumed to be 'a devout and earnest Paulinist' who acted from the highest motives he is allowed great liberty.[46] However, one must concede that we simply do not know the motives of the pseudepigrapher, nor have we any means of determining them. Whether he intended to deceive his own generation or not we simply do not know. What we do know is that he has truly deceived all the generations of scholars right up to the end of the last century at least.

In our estimation the pseudepigraphy theory does not go any distance in solving the apparent contradiction of the 'funereal' mood of 4.6-8 being followed by the optimistic tones of 4.9-21. If the pseudepigrapher gave 'historical' detail only to add verisimilitude to his own point of view, he set about his task in a most clumsy fashion.

Whether the author is thought of as an early second-century Paulinist working with real Pauline fragments before him, or a pseudepigrapher with no such aids, we are left with no choice beyond opting for a strange, if not a far-fetched reverence for the *ipsissima verba Pauli* in the case of the compiler of the fragments, and a certain ineptitude in the case of the pseudepigrapher.

(iv) The attempt to explain the coexistence of the two elements within the one letter by suggesting that Paul's conditions changed drastically in the course of writing the letter seems to strain the imagination somewhat, while the appeal to psychological considerations to explain the apparently contradictory moods of 4.6-8 and 9-21 is no more fruitful.[47]

The examples of the various types of solution proposed above seem very unsatisfactory. The supporters of authenticity play down the difficulty posed by the normal reading of 2 Tim 4.6, set alongside the more optimistic context of 2 Tim 4.9-21, while the supporters of pseudepigraphy propose a solution that does little credit to the skill of the author. The supporters of a fragments solution rely on assumptions which stretch one's credulity beyond its limits. We propose a reading of the text which requires neither the rather arbitrary literary dissection proposed by the supporters of a fragments theory, nor the assumptions required by those who favour a pseudepigraphy hypothesis. This proposal respects both the literary integrity of the letter, and takes the document to be what it presents itself to be, a personal letter of Paul to his co-worker Timothy.

We suggest that at the moment of writing to Timothy Paul did not at all consider himself to be either on the brink of the grave, as most of the commentators read the text, nor to be living a stay of execution that could last up to several months, as a small number allows (e.g. Kelly 1963 and Guthrie 1957). On the contrary, Paul was very confident about a favourable outcome to his present difficulties. It can be demonstrated that this solution meets the double requirement that the reading of 2 Tim 4.6 respects the meaning of the critical terms, and, secondly, that the context of the letter is more faithfully reflected in it.

It is difficult to avoid the strong suspicion that the conventional reading of 2 Tim 4.6-8 conflicts with what we understand to be the 'movement' of the letter. In particular, the conventional reading appears to conflict with the thrice-stated desire of Paul to see

Timothy (1.4; 4.9, 21), with the strong sense of optimism reflected in
4.17f., and with Paul's attention to specifics such as the request to
bring Mark, the cloak and the parchments (4.11, 13). Do the key
words of 2 Tim 4.6 allow of an interpretation that does less violence
to the tone of the rest of the letter? The conclusion seems to follow
that the verb σπένδομαι does not refer at all to Paul's impending
death, and the evidence for understanding the noun ἀνάλυσις
standing alone to mean 'death' is fragile, if not non-existent. Given
the wide semantic field of this noun a meaning may be found which
would suit the context of the letter. Before we propose the precise
meaning, let us first consider the context of 2 Tim 4.6-8.

B. *The Context of 2 Tim 4.6-8*
It has been argued in Chapter 4 that Second Timothy reflects Paul's
very considerable fear for Timothy's stability in the faith under
persecution, and his dissatisfaction with him as a teacher. The
exhortation to Timothy to exercise his ministry appropriately is
stated very firmly and solemnly in 4.1-5. Timothy is to be constant in
his preaching, both in favourable and unfavourable times (cf. v. 2);
although people will turn away fron the truth (vv. 3f.), Timothy is to
be vigilant in everything; he is to suffer, to do the work of an
evangelist, and to fulfil the ministry (v. 5). Notice that νῆφε is the
only imperative of the four to be in the present, which suggests that
Timothy was to exhibit a constant state of vigilance, while the Aorist
tense of the other three imperatives suggests that at the time of
writing Paul perceived Timothy to be faced with a specific, rather
than a general difficulty.

In the light of the great stress on suffering within the letter it is not
unlikely that Timothy's ministry was at a crisis, in which the choice
was between being diligent in the apostolic ministry (which would
surely bring suffering; cf. κακοπάθησον, 4.5), and taking an easier
option (such as those will do who will fall into myths, 4.5, and those
have done who have abandoned Paul, 1.15; 4.14-16). This immediate
crisis helps to explain the emphasis on suffering within the letter.[48]
The kind of fidelity required of Timothy would surely bring its
problems (2.3; 3.12). Not for the first time Paul points to his own
performance as a spur to Timothy (cf. 1.8-18; 2.1-7, 8-11; 3.10-17).

The exhortation to Timothy, which takes a new turn at 3.10, runs
right through to 4.9, and we note the continuous alternation between
σὺ δέ (3.10, 14; 4.5) and the paradigmatic behaviour of Paul (3.10f.,

14; 4.6-8). The paraenesis is framed by Paul's steadfastness in the past (3.10f.) and his long-suffering fidelity up to the present time, which will be rewarded on 'That Day' (4.6-8). Meanwhile, he is confident of a favourable resolution of his present predicament (cf. 4.16ff.).

At this point we wish to offer a translation of 4.5-9, and our translation of the critical v. 6 will be explained and justified:

5.   You, however, never cease from being vigilant in everything; do not flinch from (this present) suffering; do the work of an evangelist; carry your ministry through to its completion.

6.   For my part I am already spent, and the time for my release is at hand.

7.   I have engaged in the good struggle right to the very end; I have stayed in the race right up to the finish; I have done what was required of me (or, I have been loyal to my commitment).

8.   As for the rest, the crown of righteousness awaits me, which the Lord, the righteous judge will give me on That Day, and not only to me but to all who have loved his appearing.

9.   Do your best to come to me soon.

It has been suggested that three of the four metaphors which Paul employs in vv. 7f. come from the athletic stadium (ἀγών,[49] δρόμος,[50] and στέφανος,[51]), and that τὴν πίστιν τετήρεκα is out of place if it does not also refer to some part of the athletic activity, such as the recovery of the sum of money deposited by the runner on entering the games.[52] The evidence to support such a novel reading is slender in the extreme. There is such an abundance of evidence to support other readings of the text that it is difficult to determine with certainty the meaning here. It does not seem to refer to 'the deposit of evangelical doctrine' which has been preserved (cf. 2 Tim 1.14 and 1 Tim 1.18f.), but rather to Paul's more general fidelity in the execution of his task. Estius expressed it well in terms of the loyalty a soldier displays to his general, which is also the sense which Calvin preferred.[53]

The problem of settling for the precise images Paul had in mind is enlarged by the wide use of the terms employed. The preference for one reading rather than another is often made without the hermeneutical presuppositions being stated.[54] While the only two specific studies of the metaphors in recent times do not even once situate them within the context of the letter itself,[55] we insist that the paraenetic character of this autobiographical section of the letter is highly relevant to the understanding of the terms.

The interpreter's inability to fix with certainty the precise meaning of the images used by Paul in vv. 7f. is caused by exactly the opposite problem that attends the interpretation of ἀνάλυσις. Whereas the three words ἀγών, δρόμος and πίστις occur 16, 11, and 19 times respectively in the LXX, and 6, 3, and 243 times in the NT, ἀνάλυσις does not occur in the LXX and its only use in the NT is here. Indeed, so rare is the noun that several ancient authors do not employ it, e.g. Thucydides, Polybius, Plato, Herodotus, Pindar, Theocritus, Andocides, Lycurgus, Dinarchus, Aeschines, Demosthenes, Aristophanes, Aeschylus, Euripides.

We have argued above that nothing in that word alone suggests death. It means, in general, some kind of change or leave-taking: the change can be the resolution of a problem, or the analysis of something, or even the reduction of imperfect figures into one, and the leave-taking can be a coming-back to, as well as a going-away from. These are only some of the nuances attested in Liddell and Scott, and we have little to guide us in our choice between the various possibilities. We propose that Paul is referring to the resolution of his case, which he is confident will bring him release.[56] This reading of the noun fulfils the two criteria we have insisted upon throughout, namely, that it respects the lexicographical use of the term, and that it fits the context in which the word is employed.

With respect to the former, note that Sophocles uses the noun in the sense of deliverance from evils (*Electra* 142). Timaeus Historicus employs the noun where the sense is a release from oaths.[57] The solution of a problem is the meaning of the word in Plutarch's *Romulus* XII,4, where the problem is a geometrical one. The meaning resolution, or solution, or dissolution (of a banquet) is involved in the only use of the noun by Josephus (*Antiq.* XIX, 239). These examples of the use of ἀνάλυσις in the sense of release from, or solution of some situation stretch from Sophocles (5th cent. BC), to Timaeus (4th-3rd cent. BC), to Josephus (1st cent. AD), to Plutarch (1st-2nd cent. AD). While they can scarcely be advanced as absolutely compelling evidence, when put alongside the evidence for the meaning 'death' when the noun is alone, they are not unimpressive.[58]

The verb ἀναλύω, then, has a wide semantic field and one must therefore exercise the greatest care in opting for one meaning over another.[59]

Our translation may now be inserted into the context of 2 Tim 4.3-8.

At some future time some will not endure sound teaching and will gather teachers that suit them, and will turn away from the truth (cf. vv. 3f.). In appealing to Timothy to remain faithful, Paul points to his own steadfastness up to the present. There is a striking balance between the threefold exhortation to Timothy (v. 5) and Paul's achievement:

5.　Σὺ δὲ 　　νῆφε ἐν πᾶσιν	6.　Ἐγὼ γὰρ 　　ἤδη σπένδομαι καὶ ὁ καιρὸς 　　τῆς ἀναλύσεώς μου ἐφέστηκεν
κακοπάθησον 　　ἔργον ποίησον εὐαγγελιστοῦ 　　τὴν διακονίαν σου πληροφόρησον	7.　τὸν καλὸν ἀγῶνα ἠγώνισμαι 　　τὸν δρόμον τετέλεκα 　　τὴν πίστιν τετήρηκα
	8.　λοιπὸν ἀπόκειταί μοι 　　ὁ τῆς δικαιοσύνης στέφανος 　　ὃν ἀποδώσει μοι ὁ κύριος 　　ἐν ἐκείνῃ τῇ ἡμέρᾳ 　　ὁ δίκαιος κριτής
(8).　οὐ μόνον δὲ ἐμοι 　　ἀλλὰ καὶ πᾶσι τοῖς ἠγαπηκόσι 　　τὴν ἐπιφάνειαν αὐτοῦ.[60]	

The trilogy of specific activities is preceded in each case by a more general disposition (νῆφε ἐν πᾶσιν in the exhortation to Timothy and σπένδομαι, etc., to describe the extent of Paul's fidelity). If Timothy remains faithful he too will receive the promised crown.

Verses 6-8, then, should not be separated from 4.1-5. Together these verses form a piece, the theme of which is the exhortation to Timothy to be faithful in spending himself in his vocation, as Paul had done up to this point. The future crown will be given to both, and to all who have made their decision to love the appearance of Jesus Christ, and who have remained faithful in that decision. The focus is not at all on Paul's impending fate, but rather on present fidelity which the Lord will repay when he comes 'on that day'.[61]

5. Conclusion

This investigation began by illustrating, and commenting upon the usual designation of 2 Timothy as a farewell message. It has been pointed out that it is only 2 Tim 4.6-8 that appears to give the impression that the letter is a testament. Nothing else in the letter suggests that Paul was indulging in his final farewell to Timothy. In particular, it is very odd indeed that there are no parting words to reflect Paul's affection for Timothy (cf. Phil 2.20, 22; 1 Thess 3.2), such as one would expect in the final correspondence between Paul and one of his most energetic co-workers. One would expect a very warm, and sorrowful farewell.

Instead, we have the command to Timothy to come soon, and if possible before winter (4.9, 21), as well as the other instructions related to Timothy's future visit (4.11, 13). There are further indications in the text that Paul was confident about the future (4.16ff.).[62] Indeed, the whole tone of 4.9-21 suggests that Paul was preparing an apostolic team for further missionary activity. It is only the 'dark pessimism' of 4.6-8 that disturbs the obvious reading of the letter, and prevents several texts within the letter being given their most likely meaning (e.g. 4.11, 17f.).

Encouraged by the very weak lexicographical argument for taking the key terms of v. 6 to imply Paul's sense of imminent death, we have given an interpretation of those words that both has lexicographical support and well suits the immediate and general context of the letter. We propose that the verb σπένδομαι reflects Paul's sense of his own total dedication to his task, which he describes in three metaphors in v. 7; as a result of these efforts he is utterly spent, or exhausted.[63] We have given our reasons for understanding ἀνάλυσις to mean 'release', rather than 'death'.

Our reading has the obvious advantage of eliminating what is otherwise a great problem of reconciling 4.6-8 with the rest of the letter, and particularly with 4.9-21. Our hypothesis takes refuge neither in a fragments theory which does not respect the composition of the letter as it now stands, nor in a pseudepigraphy theory which does nothing to remove the hiatus between the two moods of the letter.

Finally, one might justifiably ask how the conventional reading of 2 Timothy gained universal acceptance? We suggest that the strong tradition of the martyrdom of Paul has been read back into the text of 2 Tim 4.6, and has imposed upon it a meaning that it does not demand, and one which creates very considerable difficulties when read against the obvious meaning of much else in the letter.

Clearly, if, as we claim, internal considerations support our understanding of the text, it has to be conceded that the external evidence of the history of scholarship is against it. But since our reading of the text both respects the lexicographical evidence, and fits the context admirably, it deserves serious consideration.

Free, then, from the burden of interpreting the rest of the letter in the shade of what appears to be the final message of Paul, the text can now be seen to be what it purports to be, namely Paul's direction to Timothy to come immediately, bringing Mark and Paul's goods with him, so that through him (Paul) the Gospel might be brought to all the nations (cf. 4.17f.).

Chapter 6

PAUL, SECOND TIMOTHY,
AND THE SALVATION OF MANKIND

It is our contention that the universal reading of 2 Tim 4.6-8, and, in particular, the understanding of the text in terms of Paul's sense of imminent death, have imposed upon a number of passages in the letter a meaning very different from the natural reading of those verses. Verses 16-18 of 2 Timothy 4, considered in themselves, seem to reflect Paul's confidence that after the first hearing of his case in the Roman court he would be acquitted and thereby enabled to carry through the next stage of his evangelical mission.

These verses seem to mark the very centre of Pauline thought, with its enthusiasm for Gospel proclamation and the universal mission.[1] Before one could enter into the new order of things it was first of all necessary to have heard the proclamation (cf. Rom 10.14f.), and at the time of the writing of 2 Timothy there were still regions in which the Gospel had not been preached. It was Paul's desire then, as indeed it also appears to have been the will of God, who rescued him from the lion's mouth, that the proclamation should be brought to a completion, and that all of the nations should hear it, through him. It was with this end in view that Paul was now assembling an apostolic team to go on the next stage of the mission. Before giving reasons to justify further this claim let us review how the commentators understand the critical verse, 2 Tim 4.17.

1. *The Commentators on 2 Timothy 4.17*

It will become clear that the conventional understanding of 2 Timothy as a final testament (due exclusively to 'the pessimism of vv. 6-8') demands that the natural meaning of 4.17 be abandoned. Verses 6-8 of ch. 4, then, determine the interpretation of vv. 16-18. The protection that Paul clearly expects in the future cannot, therefore, refer to a physical release, but must refer to some kind of spiritual deliverance. Furthermore, 'the bringing to completion of the proclamation' can refer only to Paul's performance at the first hearing in the Roman court.[2]

In that scenario the audience in the courtroom is made to function as representatives of πάντα τὰ ἔθνη, to whose evangelization Paul was so passionately committed.[3] Even though Paul himself had much wider expectations (Romans 15), many claim that he regarded his mission as complete as soon as he had proclaimed his message to the judges in Rome.[4] Spicq concedes that the ἵνα could suggest another apostolate to follow (such as in Spain), but instead he opts for the 'theological explanation' that 'lorsque l'Apôtre du monde prêche, il s'adresse au monde' (1969: 820). This is an extraodinary comment on the Apostle who had spent so much of his energy and time traversing the world, rather than adressing it from his study.

It is occasionally conceded that if πάντα τὰ ἔθνη is understood literally, the reference cannot be to Paul's defence before the judges.[5] Moreover, as Guthrie acknowledges, if the two verbs (of past, and future hope of deliverance) 'are both taken in a literal sense of deliverance in this life, there can be no doubt that Paul had a firm conviction that he would be released'. But the obvious meaning has to be abandoned because it 'seems contrary to the resignation to his fate in vv. 6-8'. The deliverance, then, has to be spiritual (as in the Lord's prayer) (Guthrie 1957: 177). If the reference to having been rescued from the lion's jaw probably means release, it 'need not do so', since the reference to the full proclamation for the whole pagan world 'could refer to witness borne on trial before the ruler of the whole pagan world'.[6]

Those who support the pseudepigraphy hypothesis do not delay over the precise historical allusions, but are content to relate everything to the conditions of the supposed pseudepigrapher's time. Brox, for example, takes the text to refer to the later estimation of Paul's death, rather than to Paul's reaction to any stage of the trial.[7] While some suggest that the language mirrors that of Psalm 22,[8] Houlden claims that the pseudepigrapher wrote the section basing it on Phil 1.12-14 and Gal 1.16 (1976: 136). If Dibelius and Conzelmann suggest that the original historical setting may have been Caesarea, and that 2 Tim 4.17, then, refers to the promise given in Acts 23.11, Karris, in his enthusiasm for the pious meaning of the letter, appears to bypass altogether the task of considering the import of the text (1979).

Several scholars, however, allow the text its natural meaning, but they do so only on condition that it be separated from 4.6-8. Scott, for example, says that the 'tone of confidence . . . is quite out of keeping with the resignation to certain death in vv. 6-8'.[9] He insists that at the time of his trial Paul was far from having completed his commission to proclaim the Gospel to the whole world, and that he was at that moment confident of acquittal. He claims that 'this would seem to be the only natural meaning of the words'. He insists that Paul, in speaking of 'all the Gentiles' hearing him, cannot very well imply that the judges on the bench were representative of the whole Gentile world, and concludes that Paul 'is not concerned with the trial itself, but with the result he now hopes from it' (Scott 1936: 141f.). Duncan also allows the text its likely meaning, but he, too, insists on the separation of vv. 6-8 from vv. 9-21 (1929: 213).

It is strange that none of the commentators mentioned seriously examines what the verse implies, and not one of them does so with reference to what is surely the key to our understanding of Paul's evangelical vocation, namely, the Letter to the Romans (especially ch. 15), a text which we shall examine in some detail.

2. *Paul's Understanding of* πάντα τὰ ἔθνη

The correct understanding of this term is a key to our comprehension of Paul's dispositions as he composed 2 Tim 4.17. Does it refer to all the peoples of the world, living in Paul's time and the future, and to every person within that category? Or does it refer to all the people of some geographical unit, such as the Roman Empire? Or is it possible that the phrase has merely a representative meaning, with only some representative parts of regions implied? Does ἔθνη here connote Gentiles, and does the πάντα, then, suggest the inclusion of the Jews as well? Does the πάντα suggest the breakdown of some barrier, such as that between Jew and Gentile, slave and freeman, citizen and non-citizen, etc.? Such theoretical questions could be multiplied.

The more relevant matter, however, is to enquire into the question of at what point Paul would consider 'all the nations' to have heard the Gospel. In particular, would that stage have been reached in Rome, either by Paul's having preached in relative freedom for two years, or by his appearing before the court officials during his trial? If one would allow Romans 15 to shed light on the question, the answer is, as we shall show, most certainly not. Rome may have been the *telos* of the Lucan gospel, but it was not so for Paul. Not only was Rome not the *terminus ad quem* of the Pauline mission, it was merely a stepping-stone, as Paul had clearly pointed out in the course of his most systematic statement of his Gospel, in his Letter to the Romans (Rom 15.24-29; cf. 11.11).

Clearly it is of great importance to know what Paul understood by 'all the nations'. Since so much of the argument here hinges on that phrase a careful examination of the terminology is called for, and it is instructive to situate Paul's use of the terminology in a wider historical context.[10] The use of ἔθνος is very extensive indeed. In the LXX it occurs some 1000 times, in Philo about 280, in Josephus more than 400, while in the NT it occurs 162 times, of which 54 are in the Pauline letters.

While the majority of the uses of ἔθνος in the LXX translate the Hebrew גוי, which normally refers to non-Jews, there are some 130 instances where it translates the Hebrew עם which is normally rendered by the Greek λαός. The terminology of the OT, then, is not rigid. What is potentially more relevant for our purpose is the fact that the phrase πάντα τὰ ἔθνη occurs some 134 times in the LXX. While πάντα τὰ ἔθνη does sometimes include the covenant people (e.g. Jer 35 [28]. 11, 14; Ps 46 [47]. 1; 48 [49]. 1; Dan 3.2, 7, 37), in the vast majority of texts in the OT it means all those peoples outside the covenant group (e.g. Deut 7.6; 10.15; Lev 20.26; Esth 4.17). Insofar, then, as the OT functions as a backdrop for Paul's use of the phrase in 2 Tim 4.17, the phrase appears not to exclude any people.

The writings of Philo of Alexandria, a somewhat older contemporary of Paul, and like Paul a diaspora Jew, provide us with the only extant significant body of diaspora Jewish literature from the first century. His 280 occurrences of the word ἔθνος fall into three broad categories: (i) some 160 times where it refers to the Jewish people/ nation, either by name, or by context (e.g. *De Vita Mosis* I, 7; *De Abr.* 57); (ii) where it is used with reference to a specific people, named, or otherwise classified, or simply as a term suggesting geographical or ethnic identity (e.g. *De Dec.* 57); (iii) some 17 times where the noun is used in a metaphorical sense (e.g. *De Som.* II, 133). Philo uses the phrase πάντα τὰ ἔθνη a surprisingly small number of times (*Leg. Ad Gaium* 240; *De Vita Mosis* II; *De Decal.* 37). We see from those three uses that when Philo uses the phrase πάντα τὰ ἔθνη he has in mind all the nations of the earth.

Although word-studies in themselves are notoriously inadequate we can say that insofar as Philo's use of the term illuminates that of his contemporary diaspora Jew, Paul's understanding of proclaiming the Gospel 'to all the nations' was hardly exhausted by his having done so among the ἔθνη he had already encountered between Arabia and Rome.[11]

Josephus was a somewhat younger contemporary of Paul, who, like Paul, was a Pharisee, but unlike Paul and Philo was not a diaspora Jew. In Josephus there is no sense of urgency in respect of an imminent end of the world, and he has no developed thought about the role of the Jews in relation to a world mission. He uses the word ἔθνος more than 400 times, and these can be put into two major categories: (i) In many cases ἔθνος refers to the Jewish nation. We read of 'the nation of the Jews' (e.g. *Bel. Jud.* 2, 197), 'the nation of the Hebrews' (e.g. *Antiq.* 7, 391), 'the nation of the Israelites' (*Antiq.* 11,3), etc. (ii) He also uses τὰ ἔθνη to refer to named individual peoples, or to other non-Jewish peoples, or districts (e.g. *Antiq.* 6,140; 13,196). Where πᾶν τό ἔθνος occurs it is almost always in the singular, and it refers either to the whole Jewish nation or to the whole nation concerned.[12] The phrase πάντα τὰ ἔθνη occurs only three times: in *Antiq.* 7,151, it refers to 'all the many great nations around them'; in *Antiq.* 12,269 the reference is to Mattathias's defiance in the face of the capitulation of 'all the other nations'; and in *Con Ap.* I, 172 Josephus records the ancient poet Choeritus's inclusion of the Jews in his enumeration of 'all the nations'. Josephus, like Philo, uses the word 'nation' without any value judgment. It is used equally of Jews and non-Jews. By way of contrast with Paul's missiology, one searches Josephus in vain for any sense of a Jewish worldwide propaganda.

The Qumran community which saw itself as 'the sole valid form of the eternal alliance between God and Israel' (Vermes 1977: 165), and considered itself to describe the parameters within which God's salvation operated had an extreme sense of exclusiveness: outside the community there was no salvation.[13] Against such a background, a linguistic study of 'the nations' is superfluous. The vast majority of the plural forms of גוי refer to the peoples in the sense of the peoples outside the covenant relationship (e.g. 1QpHab 3.5; 5.4; 1QH 6.12; 1QM 16.1), and they are often spoken of as the enemies of God's chosen people, the children of light.[14] Occasionally, however, one does find a more sympathetic attitude, but this reflects more on the omnipotence of their God than on the good of the outsiders (e.g. 1QH 6.12). If one admires the fidelity of the Covenanters, and their enthusiasm for, and joy in the Law and the Prophets, one cannot but be struck by their suffocating exclusiveness. In terms of a world mission they appear to be at the opposite pole from Paul.

In other Jewish literature spanning the period 200 BC—200 AD[15] one finds both positive and negative attitudes towards the Gentiles.[16] This period saw the resurgence of Jewish nationalism and counter- and even de-Hellenization, followed soon after by domination under the Romans, and, finally, the traumatic destruction of the Temple in the Jewish War. The major interest of the writers was to encourage somewhat down-trodden Jews, to keep alive among the people the belief that God would intervene dramatically, and to improve the moral fibre of the whole nation. It is, then, only *en passant*, that we encounter 'the nations' in the discussion. Where we do encounter the salvation of the Gentiles the emphasis is on the superiority of the Jewish legacy, rather than on the nation's love for others. Clearly Paul's enthusiastic worldwide mission stands in marked contrast to the stress in this literature, in which we do not encounter any desire in the present to bring the good news of the Jewish Law 'to all the nations'.

The extant Rabbinic material comes from a period after the death of Paul, but it is very likely that many of the insights of the Rabbis reflect traditions from Paul's period. The Rabbis have no comprehensive soteriology. Election, covenant and obedience to the Law were their central themes. According to them, salvation was available to all the Jewish-born who stayed within the covenant, and to proselytes who accepted all the conditions of the covenant. With regard to those who were neither born into the covenant, nor entered into it as proselytes there was no systematic soteriology. Although one finds among some Rabbis a sympathetic view of the Gentiles, the general assessment is not favourable.[17]

In addition to examining Jewish sources for a background against which to understand Paul in 2 Tim 4.17, it is instructive to consider the meaning of the key term 'all the nations' as it would have been understood by a Roman citizen in Paul's time. Sherwin-White discusses the designation of the Roman world as *omnes gentes* or τὰ ἔθνη (1973: 437-44). Since Paul himself was a Roman citizen, and since he could hardly have escaped the influence of its *Weltanschauung*, it is not unlikely that his understanding of 'all the nations' was influenced by the Roman view that Rome was 'dominus regum, victor atque imperator omnium gentium' (Cicero, *Or. de Domo sua* 90). The *gentes* were those people who fell within the sphere of Roman military dominance. Sherwin-White illustrates that 'always the more normal description of the Empire is not plain *gentes* but *omnes*, or *cunctae gentes*, a phrase whose persistence illustrates the recognition of both the unity and the difference of the component parts of the Empire' (p. 439). The original expansion of Rome can be summed up, he adds, by the formula, 'gentes universae in civitatem acceptae'. He does add, however, that the Greek equivalent, τὰ ἔθνη, came on the scene later as a term for the empire (p. 440).

If, then, this world-view contributed anything to Paul's understanding of πάντα τὰ ἔθνη in 2 Tim 4.17, it could hardly be claimed that the Gospel had been proclaimed by Paul to even representatives of all the nations, either before his visit to Rome or during his period there. Although it is clear that the phrase must be understood in some hyperbolic sense, it is highly unlikely that, in a world which measured eastwards and westwards from Rome, the city from which he was writing, Paul could have used it without intending to include the lands west of Rome.[18]

We have seen that the Jewish sources are at one in reflecting Israel's sense of having been especially chosen, and this election served to divide the inhabited world into two camps, those 'chosen' and 'the others'. We have seen that where the LXX uses the phrase πάντα τὰ ἔθνη it is almost always with reference to those people outside the covenant. Furthermore, the use seems to include all nations, without exception. Philo uses the phrase a surprisingly small number of times, and when he does use it he means 'all the nations of the world'. In the small number of cases in which Josephus uses the phrase 'all the nations' he, too, clearly intends to exclude no nation, even if in one of its three uses, the term is contrasted with the Jewish nation. The sense of Jewish separateness is more pronounced in the Apocalyptic Literature and among the Rabbis, and reaches a level of extremism in Qumran. In general terms the ἔθνη are those outside the covenant group. We have argued the case that for a contemporary of Paul πάντα τὰ ἔθνη could be as extensive as the boundaries of the Roman Empire, at least, and, in a document written from the capital, could hardly exclude areas to the west of Rome.

In the light of our examination of the term πάντα τὰ ἔθνη in Jewish sources, and in sources approximately contemporaneous with

Paul, it does not seem plausible that Paul could have considered the proclamation of the Gospel to have already been brought to a conclusion as a result of his missions prior to arriving in Rome, and those carried out in that city and in the Imperial courtroom.

Before examining Paul's own use of the terms, and his sense of world mission, let us consider the usage in the New Testament. Matthew uses ἔθνος fourteen times, and all refer to non-Jewish peoples.[19] πάντα τὰ ἔθνη occurs four times, with the meaning in three cases at least (Matt 24.14; 25.32; 28.19) suggesting unbounded universalism, with Matt 24.9, perhaps, being more restricted. Four of the five occurrences of ἔθνος in Mark have parallels in Matthew. The fifth occurrence is in the quotation of Isa 56.7 in Mk 11.17. As in Matthew, ἔθνη refers to non-Jews, although Jews are not to be excluded in Mk 13.10 and 11.17. The two uses of πάντα τὰ ἔθνη are noteworthy. In the scene of the cleansing of the temple Mark is the only one of the Synoptics to quote Isa 56.7 in full.[20] The other note of universalism occurs in the context of the eschatological discourse of Mark 13, where we read that the Gospel must have been preached to all nations before the trials of the disciples can begin (Mk 13.10; contrast Matt 24.14). In complete contrast to the use of ἔθνος in Matthew and Mark, John's five uses are all in the singular, and each refers to the Jewish nation (Jn 11.48, 50, 51, 52; 18.35). The term does not occur in the Johannine epistles. Unlike the other Synoptics Luke uses ἔθνος of the Jewish nation, each time on the lips of Jews (Lk 7.5; 23.2). With the exception of Lk 21.10, where the term does not exclude Jews, the other uses refer to non-Jews (Lk 18.33; 21.10, 24, 25; 22.25). The universal significance of Jesus's mission is predicted in Lk 2.32, and before ascending, Jesus instructed that repentance be proclaimed to all the nations, beginning from Jerusalem (Lk 24.47). πάντα τὰ ἔθνη occurs thrice, and it is clear that universal significance is intended.[21]

In six of the forty-three occurrences of ἔθνος in the Acts the term is used of the Jewish nation.[22] Only once are the nations spoken of in a hostile sense (21.11). Indeed, they are frequently presented as superior to the Jews in that they received the preaching.[23] If Paul's calling is to be an instrument to carry the Lord's name before the nations, the kings and the sons of Israel (9.15), it is clear that he turns to the nations only after the Jews have rejected his message (13.46; 18.6; cf. 28.28). His special task is to go to the distant nations (22.21). James describes the mission of Barnabas and Paul as one of 'making from the nations a λαός for his name' (15.14). The three uses if πᾶν τό ἔθνος suggest that 'all the nations of the earth' are in mind (2.5; 10.35; 14.16; cf. also 17.26).

Of the twenty-three occurrences of ἔθνος in the book of Revelation six appear within a quartet of plurals which clearly exclude no group of people on earth (5.9; 7.9; 11.9; 13.7; 14.6 and 17.15). In 10.11 the term is effectively synonymous with λαός. Almost all the uses of τὰ ἔθνη are neutral in themselves, but the context makes it clear as to which side of the cosmic struggle the 'nation' supports.[24] πᾶν τό ἔθνος is used nine times, and the term invariably means 'all the nations without exception' (2.9; 7.9; 12.5; 13.7; 14.6, 8; 15.4; 18.3, 23).

Apart from the letters of Paul, 1 Peter is the only NT letter that uses the term, and it does so three times. The first is an application of Exod 19.6 to the (Christian) exiles of the diaspora (1 Pet 2.9). 1 Pet 2.12 clearly refers to the non-Christian peoples, and in 4.3 the author has the bad conduct of the gentiles in mind.

We have accounted for all the uses of 'nation' and 'all the nations' in the NT (excluding Paul). Although there are some differences among the NT authors in their use of ἔθνος there is nothing to support the conclusion that the key phrase πάντα τὰ ἔθνη means anything other than 'all the nations of the earth'. Insofar as Paul's understanding of the phrase is consistent with its meaning in the documents we have examined so far, it would not seem plausible to suggest that πάντα τὰ ἔθνη in 2 Tim 4.17 could mean anything other than 'all the peoples of the world'. However, before we rest with that conclusion let us examine Paul's own use of the terms.

Moule has rightly stated that parallels from outside Paul must not be allowed to obscure the meaning of his text. Paul, he insists, is the best commentator on Paul (1974). Paul uses ἔθνος in every letter except Philippians, 2 Thessalonians, Titus, and Philemon, and in all fifty-four times.[25] None of the twenty-nine uses in Romans refers to Israel. In almost all cases it is used in the plural by way of contrast with Israel or the Jews.[26] In the other uses, however, there is no reason to think that Paul is excluding the Jews from among 'the nations'.[27] It is clear from his three uses of πάντα τὰ ἔθνη that Paul sets no narrow limits to the meaning of the term, and that he has in mind 'all the peoples of the world' (Rom 1.5; 15.11; 16.26).

The universal dimension of the Gospel reaches a high-point in this letter. The high wall of separation which Jewish thinkers erected between the chosen people and the outsiders has, according to Paul, collapsed in the revelation of God to all peoples through the activity of Jesus the Messiah. Ethnic and social distinctions disappear, in theory at least, in Christ Jesus.[28] According to Paul the human family is radically one: initially one in sin (Rom 3.22f.), but now one in righteousness (Rom 3.21).

It was this illuminating revelation that already had driven Paul in his missionary activity, 'from Jerusalem to Illyricum' (Rom 15.19), and it was that also which impelled him to bring the Good News further west than Rome, which itself, of course, had already been evangelized. In the opening salutation of the letter to the Romans he describes himself as a servant of Jesus Christ, called to be an apostle, set aside for the Gospel of God, and given grace and apostleship 'to bring about the obedience of faith among all the nations', including the Romans (Rom 1.1-6). If there could be some doubt about the extent of the meaning of τὰ ἔθνη there can be none about πάντα τὰ ἔθνη. Paul saw the Gospel was for 'all the nations', and he saw his own role in its proclamation as central.[29] Paul's emphasis on the universality of the Christian message would be all the more telling if the Roman Jewish Christians were confining their missionary efforts to converting their fellow Jews only.

In one key text Paul turns on its head the expected connection between the conversion of the Jews and that of the Gentiles. Where some elements of Jewish thought allowed for the mass conversion of the Gentiles, they saw it as taking place only after Israel had turned back to its Lord. However, Paul says that a hardening had come upon part of Israel, until such time that the fulness of the nations enters in, at which point all Israel would be saved (Rom 11.25f.). But even already Paul was happy at what God had wrought, through him, in bringing about the obedience of the nations in word and deed (Rom 15.18).[30] But clearly Rome was not to be the geographical *telos* of the Pauline preaching, but merely a transit point. His sights were fixed west of the Capital (Rom 15.24), a question to which we shall return.

Of the four occurrences of ἔθνος in 1 Corinthians one refers to the contrast between Jews and the nations (1 Cor 1.23) and the other three signify 'pagans', rather than 'foreigners' (1 Cor 5.1; 10.20; 12.2). Πάντα τὰ ἔθνη does not occur. The one occurrence of 'nation' in 2 Corinthians refers to the contrast between Paul's own people γένος and the ἔθνη (2 Cor 11.26). Each of the ten occurrences of ἔθνος in Galatians refers to the non-Jews, although the 'quotation' of Gen 12.3 at Gal 3.8 probably includes Jews also.[31] Paul refers to his own particular mission 'to the nations' as God's choice, and fundamentally God's work,[32] the separation of the spheres (cf. Gal 2.2) of activity having been agreed upon with the pillars (Gal 2.9).[33] Clearly the Pauline mission to the non-Jews is a primary theme of this letter, and the one use of πάντα τὰ ἔθνη (Gal 3.8) suggests that that mission is, by God's intention, universal.

Three of the five occurrences of ἔθνος in Ephesians refer to Paul's mission,[34] while Eph 2.11 reflects the distinction between the circumcized and the uncircumcized, and Eph 4.17 counsels against imitating pagan behaviour. Although πάντα τὰ ἔθνη does not occur in this letter, we note the stress within it on the breaking down of the barrier separating non-Jews from Jews (especially Eph 2.14ff.), and Paul's privileged and graced commission to preach that Gospel. The one occurrence of ἔθνος in Colossians is in a context reminiscent of Ephesians 3.[35] Although πάντα τὰ ἔθνη is not used, much of the letter stresses the universal salvation of mankind.[36] Each of the occurrences of ἔθνος in 1 Thessalonians is in the plural, with that in 2.16 referring to non-Jews and that in 4.5 to pagans.

In the first of the two uses of ἔθνος in 1 Timothy Paul describes himself as a (divinely appointed) 'herald and apostle ... teacher of the nations in faith and truth' (2.7; cf. 1.11). Although πάντα τὰ ἔθνη does not occur, the context makes it clear that the universal mission of the Gospel is in mind, since God, our Saviour, desires 'all men' to be saved and to come to the knowledge of the truth (2.4). The sole mediator between this one God and the man is Christ Jesus, who gave himself as a ransom 'for all' (2.6). The second use is in the christological hymn of 3.16, in which the mystery of our religion is described in terms of six aspects of the life of Jesus, with the fourth and fifth referring to the preaching among the peoples, and the believing in the world, which precede his being taken up in glory. Once again we see the emphasis on the importance of the widespread proclamation of the mystery.[37]

It was with a view to uncovering the meaning of πάντα τὰ ἔθνη in 2 Tim 4.17 that this investigation was initiated. We began by claiming that the conventional reading of 2 Tim 4.6-8 prevented 2 Tim 4.17 being given its most obvious meaning. While examining the use of the relevant terminology in many sources we have been careful to consider the underlying soteriologies of the sources.

We have seen that ἔθνος is sometimes employed to refer to the Jewish people, as well as to any other people. We have also seen that τὰ ἔθνη is often used of non-Jews, but could also mean simply 'the peoples of the world'. We have seen that Paul's use of the terminology is very consistent. Unlike Philo, John and Josephus, he never uses ἔθνος to refer to Jews. For him τὰ ἔθνη invariably designates the non-Jews of the world. But if τὰ ἔθνη meant the non-Jews did πάντα τὰ ἔθνη include the Jews also? When one keeps in mind the universal dimension of Paul's apostolic mission, and when one takes note of the strategy he employed (e.g. Romans 15), it seems clear that for him πάντα τὰ ἔθνη included all the peoples of his known world, with no exception. Only this conclusion is consistent with his sense of his own apostolic vocation 'to all men' (cf. Acts 22.15).

The question arises as to how Paul could ever imagine the *kerygma* 'to have been brought to completion', and at what stage he would be satisfied that 'all nations had heard it' (cf. 2 Tim 4.17). One must allow for some element of hyperbole. When writing to the Romans he declared that he had completed the preaching of the Gospel from Jerusalem to Illyricum (Rom 15.19). Are we expected to conclude that no inhabitant of the relevant region missed hearing the proclamation, or are we to understand only that no town or village was omitted from his programme? Neither of these alternatives is convincing. What is more likely is that Paul considered himself either personally, or through his substantial body of co-workers, to have presented the Gospel to representative groups within the region bounded by Jerusalem and Illyricum. And since that job had already been done, it was time for him to change the direction of his apostolic activity, and go westward to Spain.

Support for the common view that Paul would have considered his defence before a Roman court, or his earlier preaching in the Imperial capital to have fulfilled his apostolic goal is lacking. Our lexicographical examination of several authors who might be expected to have either influenced, or reflected Paul's thought lends no support to the common interpretation of 2 Tim 4.17. Paul's own use of the relevant terminology, and his clearly-stated evangelical goal, which we shall discuss presently, seem to rule out the common interpretation. We suggest that this interpretation has been imposed upon 2 Tim 4.17 by the usual reading of 2 Tim 4.6-8.

3. *Paul and his Mission to* πάντα τὰ ἔθνη

Since we have already argued that at the time of writing 2 Timothy Paul was in Rome, that he considered himself to be about to be released from prison, and that he was gathering his team for the next stage of his evangelization, it will be instructive to enquire into his sense of his own apostolic mission, and his evangelical strategy. This shall be done in three stages, by inquiring into Paul's sense of his vocation in general, the salvation of the Gentiles within that plan, and his intention to go to Spain.

A. *Paul's Apostolic Vocation*

As we have seen, several of the major modern commentators on 2 Timothy consider Rome to have been the theatre for the execution of Paul's task outlined in 2 Tim 4.17. It is rather surprising that such a conclusion could have been reached in the light of the evidence provided by the Letter to the Romans. But before considering that letter in detail we wish to make some observations about Paul's understanding of his mission.

No understanding of Paul's life is valid if it separates his fundamental religious experience on the way to Damascus from that of his apostolic commission. The importance of Paul for the life of the Christian Church does not lie in the fact that he had a most intense revelation of the Risen Lord, but rather in the nature of the Divine appointment and commission given as an apostle on the occasion of that revelation.[38] It is the connection between the revelation of the Risen Jesus Christ and the mission to evangelize the 'nations' that is the key to understanding Paul's life and work. The modern fascination with psychology and personalist philosophy tends to make recent generations concentrate on the personal religious experience of Paul, and give less attention to his universal mission. For Paul himself the Damascus road experience, while fundamental to his religious perception, served more to redirect his enthusiasm than merely provide him with an interior illumination. The revelation was a commission, and the commission was that Paul would communicate not merely the good news of his own conversion, but rather the Gospel of God.[39] He saw his mission as one of evangelizing, rather than merely baptizing (1 Cor 1.17), and he refers to his task as a necessity (ἀνάγκη) laid upon him.[40]

As we have seen, Paul uses the phrase πάντα τὰ ἔθνη only four times.[41] It is clear that he saw God's gift of apostleship as directed towards the bringing about of the obedience of faith 'among all the nations' (Rom 1.5), and that he understood the mystery, once hidden but now revealed, to be directed towards bringing about the obedience of faith among 'all the nations' (Rom 16.26), and that he looked forward to the time when 'all the nations' would bless God (Gal 3.8). Although in the fourth context, 2 Tim 4.17, he makes it equally clear that he wished that 'all the nations' would hear the *kerygma*, he was in no doubt that his own particular part in the universal proclamation was to preach to the non-Jews, rather than to the circumcized (Rom. 11.13). There is no necessity to conclude that Paul saw his apostolic mission as being restricted to Gentiles, as Gal 1.16; 2.2, 7ff. might suggest. The Gospel was God's power of salvation for Jew first, and then Greek (Rom 1.16). His concern for the evangelization of Jew as well as Greek is further attested in Romans 9–11, and in his identification with both Jew and Gentile in order to win them to Christ (1 Cor 9.19-23), and is particularly striking in the Act's portrayal of Paul's strategy of making his first efforts among the Jews (and proselytes) in their synagogues.[42]

But for Paul there is a causal connection between the salvation of the Gentiles and that of the Jews: Salvation has come to the Gentiles so as to make Israel jealous (Rom 11.11). He hopes that his διακονία as apostle to the Gentiles may provoke his fellow Jews, and save some of them (Rom 11.13f.). Indeed, he sees the present rejection of the Gospel by the Jews as neither permanent nor merely fortuitous, but rather as part of the mystery whereby the full number of the Gentiles will first come in, 'and thus all Israel will be saved' (Rom 11.25f.).[43] Such, then, in Paul's estimation, is the relation between the preaching of the one Gospel and the ultimate salvation of all, of Greeks first, if we may so express it, and then, as a consequence, of Jews.

B. *Paul and the Salvation of the Gentiles*
Paul's understanding of his apostolic mission is vital to a correct interpretation of 2 Tim 4.17. For that reason one must take account of his missionary goal and strategy (Munck 1954; and 1950).[44] It is central to Munck's thesis that Paul saw his calling to be that of a prophet-like apostle, who had a vital role to play in bringing about the consummation of things, now that the foretold Messiah had come

and the world awaited the completion of his ministry.[45] As a prophet of the new age, Paul saw his task as having even greater significance than that of the OT prophets (1954: 50). Munck argues from Romans 9–11 that Paul understands his mission to be an instrument to bring about the End-Time (1954: 42-49). When Paul considered his work in the East to be completed, he was free to turn his attention westward, guided more by the eschatological demand, than by the geographical strategy of the mission.[46] Munck interprets the collection as an eschatological sign: the sight of the eschatological pilgrimage of Gentiles (by way of 'representative universalism'), and of their gifts, would stimulate the Jewish people to conversion. According to Munck Paul interpreted his arrest, etc., after the failure of the pilgrimage of Gentiles, as eschatological events comparable to the Passion of Our Lord.[47]

But even if Munck overstated his case in several details, we consider that he is substantially correct in his estimate that Paul considered the evangelization of 'all the nations' to be a prelude to the advent of the End-Time, and he certainly saw himself as having a vital part to play in that enterprise (Rom 11.7-11, 25ff.; 2 Tim 4.17).[48] Clearly, if Paul considered himself to have an important part to play in such a world-wide mission considerations of strategy and geography have to be reckoned with. This would appear to be at the forefront of Paul's mind as he wrote to the Romans (Romans 15). Up to that point he was satisfied that the Gospel had been brought to completion from Jerusalem to Illyricum,[49] and now he was preparing to shift the theatre of his missionary activity from the East to the West, and in particular to Spain.

C. *Paul and the Mission to Spain*

The literature on the significance of the planned mission to Spain is not extensive.[50] Only a handful of the commentaries say anything of significance, and practically all of them do little more than make two observations, namely, that now that Paul's work was completed 'in these parts', he must move on, and since it was his practice not to build on the foundations laid by others he decided to go west.

Several commentators appear to attach little significance to the proposed visit to Spain,[51] and many other have very little to say about it.[52] Some explain the move westwards in terms of Paul's being without work (*arbeitslos*) in the west.[53] Two kinds of reasons are given for the choice of Spain. Some stress only that Paul's practice was to *found* churches, i.e., to preach to people who had not yet been evangelized, and Spain fitted that bill,[54] while others attach some special significance to the location of Spain.[55]

A few commentators question why Paul chose Spain, since there were several other places in which the Gospel had not yet been preached,[56] but most are happy to leave questions of missionary goal and strategy aside, and satisfy themselves with references to Paul's zeal.[57]

Although several commentators note that Paul's proposed visit to Rome was to be only a temporary one,[58] few seem to reflect any awareness that there might be an essential connection between the writing of the letter, the proposed visit to Rome, and the goal of the present apostolic strategy, the mission to Spain. Many seem happy with the suggestion that Rome was on the way (which it was not), and that Paul would like to see the Roman Christians more or less only in order to get to know them (*um sie kennenzulernen*).[59]

Very little attention has been given to the possible reasons for Paul's choice of Spain. Knox's proposal (as a 'bare possibility') that in Paul's mind Palestine, Syria, Asia Minor and Greece formed part of a circle (κύκλῳ Rom 15.19) and that the whole circle would not be completed until he went beyond Rome, and on to Spain itself (Knox 1964: 11) has little to commend it.[60]

Aus looks to OT Prophecy and the Jewish tradition about Gentiles coming from all the nations of the world with their gifts as the background to Paul's intention to missionize in Spain (Aus 1979: 234, 257-60). He understands Paul's collection for the poor of Jerusalem, and the procession to Jerusalem of representative Gentiles, to be an eschatological sign that the Messiah was soon to come (again), and that the delay would be shortened by his bringing additional Gentiles from Spain.

Spain was Paul's goal because of his Christian interpretation of Isaiah 66,[61] and because Tarshish (= modern Spain) was the first of the distant lands 'that have never heard of me or seen my glory' (Rom 15.20f., quoting Isa 52.15), and was followed by Put (LXX; Pul in MT), Lud, Moshech, Rosh, Tubal and Javan (LXX reads Hellas).[62] Aus argues, in a rather forced way, that the list corresponds to Paul's missionary career, and that Paul now hoped to go to the most distant land on the list, and with his helpers bring representatives of the Gentile nations, rather than diaspora Jews, to Jerusalem as an offering to the Lord Jesus, the Messiah (p. 241). Those Spanish

Gentiles would be a necessary part of the offering of the Gentiles (cf. Rom 15.16), and when representatives of all the nations mentioned in the OT eschatological prophecy had been brought to Jerusalem, the Messiah would return, and all the nations, both Gentiles and Jews would worship him (p. 242). The 'fulness of the Gentiles' would be complete only when Paul had brought Christian representatives from Spain, the most distant site in the OT vision of the End-Time events, with their gifts to Jerusalem (cf. Rom 11.25f.). It was, then, the eschatological prophecy of Isaiah 66 which determined that Spain would be the next stage of the Pauline mission, rather than Alexandria, Ethiopia, Libya, or Babylon.[63]

When writing Romans, then, Aus concludes, 'Paul firmly believed . . . that his collection enterprise would be completed during his own lifetime and primarily through his own efforts. Then the Messiah would come (again). Like the whole creation, the Apostle has until now been waiting "with eager longing for the revealing of the sons of God" (Rom 8.19; cf. v. 23). He knows that salvation is now nearer to him and the Christians of Rome than when he and they first believed (13.11)' (p. 261).

Aus's brilliant thesis, suggesting an interpretation of some key texts of Paul's letters, and of his vocation is not without its weaknesses. In particular, it is rather odd that if Isaiah 66 occupied such a crucial role in Paul's understanding of his mission, he does not quote from it in his letters (outside of 2 Thessalonians), and, moreover, in those sections of his letters dealing with the collection there is no appeal to OT apocalyptic texts. Furthermore, it is far from clear that Paul understood the collection as apocalyptically as Aus suggests.[64] The collection was primarily directed towards the alleviation of the poor in Jerusalem, but was also, obviously, a powerful statement of κοινωνία between the diaspora churches, and the mother church.[65] Moreover, neither is the thesis proved that Paul understood the 'procession' of representative diaspora believers to be comparable to the streams of nations pouring into Jerusalem at the End Time.[66]

Aus has pressed too far the influence of (some strands of) Jewish End-Time expectation on Paul. The images associated with those times are metaphors professing the authors' beliefs in the world-wide dominion of Yahweh, and should not be pressed into appearing to be literalist predictions of actual events. In our view it was Paul's grasp of the world-wide significance of Jesus, rather than a supposed

Christian interpretation and literalist reading of Isaiah 66 which was the source of his missionary dynamism.

We wish to propose that in writing to the Romans, and in planning to go out of his way to visit the community there, Paul had in mind some very significant hopes for Roman help in the next stage of his evangelical strategy. He could not have imagined that through himself alone the full number of the Gentiles would be brought in, but he was well aware of the vital role God had given him in extending the proclamation of the Gospel to all the nations (2 Tim 4.17).[67] Work in the Western end of the Empire would be a fitting reflection of that already achieved in the East. In such a development the prophetic hope for the dissemination of the news of God's glory would be further advanced through him.[68]

4. *The Romans and Paul's Planned Mission to Spain*

It is only in the Letter to the Romans that we learn of Paul's determination to bring the Gospel to Spain (Rom 15.24, 29). In the letter we also learn of his desire to visit the Roman community, and of his intention to spend some time with them (Rom 1.11-15; 15.22-24). If among the commentators there has been some shift away from reading Romans as a general theological tract,[69] and if more attention is given to the conditions of the Roman Christians as reflected in the letter,[70] very few appear to be sensitive to the connection between the letter, the proposed visit, and the next stage of the apostolic mission.[71] It is our contention that the letter, and Paul's proposal to go out of his way to visit the Roman community, are two elements in his planning for the mission to Spain, a project for the successful outcome of which he depended on the support of the Roman community. We shall now investigate Paul's expectations of the Roman community, and then enquire into the likely result of his efforts to enlist their support for the Spanish mission.

A. *Paul's Expectations of the Romans*

Our understanding of this subject is closely bound up with our estimate of the purpose of the Letter to the Romans. In our view the key to the correct understanding of the letter lies in Paul's plans as outlined in Romans 15. Paul's eyes were set on Spain, and everything in the letter is properly appreciated once one takes seriously into consideration his apostolic strategy. It was because Paul wanted the help of the Roman community for the Spanish mission that he both wrote to, and proposed to visit it. Had this mission not been uppermost in his mind, and had he not needed the help of the Romans, he would neither have written to them, nor intended to pass through.

If much of the letter deals with the fundamental theological question of justification by faith, it is framed by two sections which clearly express Paul's desire and hope to visit the Roman community. But if this desire and intention come as the second item in the thanksgiving period, and occupy all of the material from 1.9-15, Paul makes it abundantly clear that he intends merely to pass through Rome on his way to Spain. Those who have found it difficult to discern the situation context of Romans have, unwittingly, latched on to a fundamental insight, namely, that Paul is not presuming to address himself to the particular situation of the Church in Rome, but is, rather, dealing with the more general theological and missiological question of the world-wide significance of salvation in Jesus Christ, and the consequential ecclesiological question of the place of Jews and Gentiles within that mystery.[72]

Looking at the situation from Paul's standpoint, insofar as we can judge from the letter itself, it is clear that he had his heart set on evangelizing in Spain, rather than in Rome. But before he could go to Spain he had to deliver the collection to Jerusalem. Spain was the goal of his present missionary strategy, rather than of the whole mission. That mission was 'to bring about obedience ἐν πᾶσιν τοῖς ἔθνεσιν... including yourselves who are called to belong to Jesus Christ' (Rom 1.5f.). It is only in Romans that Paul states his mission in terms of bringing about the obedience among the nations, and by so doing he is from the beginning directing the attention of the Roman readers to the world-wide implications of his apostolate. And at the other end of the letter, he returns not only to the same subject, but uses the same terminology.[73] The letter, then, is framed, as it were, by references to his universal mission.

In between those frames Paul gives the most complete statement of his Gospel of the salvation of all by faith, and of the particular sequence of that missionary task as he conceived it, namely, making salvation in Christ available to the Gentiles in order to provoke Israel to jealousy (Rom 11.11, 25). In the letter he makes it clear that his work in one major region is already complete (Rom 15.23), and that he must now bring the Gospel to where it had not already been preached (cf. Rom 15.20f.). Paul writes to the Romans, then, to inform them of his immediate intentions and needs. His primary need is that the Roman community will speed him on his mission to Spain (Rom 15.24), and it is in that hope that he intends to go out of his way to visit the Roman community, after he has delivered the collection in Jerusalem.

And yet one of the recent, and most significant readings of the letter to take the *Sitz im Leben* of the Roman church seriously, does not even mention either Paul's proposed visit to Rome, or his mission to Spain.[74] Minear, however, does not make that mistake. In his view Paul's desire to effect a reconciliation between the different factions in the Roman church was intimately related to his enlisting the united support of the Roman Christians for the Spanish mission.[75] Although Beker finds it impossible to pinpoint one decisive cause for the writing of Romans, he does give first place to Paul's desire to solicit Roman help for the next stage of the circular Mediterranean evangelization.[76]

Jewett, too, opts for the view that the purpose of what he calls the 'Ambassadorial Letter' to the Romans was to advocate a cooperative mission to evangelize Spain.[77] As well as proposing that Romans was written to solicit Roman help for the Spanish mission (which we argue on other grounds), Jewett adds very considerably to our understanding of the letter, by drawing out the implications of discerning Romans to be an ambassadorial letter.[78] He claims, as we do, that the *causa* of the letter and its elaboration (1.10, 13), with its reiteration in 15.24, 'clarifies the point of the entire letter to the Romans'.[79] Jewett's reading has the great advantage of respecting the integrity of the letter, and allows each part to be interpreted in a way that coheres with the general purpose of the letter. In particular, he gives full weight to Paul's plans for Spain.[80]

The polite tone of Romans, when compared with that of Galatians, is best explained by taking seriously Paul's need of the support of the Romans for the Spanish mission. It should be added, however, that what appears in the letter is only the first stage of a process by which Paul hoped to gain the patronage of the Romans for the next stage of his plans for the world-wide spread of the Gospel. What is said in only the vaguest way in the letter about the help he wants from the Romans will be hammered out in great and precise detail when he comes to them in person.

What precisely Paul wanted of the Roman community is not, to put it mildly, clear from the text. In addition to the possibility that the importance Paul attaches to the gift of the Gentile churches for the Jerusalem poor (Rom 15.25-32) may be directed to stimulating the Romans to contribute financially to the next stage of his mission, we have the intriguing reference to Paul's hope that he would be sped on his way to Spain by the Romans (Rom 15.24).

Since few commentators make much of Paul's plans for the mission to Spain, the comments on προπεμφθῆναι (Rom 15.24) are sparse. Several content themselves with listing (some of) the NT occurrences of the verb, while others suggest that the verb included being furnished with letters of recommendation,[81] or prayers and goodwill,[82] or financial aid,[83] or provisions for the journey,[84] or with someone from Rome to accompany him to a certain point.[85] The variety of the NT uses of the verb cautions against assuming a singular meaning, and if some are suggestive, they can hardly be regarded as settling for us the meaning of the verb in Rom 15.24.[86]

Dodd suggests that the expression may have had the sense of an almost technical term, well-understood among missionaries (1932: 229; likewise Lightfoot 1885: 322), and although he devotes no space to a discussion of the Spanish mission, he suggests, on the basis of 1 Cor 16.6, 2 Cor 1.16, Acts 15.3, and 3 John 6, that both the defraying of expenses, and the appropriate accreditation were involved. Best, in addition to mentioning letters of recommendation and some money to leave Paul free to preach, hints at least that Paul may have hoped for manpower from the Romans (1967: 170). Cranfield suggests that Paul may have hoped for Roman Christians with a knowledge of Spain to accompany him thither (1979: 769). Although O'Neill does not attempt to specify Paul's hopes of the Roman community, he does recognize that in v. 24, we see more clearly and explicitly than anywhere else, that Paul did have one urgent and specific purpose in writing to Rome (1975: 245). Käsemann brings the discussion furthest by suggesting that in addition to a prayerful farewell, and someone to accompany him for part of the journey, Paul hoped that the Roman community would provide him with people who knew Spain, and that they would actively support his work, and take a certain responsibility for it.[87] But even he has not gone far enough. If the verb ('to be sped') in itself does not satisfy our curiosity about what Paul expected from the Romans, perhaps an overview of Paul's missionary practice may enlighten us.

The evidence of the Acts of the Apostles and the Pauline letters seems to point in different directions. According to the Acts it was Paul's practice to begin evangelization in the local synagogues,[88] although his activity was not confined to them.[89] However, there is no reference to a synagogue in the letters,[90] and from them we get the impression that the house assemblies were a very important means of evangelization (e.g. 1 Cor 16.19; Rom 16.5; Phlm 2; Col 4.15). His place of work also was a forum for evangelization.[91]

Although it is often claimed that there was a sizeable Jewish population in Spain during Paul's lifetime,[92] the fact remains that there is no evidence of a Jewish presence prior to the fall of Jerusalem, and that a sizeable one did not emerge until the third century.[93] If the argument from silence is valid then we have another indication of a development in Paul's missionary strategy. Spain would be Paul's first mission region without a Jewish presence. Those whose aid was being sought would, therefore, have to be all the more convinced of the universal nature of the Gospel.

Paul's dependence on others was very considerable. Local hospitality was a vital source of help in advancing the Gospel,[94] and at least one community helped to finance his mission.[95] The part played also by co-workers, both local and travelling companions was vital.[96]

We have suggested that Paul's proposed visit to the Roman community would have given him the opportunity of making his requests more explicit. For the Spanish mission to be successful Paul would need information about the country, and also a network of communities amongst whom he could evangelize and work, and from whom he could get the necessary hospitality. Given the ease of communication between Rome and Spain,[97] it is likely that some Roman Christians knew Spain, as commercial travellers, and even perhaps as part of an outreach of evangelization. It was all the more important for Paul, then, that he be well recommended by the Roman Christians.

It is very likely that the Roman community would have been in a position to provide Paul with Spanish contacts, with letters of recommendation and support, and with travelling companions who would function in the West as Barnabas, Timothy and Silvanus, etc., had done in the East. The provision of money by the Roman community might also have been vital, and would have released Paul from the burden of having to spend much of his day in the laborious work of tentmaking.[98]

We suggest then that Paul hoped that the Roman community would 'own' the mission to Spain, in the way the Antioch community did his earlier ones. That may help to explain the polite tone of Romans as compared with Galatians. Clearly Paul needed their help so badly that he considered it necessary to give the Romans the fullest account of his Gospel. Moreover, the amount of space and attention he gives in Romans 15 to the diaspora collection for the Jerusalem community may be interpreted as Paul's spur to the Romans to support his intentions for Spain, with the same generosity with which the Eastern Christians had rallied to his support for some time.

B. *Paul and the Romans: The Reality*
More than two years elapsed between Paul's writing of his missionary manifesto and his arrival in Rome, the half-way house to Spain. The circumstances of his life had taken a disastrous turn: he was now a prisoner. We should like to know how Paul fared in the company of the Roman Christians, and in particular whether his high expectations of them as reflected in Romans was matched by the reality of his reception. There is more than a little evidence to suggest that the reality fell far short of the expectation, and it is to this evidence that we now turn.

Acts 27.1–28.16 purports to describe Paul's journey from Caesarea to Rome, but the value of this account is a matter of considerable debate.[99] Among the factors which distinguish the Acts' account is the particular interest of the author in the person of Paul.[100] One is struck by the author's account of Paul's treatment at the hands of Julius. We learn immediately that he treated Paul kindly, allowing him at Sidon to go to his friends (27.3). In the subsequent references to Julius, this Roman functionary appears as a man who behaved favourably towards Paul (27.6, 11, 31), even to the extent of saving his life (27.43).

One is also struck by the frequency with which the notion of being saved occurs in the account.[101] The theme of the saving of all the passengers is very striking in 27.9–44. Moreover, it was the physical safety of all that was in question.[102] The author gives an account of two severe obstacles to the safety of the passengers: the imminent fleeing of the sailors, prevented by the intervention of Paul (27.27–32), and the threat to the lives of the prisoners at the hands of the soldiers, which was removed by the centurion's desire to save Paul (27.39–44).[103]

The theme of favour to Paul so obvious in the Acts' portrayal of Julius is taken up again in chapter 28. The author points out how the travellers were treated with unusual kindness in Malta (v. 2),[104] and that Publius entertained them 'in a friendly fashion' for three days (v. 7). Paul healed Publius's father, and many who had diseases, and when it was possible for the party to leave, the people of the island gave them many gifts, and put on board whatever they needed (v. 10).

The brethren of Puteoli, when they were found, asked them to stay with them for seven days, and the author says no more than that 'thus we went to Rome' (v. 14).

The Roman brethren did come to meet them at the Forum of Appius and the Three Taverns. On seeing them, Paul gave thanks to God, and took courage (v. 15)![105]

It is indeed very surprising that the author of Acts never mentions any activity of the Christians in Rome itself. All the more so when one remembers that it was to the Roman community that Paul addressed his most substantial letter. Luke's attention focuses only on Paul's dealings with the Jews, in two stages. The 'chief men of the Jews' (v. 17) embraced, perhaps, the *archontes*, *grammateus*, *gerousiarches* of each synagogue, as well as some *presbuteroi*, while the 'more' (v. 23) suggests the ordinary membership of the synagogues.[106]

Paul, who, as we have seen, was accustomed to the hospitality of the local brothers,[107] 'was permitted to stay by himself with the soldiers guarding him' (v. 16). The centurion of the Augustan Cohort, Julius, is the person most likely to have given Paul this permission, but when one remembers that the same Julius allowed Paul in Sidon to go to his friends to be cared for by them, one must wonder if there is not more than a suggestion that the members of the Roman community were not prepared to take Paul in.[108] But v. 16 allows of another interpretation, even less favourable to the Roman brothers, namely that they allowed Paul to stay on his own: there was no room for him in their inns. That this interpretation is not altogether eccentric is confirmed by two other references in the remaining verses of the chapter (vv. 23 and 30), each of which makes it clear that Paul was not in receipt of the normal hospitality he encountered in the course of his ministry hitherto.

Paul must have been under a considerable financial burden while in Rome.[109] His accommodation was sufficient to cater for meeting the local Jewish leaders, and the two years living at his own expense, or in his own hired quarters (v. 30), must have required some considerable income. There is no hint in the text of Acts that the Roman community made any contribution towards catering for Paul's needs. The only mention of the Roman Christians in Acts 28 is that they went to meet him at a distance from the city.[110] The account is silent about the behaviour of the Christians within the city. In particular there is not a word about any sign or gesture of hospitality which the Roman Christians proferred on Paul.[111]

When one remembers the emphasis Luke gives to the importance of hospitality in Luke–Acts in general,[112] and the four kinds of hospitality the prisoners received prior to arrival in Rome, it is difficult to escape the conclusion that Luke's account of Paul's fate in Rome can scarcely hide the fact that he was 'given the cold shoulder' by the Christian community there. One might even be justified in wondering if the reference to Paul's freedom to preach openly and unhindered is not with reference to his independence of, and even freedom from being either ostracized, or opposed by the Roman Christians.

In addition to the material in Acts 27–28 there are indications in the Captivity Letters that Paul was not well treated in Rome. If Paul was in Rome at the time of writing the Letter to Philemon we can use that letter as an indication of how he fared in Rome.[113] There is more than a hint in the letter that Paul wanted Onesimus back. If at an earlier time he was ἄχρηστος to Philemon he has now become 'to you and to me εὔχρηστος' (v. 11). Although Paul is sending him back, he would be glad to keep him 'in order that he might serve me on your behalf during my imprisonment for the gospel' (v. 13; cf. 2 Tim 4.11 of Mark). Then at the end of the letter Paul states that he knows that Philemon will do more than Paul has said (v. 20). Verse 11 and 13 suggest that Onesimus had a gospel ministry, and it seems to us that Paul is anxious to have him back. It could even be the case that Paul wanted Onesimus to join him in his mission plans for the future. It is at least plausible that help from the Roman brothers is so lacking that Paul has to depend on help from outside. The fact that there are no greetings from any Roman, such as those mentioned in Romans 16, may not be of any significance, since they may not have been known to Philemon. But the absence of any reference to help received from the Roman brethren may suggest that Paul had little good to say about the Christians in Rome.

The Letter to the Colossians gives very few clues about the

conditions in which Paul is imprisoned. If Paul acknowledges that
the Gospel is bearing fruit and growing in the whole world, as it is
among the Colossians (1.5f.), there is no indication in the letter that
the Roman Christians are helping him advance it. Paul rejoices in his
sufferings (1.24), but there is no mention of any Roman alleviating
them. Indeed, the only comfort mentioned is provided by the group
of the circumcision co-workers who advance the kingdom of God
(4.12). This could possibly suggest that others ἐκ περιτομῆς are not
advancing the Gospel. In any case, as in Philemon, there is no
greeting from the Roman brothers, but only from the same quintet as
in Philemon, and from an additional Jesus Justus.

There is very little in the Letter to the Ephesians that suggests the
circumstances of Paul's incarceration. We are told little more than
that Paul is a δέσμιος (3.1; 4.1), and an ambassador in chains (6.20).

The Letter to the Philippians gives a great deal of information
about the conditions of Paul (and also the circumstances of the
addressees).[114] There are strong signs of division within the Roman
Christian community, with most of the brethren emboldened to
speak without fear (1.4), while some preach from envy and rivalry,[115]
even if others do so out of goodwill (1.15). The Philippians had
helped Paul in his difficulties (1.7). Timothy, the co-author of the
letter, is singled out in 2.19f. for his outstanding support of Paul,
against a background of those in Rome who look to their own
interests, and not those of Jesus Christ (2.21). If 3.1-11 reflects the
Roman, rather than the Philippian, or more general scene, we have
further evidence of division, with the groups divided over Jewish
practices and dietary laws. And if 3.18 also reflects the situation in
Rome we have a reference to many living as enemies of the cross of
Christ.[116]

Paul gives no indication of how he earned his living, if that was
necessary while in captivity. He does not mention any kindness done
him by the Roman community, or by any individual in it. Instead, he
commends the generosity of the Philippians, who shared in his
suffering (4.14), and who sent Epaphroditus, their 'messenger and
minister to my needs' (2.25), to fill him with their gifts (4.18). In all,
then, Paul would appear to be rather isolated.[117] Again, none of the
people mentioned in Romans 16 is mentioned, and none of the people
named as senders of greetings in Colossians and Philemon appears.
The tone of the letter is somewhat funereal (1.21-26; 2.17), although
it is full of joy in so many places.

5. *Conclusion*

In examining the meaning of 2 Tim 4.17, we have shown that the evidence for the use of the critical phrase πάντα τὰ ἔθνη weighs very strongly against the common view that Paul would have considered himself to have brought the proclamation to the nations to completion in his appearance before a Roman tribunal. We have also drawn attention to the universal dimension of Paul's missionary enterprise. The long-term goal was that all the nations of the world would hear the proclamation.

We have noted that at the time of writing to the Romans Paul was about to make a fundamental change in his mission strategy, and was most anxious to enlist the help of the Roman Christians for his mission in Spain. We have argued that Acts 28 contains a veiled criticism of the Roman brothers, whose behaviour towards Paul was decidedly indifferent, when measured against that of several individuals and groups who by their hospitality advanced the Gospel. Insofar as the Captivity Letters, especially Philippians, reflect the situation in Rome, there is little in them to suggest that Paul was well treated. The Roman community, then, did not provide Paul with the kind of support for which he had hoped.

This scenario is consistent with the information in 2 Timothy. The Asians had abandoned him in Rome (1.5), and Onesiphorus's zeal in seeking Paul out, and Paul's praise of his efforts (1.17), may reflect the Roman Christians' indifference to his whereabouts or condition.[118] It remains now to examine other elements of 2 Timothy to illuminate further the life-setting.

Chapter 7

THE 'SITZ IM LEBEN' OF SECOND TIMOTHY

In Chapter 6 we proposed that the key text, 2 Tim 4.17, together with other texts in 2 Timothy, reflects Paul's confidence that he would be released, and that he could, therefore, embark on another stage of his missionary activity. We brought into consideration Paul's general apostolic vision and strategy, and attempted in particular to understand his concern that all the nations of the world should hear the *kerygma* through him.

We interpret Paul's desire to see Timothy (1.4), and the urgency with which this is stressed (4.9, 21) to be related to his missionary zeal. In Chapter 5 we proposed a reading of 4.6-8 that is consistent with 4.9, 21, in that it reflects Paul's confidence that he would be released from prison. Even if Alexander had done him great harm (4.14), and although he experienced many difficulties in the first hearing of his case with nobody standing by him but, rather, being abandoned by all (4.16), the Lord had taken his part and empowered him so that he could push on with his mission.[1] We propose, then, that as he writes 2 Timothy Paul is preparing himself for the next stage of his mission. What were his plans? Where did he intend going, and with whom?

Paul had hoped for so much from the Romans, but in our view he was received very badly by the Christians in Rome. If Acts 28 and the Captivity Letters suggest that Paul was not treated well in Rome, the abandonment of him by the Roman Christians is seen at its starkest in 2 Timothy. Where, one asks, were the members of the Roman community whom he addressed with such ambassadorial finesse in Romans 16? If Paul finds it hard to avoid a spirit of vindictiveness towards Alexander (4.14), the most he can bring himself to say about the Romans is the wish that the Lord may not reckon their betrayal of him against them.

If the mission to Spain depended upon the co-operation of such people it could hardly be a success. Perhaps that is why we hear nothing in any letter written from captivity of his earlier plans for a mission in Spain (Rom 15.24, 28). Insofar as Philippians and Philemon guide us about Paul's plans in Rome it is to the East that he proposes to return. And if 1 Timothy and Titus were written by Paul, and after 2 Timothy, they, too, witness to further evangelization back in the eastern part of the Empire. It may be the case that Paul had been surprised to encounter such poverty among the Roman Christians, and had to go to the east to collect funds to finance his plans for Spain.

Whatever the goal of Paul's missionary strategy he could hope for very little from the Romans. And since Demas had already taken a worldly option and gone to Thessalonica (4.10), one could hope for little more συνεργόν from him. The crown, which Paul reminds Timothy will be awarded on the Day of the Lord's coming, will be reserved for those who, like Paul himself (4.6ff.), have loved His appearing (4.8), and who, unlike Demas (4.10), have remained faithful.

Among those mentioned in the letter, Onesiphorus does not appear to be still in Rome. His being singled out for the attention he gave to Paul in Rome adds to the picture of Paul's being neglected by the Roman community. Onesiphorus, in fact, had to search diligently for Paul, who adds that he had succeeded in finding him. He seems to have been the only one (certainly among those from Asia) who was not ashamed of Paul's chains. These verses, also, suggest that the Roman Christians did not want to be associated with the prisoner, Paul.

Moreover, Titus had gone east of Rome, to Dalmatia (4.10), and Paul had sent Tychicus to Ephesus (4.12), which reflects Paul's continued interest in the east.

Of the other people mentioned in the letter little could be hoped for from the Asians. Although Crescens had gone to Gaul (Galatia) (4.10), it does not follow that he had abandoned Paul as Demas had. It is even possible that he could have been on his way to Spain.

Luke, then, is the only one of his stature with Paul in Rome, and Paul's isolation makes his desire to have Timothy come all the more understandable.[2] Only Luke is at hand for a future missionary journey, and since the Romans have neglected and even abandoned him, Paul must now assemble his own mission team. He calls his trusted co-worker, Timothy, and asks that Mark join him. In addition, he also wants Mark, and his cloak and parchments. The missionary team, then, will be Paul, Luke, both already in Rome, and Timothy and Mark who are to join them there.

Concerning the location of the mission field we can only speculate. Undoubtedly it would fall within the general vision of Paul's perception of his apostolate to bring to completion the proclamation of the Gospel, so that 'all the nations' would hear it (2 Tim 4.17). The failure to mention Spain in 2 Timothy, or in any of the letters written after Romans, suggests that he may have abandoned that plan, and if the Captivity Letters (particularly Philippians and Philemon) were written from Rome it would appear that he hoped to go to the East, rather than westward.[3] It is, of course, a possibility that the plans to go east were related to Paul's hopes to gain from the churches there the necessary support to bring to fruition his plans for a mission to Spain.

In this chapter we deal at greater length with Paul's desire that Timothy come quickly, that he bring Mark, and his cloak and parchments, and that Timothy remain steadfast in his vocation. We suggest that all four elements are related to Paul's plans for the next stage of his world-wide mission.

1. *'Oh, Come Quickly'* (*cf. 2 Tim 4.9, 21*)

Almost all of the commentaries on 2 Timothy reflect a certain unease about the place of 2 Tim 4.9-21 within a letter which virtually all take to be a farewell letter of Paul to his co-worker, Timothy.

As we pointed out in Chapter 1 Harrison solved the difficulty by extracting what he called genuine Pauline fragments of the letter, and situating them in the otherwise known framework of Paul's life. This solution involves not only extracting the elements from their present context, but also dissecting some of them in a somewhat arbitrary and doctrinaire fashion. The commentators who support a 'fragments theory' are, in the main, driven to that rather drastic solution by the difficulty of accommodating in the same letter 2 Tim 4.6-8, and 4.9-21.[4]

Those who propose a pseudepigraphic origin for the Pastorals tend to underplay the 'historical' details of the letters, and do not delay long over the difficulties posed by the proximity of 2 Tim 4.6-8 and 9-21. Dibelius, for example, has no comment on 4.9, and when he comes to 4.21, he mentions only the greetings of 21b, and says nothing of Paul's direction to Timothy in 21a to come before winter; and his comment on 1.4 does not deal with Paul's desire to see Timothy.[5] Similarly, Houlden does not comment on the instruction to come in 4.9 and 21, and he considers that Paul's desire to see Timothy (1.4) 'reproduces Rom 1.11', and 'looks to Rom 15.32' (1976: 108).

The desire to see Timothy (2 Tim 1.4; 4.9, 21) is, according to Brox, an example of one of the most common traits of correspondence (1969a: 226). For him the function of the personal details is paraenetic: Paul is presented by the pseudepigrapher as the model of fidelity to the gospel, in his being an abandoned prisoner (1969b). In like manner, Trummer sees in such passages as 4.9-21 the author's adherence to the epistolary convention of expressing the wish to see the receiver of the letter (1978: 76). Most recently, Karris avoids the many 'inconsistencies' of 4.9-21 by appealing to 'the edifying lessons Paul's life presents in this section' (1979: 40).

Among those who hold for the authenticity of the letter, we have Jeremias who does not appear to be unduly concerned about the proximity of death suggested by 4.6-8 and the time-lapse required before Timothy would get to Paul (1968:57, 60). Guthrie solves the problem by suggesting that Paul was not too optimistic that Timothy would get to him before he died (1957: 22f., 171, 179). Spicq appears to regard the letter as being finished at v. 8, so that the remainder of it appears to him to be merely the addition of some practical matters (1969: 808). Among those practical matters is the direction to Timothy to come quickly, since his solitude near death was the more profound. Hence the impatience reflected by the use of the aorist imperative, σπούδασον, followed by what Spicq calls the pleonasm, ταχέως ἐλθεῖν. Giving his usual massive textual support, especially from among the papyri, Spicq concludes that 'La formule venir "sur-le-champ, le plus vite possible",... "de suite",... "rapidement, à toute vitesse" ... est un cliché épistolaire surabondamment attesté' (1969: 810).[6]

It is necessary at this point to examine what is implied in saying that such and such is an epistolary cliché (Spicq), or an epistolary convention (Brox, Trummer, Karris).

Spicq does not explain what he means by an epistolary cliché. He gives a number of papyrus texts which use the expressions ἐν τάχει, ταχύ, ταχέως, τάχιον and εὐθέως. The dictionary meaning of cliché is, 'a fixed stereotyped expression which has lost its significance through repetition', but this meaning does not seem to us to suit the place of 1.4; 4.9 and 21 within 2 Timothy. We have already argued in Chapter 4 that Paul was very anxious that Timothy would come to him, and we have suggested reasons for his wanting him urgently.

Steen (1938) is the classic work on the epistolary cliché. He uses the term to denote those expressions which either soften or intensify epistolary imperatives. It is our contention that the suggestion that at 2 Tim 4.9, 21 we are dealing merely with an epistolary convention, such as 'I would like to see you', or with a mere ornament, robs the letter of one of its primary purposes.

Although one can adduce epistolary examples in which the writer expresses his desire to see the receiver, but does not expect his wish to be fulfilled immediately,[7] it remains true that most of the instructions and appeals to come quickly which we meet in the papyrus letters are no mere clichés, but reflect the main purpose for which the letter was written.[8] In these cases the use of such a formula as, 'as soon as you receive this letter, come . . . ', can hardly be regarded as a mere pleonasm.[9]

These examples from the papyri communicate the real urgency of requests to come quickly. We have examined all the major collections of papyrus letters, and examples of what are simply epistolary clichés are very rare.[10] The papyrus evidence for the vocabulary of 'hasten/ come quickly', etc., leads one to take the statements at their face value. In other words, when people wrote, 'Come quickly', they meant it. There is no evidence to support the view that such phrases are only epistolary clichés, if by that we mean that they are merely fixed stereotyped expressions which have lost their significance through repetition. On the contrary, the papyrus evidence suggests very strongly that where there is a request to come quickly there was a real urgency, whether due to some personal, family, legal or business crisis.

It is our contention that in 2 Timothy also Paul is expressing a real urgency that Timothy come to him. We are particularly impressed by the strategic positioning of Paul's wish to see Timothy, at the beginning of the letter, immediately after the greeting, and as the first element within the thanksgiving period (2 Tim 1.4), and also at the end of the letter, before the final greetings, and farewell (2 Tim 4.21). These two elements frame, as it were, the whole letter. Furthermore, the direction to Timothy at 4.9 to come quickly, coming immediately after the exhortations to him to be faithful to his charge, suggests that the motif was no mere afterthought.

One could also say that that section of the letter which many consider to contain genuine Pauline material also is framed, at 4.9 and 21, by the direction to Timothy to come quickly.

All of this, then, argues that Paul's request to Timothy to come quickly is one of the major concerns of the letter. Kelly does acknowledge that this motive may well have been one of Paul's main reasons for writing the letter, but he attributes the urgency to Paul's desire that Timothy pay him a visit, now that he was in such dangerous isolation in his cell (1963: 211). The earlier Hanson, for his part, recognizes that the section vv. 9-22 reflects Paul's expectation that he would be able to welcome Timothy after the long journey from Asia Minor to Rome, and he adds that Paul could not have written it with the immediate prospect of death before him (1966: 100).

We propose that Paul's urgency is real, and that it is connected with his desire, now that he was confident of his being released, that Timothy should join him and others in creating a missionary band to carry the *kerygma* further (cf. 2 Tim 4.17f.).

We suggest as a mere possibility that Paul had an additional reason for wanting Timothy by his side, namely, in order to have his support in the courtroom.[11] At the first hearing of Paul's case no one took his part, and indeed all deserted him (2 Tim 4.16). It is attractive to propose that Paul wanted Timothy to be a witness in his favour, and perhaps also Mark, and that the parchments of 2 Tim 4.13 were needed for the defence. In fact, another papyrus letter, *P. Yale* 42, provides the reader with a background against which to assess the elements of 2 Timothy.[12]

2. Μᾶρκον ἀναλαβὼν ἄγε μετὰ σεαυτοῦ
ἔστιν γάρ μοι εὔχρηστος εἰς διακονίαν *(2 Tim 4.11b)*

One of the factors which might help the reader to understand better the circumstances of Paul as he wrote 2 Timothy is Paul's request to Timothy to bring Mark along with him when he himself comes. Paul gives as his reason for wanting Mark: ἔστιν γάρ μοι εὔχρηστος εἰς διακονίαν. We would like to know precisely what Paul understood by 'useful to me' and what kind of διακονία he had in mind for Mark.

The adjective εὔχρηστος is used in only two other places in the NT: 2 Tim 2.21, and Phlm 11. The section 2 Tim 2.14–26 deals with Timothy's responsibilities to teach appropriately, 'as a workman rightly handling the word of truth' (v. 15), and vv. 20–26 are directed to Timothy in the hope that he may purify himself from what is ignoble. Having purified himself he would be a vessel 'for noble use, consecrated and useful to the master of the house, ready for any good work' (v. 21). The passage is followed by very firm admonitions to Timothy to correct his ways and to be more forbearing in his correction of opponents (vv. 22–26). It is clear that the adjective εὔχρηστος in v. 21, although used within a metaphor, suggests a sense of usefulness for the ministry, and in this case for Timothy's ministry.

In the other NT occurrence, Phlm 11 there is little that allows us to determine the sense in which Paul considered Onesimus to be useful.[13]

We shall now consider what we can learn from the use of διακονία. If Paul intended a purely private service, such as requiring Mark to keep in touch with him, or provide for him while in prison, we might expect to find such a phrase as, ἔστιν γάρ εὔχρηστος εἰς διακονίαν μοῦ. The *Revised Standard Version* and *Moffatt* translations suggest that Mark's service is to be a purely personal one to Paul in his present condition,[14] while in the *Jerusalem Bible*, the *New English Bible* and Spicq renderings one thinks more of some particular work that is to be done.[15] Jeremias, best of all, retains the ambiguity of the Greek.[16]

The noun διακονία is used of a wide range of activities, even within the NT, and hence neither an examination of the etymology of the noun, nor of the varied use of the term in the NT will answer exactly what the word means in 2 Tim 4.11. It occurs thirty-three times in the NT.[17]

In Paul, where we have the only use of the plural of the noun in the NT, we learn that there are varieties of διακονίαι but the same Lord, just as there are varieties of χαρίσματα but the same Spirit (1 Cor 12.4f.). The Pauline uses of the noun are varied.[18] However, it is clear that there is no single use in Paul which would encourage one to read the text of 2 Tim 4.11 to refer to a service to Paul himself. In fact, every use of the term by Paul is in relation to some service to the community.[19] In some instances this service is financial,[20] but it is also used of a service of God, or of Paul's service to the nations.[21]

Paul, then, never uses the term of a personal service to an individual. This conclusion weighs against taking the noun διακονία in 2 Tim 4.11 to refer to some personal service to Paul in his imprisonment. Further support for the interpretation that Paul is referring to some kind of ministry of evangelization is provided by the only other occurrence of the word in 2 Tim, at 4.5, which concludes a powerful exhortation to Timothy to preach the word, to be attentive both at suitable and unsuitable times (4.2), ... ἔργον ποίησον εὐαγγελιστοῦ τὴν διακονίαν σου πληροφόρησον (4.5).

It seems reasonable, then, to propose that Paul wants Timothy to bring Mark along with him because he is useful to Paul in the ministry of evangelization, and specifically for that new stage of missionary work on which Paul is confident of embarking.[22] If one insists that in 2 Tim 4.11 the service Paul has in mind is simply the ministry to his needs while in prison, one must recognize that such a meaning runs against the other meanings of the noun in Paul in general, and against the meaning in the only other occurrence of the noun in 2 Timothy, which is in the same chapter (4.5), as well as against the meaning in the only other occurrence of the word in the Pastorals where it refers to the work of the evangelization of the gentiles (1 Tim 1.12).

In our view it is again the common reading of 2 Tim 4.6-8 which forces a false reading upon 2 Tim 4.11. Since it is the usual view that 2 Timothy is Paul's swan-song (and it must be conceded that that view rests solely on the customary interpretation of 4.6-8), there cannot be any question of a further mission, and therefore the obvious meaning of the word διακονία must be laid aside and the term be given a meaning that it simply never has in Paul, and the obvious meaning of the present text has to be sacrificed in the interests of the common reading of 4.6-8.[23]

But even when it is used of the service of evangelization, the term διακονία does not help us to determine with any precision the service which Paul hoped for from Mark. Perhaps some little can be gleaned from the use of the cognate noun διάκονος. This term, however, is never applied to Mark in the NT, nor is it used in 2 Timothy.[24] In 1 Cor 16.15f. the co-workers and toilers are described as devoting themselves to the διακονία of the saints. The term διάκονος is associated with preaching activity in the NT.[25]

Another line of investigation is open to us. Mark is described as a συνεργός in Col 4.11 and Phlm 24, in both of which texts he features in the second place of a group, each time after a συναιχμάλωτος. The term συνεργός is not in itself very helpful in describing the nature of the contribution to the teamwork, or of the work itself.[26] However, συνεργός is the most frequent designation within the letters for Paul's associates, followed in descending frequency by ἀδελφός, διάκονος and ἀπόστολος.[27] Ellis points out that the term is not used of believers in general, and like its cognate, ἐργάτης, often, but not necessarily, refers to itinerant workers. He suggests that the two terms, συνεργός and κοπιῶν which latter occurs in the Pastorals at 1 Tim 4.10; 5.17 and 2 Tim 2.6, are equivalent expressions for a class of Christian workers. He agrees with Harnack that those who toil, govern, and admonish the brothers (1 Thess 5.12) are a specific, appointed group (Ellis 1970/1: 6f.).

We conclude, then, that Paul's choice of Mark as the one person whom Timothy is to bring with him, was dictated by the fact that Mark had already earned the title, or had been appointed to the role of συνεργός, one of a specific group within the community who carried out an exercise of hard work and toil, often as itinerant workers, for the churches.

The combination of the Pauline use of διακονία, and Mark's designation as a Pauline συνεργός seem to us to suggest that the activity which Paul had in mind for Mark was much more likely a missionary service of toil in the interests of the Gospel, than the simple one of visiting Paul in his prison cell. It could still be the case, of course, that Paul had indeed a ministry of preaching and teaching in mind for Mark (Timothy and Luke), without its being required that he himself lead that mission team. He could, perhaps, direct operations from his cell (cf. 2 Tim 4.12). The evidence of 4.16ff., however, supports our conclusion that Paul is getting things in order for another missionary activity, which he himself would lead.

3. τὸν φαιλόνην ὅν ἀπέλιπον ἐν Τρῳάδι παρὰ Κάρπῳ ἐρχόμενος φέρε καὶ τὰ βιβλία μάλιστα τὰς μεμβράνας (*2 Tim 4.13*)

In 2 Timothy Paul requests that Timothy bring his cloak and parchments. We shall briefly indicate how representatives of each of the schools of interpretation of the Pastorals understand Paul's request in 2 Tim 4.13.

(i) Writing in the early twenties (when the theory of a Second Roman Imprisonment was under strong attack) Stevenson appealed to the weight of the external evidence of tradition, and to the authenticity of at least certain passages within the Pastorals. Of all the passages where one can see Paul's handwriting, '2 Tim. 4.13 is surely the least capable of having been invented'. 'Who', he asked, 'would have thought of making that up?'

The verse fits in admirably, according to Stevenson, if one allows the traditional view of a second imprisonment. The reason he proposed for Paul's request lay in the fact that, 'in the chill of Roman prison he begins to long for the overcoat he had left behind with Carpus a few weeks before, it may be, for winter was coming on, and he had only too much experience of Roman winters, when he had felt the cold even in the comparative comfort of a hired room'.

He suggests that the parchment rolls are of the 'Sacred Scriptures or of the Saying or Doings of the Lord'. The papers, on the other hand, are his own papers, 'letters written to him and copies of his replies, and he might need them for writing some last messages to his converts'. But he needed the parchments especially, 'with their words of consolation; no doubt he never travelled without some book or other of the Old Testament in his bag, but these particular rolls that he had not thought he should require on a missionary tour he finds he needs in the Roman prison when under sentence of death' (Stevenson 1922/3: 525).

(ii) Those who opt for a fragments theory dispense with a second Roman imprisonment, and situate the fragment of which 4.13 is a portion in an earlier period of Paul's life.[28] That removes the embarrassment of having to account for a prisoner appealing for his cloak which was left behind some five or six years earlier,[29] and which might not arrive in the prison for some time, and only in the spring if Timothy did not manage to come before the winter.

(iii) If 2 Tim 4.13 is regarded by the proponents of the authenticity of the Pastorals as offering a major supporting argument,[30] it is precisely its conventional character that is appealed to by the supporters of a theory of pseudepigraphy.[31]

The precise way in which the pseudepigrapher used this epistolary convention is dealt with at great length by Trummer (1974, and 1978: 78-88). The key to the interpretation is the suggestion that the pseudepigrapher is at pains to present Paul as the model of Christian discipleship and missionary spirit. Trummer insists that the Pastorals must be interpreted as a *corpus*, and not as three independent compositions. He then uses 1 Tim 6.8 as the backdrop for viewing

2 Tim 4.13, and in the latter text he sees Paul presented by the pseudepigrapher as an example of apostolic self-sufficiency, and a practitioner of the frugality becoming a church office-holder.[32] In Chapter 4 we argued against the tendency to engage in corpus harmonization among the Pastorals. In particular, it is clear that the contexts of the two verses are very different. 1 Tim 6.8 reflects the well-attested dependence on only food and clothes,[33] in a general polemic against riches (1 Tim 6.5-10), while there is no such context in 2 Tim 4.13.

It is not at all obvious how 2 Tim 4.13 reflects Paul's apostolic poverty. The Apostle himself, after all, had boasted that he did not complain of want, but had learned to be content in whatever state he was, knowing the secret of facing plenty and hunger, abundance and want (cf. Phil 4.11ff.). Nor does the pseudepigrapher's scenario accord well with the Paul of 2 Cor 4.7-12; 4.16-5.10. Indeed one might well ask how a man who, according to Acts could afford his own rented house (Acts 28.30), was not presented by the pseudepigrapher as making other arrangements for his needs instead of requiring Timothy to search out his goods, and bring them such a distance.

Trummer suggests a paraenetic purpose for the reference to the books also: Paul, in the face of death, is presented by the pseudepigrapher as requesting the sacred books (1978: 85). It is not clear, however, how this item squares with an edifying picture of a Paul who is presented by the pseudepigrapher as having travelled without his sacred writings, and as being incapable of having some other set made available to him. If Paul had allowed himself to be without his sacred writings, as Trummer's hypothesis demands, it seems an unwarranted conclusion to suggest that his request for them now shows that 'Die heiligen Schriften sind das Buch des kirchlichen Amtsträgers' (1978: 86).

Zmijewski and Karris follow the same line of speculation as Trummer.[34] The proponents of a theory of pseudepigraphy rest their case on a wide range of assumptions that are seldom stated. These include a great deal of mind-reading of the anonymous pseudepigrapher, and the attribution to him of motives which derive from a presumed piety.

We have already given reasons for rejecting a fragments theory for 2 Timothy. We wish now to enquire into two of the assumptions of those who favour a theory of pseudepigraphy, namely that Paul's request for his cloak functions paraenetically by advocating apostolic poverty, and that the request for the parchments shows his attachment to the Scriptures right up to the end.

Where modern commentators do address the question as to why Paul wanted, or is presented as wanting, his cloak, the major reason advanced is that he needed it since winter was at hand, and his dungeon was cold.[35] Calvin offers two reasons for the request for the cloak, namely Paul's comfort, and his desire to avoid expense (1548/ 9: 340).

We would like to know why Paul needed or is presented as needing his cloak.[36] It is common to refer to the evidence of the papyri to support the view that Paul's request for his cloak reflects his poverty. This conclusion is not warranted. Much of the evidence, in fact, could equally well point in the opposite direction.

It is true that the papyri alone offer a considerable amount of interesting information concerning cloaks, and if a commentator were to put it all together a reader could easily get the impression that few letters passed hands without somebody either asking for or acknowledging the receipt of a cloak. However, despite the massive evidence which Spicq, for instance, offers on the question, the references to cloaks are actually relatively rare. On the basis of the papyrus letters and the accounts of makers of clothes, etc., one can arrive at an understanding of the kind of overgarment involved, and even some idea of the cost price, or the saleable value in the case of secondhand ones, and the texture and colour variations possible.[37] But such information from the papyri does not really enlighten us about Paul's reasons for requesting his cloak.[38]

Individual papyrus letters, then, might suggest that Paul's request for the cloak was made because he was in humble circumstances, and could not afford to get another one; or that he needed it to sell it, or to pawn it; or, simply, that he needed it to wear it. However, some other examples from the papyri reflect the writer's preoccupation with cut and colour, such as one would expect only from a dandy (e.g. *P. Oxy.* 1069), and the supporters of a pseudepigraphy theory for 2 Timothy ought to reckon with this evidence as well. One might even suggest on the basis of some papyrus evidence that we are dealing in 2 Tim 4.13 with yet another polemic,[39] in this case against some Gymnosophists, who disdain the wearing of habits, since they considered them an occasion of vanity.[40] There is, then, little in the papyrus material that enlightens us about Paul's request, and there is more than enough to caution us against the kind of speculation which is common amongst the supporters of pseudepigraphy.

Since Paul himself does not indicate why he needed his cloak, the best one can do is to suggest a reason that accords with the general context of the letter. The view that we are here dealing with an item which was composed by a pseudepigrapher in order to illustrate the frugality of Paul is not convincing. As we have indicated, Paul's request could reflect the very opposite of frugality. Neither does it seem likely that Paul wanted his cloak to keep him warm in the Roman cell. After all, he envisaged that Timothy might not be able to come before winter. And it seems unlikely that Paul's need to keep warm in a Roman prison could not have been met more simply in Rome itself, either by using the money provided by the Philippians, for example, or by borrowing from Onesiphorus or Luke, or by getting help from even one member of the Roman community.

We have already argued that at the time of writing 2 Timothy Paul was confident of being released, and that he was preparing an apostolic team for another stage of his world-wide mission. Before his hoped-for release, however, he would have to undergo the final hearing. Two future events, then, were in Paul's mind as he wrote to Timothy, the trial and the mission. Is it possible that there is a connection between either of these events and his request for his cloak and parchments?

It may be the case that in requesting his cloak Paul is stating his state of preparedness for the mission and his confidence in the successful outcome of his trial.[41] It is tempting to think that the request for the cloak is a gesture reminiscent of Elisha's reception of the prophetic mantle from Elijah, and serves as a symbol of the preparedness for going out on mission.[42] Indeed, in the religious community of itinerant preachers to which I belong the outer garment of the travelling missionary was known as 'the missioner's cloak', and when the preacher packed his cloak it was a sign that he was going out from his house on mission.

There is, however, another possibility, namely that both the cloak and the parchments were required in connection with the public hearing of Paul's case.[43] Since they are the only two items Paul requests it is an intriguing possibility that they would play a vital role in the hearing, such as providing proof of Paul's Roman citizenship.

While there is no reason to justify the suggestion that the cloak was Paul's *toga*, which would be one of the few signs showing that he was a Roman citizen,[44] it is just possible that Paul's request may be explained by his anxiety to be suitably dressed for the court hearing.[45]

It is also possible that the documents he required included his *diploma civitatis Romanae*, which served as a card of identity. A Roman who was a citizen by birth could prove it by producing a copy of the original *professio* or registration of his birth.[46] We do not know if Roman citizens carried such certificates around with them. Although they were convenient in shape and size it is more likely that they were kept in a safe place, such as the family archives, rather than carried around.[47]

It may well be the case that Paul was informed at the first hearing that he would require proof of his status as a Roman citizen, and for that reason he required Timothy to bring such proof. Paul had left it in the safe keeping of Carpus in Troas, a citizen colony, some years earlier.[48] The fact that the last visit to Troas took place some years before is, then, no problem.

4. Σὺ δὲ νῆφε ἐν πᾶσιν
κακοπάθησον, ἔργον ποίησον εὐαγγελιστοῦ,
τὴν διακονίαν σου πληροφόρησον *(2 Tim 4.5)*

In Chapter 3 we drew attention to the (double) private character of the Pastoral Letters, which separates them from the other Pauline Letters.[49] We have also insisted that each of the Pastorals must be examined in its own right, and we have emphasized the differences in content and circumstances between the three letters. It remains now to investigate more thoroughly the unique character of 2 Timothy.

We have argued that 2 Timothy presents Paul as having two major preoccupations in his mind, namely, his desire for Timothy to come to him, and his concern for the stability of Timothy, both as a believer and as an evangelist. We hope to show that these two concerns are intimately related.[50]

Exhortation and encouragement are features of the Pastoral Letters, and also of several of Paul's letters.[51] If each of the three Pastorals has a paraenetic character,[52] it is clear that 2 Timothy reflects Paul's concern for Timothy himself more than 1 Timothy does, or than Titus reflects his concern for Titus.[53]

What is the nature of this concern? Is it the case that Paul is anxious about how Timothy is faring in a climate where forms of docetism, Judaizing, and disruptive practices of worship are disturbing the unity of the community, such as afflicted some of the churches to which Ignatius wrote? Or is it the case that Timothy's authority was being undermined, as Titus's would appear to have been?

In the only anti-docetic comment in the letter (2.8) we have an affirmation of the resurrection of Jesus Christ, and a statement of his descent from David.[54] One notices in the letter the absence of any insistence on the facticity of the birth, life, especially suffering and death, and resurrection of Jesus, such as one finds in Ignatius's letters. Docetism, therefore, does not appear to have been a problem for Timothy, or for his charges, insofar as we can argue from the silence of 2 Timothy.

Moreover, 2 Timothy is devoid of any reference to Jewish practices or beliefs, such as one finds abundantly in Ignatius's letters, particularly those to the Magnesians and Philadelphians, and also in 1 Tim 1.7-11, and Tit 1.13-16; 3.8-11. We can, then, remove Judaizing also from the contenders for Paul's concern on the occasion of writing 2 Timothy.

It is our conclusion that where we encounter references to deviant doctrine and practice in 2 Timothy the focus of attention is Timothy himself, rather than the community.

Furthermore, there is no concern here, as there is in 1 Timothy and Titus, for the establishment of a hierarchical order of ministries within the community, nor any kind of *Haus-* or *Gemeindetafel*,[55] nor does Timothy's authority appear to have been subject to challenge, as Titus's seems to have been.

If, then, Timothy's problems, both those in himself as a person, and those pressing on him from without, had nothing to do with docetic deviations, Judaizing pressures, or with the weakness of his authority as a leader, what did Paul consider to be Timothy's limitations, and the obstacles to his effective leadership? We are of the view that Paul was worried about the fidelity of Timothy, and, as in the case of Ignatius's concern for Polycarp, about his performance as a minister.[56]

When in Chapter 4 we drew attention to the differences between the three Pastorals we introduced the question of Timothy's fidelity.[57] We now wish to examine in greater detail the extent of Paul's concern for Timothy both as a believer, and as an evangelist.[58] We shall proceed by going systematically through the letter, and drawing attention to the paraenetic technique of Paul. In particular we shall draw attention to Paul's use of exemplars.[59] They function as examples of either appropriate or improper behaviour. We shall see that a directive follows an example several times.[60]

A. *The Prescript (1.1f.)*
As we have noted in Chapter 3 the opening of the letter makes it clear that we are dealing with a personal letter in two senses, that is, one sent by one individual to another individual. The designation of Timothy as a 'beloved son' is consistent with Paul's perception of Timothy as a disciple whom he had brought into the Christian way of living (Acts 16.1-5).[61]

B. *Timothy's Heritage of Faith as Example (1.3-8)*
After the initial greetings Paul states that he thanks God at the memory of Timothy whom he longs to see (1.3f.). Immediately, he refers to Timothy's sincere faith, which he recognized also in Timothy's grandmother and mother (1.5).[62] However, in the light of what follows in the remainder of the letter, there is good reason to suspect that Paul's confidence about Timothy's faith was not absolute.[63] It is because of Timothy's background in faith that Paul can now issue his first exhortation, in the form of a reminder to Timothy to keep on fanning the flame (present tense) of the gift of God which he had previously received from the hands of Paul (1.6).

And because God had not given them a spirit of timidity, but of power, love and self-control (1.7), Timothy is given both a negative and a positive command, not to be ashamed of witnessing to our Lord, nor to Paul his prisoner, but to submit to the action (aorist imperative) whereby he becomes a co-sufferer for the Gospel in accordance with God's power (1.8).

C. *Paul's Fidelity in Suffering as Example (1.9-12)*
Having described some aspects of the Gospel, Paul points to himself as an example of one who was not ashamed,[64] but who was at that very moment suffering for the Gospel (v. 12), of which he had been appointed (using the punctiliar aorist) a preacher, apostle and teacher (v. 11). Paul was unshakable because of his decisive faith (perfect tense), and because of his confidence that the object of his faith would be able to guard his deposit until that Day (v. 12).[65]

D. *Paul's Teaching as Example (1.13f.)*
Having presented himself as an example to Timothy of an unashamed, suffering minister of the Gospel, Paul now points to his teaching which Timothy had already heard from him, in the faith and love in Christ Jesus. This Timothy has as a pattern of healthy words. Paul instructs him to guard the good deposit through the Holy Spirit who dwells in them both. Paul's faith was such as to be sure that he would guard his deposit (v. 12).

E. *The Negative Example of the Asians, and of Phygelus and Hermogenes (1.15)*[66]
Verses 15-18 appear between two sections which are very directive (1.13f. and 2.1-7), and they function as examples of the contrasting spirits of timidity and power, to which Paul had already referred (1.7). The Asians turned away from Paul, and are examples of the spirit of timidity.

F. *The Positive Example of Onesiphorus (1.16ff.)*
Onesiphorus, on the other hand, was not ashamed of Paul's chain, and he zealously rendered him many kindnesses, recently in Rome, and earlier at Ephesus. He, then, was an outstanding example to Timothy of the spirit of power (1.7). Paul directs Timothy's attention to the reward of such fidelity: mercy from the Lord on That Day (cf. 1.12; 4.8).

If Onesiphorus could be so faithful, how much more should Paul's son be (2.1). Against the background of the negative and positive example of the Asians and Onesiphorus (οὖν), Paul directs Timothy to be empowered in the grace that is in Christ Jesus, and he spells out what that means: he is to transmit to others (πιστοί) what he has heard from Paul. Paul's teaching, then, was not merely to be jealously guarded (1.13f.), but was to be passed on (2.2). Furthermore, Timothy's task would require fidelity to the point of co-suffering with Paul (2.3; cf. 1.8).

G. *The Positive Example of the Soldier, the Athlete and the Farmer (2.4ff.)*
Each of these three presents an aspect of the dedication that is required of Timothy. The soldier is unswerving in his fidelity to his commander. The athlete has to discipline and regulate his enthusiasm. And it is the toiling farmer who ought to be first to take the crop.

Before he gains his prize, each of the three has to strain himself, and Paul hopes that Timothy, on reflection, will emulate their devotion (v. 7).

H. *The Positive Example of Jesus Christ (2.8)*

Paul must be referring at this point to the fidelity of Jesus, who was obedient unto death, death on a cross, but who was rewarded for his fidelity (Phil. 2.8f.). Clearly, the sufferings and crucifixion of Christ were central to Paul's gospel (1 Cor 1.23ff.; 2.2f.). Timothy is reminded to keep him constantly before his mind, as with the other three examples of rewarded suffering to which he had just referred (2.4-6).

I. *The Positive Example of Paul's Own Suffering (2.9f.)*

Paul continues the theme of suffering by drawing Timothy's attention to his own present sufferings. Paul was not ashamed of the Gospel, but suffered to the point of being enchained for it. He endures everything for the sake of the elect so that they also may obtain the salvation which goes with eternal glory.

The teaching on suffering comes to a climax with Paul's quotation of the faithful word (vv. 11-13), as it were inviting Timothy to join him in suffering, and assuring him of becoming an heir of the reward God holds for those who endure.

There is so much stress on suffering at this point of the letter that it seems that Timothy's fidelity must have been threatened by a situation which would require him to suffer. There is, however, no indication within the letter as to the source of this suffering.

If up to this point Paul has concentrated on the personal fidelity of Timothy, particularly in relation to suffering, he now turns his attention to Timothy's task as an evangelist. It is clear that his performance left much to be desired.

J. ταῦτα ὑπομίμνῃσκε διαμαρτυρόμενος . . . μὴ λογομαχεῖν *(2.14)*

For the second time in the course of the letter so far Paul invites Timothy to keep constantly in his mind what he has just written (2.14; 1.7, with the imperative in each case being in the present tense).[67] The common reading of this verse, however, refers the censure to people other than Timothy, whom we consider to be the true object of the admonitions which follow.

The RSV translation, 'Remind them of this: and charge them

before the Lord...', is typical. It is clear that in the usual translations the verb ὑπομίμνῃσκε is taken to have an accusative of person understood, in addition to an accusative of object (ταῦτα). However, if one insists on supplying an accusative of person, one is left wondering who exactly is meant at this point. Translators and commentators are in obvious difficulties, and the most they can do is to opt for the vague 'them', or 'people', although some attempt to be more precise.[68]

Such a reading, however, is not required by the construction, as can be seen from the occurrence of the verb in the LXX,[69] Philo,[70] Josephus,[71] the Papyri[72] and the NT.[73] Where the verb means 'to remind somebody of something' the accusative of person is either explicit (using ὑμᾶς, αὐτήν, αὐτόν, etc.) or quite clear from the context. The use of the double accusative is abundantly attested.[74]

Where the verb occurs without an accusative of person, or without the context making it clear who is meant, it has the meaning 'to recall', 'to bring to mind', and this is clearly the case in several diverse examples,[75] and also, we propose, in 2 Tim 2.14.

Although there are not many examples of the singular imperative of the verb,[76] there is one outstanding example, and that close to the context of 2 Tim, namely, Tit 3.1. In that text the object of the verb is explicitly stated to be αὐτούς, followed by an infinitive, and there the context makes it clear that Paul is exhorting Titus in his ministry of teaching, and encouraging the different elements of the whole community in Crete.

But even if Paul had used αὐτούς in 2 Tim 2.14 we would still be left wondering to whom he is referring, and there would be as little agreement among the commentators as there is at present. The problem is solved by recognizing that it is Timothy who is to keep on remembering ταῦτα, and who is counselled to correct his ways.

There is, then, no need to demand that the verb be understood to have a double accusative in 2 Tim 2.14. Apart from the obvious difficulty of deciding who is the accusative of person, the context is better respected by understanding the verb to be directed to Timothy himself.

It is clear that the whole of ch. 2 is a counsel to Timothy personally, and that that counsel can be conveniently divided into two aspects, one dealing with his personal fidelity to his vocation even in suffering (2.1-13), and the second advising and encouraging him to be a fitting servant of the Lord, and an apt teacher (2.14-24).

To interpret 2.14 as a direction to Timothy to counsel others, then, is to break the unity of the chapter, and more seriously, to misunderstand the epistolary situation. We read the text to mean that Timothy's method of teaching was not above reproach, and was certainly not to Paul's satisfaction.[77]

The sense of 2 Tim 2.14f., is, then, 'Do not ever let these things out of your mind, Timothy, as you bear witness in the presence of God, not by engaging in word-wrangling, which is useless and brings catastrophe to those who hear you, but, rather, do your utmost to present yourself approved before God, as a worker who has no need to be ashamed, and who imparts the word of truth without deviation'.

This personal admonition to Timothy is followed by Paul's insistence that he should keep on avoiding (present imperative) empty chatterings, which will advance ungodliness even more, and will progress like gangrene.[78]

K. *The Negative Example of Hymenaeus and Philetus (2.17f.)*

Among people who are given to such excesses Paul mentions Hymenaeus and Philetus, who have gone wide of the mark with regard to the truth, holding that the resurrection is already past; such people destroy the faith of some (2.16ff.).[79] This reference to the resurrection is generally looked to as providing some definite indication of a specific kind of deviation from the truth. Indeed, it is generally grouped with other specifics in the other Pastorals, thereby giving the impression that Paul had a common enemy in mind. But this is to misunderstand the function of this reference within the wider paraenesis. The specific reference is introduced at this point, not to identify more closely the enemy, but simply to provide Timothy with an example of the kind of excesses into which word-wrangling can lead.

But even though the faith of some has been overturned (v. 18), Paul knows that God's firm foundation stands. Various interpretations have been given to the foundation (2.19).[80] Despite Timothy's difficulties Paul is confident of his ultimate welfare, since the seal of the foundation reads, 'The Lord knows those who are His': the previous warnings, then, are softened by a word of assurance that the Lord knows his own, a phrase recalling Num 16.5. In that text Korah and others were attempting to take over from Moses and Aaron, but they were rejected by God. The Lord urged

Moses and Aaron to separate themselves from among the congregation so that he might consume them in a moment (Num 16.21). Timothy, too, must distance himself from iniquity (2.19).

Paul's solicitude for Timothy continues to be reflected in what follows (2.20-26). In a great house there are both good and bad, noble and ignoble vessels. This image can be taken to refer to the community of believers, which will contain both good and bad members, and this would be consistent with the allusion to conversion in v. 21, and the repentance and escape from evil of vv. 25f. In that case, however, one has to ask why a very fundamental criticism of Timothy is interjected at v. 22. It is more likely that the whole passage is directed to the renewal of Timothy's own fidelity and commitment. For immediately after the statement that an ignoble vessel can purify itself, and become fit for noble use, Paul counsels Timothy to shun his youthful or violent[81] passions, and to aim at righteousness, faith, love, and peace, together with those who call on the Lord with a pure heart (vv. 21f.). Timothy's passions, which presumably were well known to Paul, were no mere private personality defects, but also adversely affected his presentation of the Gospel. Already Paul had advised Timothy to avoid word-wrangling (v. 14) and godless chatter (v. 16), and now he is cautioned to shun his youthful passions, which probably are opposed to the virtues he is to aim at acquiring (v. 22).

That there is something seriously astray in Timothy and in his presentation of the Gospel is confirmed by what follows. Paul appeals to him to have nothing to do with foolish and ignorant speculations, knowing that they give birth to quarrels, from which a servant of the Lord ought to be free (vv. 23f.). One can guess the nature of Timothy's excesses by noting Paul's insistence that Timothy avoid disputing.[82]

L. *The Positive Example of the Lord's Servant (2.24ff.)*

It is clear from Paul's insistence on these ways of behaviour that Timothy was in the habit of dealing with opponents in a manner which showed little forbearance, and that he preferred to match them word for word, instead of dealing with them in a more gentle fashion. Paul appeals to the example of the behaviour of the typical servant of the Lord. Only such gentleness of disposition and manner of correction will bring about that conversion which leads to true knowledge, and bring people to their senses again, thereby rescuing them from the snares of the devil, even if they have already been in captivity to him by following his will (vv. 25f.).[83]

The normal translations of 2.14, then, break the sequence of thought in this section of the letter, which is manifestly concerned with Timothy's own performance, rather than with the behaviour of others. As we have pointed out, the whole of ch. 2 is a counsel to Timothy personally, with vv. 1-13 dealing with his fidelity, and vv. 14-24 directing him to be a fitting servant of the Lord and an apt teacher. To introduce a third party at this point breaks the argument, and is not demanded by the construction. Introducing a third party, of course, deflects the attention away from Timothy, and all the commentators see in the section vv. 14-26 strong condemnations of 'the false teachers'.[84] Our reading of the text suggests that Timothy himself, rather than some group of false teachers, is the problem.

The personal admonition to Timothy continues into ch. 3. While the chapter contains lists of the vices of men (3.2-5)[85] and the virtues of Paul (3.10f.), it is framed by Paul's insistence on Timothy's behaviour (2.22-26; 3.14f.). Paul is more concerned with insisting on Timothy's more virtuous behaviour, than with describing real opponents.[86]

M. *The Negative Example of Lovers of Self (3.1-9)*
One notes references to three periods in this section: the last days (v. 1), the future (v. 2), the continuous present (v. 5, 6, 8), and again the future (v. 9).[87] Timothy is counselled to keep on avoiding those who love self, rather than God, and who have only the form, rather than the power of religion (v. 5). Such men will oppose the truth as Jannes and Jambres opposed Moses, but they will not succeed (vv. 8f.).

N. *The Positive Example of Paul's Teaching and Conduct (3.10-13)*
Paul once more appeals to Timothy to follow his teaching and his practice. He is reminded that he has followed his teaching (with the emphatic μου), his conduct, his purpose, his faith, his longsuffering, his love, his endurance, and the persecutions which he endured earlier, and from which the Lord delivered him (vv. 10f.).[88] He insists that all who desire to live piously will be persecuted (v. 12).

O. *The Positive Example of the Sacred Writings (3.14-17)*
The antidote to the dangers which will present themselves to

Timothy is to continue to adhere (present tense) to those things which he had once learned and of which he had once been convinced (aorists, v. 14). The sacred writings with which he has been acquainted from youth (cf. 1.5) will guide him, and instruct him on how to teach, reprove, and correct, so that he may be complete, and equipped for every good work (vv. 15-17).

P. *The Negative Example of Teachers who set out to please their Audience (4.1-5)*
A most solemn charge to Timothy follows immediately, with the emphasis on his responsibility for teaching, in every circumstance, and in great patience (4.2; cf. 3.10). People will inevitably not bear the sound teaching, but will seek out teachers after their own desires, who will turn away from truth and wander into myths (v. 3f.). Timothy's response must be to continue to be vigilant in everything (present), to suffer (aorist), to do the work of an evangelist (aorist), and to fulfil his διακονία (v. 5).

Q. *The Positive Example of Paul, the Negative Example of Demas and Alexander, and Paul's Present Needs (4.6-21)*
Paul once more appeals to his own fidelity as an example for Timothy. His present sufferings will ultimately bring him the crown of righteousness. The same crown awaits Timothy also (cf. v. 8).

Paul's primary concern at the moment is that Timothy would come immediately (vv. 9, 21), and that he would bring Mark (v. 11), and his parchments with him (v. 13). He gives Demas (v. 10) and Alexander (v. 14), and those who abandoned him at the first hearing (v. 16) as negative examples. Typically, Paul adds that Timothy is to guard himself against Alexander (v. 15). But despite being abandoned by human supporters Paul experienced once again the Lord's support and power (v. 17; cf. 3.11). Now that he was very hopeful of the outcome of his case (v. 18) he wished Timothy to come as quickly as possible (v. 21), so that together with Luke and Mark (v. 11) they could fulfill their apostolic plan of having τὸ κήρυγμα proclaimed fully, so that all nations would hear it (v. 17).

5. Conclusion

In this chapter we have returned to the two items which we claimed in Chapter 4 to be the two major concerns of Paul as he wrote this personal letter to Timothy from his prison in Rome. We have argued that Paul's concern for Timothy to come was a matter of great urgency for him. When seen against the background of the conventional reading of 2 Tim 4.6-8, Paul's directive to Timothy to come can only be related to a final farewell, and since Paul might be almost on the eve of his death, the message could be construed as having a somewhat perfunctory character, and thereby lose much of its urgency. But when one reads the relevant verses in terms of the overall picture which we have built up in earlier chapters one suspects that Paul wanted Timothy for some specific purpose related to his mission plans on which he hoped to embark after his release.

The papyrus material which has been examined above suggests that when a writer wrote 'come quickly' there was generally some urgent need which required the presence of the addressee. The strategic positioning of Paul's wish to see Timothy within the thanksgiving period (2 Tim 1.4), and the instruction to come quickly, coming immediately after Paul's most impassioned plea to Timothy to be vigilant, to endure suffering, to do the work of an evangelist, and to fulfil his διακονία (4.5) (in imitation of Paul's own fidelity, 4.6-8), suggest that Paul wanted Timothy very urgently indeed, and also perhaps that Timothy was somewhat reluctant to come.

That this urgency was connected with Paul's plans for the next stage of his world-wide mission is further suggested by his desire that Timothy would bring Mark with him. It is clear from Paul's use of the key term that the διακονία for which Mark was useful to Paul was that of the ministry of evangelization. This is the obvious meaning of 2 Tim 4.11. It has been argued that it was because of Paul's poor reception by the Roman Christians that Paul was left to compose his own mission team for the next stage of his evangelization.

The request for the cloak and the parchment will always remain somewhat of a mystery to exegetes. It has been proposed above that it may be related to Paul's present condition of having to appear once more in court before his final acquittal, after which he intended to lead the recently-formed mission team.

But before Timothy could be relied upon to join Paul in his mission he would have to overcome the difficulties which he appears to be enduring. Although the paraenetic character of this letter has long been recognized scholars have not taken seriously the extent to which Timothy's fidelity was under threat at the time of writing. It is clear from this intimate personal letter that Paul was very concerned about Timothy's fidelity, and that he also had serious misgivings about his behaviour as an evangelist.[89] It is no great surprise, then, that Paul should devote so much of the letter to encouraging Timothy in his faith.

The stress on suffering throughout the letter suggests that Timothy was undergoing a particular difficulty at the time of writing. The use of the aorist imperative at several key points suggests that Timothy had to take a particular stand on some question of witnessing to the Gospel. Paul's other major concern appears to be related to Timothy's manner of teaching and dealing with others.

The whole letter, then, is framed by Paul's desire to see Timothy (1.4), and by his request that Timothy come immediately (4.9-21). We contend that Paul's anxiety for Timothy and his desire to have him come were both related to his plans for the next stage of his mission. Paul wanted Timothy to come to him in Rome, and to form part of the mission-team he was assembling. Clearly Timothy's personal fidelity to the Gospel, both as a disciple and as a worker, was vital if Paul's hopes were to be realized. It was, then, all the more important for Paul to stir up in Timothy's mind the memory of his faith (2 Tim 1.5), and to encourage him to rekindle the gift of God that he had received through the laying on of Paul's hands (2 Tim 1.6).

CONCLUSION

That scholars need to widen their understanding of Paul as a letter-writer is one of the major results of this study.

After we realized that no solid conclusion could be drawn about the meaning of any pericope of the Pastoral Epistles until one had pronounced upon the question of authorship we decided to turn our attention to this very question. Recent scholarship had not gone very far beyond a restatement of the arguments for and against the Pauline authorship of the letters. At an early stage of our research we considered it desirable to contribute to breaking through the impasse which the discussion had reached.

When we first began to take notice of the variation between the first person singular and plural in the Pauline letters we wondered if some of these plurals suggested the people named in the opening verses of most of Paul's letters actually contributed to their content, expression and form. While we examined several co-authored letters of antiquity which we had uncovered, it became clear that co-authorship was always practised in those letters which had more than one name in the prescript. Our investigation of the different practice of Paul in the individual letters strongly suggests that some level of co-authorship applies in his letters also. Further investigation will be necessary to try to determine the extent of the co-authorship involved in the composition of the Pauline letters.

If the suggestion of co-authorship has not been adequately treated, the implications of Paul's use of a secretary have not been given the attention they deserve. The evidence discussed in Chapter 3 must be taken into account when one considers Paul's acknowledged use of secretarial help. While those scholars who bring Paul's use of a secretary to bear on the discussion of the authorship of the Pastorals suggest that Paul allowed the secretary in these cases more freedom than was allowed those who wrote the other letters, we suggest that because the Pastorals are personal and intimate letters Paul did not use a secretary for them.

The third factor which seemed to us to be relevant to the discussion, although it has not been given any weight in the literature, is the private nature of the Pastoral letters, both at the level of sender and addressee. Ignatius of Antioch's two letters, one to the church at Smyrna and the other to its bishop, provide an example of the radical difference between private and public correspondence.

We submit that these three factors discussed in Chapter 3 must be allowed a place in the enquiry into the concept of Pauline authorship. While it is not clear how one could quantify the extent to which these factors (or some combination of them) could account for some of the differences between the Pastorals and the Paulines, we hope to have shown that the basis on which the Pastorals are excluded from the Pauline corpus is not secure. In particular, we have argued in Chapter 2 that the model of authorship that is used in the recent application of the 'more sophisticated statistical techniques' is altogether inadequate.

Accordingly, as we examined the merits of the fragments hypothesis and the theory of pseudepigraphy we became more aware of the unlikelihood of the former, and we could not avoid questioning the many assumptions of the latter. We became increasingly unhappy about the way in which scholarship has regarded the Pastorals as one corpus. 2 Timothy appeared to us to be quite different in subject matter from 1 Timothy and Titus, and we considered it methodologically preferable to examine it in its own right. We noticed that many of the arguments by which scholars separate the Pastorals from the Paulines do not apply to 2 Timothy. We were particularly struck by the absence in it of the emphasis on church structure which is so obvious in the other two, and we were impressed by the presence of the theme of suffering which suggested to us quite a different social context from that of 1 Timothy and Titus. While we could more easily imagine a pseudepigraphic origin for these two the case for 2 Timothy being a pseudepigraphon seemed to be based on assumptions about which one could say little more than that they were possible.

The investigation carried out in this study throws new light on the whole question of Pauline authorship. Those studying the Pauline letters must take account of the relatively unusual feature of co-authorship, and also of the possibilities involved in Paul's use of secretaries. Moreover, more attention must be given to the distinction between private and public correspondence. When these three factors are taken into consideration it must be conceded that much of the conventional discussion of Pauline authorship has been seriously inadequate. We would not wish to defend an extreme conclusion of our investigation that the Pastorals, being the only letters written by Paul alone, without a secretary, and to individuals, represent his thought more faithfully that the 'authentic Paulines' do. We do claim *than* that these differences between the Pastorals and the Paulines highlight the complexity of Pauline authorship, and render less secure the basis on which the Pastorals are excluded from the Pauline corpus. The relevance of this discussion is obvious when one considers the implications of the authenticity of the Pastorals.

We hope that the evidence produced in the course of this study will encourage scholars to consider each of the Pastorals separately. Little is to be gained by applying a kind of 'pan-harmonization' to the letters, whereby a global interpretation of the corpus imposes itself on each pericope of each letter. A unique *Sitz im Leben* ought to be sought for each of the three. The reader will judge the merits of that which we propose for 2 Timothy.

When we examined 2 Timothy in terms of what it purports to be, namely a private letter of Paul to Timothy, we concluded that Paul's major reasons for writing the letter were already stated in the thanksgiving period. Paul wanted Timothy to come, and he was anxious about Timothy's fidelity and his manner of behaving. If the latter theme occupies the bulk of the material of the letter the former frames it (1.4; 4.9, 21).

Several texts in the letter suggest that Paul was confident about his future release, and 4.16f. in particular seemed to suggest that Paul had his heart set on a further mission. But the conventional reading of 4.6-8 ruled out such a possibility. We could not conceive that the real Paul could have written both 4.6-8 (understood in the conventional way) and 4.11, 13, 16f. at the same time, nor could we imagine that a pseudepigrapher would so have written. This led us into examining the key verses 4.6-8. We have demonstrated in Chapter 5 the weakness of the lexicographical case for the conventional reading of this text, and we have argued that both the lexicographical evidence and the context of the passage allow of another reading which we have proposed, and which fits the wider context of the letter. On the strength of the arguments we have produced we consider that the conventional reading of 2 Tim 4.6-8 must be abandoned, whether or not the letter is regarded as authentically Pauline or a pseudepigraphon.

It is clear from the investigation carried out in Chapter 6 that Paul saw himself about to embark on yet another stage of his world-wide mission. We have argued that the conventional reading of 4.17 has been forced upon that text by what is regarded as the 'funereal atmosphere' of 2 Tim 4.6-8. In the following chapter we showed that the same is true of 2 Tim 4.11. That Paul was building up a mission team is a much more likely reading of 4.11 and 17. The conventional reading of 2 Tim 4.11 and 17 also has to be abandoned in favour of the interpretation we propose. This also would be true whether or not the letter is viewed as authentically Pauline or as a pseudepigraphon.

In our discussion of the paraenetic character of 2 Timothy in the final chapter we have given far more stress to Timothy's condition than is customary. We have argued that Paul was very concerned about Timothy's perseverance. We have suggested that the prominence of the theme of suffering, and the use of the aorist imperative indicate that Timothy was in some particular danger. Paul's concern would have been valid at any time, but now that he had plans for a new mission it was all the more understandable.

We submit that our interpretation of various key passages of 2 Timothy coheres with the whole letter. It fits admirably the situation of Paul in Rome, as reflected in the Acts and Philippians in particular. It agrees also with what Paul is likely to have planned after his high hopes for Roman help for the Spanish mission were dashed. Whether or not Paul ever reached Spain or some place west of Rome we may never know. Whether he evangelized in Crete, as Titus suggests, after release from a Roman imprisonment, we can only surmise. We have argued that when Paul wrote 2 Timothy he was confident of being released, was building a team for a new mission, and was encouraging Timothy to come, and bring Mark with him, and join him and Luke in the next stage of the διακονία of bringing τὸ κήρυγμα to πάντα τὰ ἔθνη.

NOTES

Notes to Chapter 1

1. The quotation, which does not reflect his own view, is from Bruce (1977b: 51).

2. The Pauline authorship of all three was denied by Basilides and Marcion (Tertullian, *Adv. Marc.* v.21), and Tatian regarded only Titus as authentic (Jerome, *Prol. ad Titum*). Clement of Alexandria adds that other (unnamed) heretics rejected the letters to Timothy (*Strom.* ii.11).

3. Eichhorn (1814). Eichhorn's contribution to the subject is assessed in Schweitzer (1911: 8) and Kümmel (1970: 85).

4. Some relevant quotations are given in Kümmel (1970: 96).

5. Looking back later, Baur (1851) acknowledged that it was his study of Gnosticism in the second century that led him to his conclusion about the Pastorals, namely that they could not have been written by Paul, but that they emanated from the second century. See also Kümmel (1970: 128).

6. See Schweitzer (1911: 12) and Kümmel (1970: 21ff.).

7. Baur's historical judgment is widely attributed to the influence of the Hegelian categories of thesis/antithesis/synthesis. For a discussion of the extent to which this is true, see Hodgson (1966: 1-4); Schmithals (1965: ch. 5); Morgan (1978/9: 6); and Gasque (1975: 29f.).

8. Of that period he wrote, 'Die Zeit (ist) länger, die Kraft kürzer, die Liebe schwindsüchtiger und der Geist kurzatmiger geworden' (p. 276).

9. Ellis takes the view that it was Lightfoot (1893) that kept Anglo-American scholarship within the traditional camp (Ellis 1960: 152). However, the Lightfoot essay, although published thirteen years after that of Holtzmann's commentary, was in fact printed from lecture notes composed no later than 1862, nearly twenty years before! Despite Holtzmann's work, the traditional position continued to be defended on the continent by such as Riggen (1898), Stellhorn (1899), and Lütgert (1909), while Sabatier humbly confessed that the arguments for and against left him in a state of complete indecision (1896: 286f.).

10. He mentions in particular the arguments from the chronology, the polemic, the doctrine, the ecclesiastical organization and psychological factors, which, when taken together, 'are almost overwhelming and decisive' (Harrison 1921: 6).

11. We discuss these matters more fully in Chapter 4.

12. Although he accepts the total authenticity of the Pastorals, de Lestapis (1976) is unusual in both affirming the total authenticity of the Pastorals, and in situating them within the framework of Paul's life: 1 Timothy and Titus in 58 AD, and 2 Timothy immediately on arrival at Rome in 61 AD.

13. Both Jeremias (1968: 8f.) and Albertz (1952: 217ff.) opt for Tychicus. Luke, however, is the candidate who has gained most support. Schott was the first to propose that a disciple of Paul, *forsitan Lucas*, wrote the Pastorals (1830: 324f.). While 2 Tim 4.11 ruled out Luke for Jeremias, the same text was sufficient proof for James (1906: 154). More recently the case for Lucan authorship has been advanced by Moule, who proposed that Luke wrote during Paul's lifetime (1965: 434). Strobel (1969) argues for Lucan authorship on the basis of linguistic and theological affinities between Luke–Acts and the Pastorals. He does not, however, give any details of how Luke worked, or of the time and place of composition. Wilson (1979) improves considerably on the method of Strobel, and also deals with the objections to his thesis. He suggests that Luke (the author of Luke–Acts) was not a companion of Paul, but wrote the Pastorals after he had written the Acts, to refute the gnostic misinterpretation of Paul, and to show the churches where the source of true authority and sound teaching lay. The most ingenious suggestion comes from Quinn who holds that Luke wrote the Pastorals as the third volume of a trilogy, Luke–Acts–Pastorals. He suggests that the Pastorals are an epistolary appendix to Luke–Acts, which aims at rehabilitating the Pauline apostolate and teaching (1978. See our critique in Prior 1979: 7f.). Schmithals suggests that the *Paulus-Quelle*, the special source of Acts 13–28, may have formed one book with the Pastoral Letters (1982: 191).

14. Among commentators supporting this view are Dibelius and Conzelmann, Brox, Hasler, Easton, Gealy, Higgins, Barrett, Houlden, Karris, and the later Hanson. In many recent works on Paul the Pastorals are either excluded from the discussion (e.g. Funk 1981), or their inauthenticity is presumed (e.g. Lindemann 1979: 44-49, 134-49).

15. The introduction to the Pauline Letters in the new Irish translation of the Bible informs the reader that 'All modern scholars are of one mind: it was not Paul who wrote the Pastoral Epistles, but another person in his name. Pseudepigraphy was a common practice, which was totally accepted in the period of the New Testament'. (Our translation from *An Bíobla Naofa*, Maigh Nuad, 1981, p. 157. See Prior 1982). In a series designed to bring the best of biblical scholarship to a wide audience, Karris neither refers to the complexities of the problem, nor mentions the alternative views, but states categorically that the Pastorals are pseudepigrapha, composed about 110 AD, presenting Paul as a model for a church in transition (Karris 1979. See our review in *Heythrop Journal* 24 [1983], pp. 310ff.).

16. Brox (1969a). In Chapter 7 we deal with the paraenetic character of 2 Timothy.

17. Von Campenhausen also proposes Polycarp as the author of the Pastorals (1963).

18. Spicq (1969: 201) records the different fragments of Krenkel, Knocke, Ewald, Moffatt, Clemen, and Falconer.

19. These include: Why are there fragments in only 2 Timothy and Titus? Why are the other personal allusions in the Pastorals omitted (e.g. 1 Tim 1.3; 3.14; 5.23; 2 Tim 1.5, 15; Tit 1.5)? The fragments are not convincing separate letters. If they were parts of originally larger letters, why were they separated from them, and what has happened to the residue? How were the fragments preserved, and if they were preserved, why were they, in their original form, not incorporated in the collection of Paul's letters? If the fragments were already known to be Pauline, is it likely that the communities would have accepted such a heavily contrived redaction as we have in the surviving form? If the redactor were so versed in Paul's thought, how could he have misrepresented it so thoroughly, and how could his misrepresentation be so widely accepted?

20. One thinks of Neill's remark that 'the historical study of the New Testament has been long and widely distorted by the acceptance of assumptions which rest on no evidence whatever' (Neill 1964: 59), and of Grant's claim that 'most of the statements about the New Testament which I read are based on presuppositions which usually are not stated' (Grant 1963: 5).

21. It is true that pseudepigraphy was a well-known procedure in antiquity: 'There is scarcely an illustrious personality in Greek literature or history from Themistocles down to Alexander, who was not credited with a more or less extensive correspondence' (Metzger 1972: 10). For the practice of pseudepigraphy among Jews see Charlesworth (1979, ed. 1983-85) and Harrington (1980).

22. See James (1924) and Hennecke (1959 and 1964).

23. Examples are the *Letters of Christ and Abgarus*, the *Letter of Lentulus*, the *Correspondence of Paul and Seneca*, *Pseudo-Titus*, and the *Epistle to the Laodiceans*, the *Epistle of the Apostles*, and *3 Corinthians*. The genre is not favoured also in the Nag Hammadi collection.

24. James (1924: 477). He adds that our apocryphal epistles are few and not impressive.

25. Lightfoot adds that 'it is quite harmless, so far as falsity and stupidity combined can be regarded as harmless' (1884: 281ff.). This letter does not appear to be that referred to in the *Muratorian Canon* (lines 63-67), since it does not have a definite stance.

26. However, cf. *vaniloquia* (v. 4) with 1 Tim 1.6; 2 Tim 4.4, and 'praecavete sordidos in lucro' (v. 13) with 1 Tim 3.8; 6.10.

27. Within the NT itself there are some indications of a sensitivity towards differentiating between true and forged writing. Rev 22.18 is a warning against adding to the prophecies of the book, and in 2 Thess 2.2, although this letter is widely regarded as pseudepigraphical, we have clear testimony

to the distinction between authentic and forged writings. Paul's own insistence on adding his signature to his letters points in the same direction. In the later period, we note the *Muratorian Canon's* distinction between authentic and inauthentic letters of Paul (lines 63-67). Tertullian refers favourably to the defrocking of the Asian presbyter who had forged the Acts of Paul and Thecla, even though the author at his trial claimed to have done his writing out of love for Paul (*De Bap*. xvii). The *Apostolic Constitutions* warn against false books which were attributed to Christ and the disciples (6.16). Cyril of Jerusalem accepted the four gospels alone and rejected the rest because they were pseudepigrapha and harmful (*Catech*. 4.36). According to Justin, the manipulation of the Holy Scriptures was the worst kind of sin (*Dial*. 73, 4f.). The *Muratorian Canon* rejects the forged (*finctae*) *Letter to the Laodiceans* and the *Letter to the Alexandrians*, which are compared to the genuine Pauline Epistles as gall is compared to honey (lines 63-68).

28. Recently, Lea (1984) has concluded that there simply is no evidence that the ante-Nicene Church knowingly accepted into the NT canon a writing that was known to be pseudonymous. In the light of the early Church's careful practice he cautions against a careless use of the appeal to pseudonymity to account for differences in NT literature.

29. 'There is also a pseudonymity which is innocent, sincere and honest. . . . one may not think of malice or cowardice, but rather of modesty and natural timidity' (Deissmann 1903: 15).

30. Guthrie has surveyed the development of the idea of Canonical Pseudepigrapha. He attributes to F.C. Baur the growth of the idea of canonical 'forgeries'. Jülicher's contribution to the discussion was decisive. He made a plea not to regard pseudepigrapha as forgeries; he attributed almost unbounded credulity to the early communities. He claimed that Christians, with the best intentions and the cleanest consciences, put words into the mouth of a revered apostle; they composed letters as they did discourses; they were interested only in the message. Against such a background of unsupported assumptions, Jülicher allowed for the possibility of a pseudepigraphical canonical letter, although he cautioned against the view that regarded all the letters as pseudepigrapha (Guthrie 1962: 21f.).

31. See Cadbury's criticism of the attempts to account for Ephesians by recourse to arbitrary pseudepigraphy theories (Cadbury 1958/9: 97). Note also Kiley's lack of interest in suggesting a specific *Sitz im Leben* for the composition of Colossians by a deutero-Pauline school: 'They wrote Col sometime after Phil . . . It may have served as a letter of recommendation for Epaphras, . . . (but it also) wants to know that Paul's teaching is not strictly limited to the exigencies of time and place' (1986: 106). In a fashion typical of supporters of a theory of pseudepigraphy Fiore (1986) and Donelson (1986) too appear not to consider it necessary to suggest a specific historical context for the pseudepigraphical Pastorals.

32. In recent times several studies have been devoted to the phenomenon of pseudepigraphical writing. Torm concluded his study of a wide range of pseudepigrapha (especially the Orphic, Hermetic and Sibylline literature) with the judgment that the ancients either accepted as authentic the work of the author and regarded it highly as such, or else they saw it as a forgery, and therefore rejected it (Torm 1932: 19). Meyer gave more attention to Jewish religious pseudepigraphy, and argued that since the early Christians composed the Sermon on the Mount from Jesus' sayings, and also the discourses of the Fourth Gospel, it was not a great step to write under the name of an apostle. The criterion for acceptance of a work was apostolic truth, rather than apostolic authority (Meyer 1936: 277). Aland proposed that in the matter of canonical pseudepigrapha, ethical and psychological considerations should not have any part: 'When the pseudonymous writings of the New Testament claimed the authorship of the most prominent apostles ... this was not a skillful trick of the so-called faker ... but the logical conclusion of the presupposition that the Spirit himself was the author' (Aland 1961: 44f.). Koch proposes that the pseudonymous writer considered his master to be alive in heaven, and therefore still effective; ascribing the work to the honoured master, then, is almost the same as ascribing it to God himself (Koch 1976: 713). Brox (1973) surveys and criticizes the recent discussion concerning the usefulness of general statements concerning the practice of pseudepigraphy in antiquity, the motivation for it, the *Tendenz* of a work, etc. Brox (1977) has gathered together in one volume some of the most significant articles on the subject of pseudepigraphy (including those of Torm and Meyer) published in this century.

33. Guthrie (1962: 39). Robinson denounced the 'appetite for pseudonymity that grows by what it feeds on', and remarked that pseudonymity is a way of life among NT scholars (Robinson 1976: 186).

Notes to Chapter 2

1. Having discussed the arguments from the implied historical setting, and those dealing with the theology, the heresies and the organization of the Church, C. Spicq concludes that the only valid argument against the authenticity of the Pastorals is that of style, and particularly that of vocabulary (Spicq 1969: 179).

2. Harrison's figures for the NT and Pauline *hapax legomena* are as follows:

	Rom	1 Cor	2 Cor	Gal	Eph	Phil	Col	1 Thess
NT Hap. leg.	4	4.1	5.6	3.9	4.6	6.2	5.5	3.6
Plne Hap. leg.	10	11.1	12	10.3	10.6	12.7	9.7	7.5

176 *Second Timothy*

	2 Thess	Phlm	1 Tim	2 Tim	Tit
NT Hap. leg.	3.3	4	15.2	12.9	16.1
Plne Hap. leg.	8.7	8	27.3	24.4	30.4

For his conclusions see Harrison (1921: 22ff.). Strictly speaking, Harrison uses the term *hapax legomena* incorrectly, since many of the words occur more than once.

3. For example, he gives a list of 31 'particularly frequent and characteristic Pauline words', which are not in the Pastorals, but are in Luke–Acts. On examination, however, it is seen that no fewer than 25 of those 31 'particularly frequent Pauline words' occur no more than an average of once per Pauline letter, and no Pauline letter contains more than 28. Moreover, no less than 8 are absent from either Luke or Acts and three Paulines at least, and in one case (ὀφειλέτης) from 8 Paulines. Our calculations are based on the information in the *Computer-Konkordanz* (ed. Bachmann and Slaby 1980).

4. ἀψευδής occurs some 102 times, σωτήριος some 88 times, αἰδώς some 68 times, ῥήτως occurs some 56 times, βλαβερός some 56 times, φροντίζω some 48 times, πρόγονος some 44 times, δειλία some 38 times, and ἀνεπίλημπτος some 33 times. Our figures are based on Gunter Mayer's (incomplete) *Index Philoneus* (Mayer 1974).

5. E.g. Michaelis criticized Harrison for not having set out his graphs of the *hapax legomena* in accordance with the date of composition of the letters, and, more significantly, for having given the *hapax legomena* in terms of the number per page, rather than in terms of the total number of words in a text, which latter reckoning would show Romans to have almost the same percentage as 2 Timothy and Titus (1929: 71-74). Badcock examined each of the 175 Pastorals *hapax legomena* and showed that all but 17 can be accounted for as belonging to the Apostolic Age (e.g. 73, and 10 closely similar words, occur in the LXX; another 30 are quite classical; non-Christian writers of the Apostolic Age have 10 more words, etc.) (1937: 115-33). Hitchcock showed that while only 81% of the Pauline words occurred in Philo, no less than 87.5% of the Pastorals' did (1940: 115).

6. The bi-logarithmic type/token ratio is $\log V/\log N$, where V is the vocabulary of a text, and N is the length of text in terms of words. See Herdan (1959).

7. E.g. Kümmel applauds the 'mathematically refined statistics' of Grayston and Herdan (Kümmel 1973: 372), while Turner refers to it as a 'sophisticated modern technique' (Turner 1963: 102). Hooker judged Morton's contribution to the question of the authorship of the Pauline epistles to be 'the most sensational development of Pauline studies in the 1960s' (Hooker, 1970: 212). O'Rourke shows up some of the limitations of Harrison's method (O'Rourke 1973). Others, however, are sceptical about the method itself (e.g. Spicq 1969: 184), and Guthrie claims that mathematical

calculations can never prove linguistic affinity (Guthrie 1957: 214).

8. T.A. Robinson has shown that the difference in 'C' for the Pastorals is due to the investigators having combined the three Pastorals. When each epistle is considered individually, 'the marked difference between the "C" quantities of the Pastorals and of the Paulines all but vanishes' (Robinson 1984: 286). Robinson concludes that there may exist no relationship between the percentage of *hapax legomena* in different works that could be used to detect a difference in authorship (p. 287). But authorship in general, and Pauline authorship in particular, is very much more complicated than even Robinson seems to allow.

9. Morton and McLeman, using two criteria independently, discover two groups within the Paulines, while Grayston and Herdan, using one criterion, do not reflect this division.

10. He found that the average number of syllables per word in chapters 1–35 is 2.04, while that in chapters 40–66 is 2.11. He concluded that the second half of the book was written by at least one different author from that of the first half (Radday 1970). More recently, Radday and Shore have applied more sophisticated techniques in the investigation of the authorship of Genesis (1985). Their approach respects the interconnection between variables, and uses a pattern recognition technique (see Part Three).

11. Radday distinguishes between style (which pertains to aesthetics), and language (which is beyond the conscious control of the author). Differences in style, therefore, are not author-specifying (1970: 319f.).

12. To his credit Kenny examines no less than ninety-nine factors (1986).

13. Drake (1972) draws attention to the discussion in Casey and Nagy (1971: 56).

Notes to Chapter 3

1. Kümmel (1973: 247-52) and Martin (1978: ch. 19) ignore the presence of co-senders in the Pauline letters. Fitzmyer refers to them as 'co-senders (scribes?)' (1968a: 224).

2. With regard to the first suggestion, are we to conclude that in Romans, Ephesians and the Pastorals Paul wrote 'from his own fantasy'? Secondly, while it is not impossible that the person named at the beginning of a letter was to deliver the letter, it is not the general rule: Tychicus is the carrier of the letters in the case of Colossians and Ephesians, but is not named at the beginning of either, while Timothy is the one whose name occurs at the beginning of Colossians. Furthermore, Timothy could conceivably be the carrier of 1 Corinthians (16.10), in which case, if Doty is right, his name should be in place of that of Sosthenes (1.1). Moreover, while Timothy's name does occur in Phil 1.1, in virtue of 2.9 it can hardly be claimed that he

is the carrier of the letter. In addition, Timothy, who has just returned to the place of writing of 1 Thessalonians (3.6) is named with Paul and Silvanus (1.1), and is hardly likely to be simply the postman; indeed, to be consistent, Doty should regard both Silvanus and Timothy as the letter-carriers.

3. At the end of the NT letters we find greetings to and from groups of people: Heb 13.24, 1 Pet 5.14 and 3 John 15 send greetings to groups, while Heb 13.24, 1 Pet 5.13, 2 John 13 and 3 John 15 send greetings from groups. 1 Peter is the only non-Pauline NT letter where the writer names an individual who sends greetings (Mark, my son, 5.13). Paul's practice varies. Galatians, Ephesians, 1 and 2 Thessalonians, and 1 Timothy send no greetings, while 2 Corinthians (13.13), Philippians (4.21f.) and Titus (3.15) have general greetings. In Romans greeting are sent from eight people (16.21ff.), and in 1 Corinthians from two (16.9). In Colossians greetings are sent from Aristarchus, Mark, Jesus, Epaphras, Luke and Demas (4.10ff., 14), in Philemon from Epaphras, Mark, Aristarchus, Demas and Luke (23f.), while, in 2 Timothy Eubulus, Pudens, Linus and Claudia send greetings (4.21), and Luke is mentioned as being with Paul at the time of writing (4.11).

4. The royal plural occurs in letters 2-4; 6-8; 10-13; 15; 18-19; 22-23; 25-27; 31; 36; 44-45; 47; 50; 67; 71-72; 75. On the other hand, the following use the first singular throughout: Letters 30; 32; 34; 51-52; 54-58; 61-62; 64-66; and 68-70.

5. *P. Ryl.* 131 is a 31 AD petition from Mysthes and Pelopion. The background to the petition is as follows: 'On the 16th of Phamenoth ... as I was making an inspection of the lands which we farm ... we found that the young wheat and the barley which we have on the farm had been grazed down by the sheep of Harmiusus'. The petition itself is: 'I therefore request that he be brought before you for the ensuing punishment'. The reader is left wondering to whom the 'I' refers. One of the two, only, inspected the land, since the writer is careful to point out that a certain Aunes witnessed the damage; had both visited the property the double witness would surely have been used. It is likely that the one who visited the property and the one making the petition are the same person, but as to which of the duo so acted we can only guess. We would be in a somewhat better position to know if the bottom of the papyrus were not damaged, and if we had the document signed.

6. In a small number of letters, written to Tiro in his illness, Cicero wrote not only in his own name but in that of members of his family. However, it is clear that Cicero himself is the real author, or at least the spokesman for the concern of the family. The use of the first singular is abundant, and in some letters total. It is only when he deals with the progress of the journey, or the common solicitude for Tiro's health that he uses the first plural. The first singular is used throughout *Ad Fam.* XVI,4, 6, 7, 11, while *Ad Fam.* XVI,1, 3, 5, and 9 use both the first singular and plural.

7. In Romans there is not the slightest suggestion that Paul is writing in more than his own name. Indeed, the use of the first singular is abundant throughout the letter, and particularly in ch. 7. Where he does use the first plural it is clear that he is using it in the sense of 'you, readers, and I', or, 'we believers', or in a rhetorical fashion as in 8.31; 9.14, 30, and 10.8. All the evidence in Romans, then, confirms the fact that Paul is writing in his own name only.

8. In Ephesians Paul uses the first singular all the time, and uses the first plural only in the sense of 'you and I', or 'we believers' (e.g. 1.2f.; 2.3; 6.12, etc.). The single exception to this general rule occurs at 6.22. It is possible that this refers to Paul and Tychicus, or, perhaps, Paul and others around him in a general sense, rather as in 'how everything is here' (Col 4.9).

9. In 1 Tim 1.8 the writer is obviously referring to Timothy and himself, and nothing in the use of the first person plural suggests more than one author. 2 Timothy is a particularly personal letter, and Titus is obviously written in the name of Paul alone.

10. Note the following key verbs occurring only in the singular: εὐχαριστέω (Rom 1.8; 16.4; Eph 1.16); παρακαλέω (Rom 12.1; 15.30; 16.17; Eph 4.1; 1 Tim 1.3; 2.1); γράφω (Rom 15.15; 1 Tim 3.14); and λέγω (Rom 3.5; 6.19; 9.1; 11.1, 11, 13; 12.3; 15.8; Eph 4.17; 5.32; 1 Tim 2.7).

11. Note the following key verbs only in the plural: εὐχαριστοῦμεν (1 Thess 1.2; 2.13; 2 Thess 1.3; 2.13); παρακαλοῦμεν (1 Thess 4.1, 10; 5.14; 2 Thess 3.12); ἐρωτῶμεν (1 Thess 4.1; 5.12; 2 Thess 2.1); λέγομεν (1 Thess 4.15; 2 Thess 2.5); and κηρύσσομεν (1 Thess 2.9).

12. The final grace is in the plural (v. 25). The phrases 'our brother', 'our fellow-worker', 'our Father', and 'in us' (vv. 1-6) clearly refer to 'us believers' rather than to Paul and Timothy. As against these four uses of the first plural we have 17 uses of ἐγώ. The verbs εὐχαριστέω (4), παρακαλέω (9, 10), γράφω (19, 21) and ἐρωτάω (19, 21) occur only in the singular.

13. Lightfoot suggests that the 'us' includes Timothy, Epaphroditus and the other faithful companions known to the Philippians. He proposes that the movement from 'me' to 'us' is due to 'a shrinking from the egotism of dwelling on his own personal example' (1913: 154), which is not plausible in view of the almost exclusive use of 'I'.

14. The verb εὐχαριστέω (1.3), παρακαλέω (4.2), γράφω (3.1), ἐρωτάω (4.3) and λέγω (3.8; 4.11) occur only in the first singular.

15. Cf. 'Polycarp and the presbyters who are with him' in the opening of Polycarp *Phil*. It is clear, however, that Polycarp is the sole author since he never uses the first person plural when referring to the author, but always the first singular.

16. The verbs γράφω (1.20; 6.11) and λέγω (1.9; 3.15, 17; 4.1; 5.2, 16) occur only in the singular.

17. The verb εὐχαριστέω (1.4, 14; 10.30; 14.18), παρακαλέω (1.10; 4.16;

16.15), γράφω (4.14; 5.9, 11; 9.15; 14.37), and λέγω (1.12; 6.5; 7.6, 8, 12, 35; 10.15, 29; 11.22) occur only in the singular.

18. See the discussion in Watson (1984). The majority of this group place the composition of chs 10-13 after that of chs 1-9.

19. In the most general terms one might say that chs 1, 3-6 look like a letter from 'us', while 2, 7-9 and 11-13 have the appearance of a letter from 'me'. In more detail, 1.6f. clearly refers to the writers, while in 1.3 we find ἐλπίζω in the same sentence as γράφομεν. The first singular is emphatic at 1.23 and continues throughout ch. 2, except for the final verse, 2.17. Chs 3 and 4 are altogether in the plural, and the only exception in ch. 5 is the ἐλπίζω at 5.11. λέγω is the single exception to the same plural pattern in ch. 6. From ch. 7 the letter looks very much like one from one person, with the plural occurring at 7.13, 8.1 and 9.11. In ch. 10, where we find the person changing from the singular to the plural, we note the insistence of ἐγὼ Παῦλος in v. 1. Chs 11, 12, and 13 are very much letters from an individual, although 11.4, 21; 12.19 could refer to co-authors. 13.7-9 clearly refers to 'we writers', but immediately we find γράφω in v. 10. As another indication of the mixed nature of this letter let it be noted that 2 Corinthians is the only Pauline letter which uses both παρακαλέω (2.8; 10.1) and παρακαλοῦμεν (6.1), and likewise γράφω (2.3, 4, 9; 7.12; 9.1; 13.10) and γράφομεν (1.13).

20. In the absence of information from antiquity a modern set of (circular) letters, which we have in our possession, offers an interesting frame of reference for the composition of the Pauline letters. The writers are the three-member executive team (husband, wife, priest) of the 'Worldwide Marriage Encounter England'. All the letters carry the signature of the team. There are clear indications as to who was responsible for the different parts. For example, in eight of the letters there is a section which was clearly composed by the husband and wife. In other cases where 'we' is used there is no doubt that all three are involved. 'We' is also used of the members of the organization. 'I' is used by the priest, or one member of the couple: there is never any confusion, since they either give the name in brackets, or the context makes it clear. While there are several points of contact between these letters and those of Paul (e.g. the authors are an ecclesial team, with responsibility for the house-churches throughout the country; the writers teach, exhort, and reply to queries), the modern ones, unlike Paul's letters, leave one in no doubt as to who is responsible for each part of the letter.

21. Recently, the fact of co-authorship for 1 and 2 Thessalonians is being taken more seriously. While one author suggests that the differences between these letters and the other Paulines may be explained by Paul's having employed Silvanus or Timothy as an executive secretary for both letters (Best 1972: 53), Thurston rightly observes that 1 and 2 Thessalonians claim to have been written not by Paul alone, but by the trio, and that this fact must be taken seriously into consideration (Thurston 1973/4: 56). Most significantly of all, however, Bruce's recent commentary alerts the reader to

the possibility that Silvanus and Timothy played a responsible part along with Paul in the composition of the letters (Bruce 1982).

22. In 1 Thessalonians the first singular 'forces its way in' at 2.18; 3.5; 5.27, because in those places Paul's 'consciousness of his own leadership will out' (1952/3: 241). The reason for the singular in 2 Thess 2.5; 3.17 is that Paul is the chief speaker (p. 242). The first singular occurs in Gal 1 and 2 because 'the hidden man of the heart' writes his 'inner autobiography'. In chs 1 and 2 'sometimes the singulars are softened to the plural, when the relation between the writer and reader is felt or desired to be more intimate' (p. 242). By some strange logic he later attributes the exclusive use of the first singular in Philippians to Paul's intimacy with that community (pp. 244f.). The first singular occurs in 1 Corinthians because 'Paul takes the whole responsibility for what is asked upon himself' (p. 242). He correctly rejects the explanation that Paul is using an 'epistolary plural' in 2 Cor 1.1-14, and he suggests that such a close companion as Timothy need not be excluded from the thoughts therein. He questions if the abundant use of the plural means any more than the singular, and answers by saying, 'we cannot, obviously, be certain'. He admits that in some places 'the transitions from singular to plural and back again are more puzzling; ... and the temptation to think that they are accidental or at least irrelevant is great' (pp. 243f.). The occurrence of the first singular in both Philippians and Philemon is accounted for by the intimacy between Paul and the addressees, and two factors are combined to account for the appearance of the plurals in Colossians, namely that Paul was less intimate with the Colossians, and that they probably knew Timothy better than did the Philippians.

23. He never uses the term 'co-authors', but instead refers to the 'one or more persons with Paul' in the superscriptions (p. 286).

24. Fitzmyer has recently surveyed Aramaic epistolography (1979). In non-biblical Aramaic letters we find references to a secretary: in *AP* 26.23 (Elephantine, 412 BC) Anani, the clerk, drafted the letter, and Nabu'aqab wrote it. A scribe is also mentioned in some of the Arsames Letters (*AD* 6.6; 7.10; 8.6; 9.3; 10.5), and in some of Simon bar Kosibah's letters (5/6 *Hev* 8.7). Within the Bible Shim'shai is 'the secretary' and is a respected Persian official (Ezra 4), and Ezra himself is 'a scribe skilled in the law of Moses' (7.6, 12, 21).

25. Pardee has recently surveyed extra-biblical letters (1978). In only one of the 47 extant letters is a secretary clearly implied (*papMur* 43), since it was dictated by Simon bar Kosibah, who appears to have signed the letter in his own hand. *PapMur* 42 contains the only possible reference to a scribe (pp. 329f.). There is considerable evidence in the OT for the use of secretaries (e.g. Num 11.16; 1 Chron 4.41; 24.6). Within the OT there are several letters: David wrote to Joab by the hand of Uriah (2 Sam 11.14f.); Jezebel wrote in Ahab's name to the elders and the nobles in Naboth's city (1 Kgs 21.8-10); the king of Syria wrote to the kings of Israel, by the hand of

Naaman (2 Kgs 5.6); Jehu wrote to the elders in Samaria (2 Kgs 10.1-3, and a second letter, v. 6); the king sent messengers to Hezekiah (2 Kgs 19.9-14); Jeremiah wrote to the exiles in Babylon, by the hand of Elasah (Jer 29.4-23), and also a letter of complaint to Zephaniah (Jer 24.26-29); cf. also Neh 6.5-7; 2 Chron 2.11-15; 21.12-15; 30.1, 6; Ezra 1.1-4; Esth 1.22; 3.13; 9.21. These letters preserve only the body of the letter, and the names of the sender and the receiver are given within the text.

26. Tyrell and Purser give no less than 931 letters (1901-33). His letters differ greatly in style, and in the circumstances of composition: some were written with great care, and some in haste. His passion for letter-writing seems to have been matched only by his desire to receive letters, especially from Atticus, his friend from youth, to whom he wrote almost every day after he had left Rome in 49 BC (*Ad Att*. VII,xv,1), and even while on a journey to Cilicia in 51 BC only a few days separated his letters to him. He wrote even when he had 'nothing to write', and several times he urged Atticus to write even when he, too, thought he had nothing to say.

27. When discussing delicate political matters he sometimes declined to use his own handwriting, or even his seal, and in several places he used Greek, and a pen-name to conceal his identity (*Ad Att*. II,xix,5; VI,iv,3; v,1f.; ix,2; II,xx,5).

28. He directed him to write to Antony and others if Atticus thought it necessary, because nothing had come into his own mind worth writing (*Ad Att*. XI,xii,4). Because of his own upset of mind and body he had written only to those who had written to him, and he directed Atticus to write in his name to Basilius and even to Servilius, and to say whatever he thought fit (*Ad Att*. XI,v,4).

29. He regards the ability to write well and quickly as important: a sluggish pen delays one's thoughts, while an unformed and illiterate hand cannot be deciphered, and this necessitates the wearisome task of dictating (I,i,28).

30. He advises a slow and sure pen which does not welcome every thought which presents itself, but arranges what is approved (5). He emphasizes the need to frequently revise what has been written (6f.). He counsels care from the beginning, and condemns the practice of making a rough copy which has been written with the utmost speed of which the pen is capable (17f.). He notes with approval the practice of Cicero and others of jotting down notes and memoranda (X,iv,30f.).

31. There is abundant evidence for forms of shorthand in Latin in the first century AD (e.g. Seneca, *Ad Luc*. XC, 25), and Suetonius describes how he had heard of Titus's expertise in shorthand, and his playful contests with secretaries (*De Vita Caes, Titus* VIII,iii,2). The evidence for the use of shorthand in Greek is somewhat later (*P. Oxy*. 724, 155 AD), but Cicero's use of the phrase διὰ σημείων suggests the practice of some kind of shorthand even as early as the first century BC (*Ad Att*. XIII,xxxii,3).

32. Because he holds that the Pastorals are so different from the other letters Bahr does not consider them.

33. Since most of the subscription material is of an ethical rather than a theological character, Bahr improperly concludes that Paul is more properly regarded as the first great teacher of Christian ethics, rather than as a theologian. In fact, he suggests that a theology of Paul should be confined to the subscriptions, and that the material in the body of the letter is better regarded as 'a record of primitive Christian thinking (rather) than the theology of a particular person' (p. 41). Against Bahr it must be insisted that the support for the conclusion that an ancient author took full responsibility for what the secretary wrote is overwhelming. Manus depends heavily on Bahr, and attributes to the hand of a secretary the abrupt changes within the Pauline letters, rather than fall back on any hypothesis of Pauline fragments, or interpolations into the letters. Manus's contentions, however, are more claims than demonstrated likelihoods (Manus 1984).

34. The ambiguity of the evidence can be gauged by noting that while one author claimed that word-for-word dictation was a rarity (Roller 1933: 33), a second claimed the opposite (Hitchcock 1930: 273f.).

35. A major weakness of Bahr's thesis on the extent of Paul's subscriptions is that the non-literary letters of the period have much shorter subscriptions (see Longenecker 1974: 291).

36. If pressure of work was one reason for using a secretary (*Ad Att.* IV,xvi,1), another was the inflammation of his eyes (*Ad Att.* VII,xiiia,3). But two days later his eyes, though still slightly inflamed, did not prevent him writing in his own hand (*Ad Att.* VII,xiv,1). See also *Ad Att.* X,xvii,2; VIII,xiii,1; *Ad Quint.* II,ii,1. While travelling, he was often constrained to use a secretary, for which he apologized (*Ad Att.* V,xiv,1; cf. V, xvii,1f.; VIII,xv,3). He also confessed to laziness as the reason for not writing in his own hand, but he added, by way of chiding, that he noticed Alexis's hand in Atticus's letter to him to which he was then replying (*Ad Att.* XVI,xv,1).

37. While no other NT letter has the character of a team-letter, several do have a wide public in view: see Jam 1.1; 1 Pet 1.1; 2 Pet 1.1; 2 John 1; Jude 1; and Rev 1.4.

38. While 1 Thess 1.1, 2 Thess 1.1 and Phlm 1 may suggest that the letter in each case was written to one (house) church, Rom 1.7, Phil 1.1 and Col 1.2 suggest a plurality of house churches.

39. 1 Corinthians, while being addressed in the first instance to the church in Corinth, is also intended for all those who call upon the name of the Lord Jesus Christ (1 Cor 1.2). 2 Corinthians is addressed to the church in Corinth, but also to all the saints in the whole of Achaia (2 Cor 1.1). Galatians is addressed to all the churches of Galatia, and hence was intended by its author to have the character of a circular letter. Examples of circular letters are found in the royal Hellenistic correspondence (e.g. Letter 18 in Welles

1934), among the official letters in the Papyri (e.g. *P. Oxy.* 2108), in Daniel 4, where Nebuchadnezzar's letter to all nations, etc., is described as an 'encyclical letter' (LXX 4.37b), and also in Jam 1.1 in the NT. Ephesians is problematic because of the absence of ἐν ᾿Εφέσῳ in some manuscripts, and also because of the unexpected absence of any hint of familiarity between the writer and the receiver, such as one would expect in a letter sent by Paul to a community among whom he lived for some years.

40. Deissmann insisted that the smaller letters of Paul 'must be compared with the soldiers' letters and peasants' letters from Egypt' which were non-literary, never intended for publication, and were therefore no more than 'confidential conversation in writing' (1907: 53, 56). Having read all of the papyrus letters in almost all of the published collections we are astounded that Deissmann's thesis ever gained such prominence.

41. Deissmann's apparent disdain for the literary epistle, and his almost unlimited regard for the papyrus letters are both exaggerations: 'If the true letter might be compared to a prayer, the epistle which mimicked it was only a babbling; if there beamed forth in the letter the wondrous face of a child, the epistle grinned stiffly and stupidly, like a puppet' (1903: 10; see also 1908: 56).

42. While the papyrus letter-writer engaged in confidential conversation in writing, the writer of the epistle wrote with his eyes set on the public, cried in the market-place, and entrusted his sheets to the winds, not knowing whither they would be borne (1903: 54f.).

43. Hartman suggests that 'Paul intended his letters to be read and reread in the communities to which they were addressed, and in others as well' (1986: 139), and that the 'occasional' and particular in specific churches was so dealt with by Paul that the letter could serve as an apostolic letter to other churches as well (Phlm, 1 Cor 1.1f.; 2 Cor 2.1; 2 Thess 2.2; 3.17 and Col 4.16) (pp. 144f.).

44. E.g. the Edict of Titius Honoratus was required to be posted in public (*P. Oxy.* 2704, 292 AD); *P. Oxy.* 2108 contains an order that it be displayed in the most conspicuous places in the villages; cf. also *P. Oxy.* 3025 and *P. Oxy.* 3348.

45. C. Bradford Welles has studied 75 letters, of which 69 are strictly speaking royal letters, which come from the last three centuries BC (Welles 1934).

46. E.g. Letters 18; 19; 36; 37; 44; 47; 51; 70 in Welles (1934). Fiore gives other examples of letters which while carrying the name of a single addressee were intended for a wider audience (1986: 80 n. 6).

47. That Paul was familiar with the practice of engraving letters on *stelae* is clear from 2 Cor 3.3.

48. Paul Schubert correctly adjudged Deissmann's overestimate of the papyrus letters to be a false start (1939a: 370).

49. While for Deissmann it was the intention of the author that determined the private or public character of his letter (1908), Schubert claimed that 'the intention of the addressee to publish an epistolary document is a vastly more important criterion of its functional and formal character than the (possibly) arbitrary intention of the author' (1939b: 182).

50. Polycarp in sending to the Philippians Ignatius's letters to the Smyrnaeans provides an early example of a dissemination of letters beyond the intention of their author (Polycarp *Phil.* XIII).

51. The *Muratorian Fragment* notes how Paul, in writing to seven churches, followed the pattern of the seven letters of Revelation: 'Licet septem ecclesiis scribat, tamen omnibus dicit' (lines 59f.). The later publication of the letters shifted the focus from the historical circumstances of a letter to one church, or one region, to that of a general letter for the whole Church (see Goodspeed 1940, and Mitton 1955). Dahl deals with the movement in a Pauline letter from local to universal interest (1962).

52. See, for example, 2 Cor 10.10.

53. Barrett judges that 'Paul was the storm-centre of his age' (1974: 229).

54. Chadwick insists that Paul shows an astonishing elasticity of mind, and a greater flexibility than is usually supposed (1954/5: 275). Brown proposes 'what is virtually heresy in the eyes of many Pauline scholars ("that Paul was not always consistent in his major epistles; that he even changed his mind") and in particular that whereas he had made the mistake in Galatians of overstating his case against the Law, in 1 Corinthians he countered Gentile Christians who had no respect for the Law (1 Cor 5.1-5), and in Romans he shows that he had learned from his mistake in Galatians' (Brown 1983: 114).

55. Unfortunately, neither Lightfoot (1885) nor the most recent study to hand (Meier, in Meier and Brown 1983) pays much attention to the pre-Christian period of Antioch. The city was founded by Seleucus I in 300 BC, and reflected the influence of Greek, oriental, Jewish and later Roman civilizations. The city was in turn dominated by Zeus, Apollo, and Aphrodite, with its patron goddess, Tyche, becoming the symbol of good fortune throughout the cities of the East (Downey 1963: 5; see also his monumental study, Downey 1961). Norris, mainly on the basis of archaeological artifacts, provides evidence for the active worship of Isis, Sarapis and Demeter in Antioch (1982). The Jewish presence in Antioch is surveyed in Meeks and Wilken (1978).

56. The origin and early years of the church in Antioch are described in e.g. Downey (1963: 120–42), Meeks and Wilken (1978: 13-18), and Meier and Brown (1983: ch. 2). For an account of the second generation Christian community in Antioch see Barnard (1963), Meier and Brown (1983: chs 3 and 4), and Grant (1972).

57. V. Corwin has attempted, on the basis of the Ignatian letters, to describe the life of the Christian community at Antioch in Ignatius's time. She sees Ignatius as steering a middle course between two factions in Antioch: the Essene-Jewish Christian group, with its attachment to the Teacher of Righteousness as well as to Jesus, and the Docetic Christian group which practised a 'spiritual' form of Christianity which included a certain tendency to withdraw from the worship of the community. She, then, attributes Ignatius's eirenic spirit in his dealings with the Asia Minor communities to his experience as reconciler in Antioch (Corwin 1960: esp. 52-65). Schoedel also stresses the effect of his experience in Antioch (his alleged loss of control of the church there and the emergence of a group opposed to his authority) on his self-understanding and sense of achievement/failure (1985: 10).

58. One thinks of docetism; the Jerusalem brand of Jewish Christianity; the Matthean type (hostile to charismatic tendencies); that sympathetic to Pauline Christianity; that reflected in the Didache (itinerant, charismatic); the bishop-appointing Christianity; and that espoused by Ignatius himself. See Trevett (1981/2).

59. In his commentary (1985) Schoedel pays little attention to the religious culture obtaining in Antioch, or to the unique epistolary situation of each letter. He approaches the letters, then, with scant regard for Ignatius's origins, or of the peculiar circumstances of the addressees. It goes without saying that one's place of origin and adult experience play a significant part in shaping one's world view. It is, however, only one of the several influences that must be kept in mind if we are to understand the complexity of human experience. Ideally, one would have to reckon with a person's family background in all its dimensions, together with the person's own physical, mental and spiritual gifts, and in the case of Ignatius, his being in fetters, and a recipient of considerable comforts from several communities, and his being close to martyrdom which focused his mind in a particular way. Schoedel's major thesis, that Ignatius had suffered a major identity crisis, and had severe doubts about the efficacy of his ministry in Antioch, is more striking for the enthusiasm with which the author advances it, than for the evidence with which it is supported.

60. In particular, one notes his theological synthesis of the human and the divine in Jesus Christ, and his sense of the importance of unity between the local communities and ἡ καθολικὴ ἐκκλησία (*Smyrn.* VIII), and the unity within the local community under the threefold ministry of bishop, college of presbyters and deacons. For his assessment of the relationship between the new wine of the Gospel and the wine-skins of Judaism, see Meier and Brown (1983: ch. 5).

61. In line with the modern consensus we accept the authenticity of the Middle Recension of Ignatius's Letters (see Schoedel 1985: 2-7). It is only in Magnesia (*Magn.* VIII, IX, X) and Philadelphia (*Phld.* VI, VIII, IX) that

there is a problem of Judaizers, while docetism has made serious inroads in Ephesus (*Eph.* VII), Magnesia (*Magn.* IX), Trallia (*Trall.* IX, XI), and especially Smyrna, and much less so in Philadelphia (*Phld.* Introd.). The breakdown of community harmony is obvious in several churches: if there is some splintering of the community in Magnesia (*Magn.* VII) and Trallia (*Trall.* VII), there is disunity even in the One Bread in Ephesus (*Eph.* XX; see also V; XII), and Philadelphia (*Phld.* IV). In general one might say that Ignatius is happy enough with the community in Ephesus; is worried about the Judaizing practices under a weak bishop, Damas, in Magnesia; is worried about the bishop and the breakdown of community in Trallia; sees Philadelphia as having a major problem of disunity; and is worried about the inroads of Docetism (with its social implications), and the lack of episcopal authority among the Smyrnaeans.

62. The facticity of the circumstances of Jesus' life are spelt out more explicitly than they were even in *Trall.* (IX; X). In the letter to the Smyrnaeans, Ignatius stresses that Jesus was truly of the family of David according to the flesh, and a son of God according to the will and power of God; that he was truly born of a virgin, and was baptized by John; that he set up an ensign through his resurrection (*Smyrn.* I); that he suffered for us that we might be saved, indeed, that he truly suffered, just as truly as he had truly raised himself: his passion was no mere appearance (II); that his post-resurrection appearances were not after the fashion of a phantom, but involved eating and drinking (III); that none of the aforementioned was merely by way of appearance (δοκέω *Smyrn.* IV); and , as though the point were not already adequately made, he stresses again the reality of the humanity of Jesus (*Smyrn.* V), particularly that of his passion (V; VI), and also he advises them that the eucharist is the flesh of the Saviour (VII), finally rounding off the section with a salute in the name of Jesus Christ, in his flesh and blood, and in his passion and resurrection.

63. *Pol.* I-V is clearly a person to person letter. But in VI there is an abrupt change from singular to plural. At VII, 2 there is a return to the singular, Polycarp, but from that point to the end there is a mixture of singular and plural. While Schoedel recognizes this very strange feature, 'There seems to be no parallel in ancient letters for such a shift from singular to plural' (1985: 274), his explanation, that the church in Smyrna is addressed a second time in the form of a letter to its bishop (p. 257), is not convincing. In this he follows Lightfoot, who claims that like the Pastoral Epistles the *Letter to Polycarp* was obviously intended to be made known to the Church also (1885: 351). There is, however, no indication within the Pastorals that the author so intended. A more plausible explanation is that the *Letter to Polycarp*, as we have it, has had interpolated into it material from another letter of Ignatius to the Church at Smyrna (cf. Polycarp *Phil.* 13).

64. Schoedel is wrong in understanding *Pol.* II,2 to be 'Ignatius' description of Polycarp as the ideal bishop' (1985: 24). The context makes it clear that

Ignatius is instructing Polycarp how better to comport himself and exercise his ministry.

65. Bishop Damas of Magnesia was young, and there was a real problem of unity under him, which greatly concerned Ignatius (*Magn.* III). The community of Trallia, also, had a problem with their bishop, Polybius (*Trall.* II; VII; XII; XIII). The situation in Philadelphia also was precarious, and Onesimus of Ephesus, too, seems to have had his own problems (*Eph.* III; IV; VI; XX).

66. Note that 1 Timothy and Titus also deal with such specifics. It is not without relevance that it is only in a private letter to a church leader that Ignatius gave specific instructions about ordering the different elements of the community.

67. We do not deal here with another possible source of information on Polycarp, since we have no way of sifting the grains of truth from the huge heap of falsehood contained in the fourth-century Life of Polycarp written by a certain Pionius (see Lightfoot 1885: 419f.).

68. Irenaeus emphasizes Polycarp's familiarity with many who had seen Christ, his having sat at the feet of John, and his having been appointed Bishop of Smyrna by Apostles (*Adv. Haer.* III,3,4, and *Letter to Florinus* quoted in Eusebius *Hist. Eccles.* V, 20). Note also the great veneration with which he was held during his lifetime, in his martyrdom and afterwards (cf. *Letter of the Smyrnaeans*).

69. We must ignore the spurious fragments commenting on the Gospels, and the *Didascalia* ascribed to Polycarp (cf. Lightfoot 1885: 457, 337ff.). However, his *Letter to the Philippians* provides another source whereby we may try to assess the character, theological emphases and ministerial competence of Polycarp. However, one must bear in mind that this is not much more than a covering letter, replying to the one he had received from the Philippians, and accompanying (copies of) the letters sent by Ignatius to the Smyrnaeans, and some other letters. It should not be judged as a theological statement worked out in the calm atmosphere of a study. There is no reason to imagine that it contains a rounded picture of Polycarp's view on the Christian life. Nevertheless, when one compares this letter with those of Ignatius a number of very striking differences emerges. There are indications in his letter that Polycarp was lacking in qualities which Ignatius regarded highly. The fact that he does not introduce himself as *episkopos*, nor ever refer to the office even though he speaks at length of the duties of wives, children, widows, deacons, younger men, and presbyters (IVff.) may suggest that he did not view that ministry with the assertiveness with which Ignatius did (e.g., *Eph. VI*; *Trall.* II; *Smyr.* VIIf.; *Magn.* III; *Pol.* IIIf., VI). Perhaps he preferred a presbyterian form of government. Furthermore, he admits to not being versed in the Jewish Scriptures (XII), and this is confirmed by his never quoting them. The abundance of quotations from the New Testament writings in the letter of Polycarp witnesses to his lack of originality: 'the

author's mind is receptive and not creative' (Lightfoot 1885: 581), which is in sharp contrast to that of Ignatius. Although he clearly affirms the facticity of the incarnation, cross (VII) and resurrection (II), Polycarp's statements about the incarnation, the true humanity of Jesus, and the twofold nature of Christ are less impressive than what one finds in Ignatius (e.g., *Eph.* VII; XVIIIf.; *Magn.* VII; VIII; XI; *Trall.* IX; *Rom.* VII; *Smyr.*, *passim*; and *Pol.* III). Neither does Polycarp reflect Ignatius's insistence on the passion/blood/cross of Jesus Christ as an object of belief, a centre of unity, and a source of life (e.g., *Trall.* inscr.; *Phil.* inscr.; III; *Smyr.* I; V; *Magn.* V; *Rom.* VI; *Eph.* inscr.; XVIII; XX; cf. Polycarp's only refernces to the blood/cross, *Phil.* II; VII; XII). Polycarp also ignores another of Ignatius's emphases, namely, the unity of the Church: unity and concord are major concerns of Ignatius (e.g., *Eph.* IV; XIII; *Magn.* VI; XV; *Trall.* XII; *Phil.* inscr.; XI).

70. 'The lifetime of Polycarp was the most tumultuous period in the religious history of the world' (Lightfoot 1885: 448). In the first instance adherence to the Christian faith was prohibited, and our scant records of the period record the persecution of two Christans during Trajan's reign, Simeon of Jerusalem, recorded by Hegesippus (in Eusebius *Hist. Eccles.* III,32), as well as Ignatius himself, and the persecution of Christians in Bithynia for which Trajan himself was responsible. It is clear from the evidence of coins and inscriptions that Smyrna was conspicuous in the pagan revival within the Roman Empire (Lightfoot 1885: 451f.). Difficulties also came from the Jewish community in Smyrna (cf. the description of the Smyrnaean Jews as the 'synagogue of Satan' in Rev 3.8ff.; cf. Schürer 1986: 19f.; Hemer 1986: 57-77).

Notes to Chapter 4

1. Cf. Murphy-O'Connor (1986: 42).

2. The thanksgiving occupies an important part in Rom 1.8-15; 1 Cor 1.4-9; Phil 1.3-11; Col 1.3-14; 1 Thess 1.2-10; 2 Thess 1.3-12; Phlm 4-7 as well as in 2 Tim 1.3-5. In 2 Cor 1.3-11 and Eph 1.3-23 there is a εὐλογητὸς ὁ θεός section, while in 1 Tim 1.12-14 there is a different kind of thanksgiving. There is none in Galatians and Titus. Schubert concentrated on the occurrences of εὐχαριστέω in the letters considered to be genuinely Pauline, thereby excluding both Ephesians and the Pastorals from his examination (p. 1). He identified two types of thanksgiving: the more intimate, elaborate and personal occurring in Philemon, 1 Thessalonians, Colossians and Philippians (Type 1a), and the less elaborate, less intimate, and less personal in 1 Corinthians, Romans, and 2 Thessalonians (Type 1b) (Schubert 1939b).

3. Schubert claims that at most the Pastorals contain only fragmentary Pauline material, and that the two passages, 2 Tim 1.3-5 and 1 Tim 1.12-17

'cannot contribute to an understanding of the form and function of the genuine Pauline thanksgiving', since they are mere vestiges of the original and complete Pauline patterns (1939b: 8). O'Brien says that 'The introductory thanksgivings of the Pastoral Epistles ... have not been treated, for, apart from the question of authorship, these paragraphs do not contribute anything of significance to our study' (1977: 262). It appears that in both cases the Pastorals have been assumed to be non-Pauline, which is not uncommon. What is more reprehensible is their exclusion on the basis that they cannot contribute to the findings concerning Pauline thanksgivings.

4. See, e.g. O. Brien (1980: 61).

5. The other relevant uses of χάρις in the sense of χάριν ἔχω refer to Paul's thanks to God for graces given to the addressees (Rom 6.17; 2 Cor 9.15; cf. Col 3.16; 2 Cor 8.16), or, more generally, to believers (1 Cor 15.57; 2 Cor 2.14).

6. Timothy is not to come alone, but he is to bring Mark and Paul's parchments along with him (4.11-13). Timothy's coming will fill Paul with joy. The urgency to have Timothy visit him is precipitated by the behaviour of people who ought to have been a succour to Paul. Paul had been abandoned by the Asians (1.15), and nobody but Luke was with him (4.11). Demas had deserted him for Thessalonica, Crescens and Titus were elsewhere (4.10), Alexander the coppersmith had done him great harm (4.14), and he had gone through the first hearing of his case (4.16f.).

7. The many autobiographical references within the letter serve to reinforce this appeal to Timothy to be faithful: (a) 1.15f. contrasts the apostasy of Phygelus and Hermogenes with the service rendered Paul by Onesiphorus, both in Rome and Ephesus; (b) in 3.11, Paul reminds Timothy of the sufferings he, Paul, had to endure in Antioch, Iconium and Lystra; (c) in 4.6-8 he describes vividly his own fidelity under stress; (d) in 4.16ff. he alludes to the success of his first defense, with his confidence about the future outcome of his case. And interspersed within the letter are warnings about people's behaviour, both in the last days (3.1-9), and in the future (4.3f.). These warnings precede a personal appeal to Timothy to pay attention to the opposite virtues.

8. This theme is expanded in 2.1-8, 14, 24; 3.10f; 4.2-5.

9. Note the similarity of expression between this deliverance and that of the first defence in Rome (4.16ff.).

10. The only reference to an OT personage is to the opposition that Moses received at the hands of Jannes and Jambres. The main opposition to the upright teaching lies in useless, quarrelsome talking. One group of opponents claims that the resurrection is already past, and some group of people invites others, particularly women, to apostasy.

11. There are very few biographical details in the letter. The only places mentioned are Ephesus, in which Paul exhorted Timothy to remain, after he himself had gone to Macedonia (1.3). From the standpoint of places

mentioned, therefore, there is no difficulty in situating this letter within the otherwise known itinerary of Paul. Neither does the question of persons mentioned pose any serious problem. Unlike 2 Timothy, there is no greeting in this letter to any member of the church, nor does Paul pass on anyone's greetings. Indeed, the only people mentioned in addition to Paul and Timothy are Hymenaeus and Alexander (1.20), and Pontius Pilate (6.13).

12. We have noted that the particular concern of Paul in 1 Timothy was to counter the false teachers, and we have drawn attention to the highly developed form of community ministries in that letter also.

13. The preferred phrase is καλόν ἔργον, which occurs in Tit 2.7; 3.8, 14, and in 1 Tim 3.1; 5.10, 25; 6.18. It does not occur in 2 Timothy nor in Paul, where we find ἔργον ἀγαθόν (Rom 2.7; 13.3; 2 Cor 9.8; Eph 2.10; Phil 1.6; Col 1.10; 2 Thess 2.17, and in the Pastorals in 1 Tim 2.10; 2 Tim 2.21; 3.17; Tit 3.1).

14. The false teachers, especially the circumcision party, profess to know God, but they deny him by their deeds; they are detestable, disobedient, unfit for any good deed (1.16). Titus is urged to show himself in all respects a model of good deeds (2.7). God's grace has appeared to redeem us from iniquity and to purify for himself a people of his own, 'who are zealous for good deeds' (2.14). However, lest it appear that the holiness of man is derived from his good deeds, we have the typically Pauline warning that God has saved us, 'not because of deeds done by us in righteousness, but in virtue of his mercy . . . ' (3.5-7). This is followed by another appeal to good deeds (3.8). Indulging in stupid controversies, genealogies, dissensions, and quarrels over the Law is the opposite of good conduct (3.9ff.). Paul returns to good deeds in the final exhortation just before the farewell, 'And let our people learn to apply themselves to good deeds, so as to help cases of urgent need, and not to be unfruitful' (3.14).

15. This instruction comes as the first item in the letter, immediately after the greeting. The need for such action appears to be the presence of false teachers, people of the circumcision (1.10), who are attached to Jewish myths (1.14) and dietary practices (1.15), but who, while claiming to know God in their words, deny him by their deeds (1.16).

16. It would appear from 2.1-3.2 that Titus's authority has been under some strain. This unit is framed by references to Titus's personal responsibility for the teaching of the community, and the arrangement of the good behaviour of the various members of the community. The section is not primarily concerned with presenting a household code, but with stimulating Titus towards a better exercise of his authority.

17. Duncan (1929: 189). See also the discussion in Dibelius (1966: 106).

18. In making this suggestion Robinson acknowledged his debt to Bo Reicke whose views on the matter have since been published (Reicke 1976: 90).

19. See, e.g., the discussion in Burton (1976: 59-63).

20. We have, elsewhere, described and criticized more fully the theories of Duncan, Badcock, Johnson, Robinson, Reicke, and Wilhelm-Hooijbergh (Prior 1985: 86-89).

21. 'Despite the most careful of detailed research, it has not been found possible to define any of the sources used by the author of Acts in a way which will meet with widespread agreement among the critics... No theory has managed to impose itself by its probability and in virtue of the indications given in the text' (Dupont 1964: 166). See also the recent survey in Plümacher (1984: 120-38).

22. In his recent survey of the scholarly assessment of Acts as a source for the study of Paul, Mattill shows how central the estimation of the 'we-sections' has been (1978: 97). In the same volume, Robbins argues that the first person plural is used in Acts because it is normal within the sea voyage genre, and because the author in Rome is so familiar with the events he describes that he considers himself a participant in them (1978: 241).

23. See the surveys in Plümacher (1983; 1984); Richard (1983); and Bruce (1982).

24. Dibelius effectively bypassed the question of historicity, claiming that such a matter was fraught with subjectivity, whereas the form-critical method led to results which were universally valid, and was capable of leading to less subjective and verifiable criteria for the historicity of the tradition (1961: 91). The task of the author was a literary-theological, rather than a historical (*geschichtlich*) one (p. 98), and if Luke was a historian at all he was a 'literary historian' (*schriftstellender Historiker*), who was not above abandoning the exact reproduction of a tradition 'for a higher historical (*geschichtlich*) truth', rather than one in our modern sense (pp. 97, 107).

25. Haenchen begins his discussion of the former question with the *assumption* that when Luke wrote Acts Paul had been executed, and Christians had burned as living torches in the garden of Nero; the Holy City and the Temple lay in ruins (p. 95). Luke ends his account with a picture of Paul at work unhindered in Rome, and the complete, rounded story of the path of the gospel from Jerusalem to Rome 'brought comfort and reassurance to the faithful' (of the author's age, of course) (p. 98). Haenchen does not explain how such a half-truth could have brought comfort to his readers who knew well of Paul's fate. He judges that the other basic problem of Acts was how to deal with the mission to the Gentiles without the law. By cutting adrift from Judaism, Christianity broke the continuity with the history of salvation, on the theological side, and lost the toleration which Judaism enjoyed, on the political. Luke's solution was to show that the instigators and leaders of the Christian mission adhered steadfastly to their Jewish roots, and steered in the direction of the Gentiles only at God's bidding (p. 100).

26. 'Everything he knew concerning apostolic times, or thought himself entitled to infer, he had to translate into the language of vivid and dramatic

scenes' (p. 103). Hand in hand with his ability to enliven bare facts by transforming a simple report into action and by weaving a speech into it, went the gift of condensing events (pp. 104f.). He was no less endowed with the ability of a dramatist to produce a rapid succession of vivid and lively scenes. This skill was given all the more freedom when the author was untrammelled by tradition (pp. 106f.). As justification for Luke's alleged technique of historiography Haenchen claims only that Luke had a conception of the narrator's calling that was different from ours. Haenchen's treatment of questions of historicity is carried out with complete disregard of the high standards proposed by at least some ancient historiographers (e.g. Thucydides, Polybius, and Lucian), and of the attention to historical detail which many commentators have noticed in the Acts' account (e.g., Smith 1880, Ramsay 1915; 1930, Sherwin-White 1963, Hemer 1977/8, etc.). Haenchen's massive tome is seriously vitiated by the *Tendenzkritik* he imposes on the text of Acts.

27. If Haenchen allowed for an historical core for the journey of Paul in Acts 13-14, albeit embellished in the account, Conzelmann argues that the journey itself is an invention of the author. Moreover, he claims that the whole of Acts 27, with its account of the voyage and shipwreck, is the author's invention (1963: 72-81, 249; but see R.P.C. Hanson 1968, and his commentary 1967). For a discussion of sea voyages and the dangers associated with them see Casson 1971; 1974 and Murphy-O'Connor 1985.

28. He found that his own investigations of Acts 14 led him to the conclusion that the author was meticulously accurate in his historical setting, and he proposed that an author so exact in one point might well be expected to be accurate in others. Indeed, after many years of study and basic field-work, he claimed that Luke's history of early Christian origins was unsurpassed for its accuracy (1915: 37f., 80, 89). Although Ramsay's meticulous field-work was of the highest quality (see 1890; 1895/7), his general conclusions go well beyond the evidence (e.g. 1930: v). For even the greatest accuracy in some details (e.g. 1915: 96f.) is no guarantee of general reliability.

29. Harnack devoted three volumes of his *Beiträge* to the Lucan writings (1906; 1908; 1911). He says of the Acts: 'Es ist fast von jedem möglichen Standpunkt geschichtlicher Kritik aus ein solides und respektables, in mancher Hinsicht aber ein ausserordentliches Werk'. He went on to say that it is not only in its major features that it is a true work of history, but that it is accurate also in the majority of its details (1911: 222).

30. But while some scholars are lavish in their praise of Meyer (e.g. Olmstead 1943: 26; Gasque 1975: 158), he has been criticized for bringing 'the presuppositions of a historian of antiquity' to a study of the Acts, and thus misunderstanding it (Vielhauer 1950/1: 50, n. 37). One might say with greater justification that in his essay Vielhauer shows himself to have brought the presuppositions of his own brand of ultra-Lutheran Paulinism to

bear on the text of Acts, and to have as a consequence misunderstood both Paul and Luke.

31. E.g. Ehrhardt (1958) and (1969), Blaiklock (1970), Hemer (1977/78), van Unnik (1979), Plümacher (1979) and Hengel (1979).

32. E.g. Marshall (1970), and Drury (1976), despite the titles, pay little attention to historical questions. See our comments in Prior (1979).

33. This most recent classical historian to deal with the material in Acts writes, 'Any attempt to reject its basic historicity even in matters of detail must appear absurd' (1963: 189).

34. There is no easy solution to the problem. There is, for example, widespread scholarly disagreement concerning the nature of the Acts' account of Paul's journey to Rome (Acts 27.1–28.16). Some evaluate it as largely fictional (e.g., Conzelmann 1972: 150-59), while at the other end of the spectrum we have the view that the account is largely factual (e.g. Bruce 1977a: 498-529). In between we have those who regard it as partly factual and partly fictional (Roloff 1981: 356-69). See the discussion in Praeder (1984). While she acknowledges that the historical question merits separate study (p. 683), her investigation deals only with a literary comparison between Acts 27.1–28.16 and ancient accounts of sea voyages, and a theological comparison between the section and the remainder of Luke–Acts. The nature of Acts, and the competence of the author as a historiographer are at stake. There is a clear need to resolve the question as to what extent the account conforms to what really happened on the way between Caesarea and Rome. Did Paul have a perfectly easy, incident-free journey, or was the sea voyage frought with difficulties such as the account suggests? On the one hand nothing in the account is beyond the bounds of possibility; on the other, neither is it beyond the ability of a colourful author to have created such an account, based on the most elementary association of bad weather, high seas, forecasts, fear, prayers, etc., with the phenomenon of shipwreck.

35. No amount of literary judgments which focus on the comparison of Acts 27-28 with accounts of storms and shipwrecks in ancient novels, or in Greco-Roman, Jewish or Christian sea voyages can settle the question of what happened to Paul between Caesarea and Rome. Neither can theological judgments concerning the alleged *Tendenz* of the author solve the historical question of what really happened.

36. We emphasize conscious intentionality, to allow for the influence of subconscious motivation. The author himself is the best guide to his intentions, if he chooses to inform his readers. And it is only in the preface that he 'steps in front of the curtain. Except in this quite usual way the author nowhere explicitly discloses his self-consciousness. He does not, like many other writers, repeatedly obtrude on the reader his own labelled judgments or feelings' (Cadbury 1958: 347). It is our view that judgments concerning the historical value of Acts are the result of critical decisions taken on the basis of the supposed purpose of the author, which are made on

the basis of positions taken about developments in the Early Church, and the relative order of the Synoptic Gospels. Maddox (1982) summarizes and evaluates seven current theories of interpretation of the intentionality of Luke (1982: 19-23), and concludes that the aim of the author was to reassure the Christian community about the significance of the tradition and faith in which it stands (p. 186).

37. In his recent magisterial commentary on Luke, Fitzmyer rejects the straightforward reading of the end of Acts which suggests that the Lucan writings must have been written prior to Paul's trial or death. This obvious reading, he claims, encounters too many problems (1981: 54). Firstly, the reference to 'many' other attempts to recount the life-story of Jesus (Lk 1.1) would be difficult to understand at such an early date. Secondly, the reference to 'your house is abandoned' when addressed to Jerusalem (Lk 13.35a) 'is almost certainly a reference to the destruction of Jerusalem'. Thirdly, Luke's account of the judgment about the Temple (Lk 21.5; cf. Mk 13.2) is taken by many to be a *vaticinium ex eventu*, alluding to the taking of the city by Titus, and Lk 19.43f. reflects Luke's modification of his Marcan source 'in the light of what little he knew about the destruction of Jerusalem by the Romans' (p. 54). The argument that Lk 19.43f. and 21.20-24 presuppose a date of composition after the fall of Jerusalem is the key one for a late dating. The question at issue is whether the Lucan account of the prediction of the encirclement and capture of Jerusalem (19.43f.) and its desolation (21.20-24) *requires* that it was composed after the events of 70 AD, and in the light of the author's (or his source's) knowledge of Titus's military campaign against the city. The description of the military operations in Lk 19.43f. contains a number of details which could be read as recording what happened in the Roman siege of the city and its collapse in the war of 66-70 AD. It is our view, however, that no single detail of Luke's account is sufficiently precise as to remove it from the most commonplace account of ancient, and to some extent even modern warfare. The erection of an embankment, an encirclement, and the hemming in on every side were a normal part of laying siege to any city, a fact which the Jewish scriptures also attest abundantly (e.g., Isa 29.1-3; Jer 6.1-6; Ezek 4.1-3; cf. 1 Macc 6.51). The phrase 'they will dash you and the children to the ground' is a common one to describe the atrocities of war (e.g., Ps 137.9; Hos 10.14; 14.1; 2 Kgs 8.12; Isa 3.25f.; 13.16; Nah 3.10), and any suggestion that one is dealing with a *vaticinium ex eventu* has to contend with the fact that the 'prediction' is clearly out of harmony with Josephus's account of what happened (*Bell. Jud.* Vf.). It is, therefore, quite unnecessary to demand that the prediction of the fall of Jerusalem in Lk 19.41-44 is a *vaticinium ex eventu*, composed by the author in the knowledge of what Titus achieved in 70 AD. There simply is no reason why one must conclude from these commonplace military tactics that the author, or his source, knew what happened to Jerusalem in 70 AD (nor in 586 BC, *pace* Dodd 1947: 79). One might more reasonably have reached that

conclusion had Luke given such details as one finds in Josephus' account of the siege (the number, location and dimensions of the platforms, the flames, the famine, the details of Titus's strategy, the bandits, the faction-fighting, etc., *Bell. Jud.* V). The Lucan text reflects no more than the most general prediction of commonplace military strategy and consequent devastation.

38. Gasque (1975), although overtly partial in favour of the historicity of Acts, is the most complete survey of the *Actaforschung*.

39. Some scholars are more impressed by the arguments from tradition that the author was Luke, a fellow-traveller of Paul, and are not swayed from that conclusion by the weight of arguments which suggest that the Acts' picture of Paul is too different from Paul's own presentation of himself to come from an author who knew him well. Others, however, are so impressed by the difference between the Paul of Acts and the Paul of the Epistles that they rule out any possibility that the Acts could have been written by a companion of Paul.

40. 1. The brothers in Jerusalem related to Paul what was being said of him, and Paul performed the purification rites as requested (Acts 21.17-26). 2. 'The Jews from Asia' laid hands on Paul, but he was rescued by the tribune. Paul was arrested, bound, and carried off. The tribune ordered Paul to be scourged; Paul revealed his Roman citizenship, and all, including the tribune, were afraid. The tribune asked that a meeting of the Sanhedrin be convened (Acts 21.27-22.30). 3. Paul was brought before Lysias's *consilium*, the Sanhedrin, and was transferred to Caesarea after the Jewish death plot (Acts 22.30-23.24). 4. The tribune, Lysias, sent a *libellus* to Governor Felix in Caesarea, and Paul arrived there safely under guard (Acts 23.25-35). 5. Paul appeared before Felix in Caesarea (Acts 24), 6. before Festus in Caesarea (Acts 25.1-22), and 7. before Agrippa, Bernice, etc. (Acts 25 and 26).

41. The charge itself, of course, was a very serious one. According to Josephus (*Bell. Jud.* VI, 124-6) the Jews had been empowered to put to death anyone who violated the sanctuary, even if the culprit were a Roman citizen. Whether the alleged bringing of a Gentile into the sanctuary constituted such a violation is not clear.

42. Luke's concern to show Paul's innocence is recognized by commentators (e.g., Dupont 1967: 434, fn. 23, where the authorities proclaim Paul's innocence: Acts 16.36; 18.14; 19.37; 21.24; 23.29; 24.12, 16, 20; 25.8, 10, 18, 25, 26, 31f.; 28.17f.). The obvious inference from this is that Luke, or his source(s) considered Paul to be innocent of any crime punishable by death. O'Toole's assumption that we have little reason to assign an early date to Acts prevents him reaching the obvious conclusion, and forces him into saying that 'If at Rome Caesar found Paul innocent, Luke would certainly have written a different ending for Acts' (1978: 152). We agree with O'Toole that in chapter 26 Luke achieves the christological climax of Paul's defense on a literary level, but cannot concur with his judgment that 'anyone who

asks what actually happened leads himself astray' (p. 160). It seems to us more likely that Luke's protestation of Paul's innocence would have appeared absurd to his readers had Paul already been condemned to death by Caesar.

43. See the discussion in Sherwin-White (1963: 110ff.).

44. The matter is discussed in Sherwin-White (1963: 113ff.), and the quotation is from p. 115.

45. While several commentators have proposed that the author's intention was to produce an *apologia pro ecclesia*, Walasky suggests that part of the intention was 'to present an apologetic of the empire to his own church' (1983: 13).

46. See O'Toole (1983: 4-8).

47. With the same evidence before them critics disagree profoundly in their reading of it. We disagree with the very influential conclusion of Cadbury that, 'Readers of Acts would feel no surprise if after the gloomy predictions and close escapes it continued to carry Paul's case to a fatal outcome' (Lake and Cadbury 1933b: 338). Haenchen, in similar vein, says: 'Nowhere has he (the author) prepared his reader for a happy conclusion to the trial; he has always emphasized only that Paul deserved neither death nor imprisonment—and that is something different' (1965: 731). The remark of Brown that it is generally assumed that Paul was released (Brown and Meier 1983: 98, n. 202) is not true. There is no reason to regard the prediction of the angel (27.4), or the farewell to the Ephesian elders (20.25, 29), or the prophecy of Agabus (21.10f.) as tipping the scales against the consistent indications of Paul's innocence to which attention has been drawn. In particular, Paul's assurance that he would not see the Ephesians again need not be a *vaticinium ex eventu* since we have a record of Paul's own plans for the future, which included moving the theatre of his mission from the east to the West (Rom 15.23f., 28): irrespective of what would happen in Jerusalem, Paul did not intend to return to Ephesus.

48. If Luke were so inclined, one wonders why he did not end his account of the trial of Jesus with his appearance before Pontius Pilate, or why he did not ignore the death of Stephen, rather than give those deaths the unmistakable character of martyrdoms. Indeed, it appears that according to Luke such deaths serve to legitimate Jesus and the Christian cause, and serve as catalysts for Christian evangelization (see Talbert 1983: esp. 99f., 103). Luke spares no effort in showing the martyr-character of the death of the innocent Jesus (Lk 23.4, 14f., 22, 41, 47), and that of Stephen (Acts 6.11-14; 7.51-60), each of whom, like Paul later, appeared before the Sanhedrin (Lk 22.66f.; Acts 6.12f.). For that reason it is difficult to escape the conclusion that had Luke known about the martyrdom of Paul he would surely have reported it as a legitimation of Paul's life, and as a service to the advancement of the Gospel.

49. Among the suggestions put forward to explain the failure to carry the story further are: (i) the author died before he could finish the work; (ii) there was originally another ending, which gave an account of the death of Paul, but this element was subsequently removed to make room for the traditional later journeys and the second Roman imprisonment; (iii) the author intended a third volume, which may or may not have been executed; (iv) the author's sources were exhausted at that point; (v) the author knew he had no need to go further, since his readers knew the outcome already; and (vi) the author's alleged aim had already been achieved at this point, and there was no need, therefore, to go any further. The first five are discussed in Lake and Cadbury (1933a: 349f.), and virtually all the commentators deal with them. While some have offered rather general suggestions about the contents of a third volume (e.g. Ramsay [1930: 351f.] suggests Luke's account of the spread of Christianity to Italy and Rome; Zahn [1900: 372ff.] lists more about Paul's preaching in Rome, the outcome of his trial, the missionary activity of others, the destruction of Jerusalem, and the subsequent history of the Jerusalem church), Quinn (1980) has proposed that the Pastorals are in fact the third volume of the trilogy, Luke–Acts–Pastorals (the Pastorals, he suggests, are unreal letters composed on the basis of short notes from the historical Paul and his staff, and written about the eighties; see our remarks in Prior [1979: 7f.]).

50. Already in 1937, Goodspeed listed no less than fifteen arguments in favour of his late dating of 90 AD (pp. 191ff.). Of some recent commentators Schneider (1980/82: 121) and Weiser (1981: 40) put the date of composition between 80 and 90. Roloff, who stresses the *rapprochement* of the Acts with the Pastorals puts it at 90 (1981: 5f.). Schmithals opts for 90-100, and favours 100 (1982: 17). While Schneider concludes that the overall impression of Acts is not one of an *ecclesia pressa* (p. 120), Schmithals suggests that the apologetic or political *Tendenz* of Acts requires a context of persecution (p. 11).

51. In his 1908 work he explained how he had moved from the first to the second date (pp. 217-21), and three years later he explained what clinched the earlier date for him (1911: 65f.). He rejected the view that Paul had already left Rome, and opted instead for the proposal that Paul's relative freedom was over, and that he was being led to the praetorium for the trial proper to proceed. The reason why Luke did not give more information, then, was that the legal process was not finished before he completed his work (1911: 66-9).

52. Bruce (1952: 481) opts for early 62 AD. See also Munck (1967, 260). Robinson (1976) discusses the various options in ch. 4. Since the most recent study of the ending of the Acts, and the first full-scale one (Hauser 1979) discusses in the main only linguistic, literary and structuralist questions, the vital ones of source, tradition, redaction and historicity are deliberately left on one side.

53. Much of the argument for a later dating of Acts relies on the interpretation of Luke 1.1; 13.35a; 19.43f.; 21.20, which suggests a date after the composition of other gospels and the destruction of Jerusalem (c. 80 AD) (see the discussion in Fitzmyer 1981: 53-57, and our critique in note 37 above).

54. A different outcome to a Roman trial has been suggested by Pherigo (1951) and Gunther (1972: esp. ch. 6, 'Paul in Spain'). Paul, they suggest, was neither executed nor released, but, rather, was sent into exile to Spain, under the form of *exilium relegationis*, rather than the more severe *deportatio*. 1 Clement 5.6 is the major supporting text, but it seems to us that the critical word φυγαδευθείς does not demand a technical, formal act of expulsion. Lightfoot correctly points out that the flights from Damascus (Acts 9.25; 2 Cor 11.33), from Jerusalem (Acts 9.30), from Antioch of Pisidia (Acts 13.50), from Iconium (Acts 14.6), from Thessalonica (Acts 17.10), from Beroea (Acts 17.14), and perhaps from Corinth (Acts 20.3), or some of these, could be described by that verb (1890: 29).

55. From the second to the eighteenth century there was no challenge to Rome as the place of origin of all four Captivity Letters. As early as 1731 Oeder proposed that Paul wrote to the Philippians from Corinth c. 50 AD. In 1779 Paulus proposed that Caesarea was the place of origin of Philippians, and Lisco in 1900 was the first to suggest Ephesus. Hawthorne provides a very good summary of the facts to be accounted for, and of the strengths and weaknesses of the various hypotheses (1983: xxxvi-xliv), but in the end he concedes that his proposal that Paul wrote from Caesarea c. 59-61 AD is an assumption (xliiif.).

56. See the discussion of the various hypotheses, and the conclusion favouring the integrity of the letter in Jewett (1970).

57. Recent surveys of the arguments have led to such conclusions as, 'Recent discussion of this issue has run into an impasse. The evidence . . . is finely balanced, and a final decision is not possible' (Martin 1978: 205). Kümmel concludes his discussion of the place of origin of Philippians by acknowledging that the question cannot be answered with any certainty, although he gives his own choice in the order Ephesus, Caesarea and Rome (1973: 332). Supporters of the Roman origin of Philippians include Beare ('Taking everything into account, the ancient hypothesis that Philippians was written from Rome must be allowed to hold the field' [1973: 24]), Houlden ('Rome still has been the best chance of being right' [1970: 42]), Reicke, Harrison, Guthrie, Dodd, Schmid, while among those who prefer the Ephesian hypothesis we find the names of Duncan, Benoit, Collange, Murphy-O'Connor *et al.* (see Kümmel 1973: 325, and 329 for details). Only a small number, including Johnson (1955/6), Robinson (1976), Wilhelm-Hooijbergh (1980) and Hawthorne (1983), prefer Caesarea for Philippians.

58. We agree with Clark that the tone of Acts 28.30f. is optimistic, almost triumphant (1933: 389f.). And Loisy points to the optimism in Philemon and

Colossians, which letters, he claims, come from Rome, as confirmation of the witness of Luke (1920: 944).

59. The traditional dating has been questioned in recent times. Wilhelm-Hooijbergh argues for 69 AD (1975), and Robinson suggests early 70 AD (1976: 327-35).

60. See the discussion in Lightfoot (1890), where the author argues for Clement's personal acquaintance with Paul (Vol. 1, p. 73, and Vol. 2, p. 25).

61. Eratosthenes divided the map of the inhabited world into two parts by drawing a line from west to east, parallel to the equatorial line. At the western end προς δυσει he has the Pillars of Heracles and at the eastern επ᾽ ανατολῃ the northern boundary of India (Strabo *Geog.* Book 2, I.1). As Pherigo observes, 'Rome, when Clement wrote, was the hub, rather than the edge of the Empire' (1951: 281).

62. For a recent duscussion of the evidence for a mission to Spain see Gunther (1972: 139-50, 182ff.) and Meinardus (1978).

63. E.g. Schneemelcher claims, 'No doubt the author took this journey of Paul's to Spain from the Epistle to the Romans, as he did with a number of names' (1964b: 272). He does not, however, give any evidence.

64. Harnack did much to influence the view commonly held today. He suggested the author to be either the Roman Bishop Victor (189-199) or, less likely, his successor, Bishop Zephyrinus (199-217) (1925). In the following year Harnack's conclusions were challenged by Koch, mainly on his contention that phrases such as *in urbe Roma* and *cathedra urbis Romae ecclesiae* (lines 74ff.) would not appear in a document written from Rome (1926). More recently, Sundberg has claimed that many salient features of the text have no place in the early western church, but suit the circumstances of the eastern church in the late third or early fourth centuries (1973: 34f.), but his arguments have been comprehensively refuted in Ferguson (1982).

65. On the other hand, no other extant second-century document records a Pauline visit to Spain, not even *The Acts of Paul*. This document, however, has several pages missing before the account of Paul's arrival in Rome (from Corinth) (9).

66. As samples of contrasting evaluations consider those of Grant and Gustafsson. According to one, Eusebius was insensitive to the social, political and economic factors of the period he surveyed, and his personal bias was so strong that his judgments of persons and events are suspect (Grant 1975: 413), while the other commends Eusebius for his diligent use of sources, and for his care in basing his judgments on them (Gustafsson 1961: 429).

67. It has been suggested by Pherigo that Ignatius, in his *Letter to the Romans* (4.3), refers to Paul's having been set at liberty in Rome. In this passage Ignatius contrasts himself with Peter and Paul: they were apostles, he is a convict; they were free, he is even until now a slave. Since there is no

evidence that Ignatius was ever a slave Pherigo suggests that Ignatius is referring to Paul's having been free at Rome (1951: 282). That conclusion, however, is not valid, since the contrast is between the present state of Peter and Paul and that of Ignatius many years after their death. That Ignatius is referring to heavenly freedom is clear from the following sentence. Ignatius, therefore, does not offer any evidence in support of Paul's freedom in Rome.

68. If the three Pastorals, or any one or two of them, are genuinely Pauline, and if they, or any one, cannot be fitted into the pre-Roman period of Paul's life as known mainly from the Acts, then we have additional material in support of a release from Roman imprisonment.

69. Quinn (1980). The author then goes on to propose that the Pastorals are 'unreal' correspondence, composed as a unit, in the eighties of the first century, 'to give the reader among other things an oblique glimpse of Paul's last journey and imprisonment' (p. 291).

70. 'All possible dates for every conceivable event have found their champions' (Murphy-O'Connor 1982: 71).

71. See the arguments in Jewett (1979: 41), and Lake and Cadbury (1933b: 464).

72. For a discussion of when Pallas fell see Lake in Lake and Cadbury (1933b: 466f.). The year 55 is preferred by Lake (p. 466), Haenchen (1965) and Conzelmann (1963).

73. Lake and the authors he mentions refer the two-year period to Felix's proconsulship, rather than to Paul's imprisonment (Lake and Cadbury 1933b: 471). Haenchen considers that in the author's source it referred to Felix, but that he mistakenly referred it to Paul's imprisonment (1965: 663).

74. However, it has been argued that the year of Pallas's dismissal (55 AD) need not have been the last occasion on which he could have exercised his influence, and therefore the date of Paul's arrival in Rome need not have been so early. Pallas was an immensely rich man (Juvenal *Sat.* I,109), and according to Dio Cassius (LXII,14,3) it was because of Nero's greed for his riches that Pallas was poisoned in 62 AD. A man of such power, then, could have exercised some influence after 55 AD. Moreover, according to Tacitus, Pallas was replaced in order to weaken the position of Agrippina (*Ann.* XIII,14), and as a result of Seneca's desire to change financial policy (*Ann.* XIII,2), rather than for any personal misdemeanour.

75. See the discussion in Jewett who claims that such activity could not have taken place in the short period between October 54 (the date of Nero's accession; cf. Josephus, *Bell. Jud.* 250-270), and the summer of 55, the date of Felix's recall (Jewett 1979: 41ff.).

76. See the discussion in Jewett (1979: 43). Schürer opts for 60 (1911: 579); Plooij for 59 (1918: 58ff.), and this also is the preference of Caird, Leclercq, and Ramsay (see Jewett 1979: 130 nn. 164f. for details).

77. In favour of it is the internal evidence of Acts. Paul's sojourn in Corinth is likely to have been between autumn 50 and summer 52 (see the discussion in Hemer 1980: 6-9. But for a negative assessment of Acts 18.12 see Knox [1950: 81ff.], who held that Paul arrived in Corinth in 45 AD). According to Acts, Paul's sojourn in Corinth was from autumn 50 to summer 52, and his arrival in Jerusalem after the third missionary journey was in May 56 or 57. The two-year imprisonment in Caesarea brings us to 59 and Paul's arrival in Rome to 60, with the two-year period of Acts 28.30f. ending in 62 (see Robinson 1976 for a typical reconstruction). Against this late date Haenchen contends that the *argumentum e silentio* from Josephus concerning Festus is not decisive, since Festus's conduct was not a matter of scandal. Moreover, he claims that the argument that a new Palestinian coin came into existence in 59 and coincided with the accession of Festus does not convince, since a new Palestinian coinage did not appear until 29/30 AD, although Pilate came to power in 26 (Haenchen 1965: 71). Recently it has been suggested that Paul's instructions in Rom 13.6f. about paying taxes are made against the background of unrest in Rome over the tax-gatherers whose behaviour had to be regulated by Nero in 58 AD (Tacitus *Ann.* XIII, 50f.; Suetonius *Nero* 10). If this is so Paul was not arrested in Jerusalem before 58 (see Friedrich, Pöhlmann and Stuhlmacher 1976).

78. Those who put Festus's accession in 55 put the death of Paul in 58 (e.g. Suhl 1975: 338; Conzelmann 1963: 13; Haenchen 1965: 732), while those who put it c. 59 have Paul executed in 62, 'assuming an execution at the conclusion of the two-year imprisonment' (Jewett 1979: 132f. n. 182). We have already given our reasons for concluding that Paul was unlikely to have been executed as a result of the ('first') Roman hearing.

79. See Schneemelcher (1964c: 347).

80. Clement's purpose clearly is to correct the deviations among the community in Corinth which he attributes to jealousy and envy (3-5). It was those two vices also that led to the persecution and death of 'the greatest and most righteous pillars of the Church' (5). (James, Cephas and John also are called στύλοι in Gal 2.9; cf. 1 Tim 3.15 for the application of the term to the household of God, and Rev 3.12 where we read that the one who conquers will be made a pillar in the temple of God. It is clear that the pillars referred to had been persecuted and had striven unto death (ἕως θανάτου ἤθλησαν), but whether the striving necessarily implies martyrdom is not clear. The verb ἀθλέω is used of the striving of an athlete in 2 Tim 2.5, and the noun ἄθλησις in Heb 10.32 where it refers to a hard struggle with sufferings, but neither word is used elsewhere in the NT. Ignatius encourages Polycarp to bear the maladies of all (I). The metaphorical description of the Christian life as the striving of an athlete, then, became a favourite one, and it was later often applied to martyrs. Eusebius, speaks of the martyrs as οἱ εὐσεβείας ἀθλητοί (*Hist. Eccles.* V, introductory section). He also quotes sources in which the metaphor is applied to Christ ('the great and invincible athlete',

V, I, 42), to the martyrs collectively ('the noble athletes', V, I, 36), and to one, Blandida ('a noble athlete', V, I, 18). The verb ἀθλέω, obviously, does not demand a meaning of striving unto martyrdom, although the adverbial phrase, ἕως θανάτου, suggests that Clement was referring to those who had been martyred, although even that much cannot be insisted upon. Only Peter and Paul are singled out. The participle μαρτυρήσας (referring to Peter) does not of itself demand the meaning of being martyred, although the context may be regarded as pointing in that direction (see the arguments of Lightfoot 1890: 26f.). The witnessing in the case of Paul is somewhat more specific (μαρτυρήσας ἐπὶ τῶν ἡγουμένων), but again one does not have to interpret this as referring to martyrdom. Indeed, if we didn't have several traditions about the death of Paul in Rome we might easily read the ἡγούμενοι to refer to those rulers in τὸ τέρμα τῆς δύσεως.

81. See Warmington (1981: 124). While Suetonius has Nero, moved by the beauty of the flames, singing from the Tower of Maecenas (*Nero*, XXXVIII), Dio locates the incident on the roof of the palace (Dio LXII, 18, 1), while Tacitus merely reports the rumour that tuneful lamenting had taken place on Nero's private stage (XV, XXXIX).

82. See the discussion in Benko (1985: 14-21), Wilken (1984: 48-67), Whittaker (1984: 146-49), and Leaney (1984: 63f.).

83. This is in line with the information given by the lawyer, Sulpicius Severus (363-420): 'Afterwards, too, their religion was prohibited by laws which were enacted; and by edicts openly set forth it was proclaimed unlawful to be a Christian. At that time Paul and Peter were condemned to death, the former being beheaded with a sword, while Peter suffered crucifixion' (*Sacred History*, II,29), quoted in Finegan (1981: 23).

84. In Lüdemann's chronology an even greater amount of time is involved, for he proposes 52 AD (or 55, depending on whether the crucifixion of Jesus took place in 27 or 30) as the date of Paul's journey to Jerusalem to deliver the collection (1984: 263).

Notes to Chapter 5

1. Here are typical examples of the four types of interpretation. Pauline: 'Cette lettre est un testament' (Spicq 1969: 803); Pauline, with liberal secretary: '(Paulus) ... der sein Testament schreibt im festen Blick auf den Tod' (Jeremias 1968: 56); Pauline Fragments: 'There is not the remotest chance of his escaping alive from the hands of his enemies' (Harrison 1964: 124); and Pseudepigraphon: 3.10-4.8 is 'Paul's Last Will and Testament ... and Paul's own Expectation of Martyrdom' (Hanson 1982: 148).

2. E.g. Bengel, 'Testamentum Pauli et cygnea cantio est haec epistula' (quoted in Harrison 1964: 128). Dornier uses the familiar term *discours d'adieu*, under the heading, 'Paul au soir de sa vie' (1972: 61).

3. Several studies have concentrated on particular documents, e.g. de Jonge on the *Testament of the Twelve Patriarchs* (1953; 1975). Saldarini discusses the last words and deathbed scenes in rabbinic literature (1977). The concentration on instructions for burial, and the deathbed dialogue between disciples and master separate this rabbinic genre from that of 2 Timothy.

4. E.g. Thomas (1969), Cortès (1976) and, most importantly, Nordheim (1980 and 1985).

5. Nordheim (1980: 229). Nordheim is careful to point out that the genre allows flexibility, and that every document need not contain all the elements, nor need they always be in the same order. Moreover, the testament can contain within it other literary forms, such as wisdom sayings, covenant forms, visions, dreams, hymns, etc. (p. 231). Before a work can merit the title 'testament', he insists, more than formal characteristics must be present, such as the bringing of the past to bear on the present, and an exhortation based upon rational argument and persuasion to a particular kind of behaviour (pp. 232-37).

6. The studies on John 13–17 are mainly concerned with the origin of the material and its relation to the synoptic tradition, and do not deal in depth with the question of form. See e.g. Reim (1976); Smalley (1973); Onuki (1977); Painter (1981). Recent discussion of Acts 20.17-38 is surveyed in Lambrecht (1979), wherein also the author investigates the structure, the line of thought and the significance of the address, and the relation between tradition and redaction. See also Dupont (1962); Schürmann (1968); Barrett (1977).

7. Exum and Talbert (1967) propose that the chiastic structure of the text reaches a climax at v. 25, while Michel calls vv. 25-27 the *Kulminationspunkt* (Michel 1973: 27).

8. See e.g. the Nag Hammadi Tractate (VII,4), *The Teaching of Silvanus*.

9. See e.g. Knoch (1973). Knoch follows Brox in his judgment that the Pastorals are pseudonymous writings from a disciple of Paul, written between 90 and 100 AD (p. 44). The resemblances he notices between 2 Tim 4.1-8 and Paul's farewell in Miletus suggest to him a common tradition (p. 45). The fundamental situation of the 'apostle' in each case is his forthcoming death (pp. 45f.).

10. E.g. 'For I am already on the point of being sacrificed; the time of my departure has come' (RSV); 'As for me, already my life is being poured out on the altar, and the hour of my departure is upon me' (NEB); 'The last drops of my own sacrifice are falling; my time to go has come' (Scott 1936).

11. See e.g. Liddell and Scott (1925-40), Bailly (1950), etc.

12. See Michel (1964) for examples of the use of the verb in the OT, later Palestinian Judaism, Josephus, Philo and the NT.

13. The only three exceptions are in נסך being used once each for 'to consecrate (a king)' (Ps 2.6), 'to appoint' (Prov 8.23) and 'to weave' (Isa 25.7). Its 23 other uses all mean 'to pour out' and no less than 17 of those are rendered by σπένδομαι in the LXX: Exod 30.9; Hos 9.4; 1 Chron 11.18; Gen 35.14; Num 28.7; 2 Sam 23.16; 2 Kgs 16.13; Jer 7.18; 19.13; 32 (39).29; 44 (51).17, 19, 25; Ezek 20.28; Exod 25.29 (28); 37(38).16 (12).

14. In 8 instances the reference is to the pouring out of an unspecified liquid to an alien god (Jer 7.18; 19.13; 32.29; 44.17, 19 [twice], 25, and Ezek 20.28). In Bethel Jacob poured out an unspecified libation (Gen 35.14). In two other cases libation bowls are mentioned (Exod 25.29 [28]; 37.16). In Exod 30.9 the pouring of the unspecified libation is the third element of a trio (holocaust, oblation, libation), while in 2 Kgs 16.13 the pouring of the unspecified libation is the third element of King Ahaz's ritual (holocaust, oblation, libation, blood of the communion sacrifice), thus making it clear that the libation is separate from the blood element. In Dan 2.46 Nebuchadnezzar ordered that Daniel be offered a libation as a gesture of profound honour. In addition to those texts there remain two uses of σπένδω for which we do not have the Hebrew base: the reference in 4 Macc 3.16 is to David's refusal to drink water (cf. 2 Sam 23.16; 1 Chron 11.18), which instead he poured out to God, and in Sir 50.15 we read how Simon the High Priest poured out as a libation to God the blood of the grape (i.e. wine).

15. See Moulton and Milligan (1957) for examples.

16. E.g. Lightfoot (1913), Michael (1928), Beare (1973), Houlden (1970), Ernst (1974), Friedrich (1965), Michaelis (1935), Lohmeyer (1955), Gnilka (1968), and Getty (1980). This is merely a selection of what is virtually the unanimous interpretation of the commentators.

17. E.g. Hanson (1982), Leaney (1960), Scott (1936), Houlden (1976), Guthrie (1957), Barrett (1963), Kelly (1963), Dibelius and Conzelmann (1966), and Spicq (1969).

18. Such is Paul's orientation in Philippians towards the future apostolate that T.W. Manson went so far as to suggest that he was not even in prison while writing the letter: Paul's plans 'read like the plans of a free man' (1939: 188). And such is Collange's unease about the insistence within the letter on Paul's future plans, particularly those of seeing the Philippians again, that he proposes the bold hypothesis that rather than face death, Paul, who had been in prison for some time, decided to appeal to his Roman citizenship, a decision that was not welcomed by the Roman community (1973: 9f.). Phil 1.12-26, in his view, is Paul's apologia for his decision.

19. The much discussed question of the integrity of Philippians does not concern us here, since the relevant sections are regarded as belonging to the same letter. Recently Dalton (1979) surveyed the debate and rejected the arguments against integrity.

20. E.g. Beare (1973), Michael (1928), Bouwman (1965), Collange (1973), and Martin (1980).

21. E.g. Lightfoot (1913) and Lohmeyer (1955).

22. Sampley has given a very plausible explanation for this appeal. He suggests that Paul and the Philippians had bonded themselves into a Roman *Societas*, in which unity of purpose was a *sine qua non* (1980: 51-77).

23. See e.g. the paraphrase of Lightfoot, 'Therefore, my beloved, having the example of Christ's humility to guide you, the example of Christ's exaltation to encourage you . . . ' (1913: 115), and Martin's comment, 'The way of salvation has been depicted in the hymn' (1980: 102).

24. Likewise Lightfoot (1913), Martin (1980), Michael (1928), etc. Denis discusses the views of the two groups of scholars, and opts for the active role of the Philippians in the offering of their faith (Denis 1958: 648ff.). Note the active role of the Romans (Rom 12.1).

25. E.g. whether τῆς πίστεως is a subjective, objective, or simply an epexegetic genitive.

26. See Denis (1958: 639).

27. See Denis (1958: 649).

28. Dupont (1949: 41). Dupont's remarks deal mainly with 2 Cor 2.14, and he makes only a passing reference to Phil 2.17. He does not deal with 2 Tim 4.6.

29. The urgency of the problem of the disunity of the community is reflected in the occurrence of φρονέω in 2.2. (twice), 5, and 4.2, 10. The verb occurs 10 times in Philippians and only 11 other times in the 'undisputed' letters of Paul (and also in 1 Tim 6.17). Not all uses of the verb in Philippians, however, reflect this special concern for unity (e.g. 3.15, 19).

30. Sampley (1980: ch. 4) suggests that in the beginning of the preaching of the Gospel in Philippi Paul struck a bargain with the community there, after the fashion of the Roman relationship of *Societas*. For his part, Paul was to be their representative in his evangelizing activity, and they undertook to support him, particularly financially. Note how 1.5 and 4.15 frame the letter. One notices in this letter the absence of an appeal to apostolic authority (e.g. no ἀπόστολος in the opening verse), and also the ease with which Paul was prepared to receive financial help from the Philippians (4.10-20).

31. Paul, having spent some of his formative years in Jerusalem, was familiar with the Temple ritual. He regarded the cult as one of the privileges of the Jewish people (Rom 9.4). He saw the Christian community as the true chosen people, who inherited the responsibility of the Jewish cult, and transposed it into a spiritual key, as it were. He saw the whole of life as one of cultic service (Rom 12.1; 6.13, 19), and he described the body as the temple of the Holy Spirit (1 Cor 6.19). Other references to the relationship between Christian living and the cult include Phil 3.3; 4.18; Eph 2.19ff. Moreover, he saw his own apostolic activity in terms of the cult (Rom 15.16; cf. 1 Cor 3.16f.). The relationship between the apostle and his fellow believers in the cultic service of God is reflected in 2 Cor 2.14-17, and, as we have seen, in Phil 2.17. The relationship between Paul's apostleship and the new liturgy in

the Spirit is the subject of Denis's brilliant study (1958). The same theme is dealt with also in Corriveau (1970).

32. The Papyrus is dated 20 Nov. 131 (BC), and is published in Wilckens (1957: 219). Spicq claims that the noun is unknown in the papyri (1969: 804).

33. The text, 'Secundi Philosophi Atheniensis Sententiae, 19', is published in Mullachius (ed. 1883: 515).

34. Spicq's treatment is in his 1969: 804 ('an astonishingly learned work', in the estimation of Hanson 1982: xii). Spicq does not deal with ἀνάλυσις in his recently published volumes on NT lexicography (1978-82).

35. These include: release, deliverance, acquittal from a capital charge; getting rid of a disease; a spell for releasing a divine being; separation, parting; decease, death. The verb means: to take one's departure; to loose from; to set free, release; to acquit of a charge; to release on receipt of ransom; to let go; to discharge, to sell; to deliver; etc. (Liddell and Scott 1925-40).

36. The unsatisfactory nature of Spicq's use of the lexicographical material can be illustrated as follows. While in the LXX the noun ἀπόλυσις occurs three times, it never means 'death' (but rather, 'dismissal to their homes' in *3 Macc* 6.37, 40, and 'deliverance' in *3 Macc* 7.16). Although the corresponding verb does refer to death in Tob 3.6, 13, in each case the specific meaning is indicated by adding καὶ γένωμαι γῆ, in the case of the first, and by modifying with the adverbial phrase ἀπὸ τῆς γῆς (cf. also Ps 16 [17].14B), in the second. In 2 Macc 7.9 also the reference is to death, but again there is a modifying adverbial phrase. The verb on its own does not demand the meaning 'to die' (even if it does so in Num 20.29), since it can also mean 'to put away' (1 Esd 9.36), 'to take away' (Tob 3.17), 'to escape' (Sir 27.19), 'to return' (Exod 33.11), and 'to dismiss (troops)' (2 Macc 11.38). Indeed the verb means 'to free' in 1 Macc 10.29, 43; 2 Macc 4.47; 6.22; 10.21; 12.25, 45; etc., and in 2 Macc 6.30 it actually means 'to free from death'! The noun ἀπόλυσις does not occur in the NT. However, although the verb ἀπολύω occurs some 63 times in the NT it never means 'to die' (not even in Lk 2.29, where it has the meaning of a master dismissing his servant from service). It means, rather, 'to dismiss one's wife (Matt 1.19; 5.31, etc.) or husband (Mark 10.12)', 'to dismiss a crowd (Matt 14.15; Luke 9.12, etc.) or an individual (Matt 15.23; Acts 23.22, etc.)', 'to release a debtor' (Matt 18.27), 'to forgive' (Lk 6.37), 'to free from iniquity' (Lk 13.12), 'to send away, to send off' (Acts 13.3). But the most common of all uses of the verb in the NT is 'to release a prisoner' (Matt 27.15, 17, 21, 26; Mk 15.6, 9, 11, 15; Lk 22.16; 23.17, 18, 20, 22, 25; Jn 18.39; 19.10, 12 [twice]; Acts 3.13; 4.21, 23; 5.40; 16.35, 36; 17.9; 26.32; 28.18; and in Heb 13.12, of Timothy, which is the only occurrence of the verb outside the Gospels and Acts).

37. E.g. *P. Petr.* III, 36; *P. Tebt.* I, 5; *P. Oxy.* 237 viii; 485; 1121; 1611. It occurs some 120 times in the NT, and is used in the Gospels both for the

death of man (e.g. Matt 10.21; Lk 2.26) and of Jesus (e.g. Matt 20.18; 26.38; Jn 12.33). Paul uses the noun some 47 times, usually with reference to the death of people, but also to the death of Jesus (Rom 5.10). It is used 22 times in Romans and 6 in Philippians, but only once in the Pastorals (2 Tim 1.10). In addition it appears some 350 times in the LXX.

38. E.g. *P. Ryl.* II, 106; *P. Fay.* 30; *P. Oxy.* 68; 265; 489-494; 496; 713; 902. As well as being widely attested in classical literature it is used in the LXX also for death (e.g., Gen 27.2; Deut 31.29; 33.1; Josh 1.1; Judg 1.1; it has a different meaning in only two texts: it means 'boundary' in Bar 3.25, and 'the end of the book' in 2 Macc 15.39). Its cognate verb τελευτάω is used almost exclusively in the LXX to translate מות, and is used extensively for 'to die' in both classical literature and the papyri. The noun is used only twice in the NT (in Matt 2.15, of Herod's death), although the verb is used several times, and always with the meaning 'to die' (Matt 2.19; 9.18; 15.14; 22.25; Mk 7.10; 9.48; Lk 7.2; Jn 11.39; Acts 2.29; 7.15; Heb 11.22). The noun is also poorly attested in the Fathers: there is no reference in Goodspeed's *Index Patristicus*, and only two in his *Index Apologeticus* (1907; 1912).

39. Note the life/death terms in vv. 20, 21f., 23f.

40. Dupont has drawn attention to Paul's different perspectives on death as reflected in the Thessalonian correspondence and in Philippians and 2 Cor 5.6 (1952: especially 165-87). De Vogel notes Paul's stress on leaving the body and being with Christ (1977).

41. E.g. Cook's recent study of the two texts does not concern itself at all with the place of 2 Tim 4.6 in the context of the whole letter, nor does it discuss the critical terms (σπένδομαι and ἀναλύω/ἀνάλυσις). Unfortunately, the author's strong advocacy of Harrison's fragments theory precludes his having an alternative reading of the evidence (Cook 1982).

42. Matt 1.24; Lk 9.32; Jn 11.13; Acts 20.9 twice; Rom 13.11.

43. The exceptions are Matt 28.13; Lk 22.45; Acts 12.6, where the verb means simply 'to sleep'.

44. E.g. Scott insists that 'The request for a visit is obviously out of place in the present letter' (1936: 135). The earlier Hanson says of vv. 9-22 that 'This fragment of a letter must come fairly soon after a period of freedom, for it is full of references to recent free activity. It cannot have been written with the immediate prospect of death before him . . . ' (1966: 100). For a similar assessment see Leaney 1960: 16, and Barrett 1963: 11.

45. Trummer (1978: 81); Zmijewski (1979: 117). Karris insists that the request for the mantle, etc., simply underlines Paul as 'the model poor Christian missionary, who has the bare necessities of life' (Karris 1979: 41).

46. See e.g. Harrison (1921: 56; 1964: 14f.). De Lestapis rightly observed: 'Il n'y a pratiquement plus personne pour parler de "faussaires" ni de "falsifications"' (1976: 21).

47. Spicq, e.g., appeals to such considerations in explaining the apparently less urgent mood of 4.21 compared with that of 4.9: 'L'Apôtre étant aujourd'hui moins impatient' (1969, 823).

48. Cf. 1.8 and 4.5, of Timothy, and 1.12, 16; 3.11; 4.6-8, 14-19 of Paul.

49. It is difficult to see how the discussion about whether the first metaphor refers to a battle (fight) or an athletic contest (long race) can be resolved. Deissmann preferred the latter on the basis of a second-century AD inscription from a theatre in Ephesus (1927 edn of Deissmann 1908: 309), while Moulton and Milligan prefer the former on the basis of another inscription from 267 BC (1957: 8).

50. While most commentators regard the second metaphor as referring to a race which represents the work of Paul, Spicq, with an eye to v. 8, says that the meaning has an eschatological nuance, and he notes that the common meaning of the noun in the papyri is the 'way of access to the sanctuary' (1969: 805).

51. This fourth and final metaphor is a commonplace, and in the NT is frequently used of the reward for the victorious athlete, the faithful servant, the victor in war, and in Jam 1.12 and 1 Pet 5.4 it is used for the eschatological reward for fidelity. In the Nag Hammadi literature the metaphor is used in three different ways: (i) of the Lord himself, who has received the crown (*The Apocalypse of James* [I,2] 8.38-9.5; *The Teaching of Silvanus* [VII,4] 112.11-28; cf. *The Three Steles of Seth* [VII,5] 120.36f.); (ii) as the prize after some test (*Zostrianos* [VIII,1] 129.13-17; *The Interpretation of Knowledge* [XI,1] 21.29-35; *The Teaching of Silvanus* [VII,4] 112.11-28); and (iii) as part of the regal imagery describing the garments of the good man (*The Teaching of Silvanus* [VII,4] 87.5-26; 89.17-35 [twice]).

52. See Barton (1959). Barton refers to a letter from Lord Rankeillour to the London *Tablet* ('some years ago'), in which Rankeillour tried to smooth out what appeared to him an unacceptable break in what should have been a quartet of metaphors from the athletic arena. He searched through the examples in Moulton and Milligan (1957), and found in *P. Ryl.* I.28.187 (4th cent. AD) a use of πίστις with the meaning 'guarantee, pledge', and he proposed that meaning for the noun in 2 Tim 4.7. There is little to be said for Rankeillour's novel suggestion since in that papyrus and in those in which πίστις means 'bond, mortgage', the definite article does not occur, and the noun occurs as an adverbial phrase ἐν πίστει. Barton also, while allowing the possibility of the phrase meaning, 'I have carried out my contract', rejects Rankeillour's suggestion. It is not clear whether that letter to the *Tablet* was the source of the information ('that I heard somewhere, sometime' concerning the possibility of an entry-fee for the Greek Games) that led Twomey to suggest 'a conjectural translation that fits the situation and the imagery admirably: "I have lasted the distance; I have finished the race; I have saved my entry-fee. For the rest, there is waiting for me the victor's

crown ... which ... the just Judge will place on my brow on that day"'
(Twomey 1958: 112).

53. Estius 1843: 342 reads: 'Fidem intelligit eam quam miles imperatori quamque minister ac dispensator Domino suo debet, id est fidelitatem. . . Sed quia commissum erat ei munus evangelicae praedicationis in gentibus, de eo fideliter et perseveranter inter tot adversitates administrato gloriabitur, dicens fidem servavi' (quoted in Barton 1959: 882). Calvin wrote: 'Either sense (faithful to Captain, or faithful in right doctrine) suits well . . . (but) I have no doubt that here his allusion is to the soldier's solemn vow of loyalty' (1548/9: 338).

54. It is not clear, for example, what is the relative weight, or even relevance of a lone occurrence of a term in classical literature, on pre-Christian inscriptions, or on post-Christian papyri.

55. Barton (1959) never mentions Timothy's situation, and seems to operate on the basis that lexicographical evidence alone will settle the question, while Twomey's interest is almost entirely in making precise the athletic imagery of Paul (Twomey 1958).

56. Note the Vulgate translation of 4.6b, 'et tempus resolutionis instat'. Lewis and Scott give the meanings of *resolutio* as 'an untying, unbinding, loosening', and include in their second grouping of meanings, 'a making void, a cancelling; a solution; a release, escape' (for which they give the example Vulg. 2 Tim 4.6).

57. The text is given in Müller (1841: 197).

58. Attention has already been drawn to the use of ἀναλύω to support the meaning 'death' (in particular in Phil 1.23), and it has been shown that where the use of ἀπολύω/ἀπόλυσις insofar as it has any relevance (which is dubious), has been pressed into service, the evidence points in the direction of release, rather than death. Liddell and Scott (1925-40) reflects the wide semantic field of ἀναλύω: 'to unloose, undo; unloose, set free; relax; unloose; unwind; nullify; dissolve;. . . cancel; discharge the debt; suspend; solve the problem; . . . loose from moorings, depart, go away'. For the metaphorical use, 'to die', they give only one example (*Epig. Gr.* 340.7), and there it is the adverbial phrase, ἐς θεοὺς which makes it clear that death is the departure/ release the author has in mind. For what they call the absolute meaning 'to die' they give only two examples: Phil 1.23 and *IG*, Vol. XIV, 1794. The text of the inscription is given in Kaibel (ed. 1890). The original is written on a broken pavement stone, and the editor does not date it.

59. E.g., Josephus uses the verb four times only, all in *Antiq*. In 6.52 and 11.34 it means 'to go home', and in 19.46 it means 'to return home'; in 8.243, however, it means, 'to weaken (one's opinion of)'. In the 17 occurrences of the verb in the LXX there is no question of meaning 'to die'. It means 'to depart' (1 Esd 3.3, twice; Jdt 13.1; *3 Macc* 5.21, 44; 7.13, 20), 'to return' (Tob 2.9; Wis 2.1, to return from Hades; 2 Macc 8.25; 15.28), 'to withdraw/retreat' (2 Macc 9.1; 12.7), 'to come together' (Wis 5.12), 'to melt (of sins)' (Sir 3.15),

'to revoke a decree' (*3 Macc* 5.40), and, finally, 'to set free (the imprisoned soul)' (Wis 16.14).

60. The ἐπιφάνεια could be either the eschatological event (4.1; 1 Tim 6.14; Tit 2.13; 2 Thess 2.8), or the appearance in past history (2 Tim 1.10). In any case the use of the perfect of the verb suggests that Paul had in mind, at one and the same time, the decision taken in the past to love the 'epiphany', and the continuous fidelity to that choice.

61. See the illuminating discussion of 'The Crown of Life' in Hemer (1986: 70-76), and his use of Deissmann's suggestion that the background for the figurative language in Paul lay in the practice of a potentate himself being crowned on the occasion of his official visits (*parousiai*) (pp. 74f.).

62. 'It is clear that in funerary contexts this (ravening lion) motif symbolizes "the ravening power of death"' (Horsley 1983: 50). The meaning in 2 Tim 4.17 is 'I nearly died', and hence an allusion to Nero or the imperial power is considerably less likely (p. 51).

63. The English verb 'to spend' reflects the meaning of exhaustion that we suggest for σπένδομαι. The *Oxford English Dictionary* gives twelve uses of the transitive verb, of which 5c is 'refl. of persons or things', 'to exhaust or wear out (oneself or itself)', and gives as an example, 'Man after man spends himself in this cause (Carlyle, *Fr. Rev.* II, IV,viii)'. In its treatment of the meanings of the intransitive verb, it gives two examples, 'He never rested until he had spent himself in asserting those claims (Nestleship, *Ess. Browning* vi, 233)', and 'He spending himself . . . in his Labours of Love (Hickes and Nelson J. Kettlewell i,xx,44)'.

Notes to Chapter 6

1. One might well ask what it was about Paul's religious understanding that he was driven to travel thousands of miles, and live as an (itinerant) evangelizer in the north-eastern segment of the Roman Empire. Is it a sufficient answer to focus on Paul himself and on his convert-like enthusiasm to speak the wonders of God, or ought one to emphasize also his sense of man's requirements? Paul's joy in the Gospel and in his proclamation of it is obvious in, e.g., the thanksgiving periods of the letters, and in 1 Thess 2.8f.; 2 Cor 2.12; Gal 1.11; Phil 3.14, etc. The passion, death and resurrection of Jesus are, of course, central to the proclamation (e.g. 1 Cor 1.18, 23; 15.1-15; 1 Thess 4.14), but it is also clear that man's needs feature in Paul's thought (e.g. the enthusiasm with which he described being 'in Christ': 2 Cor 5.17; Gal 3.26; Phil 3.8f.; Rom 8.1). In Paul's understanding of his mission, then, it is unnecessary to choose between God's deed and man's need: it involved both a preaching about the facts of redemption through Christ, and an invitation to come into the new covenant (cf. 2 Cor 3.5f.).

2. Kelly attempts to explain the text in terms of Paul's very arrival in the imperial capital, or, more likely, in his having delivered his message before the imperial court. He proposes, in fact, that Paul's appearance before the august tribunal of the capital set a crown on his career as a preacher (1963: 219), which seems to us to conflict with Paul's own ambitions as stated in Romans 15.

3. Spicq gives an impressive list of the important and ordinary personnages who would be present in a Roman court on such an occasion. The critical phrase, he says, is 'évidemment hyperbolique'. He speaks of the courtroom as 'l'auditoire le plus illustre, comme représentatif de tout l'univers païen', and regards Paul's action 'de forcer cet aréopage oecuménique à écouter la révélation de Jésus-Christ ... comme l'achèvement de sa carrière de prédicateur' (1969: 820f.). See also Leaney (1960: 107).

4. Spicq regards Paul's last Roman preaching as the final achievement of his vocation as a κῆρυξ (2 Tim 1.11) (1969: 820).

5. E.g. Guthrie (1957: 176). He quotes Bernard with approval: 'the opportunity given to St. Paul of pleading his cause in the official centre of Rome, the mistress of the nations, was in a sense the "fulfilling" of the preaching of the Gospel' (p. 177).

6. Barrett (1963: 123). Jeremias, too, sees in the opportunity to preach the Gospel to the judge and the audience in the courtroom God's last gift of an opportunity to bring the Gospel to all the pagans, and he, like so many others, considers the future deliverance in a spiritual sense, as in the Lord's Prayer (Jeremias 1968: 59).

7. The later Hanson follows Brox in this interpretation (Hanson 1982: 161).

8. E.g. Lock (1924), Spicq (1969), and, with some reservation, Hanson (1982).

9. Scott (1936: 140). He considers some of the proposed interpretations of v. 16, but rejects in turn the suggestion that Paul had on a previous occasion been tried, was released, and embarked on further missionary activity (as reflected in 1 Timothy and Titus), and was now rearrested, and awaiting trial for the second time. He also rejects the view that the reference is to the first part of the present hearing, and that Paul looks forward anxiously, but not without hope, to the next sitting.

10. Israel's consciousness of its being chosen by God is central to its identity. If the first covenant, with Noah, was universal (Gen 9.1-7), the subsequent ones with Abraham (Gen 17.1-14), Moses (Exod 19f.; Deut) and Joshua (Josh 24) had a more restricted, 'national' character. Subsequent generations were frequently reminded on their covenantal roots, and when the people were unfaithful, they were called to a renewal of the covenant by their leaders, e.g. by King Josiah (2 Kgs 22f.), Scribe Ezra (Neh 8-10), and a series of Prophets (e.g. Jer 31.31-34 and Isa 54.13 promised that a new covenant would be written on the hearts of the people). For a more

comprehensive and thorough examination of the terminology, and related matters, see our Prior (1985: 170-91).

11. We discuss elsewhere Philo's soteriology (Prior 1985: 173-76). The most striking contrast between Philo and Paul is the infectious urgency of the latter as contrasted with the relative *laissez-faire* attitude of the former. Philo never gives the impression that he could contribute to bringing forward the future 'messianic' time, whereas Paul, as we shall show, thought otherwise of his role. Paul's insistence that the proclamation be brought to its completion, and that 'all the nations' would hear it through him, brought him thousands of miles in his enthusiastic mission. Philo's *Sitz*, by way of contrast, seems to have been *in der Bibliothek*.

12. E.g. *Bell. Jud.* 1, 95, 170, 648; 2, 273; *Antiq.* 1,125; 2,210; 11,203, 283, 303; 12,391; 15,248, 269, 281, 293, 295, 315; 16,115; 17,174, 181, 251.

13. 'One of the most basic views of the Qumran community was that all outside the sect were damned' (Sanders 1977: 318). If Jewish birth (or conversion) was sufficient to enter into conventional Judaism, even a Jew had to seek entrance into Qumran, be purified (e.g. 1QH 11.10ff.), undergo the various stages of the initiation process, and, having been accepted, live within the specific rules of the community (e.g. 1QS 3.13f.; cf. 1QH 16.11f.).

14. E.g. 1QM 4.12; 6.6; 9.9; 12.11; and *passim* for the forty-year war between the sons of light (the Qumran Covenanters), the victors, and the sons of darkness (all others), the vanquished; 1QpHab 13.1.

15. No attempt is made here to do justice to a very complex body of material. There is a vast amount of material to be taken into account, and there is no substitute for studying carefully each of the thirteen documents of the Apocrypha, the fifty-two in the Pseudepigrapha proper, and the thirteen in the Supplement (Charlesworth 1983 and 1985a). The disparate nature of the documents warns the reader against any facile overview, and corrects any misapprehension that there was a normative Judaism in the period of the New Testament (see the comments of Charlesworth 1985b: esp. 21f., 44, 56ff., 63-68, 81ff., 92f.).

16. Positive views include *1 Enoch* (10.21; 91.14; cf. 90.3), *The Testament of the Twelve Patriarchs* (e.g. *T. Benj.* 9.2; *T. Naph* 2.5; 8.1-6; *T. Levi* 14.4; 18.9), and several texts foretell the salvation of the Gentiles (*T. Sim.* 6.5; *T. Levi* 2.11; 4.4; 5.7; 8.14; 18.9; *T. Jud.* 25.5; *T. Dan.* 6.2, 7; *T. Asher* 7.3; *T. Benj.* 10.5). The *Sibylline Books*, too, rather like Philo (*De Vita Mos.* II, 43-48; *De Praem. et Poen.* 162-168), predict a future time of great prosperity for the Jewish nation, which will attract the other nations to their moral way of life (3, 194f.), a time when the nations will make procession to the Temple and ponder the Law of the Most High God (3, 10-19), and bring frankincense and other gifts (3, 772-75; cf. Isa 60; Tob 13.11; Rom 15.15f.). Several other texts, however, are far less sympathetic towards the Gentiles (e.g., *Jubilees* 15.26; 33f.; 22.16; 23.23f., 30; *Assumption of Moses* (especially 10.5-

10); 2 Esdras (especially 7.20f., 36ff.; but see 13.13); Daniel (2.14, but see 7.14); and some of the *Psalms of Solomon* (e.g. 17.4, 27, 32).

17. On one side we have R. Eliezer: 'None of the heathens has any share in the world to come', but see the more compassionate point of view in R. Jehoshua (Tr. *Sanhedrin* 2). Note the very positive assessment in *Sifra Ahare pereq* 13.13 which states that even a foreigner who does the Torah is like a high priest, and *Mek. Shirata* 3 (126; II,24 to 15.2), which unites a view of God's universal salvific designs with the special place of the Jew.

18. Strabo's world, for instance, stretched from Scythia and Celtica in the north to the remotest confines of Ethiopia in the south, and from India, the far east, to Iberia the far west (*Geog.* Bk 1, I.13). In another place he refers to a map of his predecessor, Eratosthenes, in which he divided the inhabited world into two parts by a line drawn from west to east, with the westerly extremity at the Pillars of Heracles, and that of the east, the more remote peaks of the mountain chain that forms the northern boundary of India (*Geog.* Bk 2, I.1). But even further to the west he locates the Sacred Cape as 'the most westerly point of the inhabited world' (*Geog.* Bk 2, V, 14). Furthermore, long before Paul's time, the Romans had a very strong presence in Britain.

19. Matt 4.15; 12.18, 21 are fulfillment quotations from Isa 8.13 and 52.1-4, respectively. Practices of the Gentiles are referred to perjoratively (Matt 6.32; 20.25). The disciples are warned of difficulties at their hands (Matt 10.18; 20.19; 24.9). Matt 24.7, 14 and 25.32 refer to the eschaton.

20. The parallels in Matt 21.13 and Lk 19.46 omit 'for all the nations', which is in both the MT and the LXX.

21. Lk 21.24; 24.47; and 12.30, where Luke adds πάντα (cf. Matt 6.32).

22. Once (10.22) by name; on the lips of Tertullus in 24.2, and of Paul in 24.10, 17; 26.4; 28.19.

23. E.g. 4.27; 10.45; 11.1, 18; 13.48; 14.2, 5, 27; 26.17, 20, 23; 28.18.

24. For the 'hostile' nations see Rev 11.9, 20 (cf. 11.18); 12.5; 13.7; 14.8; 16.19; 17.15; 18.3, 23; 20.8; 19.5. For the 'victorious' nations see Rev 5.9; 7.9; 14.6; 15.3, 4; 20.3; 21.24, 26; 22.2.

25. The distribution is: in Romans, 29; 1 Corinthians, 3; 2 Corinthians, 1; Galatians, 10; Ephesians, 5; Colossians, 1; 1 Thessalonians, 2; 1 Timothy, 2; 2 Timothy, 1.

26. Rom 2.4; 3.9 (twice); 9.24, 30; 11.11, 13, 25, 26; 15.9, 10, 11, 12, 27; 10.9; 2.24.

27. E.g. Rom 1.5, 13; 4.17f.; 15.16, 18; 16.4, 26.

28. Rom 10.11. See also Gal 3.28; Col 3.11; 1 Cor 12.13.

29. Note the emphatic οὖν εἰμι ἐγὼ ἐθνῶν ἀπόστολος in Rom 11.3. See also his understanding of his mission as reflected in Rom 15.15ff., 26.

30. Paul's consciousness of his own particular contribution is highlighted in the use of the same phrase, δι' ἐμοῦ, occurring in 2 Tim 4.17.

31. Note, in the event of Gal 3.8 being a quotation of Gen 12.3, Paul's (?)

change in the text of the LXX (=MT) from πᾶσαι αἱ φυλαὶ τῆς γῆς to πάντα τὰ ἔθνη.

32. Gal 1.16 (cf. Rom 1.1-5); 2.2, 8, 9. Note that in Gal 2.8 we have ἐνεργήσας... εἰς τὰ ἔθνη, and in 2 Tim 4.17 ἐνεδυνάμωσέν με ἵνα...

33. The use in Gal 2.12 is to Peter's eating with Gentiles, and in Gal 2.14 to the unreasonableness of expecting Gentiles to live like Jews.

34. He is a prisoner, for the sake of the ἔθνη (Eph 3.1), and his mission is to announce God's mystery (hidden before, etc.; cf. Rom 16.25f.) that the Gentiles are fellow heirs, etc. (Eph 3.6). Paul, by God's grace (cf. Rom 1.5), was given the power (3.7; cf. ὁ δυναμένος in 3.20, and 2 Tim 4.17) to proclaim to the nations the unsearchable riches of Christ (Eph 3.8).

35. Note how Paul stresses his own position of being God's διάκονος (1.23, 25) to bring to completion among the Colossians the word of God (cf. 2 Tim 4.17).

36. See in particular Col 1.28. Note, also, the terminology of the following verse: 'For this I toil' κοπιάω (cf. 2 Tim 2.6; 1 Tim 4.10; 5.17), 'struggling' ἀγωνιζόμενος (cf. 2 Tim 4.7; 1 Tim 6.12) κατὰ τὴν ἐνέργειαν αὐτοῦ τὴν ἐνεργουμένην ἐν ἐμοὶ ἐν δυνάμει (cf. 2 Tim 4.17).

37. The world-wide dissemination of the mystery is further illustrated if Murphy-O'Connor is correct in his suggestion that the phrase is an interpolation of the author, and if ἄγγελοι refers to the apostles, rather than to heavenly figures (Murphy-O'Connor 1984).

38. It is widely held that the Damascus road experience, although described in some detail no less than three times in Acts (9.1-9a; 22.1-21; 26.1-29), is rather played down in Paul's own letters. Recently, Kim has argued for the centrality of that experience in the letters also: 'The essential elements and main lines of his theology have their origin in the fundamental revelation... Further reflections on the revelation in the light of the Old Testament Scriptures, his experience in the mission field and his controversies with his opponents led him to deepen and sharpen his understanding of the gospel revealed on the Damascus Road' (1982: 334f.). Paul mentions his experience of conversion/call to apostleship in 1 Cor 9.1; 15.8ff.; Gal 1.13-17; and Phil 3.4-11. Some interpreters see an allusion to it in Rom 10.2ff.; 1 Cor 9.16f.; 2 Cor 3.4-4.6; 5.16; Eph 3.1-13; Col 1.23-29. The use of the formula χάρις and the aorist passive of δίδωμι plus μοι in Rom 12.3; 15.15; 1 Cor 3.10; Gal 2.9; Eph 3.2, 7, 8 also suggests a definite occasion on which Paul received his call to apostleship. Furthermore, Paul's insistence on his having been called to be an apostle (Rom 1.1; 1 Cor 1.1; cf. 2 Cor 1.1; Eph 1.1; Col 1.1) suggests an allusion to the Damascus event. Although many of these references and allusions occur in the polemical context of defending his gospel and apostleship (e.g., 1 Cor 9.1; 15.5-10; Gal 1.13-17; Phil 3.4-11; 2 Cor 3.4-4.6; 5.16-21) it is clear that the Damascus road experience was central to Paul's theology and apostleship (see Kim 1982: 3-31). In Gal 1.11-17 Paul is anxious to insist that the Gospel preached by him was not human

in its origin, but came as a revelation of Jesus Christ. God had set him apart (cf. Rom 1.1) from his mother's womb, called him through his grace (Gal 1.15; cf. Jer 1.5; Isa 49.1), was pleased to reveal His Son to him (indeed, ἐν ἐμοί), not for any merely personal reasons, but that he might preach him among the Gentiles (Gal 1.16).

39. Stendahl (1977: 7-23) prefers to refer to the experience as a 'call', rather than a conversion. Paul himself refers to his appointment in relation to the Gospel of God (Rom 1.1; 15.16; 2 Cor 11.7; 1 Thess 2.2, 8f.), or the Gospel of Christ (Rom 15.19; 1 Cor 9.12; 2 Cor 2.12; 9.13; 10.14; Gal 1.7; Phil 1.27; cf. 1 Thess 3.2 where he refers to Timothy as a διάκονος of God in the Gospel of Christ, and 2 Thess 1.8 for the designation 'the Gospel of our Lord Jesus'), or 'my Gospel' (Rom 2.16; 16.25; 2 Tim 2.8), and 'our Gospel' (2 Cor 4.3; 1 Thess 1.5; 2 Thess 2.14).

40. In 1 Cor 9.16 he says, 'Woe to me if I do not preach the Gospel'.

41. Or five, if one includes the quotation from Ps 117.1 in Rom 15.11.

42. See the recent discussion of the division of labour between Paul and Barnabas, and the Jerusalem pillars in Sampley (1980). The solemn sealing of the contract by handshake (p. 27), signalled that each side was free to go out as representatives of the same gospel with a division of labour; there was no question of a parting of the ways (p. 30). Sampley's societal model for the subsequent relationship between Paul and his group, and Peter and his, avoids many of the excesses of those who see only friction between the two strands of early Christianity. The division of responsibilities was freely entered into; the preaching of the same Gospel was the shared goal and focus of the energies of both groups; the Gospel was one, even if the audiences were different (see Gal 2.1-10). Sampley does, however, venture to suggest that the gesture of sealing the contract (the handshake) may have been understood differently by the two groups: the Pillars seeing it from a Jewish background of superiors acknowledging inferiors, with Paul, more familiar with Roman Law, seeing the gesture as a sealing of a consensual *Societas* (pp. 49f. n. 50).

43. A recent examination of Rom 11.25-32 concludes that Paul did not conceive of the conversion of all the Jews, but only of the pious ones (*hassidim*) among them (Refoulé 1984: esp. 273).

44. His thesis can be summarized as follows (the numbers in brackets after each section refer to those pages of the original German, *Paulus und die Heilsgeschichte*, in which the relevant element of Munck's thesis is emphasized). (i) By way of contrast with the approach of the Jerusalem community, which addressed itself almost exclusively to Jews in Jerusalem, Paul began in foreign parts, and gradually conceived of his role as critical to salvation history (pp. 268, 113f.). (ii) In line with much of contemporary Judaism, the Jerusalem community saw the ultimate conversion of the Gentiles to be conditional upon that of the Jews. In Paul's scheme the order was reversed (pp. 230, 253-58, 36f.). (iii) Paul, then, considered the End-

Time conversion of all Israel as dependent upon the conversion of (representatives of) all the Gentiles (pp. 28-53, 242-76). (iv) Paul saw himself as *the* Apostle of the Gentiles, and that was the source of the exceptional drive in his missionary activity (cf. pp. 53-60). (v) Paul's view of the salvation of mankind was accepted by the Jerusalem community, and between them they hammered out a division of territories, with the Jerusalem community being responsible for areas in which the majority of Jews lived (Palestine, Cilicia, Syria, Mesopotamia and Egypt), while Paul took on the responsibility of evangelizing in the remainder of the Roman Empire (pp. 111-14, 226-32). (vi) Because there was such a division of territorial responsibility, there was no real conflict between Paul and Peter/James. The (Tübingen) emphasis on a Jewish/Gentile split is altogether exaggerated (pp. 61-78). (vii) Paul hoped to speed on the coming of the End-Time by bringing both the Gentiles and their gifts to Jerusalem (in fulfilment of such prophecies as Isa 2.2; 60.5f., etc.), and thus precipitate the conversion of the Jews also (p. 298). (viii) Paul's arrest, however, forced a change in his strategy, and he saw in his appealing to Caesar an opportunity of bringing the Gospel to the completion he desired (pp. 303-29).

45. We discuss this matter in greater detail in Prior (1985: 194-200).

46. Munck (1954: 49-55). Munck insists that Paul considered his work to be complete in the sense that a 'representative number' of people had heard the message, from Jerusalem to Illyricum (see 1950: 31f.).

47. Munck uses Matt 10.18ff., Mk 13.9ff., and 2 Tim 4.16ff. to strengthen his suggestion that Paul saw it as necessary that preachers would have to bear witness before the authorities in order to bring the Gospel to the Gentiles. In particular he saw his own appearance before Caesar as critical to the eschatological fulfilment. Munck ends his book by claiming that because Paul considered himself to have completed his task of bringing the Gospel to all the nations (after his appearance before Caesar), he could write 'I have fought the good fight, I have finished the race, I have kept the faith' (1954: 324).

48. He can be criticized for not giving due weight to what appears to be the waning of Paul's eschatological fervour, for his appearance of harmonizing and unifying the metaphorical language and images of disparate Jewish theologies, and in particular for his interpretation of the significance of the Collection as the fulfilment of the End-Time. Furthermore, in his insistence that Paul considered himself *the* Apostle of the Gentiles and in his stress on a territorial division of labour as between Paul and the other camp Munck has gone further than the evidence requires. For details of our criticisms see Prior 1985: 194-200.

49. 'πεπληρωκέναι the Gospel of Christ' (Rom 15.19; note the use of the same verb with δι' ἐμοῦ τὸ κήρυγμα in 2 Tim 4.17).

50. E.g. the renowned *Ecole Biblique* catalogue, which includes all articles on each verse of the biblical books, has no entry for Rom 15.24, which means

that the library does not have even one article that focuses on this verse alone.

51. E.g. Zahn (1925), Lietzmann (1933), Kühl, (1913), Cerfaux (1947), Althaus (1949), Manson (1962), Maddelena (1975), Theissen and Byrne (1969), and Harrisville (1980). The argument that the geographical references in Rom 15.19-28 are either a later insertion into the text, or are simply part of a wider forgery can safely be dismissed, since it has been effectively refuted in the past and is not taken seriously today. Lipsius (1892) excised some of vv. 19f., all of vv. 22-24, and the reference to Spain in v. 28. Pallis (1920) dismissed the proposed visit to Spain as a plagiarism after 1 Corinthians 16 and 2 Corinthians 1. For counter-arguments see Sanday and Headlam (1896: 411); O'Neill (1975: 245).

52. Murray (1965) simply refers to Spain as the western limit of Europe, while Fitzmyer (1968b) says no more that that the relevant verses reveal the breadth of Paul's zeal. Cranfield (1979) deals mainly with the help Paul expects.

53. E.g. Wilckens (1983), Michel (1978), Lagrange (1922), and Huby (1940).

54. E.g. Huby (1940), Nygren (1951), Ridderbos (1959), Rousseau (1960).

55. E.g. 'Nothing will stop him but the end of his own life or the barrier of the ocean' (Sanday and Headlam 1896: 412); Spain is the 'Ende der bekannten Erde' (Schlatter 1935: 389), which, incidentally, was certainly not true; 'Sa vision des tâches apostoliques embrassait "les confins du monde habité"' (Leenhardt 1957: 209), and Murray (1965) states that Spain marks the western limits of Europe.

56. E.g. Barrett, one of the few commentators to deal with the geographical options, points out that since there was no more scope for Paul in the east, there remained the north coast of Africa, from Alexandria to the province of Africa, Gaul and Spain. 'Strangely', he says, 'Paul never alludes to African territory' (1957: 277). Best suggests that Paul chose Spain rather than North Africa or Gaul, because 'Spain had many trading connections with the East and there were a number of synagogues there' (1967: 169), for which latter claim, incidentally, there is no evidence whatever. Schlatter (1935: 389) has a similar view. Nygren suggests that it was the worldwide task of Paul that drove him west (1951: 321f.).

57. E.g. Sanday and Headlam (1896) refer to the width and boldness of St Paul's schemes: 'He must carry his message ever further' (p. 412); cf. Fitzmyer (1968b: 329).

58. E.g. Godet speaks of a visit *en passant*, with the emphasis on εἰς Σπανίαν rather than on δι' ὑμῶν (v. 28; Godet 1890: 570). Kühl (1913) refers to Rome as a *Durchgangsstation* (p. 474); similarly, Schlatter (1935: 389).

59. Godet does point out that Paul could have gone directly from Asia to Spain, but he misses the real significance of the visit by attributing the stop-

over in Rome to Paul's 'faim et soif d'entrer en communication personnelle avec les chrétiens de Rome, et il fera un détour pour les visiter en passant' (1890: 571).

60. See our critique in Prior 1985: 202f.

61. 'I ... maintain that Isaiah 66 played a major role in Paul's entire collection exercise, and it provided him with the urgency of missionizing in Spain' (Aus 1979: 237f.). He points to the fact that Jewish and Jewish Christian circles interpreted v. 9 to refer to the messianic King, and he suggests that Paul would have understood this to be fulfilled at the parousia of Christ. Moreover, v. 12 predicts the flow to Jerusalem of the wealth of the nations, and v. 18 that of the gathering of 'all the nations', while v. 19 speaks of God sending some of those who have survived to the nations. Paul, according to Aus, would understand the survivors (whom he calls 'the saved') of v. 19 to be those who believed in the redemption found in Jesus the Messiah (cf. Paul's use of the term in 1 Cor 1.18 and 2 Cor 2.15), and who would now embark on the worldwide mission foreseen by Isaiah. He points to Westermann's comment on Isa 66.19 (Aus 1979: 240): 'Hier ist zum erstenmal ganz eindeutig von Mission in unserem Sinne die Rede: Sendung einzelner Menschen zu den fernen Völkern, um dort die Herrlichkeit Gottes zu verkündigen. Es entspricht genau der apostolischen Mission am Anfang der christlichen Kirche' (Westermann 1966: 377).

62. The identification of Tarshish with modern Spain is widely attested, and Aus gives abundant evidence of where it occurs in the context of Yahweh's universal dominion (e.g. Ps 122.8-11; cf. *Ps. Sol.* 8.16 (15)-17, and Rabbi Simlai's identification of Spain with the end of the world [*b. Nid.* 30b]. Aus claims that Paul, too, would have made this identification (pp. 245f.).

63. Aus points out that other OT passages, and rabbinic interpretation, associate Tarshish with the universal dominion of Yahweh, and with the eschatological pilgrimage to the messianic King. Such texts as Ps 68.30; 72.10; Isa 60.11; Jer 3.14, then, provided Paul with the background for his own idea of a procession of Gentile converts, bearing gifts, to Jerusalem. Paul's hope was that such a triumphal procession (cf. 2 Cor 2.14) would arouse jealousy in the Jews, and that, thus, all Israel would be saved (Rom 10.19; 11.11, 14). *B. Pesah* 118b supports the jealousy strategy: Egypt's gift would be accepted by the Messiah; Ethiopia, next, would be encouraged to bring its gift, which it knew would be acceptable, since it had never harmed the Israelites as the Egyptians had. Finally, it would be the Roman State's turn to reason, 'If the Messiah accepts gifts from those who are not his brothers, how much so will he accept my gifts, since I am his brother'. Paul hoped that the sight of the Gentiles, who are not a nation (Rom 10.19), and did not seek the Lord (Rom 10.20), having their offering accepted in Jerusalem would stimulate the Jews, too, to accept Jesus as Messiah, and then He would come again. Such was 'the main purpose of Paul's collection

enterprise, which was designed not merely to alleviate poverty in the Jerusalem Christian congregation' (Aus, pp. 255f.).

64. It is not at all clear that Paul saw in the collection anything more than an act of kindness on the part of the scattered churches for the poor in the mother-church, which gesture, of course, had obvious relevance to the fellowship in the one Gospel of the two distinct groups, Gentiles and Jews (cf. Gal 2.1-10). Neither is it clear that Paul saw in the collection and the pilgrimage of representatives to Jerusalem the fulfilment of such precise messianic expectations as the rather literalist interpretation Aus gives to the metaphorical language of Isaiah 66. In those texts which speak of the final time, such processions occur after the new order has been inaugurated, and are not presented as acts which bring it about. It is not easy to imagine that Paul presumed that his own 'messianic' activities would force the hand of the Messiah to come again. If Paul had so understood the significance of his collection enterprise one would expect him, when appealing to the OT for support, to use passages which have an eschatological dimension. Instead, he chooses texts which recommend generosity of giving, and even promise an abundant reward to those who are generous. E.g. 2 Cor 8.15, quoting Exod 16.18; 2 Cor 9.6, alluding to Prov 11.24f.; 2 Cor 9.7, alluding to Prov 22.8 (LXX); 2 Cor 9.9, quoting Ps 112.9; 2 Cor 9.10, quoting Isa 55.10, and alluding to Hos 10.12.

65. That the alleviation of the needs of the Jerusalem community was the primary motive for the collection is clear from 2 Corinthians 8–9. 2 Cor 8.4 describes it as ἡ κοινωνία τῆς διακονίας τῆς εἰς τοὺς ἁγίους while 9.12 says it makes up for the needs of the saints. In 8.12f. Paul wants equality of provisions, with the promise that in the future those who are helped now may supply the present contributors' future needs (8.14). Notice also the profit-motive in 9.6ff. Moreover, Acts 11.27-30 provides evidence that the disciples in Jerusalem (and Judea) were in need of material relief, and it and Acts 24.17 attest to the role of the diaspora communities in responding to their suffering. In Gal 2.10 we read of a major condition in the agreement, laid down by the Jerusalem pillars, that Paul and Barnabas would remember the poor, which Paul (at least: does the change from plural to singular suggest that Barnabas was not?) was anxious to do. Nickle argues that 'Paul's collection was instigated ostensibly as a simple act of Christian charity, at the Jerusalem meeting' (1966: 72), and that while reflecting several aspects of contemporary Judaism, 'he borrowed most heavily for the organization of his collection from the Jewish Temple tax' (p. 99). He does, however, allow for an eschatological dimension in his proposed three levels of theological significance for the collection: an act of Christian charity among fellow believers motivated by the love of Christ; a sign of solidarity with the Jerusalem church, emphasizing the common fellowship of Jew and Gentile; and thirdly and rather vaguely, 'an eschatological pilgrimage of the Gentile Christians to Jerusalem by which the Jews were to be confronted with the

undeniable reality of the divine gift of saving grace to the Gentiles and thereby be themselves moved through jealously to finally accept the gospel' (p. 142). He allows that the gesture was a dramatic expression of the first two, but that 'as an instrumental event of the *Heilsgeschichte*, intended to prod the unbelieving Jews to profess faith in Christ, Paul's project was a crashing failure' (p. 155).

66. Paul himself was not sure that it was worth his while going with those chosen (1 Cor 16.4). To suggest that a tiny group of believers from the diaspora churches would be interpreted 'messianically' by the Jews in Jerusalem is to stretch one's imagination rather too far. Whatever may be alleged about Paul's expectations, there is nothing to suggest that Jerusalem Jews would have interpreted the arrival of a modest number of alms-carriers from the diaspora messianically, and that they would have been seen by them as a prelude to the arrival of the End-Time.

67. Even if Paul sometimes appears to have an exaggerated sense of his own contribution, he was not unappreciative of the work of both itinerant co-workers, and the good witness of the local communities as agents of wider evangelization, as his letters show.

68. E.g. Isa 66.19; Gen 10; Ezek 27.10-25; 38; Isa 45.22f.; Ps 65.5; Rom 10.12; 1 Cor 9.16.

69. Melanchton, for example, described the letter as a *christianae religionis compendium*. The aspect of theological tract is reflected in the commentaries of, e.g. Dodd, Nygren, and Cranfield. It has been called Paul's 'last will and testament' (Bornkamm 1971: ch. 2). Even Stendahl (1977) tends to regard it as a theological treatise, even if it has immense implications for mission. Kümmel is sensitive to both Romans' 'testament' character, and to its concrete message to the Roman church, which he relates to the world mission (Kümmel 1973: 312ff.).

70. Outstanding in this respect is Minear (1977), who sees the letter as directed to the reconciliation of the five disparate factions the author finds in Rome.

71. E.g. Dahl, in a chapter devoted specifically to the missionary theology in Romans, mentions the mission to Spain almost as an afterthought, and gives the impression that the Roman community itself was Paul's primary concern at that time.

72. On the basis of Rom 15.20f. alone one would presume that Paul would have been particularly sensitive not to interfere with the church situation in Rome. There is no reason to think that he had any part to play in its foundation, or that anyone there looked to him for guidance about its domestic affairs. It may be the case that he was aware of tensions within the community, but it is not likely that Paul would have taken it upon himself, unasked as far as we can judge, to suggest a solution without some pressing reason.

73. Note the almost identical phrase, εἰς ὑπακοὴν εἰς πάντα τὰ ἔθνη, in 16.26, and εἰς ὑπακοὴν ἐθνῶν in 15.18, speaking of what Christ had worked in him so far. Paul uses ὑπακοή four more times in Romans (16.19 of the obedience of the Romans known to all; 5.19 speaks of the obedience of Christ, and 6.16, twice, of the obedience which leads to righteousness). He uses ὑπακοή four times in the other letters, but it is never related to the goal of his vocation and mission (2 Cor 7.15; 10.6; Phlm 21 refer to the obedience of the people addressed, while 2 Cor 10.5 has the ambiguous εἰς τὴν ὑπακοὴν τοῦ Χριστοῦ). The contrast, then, between Paul's use of 'your obedience' (when addressing a congregation), and 'obedience among the nations' in Romans advances further the view that Paul's concerns at the time of writing Romans went beyond the problems of the Roman community, whose obedience, in any case, was already well known (Rom 16.19).

74. Wiefel (1977) situates the letter in a very definite historical context. Before Claudius's expulsion of the Jews (including Jewish Christians) from Rome, the Christian community there was organized within the synagogue (p. 109). When they were allowed back (cf. Dio Cassius, *Historia Romana* 60, 6, 6), the returning Jewish Christians found the Gentile Roman community with a form of organization based on house churches, rather than on the synagogue. Romans, then, was written 'to assist the Gentile Christian majority, who are the primary addressees of the letter, to live together with the Jewish Christians in one congregation, thereby putting an end to their quarrels about status' (p. 113). Paul (strangely, if Wiefel is correct) never aludes to such a precise historical setting, but instead he frames his message with news of his intended visit, and his hopes to be sped on his way to Spain by the Romans, neither of which facts does Wiefel mention. In restricting Paul's concern to the supposed divisions within the Roman church, Wiefel, in addition to ignoring vital evidence, reduces the overriding thrust of Romans, namely that salvation is possible in Jesus Christ for 'all the nations', to the domestic squabbles within one church.

75. Note the plural in the subtitle of Minear (1971), 'The Purposes of Paul in the Epistle to the Romans'; cf. 'The Purposes of the Letter' in Martin (1978: 189-92). Minear writes: 'The reconciliation of the Roman saints held top priority in his preparation for a mission to Spain. Thus a very simple fact—the plans to go to Spain—prompted a very obvious intention: the desire to secure full Roman support. And this intention evoked a strong concern for reconciling the antagonists among the Roman Christians' (p. 3). We wish to emphasize that Paul's polemic in Romans is not fully explained by regarding it as directed to the reconciliation of the Roman factions only, but also springs from the kernel of his own experience which is reflected in the general, catholic character of the letter (cf. Manson 1938: 'St. Paul's Letter to the Romans—and Others'). Moreover, we find Donfried's methodological principle I, 'Any study of Romans should proceed on the

initial assumption that this letter was written by Paul to deal with a concrete situation in Rome' (1977: 122), too narrow in its perspective. Those who have found difficulty in identifying the specific situation in Rome have touched on a fundamental difference between this letter and the other Paulines, even if they have failed to relate Paul's missiological testament to the immediate strategic goal of his evangelization, the mission to Spain. Wuellner (1976) rightly draws attention to the argumentative aspect of Romans, and sees in the conclusion (Rom 15.14–16.23) the 'peroration' of Paul's argument, namely, a statement of his future plans and his expectations of the Romans (15.24b), and his present preoccupations (the bringing of the collection to Jerusalem, and his plans for a mission to Spain) (15.25ff.). Watson (1986), on the other hand, while stressing Paul's aim to entice the Jewish Christians in Rome to break with their synagogues, and to join the supporters of his brand of Gentile Christianity, does not relate it to Paul's wider mission plans, and in particular his strategy to evangelize in Spain.

76. Beker speaks of 'A Convergence of Motivations'. The other three motives are: to solicit Roman prayers for the reception of the collection, etc.; to defuse the situation that may have been occasioned by the Galatian letter (with its apparent hostility to Judaism) in Jerusalem, and perhaps in Rome, and to address himself to the reconciliation of the weak and the strong in Rome (Beker 1980: 71-74; 1986: 12).

77. Jewett is rightly cautious about opting for one fixed genre, and he prefers to describe Romans as 'a unique fusion of the "ambassadorial letter" with several of the other subtypes in the genre: the paraenetic letter, the hortatory letter, and the philosophical diatribe' (1982: 9; cf. the 27 sub-types in epideictic literature in Burgess 1902).

78. In particular he notes that the Christian ἀπόστολος has many functions in common with that of an ambassador (Jewett 1982: 10ff.). Moreover, the introduction, Rom 1.1-5, resembles the presentation of diplomatic credentials, and Jewett notes the diplomatic finesse of 1.8-12 (p. 12 n. 1). In the key verses, 1.16ff., Jewett sees Paul as presenting himself 'as an ambassador of the δύναμις θεοῦ . . . extending the sovereign's cosmic foreign policy through the preaching of the gospel' (p. 15). Then there is the 'politically astute' reference to Paul's confidence in the maturity of the Romans (15.4), the use of the term λειτουργός (v. 16), which has ambassadorial, rather than liturgical resonances, the 'diplomatic thrust' in 15.17-21, and the diplomatic sense of 'I have fulfilled my obligations and directives' in 15.19. To this can be added Käsemann's explanation for the apparent change in goal as reflected between 1.11f. and 15.24, as an application of *diplomatische Vorsicht* (1973, original German, p. 379). The model of ambassadorial letter helps the reader to understand the place of ch. 16 also, as being an attempt to enlist allies for the planned mission, while the exhortation to tolerance between the weak and the strong (14.1–15.13) also is

integral to the letter, in that it stresses the equality of Jews and Gentiles, while such passages as 1.3f.; 3.5; 7.15-24 serve the diplomatic purpose of respecting the various strands within the early church. 'The entire letter', he rightly claims, 'coheres when one takes seriously Paul's own statement about his goals' (Jewett 1982: 19). Finally, he draws attention to the potential of 'evangelical diplomacy' in dealing creatively with diversity: Paul 'views the gospel not so much as an ideology to be imposed in an authoritarian manner but as a divine power that transforms everything' (p. 20).

79. Jewett (1982: 15). He adds that Paul's caution in the letter was 'because the mission requires the full cooperation of the Roman churches, which in turn depends on their having accepted the argument of Romans concerning the unifying imperative of the gospel' (p. 17).

80. In his recent commentary on Romans Zeller likewise suggests that Paul's intention in writing the letter was to win over the Roman Christians to his universal gospel so that they would support him in his next task, the mission to Spain. Neither the situation in Rome, nor Paul's request for prayers concerning his visit to Jerusalem is sufficient to account for such a detailed statement of his theology (1985).

81. E.g. Lagrange (1922), Michel (1978), and Best (1967). In the OT, letters of recommendation are mentioned, but in addition to the verb (1 Esd 4.47; 1 Macc 12.4). The verb is not used to translate any MT word, but occurs three other times in the LXX, meaning 'to escort' (to his tent, in Jdt 10.15), and 'to send' ('forth', in Wis 19.2, and 'to Hades', in 2 Macc 6.23).

82. E.g. Fitzmyer (1968b), Murray (1965), Wilckens (1982).

83. E.g. Fitzmyer (1968b), Best (1967), Wilckens (1982), Dodd (1932).

84. E.g. Lagrange (1922), Michel (1978), Godet (1890).

85. Lagrange (1922) and Michel (1978) suggest 'for a certain distance', while Wilckens (1982) nominates the first station. The meaning 'to conduct, to escort (especially a departing traveller)' occurs in, e.g., Herodotus Bk. I, III.50; Sophocles, *Oed. Col.* 1667, and *P. Flor.* II, 206, 2, and Acts 21.5, while that of 'to send before, to send forward, or forth' is widely attested (Moulton and Milligan 1957, Liddell and Scott 1925-40, etc.), and the verb is used of Paul's 'send-off' by the Ephesian elders (Acts 20.38).

86. In addition to occurring in Acts 20.38 ('to send off'), and Acts 21.5 ('to accompany for a certain distance'), the verb appears in six texts, in addition to Rom 15.24. The sense of providing all that was needed seems to be behind the exhortation to Titus to speed Zenas and Apollos on their way (Tit 3.13), and perhaps also in Paul's exhortation to the Corinthians to speed Timothy on his way in peace (1 Cor 16.11). Hospitality and financial assistance to itinerant brethren is commended as worthy of God in 3 John 6. This is also the sense in the single occurrence of the verb in the Apostolic Fathers (Polycarp, *Phil.* 1.1; Goodspeed 1907); the word does not occur in the Apologists (Goodspeed 1912). 1 Cor 16.6 seems to suggest that the

Corinthian community should contribute to Paul's mission 'wherever he goes', while the use in 2 Cor 1.16 is as tantalizingly vague as is that in Rom 15.24. However, when Paul, Barnabas, and some of the others were sped on their way to the Jerusalem Conference, they appear to have been given the status of officially appointed representatives going up with the church's authority as ambassadors (Acts 15.3).

87. He concludes, 'The epistle is written with this as at least one of its purposes' (1973: 398). Käsemann rightly notes that if Rome is only a *Durchgangs-* or *Zwischenstation* (the quartet, διαπορευόμενος, θεάσασθαι ὑμᾶς, πρῶτον, and ἀπὸ μέρους make Paul's intentions obvious), it could be Paul's basis for his next evangelical operation (pp. 397f.). If, then, Spain is the goal of Paul's journey, Rome should be the bridgehead.

88. E.g. in Salamis (13.5), Pisidian Antioch (13.14-43), Iconium (14.1), Thessalonika (17.1-4), Beroea (17.10-12), Athens (17.17), Corinth (18.4), and Ephesus (18.19; 19.8; cf. 24.12).

89. He evangelized also 'in the place of prayer' in Philippi (16.13), in people's houses (Lydia's in Philippi, 16.15; Jason's in Thessalonika, 17.5-9; Priscilla and Aquila's in Corinth, 18.2-4; Justus's in Corinth, 18.7), in a (public) meeting room (Tyrannus's in Ephesus, for two years, 19.9f.), and in his own lodgings in Rome (28.16, 30). He also availed of opportunities of speaking more publicly, as in the agora and Areopagus in Athens (17.17-34), and in Lystra (14.8-18), Philippi (16.16-34), and Ephesus (19.11-20). The courtroom also provided opportunities.

90. Although some of Paul's earlier activity took place before the Jerusalem conference, much of it was later, and the Acts picture appears to conflict with the fundamental division of labour agreed upon (Gal 2.7ff.). Such a division of labour, however, was hardly likely to exclude Paul from some contact with the synagogues.

91. Hock has drawn attention to Paul's trade as a medium of evangelization. See his most recent and complete account (1980).

92. E.g. in connection with Paul's plans for his mission Käsemann says of Spain that 'There were certainly some synagogues there' (1973: 398).

93. Bowers provides 'a comprehensive review of the evidence', both material and literary (1975: 400). Spain signified 'the remotest land' in rabbinic literature (e.g. *Yeb* 63a; *Midr Rab* Ps xxii; *Ber* 62a; *Nid* 30b), and the lists of the lands to which the Jews spread always stop short of the western Mediterranean beyond Rome (pp. 398-401).

94. Acts mentions the hospitality of Judas (9.11, 17), of the Jerusalem church (15.3f.; 21.17), of the jailer in Philippi (16.33f.), and of the churches on the way to Jerusalem (21.4, 7, 8, 16), and at Puteoli (28.14). Paul himself looked forward to receiving hospitality in Corinth (1 Cor 16.6), and Rome (Rom 15.23f.), and asked Philemon that a room be made ready for him (Phlm 22).

95. Paul had received financial help from the Philippians at least three times (Phil 2.25-30; 4.10-20), even though he refused help from the Corinthians. See the discussion in Sampley (1980: ch. 4).

96. Some 100 names are associated with Paul in Acts and the letters, and no less than 36 associates are mentioned by him under nine different designations. See Ellis (1970/1, and the chart on p. 438). Ellis concludes: 'In summary, the picture that emerges is that of a missionary with a large number of associates. Indeed Paul is scarcely ever found without companions. Yet few of them are included in his immediate and subordinate working circle, still fewer work with him on a continuing, long-term basis' (p. 5).

97. Pliny relates that Hispania Citerior could be reached from Ostia in as little as four days, and Cadiz in seven (*Hist.* XIX, 19.1; cf. Strabo, *Geog.* iii,2.5-6.).

98. Hock notes that if working as a tentmaker made Paul economically independent, and provided him with some means of conversation with fellow-workers (e.g. with Aquila and Priscilla, Acts 18.2f.), and provided an opportunity of informal evangelization with customers, the work was wearying, and was a source of personal hardship and social humiliation (1980: 67).

99. See Praeder (1984). Predictably all travelogues have some features in common, but the surviving ancient ones display a great variety of interest. To treat the Acts account as if it conformed to a set pattern of travel reporting is to ignore the great variety within ancient literature, as well as to ignore some of the sober elements in the account in Acts. For the omission of some of the more characteristic elements found in the epic accounts, see Praeder (1984: 694).

100. See the discussion in Praeder (1984: 686ff.).

101. In the story of the storm and shipwreck itself there are no less than seven references to being saved (27.20, 31, 34, 43, 44; 28.1, 4). Being saved from the dangers posed by the sea is, of course, well established in the Jewish-Christian tradition: one thinks immediately of the rescue of Noah (Gen 8.1-14), Jonah (Jon 1-2), Jesus' disciples (Matt 8.25f.), and of Peter (Matt 14.30ff.)—cf. Ps 10.23-32 (LXX); Wis 14.1-6. It is pointed out that Paul's speech of hope in 27.21-26 is unusual, if not unique in ancient accounts, all of which speak of the certainty of dying (Praeder 1984: 696).

102. This is expressed strikingly in the phrase 'not a hair from your head shall perish' (27.34), a phrase almost identical with the Lord's assurance to his disciples when he spoke of persecution, recorded only by Luke (21.18).

103. Would not this stress on the promise of the safety of all, and their subsequent deliverance, ring hollow if the author and readers of Acts knew that some two years after the events he records Paul was condemned to die?

104. Another aspect of the safety theme enters in here. The Maltese are presented as interpreting Paul's snake-bite as a sign of justice, despite his having been saved at sea (28.4). One may observe again that if the Acts were completed after Paul's execution in Rome, his known death would make the earlier deliveries rather ironic.

105. This incident is interpreted very favourably by Prete. As well as assuring the reader that there already existed an organized Christian community in Rome the incident shows that it was 'piena di zelo'. He argues that the whole section, vv. 16-31, is 'stage managed' by Luke so that Paul can be seen to focus on the Jewish community in Rome, rather than deal with the Christians, or the remainder of the 1.5 million other inhabitants: obviously, he claims, such contacts with the Christians and pagans of Rome did not enter into the scheme of things of the author of Acts (Prete 1983: 151f.). Prete proposes that the author's aim in vv. 16-31 was to show how the Gospel was to be made available to the Gentiles since the Jews rejected it (p. 166).

106. See Penna (1982: 328ff.). From the more than 534 inscriptions in the Jewish catacombs we know the names of eleven Roman synagogues, of which perhaps five can be dated as early as the time of Paul's sojourn in Rome. The estimates of the numbers of Jews in Rome vary from 40-60,000 (Leon 1960: 135f., and 1964: 154), to 10,000, with the most recent estimate being put at 20,000 (Penna 1982: 328; see also 341, note 53). The absence up to recently of any evidence of a central administration (contrast the situation of the Jews in Alexandria) has been taken as indicating that each community was independent. However, the discovery of the term *archigerousiarches* in an epitaph in the Jewish catacomb on the Via Nomentana (c. III-IVth century AD) makes it possible that one person had authority over the entire Jewish community in the city (see Schürer 1986: 80f.). The evidence suggests that the Roman Jews were poor, and had a low level of literacy (Leon 1964: 162). The Roman Jews did not live in one ghetto, and since they came from several different regions, and used different languages we can presume that they reflected a wide spectrum of social and religious identity. According to Luke 'some were persuaded' by what Paul said about Jesus (v. 24), and clearly others were not (v. 25). It may be the case that the different synagogues in Rome gave different responses to the Gospel (see Drane 1980). Since some of the Roman Christians would have come from their ranks perhaps we can suppose that some of the difficulties within the Roman Christian communities may have already existed within the diversity of the original Jewish communities. Paul's eirenic letter, then, may also have aimed at healing the rifts among the Jewish communities, and inviting more of their members to accept Jesus as Messiah.

107. In addition to the hospitality Paul expected for himself, note also his request that the Romans treat Phoebe hospitably (Rom 16.1f.). See also his concern that others be welcomed (e.g., Phil 2.25-30; Col 4.7-9; Eph 6.21f.).

108. The same critical verb, ἐπιτρέπω, is used of the permission in each case (27.3; 28.16), and when one compares Paul's being isolated in Rome with his being cared for by the brothers in Sidon, the contrast appears all the more stark.

109. The question of Paul's means of support has been much discussed. Cadbury argued that Paul worked in Rome, and he took the phrase of v. 30 to mean 'on his own earnings' (1926: 321f.). Bruce agrees with this understanding, noting that Paul's *libera custodia* would have permitted him to carry on his trade of tent-making (1952: 480). On the other side, both Conzelmann (1963: 96) and Haenchen (1965: 726) prefer the reading, 'in his own rented quarters'. Hock also discusses the matter (1980: ch. 3).

110. Haenchen reads the evidence in terms more favourable to the Romans than we do. He interprets Luke's account of this incident in terms of Luke setting up for the Roman Christians an honourable though modest monument (1965: 719). He rightly castigates Bauernfeind's romanticization of v. 15 ('In Rome a community was awaiting him which knew very well how to support its shepherds . . . the bonds of love, etc.', quoted in Haenchen, pp. 719f.), and notes that Luke is much more reserved in his description of Paul's welcome.

111. Haenchen acknowledges that one could interpret Luke's silence critically, but he affirms that Luke has avoided even hinting at such a tension. He interprets Luke's virtual elimination of the Roman community by his silence as being due to his desire to present Paul proclaiming in Rome the gospel up to that time unknown (1965: 720). We hope to have shown that there is much more than a hint of criticism in Luke's silence.

112. See, e.g., the recent discussion of the importance of hospitality in Luke–Acts in Malherbe (1977a: 65-68).

113. Note that three of the five people mentioned in Philemon occur also in 2 Tim 4.10f., and all five in Colossians. This suggests a common origin for the three letters.

114. We have argued in Chapter 4 that Rome is the most likely provenance of the letter.

115. Clearly Paul did not have things his own way in Rome. If he could complain that some were preaching Christ διὰ φθόνον καὶ ἔριν, some forty years later Clement of Rome recalls that the greatest and most righteous pillars of the church were persecuted διὰ ζῆλον καὶ φθόνον and while he says that Peter endured many labours διὰ ζῆλον ἄδικον, Paul διὰ ζῆλον καὶ ἔριν showed great endurance (V; see the seven examples of OT victims of ζῆλος in IV). This evidence suggests that some Roman Jewish Christian preachers may have been responsible even for Paul's death! (See Cullmann 1930 and 1962: 102-10; Matt 24.10.)

116. Harrison paints a very bad picture of the church in Rome in respect of its treatment of Paul: 'When he was awaiting his trial, some members of the church at Rome, so far from even trying to help him, had been active in

making of the Gospel itself a tool to damage his case... Some, who had seemed to favour his cause, had withdrawn their support in these last critical days. Alarmed by ominous signs of coming storm, they had openly disclaimed any sympathy with him and his aims, proving only too conclusively that in their minds, after all, their own interests came first, not the things of Jesus Christ' (1964: 119f.).

117. Two groups, however, do send greetings (4.21f.) and it is probably fanciful to suggest that the reference to the brothers with me may imply that other brothers were not on his side.

118. Jeremias comments: 'in Rom, wo die christliche Gemeinde, nicht ohne Geduld (vgl. 4.16) die Verbindung mit Paulus offenbar verloren hatte...' (1968: 46).

Notes to Chapter 7

1. In the time between the first favourable hearing, and the second hearing to be held, at which he confidently hoped to be acquitted, Paul wished Timothy not to tarry, but to come quickly for there was much to be done in the διακονία (4.11) of bringing the *kerygma* to its completion, at which time 'all the nations' would have heard it (4.17).

2. Since we hold that among the Captivity Letters at least 2 Timothy and Philippians were written from the imperial capital, it should be of considerable interest to enquire into Paul's situation as reflected in 2 Timothy as compared with that in Philippians. As between Colossians, Philemon and Philippians there appears to be an increase in Paul's isolation, and in his facing up to the prospect of death. In 2 Timothy the situation is even worse, at least as far as the isolation goes. If in Philemon we have the presence of Timothy (v. 1), Epaphras (v. 23), Mark, Aristarchus, Demas and Luke (v. 24), and in addition to those Jesus Justus in Colossians (Col 4.11), 2 Timothy presents us with a sad list of absent friends and deserters, relieved only by the stark sentence, 'Luke alone is with me' (4.11). The meaning of the text is probably that Luke is the only one of the intimate circle of co-workers still with Paul, and there is no reason to infer (as Freeborn does, 1973: 128) that Luke also is in prison.

3. The departure of Demas would seem to place 2 Timothy later than Philemon and Colossians. The absence of Timothy in 2 Timothy would agree with placing the letter later than Philemon, Colossians and Philippians, since he is a co-writer of all three (Phlm 1; Col 1.1; Phil 1.1). It is clear in Philippians that Paul intended sending Timothy to Philippi, but that he hesitated to do so until he found out how things would go with himself (Phil 2.23). It seems to us that Paul became sufficiently secure before the first hearing, and that he dispatched Timothy to Philippi, some time after which

he also dispatched Tychicus to Ephesus (2 Tim 4.12), and others had gone elsewhere (2 Tim 4.9f.).

4. Scott said flatly of 2 Tim 4.9: 'The request for a visit is obviously out of place in the present letter. . . . This request is indeed surprising after the previous part of the letter. Nothing has been said as to an expected visit from Timothy' (Scott 1936: 135). However, that Paul had in his mind to see Timothy again is stated at the very outset of the letter and we have argued in Chapter 4 that the strategic positioning of Paul's desire to see Timothy and his instructions to him to come quickly (2 Tim 1.4; 4.9, 21) suggests that this matter was a major reason for Paul's writing the letter. Barrett, although not at all convinced by Harrison's suggestions (Barrett 1963: 11f.), also regards 4.9 as inconsistent with 4.6-8, which, he says, speaks of Paul's death as imminent, and he goes on to say that the verses 'were not necessarily all written at the same time' (pp. 119f.). See also Hanson, in his earlier commentary (1966: 6f., 99f.). Hanson has since abandoned the theory of fragments (1981: 402f.; 1982: 10f.).

5. Dibelius and Conzelmann (1966: 122, 125, 98). Even though there is an excursus on 2 Tim 4.20f. the instruction to come is not dealt with.

6. See also the discussion in White (1978).

7. E.g. in *P. Oxy.* 1676, in which a mother complains to the receiver that he had not come to her son's birthday. She expresses her desire that he come in the near future, but is realistic enough to realize that he may not come for some time.

8. In a great number of papyrus letters the phrase 'as soon as you receive this letter . . . ' follows the greeting (e.g. *P. Hibeh* 44, 45, 58, 59, 61; *P. Tebt.* 748, 749). A very specific instruction follows and in many cases this is the main, if not the only purpose of the letter. This is clearly the case of the second century AD *P. Köln* 107, which is one of the shortest of all the papyrus letters, consisting of only seven very short lines. It reads, 'From Servilius Pudens, centurion. On receipt of my letter immediately come to me to the metropolis, or to Arabia. Farewell' (cf. *P. Oxy.* 1065).

9. E.g. in a very poignant letter of October 64 AD, Thaubas writes to her father that he would do well to come immediately on receipt of the letter because his daughter, her sister Herennia, died in childbirth (*P. Fouad* I, 75). In the 4th cent. AD, Judas wrote to his wife (mainly) describing his fragile condition after a riding accident; he appeals that she send her brother immediately (*P. Oxy.* 3314). Apion wrote to Didymus (3rd cent. AD), telling him to put off everything and come immediately on receipt of the letter, because his sister was sick (*P. Tebt.* 421). Other reasons for the urgency include: to prevent a poor man being beaten again by the strategus (*P. Ups. Frid* 9): to give evidence in a lawsuit (*P. Yale* 34); and often the reason is one of business (e.g., *P. Oxy.* 1215, 1840, 1844, 1770, 3407, 2844; *P. Fayum* 126, 135; *P. Yale* 40). See also *P. Yale* 42; 48; 84; *P. Oxy.* 123; 3407; *P. Cair. Zen.* 59831; *B.G.U.* IV 1204; 1209.

10. Taueris's ending of his letter with ταχὺ ἔρχῃ εινα ειδομεν συ, is rather hollow, especially after he had requested his brother, Theodore, to do him no less than six favours (*P. Oxy.* 2599).

11. It was for such a purpose that a certain Skythes wanted the *comogrammateus*, Ptolemaios, to come quickly, and bring a certain shepherd with him. If this were done Skythes was confident that the outcome of the case would be favourable: 'Skythes to Ptolemaios, greeting. Come to Talao immediately, bringing also the shepherd who is to give evidence about the matters of which you spoke to me. If you do this slowly you will harm yourself, for I am not at leisure to remain longer. Farewell' (*P. Yale* 34).

12. *P. Yale* 42 provides an intriguing comparison with 2 Timothy. The writer of the letter, Nechthosiris, is in Alexandria, where he has been detained by the diocetes. He and his servants have been in need of food and clothing, but he had not heard anything from Philadelphia, and so he was worried. Finally, a certain Protolaos had brought news, but the request for the supplies had not so far been answered. In the letter he gives Leon good news about the condemnation of their opponents by the chrematists, and states that the king will hear the case. He is confident that if Apollonius comes to the city he will be cleared. The letter falls into four natural divisions: (i) Nechthosiris's solicitude for Leon, and the reassurance brought through Protolaos (5-9, 10f.); (ii) a request, with the background information that Dionysios had not delivered the cloak and food (12-16); and the petition itself, asking Leon to see to it that these matters be set right (16-22); (iii) information about Nechthosiris's situation and that of his associates: Leon is not to worry, for all is well (23f.); 'they' have been convicted by the chrematists (24f.), and he has himself been detained by the diocetes (26-29); the king will hear the case (30f.), and the outcome is up to the gods (31f.); and, finally, in (iv) we have the advice that Leon's brother should come to the city, and the assurance that he would be released as soon as he is cleared in the suit against 'them' (32-37). One notes a certain correspondence between this letter and 2 Timothy. The concern of Paul in 2 Tim 4.13 mirrors that in *P. Yale* 42, 12-22. Paul's concern for Timothy, both as a believer in the face of difficulty, and as a minister, is reflected throughout 2 Timothy, and mirrors the concern of the writer of *P. Yale* 42, 5-10. 2 Tim 4.14-17 mirrors *P. Yale* 42, 23-32. This papyrus letter, then, indicates, by analogy, how the various elements of 2 Timothy could be construed— without distortion—as belonging together. By comparing 2 Timothy with *P. Yale* 42 we can more easily imagine the legal process of Paul, and his preoccupations at that time. We learn from the papyrus letter that Apollonios (together with Leon and Necthosiris) was engaged in a controversy with another group, and was in danger of being arrested by his immediate superior, the diocetes. Nechthosiris was detained by the diocetes, but not arrested, so that a plea to the jurisdiction might not be entered on his behalf. Meanwhile, the other party had been brought before the king's superior

judges, the chrematists, and found guilty. The chrematists, however, could only judge; they could not sentence. Nechthosiris informs Leon of the king's interest in the case, and, despite his cautionary phrase, 'it is up to the gods', he is quite confident of Apollonios being cleared. Meanwhile, some time would elapse before the hearing in the presence of the king, and during that period the cloak, tunic and food would be necessary.

13. Paul sends Onesimus back to Philemon. If before he was useless to Philemon, he had since become useful to both Philemon and Paul. It is clear that Paul would like to keep Onesimus with him, ἵνα ὑπὲρ σοῦ μοι διακονῇ ἐν τοῖς δεσμοῖς τοῦ εὐαγγελίου (v. 13), and there is more than a hint in the following verse that Paul actually wants Onesimus back.

14. The RSV reads, 'for he is very useful in helping me', and Moffatt's translation is, 'for he is useful in helping me'.

15. The JB is a rather free rendering: 'I find him a useful helper in my work'. The NEB has, 'for I find him a useful assistant', which is also the translation of Kelly 1963 (p. 211). Spicq translates it, 'car il m'est utile pour le ministère' (1969: 815). Dibelius and Conzelmann prefer the phrase, 'for I can make good use of his services' (1966: 122).

16. 'denn ich kann ihn sehr gut zum Dienst brauchen' (1968: 57).

17. It refers to the serving at tables in Lk 10.40. In Acts 1.25 (cf. 1.17) it is associated with apostleship. In Acts 6.4 it is used of the ministry of the word. In 20.24 the ministry is in relation to the witnessing to the gospel. In 21.19 Paul is recalled as declaring what God had done among the gentiles through his ministry. In the other uses in Acts the noun refers to the daily distribution (6.1), and to the financial aid for the church in Judea (11.29; 12.25). The noun is used of the ministry of angels in Heb 1.14, and in Rev 2.19 it describes the works of the church in Thyatira (works, love, faith, διακονία and endurance).

18. In 1 Cor 16.15 we read that the household of Stephanas appointed themselves εἰς διακονίαν τοῖς ἁγίοις. Although we cannot be sure what the term means, the following verse suggests that such people exercised some authority within the community, after the fashion of those who were συνεργοί and κοπιῶντες. In Eph 4.11f. we read that Christ gave apostles, prophets, evangelists, shepherds and teachers for the perfecting of the saints, the work of the ministry, the building up of the body of Christ. The unspecified character of διακονία is reflected also in Rom 12.6ff., where we have a list of the different χαρίσματα: prophecy, διακονία, followed by teaching, exhorting, sharing, leading, and showing mercy. In 2 Corinthians alone the breadth of the meaning of the term is obvious. In 2 Cor 8.1-7 the financial support for the Jerusalem community is described as a διακονία to the saints (v. 4; cf. 9.1, 12f.). The financial support of the Corinthians themselves is the obvious meaning of διακονία in 2 Cor 11.8, and the collection for the Jerusalem church is probably the meaning of the noun also in Rom 15.31 (cf. Acts 11.29; 12.25). In 2 Corinthians we have four

altogether differently qualified διακονία (of death, of the spirit, of condemnation, and of righteousness, 2 Cor 3.7ff.). Again, it is a gospel ministry (2 Cor 4.1-3), and a ministry of reconciliation (2 Cor 5.17f.), a service to God which brings many difficulties (cf. 2 Cor 6.1-10). In Rom 11.13 Paul refers to his being an apostle of the nations as ἡ διακονία μου. In Col 4.17 Paul and Timothy send a message to be delivered to Archippus: 'See that you fulfill the ministry which you received in the Lord'. In 1 Tim 1.12 Paul gives thanks to God who judged him faithful, θέμενος εἰς διακονίαν.

19. E.g. Rom 12.7; 1 Cor 12.5; 16.15; 2 Cor 4.1; 5.18; Eph 4.12.

20. E.g. Rom 15.31; 2 Cor 8.4; 9.1, 12f.; 11.8.

21. E.g. Rom 11.13; cf. 1 Tim 1.12.

22. The Acts of Peter have a heavenly voice say, with regard to Paul's visit to Spain: 'Paul the servant of God is chosen for (this) service for the time of his life' (1), and Eusebius records that tradition has it that after defending himself the Apostle was again sent on the ministry of preaching (ἐπὶ τὴν τοῦ κηρύγματος διακονίαν λόγος ἔχει), and coming a second time to the same city suffered martyrdom under Nero (*Hist. Eccles.* II,xxii).

23. One can easily see the difficulties of the commentators. Scott notes that it is doubtful if διακονία refers to personal service or to work in the mission, and he concludes that the vagueness is probably intentional (1936: 136). Guthrie goes no further than to say that the word is a quite general term expressing any kind of service (1957: 172), while Barrett says only that Mark was useful for Christian service (1963: 120). Kelly notes that διακονία means either personal service to Paul or public ministering. Either interpretation is possible, he says, but the tone of the passage 4.9-21 very much favours the former (1963: 214). It is our firm view that the tone favours the latter, as does every other use of the word in Paul. Houlden, Karris, Hanson and Leaney do not deal with the matter, while Dibelius raises the possibility that the phrase πάντα τὰ ἔθνη of v. 17 might suggest that the first defence was successful and that Paul was making plans for a visit to Spain; but he rejects the hypothesis as entirely impossible in the light of 4.20 (1966: 126). Jeremias goes furthest in his remark that, 'Nicht an sich denkt Paulus, sondern an die Arbeit; die Ernte ist gross und erfordert Arbeiter' (Jeremias 1968: 58), but he, too, cannot contemplate a new phase in Paul's missionary activity, since Paul 'sein Testament schreibt im festen Blick auf den Tod (v. 6)' (1968: 56). Spicq is forced into an exegetical somersault: 'Normalement, la διακονία serait le ministère (Chrysostome, Belser, Jeremias; dans les inscriptions et les papyrus, l'accent est sur les services rendus à la collectivité, *Inscriptions de Priene*, 102, 5; *PSI* 361, 24; cf. Moult. Mil.), mais ici il porte d'abord sur l'aide personnelle apportée à Paul (Theod. de Mop., Bernard, Wohlenberg, Parry), sans oublier que celui-ci est avant tout Apôtre, et qu'il aura Marc sous la main "pour le ministère" (cf. Onésiphore, 2 Tim 1.18): Amène-le, il me sera utile . . . ' (1969: 814).

24. The two terms διάκονος and συνεργός are used of Paul himself (1 Cor

3.5, 9), Apollos (1 Cor 3.5, 9), and Timothy (2 Cor 3.6; 6.4; cf. Rom 16.21 and 1 Thess 3.2). One could also argue the case for Achaicus, Fortunatus and Stephanas (1 Cor 16.15ff.).

25. E.g. Eph 3.5-10; Col 1.23-29. See also Georgi (1964: 32-36).

26. It occurs 13 times in the NT, and with the sole exception of 3 John 8 only in Paul. The noun, or its cognate verb, is not found either in Acts, or in the Pastorals. In six of the occurrences in Paul the noun is in the plural, as it is also in 3 John 8. As well as describing Paul himself (1 Cor 3.9), it is also applied to Apollos (1 Cor 3.9), Aquila and Prisca (Rom 16.3ff.), Aristarchus (Phlm 24; cf. Col 4.10), Clement (Phil 4.2f.), Demas (Phlm 24; cf. Col 4.11, 14), Philemon (Phlm 1), Timothy (Rom 16.2; 1 Thess 3.2; cf. 1 Cor 16.10), Titus (2 Cor 8.23), Urbanus (Rom 16.9), as well as Mark himself (Phlm 24; Col 4.11). It can also be taken to include Achaicus (1 Cor 16.15ff.), and perhaps Euodia and Syntyche (Phil 4.2f.), Fortunatus (1 Cor 16.15f.), Silas (1 Thess 3.2), and Stephanas (1 Cor 16.15ff.). Little is learned from its two uses in the LXX, 2 Macc 8.7, and 14.5, where it means 'attack', and 'purpose', respectively.

27. See Ellis 1978 (= Ellis 1970/1), p. 6, and the chart on p. 438 of the original publication (1970/1).

28. E.g. Harrison (1964: 108-17).

29. The five or six years is arrived at by identifying Paul's visit to Troas with that mentioned in Acts 20.6. Conscious of the problem, Guthrie rules out the possibility that Acts 20.6 is the incident Paul refers to, and suggests instead that Paul had made a recent visit to Troas (1957: 173).

30. Jeremias says, 'Das Einmalige der Lage, das sich namentlich in v. 13 spiegelt, und das Einmalige des Verhältnisses zwischen Schreiber und Empfänger wird stets . . . das Hauptargument für die Echtheit der Pastoralbriefe bleiben' (1968: 60). Likewise, Kelly: 'It is extremely unlikely that an imitator in the ancient world would have thought of inventing banal details like these' (1963: 215). Guthrie says that the references to cloak, books and parchments 'are so incidental that they bear strong marks of authenticity' (1957: 173). But Spicq, who in the previous edition of his commentary agreed with Stevenson that of all the authentic passages 2 Tim 4.13 was the least capable of having been invented (1947: 392), was later less sure of this judgment, 'tant ce verset, relu dans son contexte folklorique, fait figure de cliché' (1964: 389 n. 2). Attention has already been drawn to our dissatisfaction with Spicq's use of the word cliché.

31. E.g. Brox (1969a: 273): 'Ein pseudonymer Briefschreiber konnte sich ohne weiteres auch einer solchen Aufforderung als eines literarischen Mittels bedienen'.

32. Cf. the requirement that an officer be ἀφιλάργυρος (1 Tim 3.3, 8; Tit 1.7); and also 1 Tim 6.5, with its polemic against money-making in the ministry.

33. E.g. Cicero, *De Off.* I, 4, 12; Epictetus III,22, 46f.; Matt 6.25-29, etc.

34. Zmijewski insists that the Pastorals are neither a forgery nor a holy cheat, but the (pseudepigraphical) letters which substitute for the physical absence of Paul (1979: 113). They make present and give a future in the Church to the deposit of Paul (p. 112). He makes his own the pious assumption of Trummer: 'Der Mantel, das "ist alles, was er hat, und alles was er braucht—, ausser den Schriften"' (p. 117, quoting Trummer 1978: 82), and he affirms that 'Die Schriften sind das, was Paulus selbst—bis zu seinem Tod—benötigt, was für ihn unverzichtbar ist' (p. 117). Similarly, Karris says that the papyrus evidence suggests that poor people frequently requested friends to bring or send them their winter mantle, and he adds, 'The details of verse 13 are drawn from this common feature of a letter from a person who is away from home. The author uses these details to give life to two general principles. The example of Paul requesting his mantle illustrates the truth of the teaching found in 1 Tim. 6.6-8 . . . Paul is the model poor missionary, who has the bare necessities of life. By requesting the sacred writings in parchment Paul gives the approval of his life to the teaching of 2 Tim. 3.15-17. His preaching stems from his meditation on the sacred writings of the Old Testament' (1979: 41).

35. E.g. 'Der Winter steht vor der Tür, und das Gefängnis ist kalt' (Jeremias 1968: 58). Similarly, Kelly (1963: 215). Several commentators do not deal with the question (e.g. Scott, Hanson, Guthrie and Houlden), and Dibelius and Conzelmann confine themselves to discussing the morphology of the noun.

36. For the view that Paul wanted his own cloak in particular because he had made it himself, see Spicq (1964: note 33). Newman, closer to our own time, confessed to having been particularly attached to his cloak: 'I have it (i.e. the old blue cloak that he had worn during his Mediterranean trip) still. I have brought it here to Littlemore, and on some cold nights I have had it on my bed. I have so few things to sympathize with me that I take to cloaks' (*Letters and Correspondence of John Henry Newman*, ed. Anne Mozley, Vol. 1, 9, 429).

37. See Spicq (1964). However, even if we had much more information about the value of cloaks we would not be sure of the value of Paul's one, since so much would depend on the quality, age, colour, fit, etc. For example, according to a petition written in 29 AD the material for a cloak stolen was stated to be worth eighteen silver drachmas (*P. Ryl.* II, 127), while from the following year we have another petition complaining of the robbery of a finished cloak worth no more than four silver drachmas (*P. Ryl.* II, 128).

38. Most of the papyrus letters which mention a cloak do not give the reason for requesting or sending it; presumably both sender and receiver would have no doubt why. Some, however, do give reasons, ranging from the fact that the cloak is a precious possession (e.g. *P. Oxy.* 929; 2149), or that, at the other extreme, the one requesting it is in humble circumstances and

needs it (*P. Oxy.* 2682; *P. Oxy.* 3060 tells of a Ptolemaeus who had to pawn his cloaks, 'so that we may eat'). In other cases the writer of a letter has more pressing requests, and adds that the cloak is to be brought along when the receiver comes (e.g. *P. Tebt.* 421; *P. Cornell Inv.* I, 11).

39. The exhortation to drink wine (1 Tim 5.23) is sometimes taken to be a polemic against asceticism, and 1 Tim 2.15; 3.2; Tit 1.6 are sometimes interpreted as a polemic against sexual asceticism.

40. See Philo, *De Somn.* II, 56.

41. In *Padua Papyrus* 1 Osea wrote to his son, Sheloman, who had gone off on a caravan. The son had requested a tunic and clothing, and at the time of his father's writing the son was about to be released (see Fitzmyer 1979: 220).

42. The most that we would suggest is that there may have been in Paul's and/or Timothy's mind an association between (prophetic) garment and mission, as there was in the case of Elisha (1 Kgs 19.19), and in that of John the Baptist (Mark 1.6). However, Paul's choice of word, φαιλόνης, occurs neither in the LXX nor elsewhere in the NT. For the significance of Elijah's mantle and the clothes of John the Baptist, see, e.g., Hengel 1968, ch. 2, especially p. 36 n. 71.

43. What the books and parchments contained has been the subject of much speculation in the history of exegesis. Spicq summarizes the suggestions of scholars: OT texts; collections of logia etc. of Christ; testimonia; Paul's personal notes; copies of his letters; drafts of his writings; lecture notes; 'my papers', including, e.g., a certificate of Roman citizenship. Spicq himself, quoting Aquinas and Nicholas of Lyra in support, opts for the view that the request reflects Paul's desire to be instructed by, and to teach, the Sacred Scriptures. The fact is, however, that we have no way of knowing for certain what documents Paul required. If it were the Scriptures we must conclude that he had travelled without them, and did not get a copy from such as Onesiphorus, Luke, or a Roman Christian or Jew. An important observation has been made by Skeat. He argues that the μάλιστα in τὰ βιβλία μάλιστα τὰς μεμβράνας introduces a definition, or a particularization, rather than an addition. The meaning, then, is 'bring . . . the books—I mean the parchment notebooks'. He argues his case from the use of μάλιστα in Tit 1.10f. and 1 Tim 4.10, and in four papyri (Skeat 1979). If he is correct, we know that it was the parchment books alone that Paul requested, and not two sets of documents. However, this does not leave us any better informed about the contents of Paul's μεμβράναι.

44. The *toga* was, of course, the formal and official dress of a Roman citizen, and was the only external sign of his status. The garment was cumbersome, and was not popular even in Rome, with several Emperors having to issue decrees to enforce its use on public occasions: Augustus directed the *aediles* never again to allow anyone to appear in the Forum or its neighbourhood except in the *toga* (Suetonius XL,5; see also the criticism of

Christians of a later period not wearing the *toga*: Tertullian *De Pallio* 5). It is not likely that Paul would have used his in the East, and certainly not in Palestine where he would have wanted to emphasize his Jewish character. However, Paul's term for the garment corresponds to the *paenula*, rather than the *toga*. See the discussion in Sherwin-White (1963:149f.).

45. Quintilian devotes the third and final chapter of Book XI to the dress, gestures, and delivery of an orator. He deals at length with the dress of an orator, and gives precise instructions as to how the *toga* is to be worn (XI,iii,137-143), and how one is to vary one's voice, gesture and gait in the presence of emperor, senate, people, magistrates, or in public and private trials (XI,iii,151). Pliny, writing to Cornelius Minicianus of the demotion of Senator Valerius Licinianus, describes how he made his entry clad in a Greek cloak (*cum Graeco pallio amictus*), since those who had been ritually banished were not allowed to wear the *toga* (*Ep.* IV. 11.3).

46. Only legitimate children and Roman citizens were registered. The *professio liberorum* was a declaration before a magistrate, either in Rome, or at the *tabularium publicum* in the provinces, within thirty days of the birth. It consisted of the names of the parents, the sex of the child, the date of birth, the birthplace and domicile of the parents, and a declaration that the child was both legitimate and a Roman citizen. The professions were registered and the register was displayed publicly. Birth certificates were copies from the *album professionum*, certified by (usually seven) witnesses, and written by professional scribes on the familiar diptych (see Schulz 1942). Although the birth certificate offered only *prima facie* evidence of Roman citizenship (it was left to the judge to assess the reliability of the evidence), the value of such a document is obvious. When Paul appealed to his being a Roman citizen (Acts 16.37; 22.25-29; 25.11) he may have been required to produce his birth certificate; both Schulz (pp. 63f.) and Cadbury before him (Lake and Cadbury 1933b: 316) allege that Paul always carried such a document with him, but there is no way of knowing if this was the case.

47. This is the judgment of Sherwin-White (1963: 148f.).

48. Whether or not Skeat is correct in suggesting that μάλιστα means 'that is', rather than 'especially', it is clear from the use of the plural, 'the parchments', that Paul required more than a document proving Roman citizenship. Perhaps other documents helpful for his defence were in the collection (see Jeremias 1968: 58).

49. The *Muratorian Canon* already reflects the distinction between the ecclesial and the personal letters of Paul. The MS P[46] groups the Pauline ecclesial letters, and includes Hebrews, presumably because of its ecclesial character. Quinn suggests that there were also separate codices that contained the letters purporting to be to individuals. He sees in the present order of the Paulines the old seam joining the personal (Pastorals and Philemon) to the nine Pauline ecclesial letters (Quinn 1981: 495).

50. The papyri illustrate the great variety of reasons for writing letters (to

maintain contact, to disclose and/or seek information, and to give instructions and make requests, etc.). In most cases the main reason is obvious. No reader could fail to see the reason for the writing of *P. Oxy.* 3063: the receiver is to cut down the vines—the writer complains of having written 'a thousand times' already, and now issues the instruction, 'cut them down, cut them down, cut them down, cut them down'. On the other hand, *P. Oxy.* 3406 is a mere eleven-line note, but it contains no less than six quite specific instructions. Exler put ancient Greek letters into four categories: familiar, business, petitions/applications, and official letters (1923). More recently White and Kensinger divide them into orders/instructions, letters of request, and letters imparting information (1976: 79). See also Koskenniemi (1956), Doty (1969), and White (1983).

51. It is clear that paraenesis plays an important part in all of Paul's letters. It was one of the major aims of his ministry to bring about an improvement in people's lives, and to help them prepare for the End-Time (e.g., 1 Thess 5.23; Phil 4.4-7; Rom 16.20; Gal 6.15; 2 Cor 13.11). See Malherbe (1983), and the discussion of Paul's 'enabling language' in Sundberg (1986). Fiore devotes a whole chapter to aspects of Paul's manner of exhortation, and draws particular attention to his use of personal example (1986: 164-86).

52. Pseudo-Libanius (300-600 AD) gives the paraenetic letter the first place among over forty types of ancient letter. He defines the paraenetic style to be that which persuades the reader to pursue something, or avoid something. It involves two parts: persuasion and dissuasion. Paraenesis, he insists, does not allow of a counter-statement, as does mere advice (see Malherbe 1977b: 62f., 70f. for the text and translation). Clearly 2 Timothy fits pseudo-Libanius's description of the paraenetic epistolary style (see Quinn 1981: 499). Verner discusses the wider issues of paraenesis in his excursus 'Paraenetic Discourse' (1983: 112-25). Fiore rightly states that 'The Pastoral letters speak the language of exhortation from start to finish' (1986: 14), and his whole form critical study situates them in the genre of epistolary paraenesis. Because his sympathies lie with the pseudepigraphic theories of the authorship of the Pastorals (p. 7) he frees himself from the burden of situating them in a real life context. He regards them as fictional letters, and he appears not to consider it necessary to suggest any more definite time of composition than 'the late first or early second century A.D.' (p. 234), or any place of origin, or any real specification of the addressees. We cannot accept as adequate his very vague 'outlines of a likely historical situation for the letters' (p. 234). While commending Fiore for his examination of the literary genre, and his thorough treatment of the function of personal example in the Pastorals and elsewhere, we do not accept the validity of his painless movement from an analysis of the literary form to what he presumes to regard as a historical reconstruction of the circumstances of composition.

53. Calvin noted that the chief purpose of 2 Timothy was 'to confirm

Timothy both in the faith of the Gospel and in his pure and constant preaching of it' (1548/9: 287). Of 1 Timothy he said, 'In my view this epistle was written more for the sake of others than for Timothy himself' (p. 184), while he concluded that Paul's purpose in writing to Titus was to arm him with his authority to help Titus bear the burden of dissent from those who wanted for reasons of selfish ambition to be raised to the rank of Pastors, etc. (p. 349).

54. One must recognize the function of such a statement in the letter. The context here is the material of 2.1-13. This section is concerned with Paul's appeal to Timothy to be steadfast, to suffer as a soldier of Jesus Christ, to compete according to the rules, like an athlete looking for the crown, and to work hard like the farmer, and to take Jesus Christ, risen from the dead, descended from David, as an example of one who triumphed. In the same section Paul points to his own alignment with the demands of the Gospel, even to the point of wearing fetters like a criminal, and enduring all that came his way. The section reaches a climax in vv. 11-13, in which Paul quotes a hymn, or a creedal statement, which stresses and lauds the life of endurance.

55. Contrast 1 Tim 2.8-15; 6.1-2; Tit 2.1-10; cf. Tit 3.1-8.

56. See our discussion of the Ignatian correspondence in Chapter 3.

57. Supporters of theories of pseudepigraphy for the Pastorals do not take seriously the differences between the letters. The general categorization of the letters as 'fictitious correspondence' is taken as sufficient justification for ignoring the most striking differences of context, and disregarding many of the striking features of the individual letters. In any enquiry into the epistolary character of any letter we consider it essential to respect its individuality, and our study attempts to give due respect to the text of 2 Timothy.

58. Although the paraenetic character of Second Timothy has long been recognized (see, for example, Dibelius and Conzelmann 1966: 7; Schroeder 1976a and 1976b, Donelson 1986, Fiore 1986, and the literature cited), scholars have not taken seriously the extent to which Timothy's fidelity was under threat, at the time of writing. In our view two tendencies within the study of the Pastorals have contributed to that state of affairs, namely, the failure to recognize the integrity and individuality of each of the three letters, and the fascination with the attempt to identify the false teachers implied in the letters. These two tendencies can be seen to operate in two of the most recent comments of the polemic of the Pastorals. Neither Cranford (who holds that the Pastorals are authentically Pauline, 1980: 26, n. 10), nor Karris (who supports the theory of pseudepigraphy, 1973; see our critique of Karris 1979 in Prior 1983) allows for any specificity in the *raison d'être* of each letter. Furthermore, each of them separates the false teaching sections of the letters from their individual epistolary contexts, and they treat the matter as though 'Paul' were dealing with one general enemy (e.g., Sell 1982,

Hoffmann 1984, and Fiore 1986). Moreover, many scholars do not take seriously the likelihood that each of the letters reflects a particular epistolary situation, with the result that the unwary reader is easily drawn into interpreting 2 Timothy in terms of information drawn from the other two. For example, little is ever made of the fact that 1 Timothy purports to be concerned with the situation of Timothy in Ephesus (1.3), and Titus deals with the situation in Crete (1.5), while 2 Timothy does not appear to concern itself with any particular region, but concentrates instead on Paul's concern for Timothy himself. Nor do commentators give sufficient attention to the sequence of the letters, nor to the much more fundamental fact that it is only in 2 Timothy that Paul is in prison.

59. While dealing with many other forms of exhortation (admonitions, prescriptions, lists of qualities, catalogues of vices and virtues, etc.) Fiore's study (1986) pays particular attention to the function of personal example in the Pastorals, and in doing so brings together a great deal of most interesting material. However, the author's assumptions (especially those concerning the pseudonymity of the Pastorals), methodology (chiefly his failure to respect the individuality of each of the three letters), and conclusions (particularly the vagueness of his historical reconstruction) are very different from ours.

60. The example in 1.5 is followed by the directive in vv. 6-8; that in 1.11f., by the directive in 1.13f.; that in 1.15 (bad) and 1.16-18 (good) by the directives in 2.1-3; that of 2.14 by the directives in 2.15f.; 2.20f. by the directives in 2.22-26; 3.2-5 by the directive in 3.5; 3.10-13 by the directives in 3.14–4.5; 4.6-8 by the directives in 4.9, 11, 13, 21; and 4.14 by the directive in 4.15.

61. Paul regards converts to Christianity as a new creation (2 Cor 5.17; cf. *b. Yebam* 22a; and for the Jewish tradition to this day see Daube 1986:40). In the Greek, and particularly in Hellenistic rhetorical and philosophical tradition it was common to describe the teacher/pupil relationship in terms of that of father/son (see Fiore 1986: 34ff., 214 for examples). Paul's sense of spiritual fatherhood was very strong (1 Cor 4.14ff.; 1 Thess 1.6 [cf. 2.7-12]; Gal 4.12 [cf. v. 19]), and gave him the authority to present himself as a model to his spiritual children (see Boer 1962: 214).

62. The appeal to personal example, and especially to the *oikeia paradeigmata (exempla domestica)*, is a feature of the paraenetic tradition (see Fiore 1986: 23 and *passim*).

63. πέπεισμαι δὲ ὅτι καὶ ἐν σοί (1.5). The phrase itself can, of course, be read as indicating Paul's absolute confidence in Timothy, but it seems to us that the overall tone of the letter betrays Paul's fears for Timothy, both with respect to his ability to bear patiently the necessary suffering, and to perform satisfactorily his function as evangelist.

64. The appeal to personal example is a feature of the paraenetic genre: 'non auribus modo, verum etiam oculis'. For the preference for example over

precept see, e.g., Seneca *Ep.* 6.5 ('longum iter est per praecepta, breve et efficax per exempla'), and Pliny's description of example as the surest method of instruction (Letter to Titius Aristo 8.14), together with numerous other examples quoted in Fiore (1986: 33-37). For a discussion of Paul's use of himself as an example see Fiore (1986: 164-83 [on 1 Cor], 184ff. [on 1 Thess 1.6; 2.14; Phil 3.17; 2 Thess 3.7; Eph 5.1; Gal 4.12], and 198-208 [on 1 Tim 1.3-20; 2 Tim 1.3-18; 3.1-4.8]).

65. Note the association of 'not being ashamed' and 'suffering', with respect to both Timothy (v. 8), and Paul (v. 12).

66. The use of antithetical examples is a feature of the paraenetic genre (see Fiore 1986: 69, 72, 137-42, 146-61).

67. The majority of the commentators refer ταῦτα to what precedes it, although Falconer (1937: 84) and Bratcher (1983:81) take it to refer to what follows. We suggest that it is the section vv. 8-13, which focuses on suffering, that Paul has in mind, although many commentators would wish it to be extended to include the Christian message as learned from Paul (2.2) (Spicq 1969, Scott 1936, and Kelly 1963).

68. 'Them' is favoured by the RSV, JB, and the New JB, while Scott (1936) prefers 'men'. 'The people' is the choice of Kelly (1963) and Dibelius–Conzelmann (1966). Karris (1979) takes it to refer to 'church leaders' and Houlden (1976) claims that the understood accusative refers back to 'the elect' of v. 10, while Barrett (1963) observes that the connection between this section and the preceding paragraph is not close.

69. The verb occurs only four times in the LXX. Where it means 'to remind someone' there is the double accusative (Wis 12.2; *4 Macc* 18.14), and in the one instance where the meaning is 'to recall' there is an accusative of thing only (Wis 18.22). Its fourth appearance is as a participial noun (3 Kgdms 4.3).

70. Mayer's Index (1974) instances 29 uses. There is only one imperative, and that in the first singular (*De Vita Mosis* II,139). The meaning, 'to call to mind' is attested in several places (*Leg. Alleg.* III,17; *De Ebr.* 154; *De Con. Ling.* 3; *De Congressu* 41; 42; *De Som.* I,93; *De Leg. Spec.* II,237; III,128). It means 'to remember' in *De Ebr.* 208; *De Ios.* 92; 98; *De Vita Mos.* I,193; *De Leg. Spec.* II,68; *De Vita Contem.* 35. Where the verb means 'to remind' the accusative of person is either clearly stated (as in *De Praem. et Poen.* 119), or, more generally, is clear from the context (*De Plant.* 108; *De Abr.* 229; *De Leg. Spec.* I,264; II,21, 131, 152). The stronger form of reminder, 'to warn', is the meaning in *De Leg. Spec.* I,193. Nowhere is there any doubt about who is being reminded, nor of what someone is being reminded.

71. Josephus uses the verb 20 times. There is no use of the imperative. Several times we meet the participle where the accusative of person is clear in the sentence (*Bell. Jud.* 2,292; *Antiq.* 7,53, 258; 8,304; 13,216; 14,152; 16,57; *Vita* 60; 377). The accusative of person is very explicit in many cases (ὑμᾶς in *Bell. Jud.* 3,472; αὐτήν in *Antiq.* 2,51; αὐτόν in *Antiq.* 6,131; 11,58;

τούς . . . in *Vita* 254; and with the person named in *Vita* 177). Where it is not so explicit the context makes it crystal clear who is the accusative of person (e.g. *Antiq.* 5,3). Where the meaning is 'to remind somebody of something', then, there is no difficulty in recognizing who is being reminded.

72. We are not, of course, dealing here with either one author, one genre, or one period. We have examined eleven uses of the verb in the Oxyrhynchus collection (*P. Oxy.* 125; 1414; 1610, fr. 1; 1870; 1877 twice; 1886; 2152; 2924; 3023; 3350). The meaning is 'to remind', and there is never any doubt about the identity of the one being reminded (ὑμᾶς in 1414; αὐτόν in 1610; 2152; τούς. . . in 2924; 'your aptitude' in 3350; 'his piety' in 1877).

73. In addition to its occurrence in 2 Tim 2.14, the verb is used seven times in the NT, and in four cases we have a double accusative, with the accusative of person explicit (ὑμᾶς in John 14.26; 2 Pet 1.12; Jude 5, and αὐτούς in Tit 3.1). The subject of the verb is clear in the other two cases (Peter in Luke 22.61, and the Elder in 3 John 10).

74. E.g. in addition to the examples above, Xenophon, *Cyr.* III,3, 37; Thucydides VII.64.1; Plato *Phil.* 31, c.

75. E.g. *P. Chr.* I,238, 1; Wis 18.22; Luke 22.61; 2 John 10; Philo, *Leg. Alleg.* III,17; *De Sac. Abel. et Caini* 31; *De Ebr.* 1; *Quis Rerum* 141; *De Congressu* 41f.

76. There is none in Josephus, nor in the LXX, nor in the Oxyrhynchus papyri, and only one, in the first singular, in Philo.

77. Despite much searching we failed to find this reading of 2 Tim 2.14 in any literature prior to our Prior 1985: 263-67. It is, then, with considerable surprise that we see the reading we propose being taken as the natural one in Fiore 1986: 218 ('Timothy is cautioned to avoid . . . '). Fiore does not appear to be aware of the 'unique' character of his interpretation, since he does not discuss an alternative reading nor give arguments justifying his own.

78. Compare Seneca's caution against enquiring into useless knowledge, which he claims renders a person a troublesome, wordy, tactless, and self-satisfied bore (*Ep.* 88.35, 37. See the discussion in Fiore 1986: 199 n. 18).

79. Sellin, who assumes that Paul did not write 2 Timothy, suggests that in the author's period the apocalyptic elements of Paul's theology (e.g. Rom 6.1-4), already modified in the Pauline school (Col 2.11ff.), had gone into the background. He suggests that the Pastor's polemic against the spiritualizing of the resurrection is related to the presence of persecution, and that the author wishes to restore to the concept its apocalyptic character (1983: 234).

80. These have included Christ and his Apostles (cf. Eph 2.19f.), or the truth of the Gospel, or the truth of the Church or of the local church.

81. Spicq notes that the *hapax* νεωτερικός is used with a nuance of violence (1969: 764).

82. The section 2.14-26 begins with the instruction not to engage in word-

wrangling (v. 16), and towards the end we have two more references to wrangling (vv. 23f.).

83. Note the insistence on the qualities of the teacher in Quintilian *Inst.* 2.1-8 (cf. Pliny *Ep.* 8.32.2).

84. Johnson argues that the author's method in 2.14-4.8 is to contrast Timothy's behaviour with that of the false teachers, and he makes the third person plural verbs in 2.16, 18 refer to such teachers (1978: 9).

85. The vice list begins with φίλαυτοι, and ends with φιλήδονοι μᾶλλον ἤ φιλόθεοι. This polarity between φίλαυτος and φιλόθεος is employed also by Philo in his allegorical exegesis of the sacrifice of Cain and Abel: the soul contains within itself the two tendencies of love of God, and love of self; if it does not bring forth the former (Abel) it will bring the latter (Cain) (*De Sac.* 2f.; *Quod Det.* 32; cf. *Quod Det.* 78, and *De Post.* 21). Of those who attribute the responsibility of sinning to the Deity he says that they have made self-love their aim, rather than love of God (*De Fuga* 81). In only one place in his writings does Philo express the tendencies in the soul in terms of the polarity of φιλήδονος and φιλόθεος. He also contrasts the two poles of behaviour, whereby the soul tends in an irrational, unmeasured, and unruly movement to forcibly render the body φιλήδονος and φιλοπαθής rather than φιλάρετος and φιλόθεος (*De Agric.* 87). Only here does Philo express the tendencies in the soul in terms of the polarity of φιλήδονος and φιλόθεος. 2 Tim 3.4 is the only occasion on which Paul also does so. Philo also describes the Essenes as an example of a people who practised a three-fold devotion to God (φιλόθεος), virtue (φιλάρετος) and man (φιλανθρώπος) (*Quod Omnis* 83f.). The list of vices in 2 Tim 3.2f. can be regarded as an expansion of the basic condition of φίλαυτος. Although six of the list do not occur elsewhere in the NT, five are not uncommon in Hellenistic Judaism: φίλαυτος occurs 18 times in Philo, ἄσπονδος 32 times, ἀκρατής 14 times, ἀνήμερος 12 times, and φιλήδονος 23 times; Philo does not use ἀφιλάγαθος (nor ὑπερήφανος which occurs 5 times in the NT, nor ἄστοργος, which occurs in the NT only in 1 Timothy.

86. Philo lists no less than 144 vices to characterize the φιλήδονος, including φίλαυτος, ἀλαζών, ἀπειθής, ἄσπονδος, and διάβολος of the list of 2 Tim 3.2ff. The rather arbitrary character of such a list is suggested by the fact that although φιλήδονος occurs no less than 23 times in Philo it occurs only once more in association with any of the five it has in common with 2 Tim 3.2ff. (*De Som.* II, 210 with ἄσπονδος). Morover, although only three of the 2 Timothy list do not occur in Philo, the terms never appear as a group of vices, with the exception of the six which are included among the 144 in *De Sac.* 32, and the association of ἀνόσιος with φιλόθεος in *De Dec.* 63. Philo, then, although he has multiple lists of vices, gives little support to the suggestion that the list of 2 Tim 3.2ff. is borrowed from a conventional list of vices. Note, however, that while the list of 29 terms in Rom 1.18-32 includes only three which occur also in 2 Timothy 3 (ὑπερήφανος, ἀλαζών, γονεῦσιν

ἀπειθής) these three appear in almost the same order in the two. Various attempts have been made to find a rationale for the order of the terms in 2 Tim 3.2ff. Perhaps assonance was a factor in the composition of the vice list of 2 Tim 3.2ff.: φίλαυτοι and φιλάργυροι at the beginning, and φιλήδονοι and φιλόθεοι at the end, and the list of seven terms beginning with ἀ-, separated only by διάβολοι and then followed by two terms beginning with προ- (cf. the assonance in Philo *De Sac.* 15; 22; 32).

87. The movement from the last days, to the future, to the present is indeed confusing. Part of the difficulty is solved if one relates 3.1 to the preceding verses, rather than to what follows. The immediately preceding verses are concerned with the repentance which will follow Timothy's ministry, if only he behaves gently. Invoking the stressful times which will attend the last days would serve as a further spur to Timothy to deal kindly with those who err. Furthermore, one notes the succession of the adversative δέ which occurs in 2.22 (twice), 23, 24 and 3.1, suggesting a link stretching from 2.20 to 3.1. If one insists on linking 3.1 with what follows it is difficult to understand the present imperative of v. 5, unless one understands the last days to have come already.

88. In encouraging Timothy to bear with suffering Paul is determined to emphasize that suffering will be rewarded (cf. 2.4-13; 4.8, 16-18). Suffering, therefore, is of temporary duration, and brings the Lord's deliverance.

89. 'It is inconceivable that the apostle should so often have urged him (Timothy) to take a bold stand, if he had evidently possessed a dauntless courage; nor would he so often have warned him against the claims of a false knowledge, if he had not been over-inclined to listen to them; nor would he have bidden him to see to it that no man despised his youth, if it had been a needless injunction' (Medley 1895: 233). Medley speculates that Timothy may have been the angel of the church in Ephesus who has left his first love (Revelation 2) (pp. 233f.).

BIBLIOGRAPHY

I. Ancient Authors Cited

Apostolic Constitutions. In F.X. Funk, *Didascalia et Constitutiones Apostolorum*. 2 Vols. Paderborn, 1905.

Appian (*Appianus Historicus*). *Appian's Roman History*. Text, and English translation by H.E. White (Loeb, 4 Vols.: 2-5) (*Bell. Civ.* = Bella Civilia in Vol 3 & 4), 1912-13.

Chrysostom, John. *Homiliae in 1 Tim, 2 Tim, et Tit*. Migne *PG* 62:501-700.

Cicero, M. Tullius. (*Ad Att.* = *Epistulae ad Atticum*). *Letters to Atticus*. Text, and English translation by E.O. Winstedt (Loeb, 3 Vols.: 7, 8, 97), 1912-18.

—(*Ad Fam.* = *Epistulae ad Familiares*). *Letters to his Friends*. Text, and English translation by W.G. Williams (Loeb, Vols. 1 and 2: 205, 216, 1927-9), and W.G. Williams and M. Cary (Vol. 3: 230, 1929), and Vol. 4, 1954.

—*De Off.* = *De Officiis*. Text, and English translation by W. Miller (Loeb 30), 1913.

—'De Domo Sua'. In *The Speeches*. Text and English translation by N.H. Watts (Loeb, Cicero, Vol. XI), 1923.

Clement of Alexandria. *Strom.* = *Stromata 1-6*, ed. O. Stählin and L. Fruchtel (Die griechischen christlichen Schriftsteller 52/15). Berlin, 1960.

Clement of Rome. See Lightfoot 1890, below.

Cyril of Jerusalem, Saint. *Catech.* (1-18) = *Catecheses Illuminandorum. Catecheses. Lectures on the Christian Sacraments: the Protocatechesis and the Five Mystagogical Catecheses* (Greek and English text), ed. F.L. Cross. London, 1951.

Dio Cassius. *Dio's Roman History*. Text, and English translation by E. Cary (Loeb, 9 Vols.: 32, 37, 53, 66, 82, 83, 175-7), 1914-27.

Dio Chrysostom. *Discourses*. Text, and English translation by J. Cohoon and H.L. Crosby (Loeb, 5 Vols.: 257, 339, 358, 376, 385), 1932-51.

Epictetus. *Discourses*. Text, and English translation by W.A. Oldfather (Loeb, 2 Vols.: 131, 218), 1926.

Eusebius. *Hist. Eccles.* = *Historia Ecclesiastica*. Text, and English translation by Kirsopp Lake and J.E.L. Oulton (Loeb, 2 Vols.: 153, 265), 1926-32.

Fragmentum Muratorianum. In T. Zahn, *Geschichte des neutestamentlichen Kanons*, 1890/92. Vol. 2: 1-143 (with commentary). Erlangen/Leipzig. English translation in Hennecke 1959, 42-45, and B.M. Metzger, *The Canon of the New Testament, Its Origin, Development, and Significance*. Oxford, 1987: 305ff.

Herodotus, *History*. Text, and English translation by A.D. Godley (Loeb, 4 Vols.: 117-120) 1920-25.

Homer *Il.* = *Iliad*. Text, and English translation by A.T. Murray (Loeb, 2 Vols.: 170-71), 1924-5.

—*Od.* = *Odyssey*. Text, and English translation by A.T. Murray (Loeb, 2 Vols.: 104-105), 1919.

Ignatius of Antioch, Saint. See Lightfoot 1885 below.

Jerome, Saint. *In Epistolam ad Titum*. In *Opera Exegetica*, cura et studio M. Adriaen (& F. Gloriae) (Corpus Scriptorum Ecclesiasticorum Latinorum, 9 Vols.). Vienna, 1959-70.

Josephus. Text, and English translation by H.St.J. Thackeray (Vols. 1, *Vita*, 186; Vols. 2-3: *Bell. Jud.* = *Bellum Judaicum*, 203, 210; Vol. 4: *Antiq.* = *Antiquitates* 242), H.St.J. Thackeray and R. Marcus (Vol. 5.281, *Antiq.*), R. Marcus (Vol. 6-7: 326, 365, *Antiq.*), R. Marcus and A. Wikgren (Vol. 8.410, *Antiq.*) and L.H. Feldman (Vol. 9: 433, *Antiq.*) (Loeb, 9 Vols.), 1925-65.

Justin Martyr, Saint. *Dial.* = *Dialogus cum Tryphone*. In *An Early Christian Philosopher: Justin Martyr's 'Dialogue with Trypho'*, *Chapters 1-9*. Introduction, text and commentary, ed. J.C.M. van Winden. Leiden, 1971.

Juvenal. *Sat.* = *Satires*. In *Juvenal and Persius*. Text, and English translation by G.G. Ramsay (Loeb, Vol. 91), 1918.

Lactantius, Lucius. *De mort. persec.* = *De Mortibus Persecutorum*. In *De la mort des persécuteurs*. Introduction, texte critique et traduction, et commentaire de J. Moreau. (Sources Chrétiennes, 39). Paris, 1954.

Philo. Text, and English translation of Vols. 1-5 (226-27, 247, 261, 275) by F.H. Colson and G.H. Whitaker, and of Vols. 6-10 (289, 320, 341, 363, 379) by F.H. Colson (Loeb, 10 Vols.). Two supplementary Vols. (380, 401), with translation from an Armenian text by J.W. Earp. 1929-51.

Pliny the Elder. *Hist. Nat.* = *Historia Naturalis*. *Natural History*. Text, and English translation by H. Rackham, etc. (Loeb, 10 Vols.: 330, 352-53, 370-71, 392-93, 418, 394, 419; index Vol.: 435), 1938-1963.

Pliny the Younger. *Letters*. Text, and English translation by W. Melmoth, rev. W.M.L. Hutchinson (Loeb, 2 Vols.: 55, 59), 1915.

Plato. *Phil.* = *Philebus*. In *The Statesman*. *Philebus*. Text, and English translation by H.N. Fowler (Loeb 164), 1925.

Plutarch. *Plutarch's Moralia*. In 15 Vols., with text, and an English translation by F.C. Babbitt, *et al.* 'Consolatio ad Apollonium' (Vol. 2, Loeb 222), 'De Alexandri Magni Fortuna aut Virtute' (Vol. 4, Loeb 305), 1927. *Plutarch's Lives*. In 10 Vols, with text, and English translation by B. Perrin. 'Romulus' (Vol. 1, Loeb 46), 1914-26.

Polybius. *The Histories*. Text, and English translation by W.R. Paton (Loeb, 6 Vols.: 128, 137-38, 159-61), 1922-27.

Quintilian. *Institutio Oratoria*. Text, and English translation by H.E. Butler (Loeb, 4 Vols.: 124-27), 1920-22.

Seneca. *Ad Luc.* = *Ad Lucilium Epistulae Morales*. Text, and English translation by R.M. Gummere (Loeb, 3 Vols.: 75-7), 1917-25.

Sophocles. *Sophocles*. Text, and English translation by F. Storr (*Loeb*, 2 Vols.: 20-21). *Oed. Col.* = *Oedipus Coloneus* (Vol. 1); *Electra* (Vol. 2), 1912.

Strabo. *Geog.* = *The Geography of Strabo*. Text, and English translation by H.L. Jones (Loeb, 8 Vols.: 49, 50, 182, 196, 211, 223, 241, 267), 1916-32.

Suetonius. *De Vita Caes.* = *De Vita Caesarum*. *The Lives of the Caesars*. Text, and English translation by J.C. Rolfe (Loeb, 2 Vols.: 31, 38), 1914.

Tacitus, *Dialogues*, etc. Text, and English translation by W. Peterson (Loeb 35). *The Histories*. Text, and English translation by C.H. Moore (Loeb 111, 249). *Ann.* = *The Annals*. Text, and English translation by J. Jackson (Loeb: 249, 312, 322), 1931-37.

Tertullian. *Adv. Marc.* = *Adversus Marcionem*, ed. E. Evans. 2 Vols. (Oxford Early Christian Texts). Oxford, 1972.

—*De prescriptione haereticorum*, ed. E. Kroymann (Corpus Scriptorum Ecclesiasticorum Latinorum, 47). Vienna 1906. *De Bap.* = *De Baptismo*, ed. A. Reifferscheid (Corpus Scriptorum Ecclesiasticorum Latinorum, 20). *De pallio* (Corpus Scriptorum Ecclesiasticorum Latinorum, 76). Vienna.

Thucydides. *History of the Peloponnesian War.* Text, and English translation by C.F. Smith (Loeb, 4 Vols.: 108-10, 169), 1921-30.

The Nag Hammadi Library in English, ed. J.M. Robinson, M.W. Meyer, *et al.* Leiden 1977.

Xenophon. *Cyr.* = *Cyropaedia.* Text, and English translation by W. Miller (Loeb 51-52), 1914.

II. *Papyri Cited*

B.G.U. = *Berliner griechische Urkunden* (Ägyptische Urkunden aus den Königlichen Museen zu Berlin). Berlin, 1895.

P. Amh. = *Amherst Papyri*, ed. B.P. Grenfell and A.S. Hunt. 2 Vols. London, 1900-1901.

P. Cair. zen. = *Zenon Papyri*, 4 Vols., ed. C.C. Edgar. Catalogue gen. des Antiq. Egypt. du Musée du Caire, 79, 1925-31.

P. Chr. = *Grundzüge und Chrestomathie der Papyruskunde*, ed. L. Mitteis (and U. Wilcken). Leipzig and Berlin, 1912.

P. Cornell = *Greek Papyri in the Library of Cornell University*, ed. W.L. Westermann and C.J. Kraemer. New York, 1926. *P. Cornell Inv.* I, 11, ed. H.C. Youtie, in *Zeitschrift für Papyrologie und Epigraphik* 22 (1976) 53-56.

P. Fayum = *Fayum Towns and their Papyri*, B.P. Grenfell, A.S. Hunt and D.G. Hogarth. London, 1900.

P. Flor. = *Papiri Fiorentini documenti pubblici e privati dell'età romana e bizantina*: I, ed. G. Vitelli, Milan 1906; II, ed. D. Comparetti, 1908-11; III, ed. G. Vitelli, 1915.

P. Fouad = *Les papyrus Fouad* I, nos. 1-89. Publications de la Société Fouad I de Papyrologie. Textes et Documents III, ed. A. Bataille, *et al.* Cairo, 1939.

P. Gen. = *Les Papyrus de Genève*, transcrits et publiés par Jules Nicole. Geneva, 1896, 1900.

P. Giess. = *Griechische Papyri im Museum des oberhessischen Geschichtsvereins zu Giessen*, I/1-3, ed. O. Eger, E. Kornemann and P.M. Meyer. Leipzig, etc. 1910-12.

P. Haun. = *Papyri Graecae Haunienses. Fasciculus Secundus (P. Haun. II, 13-44). Letters and Mummy Labels from Roman Egypt.* (Papyrologische Texte und Abhandlungen, 29), ed. by Adam Bülow-Jacobsen. Bonn, 1981.

P. Hibeh = *Hibeh Papyri*, part I, ed. B.P. Grenfell and A.S. Hunt. London, 1906.

P. Köln = *Kölner Papyri (P. Köln)*, Band 2, bearbeitet von Barbel Kramer und Dieter Hagedorn (Papyrologica Coloniensia, Vol. (VI) I. Openladen, 1978.

P. Lond. = *Greek Papyri in the British Museum*, Vols. 1 & 2 ed. F.G. Kenyon, Vol. 3 ed. F.G. Kenyon and H.I. Bell; Vol. 4 and 5 ed. H.I. Bell. London, 1893.

P. Lond. ined. = 'Unpublished' *P. Lond.* Nr. 1561 is published in B. Olsson, *Papyrusbriefe aus der frühesten Römerzeit*, no. 80. Uppsala, 1925.

P. Madg. = *Papyrus de Magdola*, rééd … par Jean Lesquier. Paris, 1912.

P. Mich. Inv. 241, er. H.C. Youtie, in *Zeitschrift für Papyrologie und Epigraphik* 22 (1976), 49-52.

P. Oxy. = *Oxyrhynchus Papyri*, ed. B.P. Grenfell and A.S. Hunt, *et al.* London, 1898.

P. Petr. = *The Flinders Petrie papyri.* part 1, ed. J.P. Mahaffy (Royal Irish Academy, Cunningham Memoirs, no. 8); part 2, ed. J.P. Mahaffy (*ibid.*, no. 9); part 3, ed. J.P. Mahaffy and J.G. Smyly (*ibid.*, no. 11). Dublin, 1891-1905.

P. Princ. = *Papyri in the Princeton University Collections.* Vol. 3, ed. A.C. Johnson, and S.P. Goodrich. Princeton University Press 1942.

P.Ross.-Georg. = *Papyri Russischer und Georgischer Sammlungen*, herausgegeben von Gregor Zereteli, bearbeitet von G. Zereteli, O. Krüger, and P. Jernstedt. Tiflis, 1925-35.

P. Ryl. = *Catalogue of the Greek Papyri in the John Rylands Library at Manchester*, Vol. 1, 1911, ed. A.S. Hunt; Vol. 2, 1915, ed. A.S. Hunt, J. de M. Johnson and V. Martin; Vol. 3, 1938, ed. C.H. Roberts.

P. Tebt. = *Tebtunis Papyri*, ed B.P. Grenfell, A.S. Hunt, J.G. Smyly and E.J. Goodspeed. London and New York. Vol. 1, 1902; Vol. 2, 1907; Vol. 3, part 1, 1933, part 2 (ed. A.S. Hunt, J.G. Smyly, C.C. Edgar; London and Univ. of California Press) 1938.

P. Thead. = *Papyrus de Théadelphie*, ed. par Pierre Jouguet. Paris, 1911.

P. Ups. Frid = *Ten Uppsala Papyri*, ed. with trans. and notes by Bo Frid. Bonn, 1981.

P. Yale = *Yale Papyri in the Beinecke Rare Book and Manuscript Library*, I. (American Studies in Papyrology, Vol. 2), ed. J.F. Oates, A.E. Samuel and C. Bradford Welles. New Haven-Toronto, 1967. (The papyri are known also by the designation *P. Yale Inv.*, and some of them were published earlier: details in this Vol.)

P. Zen. Col. = *Zenon Papyri: business papers of the 3rd century B.C.*, ed. W.L. Westermann and E.S. Hasenoehrl. New York, Vol. 1 (*Columbia papyri, Greek Series*, Vol. 3), 1934.

III. *Secondary Literature*

Achtemeier, P.J.
1986   'An Elusive Unity: Paul, Acts and the Early Church', *CBQ* 48:1-26.
Aland, K.
1961   'The Problem of Anonymity and Pseudonymity in Christian Literature of the First Two Centuries', *JTS* n.s. 12:39-49.
Albertz, M.
1952   *Die Botschaft des Neuen Testaments*, Zollikon-Zürich.
Alexander, P.S.
1984   'Epistolary Literature', in Stone 1984, pp. 579-96.
Althaus, H.
1949   *Der Brief an die Römer*, Das Neue Testament Deutsch, 6; Göttingen.
Amir, Y.
1970   'The Messianic Idea in Hellenistic Judaism', *Immanuel* 2:58-60. This is a summary of the original Hebrew article in *Machanayim* 124 (1970): 54-67.
Aus, R.D.
1979   'Paul's Travel Plans to Spain and the "Full Number of the Gentiles" of Rom. XI, 25', *NovT* 29: 232-62.
Bachmann, H. and W.A. Slaby, eds.
1980   *Computer-Konkordanz zum Novum Testamentum Graece: von Nestle-Aland, 26. Auflage und zum Greek New Testament, 3rd edition*, Berlin/New York.
Badcock, F.J.
1937   *The Pauline Epistles and the Epistle to the Hebrews in their Historical Setting*, London.

Bahr, G.J.
1966   'Paul and Letter Writing in the Fifth [for First] Century', *CBQ* 28: 465-77.
1968   'The Subscriptions in the Pauline Letters', *JBL* 87: 27-41.
Bailly, A.
1950   *Dictionnaire grec français* (rev. by L. Sechan and P. Chantraine), Paris.
Barnard, L.W.
1963   'The Background of St. Ignatius of Antioch', *VC* 7: 193-206.
Barrett, C.K.
1957   *A Commentary on the Epistle to the Romans*, Black's New Testament Commentary; London.
1963   *The Pastoral Epistles*, The New Clarendon Bible; Oxford.
1971   *The First Epistle to the Corinthians*, Black's New Testament Commentary, 2nd edn; London.
1974   'Pauline controversies in the Post-Pauline Period', *NTS* 20: 229-45.
1977   'Paul's Address to the Ephesian Elders', In *God's Christ and his People. Studies in Honour of N.A. Dahl*, ed. J. Jervell and W.E. Meeks; Oslo/Bergen/Tromsoe.
Barton, J.M.
1959   'Bonum certamen certavi . . fidem servavi', *Bib* 40: 878-84.
Bauer, W.
1958   (also 1971, 5th edn) *Griechisch-deutsches Wörterbuch zu den Schriften des Neuen Testaments und der übrigen urchristlichen Literatur*, Berlin.
Bauer, W., F.W. Gingrich and F.W. Danker
1979   *A Greek-English Lexicon of the New Testament and Other Christian Literature* (2nd edn), Chicago/London.
Baur, F.C.
1835   *Die sogenannten Pastoralbriefe des Apostels Paulus aufs neue kritisch untersucht*, Stuttgart/Tübingen.
1838   'Über den Ursprung des Episcopats in der christlichen Kirche. Prüfung der neuesten von Hrn. Dr. Rothe hierüber aufgestellten Ansicht', *Tübinger Zeitschrift für Theologie* 11, 3: 1-185.
1845   *Paulus, der Apostel Jesu Christi*, Stuttgart.
1851   'Die Einleitung in das Neue Testament als theologische Wissenschaft', *Theologische Jahrbücher*, ed. F.C. Baur and E. Zeller, 10: 294-96.
Beare, F.W.
1973   *The Epistle to the Philippians*, Black's New Testament Commentaries; 3rd edn, London.
Beker, J.C.
1980   *Paul the Apostle, The Triumph of God in Life and Thought*, Edinburgh.
1986   'The Faithfulness of God and the Priority of Israel in Paul's Letter to the Romans', in *Christians among Jews and Gentiles: Essays in Honor of Krister Stendahl on His Sixty-fifth Birthday*, ed. G.W.E. Nickelsburg with G.W. MacRae, S.J.; *HTR* 79: 10-16.
Benko, S.
1985   *Pagan Rome and the Early Christians*, London.

Bertram, G.
1932 'ἔθνος' in Kittel/Friedrich 1933-73, *TDNT* II: 364-69.
Best, E.
1967 *The Letter to the Romans*, Cambridge Biblical Commentary on the New English Bible; Cambridge.
1972 *A Commentary on the First and Second Epistles to the Thessalonians*, Harper's New Testament Commentaries; New York.
Bietenhard, H.
1976 'Ethnos', in *The New International Dictionary of New Testament Theology*, ed C. Brown; Exeter; Vol. II, pp. 790-95.
Blaiklock, E.M.
1970 'The Acts of the Apostles as a Document of First Century History', in *Apostolic History and the Gospel. Biblical and Historical Essays Presented to F.F. Bruce on his 60th Birthday*, ed. W.W. Gasque and R.P. Martin; Exeter, pp. 41-54.
Boer, Willis Peter de
1962 *The Imitation of Paul. An Exegetical Study*, Kampen.
Bornkamm, G.
1971 'Der Römerbrief als Testament des Paulus', in *Geschichte und Glaube, II*. The references are to the translation in Donfried, ed. 1977.
Bouwman, G.
1965 *De Brief van Paulus aan de Filippiërs*, Het Nieuwe Testament; Uitgevers.
Bowers, W.P.
1975 'Jewish Communities in Spain in the Time of Paul the Apostle', *JTS* n.s. 26: 395-402.
Bratcher, R.G.
1983 *A Translator's Guide to Paul's Letters to Timothy and to Titus*, London/New York/Stuttgart.
Brown, R.E. and J.P. Meier,
1983 *Antioch and Rome. New Testament Cradles of Catholic Christianity*, London.
Brox, N.
1969a *Die Pastoralbriefe*, Regensburger Neues Testament 7.2, 4th edn, Regensburg.
1969b 'Zu den persönlichen Notizen der Pastoralbriefe', *BZ* 13:76-79.
1973 'Zum Problemstand in der Erforschung der altchristlichen Pseudepigraphie', *Kairos* 15: 10-23.
Brox, N., ed.
1977 *Pseudepigraphie in der heidnischen und jüdisch-christlichen Antike* (Wege der Forschung 484), Darmstadt.
Bruce, F.F.
1952 *The Acts of the Apostles*, 2nd edn, London.
1977a *Commentary on the Book of Acts*, The New International Commentary on the New Testament; Grand Rapids.
1977b 'The History of New Testament Study', *in New Testament Interpretation. Essays in Principles and Methods*, ed. I.H. Marshall; Exeter, pp. 21-59.
1982a *1 & 2 Thessalonians*, The Word Biblical Commentary, 45; Waco.
1982b 'The Acts of the Apostles Today', *BJRL* 65: 36-56.

1984 *The Epistles to the Colossians, to Philemon, and to the Ephesians*, The New International Commentary on the New Testament; Grand Rapids.

Büchsel, F.
1964 'ἀναλύω, ἀνάλυσις', in Kittel/Friedrich 1933-73, *TDNT* IV: 337.

Bultmann, R.
1949 *Das Urchristentum im Rahmen der antiken Religionen*, Zürich. The references are to the translation by R.H. Fuller, *Primitive Christianity in its Contemporary Setting*, London/New York, 1956.

Burgess, T.C.
1902 'Epideictic Literature', *Studies in Classical Philology* 3: 110-13.

Burton, E. de Witt
1976 *Syntax of the Moods and Tenses in New Testament Greek*, Grand Rapids.

Cadbury, H.J.
1926 'Lexical Notes on Luke-Acts III: Luke's Interest in Lodging', *JBL* 45: 305-22.
1958 *The Making of Luke-Acts*, a very slightly revised edition of the 1927 first edition. London.
1958/59 'The Dilemma of Ephesians', *NTS* 5: 91-102.

Calvin, J.
1548/9 *Commentarii in utramque epistolam ad Timotheum*. Geneva, 1548. *Commentaire sur l'Épître de S. Paul à Tite*, Geneva, 1549. References are to the translation by T.A. Smail, *The Second Epistle of Paul the Apostle to the Corinthians and the Epistles to Timothy, Titus and Philemon*, Edinburgh/London, 1964.

Calvino, R.
1980 'Cristiani a Puteoli nell' anno 61. Riflessioni sull' importanza della notizia concisa degli 'Atti' (28, 13b-14a) e riposta all' interrogativo sulle testimonianze monumentali coeve', *Rivista di Archeologia Cristiana* 56: 323-30.

Campenhausen, H. von
1963 'Polykarp von Smyrna und die Pastoralbriefe', in *Aus der Frühzeit des Christentums. Studien zur Kirchengeschichte des ersten und zweiten Jahrhunderts*, Tübingen, pp. 197-252.
1968 *Die Entstehung der christlichen Bibel*, Beiträge zur historischen Theologie 39; Tübingen. References are to the translation by J.A. Baker, *The Formation of the Christian Bible*, London, 1972.

Casey, R.G., and G. Nagy
1971 'Advances in Pattern Recognition', *Scientific American* 224: 56-71.

Casson, L.
1971 *Ships and Seamanship in the Ancient World*, Princeton.
1974 *Travel in the Ancient World*, London.

Cerfaux, L.
1947 *Une lecture de l'Épître aux Romains*, Tournai/Paris.

Chadwick, H.
1954/5 'All Things to All Men' (1 Cor 9.22)', *NTS* 1: 261-75.

Charlesworth, J.H.
1979 'A History of Pseudepigrapha Research: The Re-emerging Importance of the Pseudepigrapha', in *Aufstieg und Niedergang der römischen*

Welt, II, ed. H. Temporini and W. Haase, Berlin/New York, pp. 54-88.

Charlesworth, J.H., ed.
1983-85 *The Old Testament Pseudepigrapha. Volume 1: Apocalyptic Literature and Testaments. Volume 2: Expansions of the 'Old Testament' and Legends, Wisdom and Philosophical Literature, Prayers, Psalms and Odes, Fragments of Lost Judeo-hellenistic Works*, London.

Clark, A.C.
1933 *The Acts of the Apostles*, Oxford.

Collange, J.-F.
1973 *L'Épître de Saint Paul aux Philippiens*, Commentaire du Nouveau Testament; Neuchâtel-Paris. References are to the translation by A.W. Heathcote, *The Epistle of Saint Paul to the Philippians*, London, 1979.

Conzelmann, H.
1963 *Die Apostelgeschichte*, Handbuch zum Neuen Testament, 7 (2nd edn, 1972), Tübingen.

Cook, D.
1982 '2 Timothy 4.6-8 and the Epistle to the Philippians', *JTS* n.s. 33: 168-71.
1984 'The Pastoral Fragments Reconsidered', *JTS* n.s. 35: 120-31.

Corriveau, R.
1970 *The Liturgy of Life. A Study of the Ethical Thought of St. Paul in his Letters to the Early Christian Communities*, Brussels/Paris.

Cortès, E.
1976 *Los Discursos de Adiós de Gn 49 a Jn 13-17. Pistas para la historia de un género literario en la antigua literatura judía*, Barcelona.

Corwin, V.
1960 *St. Ignatius and Christianity in Antioch*, New Haven/London.

Cranfield, C.E.B.
1980 *The Epistle of Paul to the Romans*, The International Critical Commentary; Edinburgh.
1982 'Changes in Person and Number in Paul's Epistles', in *Paul and Paulinism*, ed. M.D. Hooker and S.G. Wilson; London, pp. 280-89.

Cranford, L.
1980 'Encountering Heresy: Insight from the Pastoral Epistles', *Southwestern Journal of Theology* 22: 23-40.

Cullmann, O.
1930 'Les causes de la mort de Pierre et de Paul d'après le témoignage de Clement Romain', *RHPR* 10: 294-300.
1936 'Le caractère eschatologique du devoir missionaire et de la conscience apostolique de S. Paul sur le κατέχον(-ων) de II Thess. 2.6-7', *RHPR* 16: 210-45.
1962 *Peter: Disciple, Apostle, Martyr*, 2nd edn, London.

Dahl, N.A.
1962 'The Particularity of the Pauline Epistles as a Problem in the Ancient Church', in *Neotestamentica et Patristica: Eine Freundesgabe, Herrn Professor Dr. Oscar Cullmann zu seinem 60. Geburtstage überreicht*, NovT Supp. 6; Leiden pp. 261-71.
1977 'The Missionary Theology in the Epistle to the Romans', in his *Studies in Paul*, Minneapolis, pp. 70-94.

Dalton, W.J.
1979   'The Integrity of Philippians', *Biblica* 60: 97-102.
Daube, D.
1986   'Onesimus', in *Christians among Jews and Gentiles: Essays in Honor of Krister Stendahl on his Sixty-fifth Birthday*, ed. G.W.E. Nickelsburg with G.W. MacRae, S.J.; *HTR* 79: 40-43.
Davies, W.D.
1955/6   Review of J. Munck, *Paulus und die Heilsgeschichte* (Munck 1954), in *NTS* 2: 60-72.
Deissmann, A.
1903   'Prolegomena to the Biblical Letters and Epistles', in *Bible Studies. Contributions chiefly from Papyri and Inscriptions to the History of the Language and Literature, and the Religion of Hellenistic Judaism and Primitive Christianity*, Edinburgh, pp. 3-59. This is the authorized translation by A. Grieve, incorporating recent changes and additions to *Bibelstudien. Beiträge, zumeist aus den Papyri und Religion des hellenistischen Judentums und des Urchristentums*, Marburg, 1895.
1907   *New Light on the New Testament. From Records of the Graeco-Roman Period*, revised from *ExpTim* 18 (1906/7), and translated from the author's MS by L.R.M. Strachan; Edinburgh.
1908   *Licht vom Osten*, Tübingen. References to the translation by L.R.M. Strachan, *Light from the Ancient East. The New Testament Illustrated by recently discovered Texts of the Graeco-Roman World*, London, 1912.
1923   'Zur ephesinischen Gefangenschaft des Apostels Paulus', in *Anatolian Studies: Presented to Sir W.M. Ramsay*, ed. W.H. Buckler and W.M. Calder; Manchester, pp. 121-27.
1929   *The New Testament in the Light of Modern Research*, The Haskell Lectures 1929; London.
Delling, G.
1973   'Das letzte Wort der Apostelgeschichte', *NovTest* 15: 193-204.
Denis, A.-M.
1957   'Versé en Libation (Phil 2.17) = Versé son Sang? A propos d'une référence de W. Bauer', *RSR* 45: 567-70.
1958   'La Fonction apostolique et la liturgie nouvelle en esprit. Étude thématique des métaphores pauliniennes du culte nouveau', *RSPT* 42: 401-36, 617-56.
Dibelius, M.
1961   *Aufsätze zur Apostelgeschichte*, Forschungen zu Religion und Literatur des Alten und Neuen Testaments n.F. 42; ed. H. Greeven; 4th edn; Göttingen. The collected essays were first published between 1932 and 1947.
Dibelius, M. and H. Conzelmann
1966   *Die Pastoralbriefe*, Handbuch zum Neuen Testament, 13; 4th edn; Tübingen. The references are to the translation by B. Buttolph, and A. Yarbro, *The Pastoral Epistles*, Hermeneia; Philadelphia, 1972.
Dodd, C.H.
1932   *The Epistle of Paul to the Romans*, The Moffatt New Testament Commentary; London.
1934   'The Mind of Paul: II', *BJRL*. References are to the corrected reprint

in his *New Testament Studies*, Manchester, 1967, pp. 83-128.

1947 'The Fall of Jerusalem and the "Abomination of Desolation"', *Journal of Roman Studies* 37: 47-54; reprinted in *More New Testament Studies*, Manchester, 1968, pp. 69-83, to which reference is made here.

Donelson, L.R.
1986 *Pseudepigraphy and Ethical Argument in the Pastoral Epistles*, Tübingen.

Donfried, K.P.
1977 'False Presuppositions in the Study of Romans', in Donfried, ed. 1977, pp. 120-48.

Donfried, K.P., ed.
1977 *The Romans Debate*, Minneapolis.

Dornier, P.
1972 'Paul au soir de sa vie', *Assemblées du Seigneur* 60-65.

Doty, W.G.
1969 'The Classification of Epistolary Literature', *CBQ* 31: 183-99.
1973 *Letters in Primitive Christianity*, Guides to Biblical Scholarship: New Testament Series; Philadelphia.

Downey, G.
1961 *A History of Antioch in Syria from Seleucus to the Arab Conquest*, Princeton.
1963 *Ancient Antioch*, Princeton.

Drake, B.
1972 'Unanswered Questions in Computerized Literary Analysis', *JBL* 91: 241f.

Drane, J.W.
1980 'Why did Paul Write Romans?', in *Pauline Studies. Essays Presented to F.F. Bruce*, ed D.A. Hagner and M.J. Harris, pp. 208-27.

Drury, J.
1976 *Tradition and Design in Luke's Gospel. A Study in Early Christian Historiography*, London.

Duncan, G.S.
1929 *St Paul's Ephesian Ministry*, London.
1956/7 'Paul's Ministry in Asia—The Last Phase', *NTS* 3: 211-18.

Dupont, J.
1949 *Gnosis. La Connaisssance religieuse dans Les Épîtres de Saint Paul*, Louvain/Paris.
1952 σὺν Χριστῷ. L'Union avec le Christ suivant Saint Paul, première partie, 'Avec le Christ' dans la Vie Future, Bruges.
1962 *Le Discours de Milet. Testament pastoral de Saint Paul (Actes 20.18-36)*, Lectio Divina 32; Paris.
1964 *The Sources of Acts. The Present Position*, London. The translation by Kathleen Pond has been made from a revised text of *Les Sources du livre des Actes. État de la question*, Bruges, 1960, and 'must be considered as a new edition' (p. 6).
1967 *Études sur les Actes des Apôtres*, Paris.

Easton, B.S.
1948 *The Pastoral Epistles*, London.

Eden, G.R., and F.C. MacDonald
1932 *Lightfoot of Durham*, London.

Ehrhardt, A.
1958 'The Construction and Purpose of the Acts of the Apostles', *ST* 12: 48-79.
1969 *The Acts of the Apostles: Ten Lectures*, Manchester.

Eichhorn, J.G.
1814 *Einleitung in das Neue Testament*, Vol. 3; Leipzig.

Ellis, E. Earle
1960 'The Authorship of the Pastorals: A Résumé and Assessment of Current Trends', *EvQ* 32: 151-61.
1970/1 'Paul and his Co-Workers', *NTS* 17: 435-52. The article is reprinted without the chart of p. 438, in the author's *Prophecy and Hermeneutic*, WUNT 18; Tübingen, 1978, pp. 3-22, to which the references are made.

Enslin, M.S.
1979 'Once More, the Messiah', in *Essays on the Occasion of the Seventieth Anniversary of the Dropsie University. 1909-1979*, ed. A.I. Katsh and L. Nemoy; Philadelphia, pp. 49-61.

Ernst, J.
1974 *Die Briefe an die Philipper, an Philemon, and die Kolosser, an die Epheser*, Regensburger Neues Testament, 6; Regensburg.

Estius, G.
1843 *In Omnes B. Pauli epistolas, item in catholicas commentari*, Moguntiae.

Exler, F.X.J.
1923 *The Form of the Ancient Greek Letter. A Study in Greek Epistolography* (Dissertation: Washington) Chicago, 1976.

Exum, C. and Talbert, C.
1967 'The Structure of Paul's Speech to the Ephesian Elders (Acts 20.18-35)', *CBQ* 29: 233-36.

Falconer, R.
1937 *The Pastoral Epistles*, Oxford.

Ferguson, E.
1982 'Canon Muratori. Date and Provenance', *Studia Patristica* (ed. E.A. Livingstone) 18: 677-83.

Finegan, J.
1981 *The Archaeology of the New Testament. The Mediterranean World of the Early Christian Apostles*, Boulder/London.

Fiore, B.
1986 *The Function of Personal Example in the Socratic and Pastoral Epistles*, Analecta Biblica 105; Rome.

Fitzmyer, J.A.
1968a 'New Testament Epistles', in *Jerome Biblical Commentary*, ed. R.E. Brown, J.A. Fitzmyer, and R.E. Murphy; London/Dublin/Melbourne, pp. 223-26.
1968b 'The Letter to the Romans', in *Jerome Biblical Commentary*, ed. R.E. Brown, J.A. Fitzmyer, and R.E. Murphy; London/Dublin/Melbourne, pp. 291-331.
1979 'Aramaic Epistolography', pp. 183-204, and 'The Padua Aramaic Papyrus Letters', pp. 219-30, in his *A Wandering Aramean: Collected Aramaic Essays*, Missoula.
1981-85 *The Gospel According to Luke (I-IX)* (1981), *(X-XXIV)* (1985), The Anchor Bible; New York.

Foakes-Jackson, F.J. and K. Lake
1920-33   *The Beginnings of Christianity*. Part I. *The Acts of the Apostles*. Vol. 1:
           Prolegomena I. The Jewish, Gentile and Christian Backgrounds.
           London, 1920. Vol. 2: *Prolegomena II. Criticism*, London, 1922. Vol. 3:
           The Texts of Acts, London, 1926. Vol. 4: *English Translation and
           Commentary*, London, 1933. Vol. 5: *Additional Notes*, London,
           1933.
Freeborn, J.C.K.
1973   '2 Timothy 4, 11: "Only Luke is with me"', in *SEv* (Papers presented
           to the Fourth International Conference on New Testament Studies,
           Oxford 1969), ed. E.A. Livingstone; Berlin.
Friedrich, G.
1965   *Der Brief an die Philipper*, Neues Testament Deutsch; 8th edn,
           Tübingen/Göttingen.
Friedrich, J., W. Pohlmann and P. Stuhlmacher
1976   'Zur historischen Situation und Intention von Röm. 13:1-7', *ZTK* 73:
           131-66.
Funk, A.
1981   *Status und Rollen in den Pastoralbriefen. Eine inhaltsanalytische
           Untersuchung zur Religionssoziologie*, Innsbrucker theologische Studien
           7; Innsbruck/Wien/München.
Funk, R.W.
1967   'The Apostolic Parousia: Form and Significance', *in Christian History
           and Interpretation: Studies Presented to John Knox*, ed. W.R. Farmer,
           C.F.D. Moule and R.R. Niebuhr; Cambridge, pp. 249-68.
Gaertner, B.
1955   *The Areopagus Speech and Natural Revelation*, Uppsala.
Gasque, W.W.
1966   *Sir William Ramsay: Archaeologist and New Testament Scholar*,
           Grand Rapids.
1975   *A History of the Criticism of the Acts of the Apostles*, Grand Rapids.
Gealy, F.D.
1955   *The Pastoral Epistles*, Interpreter's Bible 11; New York.
Georgi, D.
1964   *Die Gegner des Paulus im 2. Korintherbrief. Studien zur religiösen
           Propaganda in der Spätantike*, WMANT; Neukirchen-Vluyn.
Getty, M.A.
1980   *Philippians and Philemon*, New Testament Message 14; Dublin.
Gnilka, J.
1968   *Der Philipperbrief*, Herders Theologischer Kommentar zum Neuen
           Testament 10/3; Freiburg-im-Breisgau.
Godet, F.
1890   *Commentaire sur l'Épître aux Romains*, Vol. 2; 2nd edn. Neuchâtel/
           Paris.
Goodspeed, E.J.
1907   *Index Patristicus sive Clavis Patrum Apostolicorum Operum* ex
           editione Gebhardt, Harnack, Zahn lectionibus editionum minorum
           Funk admissis, Leipzig.
1912   *Index Apologeticus sive Clavis Iustini Martyris Operum aliorumque
           apologetarum pristinorum*, Leipzig.

1937   *An Introduction to the New Testament*, Chicago.
1940   *Christianity Goes to Press*, New York.

Grant, R.M.
1963   *A Historical Introduction to the New Testament*, New York.
1972   'Jewish Christianity at Antioch in the Second Century', *RSR* 60: 97-
          108.
1975   'The Case Against Eusebius. Or, Did the Father of Church History
          Write History?', in *Studia Patristica 12*, Texte und Untersuchungen
          115; Berlin, pp. 413-21.

Grayston, K., and G. Herdan
1959   'The Authorship of the Pastorals in the Light of Statistical Linguistics',
          NTS 6: 1-15.

Gunther, J.J.
1972   *Paul: Messenger and Exile. A Study in the Chronology of his Life and
          Letters*, Valley Forge.

Gustafsson, B.
1961   'Eusebius' Principles in Handling his Sources, as Found in his Church
          History, Book I-VII', *Studia Patristica 4*, Texte und Untersuchungen
          79; Berlin, pp. 429-41.

Guthrie, D.
1956   *The Pastoral Epistles and the Mind of Paul*, London.
1957   *The Pastoral Epistles*, The Tyndale New Testament Commentaries;
          London.
1962   'The Development of the Idea of Canonical Pseudepigrapha in New
          Testament Criticism', *Vox Evangelica* 1. The References are to the
          reprint in *The Authority and Integrity of the New Testament*,
          Theological Collections 4; London, 1965, pp. 14-39.

Haenchen, E.
1965   *Die Apostelgeschichte*, Kritisch-exegetischer Kommentar über das
          Neue Testament; Göttingen. The references are to the translation by
          B. Noble, G. Shinn, H. Anderson and R. McL. Wilson, *The Acts of the
          Apostles*, Philadelphia/Oxford, 1971.

Hansack, E.
1975   'Er lebte . . . von seinem eigenen Einkommen' (Apg 28, 30)', *Biblische
          Zeitschrift* 19: 249-53.
1978   'Nochmals zur Apostelgeschichte 28, 30. Erwiderung auf F. Saums
          kritische Anmerkungen', *Biblische Zeitschrift* 21: 118-21.

Hanson, A.T.
1966   *The Pastoral Letters*, The Cambridge Bible Commentary; Cambridge.
1968   *Studies in the Pastoral Epistles*, London.
1981   'The Domestication of Paul: A Study in the Development of Early
          Christian Theology', *BJRL* 63: 402-18.
1982   *The Pastoral Epistles*, New Century Bible Commentary; Grand
          Rapids/London.

Hanson, R.P.C.
1967   *The Acts of the Apostles*, New Clarendon Bible; Oxford.
1968   'The Journey of Paul and the Journey of Nikias. An Experiment in
          Comparative Historiography', in *SEv* Vol. 4, part 1, Texte und
          Untersuchungen, 102; Berlin, pp. 315-18.

Harnack, A. von

1906 *Beiträge zur Einleitung in das Neue Testament.* Vol. 1, *Lukas der Arzt: Der Verfasser des dritten Evangeliums und der Apostelgeschichte*, Leipzig.

1908 *Beiträge zur Einleitung in das Neue Testament*, Vol. 2, *Die Apostelgeschichte*, Leipzig.

1911 *Beiträge zur Einleitung in das Neue Testament, IV. Neue Untersuchungen zur Apostelgeschichte und zur Abfassungszeit der synoptischen Evangelien*, Leipzig.

1925 'Über den Verfasser und den literarischen Charakter des Muratorischen Fragments', *ZNW* 25: 154-60.

Harrington, D.J.

1980 'Research on the Jewish Pseudepigrapha during the 1970s', *CBQ* 42: 147-59.

Harrison, P.N.

1921 *The Problem of the Pastoral Epistles*, Oxford.

1955/6 'Important Hypotheses Reconsidered, III. The Authorship of the Pastoral Epistles', *ExpTim* 67: 77-81.

1964 *Pauline and Pastorals*, London.

Harrisville, R.A.

1980 *Romans*, Augsburg Commentaries on the New Testament; Minneapolis.

Hartman, L.

1986 'On Reading Others' Letters', in *Christians among Jews and Gentiles: Essays in Honor of Krister Stendahl on his Sixty-fifth Birthday*, ed. G.W.E. Nickelsburg with G.W. MacRae, S.J.; *HTR* 79: 137-46.

Hasler, V.

1978 *Die Briefe an Timotheus und Titus*, Zürcher Bibel Kommentar, Zurich.

Haupt, E.

1902 *Die Gefangenschaftsbriefe*, Kritisch-exegetischer Kommentar 9; 7th edn; Göttingen.

Hauser, H.J.

1979 *Strukturen der Abschlusserzählung der Apostelgeschichte (Apg. 28.16-31)*, Analecta Biblica 86; Rome.

Hawthorne, G.F.

1983 *Philippians*, Word Biblical Commentary; Waco.

Hemer, C.J.

1977/8 'Luke the Historian', *BJRL* 60: 28-51.

1980 'Observations on Pauline Chronology', in *Pauline Studies. Essays Presented to F.F. Bruce*, ed. D.A. Hagner and M.J. Harris; Exeter, pp. 3-18.

1986 *The Letters to the Seven Churches of Asia in their Local Setting*, JSNT Supplement Series 11; Sheffield.

Hengel, M.

1968 *Nachfolge und Charisma*, Berlin. References are to the translation by J.C.G. Greig, *The Charismatic Leader and his Followers*, Edinburgh, 1981.

1971/2 'Die Ursprünge der christlichen Mission', *NTS* 18: 15-38. John Bowman's translation, 'The Origins of the Christian Mission' is published in Hengel's *Between Jesus and Paul*, London, 1983, pp. 48-64.

1979   *Zur urchristlichen Geschichtsschreibung*, Stuttgart. References are to the translation by J. Bowden, *Acts and the History of Earliest Christianity*, London/Philadelphia, 1980.

Hennecke, E.

1959   *Neutestamentliche Apokryphen*, I, ed. W. Schneemelcher; Tübingen. The references are to the translation by A.J.B. Higgins, G. Ogg, R.E. Taylor and R.McL. Wilson, *New Testament Apocrypha*, 1, London, 1963.

1964   *Neutestamentliche Apokryphen*. II, ed. W. Schneemelcher; Tübingen. References are to the translation by E. Best, D. Hill, G. Ogg, G.C. Stead and R.McL. Wilson, *New Testament Apocrypha*, II, London, 1965.

Herdan, G.

1959   *Type-Token Mathematics, A Text-Book of Mathematical Linguistics*, The Hague.

Higgins, A.J.B.

1962   'The Pastoral Epistles', in *Peake's Commentary on the Bible*, London.

Hilgert, E.

1984   'Bibliographia Philoniana 1935-1981', in *Aufstieg und Niedergang der römischen Welt*, Principat 21/1; Berlin/New York, pp. 47-97.

Hitchcock, F.R.M.

1929   'Tests for the Pastorals', *JTS* 30: 272-79.

1930   'The Use of *graphein*', *JTS* 31: 271-75.

1940   'Philo and the Pastorals', *Hermathena* 56: 113-35.

Hock, R.F.

1980   *The Social Context of Paul's Ministry. Tentmaking and Apostleship*, Philadelphia.

Hodgson, P.C.

1966   *The Formation of Historical Theology. A Study of Ferdinand Christian Baur*, New York.

Hoffmann, R.J.

1984   *Marcion: On the Restitution of Christianity. An Essay on the Development of Radical Paulinist Theology in the Second Century*, American Academy of Religion Academy Series; Chico.

Holtzmann, H.J.

1880   *Die Pastoralbriefe kritisch und exegetisch behandelt*, Leipzig.

Hooker, M.

1970   'New Testament Scholarship in the 1960s', *The Church Quarterly* 2: 207-14.

Horsley, G.H.R.

1981 (2,3)   *New Documents Illustrating Early Christianity. A Review of the Greek Inscriptions and Papyri published in 1976 (7, 8)*, North Ryde.

Houlden, J.L.

1970   *Paul's Letters from Prison. Philippians, Colossians, Philemon and Ephesians*, The Pelican New Testament Commentaries; London.

1976   *The Pastoral Epistles*, Penguin New Testament Commentaries; London.

Huby, J.
    1940   *Saint Paul: Épître aux Romains*, Verbum Salutis; Paris.
James, J.D.
    1906   *The Genuineness and Authorship of the Pastoral Epistles*, London.
James, M.R.
    1924   *The Apocryphal New Testament. Being the Apocryphal Gospels, Acts,
                Epistles, and Apocalypses with Other Narratives and Fragments*,
                Oxford. The page references are to the corrected 1953 edn.
Jeremias, J.
    1968   *Die Briefe an Timotheus und Titus* (With H. Strathmann, *Der Brief an
                die Hebräer*), 9th edn; Das Neue Testament Deutsch 9; Göttingen.
Jervell, J.
    1984   *The Unknown Paul. Essays on Luke–Acts and Early Christian History*,
                Minneapolis.
Jewett, R.
    1970   'The Epistolary Thanksgiving and the Integrity of Philippians', *NovT*
                12: 40-53.
    1979   *Dating Paul's Life*, London.
    1982   'Romans as an Ambassadorial Letter', *Int* 36: 5-20.
Johnson, D.G.
    1984   'The Structure and Meaning of Romans 11', *CBQ* 46: 91-103.
Johnson, L.
    1956/7   'The Pauline Letters from Caesarea', *ExpTim* 68: 24-26.
Johnson, L.T.
    1978   'II Timothy and the Polemic against False Teachers: A Re-examination',
                Ohio Journal of Religious Studies 6: 1-26.
Johnson, P.F.
    1974   'The Use of Statistics in the Analysis of the Characteristics of Pauline
                Writing', *NTS* 20: 92-100.
Jonge, M. de
    1953   'The Testaments of the Twelve Patriarchs. A Study of their texts,
                composition and origin' (unpublished dissertation, University of
                Assen).
Jonge, M. de, ed.
    1975   *Studies on the Testaments of the Twelve Patriarchs. Texts and
                Interpretation*, Leiden.
Kaibel, G., ed.
    1890   *Inscriptiones Graecae, Vol. XIV Italiae et Siciliae*, Berlin.
Karris, R.J.
    1973   'The Background and Significance of the Polemic of the Pastoral
                Epistles', *JBL* 92: 549-64.
    1979   *The Pastoral Epistles*, New Testament Message; Vol. 17; Dublin.
Käsemann, E.
    1973   *An die Römer*, Handbuch zum Neuen Testament, 8a; Tübingen.
                References are to the translation by G.W. Bromiley, *Commentary on
                Romans*, London, 1980.
Katsh, A.I., and L. Nemoy, ed.
    1979   *Essays on the Occasion of the Seventieth Anniversary of the Dropsie
                University (1909-1979)*, Philadelphia.

Kelly, J.N.D.
    1963   *The Pastoral Epistles*, Black's New Testament Commentaries; London.
Kenny, A.
    1986   *A Stylometric Study of the New Testament*, Oxford.
Kiley, M.
    1986   *Colossians as Pseudepigraphy*, The Biblical Seminar; Sheffield.
Kim, S.
    1982   *The Origin of Paul's Gospel*, Grand Rapids.
Kittel, G. and G. Friedrich
    1933-73   *Theologisches Wörterbuch zum Neuen Testament*. Begründet von Gerhard Kittel, herausgegeben von Gerhard Friedrich; 9 vols; Stuttgart. The references are to the translation by Geoffrey W. Bromiley, *Theological Dictionary of the New Testament*, 9 volumes; Grand Rapids, 1964-1974.
Knoch, O.
    1973   'Das Testament des Paulus nach dem zweiten Timotheusbrief', in *Die 'Testamente' des Petrus und Paulus. Die Sicherung der apostolischen Überlieferung in der spätneutestamentlichen Zeit*, Stuttgart, pp. 44-64.
Knox, J.
    1950   *Chapters in a Life of Paul*, New York/Nashville.
    1964   'Romans 15.14-33 and Paul's Conception of his Apostolic Mission', *JBL* 83: 1-11.
Koch, H.
    1926   'Zu A. von Harnacks Beweis für amtlichen römischen Ursprung des Muratorischen Fragments', *ZNW* 25: 154-60.
Koch, K.
    1976   'Pseudonymous Writing', *The Interpreter's Dictionary of the Bible* Supp. Vol., pp. 712-14.
Koester, H.
    1980   *Einführung in das Neue Testament*, Berlin/New York. The references are to the author's translation, *Introduction to the New Testament*. Vols 1 and 2; Philadelphia, 1982.
Koskenniemi, H.
    1956   *Studien zur Idee und Phraseologie des griechischen Briefes bis 400 n. Chr.*, Helsinki.
Kühl, E.
    1913   *Der Brief des Paulus an die Römer*, Leipzig.
Kümmel, W.G.
    1970   *Das Neue Testament: Geschichte der Erforschung seiner Probleme*, Freiburg/Munich. References are to the translation by S. McLean Gilmour and Howard C. Kee, *The New Testament. The History of the Investigation of Its Problems*, London, 1973.
    1973   *Einleitung in das Neue Testament*, 17th edn; Heidelberg. References are to the translation by Howard C. Kee, *Introduction to the New Testament*, London, 1975.
Kuss, O.
    1940   *Die Briefe an die Römer, Kor, und Gal*, Regensburger Neue Testament; Regensburg.

Lagrange, M.-J.
1922   *Saint Paul: Épître aux Romains*, Études Bibliques; 2nd edn; Paris.
Lake, K.
1909   'What was the End of St. Paul's Trial?' *Interpreter* Jan., 5, 146-56. The
         reference is to the reprint in Lake 1933a: 326-32.
Lake, K. and H.J. Cadbury
1933a   *English Translation and Commentary*, Vol. 4 of *The Beginnings of
         Christianity*, Part 1, *The Acts of the Apostles*, ed. F.J. Foakes-Jackson
         and Kirsopp Lake; London.
1933b   *Additional Notes*, Vol. 5 of *The Beginnings of Christianity*, Part 1, *The
         Acts of the Apostles*, ed. F.J. Foakes-Jackson and Kirsopp Lake;
         London.
Lambrecht, J.
1979   'Paul's Farewell-Address at Miletus (Acts 20.17-38)', in *Les Actes des
         Apôtres. Traditions, Rédaction, Théologie*, Bibliotheca Ephemeridum
         Theologicarum Lovaniensium; ed. J. Kremer; Gembloux/Louvain,
         pp. 307-37.
Lampe, G.W.H., ed.
1961   *A Patristic Greek Lexicon*, Oxford.
Lea, T.D.
1984   'The Early Christian View of Pseudepigraphic Writings', *Journal of
         the Evangelical Theological Society* 27: 65-75.
Leaney, A.R.C.
1960   *The Epistles to Timothy, Titus and Philemon*, London.
1984   *The Jewish and Christian World 200 BC to AD 200*, Cambridge
         Commentaries on Writings of the Jewish and Christian World 200 BC
         to AD 200, VII; Cambridge.
Leenhardt, F.-J.
1957   *L'Épître de Saint Paul aux Romains*, Neuchâtel/Paris.
Lekebusch, E.
1854   *Die Composition und Entstehung der Apostelgeschichte*, Gotha.
Leon, H.J.
1960   *The Jews of Ancient Rome*, Philadelphia.
1964   'The Jews of Rome in the First Centuries of Christianity', in *The
         Teacher's Yoke. Studies in Memory of Henry Trantham*, ed. J.
         Vardaman, J.L. Garrett, Jr and J.B. Adair; Waco.
Lestapis, S. de
1976   *L'Énigme des Pastorales de Saint Paul*, Paris.
Levison, M., A.Q. Morton, and W.C. Wake
1966   'On Certain Statistical Features of the Pauline Epistles', *The
         Philosophical Journal* 3: 129-48.
Liddell, H.G. and R. Scott
1925-40 *A Greek-English Lexicon: A New Edition Revised and Augmented
         Throughout* by H.S. Jones, assisted by R. McKenzie (9th edn,
         reprinted 1966); Oxford. A Supplement by E.A. Barber was published
         in 1968.
Lietzmann, H.
1913   *An die Römer*, Handbuch zum Neuen Testament; Tübingen.
Lightfoot, J.B.
1884   *St Paul's Epistles to the Colossians and to Philemon*, 7th edn;
         London.

1885   *The Apostolic Fathers*, Part 2. Vol. 1, and Vol. 2, section 1 and 2, *S. Ignatius. S. Polycarp*, London.

1890   *The Apostolic Fathers*, Part 1. Vols 1 and 2, *S. Clement of Rome*, 2nd edn, London.

1893   'The Date of the Pastoral Epistles', in his *Biblical Essays*, London, pp. 397-410.

1913   *St. Paul's Epistle to the Philippians*, London.

Lindemann, A.

1979   *Paulus im ältesten Christentum. Das Bild des Apostels und die Rezeption der paulinischen Theologie in der frühchristlichen Literatur bis Marcion*, Beiträge zur historischen Theologie 58; Tübingen.

Lipsius, R.A.

1892   *Der Brief an die Römer*, Handkommentar zum Neuen Testament; 2nd edn; Freiburg.

Lock, W.

1924   *The Pastoral Epistles*, The International Critical Commentary; Edinburgh.

Lofthouse, W.F.

1946/7   'Singular and Plural in St. Paul's Letters', *ExpTim* 58: 179-82.

1952/3   '"I" and "We" in the Pauline Letters', *ExpTim* 64: 241-45.

Lohmeyer, E.

1955   *Die Briefe an die Philipper, Kolosser, und an Philemon*, Kritisch-exegetischer Kommentar 9; 11th edn; Göttingen.

Lohse, E.

1968   *Die Briefe an die Kolosser und an Philemon*, 14th edn; Kritisch-exegetischer Kommentar über das Neue Testament, 9.2; Göttingen. References are to the translation by W.R. Poehlmann and R.J. Karris, *Colossians and Philemon: A Commentary on the Epistles to the Colossians and Philemon*, Hermeneia; Philadelphia, 1971.

Loisy, A.

1920   *Les Actes des Apôtres*, Paris.

Longenecker, R.N.

1974   'Ancient Amanuenses and the Pauline Epistles', in *New Dimensions in New Testament Study*, ed. R.N. Longenecker and M.C. Tenney; Grand Rapids, pp. 281-97.

Lüdemann, G.

1984   *Paul, Apostle to the Gentiles: Studies in Chronology*. London. 'The present English translation (by F. Stanley Jones) can . . . be regarded as a second edition' of *Paulus, der Heidenapostel, Vol. 1: Studien zur Chronologie*, Göttingen, 1980 (p. 289).

Lütgert, W.

1909   *Die Irrlehrer der Pastoralbriefe*, Gütersloh.

Maddelena, A.

1974/5   *La lettera ai Romani*, Bologna.

Maddox, R.

1982   *The Purpose of Luke–Acts*, Studies of the New Testament and its World; Edinburgh.

Malherbe, A.J.

1977a   *Social Aspects of Early Christianity*. Rockwell Lectures of 1955; Baton Rouge/London.

| 1977b | 'Ancient Epistolary Theorists', *Ohio Journal of Religious Studies* 5: 3-77. |

1977c   *The Cynic Epistles. A Study Edition*, SBL Sources for Biblical Studies 12; Missoula.

1983   'Exhortation in First Thessalonians', *NovT* 35: 238-56.

1984   'In Season and Out of Season': 2 Timothy 4.2', *JBL* 103: 235-43.

Maly, E.H.

1979   *Romans*, New Testament Message 9; Dublin.

Manson, T.W.

1938   'St. Paul's Letter to the Romans—and Others'. Reprinted in Donfried, ed. 1977, pp. 1-16.

1939   'St. Paul in Ephesus. The Date of the Epistle to the Philippians', *BJRL* 23: 182-200.

1962   'Romans', in *Peake's Commentary on the Bible*, ed. M. Black and H.H. Rowley; London, pp. 940-53.

Manus, C.U.

1984   '"Amanuensis Hypothesis": A Key to the Understanding of Paul's Epistles in the New Testament', *Bible Bhashyam* 10: 160-74.

Marshall, I.H.

1970   *Luke, Historian and Theologian*, Exeter.

Martin, R.P.

1959   *The Epistle of Paul to the Philippians*, Tyndale New Testament Commentaries; London.

1978   *New Testament Foundations*, II: Acts–Revelation; Exeter.

1980   *Philippians*, The New Century Bible Commentary; rev. edn; Grand Rapids.

Mattill, A.J.

1978   'The Value of Acts as a Source for the Study of Paul', in *Perspectives on Luke–Acts*, ed. C.H. Talbert; Danville/Edinburgh.

Mayer, G.

1974   *Index Philoneus*, Berlin/New York.

Medley, E.

1895   'The Character of Timothy as Reflected in the Letters Addressed to him by the Apostle Paul', *Expositor*, 5th series, 2: 223-34.

Meeks, W.A. and R.L. Wilken

1978   *Jews and Christians in Antioch in the First Four Centuries of the Common Era*, SBL Sources for Biblical Study, 13; Missoula.

Meier, J.P. and R.E. Brown

1983   *Antioch and Rome. New Testament Cradles of Catholic Christianity*, London.

Meinardus, O.F.A.

1978   'Paul's Missionary Journey to Spain: Tradition and Folklore', *Biblical Archaeologist* 41: 61-63.

1979   'Dalmatian and Catalanian Traditions about St. Paul's Journeys', Εκκλησιαστικός Φάρος 61: 221-30.

Metzger, B.M.

1958/9   'A Reconsideration of Certain Arguments Against the Pauline Authorship of the Pastoral Epistles', *ExpTim* 70: 91-94.

1972   'Literary Forgeries and Canonical Pseudepigrapha', *JBL* 19: 3-24.

Meyer, A.
1936   'Religiöse Pseudepigraphie als ethisch-psychologisches Problem', *ZNW* 35: 262-79.
Meyer, E.
1921a   *Ursprung und Anfänge des Christentums.* I, *Die Evangelien,* Stuttgart/ Berlin.
1921b   *Ursprung und Anfänge des Christentums.* II, *Entwicklung des Judentums und Jesus von Nazareth,* Stuttgart/Berlin.
1923   *Apostelgeschichte und die Anfänge des Christentums,* Stuttgart/Berlin.
Michael, J.H.
1928   *The Epistle of Paul to the Philippians,* Moffatt New Testament Commentaries; London.
Michaelis, W.
1929   'Pastoralbriefe und Wortstatistik', *ZNW* 28: 69-76.
1935   *Der Brief an die Philipper,* Theologisches Handkommentar zum Neuen Testament 11; Leipzig.
Michaelson, S. and A.Q. Morton
1971-72 'Last Words. A Test of Authorship for Greek Writers', *NTS* 18: 192-208.
Michel, H.-J.
1973   *Die Abschiedsrede des Paulus an die Kirche Apg 20,17-38. Motivge-schichte und theologische Bedeutung.* München.
Michel, O.
1964   'σπένδομαι', in Kittel/Friedrich 1933-73. *TDNT* VII: 528-36.
1978   *Der Brief an die Römer.* Meyer. 14th edn, Göttingen.
Minear, P.S.
1971   *The Obedience of Faith. The Purposes of Paul in the Epistle to the Romans,* Studies in Biblical Theology, Second Series 19; London.
Mitton, C. Leslie
1955   *The Formation of the Pauline Corpus,* London.
Morgan, R.
1978/9 'Biblical Classics II. F.C. Baur: Paul', *ExpTim* 90: 4-10.
Morton, A.Q. and J. McLeman
1966   *Paul, the Man and the Myth. A Study in the Authorship of Greek Prose,* London.
Moule, C.F.D.
1965   'The Problem of the Pastoral Epistles: A Reappraisal', *BJRL* 47: 430-52.
1974   'Interpreting Paul by Paul. An Essay in the Comparative Study of Pauline Thought', in *New Testament Christianity for Africa and the World. Essays in Honour of Harry Sawyerr,* ed. M.E. Glasswell and E.W. Fashoule-Luke; London, pp. 78-90.
Moulton, J.H. and G. Milligan
1957   *The Vocabulary of the Greek Testament Illustrated from the Papyri and Other Non-Literary Sources,* 2nd edn; London.
Mullachius, F.G.A., ed.
1883   *Fragmenta Philosophorum Graecorum,* I, Paris.
Müller, C., ed.
1841   *Fragmenta Historicorum Graecorum,* I, Paris.

Munck, J.
  1950   'Israel and the Gentiles in the New Testament', in *Bulletin of the SNTS* I: 26-38.
  1954   *Paulus und die Heilsgeschichte*, Copenhagen. References are to the translation by F. Clarke, *Paul and the Salvation of Mankind*, London, 1959.
  1967   *The Acts of the Apostles*, The Anchor Bible; New York.
Murphy-O'Connor, J.
  1964   *Paul on Preaching*, London/New York.
  1982   'Pauline Missions Before the Jerusalem Conference', *RB* 89: 71-91.
  1984   'Redactional Angels in 1 Tim. 3.16', *RB* 91: 178-87.
  1985   'Traveling Conditions in the First Century. On the Road and on the Sea with St. Paul', *Bible Review* 1: 38-47.
  1986   'Pneumatikoi and Judaizers in 2 Cor 2.14–4.6', *Australian Biblical Review* 34: 42-58.
Murray, J.
  1965   *The Epistle to the Romans*, II, The New International Commentary on the New Testament; Grand Rapids.
Neill, S.
  1964   *The Interpretation of the New Testament, 1861-1961*, Oxford.
Nickle, K.F.
  1966   *The Collection. A Study in Paul's Strategy*, London.
Nikiprowetzky, V.
  1967   'La Spiritualisation des sacrifices et le culte sacrificiel au temple de Jérusalem chez Philon d'Alexandrie', *Sem* 17: 97-116.
Nordheim, E. von
  1980   *Die Lehre der Alten. I. Das Testament als Literaturgattung im Judentum der hellenistisch-römischen Zeit*, Leiden.
  1985   *Die Lehre der Alten. II. Das Testament als Literaturgattung im Alten Testament und im Alten Vorderen Orient*, Leiden.
Norris, F.W.
  1982   'Isis, Sarapis and Demeter in Antioch of Syria', *HTR* 75: 189-207.
Nygren, A.
  1951   *Der Römerbrief*, Göttingen.
O'Brien, P.T.
  1974/5 'Thanksgiving and the Gospel in Paul', *NTS* 21: 144-55.
  1977   *Introductory Thanksgivings in the Letters of Paul*, Leiden.
  1980   'Thanksgiving within the Structure of Pauline Theology', in *Pauline Studies. Essays Presented to F.F. Bruce*, ed. D.A. Hagner and M.J. Harris; Exeter, pp. 50-66.
Ollrog, W.H.
  1979   *Paulus und seine Mitarbeiter. Untersuchungen zu Theorie und Praxis der paulinischen Mission*, WMANT 50. Neukirchen.
Olmstead, A.T.
  1943   'History, Ancient World, and the Bible: Problems of Attitude and Method', *JNES* 2: 1-34.
O'Neill, J.C.
  1975   *Paul's Letter to the Romans*, Penguin New Testament Commentaries; London.

Onuki, T.
1977   'Die johanneischen Abschiedsreden und die synoptische Tradition.
        Eine traditionskritische und traditionsgeschichtliche Untersuchung',
        Annual of the Japanese Biblical Institute 3: 157-268.
Oppenheim, A.L.
1967   *Letters from Mesopotamia. Official, Business and Private Letters on
        Clay Tablets from Two Millennia*, Chicago/London.
O'Rourke, J.J.
1973   'Some Considerations about Attempts at Statistical Analysis of the
        Pauline Corpus', *CBQ* 35: 483-90.
O'Toole, R.
1978   *The Christological Climax of Paul's Defense (Ac 22.1–26.32)*, Analecta
        Biblica 78; Rome.
Painter, J.
1981   'The Farewell Discourses and the History of Johannine Christianity',
        NTS 27: 525-43.
Pallis, A.
1920   *To the Romans*, Liverpool.
Pardee, D.
1978   'An Overview of Ancient Hebrew Epistolography', *JBL* 97: 321-46.
Penna, R.
1982   'Les Juifs à Rome au temps de l'Apôtre Paul', *NTS* 28: 321-47.
Penny, D.N.
1979   'The Pseudo-Pauline Letters of the First Two Centuries' (unpublished
        doctoral dissertation, Emory University).
Pherigo, L.J.
1951   'Paul's Life after the Close of Acts', *JBL* 70: 277-84.
Plooij, D.
1918   *De Chronologie van het Leven van Paulus*, Leiden.
Plümacher, E.
1979   'Die Apostelgeschichte als historische Monographie', in *Les Actes des
        Apôtres. Traditions, Rédaction, Théologie*, Bibliotheca Ephemeridum
        Theologicarum Lovaniensium; ed. J. Kremer; Gembloux/Louvain,
        pp. 457/66.
1983   'Acta-Forschung 1974-1982', *TRu* 48: 1-56.
1984   'Acta-Forschung 1974-1982. (Fortsetzung und Schluss)', *TRu* 49: 105-
        69.
Praeder, S.M.
1984   'Acts 27.1–28.16. Sea Voyages in Ancient Literature and the Theology
        of Luke–Acts', *CBQ* 46: 683-706.
Preisigke, F.
1925-31 *Wörterbuch der griechischen Papyruskunden mit Einschluss der
        griechischen Inschriften, Aufschriften, Ostraka, Mumienschilder usw.
        aus Ägypten*, vollendet und herausgegeben von E. Kiessling (3 Vols.);
        Berlin. Three fascicles of Vol. 4 have appeared (1958, 1966, 1971). In
        addition *Supplement I*, ed. W. Rubsam; Amsterdam 1969-71.
Prete, B.
1983   'L'Arrivo di Paolo a Roma e il suo Significato secondo Atti 28,16-31',
        RivB 31: 147-87.

Prior, M.
    1979   'Revisiting Luke', *ScrB* 10: 2-11.
    1982   'The Bible in Irish', *ScrB* 13: 2-4.
    1983   Review of R.J. Karris, *The Pastoral Epistles*, *Heythrop Journal* 24: 310ff.
    1985   'Second Timothy: A Personal Letter of Paul' (unpublished doctoral dissertation, University of London).

Quinn, J.D.
    1978   'The Last Volume of Luke: The Relation of Luke–Acts to the Pastoral Epistles', in *Perspectives on Luke–Acts*, ed. C.H. Talbert; Danville/Edinburgh, pp. 62-75.
    1980   'Paul's Last Captivity', *Studia Biblica 1978: III*, JSNT Supp. 3; Sheffield, pp. 289-99.
    1981   'Paraenesis and the Pastoral Epistles', in *De la Tôrah au Messie. Mélanges Henri Cazelles*, ed. M. Carrez, J. Doré, and P. Grelot; Paris, pp. 495-501.

Radday, Y.T.
    1970   'Two Computerized Statistical-Linguistic Tests Concerning the Unity of Isaiah', *JBL* 89: 319-24.

Radday, Y.T., H. Shore, *et al.*
    1985   *Genesis. An Authorship Study in Computer-Assisted Statistical Linguistics*, Analecta Biblica 103; Rome.

Ramsay, W.M.
    1890   *Historical Geography of Asia Minor*, London.
    1895/7   *Cities and Bishoprics of Phrygia*, 1 (1895), 2 (1897), Oxford.
    1915   *The Bearing of Recent Discovery on the Trustworthiness of the New Testament*, London/New York/Toronto.
    1930   *St Paul the Traveller and the Roman Citizen*, 17th edn; London.

Refoulé, F.
    1984   '. . . *Et ainsi tout Israël sera sauvé,' Romains 11.25-32*, Lectio Divina 117; Paris.

Reicke, Bo
    1970   'Caesarea, Rome and the Captivity Epistles', in *Apostolic History and the Gospel: Biblical and Historical Essays Presented to F.F. Bruce*, ed. W.W. Gasque and R.P. Martin; Exeter, pp. 277-86.
    1973   'The Historical Setting of Colossians', *RevExp* 70: 429-38.
    1976   'Chronologie der Pastoralbriefe', *TLZ* 101: 82-94.

Reim, G.
    1976   'Probleme der Abschiedsreden', *BZ* 20: 117-22.

Rengstorf, K.H.
    1973-1983   *A Complete Concordance to Flavius Josephus*, I, 1973; II, 1975; III, 1979; IV, 1983, Leiden.

Richard, E.
    1983   'Luke—Writer, Theologian, Historian. Research and Orientation of the 1970's', *BTB* 13: 2-15.

Riciotti, G.
    1958   *Gli Atti degli Apostoli e le lettere di San Paolo*, Arnoldo Mondatori Editore.

Ridderbos, H.
    1959   *An die Romeinen*, Kampen.

Riggen, E.
 1898   *Die Pastoralbriefe des Apostels Paulus*, Munich.
Rius-Camps, J.
 1979   *The Four Authentic Letters of Ignatius, The Martyr*, Christianismos 2;
          Rome.
Robbins, V.K.
 1978   'By Land and by Sea: The We-Passages and Ancient Sea Voyages', in
          Perspectives on Luke–Acts, ed. C.H. Talbert; Danville/Edinburgh,
          pp. 215-42.
Robinson, J.A.T.
 1976   *Redating the New Testament*, London.
Robinson, T.A.
 1984   'Grayston and Herdan's 'C' Quantity Formula and the Authorship of
          the Pastoral Epistles', *NTS* 30: 282-88.
Roller, O.
 1933   *Das Formular der paulinischen Briefe. Ein Beitrag zur Lehre vom
          antiken Briefe*, Beiträge zur Wissenschaft vom Alten und Neuen
          Testament 4/5 (58); Stuttgart.
Roloff, J.
 1981   *Die Apostelgeschichte. Übersetzt und erklärt*, Das Neue Testament
          Deutsch 5; Göttingen.
Ropes, J.H.
 1926   *The Text of Acts*, Vol. 3 of *The Beginnings of Christianity*, Part 1, *The
          Acts of the Apostles*, ed. F.J. Foakes-Jackson and Kirsopp Lake;
          London.
Sabatier, A.
 1896   *L'Apôtre Paul, esquisse d'une histoire de sa pensée*, Fischbacher.
Saldarini, A.J.
 1977   'Last Words and Deathbed Scenes in Rabbinic Literature', *Jewish
          Quarterly Review* (n.s.): 68: 28-45.
Sampley, J.P.
 1980   *Pauline Partnership in Christ. Christian Community and Commitment
          in Light of Roman Law*, Philadelphia.
Sanday, W. and A.C. Headlam
 1896   *The Epistle to the Romans*, International Critical Commentary; 2nd
          edn; Edinburgh.
Sanders, E.P.
 1977   *Paul and Palestinian Judaism. A Comparison of Patterns of Religion*,
          London.
Sandmel, S.
 1979   'Apocalypse and Philo', in *Essays on the Occasion of the Seventieth
          Anniversary of the Dropsie University (1909-1979)*, ed A.I. Katsh and
          L. Nemoy; Philadelphia, pp. 383-87.
Saum, F.
 1976   'Er lebte . . . vom eigenen Einkommen' (Apg 28, 30)', *Biblische
          Zeitschrift* 20: 226-29.
Schenk, W.
 1984   *Die Philipperbriefe des Paulus. Kommentar*, Stuttgart/Berlin/Cologne/
          Mainz.

Schlatter, A.
1935   *Gottes Gerechtigkeit. Ein Kommentar zum Römerbrief*, Stuttgart.
Schleiermacher, F.
1807   *Über den sogenannten ersten Brief des Paulus an den Timotheus*, Berlin.
Schlier, H.
1977   *Der Römerbrief*, Freiburg/Basel/Wien.
Schmithals, W.
1965   *Paulus und die Gnostiker*, Hamburg. References are to the translation by J.E. Steely, *Paul and the Gnostics*, Nashville/New York, 1972.
1982   *Die Apostelgeschichte des Lukas*, Zürcher Bibelkommentare Neues Testament 3/2; Zürich.
Schneemelcher, W.
1964a   'Apostolic Pseudepigrapha', in Hennecke 1964. References are to the translation by G. Ogg, pp. 88-94.
1964b   'The Acts of Peter', in Hennecke 1964. References are to the translation by G.C. Stead, pp. 259-322.
1964c   'The Acts of Paul', in Hennecke 1964. References are to the translation by R.McL. Wilson, pp. 322-87.
Schneckenburger, M.
1841   *Über den Zweck der Apostelgeschichte*, Bern.
Schneider, G.
1980-82   *Die Apostelgeschichte. I. Teil. Einleitung. Kommentar zu Kap. 1,1– 8,40. II. Teil. Kommentar zu Kap. 9,1–28,31*, Herders theologischer Kommentar zum Neuen Testament, V/1-2; Freiburg/Basel/Wien.
Schoedel, W.R.
1985   *Ignatius of Antioch. A Commentary on the Letters of Ignatius of Antioch*, Hermeneia; Philadelphia.
Schroeder, D.
1976a   'Exhortation in the New Testament', *The Interpreter's Dictionary of the Bible, Supp. Vol.*, Nashville, pp. 303f.
1976b   'Parenesis', *The Interpreter's Dictionary of the Bible, Supp. Vol.*, Nashville, p. 643.
Schott, H.A.
1830   *Isagoge historico-critica in libros Novi Foederis sacros*, Jena.
Schubert, P.
1939a   'Form and Function of the Pauline Letters', *Journal of Religion* 19: 365-77.
1939b   *Form and Function of the Pauline Thanksgivings*, Berlin.
Schulz, F.
1942   'Roman Registers of Birth and Birth Certificates', *Journal of Roman Studies* 32: 78-91, and part II in 33 (1943): 55-64.
Schürer, E.
1911   *Geschichte des jüdischen Volkes im Zeitalter Jesu Christi*, I, 4th edn; Leipzig.
1986   *The History of the Jewish People in the Age of Jesus Christ (175 B.C.— A.D. 135)*. Vol. III.1. Revised and edited by G. Vermes, F. Millar, and M. Goodman; Edinburgh.
Schürmann, H.
1968   'Das Testament des Paulus für die Kirche. Apg. 20.18-35', in his

Traditionsgeschichtliche Untersuchungen zu den synoptischen Evangelien, Düsseldorf, pp. 310-40.

Schwegler, A.
1846   *Das nachapostolische Zeitalter in den Hauptmomenten seiner Entwicklung*, I, Tübingen.

Schweitzer, A.
1911   *Geschichte der Paulinischen Forschung von der Reformation bis auf die Gegenwart*. References are to the translation by W. Montgomery, *Paul and His Interpreters. A Critical History*, London, 1912.

Schweizer, E.
1976   *Der Brief an die Kolosser*. Evangelisch-Katholischer Kommentar zum Neuen Testament; Neukirchen-Vluyn/Einsiedeln/Cologne/Zurich. The references are to the translation by A. Chester, *The Letter to the Colossians. A Commentary*, Minneapolis, 1982.

Scott, E.F.
1936   *The Pastoral Epistles*, The Moffatt New Testament Commentaries; London.

Sell, J.
1982   *The Knowledge of Truth—Two Doctrines. The Book of Thomas the Contender (CG II, 7) and the False Teachers in the Pastoral Epistles*, European University Studies, Series 23, 194; Frankfurt am Main.

Sellin, G.
1983   'Die Auferstehung ist schon geschehen'. Zur Spiritualisierung apokalyptischer Terminologie im Neuen Testament', *NovT* 25: 220-37.

Sherwin-White, A.N.
1963   *Roman Society and Roman Law in the New Testament*, Oxford.
1973   *The Roman Citizenship*, 2nd edn; Oxford.

Skeat, T.C.
1979   '"Especially the Parchments". A Note on 2 Tim. 4.13', *JTS* n.s. 30: 173-77.

Smalley, S.S.
1973   'The Testament of Jesus: Another Look', in *SEv* Vol. VI, Texte und Untersuchungen 112; ed. E.A. Livingstone; Berlin, pp. 495-501.

Smith, J.
1880   *The Voyage and Shipwreck of St. Paul*, 4th edn; London.

Spicq, C.
1964   'Pèlerine et Vêtements. A propos de 2 Tim. 4.13 et Act. 20.33', in *Mélanges Eugène Tisserant*. I. Écriture Sainte—Ancien Orient; Studi e Testi 231; Vatican, pp. 389-417.
1969   *Saint Paul. Les Épîtres Pastorales*. Tome I & II. Études Bibliques; Paris.
1978-82   *Notes de Lexicographie Néo-Testamentaire*, Tome I, II (1978), Supp. (1982), OBO 22/1,2,3; Fribourg/Göttingen.

Steen, H.A.
1938   'Les Clichés épistolaires dans les lettres sur papyrus grecques', *Classica et Medievalia* 1: 119-76.

Stellhorn, F.W.
1899   *Die Pastoralbriefe Pauli*, Gütersloh.

Stendahl, K.
    1977   *Paul among the Jews and Gentiles*, London.
Stenger, W.
    1974   'Timotheus und Titus als literarische Gestalten (Beobachtungen zur Form und Funktion der Pastoralbriefe)', *Kairos* 16: 252-67.
Stevenson, J.S.
    1922/3 'II Timothy 4.13 and the Question of St. Paul's Second Captivity', *ExpTim* 34: 524f.
Stone, M.E., ed.
    1984   *Jewish Writings of the Second Temple Period. Apocrypha, Pseudepigrapha, Qumran Sectarian Writings, Philo, Josephus* (Compendia Rerum Judaicarum ad Novum Testamentum, Section Two, Vol. II); Assen/Philadelphia.
Stowers, S.K.
    1981   *The Diatribe and Paul's Letter to the Romans*, SBL Dissertation Series 57; Chico.
Strobel, A.
    1969   'Schreiben des Lukas? Zum sprachlichen Problem der Pastoralbriefe', *NTS* 15: 191-210.
Suhl, A.
    1975   *Paulus und seine Briefe. Ein Beitrag zur paulinischen Chronologie*, Gütersloh.
Sundberg, A.C.
    1973   'Canon Muratori: A Fourth-Century List', *HTR* 66: 1-41.
    1986   'Enabling Language in Paul', in *Christians among Jews and Gentiles: Essays in Honor of Krister Stendahl on His Sixty-fifth Birthday*, ed. G.W.E. Nickelsburg with G.W. MacRae, S.J.; *HTR* 79: 270-77.
Talbert, C.H.
    1983   'Martyrdom in Luke–Acts and the Lukan Social Ethic', in *Political Issues in Luke–Acts*, ed. R.J. Cassidy and Philip J. Scharper; New York, pp. 99-110.
Theissen, A.
    1969   revised by P. Byrne. 'Romans', in *A New Catholic Commentary on Holy Scripture*, ed. R.C. Fuller, *et al.*, London: Nelson, pp. 1103-42.
Thomas, J.
    1969   'Die gattungsgeschichtliche Frage', pp. 133-38 of 'Aktuelles im Zeugnis der zwölf Väter', in *Studien zu den Testamenten der zwölf Patriarchen*, ed. C. Burchard, J. Jervell and J. Thomas; BZNW 36; Berlin.
Thurston, R.W.
    1973/4 'The Relationship between the Thessalonian Epistles', *ExpTim* 85: 52-56.
Torm, F.
    1932   *Die Psychologie der Pseudonymität im Hinblick auf die Literatur des Urchristentums*, Gütersloh.
Trevett, C.
    1981/2 'The Much-maligned Ignatius', *ExpTim* 93: 299-302.
Trummer, P.
    1974   '"Mantel und Schriften" (2 Tim. 4.13). Zur Interpretation einer persönlichen Notiz in den Pastoralbriefen', *BZ* n.s. 18: 193-207.

1978 *Die Paulustradition der Pastoralbriefe*, Beiträge zur biblischen Exegese und Theologie, 8; Frankfurt/Bern/Las Vegas.

1981 'Corpus Paulinum—Corpus Pastorale. Zur Örtung der Paulustradition in den Pastoralbriefen', in *Paulus in den neutestamentlichen Spätschriften*, herausgegeben von Karl Kertelge; Quaestiones Disputatae; Freiburg/Basel/Wien, pp. 122-45.

Turner, N.
1963 *A Grammar of New Testament Greek*, by J.H. Moulton. III, *Syntax*, by Nigel Turner; Edinburgh.

Twomey, J.J.
1958 'I Have Fought the Good Fight', *Scripture* 10: 110-15.

Tyrrell, R.Y. and L.C. Purser
1901-33 *The Correspondence of M. Tullius Cicero*, Dublin/London (=Hildesheim 1969).

Unnik, W.C. van
1979 'Luke's Second Book and the Rules of Hellenistic Historiography', in *Les Actes des Apôtres. Traditions, Rédaction, Théologie*, Bibliotheca Ephemeridum Theologicarum Lovaniensium; ed. J. Kremer; Gembloux/Louvain, pp. 37-60.

Usteri, L.
1824 *Entwicklung des Paulinischen Lehrbegriffs mit Hinsicht auf die übrigen Schriften des Neuen Testaments. Ein exegetisch-dogmatischer Versuch*, Zurich.

Vermes, G.
1977 *The Dead Sea Scrools. Qumran in Perspective*, London.

Verner, D.C.
1983 *The Household of God. The Social World of the Pastoral Epistles*, SBL Dissertation Series 71; Chico.

Vielhauer, P.
1950/1 'Zum 'Paulinismus' der Apostelgeschichte', *Evangelische Theologie* 10: 1-15. The references are to the translation by W.C. Robinson, Jr, and V.P. Furnish, 'On the "Paulinism" of Acts' in *Studies in Luke-Acts*, ed. L.E. Keck and J.L. Martyn; New York/Nashville, 1966, pp. 33-50.

Vine, V.E.
1984-5 'The Purpose and Date of Acts', *ExpTim* 96: 45-48.

Vogel, C.J. de
1977 'Reflexions on Philipp. 1.23-24', *NovT* 19: 262-74.

Vollmer, F., ed.
1900 *Thesaurus Linguae Latinae editus auctoritate et consilio Academiarum quinque Germanicarum*, etc. Leipzig.

Walaskay, P.W.
1983 *'And So We Came to Rome': The Political Perspective of St. Luke*, SNTS Monograph Series 49; Cambridge.

Warmington, B.H.
 Nero: Reality and Legend, London.

Watson, F.
1984 '2 Cor. X-XIII and Paul's Painful Letter to the Corinthians', *JTS* n.s. 35: 324-46.

1986 *Paul, Judaism and the Gentiles. A Sociological Approach*, SNTS Monograph Series 56; Cambridge.

Weiser, A.
1981   *Die Apostelgeschichte Kapitel 1–12*, Ökumenischer Taschenbuchkommentar zum Neuen Testament 5/1; Gütersloh/Würzburg.

Welborn, L.L.
1984   'On the Date of First Clement', *Biblical Research* 29: 35-54.

Welles, C. Bradford
1934   *Royal Correspondence in the Hellenistic Period. A Study in Greek Epigraphy*, New Haven.

Westermann, C.
1966   *Das Buch Jesaja. Kapitel 40–66*, Das Alte Testament Deutsch 19; Göttingen.

Wette, W.M.L. de
1826   *Lehrbuch der historischen-kritischen Einleitung in die Bibel Alten und Neuen Testament. Zweyter Teil: Die Einleitung in das Neue Testament enthaltend*, Berlin.

White, J.L. and K.A. Kensinger
1976   'Categories of Greek Papyrus Letters', in *Society of Biblical Literature Seminar Papers*, Missoula, pp. 79-91.

White, J.L.
1978   'Epistolary Formulas and Clichés in Greek Papyrus Letters', *Society of Biblical Literature Seminar Papers*, II (no. 14), Missoula, pp. 289-319.
1983   'Saint Paul and the Apostolic Letter Tradition', *CBQ* 45: 433-44.
1984   'New Testament Epistolary Literature in the Framework of Ancient Epistolography', in *Aufstieg und Niedergang der römischen Welt*, II Principat 25.2, ed. W. Haase; Berlin/New York, pp. 1730-56.
1986   *Light from Ancient Letters*, Foundations and Facets: New Testament; Philadelphia.

Whittaker, M.
1984   *Jews and Christians: Graeco-Roman Views*, Cambridge Commentaries on Writings of the Jewish and Christian World 200 BC to AD 200, VI; Cambridge.

Wiefel, W.
1977   'The Jewish Community in Rome', in Donfried, ed. 1977, pp. 100-119.

Wilckens, U.
1957   *Urkunden der Ptolemäerzeit (Ältere Funde)*, ed. Ulrich Wilcken, *Papyri aus Oberägypten*, Berlin.
1982   *Der Brief an die Römer*, Evang.-Kath. Kommentar zum Neuen Testament, Vol. III; Neukirchen.

Wilhelm-Hooijbergh, A.E.
1975   'A Different View of Clemens Romanus', *Heythrop Journal* 16: 266-88.
1980   'In 2 Tim. 1.17 the Greek and Latin Texts may have a different meaning', *Studia Biblica 1978: III*, JSNT Supp. 3; Sheffield, pp. 435-38.

Wilken, R.L.
1984   *The Christians as the Romans Saw Them*, New Haven/London.

Wilson, S.G.
1979   *Luke and the Pastoral Epistles*, London.

Wolfson, H.A.
1948   *Philo. Foundations of Religious Philosophy in Judaism, Christianity, and Islam.* II, 2nd revised printing; Cambridge, Mass.

Wuellner, W.
1976   'Paul's Rhetoric of Argument in Romans: An Alternative to the Donfried-Karris Debate over Romans', *CBQ* 38: 330-51.

Zahn, T.
1900   *Einleitung in das Neue Testament*, II, 2nd edn; Leipzig.
1910   *Der Brief des Paulus an die Römer*, Leipzig.

Zeller, D.
1985   *Der Brief an die Römer*, Regensburger Neues Testament; Regensburg.

Zeller, E.
1854   *Die Apostelgeschichte nach ihrem Inhalt und Ursprung kritisch untersucht*, Stuttgart.

Zmijewski, J.
1979   'Die Pastoralbriefe als pseudepigraphische Schriften', in *Studien zum Neuen Testament und seiner Umwelt* 4, ed. Albert Fuchs; Linz, pp. 97-118.

INDEX

INDEX OF BIBLICAL AND OTHER ANCIENT REFERENCES

OLD TESTAMENT

NEW TESTAMENT

PSEUDEPIGRAPHA

RABBINIC LITERATURE

OTHER ANCIENT LITERATURE

PAPYRI

INDEX OF MODERN AUTHORS

Robinson, J.A.T. 68, 175n33, 191n18,
192n20, 198n52, 199n57, 200n259,
202n77, 269
Robinson, T.A. 177n8, 269
Roller, O. 17, 183n34, 269
Roloff, J. 194n34, 198n50, 269
Ropes, J.H. 269

Sabatier, A. 171n9, 269
Saldarini, A.J. 203n1, 269
Sampley, J.P. 206nn22,30, 216n42,
266n95, 269
Sanday, W. 218nn51,55,57, 269
Sanders, E.P. 213n13, 269
Sandmel, S. 269
Saum, F. 269
Schenk, W. 41, 269
Schlatter, A. 218nn55,56,58, 270
Schleiermacher, F. 14, 270
Schlier, H. 270
Schmithals, W. 171n7, 172n9,
198nn50,51, 270
Schneckenburger, M. 270
Schneemelcher, W. 20, 200n63, 202n79,
270
Schneider, G. 198n50, 270
Schoedel, W.R. 55, 186nn57,59,61,
187nn63,64, 270
Schott, H.A. 172n13, 270
Schroeder, D. 239n58, 270
Schubert, P. 52, 61, 184n48, 185n49,
189nn2,3, 270
Schulz, F. 237n46, 270
Schürer, E. 189n70, 201n76, 227n106,
270
Schürmann, H. 204n6, 270f.
Schwegler, A. 271
Schweitzer, A. 171nn3,6, 271
Schweizer, E. 45, 271
Scott, E.F. 61, 204n10, 205n17, 208n44,
212n9, 230n4, 233n23, 235n35,
241nn67,68, 271
Scott, R. 98f., 109, 115, 204n11, 207n35,
210nn56,58, 224n85, 262
Sell, J. 239n58, 271
Sellin, G. 242n79, 271
Sherwin-White, A.N. 71, 76, 118f.,
193n26, 197nn43,44, 237nn44,47,
271

Shore, H. 177n10, 268
Skeat, T.C. 236n43, 237n48, 271
Slaby, W.A. 176n3, 248
Smalley, S.S. 204n6, 271
Smith, J. 193n26, 271
Spicq, C. 14, 99ff., 104, 144, 147, 152,
173n18, 175n1, 176n7, 203n1,
205n17, 207nn32,34,36, 209nn47,50,
212nn3,4,8, 232n15, 233n23,
234n30, 235nn36,37, 236n43,
241n67, 242n81, 271
Steen, H.A. 145, 271
Stellhorn, F.W. 171n9, 271
Stendahl, K. 216n39, 221n69, 272
Stenger, W. 19, 272
Stevenson, J.S. 149f., 234n30, 272
Stone, M. 272
Stowers, S.K. 272
Strobel, A. 172n13, 272
Stuhlmacher, P. 202n77, 272
Suhl, A. 202n78, 272
Sundberg, A.C. 200n64, 238n51, 272

Talbert, C.H. 197n48, 204n7, 272
Thomas, J. 1969. 203n4, 272
Thurston, R.W. 180n21, 272
Torm, F. 175n32, 272
Trevett, C. 168n58, 272
Trummer, P. 19, 144, 150f., 208n45,
235n34, 272f.
Turner, N. 276n7, 273
Twomey, J.J. 209n52, 210nn52,55, 273
Tyrrell, R.Y. 182n27, 273

Unnik, W.C. van 194n31, 273
Usteri, L. 14, 173

Vermes, G. 117, 273
Verner, D.C. 238n52, 273
Vielhauer, P. 193n30, 273
Vine, V.E. 273
Vogel, C.J. de 208n40, 273
Vollmer, F. 273

Wake, W.C. 30, 273
Walaskay, P.W. 197n45, 273
Warmington, B.H. 203n81, 273
Watson, F. 180n18, 223n75, 273
Weiser, A. 198n50, 273

JOURNAL FOR THE STUDY OF THE NEW TESTAMENT
Supplement Series

Preface

Keith S. Cox and Zealure C. Holcomb

The starting point of this book is the idea that understanding statistics in the context of a statistics course or textbook is quite different from understanding statistics in the context of a research article. Indeed, we see the latter, understanding statistics in a research article, as a skill that must be learned, and one that is often underdeveloped in introductory statistics coursework. Thus, a student might earn a high grade in an introductory statistics course but not be able to make heads or tails of statistical procedures from that course when they appear in a research article. This book aims to help students avoid that unfortunate outcome. Our goal is to give students the opportunity to translate their understanding of statistics from the classroom to the journal article.

This book presents brief excerpts from research journals representing a variety of fields, with an emphasis on the social and behavioral and health sciences. The questions that follow each excerpt allow students to practice interpreting published research results.

The questions require students to apply a variety of skills, including:

- locating specific information in statistical tables, figures, and discussions of results;
- performing simple calculations to determine answers to questions not directly answered in the excerpts;
- discussing the authors' decisions regarding reporting techniques;
- describing and interpreting major trends revealed by data, including evaluating the authors' interpretations; and
- evaluating procedures used to collect the data underlying the statistics presented.

Excerpts are drawn from the method and result sections of journal articles, and when needed for clarity, we preface an excerpt with background information so that students will be able to better comprehend the material in the excerpt.

SOME ASSUMPTIONS UNDERLYING THE DEVELOPMENT OF THIS BOOK

A major assumption is that students will find materials based on actual research reports inherently more interesting than the hypothetical examples typically presented in research methods and statistics textbooks.

It is also assumed that students will benefit from practicing with materials written by numerous authors. This allows them to see variations in the uses of statistics and in reporting techniques as they are actually used by researchers.

A statistical guide at the beginning of each exercise provides highlights that help in the interpretation of the associated excerpt. The guides are not comprehensive because it is assumed that students using this book are enrolled in statistics and research courses in which theoretical and computational concepts are covered in greater detail. Thus, the statistical guides should be thought of as reminders of basic points to be considered when attempting the exercises.

Finally, it is assumed that a collection of complete research reports would be too much material to integrate into traditional statistics and research methods courses. Instructors are often pressed for time when just covering the essentials. Hence, this book presents brief article excerpts to conserve instructional time.

CAUTIONS WHEN USING THIS BOOK

Students should be aware that the exercises are based on excerpts from journal articles. Although the excerpts are in the original authors' own words, many important details presented in the complete articles are omitted in this book for the sake of brevity. Before generalizing from the excerpts, students should read the full research articles, which are available through most large academic libraries.

Although answers to the Factual Questions are either right or wrong, there may be more than one defensible answer to each of the Questions for Discussion. At first, some students are surprised to learn that the interpretation of data does not always yield one answer. Yet it is precisely because of this circumstance that practice is needed in interpreting research results as they actually appear in journals.

Finally, students will discover occasional inconsistencies between what is recommended by their textbook authors and the analysis and reporting techniques employed by the authors of the excerpts. Variations are permitted by journal editors, and the excerpts in this book will help students prepare for reading published research articles that are not always "textbook perfect." When taking tests in class, however, students should follow the recommendations made by their textbook authors and their instructors.

ABOUT THE NINTH EDITION

The ninth edition of this book includes two major changes. (1) New statistical topics have been added to the text to better reflect contemporary thinking on statistical subjects, e.g., exercises on p-hacking and the replication crisis. (2) The book includes supplementary materials on how

to perform some of the statistical techniques covered in the text. Data sets, statistical guides, and videos will help instructors and students get comfortable completing some of the classics of statistical analysis (e.g., correlation, regression, *t*-tests, and ANOVA) employing one of the most commonly used statistical packages, SPSS.

Acknowledgments

We are grateful for editorial direction and guidance by Hannah Shakespeare, Matt Bickerton, and Danielle Dyal. Finally, we are grateful for technical reviews by Martin Pettitt and Philip Stirups.

Unit 1

Basic Descriptions of the Data: Measurement and Frequency

CHAPTER INTRODUCTION

Most of today's research is based on numbers in one way or another. The numbers might be heartbeats per minute, or represent DNA type, or they might reflect beliefs about the afterlife. No matter what the numbers are about, they are still numbers. And numbers have standard ways of working.

Statistics is the branch of math that deals with how groups of numbers behave. And since most research today involves groups of numbers, most research involves statistics. For some people, this is pretty intimidating. Research is hard enough to understand, but then statistics get thrown into the mix! We could tell you to not be intimidated, but you probably would not believe us. In fact, at multiple points in our careers, we have been intimidated by the combination of research and statistics. So we probably should not be too preachy about not being intimidated. Instead, the aim of this workbook is to *show* you how to defang the complexity of statistics in research articles. With that skill, you can make sense of research findings across the behavioral and health sciences and beyond.

One thing to notice about this workbook is that we bite off a small bit of a research article and really chew on it. We do not worry about the full article because you do not have to understand *everything* in an article to understand *anything* in an article. We think this is a great way to approach the complexity of statistics in research articles. Take one thing at a time, and stick with it until you get it. We will illustrate this method throughout the book.

The big idea in Unit 1 I is how to understand the basic aspects of a set of numbers, often called a dataset. A short list of straightforward math ideas can go a long way in revealing important features of a dataset, ideas like *percentage* or *cumulative percentage*. To boot, these ideas do not rely on technical or sophisticated math. In fact, you probably learned the math for calculating a percentage in elementary school. This is a point to be encouraged about. Hopefully, you will feel that way after you have worked through Unit 1.

1

DOI: 10.4324/9781003096764-1

Percentage I

Adolescent Substance Abuse

STATISTICAL GUIDE

Percent means "per 100." For instance, say there are 100 residents in a town and 60% are left-handed. This means 60 per 100 are left-handed, or 60 in total are left-handed. Now, you do not have to have a group size of 100 to use the idea of percent. Say the town down the road has 212 residents and 50% are left-handed. To figure out the total number of left-handed residents in this town translate the 50% into a decimal. (Do this by moving the decimal place over two places to the left: from 50.0% to 0.50.) Now multiply 0.50 times the total number of residents in the town (0.50 × 212), which equals 106.

To calculate a percentage, divide the part by the whole and multiply by 100. For instance, say there was a survey given to high schoolers at a mental health treatment center (like in the excerpt below), and 8 of the 234 respondents reported having tried cocaine, then 3.4% reported cocaine use (8/234 = 0.0342; 0.324 × 100 = 3.42, which is written as 3.42% or 3.4%).

EXCERPT FROM THE RESEARCH ARTICLE[1]

> The adolescent clients within three sites of a [substance abuse] residential treatment community (TC) were surveyed . . .
>
> The questionnaire used in this study consisted of 102 questions and was divided into four sections . . . The third section inquired
>
> *(continued)*

1 Solhkhah, R., Galanter, M., Dermatis, H., Daly, J., & Bunt, G. (2009). Spiritual orientation among adolescents in a drug-free residential therapeutic community. *Journal of Child & Adolescent Substance Abuse, 18*, 57–71. Reprinted by permission of Taylor & Francis LLC.

(continued)

about past drug use, including lifetime history[2] and perceived greatest problem drug . . . The youths were queried as to the greatest problem drug among 12 substances (marijuana, hallucinogens, alcohol, benzodiazepines, depressants, noncocaine stimulants, cocaine, heroin, prescription opiates, inhalants, "club drugs," and nicotine).

Table 1
Drug Use Characteristics of Adolescent TC Sample (N = 181)

Substance	Greatest problem drug %	Lifetime use[a] %
Marijuana	65.7	99.4
Nicotine	11.0	81.8
Alcohol	6.1	94.5
Cocaine/crack	5.5	34.8
Club drugs	3.9	32.0
Heroin/illicit methadone	3.3	13.8
Hallucinogens	3.3	31.5
Benzos/depressants	1.2	31.5
Inhalants	0	9.4
Prescription opiates	0	25.4

[a] Percent of sample reporting any use prior to TC admission.

STUDY QUESTIONS

Factual Questions

1. What percentage of the clients reported ever using inhalants?
2. What percentage of the clients reported alcohol as their greatest drug problem?
3. Which substance has the highest percentage for lifetime use?
4. Expressed as a percentage, what was the difference between marijuana and nicotine as the greatest drug problem?
5. How many of the 181 study participants reported nicotine as their greatest drug problem? (Round your answer to the nearest whole number.)
6. How many of the 181 study participants reported ever

---

2   Lifetime use means the adolescent used this substance at least once in their entire life before coming to the treatment center.

using alcohol in their lifetime? (Round your answer to the nearest whole number.)

7. How many of the 181 study participants reported ever using inhalants in their lifetime? (Round your answer to the nearest whole number.)

8. What is the sum of the percentages for the greatest drug problem?

Questions for Discussion

9. If you sum the percentages under the column labeled "Lifetime use," you get considerably more than 100%. Does this make sense? How is this possible?

10. Would you feel comfortable generalizing the results reported here to the general population of adolescents in upstate New York? Explain.

11. Do any of the response rates for "Greatest problem drug" or "Lifetime use" surprise you? Why? Why not?

Percentage II

Nonsuicidal Self-Injury

EXCERPT FROM THE RESEARCH ARTICLE[1]

To review percent, see Exercise 1.1.

Participants included 508 students (51% female) in Grades 6 (35%), 7 (30%), and 8 (35%) at the outset of the study attending a middle school in a moderately sized, middle-class community in the northeastern United States.

Engagement in NSSI (nonsuicidal self-injury) was determined by an affirmative response to the item "Have you harmed or hurt your body on purpose (e.g., cutting or burning your skin, hitting yourself, or pulling out your hair)?" For participants who endorsed engaging in NSSI, follow-up questions were provided to assess frequency of the behavior within the past year and to inquire whether the participant had made a suicide attempt in the past year (90% reported they did not, suggesting that NSSI indeed involves nonsuicidal self-injury).

It was anticipated that engagement in NSSI would be associated with engagement in other health-risk behaviors, including substance use, eating pathology, and sexual risk behaviors.

Table 1
Correlates of Nonsuicidal Self-Injury (NSSI) in Percentages

	NSSI group ($n = 49$)	Non-NSSI group ($n = 459$)
Ever used drugs to get high	46.7	4.4
Smoked cigarettes in the past year	73.3	28.0

1 Hilt, L. M., Nock, M. K., Lloyd-Richardson, E. E., & Prinstein, M. J. (2008). Longitudinal study of nonsuicidal self-injury among young adolescents: Rates, correlates, and preliminary test of an interpersonal model. *Journal of Early Adolescence*, *28*, 455–469. Reprinted by Permission of SAGE Publications, Inc.

	NSSI group (n = 49)	Non-NSSI group (n = 459)
Had sexual intercourse in the past year involving drinking or using drugs beforehand	33.3	11.9
Describe self as overweight	45.9	25.8
Fasted to lose weight or keep from gaining weight in the past month	43.3	7.9
Binged in the past year	76.3	41.1

STUDY QUESTIONS

Factual Questions

1. Which grade level had the smallest number of participants?
2. How many of the 508 students were female? (Round your answer to the nearest whole number.)
3. As a percent of the sample, how many more sixth graders are there than seventh graders? As a whole number, how many more sixth graders are there than seventh graders?
4. Of the six categories of health-risk behaviors in Table 1, which category was reported most often by the NSSI group?
5. For how many of the six categories of health-risk behaviors did the NSSI group have a higher percentage than the non-NSSI group? (Answer this question just by looking and don't worry about a statistical test to show if one percentage is higher than another.)
6. What is the percentage difference between the two groups for "Ever used drugs to get high"?
7. What number of participants in the NSSI group reported they smoked cigarettes in the past year? (Round your answer to the nearest whole number.)
8. What number of participants in the non-NSSI group reported they smoked cigarettes in the past year? (Round your answer to the nearest whole number.)
9. In terms of the numbers of participants, did more of the students in the NSSI group or more of the students in the non-NSSI group report having binged in the past year?

Questions for Discussion

10. For the non-NSSI group, the percentages in Table 1 sum to more than 100%. Explain how this is possible.

11. Does it surprise you that higher percentages of the participants in the NSSI group engaged in health-risk behaviors than participants in the non-NSSI group? Explain.

Frequency Distribution with Percentages

Frequency of Dream Content

STATISTICAL GUIDE

A *frequency distribution table* helps to organize and summarize a distribution. It gives a bird's eye view of the scores in the distribution. It is a table that shows the number of times (or frequency of cases) a score occurred in a distribution. Typically, the scores are listed in order (like low to high) in the first column, and the numbers of cases are listed in the second column. Often, the percentage of times a score occurred is also provided as part of a frequency table.

Excerpt From the Research Article[1]

> Previous studies indicated that various dream topics were reported by a relatively large portion of the sample. These so-called "typical dream themes" could be defined as dreams with similar contents reported by a high percentage of the people . . . Nielsen et al. (2003) developed the Typical Dream Questionnaire (TDQ) that, in the latest version, encompasses 56 dream items . . .
>
> Overall, 2,015 women and 878 men participated in the study (total sample size: $N = 2893$) . . .
>
> [T]he participants were instructed to report their last recent dream in a way as detailed as possible . . .
>
> *(continued)*

---

1 Mathes, J., Schredl, M., & Göritz, A. S. (2014). "Frequency of typical dream themes in most recent dreams: An online study." *Dreaming*, 24(1), 57. Copyright © 2014 by the American Psychological Association. Reproduced with permission.

(continued)

The dream reports were evaluated by a judge using the 56 dream themes of the TDQ. If a TDQ theme was present at least once, the dream was coded with 1, otherwise 0. Multiple themes per dream were possible . . .

Table 1
Number of Typical Dream Themes Per Dream Report

Number of typical dream themes per dream report	Frequency	Percent
0	1,195	41.31%
1	1,045	36.12%
2	443	15.30%
3	150	5.18%
4	47	1.62%
5	13	0.45%

Table 2
Frequency Ranks of Typical Dream Themes (N = 2,893)

Themes	Total sample	Ranks (N = 2,893)
Flying or soaring through the air (11)	11.69%	1
Trying something again and again (3)	11.34%	2
Being chased or pursued (1)	8.95%	3
Sexual experiences (32)	7.29%	4
School, teachers, studying (31)	6.12%	5
Arriving too late (6)	3.98%	6
A person now dead being alive (35)	3.54%	7
A person now alive being dead (36)	3.46%	8
Being physically attacked (2)	3.15%	9
Swimming (7)	2.73%	10

Note: Only the top ten most frequent dream themes are shown from the original version of Table 2.

STUDY QUESTIONS

Factual Questions

1. How many participants are in the study?
2. What percentage of participants identified as men and what percentage identified as women?
3. According to Table 1, what is the most common number of typical dream themes per dream report?
4. What is the frequency and percentage for your answer to Question 3?
5. What percentage of the sample had three or more typical dream themes per dream report?
6. What percentage of the sample had 1 or fewer dream themes per dream report?
7. What dream theme occurred with the highest frequency? What percentage of the sample had this dream theme?
8. What percentage of the sample, at most, had one of the top three ranked dream themes?

Questions for Discussion

9. Table 1 reports that the most common number of typical dream themes per dream report is 0. How can this be?
10. If you add up the percentages in Table 1, they sum to 99.98%. Why do you think they do not sum to 100%?

Cumulative Percentage and Percentile Rank

Norms for a Spelling Test

STATISTICAL GUIDE

A *cumulative percentage* helps to illuminate where a score falls in a distribution. It indicates the percentage of participants that scored at and below a given score. A cumulative percentage is also known as a *percentile rank*. For instance, if 40% of a group had scores equal to or lower than a participant's score, then that participant has a percentile rank of 40; so we say, "they scored in the 40th percentile".

> To review percentage, see Exercise 1.1.

Test makers often try out a test with a large group of participants (known as the *norm group*) and then build a table such as the one in the excerpt below (known as a *norms table*). Those who subsequently take the test can convert their raw score (number of right answers) to a percentile rank using the table. In this way, the scores of later test takers are interpreted in relationship to how the norm group performed.

EXCERPT FROM THE RESEARCH ARTICLE[1]

> This test is composed of 76 words with one or more letters missing. A short line indicates where the letter(s) should be inserted (e.g., exper_ment). Words were selected from lists of the words most frequently misspelled by college students. Brief hints are provided in ambiguous or potentially difficult situations (e.g., capt n/ military rank). The test is timed at 10 minutes.
>
> *(continued)*

---

1 Coren, S. (1989). The Spelling Component Test: Psychometric evaluation and norms. *Educational and Psychological Measurement*, *49*, 961–971. Reprinted by Permission of SAGE Publications, Inc.

A sample of 316 undergraduate university students was tested on the Spelling Component Test. Results from this administration were combined with the 386 subjects tested [earlier] to furnish a normative sample of 702 university students (407 females and 295 males).

The normative distribution of scores, for the full sample and separated by gender, is given in Table 1, in terms of cumulative percentages.

Table 1

Norms for the Spelling Component Test Based on 702 University Undergraduate Students

	Cumulative Percentage		
Raw score	Females ($N = 407$)	Males ($N = 295$)	Total ($N = 702$)
69–70	99.4	99.6	99.5
67–68	98.6	99.6	99.0
65–66	97.1	99.6	98.2
63–64	94.8	97.1	95.9
61–62	92.5	95.5	93.9
59–60	88.0	93.0	90.5
57–58	83.0	87.6	85.2
55–56	76.1	84.7	79.8
53–54	70.9	79.3	74.7
51–52	67.4	76.0	71.4
49–50	63.4	72.3	67.5
47–48	59.0	68.2	63.2
45–46	53.0	61.2	56.7
43–44	45.0	53.3	48.8
41–42	36.9	49.2	42.5
39–40	31.7	43.8	36.8
37–38	25.6	38.2	31.0
35–36	20.5	30.2	25.0
33–34	16.4	24.4	20.4
31–32	11.2	17.8	14.3
29–30	8.1	14.5	11.2
27–28	6.1	11.2	7.9
25–26	4.0	8.7	5.7
23–24	2.0	6.2	3.6
21–22	1.4	4.1	2.5
19–20	0.9	3.7	2.0
17–18	0.3	1.2	1.0
15–16	0.3	0.4	0.3

STUDY QUESTIONS[2]

Factual Questions

1. What percentage of the females had scores at or below 27–28?

2. What percentage of the males had scores at and below 27–28?

3. Compare your answers to Questions 1 and 2. Considering only raw scores up to 28, who is performing better, females or males? Explain.

4. Based on the total sample, what is the percentile rank for a person with a raw score of 34?

5. Based on the norms for males, what is the percentile rank for a male with a raw score of 34?

6. Based on the total sample, a percentile rank of about 85 corresponds to which raw scores?

7. What percentage of the females had scores of 38 or less?

8. What percentage of the males had scores of 38 or less?

9. If the test were being used for college admissions, would a female who had a raw score of 38 be better off if her percentile rank were derived from the female norms or the norms for the total sample (both males and females)? Explain.

10. If the test were being used for college admissions, would a male who had a raw score of 38 be better off if his percentile rank were derived from the male norms or the norms for the total sample (both males and females)? Explain.

Questions for Discussion

11. The researcher states that there were 76 words on the test, but the highest score in Table 1 is 70. Speculate on the reason for this apparent discrepancy.

12. Suppose your professor administered this spelling test to you and offered to give you either your raw score only or your percentile rank based on your gender only. Which would you choose? Why?

13. The norms for the total sample are based on the responses of more females than males. Is this a problem? Explain.

---

2   The researchers used a binary concept for gender/sex in this study. In addition, they did not highlight that female and male were self-identified by the participants.

Rate per 100,000: Alternatives to Percentage

Annual US Homicide Rates

STATISTICAL GUIDE

To review percent, see Exercise 1.1.

Recall that percent is a *rate per 100*. When a characteristic is very rare, percentages can be awkward to read and interpret. For instance, 0.023% of the males in Canada committed suicide in a recent year. This is read as "twenty-three thousandths of one percent," which is awkward to say and even more awkward to understand. Using *rate per 100,000* makes this number more understandable: For males in Canada, in a recent year, the suicide rate was 23 per 100,000. Researchers often present behaviors with very low frequencies using rate per 100,000 for ease of under-standing and comparison.

To convert a very small percentage to a different rate, use the follow-ing multipliers:

If you want to convert a percentage to this rate:	Multiply the percentage by this number: (Multiplier)	Example (Canadian male suicide rate)
Per 1,000	10	0.023% × 10 = 0.23 per 1,000
Per 10,000	100	0.023% × 100 = 2.3 per 10,000
Per 100,000	1,000	0.023% × 1,000 = 23 per 100,000
Per 1,000,000	10,000	0.023% × 10,000 = 230 per 1,000,000

To convert some other rate to a percentage, use the following divisors:

If you have one of the following rates and want to convert it to a percentage:	Divide the rate by this number: (Divisor)	Example (Canadian male suicide rate)
Per 1,000	10	0.23 per 1,000 becomes: 0.23 ÷ 10 = 0.023%
Per 10,000	100	2.3 per 10,000 becomes: 2.3 ÷ 100 = 0.023%
Per 100,000	1,000	23 per 100,000 becomes: 23 ÷ 1,000 = 0.023%
Per 1,000,000	10,000	230 per 1,000,000 becomes: 230 ÷ 10,000 = 0.023%

EXCERPT FROM THE RESEARCH ARTICLE[1]

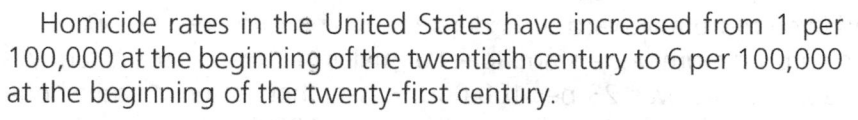

Homicide rates in the United States have increased from 1 per 100,000 at the beginning of the twentieth century to 6 per 100,000 at the beginning of the twenty-first century.

Figure 1. US homicide rates from 1900–2004.

1   Zagar, R. J., Busch, K. G., Hughes, J. R., & Arbit, J. (2009). Comparing early and late twentieth-century Boston and Chicago male juvenile offenders: What changed? *Psychological Reports*, *104*, 185–198. Reprinted by Permission of SAGE Publications, Inc.

STUDY QUESTIONS

Factual Questions

1. The homicide rate in 1920 was approximately 6 per 100,000. Expressed as a percentage (per 100), what was the homicide rate in 1920?

2. Is your answer to Question 1 more or less than 1%?

3. The homicide rate in 1909 was approximately 4 per 100,000. Expressed as a percentage (per 100), what was the homicide rate in 1909?

4. Convert your answer to Question 3 to a rate per 1,000,000.

5. Suppose 0.15% of individuals committed a particular crime in a given year. How many individuals per 1,000 committed that crime?

6. For the percentage in Question 5, how many individuals per 10,000 committed that crime?

Questions for Discussion

7. There is considerable fluctuation in the homicide rates from 1900 to 2000. How would you describe the homicide rate in 2000 in relation to rates across the twentieth century? What do you make of the variations in the homicide rate in America?

8. If you were the director of the FBI's Homicide Taskforce (a national agency in the US), how might you use the information in Figure 1 to try to lower the homicide rate in the United States?

Nominal and Rank Order Data: Scale of Measurement I

PTSD, Substance Use, and Risky Sexual Behaviors

STATISTICAL GUIDE

There is a question that is often overlooked when starting a statistical analysis. It is a key question whenever data is involved. The question is simple: what kind of data is it? This question is sometimes referred to as *scale of measurement* or *level of measurement* because it relates to how a variable or outcome is measured. There are four typical answers to this question in quantitative social sciences. This exercise will look at the first two, *nominal* and *rank order*, and the next exercise will look at the other two.

Scale of measurement is important for two reasons. First, you need to know how something is measured, the scale of it, to understand what the measurement means. Second, the scale of measurement determines what kind of statistical tests can be run with a variable (but we'll cover that in more detail later in the book).

A *nominal* variable is one that puts responses in a limited set of categories. For example, blood type is a biological variable that is nominal (i.e., O, A, B, AB). Affiliation with a political party is another example of a commonly measured nominal variable. In America, for instance, respondents are given the option of selecting Republican, Democrat, Green, Libertarian, or Other. The central feature of nominal data is that it puts responses into categories. It allows you to answer questions like "What percentage of Americans are in the Green Party?"

A major limitation to nominal data is that there are a lot of statistical procedures you cannot use with nominal variables. Many procedures require that the data contain an idea of *more and less*, *higher or lower*. For example, gender is a nominal variable, and it does not make a lot of sense to think of a man as having more gender than a woman. No, man and woman are two examples of gender, but we do not think of them in terms of more and less gender. In contrast, *rank order* data does exactly this: the data tells you which responses are higher or lower, greater or

lesser. During the fall, American college football has a weekly ranking of the top 25 teams. These rankings are an example of rank order data. The number one team is thought to be better than all the other teams, and the number two team is thought to be better than all other teams apart from the number one team, and so on. Rank order data is also called *ordinal* data because you are putting the data in an order.

You might sometimes hear a variable described as *dichotomous*. This means that the variable has two levels or two options. If the two levels are categories without ranking, like cat-lover (yes or no), then the variable is nominal. If the two levels include information about rank, then the variable is rank order.

Watch out! Terminology warning! Some stats folks use these terms slightly differently. Some stat folks use nominal and categorical interchangeably. Others use categorical to mean nominal or ordinal. So you have to read the fine print on this sometimes.

Each of the following article excerpts contains examples of at least one nominal or rank order variable. Read the excerpts and find all examples of nominal and rank order variables. Caution: some of the variables in the excerpts are neither nominal nor rank order.

EXCERPTS FROM RESEARCH ARTICLES

1. The final sample ($n = 289$) was 89% male, 13% African-American, 1.5% Hispanic, 0.5% Native Hawaiian or other Pacific Island, and 85% White. The average age of study participants was 50.4 years ($SD = 15.10$). Service era included 0.3% World War II, 0.8% Korea, 37.7% Vietnam, 16.9% Desert Storm/Desert Shield, 30.4% OEF/OIF, and 11.5% Other.[1]

2. Considering smoking status, we created a . . . variable coding four groups, namely (1) stable smokers who smoked both at T1 and T2; (2) quitters who smoked at T1 and did not smoke at T2; (3) starters who initiated smoking by T2 but did not smoke at T1; (4) stable non-smokers who smoked neither at T1 nor T2.[2]

(continued)

---

1 Cox, K. S., Mouilso, E. R., Venners, M. R., Defever, M. E., Duvivier, L., Rauch, S. A., . . . & Tuerk, P. W. (2016). Reducing suicidal ideation through evidence-based treatment for posttraumatic stress disorder. *Journal of psychiatric research*, 80, 59–63.

2 Thege, B. K., Urbán, R., & Kopp, M. S. (2013). Four-year prospective evaluation of the relationship between meaning in life and smoking status. *Substance abuse treatment, prevention, and policy*, 8(1), 1. © 2013 Konkolÿ Thege et al. Published by Biomed Central Ltd

(continued)

3. *Demographic Characteristics*. These items included age (in years), gender, ethnicity (indicator coded as Non-Hispanic White, Hispanic, African-American, Mixed Ethnicity, or Other [Asian, American Indian/Native American, or "other"]), and whom the student lives with (both parents, only mother, only father, sometimes mother and sometimes father, other, or alone; coded as living with both parents or not). Socio-economic status was assessed by parent education and rooms-per-person in the home. Parent education was measured as the single highest value considered across both parents, as a six-level variable ranging from "did not complete 8th grade" to "attended or completed graduate school." Rooms-per-person was calculated as the quotient of the total number of rooms (except kitchen, bathrooms, closets, or laundry rooms) divided by the number of people living in the home.

   Risky Sexual Behavior. Participants also were asked about risky sexual behavior . . . Participants were asked, "Was a condom used the last time you had sexual intercourse?" This item was coded as "yes," "no," or "I have not had sexual intercourse." A second nominal variable was created for sexual intercourse while using alcohol or other drugs. Specifically, participants were asked: "During the past 30 days, how many times did you have sexual intercourse while using alcohol or other drugs?" (in increments of 5, from "0 times," "1–5 times," "6–10 times," to "More than 30 times," or "I did not have sexual intercourse." This item was coded as "0 times," "1 or more times," or "I have not had sexual intercourse").[3]

4. Lifetime use of alcohol without parental permission, cigarettes, and marijuana were each assessed with a dichotomous item (0 = no, 1 = yes) . . . Past year use of each substance was assessed with open-ended frequency (e.g., "How many times

---

3 Sussman, S., Sun, P., Rohrbach, L. A., & Spruijt-Metz, D. (2012). "One-year outcomes of a drug abuse prevention program for older teens and emerging adults: evaluating a motivational interviewing booster component." *Health Psychology, 31*(4), 476. Copyright © 2014 by the American Psychological Association. Reproduced with permission.

in the past year have you used alcohol/cigarettes/marijuana?")
and quantity items for alcohol and cigarettes (e.g., "On the
days you drink alcohol/smoked cigarettes, about how many
drinks/cigarettes do you have/?") . . .[4]

4   Colder, C. R., Scalco, M., Trucco, E. M., Read, J. P., Lengua, L. J., Wieczorek, W. F., &
Hawk Jr, L. W. (2013). Prospective associations of internalizing and externalizing
problems and their co-occurrence with early adolescent substance use. *Journal of
abnormal child psychology*, *41*(4), 667–677. With permission of Springer.

Interval and Ratio Data: Scale of Measurement II

Depression, Life Satisfaction, and Reaction Time

STATISTICAL GUIDE

Beyond nominal and rank order, there are two further types of data—*interval* and *ratio*.

Interval data can be more informative than rank order data because with interval data the distance between levels is quantified and consistent. For example, the Fahrenheit temperature scale is an interval scale. Going from 45 degrees Fahrenheit to 50 degrees Fahrenheit is the same interval as going from 53 degrees Fahrenheit to 58 degrees Fahrenheit. Each interval is five degrees, and five degrees means the same thing in each instance. Rank ordering does not tell you this kind of information. If Wednesday was hotter than Tuesday, you can rank order them in terms of temperature, but you do not know how much hotter Wednesday was than Tuesday. You need to have set *intervals* of measurement to do this. Many scales in the social sciences produce interval data.

Ratio data can be more informative than interval data because it adds the idea that zero on the scale means total absence of the thing the scale is measuring. For many scales, either there is not a zero or the score of zero does not mean a total absence of the thing. For example, many self-report scales in psychology are constructed so that the lowest possible score is 5 or 10 or even 17. Or take temperature. Zero degrees Fahrenheit is not the total absence of heat. There are negative temperatures below zero. So why does this matter? Consider an example. If a measure is on a ratio scale, then scoring a 10 is twice as much as scoring a 5. In this case it is easy to understand the relationship between a score of 5 and 10. But if the lowest possible score on a measure is a 5, then 10 is not really twice as much as 5, because 5 means something like zero. So what then is the relationship between a score of 5 and 10? It is harder to say if the measure is on an interval scale. In general, ratio scores are easier to interpret because they include the idea of zero.

To sum up, there are four types of data: nominal, rank order, interval, and ratio. And each one gives you more quantitative information than the next: nominal < rank order < interval < ratio.

One final point: people often refer to the type of data as the *scale of measurement* or *level of measurement*. When someone asks, "What is the scale of measurement?" they are asking if the data is nominal, rank order, interval, or ratio.

Below there are further examples of the different kinds of data that are present in research articles. In each of the examples, identify every variable that has an interval or ratio scale of measurement.

One quick and a bit wonky note before you get to the exercise. Below there are several self-report scales that have number ratings for item answers (e.g., 1 means "a little," 3 "moderately," and 5 "a lot"). Researchers often treat such scales as having interval consistency, which we will do for this exercise. Other researchers disagree and treat such data as ordinal as they believe the intervals between such number responses aren't equal, e.g., in our example the distance between 1 ("a little") and 3 ("moderately") is not the same distance as between 3 ("moderately") and 5 ("a lot"). If this sounds complicated, it can be.

EXCERPTS FROM RESEARCH ARTICLES

1. Participants and partners were assessed at baseline, 6, and 18 months via clinic and home visits. The primary outcome was body weight, measured in street clothes with shoes removed using a calibrated digital scale (Tanita BWB 800) and recorded to the nearest 0.1kg. Height was measured at baseline to the nearest centimeter using a calibrated, wall-mounted stadiometer.[1]

2. The mean duration of on-task behavior during the math task was generated from continuous behavioral codings of children's on-task behavior during the math task. On-task behavior

(continued)

---

1 Gorin, A. A., Raynor, H. A., Fava, J., Maguire, K., Robichaud, E., Trautvetter, J., Crane, M. & Wing, R. R. (2013). Randomized controlled trial of a comprehensive home environment-focused weight-loss program for adults. *Health Psychology*, *32*(2), 128. Copyright © 2013 by the American Psychological Association. Reproduced with permission.

(continued)

was defined as visual attention directed toward the math worksheet . . . Any time a participant's gaze left the worksheet, he/she was considered off-task.[2]

3. The PTSD Checklist (PCL)-military version . . . is a 17-item self-report measure of PTSD symptoms . . . PCL scores range from 17 to 85 with higher scores indicating greater symptom severity.[3]

4. The Beck Depression Inventory-II (BDI-II . . .) is a 21-item . . . self-report depression inventory designed to assess symptoms and level of depression. The questionnaire consists of 21 items comprising a list of four statements each about a particular symptom of depression. Scores on the individual items range from 0 to 3. The respondent has to choose the statement that best represented his or her mood during the last two weeks. Total scores can range between 0 and 63, with higher scores reflecting higher levels of depression.[4]

5. The Satisfaction With Life Scale (SWLS) . . . assesses an individual's global satisfaction with his or her life. The scale is composed of five questions that are rated on a 7-point Likert scale. An example of an item is: "In most ways my life is close to my ideal." Total scores on the SWLS range from 5 to 35.[5]

2 Antonini, T. N., Narad, M. E., Langberg, J. M., & Epstein, J. N. (2013). Behavioral correlates of reaction time variability in children with and without ADHD. *Neuropsychology, 27*(2), 201. Copyright © 2013 by the American Psychological Association. Reproduced with permission.

3 Cox, K. S., Mouilso, E. R., Venners, M. R., Defever, M. E., Duvivier, L., Rauch, S. A., . . . & Tuerk, P. W. (2016). Reducing suicidal ideation through evidence-based treatment for posttraumatic stress disorder. *Journal of Psychiatric Research, 80*, 59–63. © Elsevier.

4 Roelofs, J., van Breukelen, G., de Graaf, L. E., Beck, A. T., Arntz, A., & Huibers, M. J. (2013). Norms for the Beck Depression Inventory (BDI-II) in a large Dutch community sample. *Journal of Psychopathology and Behavioral Assessment, 35*(1), 93–98. With permission of Springer.

5 Cox, K., & McAdams, D. P. (2014). Meaning making during high and low point life story episodes predicts emotion regulation two years later: How the past informs the future. *Journal of Research in Personality, 50*, 66–70. © Elsevier.

6. According to both the scientific literature and popular media, all one needs to win a US presidential election is to be taller than one's opponent . . . We collected the heights of the US presidents and their opponents from [an encyclopedia source]. Since 1789, there have been 56 US presidential elections.[6]

6 Stulp, G., Buunk, A. P., Verhulst, S., & Pollet, T. V. (2013). Tall claims? Sense and non-sense about the importance of height of US presidents. *The Leadership Quarterly*, 24(1), 159–171. © Elsevier.

Describing the Data

CHAPTER INTRODUCTION

When you want to understand a dataset, the first task is describing the basic features of the data. That is what *descriptive statistics* do. They give you the big picture of what is going on with variables in a dataset. Researchers start investigating a dataset by calculating descriptive statistics. Then they go on to fancier stuff we will cover in later units.

Most variables in a dataset will have a *distribution* of scores. This means there are a range of scores for that variable. The variable might be a math test, and the distribution is the list of the scores a group of students got when they took the math test. We will use the idea of distribution throughout the workbook.

Central tendency and *dispersion* are two crucial ideas for describing a distribution. *Central tendency* sounds like what it means—the central or common tendency of a set of scores. *Dispersion* means how dispersed or spread out a set of scores is. Unit 2 takes you through a series of exercises on both of these concepts. Unit 2 will give you a good idea of how research articles use ideas like *mean* and *median* and *standard deviation* to describe a dataset.

If Unit 1 covered math concepts that are straightforward to calculate, Unit 2 continues this trend. For example, the *mean* or *average* is not overly difficult to calculate (with a small set of numbers). Still, Unit 2 brings online a few math ideas that are more complicated to calculate. But don't worry about this. Your goal should not be to understand exactly how every statistical concept is calculated.* Instead, it is more important to have a general sense of what a statistical concept means or describes. The nice thing about Unit 2 is that pretty much all the statistical concepts describe the central tendency or dispersion of a variable. So those are the two big ideas you will be working with in Unit 2.

---

* Okay, so your statistics professor might give you a test where you have to exactly calculate some of the ideas in Unit 2. If so, then, yeah, you probably should make it your goal to learn how to do that.

DOI: 10.4324/9781003096764-2

Mean, Median, Mode, and Cumulative Percentage

Counseling Duration

STATISTICAL GUIDE

To review frequency, percent, and cumulative percentage, see Exercises 1.1–1.4.

If you want to know the most typical score in a distribution, there are three different ways to calculate it: the mean, the median, and the mode. These are three different ways to describe the *central tendency* of a distribution. Researchers want to know the central tendency because they like to have one score that best represents all the scores in a distribution.

When someone says, "the average," they typically have the idea of the *mean* (*M*) in mind. The mean often is a good representative for the central tendency of a distribution. The mean is calculated by summing all the scores and dividing by the number of scores. One drawback of the mean is that it is pulled toward extreme scores in an unbalanced distribution (i.e., a skewed distribution, with extreme scores on one side and without extreme scores on the other side to balance it). So in unbalanced distributions, the mean can be a poor representative of the central tendency.

The *median* (*Mdn*) is the score that shows the middle value in the distribution. Half of the scores are above it, and the other half are below it. For instance, if the median for a group is 10.0, then 50% of the cases lie below 10.0, and 50% are above 10.0. The median is *not* pulled toward extreme scores in a skewed distribution.

The *mode* is the most frequent score in a distribution. For instance, if a set of test scores includes the following values 82, 84, 84, and 98, the mode is 84. It appears twice while the other scores appear only once.

Cumulative percentage sometimes appears along with other descriptions of a distribution, like frequency, percent, and central tendency.

The research article below includes cumulative percentage in describing the distribution of counseling duration. A common symbol for cumulative percentage is *cum%*, but another symbol for cumulative percentage is $\Sigma\%$. This second symbol is used because the cumulative percentage is calculated by summing percentages, and the Greek letter Σ means *sum of* in statistics.

The *f* in the table in the excerpt means *frequency*, which indicates how many individuals had each score.

One more note, "scores" are not always "test scores" in statistics. In the excerpt, the scores are "number of sessions completed." Thus, if a client completes ten sessions, their score is 10.

EXCERPT FROM THE RESEARCH ARTICLE[1]

During an academic year, new clients at a university counseling center were recruited to participate in this study. All new clients requesting individual counseling services were eligible to participate. Ninety-four new clients (the majority of new clients at the center) agreed to participate . . . The ages of the participants ranged from 18 years to 47 years (*Mdn* = 21.00, *M* = 22.4 . . .).

Table 1 presents a frequency distribution of counseling duration. Participants completed from 1 to 28 sessions (*Mdn* = 3.0, *M* = 4.6 . . .). As evident in the table, most participants completed a relatively small number of sessions.

Table 1
Frequency Distribution of Counseling Duration

No. of sessions completed	f	%	$\Sigma\%$
1–3	54	57.4	57.4
4–6	22	23.4	80.8
7–9	8	8.5	89.3
10–12	4	4.3	93.6
14–17	3	3.2	96.8
18–28	3	3.2	100.0

Note: *Mdn* = 3, Mode = 1, *M* = 4.6.

---

1 Hatchett, G. T. (2003). Does psychopathology predict counseling duration? *Psychological Reports, 93*, 175–185. Reprinted by Permission of SAGE Publications, Inc.

STUDY QUESTIONS

Factual Questions

1. What is the median age of the clients?
2. What percentage of clients are under 21 years of age?
3. Are the mean and median number of sessions completed the same? Explain.
4. The footnote to the table states: "Mode = 1." What does this mean?
5. How many clients completed 7–9 sessions?
6. What percentage of the clients completed 7–9 sessions?
7. What is the cumulative percentage for 7–9 sessions?
8. What percentage completed at least one session but not more than nine sessions?
9. Which group of scores has the highest percentage of clients?
10. Is the following statement true or false? "57.4% of the clients completed more than 3 sessions."
11. Is the following statement true or false? "100% of the clients completed between 18 and 28 sessions."
12. Is the following statement true or false? "80.8% of the clients completed six or fewer sessions."

Questions for Discussion

13. In the excerpt, the researcher states that "most participants completed a relatively small number of sessions." Do the statistics in the table support this statement? Explain.
14. The researcher chose to group the scores in the first column (i.e., 1–3, 4–6, and so on). An alternative would be to list all the scores individually (i.e., 1, 2, 3, 4, 5, and so on) without grouping. If you had prepared the table, how would you have grouped the scores? Why?

Mean and Range

Cancer Risk-Reduction Behaviors

STATISTICAL GUIDE

The *range* is the difference between the highest and the lowest values in a set of scores. So, if the highest score in a distribution is 7, and the lowest is 4, the range is 3. Sometimes researchers merely report the highest and lowest values (without subtracting) and refer to the two values as the range, e.g., check out Table 1 below.

To review mean, see Exercise 2.1.

The range is one indicator of how dispersed or spread out a set of scores is. The range is important because it gets at the idea of *variation* or *variability* in a distribution—one of the key features of a distribution. If the range is small, the variation is small and vice versa.

By the way, the terms *variation*, *spread*, and *dispersion* are often used interchangeably. They all point toward a central idea—the amount of difference in the scores, one from another, in a distribution. The range is the most straightforward way to calculate the variation or spread in a distribution. It is also the most conceptually simple way to think about variation in a distribution. Still, the range as a description of variation has its limitations, which is why other methods to calculate variation are needed, like standard deviation.

BACKGROUND NOTE

The researchers who reported the information below were studying the physical activity of women who had survived breast cancer. The women in the study self-reported their levels of physical activity (i.e., their activities were *not* observed by the researchers).

Excerpt from the Research Article[1]

Table 1
Physical Activity (Mean Hours/Day Averaged Over Seven Days)

Activity Level	M	Range
Sleep	7.35	5.5–8.8
Light physical activity	8.71	3.0–16.0
Moderate physical activity	3.36	.71–8.3
Hard physical activity	.78	0–4.1
Very hard physical activity	.14	0–1.05

STUDY QUESTIONS

Factual Questions

1. On average, how many hours per day did the women sleep?
2. On average, how many hours a day did the women engage in "Light physical activity"?
3. On average, which type of physical activity was done for the least amount of time?
4. Did the women average more than an hour a day of "Hard physical activity"?
5. Which physical activity had the largest range? Why do you think this activity had the largest range of responses?
6. What is the smallest number of hours of sleep reported?
7. Did some of the women report engaging in no "Hard physical activity"? Explain.
8. Did any of the women report engaging in more than an hour of "Hard physical activity"? Explain.
9. Is there more variation in "Hard physical activity" or in "Very hard physical activity"? Explain.
10. Is the mean for "Hard physical activity" closer to one end of the range than the other? If so, which one?
11. What explains your answer to Question 10?

---

1 Lindsey, A. M., Waltman, N., Gross, G., Ott, C. D., & Twiss, J. (2004). Cancer risk-reduction behaviors of breast cancer survivors. *Western Journal of Nursing Research*, *26*, 872–890. Reprinted by Permission of SAGE Publications, Inc.

Questions for Discussion

12. In your opinion, what are the advantages and disadvantages of using self-reports for gathering data on physical activities instead of directly observing the participants' activities? Explain.

13. The women were asked about their activities over a seven-day period. In your opinion, do you think people can accurately report on these activities going back seven days? Explain.

Median and Interquartile Range

Physical Function in Injured Older Adults

STATISTICAL GUIDE

To review median, see Exercise 2.1. To review range, see Exercise 2.2.

Many variables in the social sciences are distributions, and one important feature of a distribution is *variability*—the spread or dispersion in the scores in the distribution. Looking at the range of a distribution of scores helps to define the variability in that distribution. The *interquartile range* is a further way to specify the variability in a distribution. If the scores in a distribution are ranked from highest to lowest, they can be divided into four equally-sized groups. These groups are called quartiles. The first quartile contains the lowest 25% of scores. The second quartile contains the scores that fall between the 25th percentile and the 50th percentile. The third quartile contains the scores that fall between the 50th percentile and the 75th percentile, and the fourth quartile contains the scores that fall between the 75th percentile and the 100th percentile.

The *interquartile range* is the difference between the 25th and 75th percentile (or the lowest score in the 2nd quartile and the highest score in the 3rd quartile). It contains the middle 50% of the distribution. The interquartile range is helpful to know because it reveals the dispersion of the middle 50% of the distribution. If there is one extreme score in a distribution, the range will be large, even if the rest of the scores are not very spread out from each other. The interquartile range avoids this pitfall because it does not include extreme scores. Instead, the interquartile range shows where the middle of the pack is located.

The *median* falls exactly between the 25th percentile and the 75th percentile, so the median is in the middle of the interquartile range.

If the interquartile range is large, we know that the distribution is spread out, at least in the middle. If the interquartile range is small, the distribution is clumped together around the median.

EXCERPT FROM THE RESEARCH ARTICLE[1]

Although the prevalence of frailty is high in injured older adults, the process of screening is difficult, because they are in pain and may also have altered consciousness . . . Barriers encountered because of injury can preclude the ability to collect important admission information. Thus, a proxy respondent is often called upon to provide information on behalf of the injured older adult . . . The aim of this study was to compare self-reported preinjury physical frailty measures with proxy-reported measures.

Three brief physical function screening instruments were selected, based on the study's interest in multiple domains (strength, function, mobility, activities of daily living (ADLs)). The Vulnerable Elders Survey (VES-13) assigns points to 13 items in four categories (age, self-rated health, common physical tasks, ADLs).

The modified Barthel Index (mBI) assesses 10 ADLs . . . A score of 20 indicates no disability, and lower scores indicate greater levels of dependence.

The Life Space Assessment (LSA) examines an individual's usual patterns of mobility during the month preceding assessment [with higher scores indicating greater independence].

Table 1

Comparisons of Older Adult and Proxy Scores for Screening Instruments for Physical Frailty

Instrument	Median (Interquartile Range)	Perfect Agreement	90% Agreement[a]	Intraclass Correlation
			n (%)	
VES (range 0–12)[b]				
Older adult	3 (1–6)	39 (51)	66 (86)	0.88
Proxy	3 (1–7)			
mBI (range 0–20)[c]				
Older adult	20 (18–20)	48 (62)	69 (89)	0.90
Proxy	20 (19–20)			

1 Maxwell, C. A., Dietrich, M. S., Minnick, A. F., & Mion, L. C. (2015). Preinjury Physical Function and Frailty in Injured Older Adults: Self-Versus Proxy Responses. *Journal of the American Geriatrics Society, 63*(7), 1443–1447. Reprinted with permission of John Wiley and Sons, Inc. © (2015) Maxwell, C. A., Dietrich, M. S., Minnick, A. F., & Mion, L. C.

Instrument	Median (Interquartile Range)	Perfect Agreement	90% Agreement[a]	Intraclass Correlation
			n (%)	
LSA (range 0–120)[d]				
Older adult	62 (39–82)[e]	27 (35)	55 (71)	0.84
Proxy	68 (42–84)			

[a] Percentage agreement within 90% of the possible instrument range. Vulnerable Elders Survey (VES) ± 1 point, Modified Barthel Index (mBI) ± 2 points, Life Space Assessment (LSA) ±12 points.

[b] Higher scores indicate greater vulnerability and frailty.

[c] Lower scores indicate greater dependency.

[d] Higher scores indicate greater independence.

[e] Wilcoxon signed rank, $z = 2.15$, $P = .03$.

STUDY QUESTIONS

Factual Questions

1. What is the median score on the VES for the older adults? For the proxy respondents? What is the interquartile range for the older adults? For the proxy respondents?
2. For older adult respondents, a VES score of 5 is:
   A. above the 75th percentile
   B. below the 75th percentile
3. What is the range of possible scores on the VES? Does much of the range of possible scores on the VES fall outside of the interquartile range for this sample?
4. On the LSA, is the interquartile range similar for the older adult and proxy respondents?
5. For the older adult sample, on the LSA, is the median score close to the middle of the full range of the LSA measure?
6. What is the median score on the mBI for the older adult respondents? For the proxy respondents?
7. Are there any mBI scores in the sample that are higher than the median score?
8. What is the range of possible scores on the mBI? Are the interquartile ranges for the mBI in this sample in the middle of the possible scores on the mBI scale?
9. For an older adult respondent, a score of 27 on the LSA will be in what quartile of scores?
   A. First
   B. Second
   C. Third
   D. Fourth

Questions for Discussion

10. Consider your answer for number 7. How is it that the median is also the highest possible score on a measure?

11. Are the medians and interquartile ranges similar between the older adult and proxy respondents for all three measures? What does this tell us?

Mean, Standard Deviation, and 68% Rule

Asian Values

STATISTICAL GUIDE

To review mean and median, see Exercise 2.1. To review range, see Exercise 2.2. To review normal distribution, see Exercise 3.8.

The amount of *variability* in a distribution is a very important feature of a distribution. It's so important, in fact, that it has multiple names, like *dispersion* or *spread*. The *standard deviation* (*SD*) is a yardstick for measuring variability in a distribution. If the standard deviation is small, the scores in a distribution will mostly huddle close to the mean. If the standard deviation is large, the scores in a distribution will be more widely dispersed from the mean. In fact, you can think of the standard deviation as the *average* amount scores differ, or deviate, from the mean.

In a normal distribution (i.e., a type of symmetrical, bell-shaped distribution), about 34% of cases are within one standard deviation above the mean and about 34% are within one standard deviation below the mean. For instance, if the mean equals 50.00 for a normal distribution and one standard deviation unit equals 10.00, then 34% of the cases lie between 40.00 and 50.00, and 34% lie between 50.00 and 60.00. Thus, 68% of the cases lie within 10 points of the mean (i.e., 68% lie between 40.00 and 60.00).

EXCERPT FROM THE RESEARCH ARTICLE[1]

This study was conducted at a Chinese community center in a southwestern city of the United States . . .

---

1 Lau, M., Markham, C., Lin, H., Flores, G., & Chacko, M. R. (2009). Dating and sexual attitudes in Asian American adolescents. *Journal of Adolescent Research*, *24*, 91–113. Reprinted by Permission of SAGE Publications, Inc.

A convenience sample of youths aged 14 to 18 years old was recruited via posters and word of mouth at the center's after-school volunteer program and Chinese-language school for high school students.

The AVS [Asian Values Scale] uses a modified Likert-type scale in which 1 = *strongly disagree*, 2 = *moderately disagree*, 3 = *mildly disagree*, 4 = *neither agree nor disagree*, 5 = *mildly agree*, 6 = *moderately agree*, and 7 = *strongly agree*. Scores were based on responses to 36 statements written at a middle school reading level . . . The six Asian cultural values themes explored were (1) collectivism, (2) conformity, (3) emotional self-control, (4) family recognition, (5) filial piety, and (6) humility.

Each statement in the scale reflected one of the above themes.

Using the AVS as a continuous scale, scores for level of adherence to Asian values can range from 36 to 252; those with lower scores demonstrate a lower adherence to Asian values, whereas those with higher scores demonstrate a higher adherence.

Fifty-two youths were interested in participating in the study, and 31 youths completed the entire study. The most common reasons for nonparticipation were the time commitment and lack of interest.

AVS scores for the study population ranged from 109 to 206; the mean score was 155.1 (± *SD* 20.7), and the median score was 152. For boys, the mean score was 152.7 (± *SD* 17.6), with a range of 109 to 176 and a median score of 154.5. For girls, the mean score was 158.3 (± *SD* 24.7), with a range of 127 to 206 and a median of 151.

STUDY QUESTIONS[2]

Factual Questions

1. In the excerpt, the mean is reported as a measure of central tendency. What other measure of central tendency is also reported?

2. Which two statistics in the excerpt are measures of the variability in the scores?

3. Assuming that the distribution of scores for the study population is normal, what percentage of participants had scores between 134.4 and 175.8?

4. Assuming that the distribution of scores for the study population is normal, what

---

2 The researchers used a binary concept for gender/sex in this study. In addition, they did not highlight that female and male were self-identified by the participants.

percentage of participants had scores between 155.1 and 175.8?

5. Assuming that the distribution of boys' scores is normal, what percentage of boys had scores between 135.1 and 152.7?

6. Based on the standard deviations, do boys *or* girls have greater variability in their scores?

7. Assuming that the distribution of scores is normal, the middle 68% of boys had scores between what two values?

8. Assuming that the distribution of scores is normal, the middle 68% of girls had scores between what two values?

Questions for Discussion

9. The researchers state that they used a "convenience sample." What is your understanding of the meaning of this term? Is such a sample the best type to use in social science research? Explain.

10. Does the fact that only 31 of the 52 youths completed the study affect your confidence in the results of this study? Explain.

Mean, Standard Deviation, and 95% and 99% Rules

College Student Alcohol Knowledge

STATISTICAL GUIDE

The *standard deviation* (*SD*) gives a numerical value for the amount of variability or spread in a distribution. If a distribution is normal, the standard deviation can be used to gain a lot of information about a distribution quickly:

To review mean, see Exercise 2.1. To review standard deviation, see Exercise 2.4. To review normal distribution, see Exercise 3.8.

- 68% of scores are within 1 SD of the mean of the distribution
- 95% of scores are within 1.96 SDs of the mean of the distribution
- 99% of scores are within 2.58 SDs of the mean of the distribution
- 99.7% of scores are within 3 SDs of the mean of the distribution.

Since 1.96 SDs is very close to 2 SDs, researchers often use 2 SDs as a benchmark. Researchers will say that 2 SDs from the mean (above and below) captures *approximately* 95% of the scores in a distribution (even when 2 SDs actually captures a little more than that). Also notice that 2 SDs from the mean captures the middle 95% of a normal distribution. The most extreme 5% of scores, 2.5% above and 2.5% below, are outside this range.

BACKGROUND NOTE

The study below investigated alcohol education for incoming college freshman. The researchers investigated if the timing of the education had an impact—during the summer before college vs. during the first year of college. The intervention group completed the alcohol education during the summer, and the control group completed the alcohol education during their freshman year.

EXCERPT FROM THE RESEARCH ARTICLE[1]

The authors assessed the short-term effectiveness of a Web-based alcohol education program on entering freshmen.

Study participants were incoming first-year students at a mid-sized, rural, elite, private university in the Northeast . . .

In June of 2006, all incoming first-year students were randomly assigned to either an intervention . . . or control . . . group . . . In mid-July, students in the intervention and control groups received a letter, mailed to their home address, detailing the expectations for completing the online program. Both groups also received printed materials highlighting the university's alcohol policy. Students in the intervention group were expected to complete the precourse knowledge test . . . the Web-based course, and the postcourse examination prior to arrival on campus. The control group participants were expected to complete only the precourse knowledge test and the precourse survey prior to coming to campus . . . The control group was . . . invited to complete the online course during the academic year.

Table 1

Pre- and Postintervention Knowledge Test Scores

		Control group test scores				Intervention group test scores			
		Pre		Post		Pre		Post	
	n	M	SD	M	SD	M	SD	M	SD
All student participants	1,891	73.3	9.9	83.2	12.8	74.0	8.7	88.4	6.2

1   Croom, K., Lewis, D., Marchell, T., Lesser, M. L., Reyna, V. F., Kubicki-Bedford, L., Feffer, M., & Staiano Coico, L. (2008). Impact of an online alcohol education course on behavior and harm for incoming first-year college students: Short-term evaluation of a randomized trial. *Journal of American College Health*, *57*, 445–454. Reprinted by permission of Taylor & Francis LLC.

STUDY QUESTIONS

Factual Questions

1. Just by visual inspection, which group had slightly higher pretest scores, on average?

2. On the pretest, which group had greater variability in their scores?

3. On the posttest, which group had less variability in their scores?

4. Just by visual inspection, which group showed a greater gain from pretest to posttest on the Knowledge Test?

5. Assuming that the distribution of pretest scores for the control group is normal, between what two values are the middle 95% of participants?

6. Does the mean pretest score for the intervention group fall within the range of the two scores that you gave as your answer to Question 5?

7. Assuming that the distribution of posttest scores for the control group is normal, between what two values are the middle 95% of participants?

8. Assuming that the distribution of posttest scores for the control group is normal, between what two values are the middle 99.7% of participants?

9. Assuming that the distribution of pretest scores for the control group is normal, between what two values are the middle 99.7% of participants?

10. Assuming a normal distribution of the pretest intervention group scores, what percentage of the participants had a pretest score between 56.6 and 91.4?

Questions for Discussion

11. If your work is correct, the interval you calculated for Question 8 should be larger than the interval you calculated for Question 7. Does this make sense? Explain.

12. In addition to increases in knowledge, what other outcomes might a researcher consider in a study of an alcohol intervention program for college students?

13. Would you be willing to generalize the results of this study at a private university to public universities? Explain.

z Scores I

BMI around the World

STATISTICAL GUIDE

To review the mean, see Exercise 2.1. To review the standard deviation, see Exercise 2.4. To review normal distribution, see Exercise 3.8. To review percentile rank, see Exercise 1.4.

The *z* score is a helpful tool to quickly understand how far a particular score is from the mean of a sample. Every score in a distribution has a corresponding *z* score. The *z* score for the mean of a distribution is set at 0. If a particular score is larger than the mean, then the *z* score will be positive, and if the particular score is smaller than the mean, then the *z* score will be negative. As scores get farther from the mean, the absolute value of their *z* scores gets larger. So a *z* score of 2 is farther from the mean than a *z* score of 1. Similarly, a *z* score of −2 is farther from the mean than a *z* score of −1.

A *z* score is calculated in a straightforward way. Step 1: Find the difference between a particular score and the sample mean. Step 2: Divide the difference by the standard deviation. Step 3: Proudly display your newly calculated *z* score.

If you think about how a *z* score is calculated, you might realize that a *z* score shows how many standard deviation units a score is from the mean of the sample. For example, if the mean is 50, and the standard deviation is 10, a score of 60 will have a *z* score of 1, as 60 is one standard deviation away from the mean. A score of 40 will have a *z* score of −1, as 40 is one standard deviation below the mean. Also, *z* scores can be decimals, so a score of 57.5 will have a *z* score of 0.75.

Finally, *z* scores tend to range from −3 to +3, as most scores fall within three standard deviations of the mean.

BACKGROUND NOTE

The excerpt below includes Table 1, which shows that if a variable is normally distributed, *z* scores correspond to percentile ranks. Review Table 1 to get a sense of how *z* scores can relate to percentiles.

The excerpt presents data on *anthropometry*, or physical measures of the human body. In particular, Table 2 presents data on the Body Mass Index (BMI) of children and adolescents from around the world. This table presents the percentiles and corresponding *z* scores for different BMI cut points. The three BMI cut points are 17 and below for excessive thinness, 25–30 for overweight, and 30 and above for obesity.

EXCERPT FROM THE RESEARCH ARTICLE[1]

Table 1
Comparison of Percentiles and z scores in Anthropometry

Percentiles	*z* scores
Under normal distribution, a percentile must correspond to a fixed *z* score. Following is a list of usually used percentile–*z* score conversion values.	
0.2nd	−3
2.3rd	−2
2.5th	−1.96
5th	−1.64
15th	−1.04
16th	−1
50th (median)	0
84th	+1
85th	+1.04
95th	+1.64
97.5th	+1.96
97.7th	+2
99.8th	+3

---

1 Wang, Y., & Chen, H. (2014). Use of Percentiles and Z scores in Anthropemtry. In Preedy, V. R. (Ed.), *Handbook of anthropometry: Physical measures of human form in health and disease*. Spring Science & Business Media. Table 1 reprinted with permission of Springer. Table 2 reprinted under Fair Use.

Table 2

Estimated Children/Adolescents' Percentiles and z scores Corresponding to the Recommended BMI Cut Points for Adults for the Classification of Thinness Grade 2 (BMI <= 17), Overweight (BMI >= 25), and Obesity (BMI >= 30)

		Boys						Girls					
		Percentiles corresponding to			Z scores corresponding to			Percentiles corresponding to			Z scores corresponding to		
Data Source		BMI = 17	BMI = 25	BMI = 30	BMI = 17	BMI = 25	BMI = 30	BMI = 17	BMI = 25	BMI = 30	BMI = 17	BMI = 25	BMI = 30
WHO (2007)[a]	USA	—	—	—	—	1	2	—	—	—	—	1	2
IOTF (2000, 2007)[b]	Brazil	3	95.3	99.9	-1.9	1.7	3.1	2	84.8	98.0	-2.0	1.0	2.1
	Hong Kong	9	88.3	96.9	-1.3	1.2	1.9	6	90.2	98.2	-1.6	1.3	2.1
	The Netherlands	2	94.5	99.7	-2.2	1.6	2.7	3	93.5	99.7	-1.9	1.5	2.7
	Singapore	6	89.5	98.3	-1.5	1.3	2.1	9	93.0	99.0	-1.3	1.5	2.3
	UK	2	90.4	99.1	-2.2	1.3	2.7	2	88.3	98.8	-2.0	1.2	2.3
	USA	1	81.9	96.7	-2.4	0.9	1.8	3	83.5	96.0	-2.0	1.0	1.8

Note: This table summarizes the corresponding percentiles and z scores, which correspond to the specific BMI cut points at the age (e.g., 18 or 19 years old) of transitioning to adulthood.

[a] WHO (2007)2007 growth reference, BMI equal to these cut points at age 19 years old (de Onis et al. 2007)

[b] The IOTF reference, at age of 18 years on each country's data set (Cole el al. 2000, 2007)

STUDY QUESTIONS[2]

Factual Questions

1. For a normal distribution, a z score of +1 is at what percentile? How many standard deviations is this score from the mean?
2. For a normal distribution, a z score of −1 is at what percentile? How many standard deviations is this score from the mean?
3. For a normal distribution, what z scores correspond to the 99.8th and .2nd percentiles? How many standard deviations are these two scores from the mean?
4. For boys in Singapore, what percentile and z score correspond to a BMI of 17?
5. For girls in Brazil, what percentile and z score correspond to a BMI of 25?

6. For boys, which country has the smallest z score corresponding to a BMI of 30? What is that z score?
7. Write out an interpretation of what your answer in Question 6 means.
8. Which country has the largest percentage of girls with a BMI that is 17 or below? What z score and percentile correspond to this BMI for this country?
9. For Table 2, a BMI between 17 and 25 is considered most healthy. Which country had the most boys in this range? For this country, what z scores correspond to this range?

Questions for Discussion

10. Suppose you had only been given the mean BMI for each of the countries in Table 2, and you had not been given Table 2 itself. Would that information have been more or less helpful in understanding BMI in these countries than the information presented in Table 2?

11. What is the largest z score in Table 2? Give an interpretation of what that z score means.
12. Do you agree with the labeling of BMI scores in this study, in which BMI ranges are labeled as excessive thinness, healthy, overweight, and obesity?

---

2 The researchers used a binary concept for gender/sex in this study. In addition, they did not highlight that female and male were self-identified by the participants.

z Scores II

Depression Levels in a Dutch Sample

STATISTICAL GUIDE

To review z scores, see Exercise 2.6.

As discussed before, when a distribution is normal, z scores correspond to particular percentile ranks.

BACKGROUND NOTE

The Beck Depression Inventory (BDI-II) is a standard self-report scale for depression symptoms. Since the scale, and its norms, were developed with samples in the United States, it is important to establish norms for the scale when using it outside the US. The excerpt below reports on an attempt to establish norms for the scale with a Dutch sample.

The BDI-II contains 21 items, and scores range from 0 to 63, with higher scores indicating more depression symptoms. Scores in the 20s are generally considered to be suggestive of the presence of moderate depressive symptoms. Scores in the 30s and above are usually considered to indicate the presence of severe depressive symptoms.

EXCERPT FROM THE RESEARCH ARTICLE[1]

> A random selection of individuals in the general population (age range: 18–65 years) received an invitation letter to complete a screening questionnaire via the internet. Six municipalities in the Southern part of the Netherlands cooperated by providing . . . a total of 217,816 names and addresses, and letters were sent to
>
> *(continued)*

1   Roelofs, J., van Breukelen, G., de Graaf, L. E., Beck, A. T., Arntz, A., & Huibers, M. J. (2013). Norms for the Beck Depression Inventory (BDI-II) in a large Dutch community sample. *Journal of Psychopathology and Behavioral Assessment, 35*(1), 93–98. With permission of Springer.

(continued)

Table 1

Norms of the BDI-II total score in a community sample breakdown by gender and education level

		5th Percentile (z = −1.64)	20th Percentile (z = −.84)	40th Percentile (z = −.25)	60th Percentile (z = .25)	80th Percentile (z =.84)	95th Percentile (z = 1.64)
Males	Low education	0	3	8	14	22	36
	Medium education	0	2	5	10	17	30
	High education	0	1	3	7	13	25
Females	Low education	0	4	10	15	24	39
	Medium education	0	2	6	11	19	32
	High education	0	1	4	7	15	27
Total sample		0	2	6	11	18	32

these addresses with the request to participate in this study . . . A total number of 7,500 individuals completed the BDI-II . . . 57.3 % was female (N = 4,300) and 42.7 % male (N = 3,200). Mean age was 43.3 years (SD = 13.3 years, range 18–65 years) . . .

[T]he highest completed level of [education] was rated on an 8-point scale with 1 = no education, 2 = elementary school, 3 = lower technical and vocational training, 4 = medium technical and vocational training, 5 = higher general secondary education, 6 = pre-university education, 7 = bachelor's degree, 8 = master's degree. Education level was further categorized as follows: low education (1, 2, 3: 14.7 %), medium education (4, 5, 6: 50.4 %), and high education (7, 8: 35 %).

STUDY QUESTIONS[2]

Factual Questions

1. How many individuals are in this sample?
2. What percentage of the sample was categorized as low education? Medium education? High education?
3. For all levels of education and gender identifications, a z score of –1.64 corresponded with what score on the BDI?
4. For males with low education, how many standard deviation units from the mean is a BDI score of 14?
5. For females with medium education, how many standard deviation units below the mean is a BDI score of 2?
6. For which group did the highest z score (i.e., 1.64) correspond to the lowest BDI score?
7. For medium education females, what is the difference in standard deviation units between a BDI score of 2 and a BDI score of 19?
8. For your answer in Question 7, what percentage of that subgroup does your answer represent?
9. For low education females, what z scores correspond with BDI scores above 15 and below 10?
10. Which groups have BDI scores higher than or equal to the sample total, for all six reported z scores?

Question for Discussion

11. If you were a clinician in the Netherlands, how might Table 1 be helpful to you?

---

2 The researchers used a binary concept for gender/sex in this study. In addition, they did not highlight that female and male were self-identified by the participants.

T Scores

Treatment of Problem Behaviors in Children

STATISTICAL GUIDE

T scores are similar to *z* scores, as both are standardized ways to show where an individual score falls in relation to the mean of a distribution. *T* scores are most often used with standardized tests or measures as part of psychological and educational assessment. In developing a standardized test, researchers give their test to a large sample and see how the sample performs. This sample is called the *norm group*. Later, when other samples or individuals take the same test, their scores are compared to the norm group sample. *T* scores help to make the comparisons between the norm group and later test takers.

As a rule, *T* scores have a mean of 50.00 and a standard deviation of 10.00 for the norm group on which a new test is standardized. Test makers prepare norms tables that allow a later test taker's raw score (points earned) to be converted to the *T* score equivalents that would have been obtained if the later test taker had been in the norm group.

Because there are about three standard deviation units on both sides of the mean in a normal distribution, in practice, *T* scores range from 20.00 to 80.00 (i.e., three times the standard deviation of 10.00 ± the mean of 50.00).

Note that the mean of 50.00 and the standard deviation of 10.00 are true of the *norm group* but not necessarily true of a subsequent group that is studied. Hence, if a study group has a mean of 55.00, the reader will immediately know that their mean is higher than the norm group's mean. Also, for instance, if the study group's standard deviation is 9.00, the reader will immediately know that their standard deviation is lower than the norm group's standard deviation.

EXCERPT FROM THE RESEARCH ARTICLE[1]

The immediate and long-term effects of a Parent-Child Interaction Therapy-derived program offered at a Kaiser Permanente [HMO] facility were evaluated.

Data were gathered from a Northern California Kaiser Permanente, serving a mostly middle-class, suburban community. Participants were self-referred or referred by their pediatrician or school due to problem behaviors . . .

Eyberg Child Behavior Inventory (ECBI). This self-report measure has two scales: The Intensity Scale measures the frequency of misbehavior; the Problem Scale measures the number of behaviors the parents identify as a problem for them.

Table 1

Mean Raw Scores (and Corresponding T Scores) on the ECBI Measure at Pretreatment and Posttreatment

	Pretreatment	Posttreatment
ECBI Intensity Scale[a]	140.36	114.53
	$T = 62$	$T = 55$
ECBI Problem Scale[a]	15.66	9.00
	$T = 61$	$T = 52$

[a] Clinically significant scores (i.e., above-norm cutoff scores); Intensity score > 131 or $T > 60$; Problem score > 15 or $T > 60$ (Eyberg & Pincus, 1999).

$N = 73$

STUDY QUESTIONS

Factual Questions

1. Which of the four mean T scores in the table is closest to the mean of the norm group?
2. Which of the four mean T scores in the table is farthest from the mean of the norm group?
3. How many of the four mean T scores in the table are above the mean for the norm group?

1 Pade, H., Taube, D. O., Aalborg, A. E., & Reiser, P. J. (2006). An immediate and long-term study of a temperament and Parent-Child Interaction Therapy based community program for preschoolers with behavior problems. *Child & Family Behavior Therapy*, 28, 1–28. Reprinted by permission of Taylor & Francis LLC.

4. By how many raw score points did the average participant decline from pretreatment to posttreatment on the Intensity Scale?

5. By how many T score points did the average participant decline from pretreatment to posttreatment on the Intensity Scale?

6. By how many raw score points did the average participant decline from pretreatment to posttreatment on the Problem Scale?

7. By how many T score points did the average participant decline from pretreatment to posttreatment on the Problem Scale?

8. In terms of raw scores, was there a greater decline on the "Intensity Scale" *or* "Problem Scale"?

9. In terms of T scores, was there a greater decline on the "Intensity Scale" or "Problem Scale"?

Questions for Discussion

10. Are the mean raw scores *or* the mean T scores more informative? Explain.

11. Are the mean scores on the two scales ever in the "clinically significant range"? (See superscript a.) Are the scores in that range at post-treatment? What does this suggest about the treatment?

Displaying Data: Visualizing What Is There

CHAPTER INTRODUCTION

Try to imagine how you would describe a particular apple without seeing it. You could do it (describe how it feels and smells . . .), but it might be hard. The same is true with data. You can describe data without visualizations, but it is hard to do. Since the description is one of the first tasks in working with a dataset, visualizations are a great place to start. Unit 2 covered the basics of *descriptive statistics*. Unit 3 takes the same ideas (e.g., mean and standard deviation) and shows how researchers visualize these concepts with graphs and figures. In essence, you get to *see* the description, instead of just reading about it.

Graphs and figures can be some of the most important features in a research article. In fact, for many researchers, the graphs and the figures (and maybe the tables) are the first things they focus on when reading an article. Unit 3 covers some of the most frequent kinds of graphs and figures that show up in research articles. You can think of these as the greatest hits of visual description of data.

Unit 3 introduces a new wrinkle to thinking about data. So far in the workbook, we have only considered one variable at a time. We discussed the *mean* for the Asian Values Scale or the *range* in hours of sleep per night. In each case, we were focusing on one variable at a time. When we discuss *scatterplots* in Unit 3, we will look at two variables at the same time. For example, we will look at drunk driving rates (variable 1) and alcohol consumption (variable 2) at the same time. Here we are starting to consider the *relationship* between two variables—something we could not do when only considering one variable at a time. Most of the rest of this workbook, and indeed, a lot of statistics, is about relationships between variables.

DOI: 10.4324/9781003096764-3

Histogram

Reading Improvement

STATISTICAL GUIDE

A *histogram* is a standard way to visually display the frequency of the scores of a distribution. In a histogram, the scores on a variable are placed on the horizontal axis (i.e., *x*-axis), and the frequency of those scores are shown on the vertical axis (i.e., *y*-axis). For instance, take a look at the histograms below. The reading scores for the sample are on the *x*-axis, and the frequency of each score is on the *y*-axis.

Recall that the *mode* is the most frequently occurring score in a distribution. The mode is easy to identify in a histogram because it is the tallest bar. So you can find the ten modes in the histograms below in about 7 seconds.

A histogram can be helpful in identifying *outliers*, scores that are very different than almost all other scores. For instance, look at the histogram below, on the right side, second from the top. Most of the scores are 50 and above, but way to the left there are a few outliers around 40.

The histograms of some distributions are *symmetrical* around the mode. The histograms of some distributions are somewhat symmetrical around the mode. And the histograms of some distributions are really not symmetrical around the mode. These latter histograms are called *skewed*. Skew comes in two varieties, positive and negative. *Positive skew* has a long tail to the right and the bulk of scores pushed to the left. *Negative skew* has a long tail to the left and the bulk of scores pushed to the right.

EXCERPT FROM THE RESEARCH ARTICLE[1]

The Observation Survey of Early Literacy Achievement (OS; Clay, 2002) is an individually administered assessment tool that is used extensively in the United States and other countries.

FIGURE 1
FREQUENCY DISTRIBUTIONS OF CLAY'S OBSERVATION SURVEY SCALES
AT BEGINNING AND END OF GRADE 1 (n = 182)

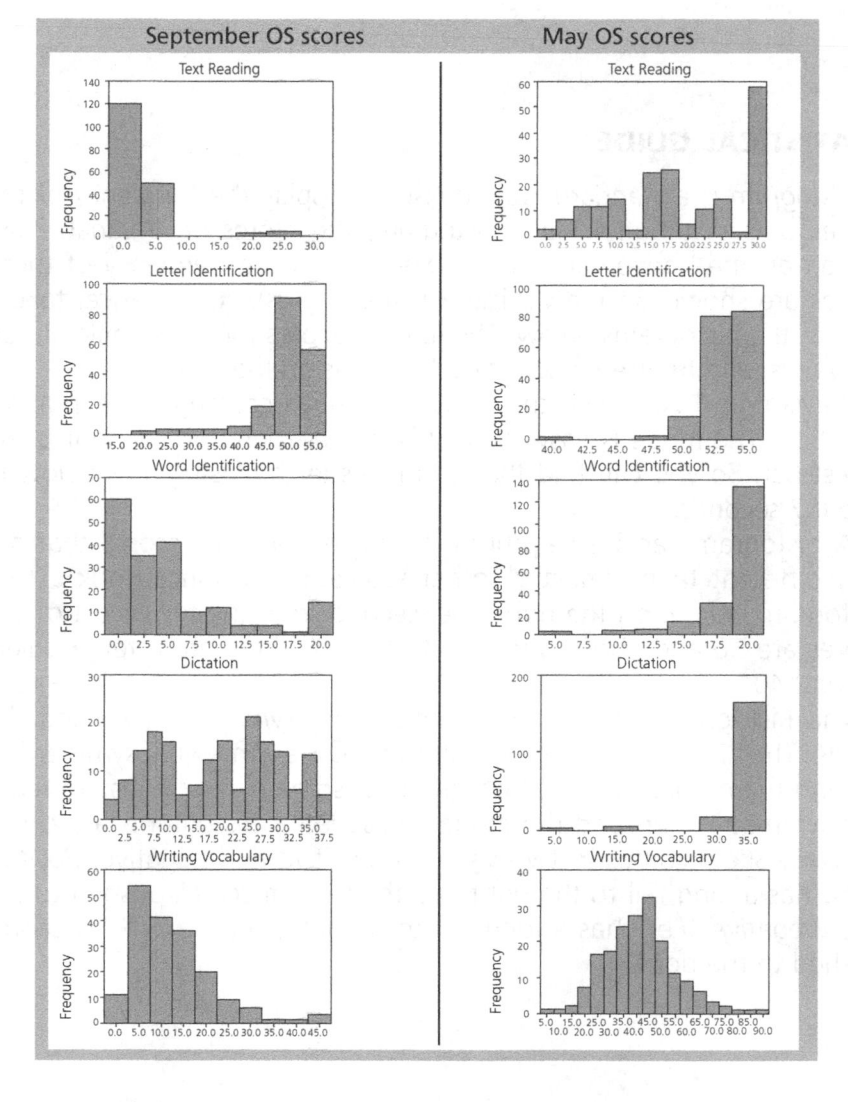

1 Denton, C. A., Ciancio, D. J., & Fletcher, J. M. (2006). Validity, reliability, and utility of the Observation Survey of Early Literacy Achievement. *Reading Research Quarterly*, *41*, 8–34. With Permission of John Wiley & Sons, Inc. © 2006 International Reading Association.

The participants in the current study . . . were 182 first-grade students . . . Of these students, 130 had been identified as being at risk for reading difficulty, and 52 were typically developing readers from the same classrooms.

At the beginning and end of first grade, all students ($n = 182$) were individually assessed . . . We administered the OS to the participating first graders in September [the pretest] and early May [the posttest] of the same school year. Figure 1 presents the score distributions for the 182 students . . .

STUDY QUESTIONS

Factual Questions

1. What is the mode for Writing Vocabulary on the pretest (September OS Scores)?
2. What is the mode for Writing Vocabulary on the posttest (May OS Scores)?
3. Does the distribution for Word Identification on the pretest have a positive skew *or* negative skew?
4. Does the distribution for Word Identification on the posttest have a positive skew *or* negative skew?
5. Which one of the pretests clearly has a negative skew?
6. Which one of the posttests has the least skew (i.e., is most symmetrical)?
7. For which one of the tests is there the least change from pretest to posttest?
8. Which one of the following is more skewed?
   A. Dictation pretest
   B. Dictation posttest
9. Which one of the distributions comes closest to having a bell shape (i.e., being a normal curve)?
10. What is the approximate frequency for a score of 50.0 on the Letter Identification pretest?

Questions for Discussion

11. In your opinion, which test is the least useful for measuring reading improvement at the first-grade level?
12. Suppose the researchers presented only the mean score on each pretest and the mean score on each posttest (without presenting histograms). Would this be a better way to present the results?

Mean, Median, and Histogram
Mental Health Contact Hours

STATISTICAL GUIDE

The mean, median, and mode, the *measures of central tendency*, have important relationships with a histogram. Understanding these relationships helps to illuminate the basic contours of a distribution. As we saw in the previous exercise, the mode is the highest bar in a histogram. In this exercise, we will focus on how the mean and median relate to the histogram. (*Note*: the mean is sometimes referred to as the *average*.)

To review histogram, see Exercise 3.1. To review mean and median, see Exercise 2.1.

And just as a quick review, two points: (1) Small numbers of scores that are far from the bulk of the scores are called *outliers*. (2) A distribution with extreme scores to the right (but not the left) is said to have a positive skew, while one with extreme scores to the left (but not to the right) is said to have a negative skew.

EXCERPT FROM THE RESEARCH ARTICLE[1]

This study surveyed a sample of . . . mental health professionals employed by two community mental health agencies in rural northern and central Michigan . . . The survey sample included social workers (65.8%), psychologists (11%), counselors (8.2%), and other professionals (4%).

1 Riebschleger, J. (2005). Mental health professionals' contact with family members of people with psychiatric disabilities. *Families in Society: The Journal of Contemporary Social Services, 86*, 9–16. Reprinted under Fair Use.

   Figure 1 demonstrates that community mental health professionals reported 0 to 16 hours/week of family contact time [i.e., contact
time with family members of those with psychiatric disabilities]. The
mean of reported family contact hours per week was 3.5; the mean
was 3.02 with two large outliers omitted. Given the large positive
skew of the distribution . . . a useful measure of central tendency
is the median of 2 hours/week of reported family contact time.
The average number of hours per week of family contact time for
professionals who served children was 7.39; the average number of
hours per week of family contact time for professionals who served
adults was 2.58.

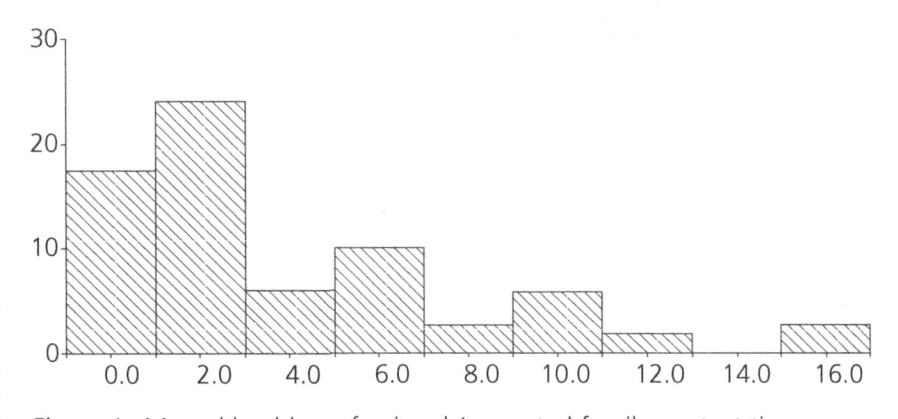

Figure 1. Mental health professionals' reported family contact time.

Note: Professionals' family contact hours per week (*N* = 69); Mean = 3.5; Adjusted
Mean = 3.02; Median = 2.0.

STUDY QUESTIONS

Factual Questions

1. What is the sample size?
2. In the histogram, are the outliers far to the left or far to the right?
3. By how many points do the mean of 3.5 and the median differ?
4. How have the outliers influenced the mean relative to the median?
5. Going by Figure 1, what is the mode of the distribution? What is the relationship between the mode and the median in this case?
6. Is the distribution in the histogram skewed? Explain.

Questions for Discussion

7. Do you think that the mean of 3.5 or the median of 2.0 is better for describing the central tendency of the distribution in the histogram? Explain.

8. What kind of information does the adjusted mean provide that the mean of 3.5 does not provide? (See the text and the figure to determine what the adjusted mean is.)

9. In the last sentence, the researcher reports two averages (7.39 and 2.58). Do you think these are means or medians?

10. The sample included various subgroups of mental health professionals (e.g., social workers and psychologists). In your opinion, would it have been more informative to provide separate histograms for each type of professional?

Stem and Leaf Plot

Competency to Stand Trial

STATISTICAL GUIDE

A *stem and leaf plot* is one among many ways to visualize a set of scores. Check out the stem and leaf plot below (Figure 1) to see what they typically look like. The strength of the stem and leaf plot is that it quickly summarizes the data, while presenting every data point in the distribution. Take Figure 1. The stem column is the tens place for scores, and the leaf column is the ones place for scores. Start at the bottom. The stem column has a 5 in it, and the leaf column also has a single 5 in it. This means there was one score of 55 in the dataset. (Disregard the decimal point.) Now go up to the second 5 in the stem. It has a 0 (zero) next to it in the leaf column. This means there is one score of 50 in the dataset. Continuing up the stem column, there is a 48, and a 42, and 36, and 30. Now, things get more interesting in the 20s. There are seven scores from 25 to 29: 25, 25, 25, 26, 27, 27, and 29. Notice that 5 is repeated three times next to the stem of 2, and this means there were three scores of 25.

A stem and leaf plot can be thought of as a way to visualize the frequency of scores, while maintaining the individual scores. In fact, stem and leaf plots often include a frequency column, as in Figure 1. But notice that the information in the frequency column is redundant, as one could count the number of scores in each row of the leaf to determine the frequency.

BACKGROUND NOTE

The stem and leaf plot in Figure 1 has one confusing detail. Each stem has a decimal point after it. This suggests that the stem is the ones place, and the leaf is the tenths place. The article itself makes it clear this is the wrong way to interpret this figure. The stem is the tens place, and the

leaf is the ones place. In addition, the data in the stem and leaf plot are percentages, so the bottom row should be read as 55%. The second bottom row should be read as 50% and so on. This is one tricky part about stem and leaf plots. You have to figure out the value of the stem and of the leaf to interpret the figure.

EXCERPT FROM THE RESEARCH ARTICLE[1]

This study examined clinician variation in Competency to Stand Trial (CST) opinions within two statewide samples of clinicians: Virginia and Alabama.

Virginia. Sample 1 featured 55 Virginia clinicians (42 psychologists, nine psychiatrists, and four social workers) who each conducted at least 20 competence evaluations ($M = 121.5$, $SD = 200.4$, range = 20–963), for a total of 6,680 evaluations, between 1993 and 2003 . . .

We first calculated, for each clinician, the percentage of cases in which that clinician rendered an opinion of incompetent to stand trial (IST). In Virginia, rates of IST findings varied considerably among the evaluators, ranging from 0% to 62% with an average of 20.4% ($SD = 15.7$).

.Rates of IST findings differed substantially by the evaluator's profession. Among the four social workers . . . the IST rate was consistently above 40% ($M = 46.1\%$, $SD = 2.1$). Among the nine psychiatrists, seven had IST rates lower than 8%, while one had a rate of 20.0% and another had a rate of 62.5%. After removing the one clear outlying psychiatrist (IST = 62.5%), the mean rate of IST opinions among psychiatrists was 5.8% ($SD = 6.0$). Psychologists' rate of IST opinions fell between the other groups, with a mean rate of 20% ($SD = 13.0$). The distribution of IST rates for psychologists was positively skewed . . . with most tending to find fewer than 30% to be IST (see Figure 1).

1   Murrie, D. C., Boccaccini, M. T., Zapf, P. A., Warren, J. I., & Henderson, C. E. (2008). "Clinician variation in findings of competence to stand trial." *Psychology, Public Policy, and Law*, 14(3), 177. Copyright © 2008 by the American Psychological Association. Reproduced with permission.

Frequency	Stem	Leaf
5.00	0.	02344
6.00	0.	566799
4.00	1.	0034
8.00	1.	55667889
6.00	2.	001133
7.00	2.	5556779
1.00	3.	0
1.00	3.	6
1.00	4.	2
1.00	4.	8
1.00	5.	0
1.00	5.	5

Figure 1. Stem and leaf plot of incompetent to stand trial rates for psychologists in Virginia who had performed 20 or more evaluations.

STUDY QUESTIONS

Factual Questions

1. Data on how many psychologists is displayed in Figure 1?
2. What is the mean rate for Incompetent to Stand Trial (IST) opinions for psychologists?
3. Inspecting the stem and leaf plot, does the answer to Question 2 make sense?
4. What is the mode in Figure 1?
5. Write out all the IST rates that fell between 20% and 24%.
6. Write out all the IST rates that fell between 5% and 9.99%.
7. Can you find the IST rate for all 42 psychologists just by looking at Figure 1?
8. Without looking at the Frequency column, can you tell which bins (i.e., 0% to 4.99%, 5% to 9.99%, etc.) have more data points in them? Explain.
9. Which two bins (i.e., 0% to 4.99%, 5% to 9.99%, etc.) have the greatest number of data points in them?

Questions for Discussion

10. Why might it matter that clinicians have widely varying rates of IST opinions?
11. Why might psychiatrists, psychologists, and social workers have such markedly different rates of IST opinions?

Box and Whisker Plot

Serotonin Transporter Gene and Anti-Depressant Response

STATISTICAL GUIDE

The *box and whisker plot* is a simple way to visualize the spread or dispersion of a set of scores. Three box and whisker plots can be seen below in Figure 1. You will notice that there are three rectangles. This is the *box*. The *whiskers* are the lines that extend out from the top and bottom of the three rectangles. Here's a guide for interpreting a typical box and whisker plot:

To review median and interquartile range, see Exercise 2.3.

Median score	Line in the rectangle
75th percentile score	Top of the rectangle
25th percentile score	Bottom of the rectangle
Highest score	Top whisker
Lowest score	Bottom whisker

BACKGROUND NOTE

Serotonin is an important chemical in the brain. (It's a neurotransmitter to be technical about it.) It helps communicate signals between brain cells. For depressed individuals, serotonin is not as efficient in communicating signals between brain cells. The study below investigates serotonin genes and the uptake of serotonin in the blood when individuals are given a drug that boosts serotonin levels.

Figure 1 has three groups: *l/l*, *l/s*, and *s/s*. The *l* stands for long, and the *s* stands for short. Each group has a different version, or *genotype*, of a serotonin-related gene. The *x*-axis in Figure 1 gives the three genotypes. The *y*-axis (Vmax) is the rate of serotonin uptake in the blood.

EXCERPT FROM THE RESEARCH ARTICLE[1]

We enrolled 99 depressed patients [in Korea]. The baseline clinical evaluation was completed in close proximity to the biological studies. Blood was drawn between 0800 and 1000 hours for genotyping and 5-HT uptake measures . . .

Eighty-eight of the 99 enrolled patients (88.8 %) completed the six-week treatment trial . . .

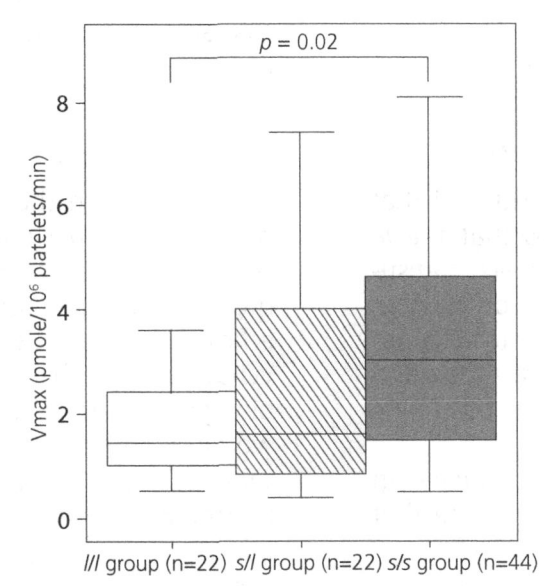

lll group (n=22) *s/l* group (n=22) *s/s* group (n=44)

5-HTTLPR in Depressive Patients

Fig. 1 Box and whisker plot comparison of serotonin uptake rates (Vmax values, pmoles/10^6 platelets/minute) among the different variants of 5-HTT gene promoter polymorphism in depressed patients. Each box displays the median, 75th percentile, and 25th percentile values; *horizontal bars* indicate the highest and lowest observed values

STUDY QUESTIONS

Factual Questions

1. How many individuals are in each group?
2. What is the median Vmax rate for each group?
3. Which box has the smallest spread in Vmax rates? What is that spread?

1 Myung, W., Lim, S. W., Kim, S., Kim, H., Chung, J. W., Seo, M. Y., . . . & Kim, D. K. (2013). Serotonin transporter genotype and function in relation to antidepressant response in Koreans, *Psychopharmacology*, *225*(2), 283–290. With permission of Springer.

4. Which group has the widest whiskers for Vmax scores? What is that spread?
5. What are the 75th percentile Vmax scores for the three groups?
6. The median score for Vmax rate for the *l/l* group would be in about what percentile in the *s/s* group?

7. Which group has the largest standard deviation in its Vmax rates?
8. Which group has the smallest standard deviation in its Vmax rates?
9. Which group has the largest mean value for Vmax?
10. Estimate what percentage of the *s/s* group has Vmax scores that are higher than the scores of every *l/l* individual.

Questions for Discussion

11. The statement in Figure 1 that $p = .02$ indicates that the *l/l* and *s/s* groups have statistically significant differences in their Vmax rates. Given what you see in the box and whisker plots, does this make sense? Explain.
12. This study was conducted in Korea. The authors note that the findings are the opposite of what is usually found in American samples, where *l/l* groups uptake serotonin more efficiently than *s/s* groups. What do you think about a biological finding in psychiatry working one way in Korean samples and the opposite way in American samples?

Line Graph with Rate per 100,000

International Homicide Rates

STATISTICAL GUIDE

To review rate per 100,000, see Exercise 1.5.

A line graph can be a useful way to visually display changes in the frequency of a variable over time. Check out Figure 1 below. The y-axis is the frequency of the variable and the x-axis is the relevant measure of time, i.e., years. The frequency of intentional homicide is very low, and so Figure 1. displays it in terms of rate per 100,000 people. Line graphs often include such adjustments when the frequency of a variable is very low, so that changes in frequency can be more easily seen.

EXCERPT FROM THE RESEARCH ARTICLE[1]

In 1983 Freda Adler published Nations Not Obsessed with Crime, a unique monograph that aimed to identify the common characteristics of countries with relatively low crime rates . . .

The main data source for this paper is the Crime Trends Surveys (CTS) of the United Nations. . . .

Figure 1 shows the trends in intentional homicide rates for Adler's low-crime countries using the available CTS data from 1970 to 2010, supplemented with other national police data gathered in the UN Global Study on Homicide.

(continued)

---

1   Stamatel, J. P. (2014). Revisiting nations not obsessed with crime. *Crime, Law and Social Change*, *62*(2), 113–129. With permission of Springer.

(continued)

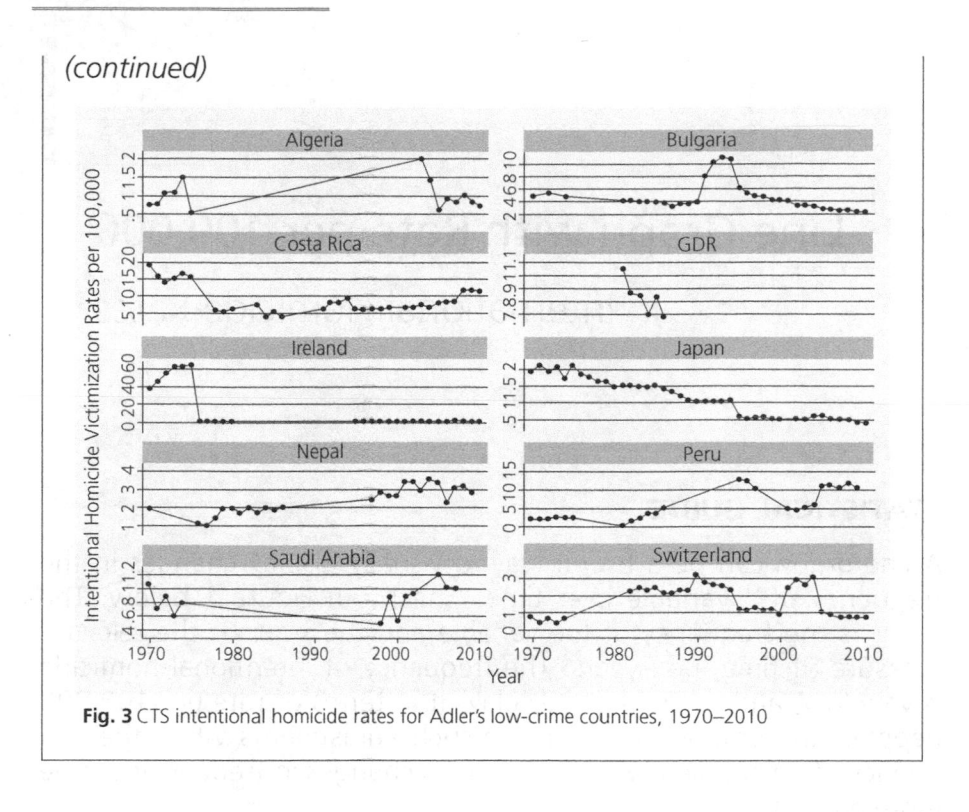

Fig. 3 CTS intentional homicide rates for Adler's low-crime countries, 1970–2010

STUDY QUESTIONS

Factual Questions

1. Are the values on the *y*-axes the same for each country in Figure 1?
2. What explains the answer to Question 1?
3. Which country has the highest homicide victimization rate? What year was it, approximately?
4. What was the rate per 100,000 for your answer in Question 3?
5. Which country had a steadily decreasing homicide victimization rate from 1970 to 2010?
6. For Japan, what was the homicide victimization rate in 1970 and what was it in 2010?
7. How many times greater is the homicide victimization rate in Japan in 1970 when compared with Japan in 2010?
8. Suppose there were 200,000 people in Japan in 2010. How many murders would have occurred in 2010 in Japan?
9. Suppose there were 1,000,000 people in Nepal in 1970. How many murder victims would there have been in 1970 in Nepal?

Questions for Discussion

10. For the difference in murder victimization between 1970 and 2010, categorize each country as either *clearly lower*, *clearly higher*, or *about the same*? Why did you put each country in each category?

11. If you were a policymaker trying to understand how to decrease the murder rate, what country and time period would you most like to study?

12. Are there any overall trends you see across all ten countries? Explain your answer.

Scatterplot

Population Drinking and Drunk Driving

STATISTICAL GUIDE

A *scatterplot* (also known as a *scattergram* or *scatter diagram*) visually depicts the relationship between two variables on the *xy*-coordinate plane (see Figure 1 below). One variable is on the *x*-axis, and the other variable is on the *y*-axis. For each case or participant, a dot is placed to show where the case stands on both variables. So if there are 25 participants, there will be 25 dots on the *xy*-coordinate plane.

Patterns in the dots speak to the nature of the *relationship* between the two variables. Diagonal patterns of dots, from the lower left to the upper right, indicate a *direct* or *positive* relationship. Diagonal patterns, from the upper left to the lower right, indicate an *inverse* or *negative* relationship. If there is no clear pattern, and the dots just appear scattered, there is likely a weak relationship, or none at all, between the two variables.

BACKGROUND NOTE

For the excerpt below, DWI stands for "driving while intoxicated," and BAC stands for "blood alcohol content." Also note that the rates of DWI are given per 100,000 inhabitants. See Exercise 1.5 for a review of rates per 100,000. Also note that both the *x* and *y*-axis in the diagrams have the symbol (Ln) on them. This indicates that the natural log of each variable is being displayed.

EXCERPT FROM THE RESEARCH ARTICLE[1]

We focused on the period 1957–1989, during which the DWI leg-islation remained unchanged in Norway, as well as in Sweden. For

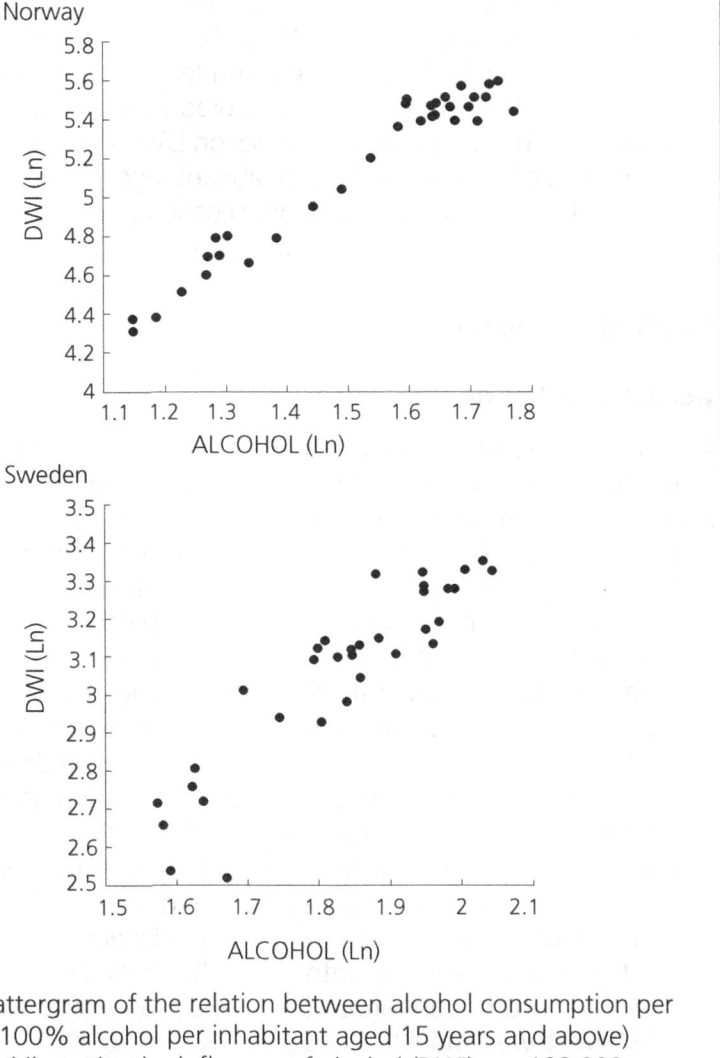

Figure 1. Scattergram of the relation between alcohol consumption per capita (liters 100% alcohol per inhabitant aged 15 years and above) and driving while under the influence of alcohol (DWI) per 100,000 inhabitants aged 15–69 years in Norway and Sweden.

(continued)

1 Norström, T., & Rossow, I. (2013). Population drinking and drink driving in Norway and Sweden: an analysis of historical data 1957–89. *Addiction*, *108*(6), 1051–1058. With Permission of John Wiley & Sons, Inc. © 2013 The Authors, *Addiction* © 2013 Society for the Study of Addiction.

(continued)

Norway, annual data on convictions for DWI (i.e., with a BAC > .05%) per 100,000 inhabitants (15–69 years) were obtained from Statistics Norway. The DWI proxy for Sweden comprised the number of people suspected of DWI per 100,000 inhabitants (aged 15–69 years) (source: Traffic Injuries, various issues, Statistics Sweden). These data are based on the information gathered by the police at the scene of the crash. A driver suspected by the police to be under the influence of alcohol is screened by means of breathalyzer or blood sample tests. These data comprise the basis for official statistics on DWI. Data on total alcohol sales in liters of pure alcohol per inhabitant (aged 15 years and older) were used as a proxy for total alcohol consumption . . .

STUDY QUESTIONS

Factual Questions

1. What are the two variables in the scatterplots in Figure 1?
2. Are the values on the *x*- and *y*-axes the same for the scatterplot for Norway and the scatterplot for Sweden? Explain why or why not.
3. Data from how many distinct years are represented in each scatterplot?
4. How many DWI rates are represented in each scatterplot?
5. How many years of total alcohol sales per capita are represented in the scatterplots?
6. For the year in Norway with alcohol consumption around 1.45, what was the DWI rate per 100,000?

7. For Sweden, if the alcohol consumption was above 2, then the DWI rate per 100,000 was which of the following?
   A. above 3
   B. below 3
   C. exactly 3
8. Do the two scatterplots look generally similar in their shape or generally dissimilar?
9. The scatterplots suggest which of the following relationships between alcohol consumption and DWI rate?
   A. Direct
   B. Indirect
   C. No relationship

Questions for Discussion

10. This study uses alcohol sales per capita as a proxy for alcohol consumption per capita. Do you think this is valid? In other words, do you think that alcohol purchases per capita are a good approximation of alcohol consumption per capita?
11. Do you think scatterplots with these variables would look similar in other countries? Why or why not?

Scatterplot and Regression Line

Child Poverty and Mortality

STATISTICAL GUIDE

To review scatterplots, see Exercise 3.6. To review rate per 100,000, see Exercise 1.5.

A *regression line* drawn through a scatterplot shows the overall pattern of the data points using a single straight line (see Figure 1 below). The line is an attempt to give a best estimate of all the data points. The line will not be a perfect estimation but rather an approximation. This line is usually referred to as a "best-fit line." It is drawn to minimize the distance between it and each data point.

As with correlation, when the line rises from the lower left to the upper right, it indicates that the relationship is *direct* (i.e., positive). When the line falls from the upper left to the lower right, it indicates that the relationship is *inverse* (i.e., negative). If the dots on the scatterplot all fall exactly on a regression line, then the line does a perfect job approximating the real data (the dots). If the dots are widely scattered, and far from the line, then the regression line does a worse job of approximating the real data. In addition, scatterplots with widely scattered dots, without a clear pattern, will represent smaller correlations.

The slope of a regression line tells you about the size of the correlation between the two variables. The steeper the slope, the larger the correlation. A flat regression line means a correlation near zero.

Note that the "participants" in the study that follows are states within the United States.

EXCERPT FROM THE RESEARCH ARTICLE[1]

The federal poverty line, an absolute measure of childhood deprivation that provides a common standard for all US children, was . . . designed to represent roughly three times the average cost of the least expensive nutritionally adequate food plan, as determined by the Department of Agriculture.

We obtained estimates of the percentage of children living below the federal poverty level in each state from the . . . poverty estimate files prepared by the U.S. Bureau of the Census [and examined their relationship with child mortality rates].

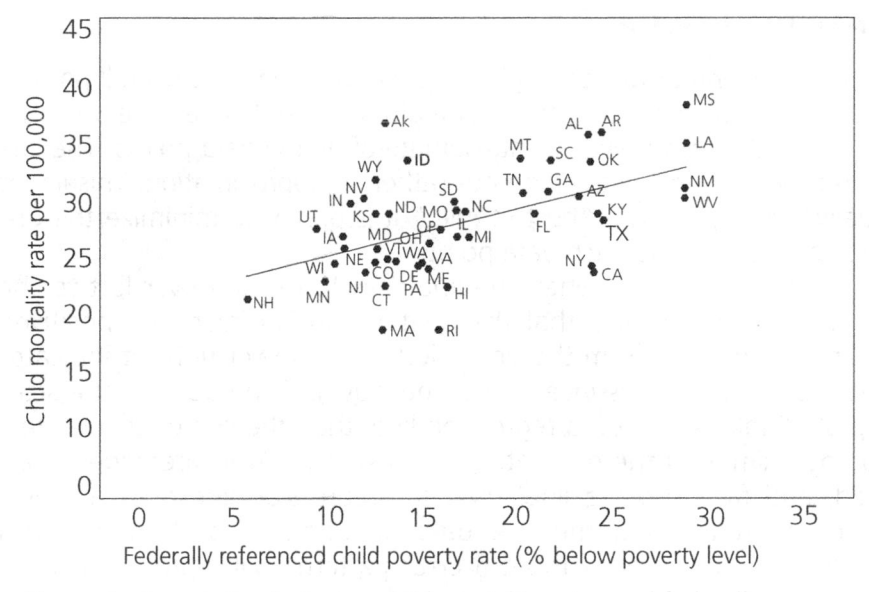

Figure 1. Association between child mortality rates and federally referenced child poverty rates.

STUDY QUESTIONS

Factual Questions

1. Compared with other states, does New Hampshire (i.e., NH) have a high or low child poverty rate? Explain.

2. Compared with other states, is New Hampshire near the top or near the bottom in its child mortality rate? Explain.

1 Hillemeier, M. M., Lynch, J., Harper, S., Raghunathan, T., & Kaplan, G. A. (2003). Relative or absolute standards for child poverty: A state-level analysis of infant and child mortality. *American Journal of Public Health*, *93*, 652–657. Reprinted with permission of Sheridan Content Solutions.

3. Do states with high child poverty rates also have high mortality rates? If yes, give an example.

4. Do states with low child poverty rates also have low mortality rates? If yes, give an example.

5. Considering your answers to Questions 3 and 4, does the relationship seem to be direct (i.e., positive) or inverse (i.e., negative)? Explain.

6. Rhode Island (RI) has one of the lowest child mortality rates. Does it also have one of the lowest child poverty rates? Explain.

7. Consider the four states at the far right of the scatterplot (i.e., MS, LA, NM, and WV). In terms of child mortality rates, a child would have a better chance of surviving childhood in which of these four states?

8. Is Alaska (AK) a good example of a state conforming to the overall trend indicated by the regression line or is it an exception? Explain.

9. New Hampshire has a child mortality rate of about 21 per 100,000. Is this mortality rate more or less than 1%? Explain.

Questions for Discussion

10. If you were describing the results of this study to another student, would you describe the relationship between child mortality and poverty as *very strong*? Explain.

11. Do the results of this study clearly confirm the conclusion that child poverty *causes* child mortality? Explain.

12. There is considerable variation from state to state in child poverty rates, from about 8% for NH to about 30% for MS, LA, NM, and WV. Does this amount of variation surprise you? Explain.

13. Based on the data reported in this study, do you agree with the conclusion that the researchers stated as the last sentence of their paper? "In view of the association demonstrated here between child deprivation levels and mortality risk, failure to identify and ameliorate conditions in which families possess inadequate resources may have serious consequences for children's health and for their life chances."

The Normal Distribution

Muscular Dystrophy and Intelligence

STATISTICAL GUIDE

The *normal distribution* is a key idea that shows up all over statistics. Most importantly, many statistical tests (like *t*-tests and ANOVA) assume that variables are normally distributed, i.e., look like a normal distribution. If variables are not sufficiently normal, alternative statistical tests have to be used. These alternatives are called *nonparametric*. (Check out Unit 6 to get a sense of nonparametric tests.)

To review histogram, see Exercise 3.1. To review the 1-2-3 rule and the normal distribution, see Exercise 2.5.

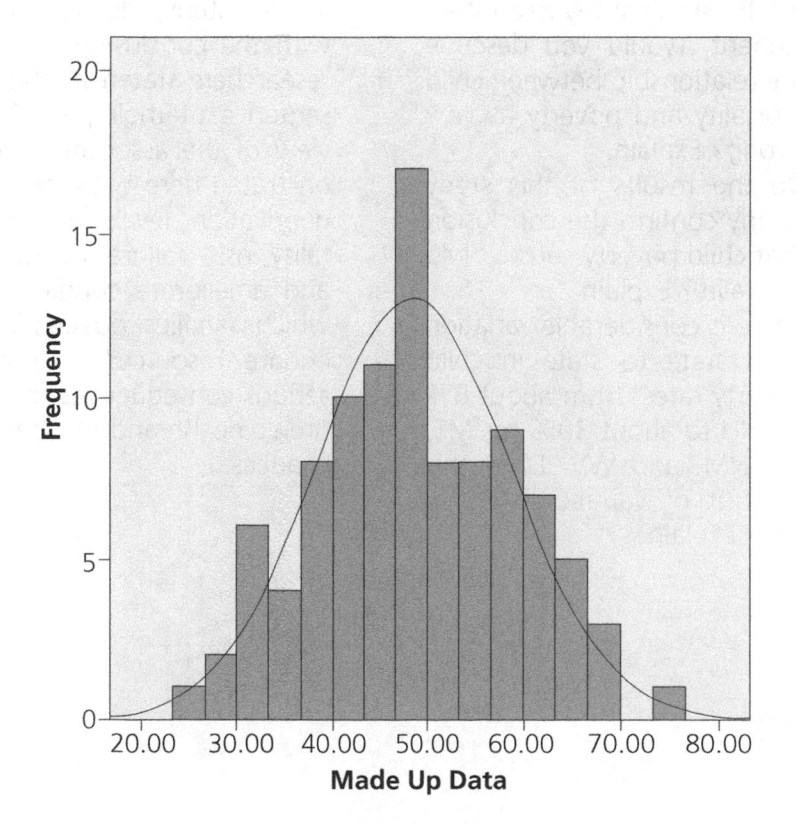

The figure above is a histogram of made-up data. A normal curve is laid over the histogram. The normal curve has one peak; it is symmetrical around that peak; and the tails decrease to zero. There are more technical features to the normal distribution (check out Exercise 2.5 for some of those), but those three features give the general gist. You can tell if a distribution is approximately normal by visually inspecting a histogram. Few variables in nature, or in the social or health sciences, are perfectly normal. Fortunately, most statistical tests that assume normally distributed data do not require the data to be perfectly normal. In fact, a distribution can appear to be fairly non-normal and still be workable for many of the standard statistical procedures. There are precise statistical tests that reveal if data is so non-normal that alternative (and less commonly used) statistical procedures are needed. The distribution in the histogram below is fairly close to normal by visual inspection, and a statistical test (the Kolmogorov–Smirnov test of normality) confirms it is sufficiently normal for standard statistical tests.

BACKGROUND NOTE

The excerpt below discusses intelligence tests. Such tests are often broken down into three scores: full-scale intelligence quotient (FIQ), verbal intelligence quotient (VIQ), and processing intelligence quotient (PIQ). 100 is the average IQ score and 15 is the standard deviation for the intelligence tests used in the excerpt below.

This paper uses the Kolmogorov–Smirnov test of normality to see if the distributions in the study are close enough to normal to be considered normal.

EXCERPT FROM THE RESEARCH ARTICLE[1]

Duchenne muscular dystrophy (DMD) is a disease that has as its hallmarks progressive muscle weakness and degeneration of skeletal muscle. Also observed among those with DMD is a higher rate of mental retardation than in the normally developing population . . .

(continued)

1 Cotton, S., Voudouris, N. J., & Greenwood, K. M. (2001). Intelligence and Duchenne muscular dystrophy: Full-Scale, Verbal, and Performance intelligence quotients. *Developmental Medicine & Child Neurology*, *43*(7), 497–501. Reprinted with permission of John Wiley & Sons, Inc. © 2001 The authors.

(continued)

While estimates for the prevalence of mental retardation in the normally developing population are approximately 9%, estimates of mental retardation . . . [for] children with DMD have ranged from 20% to as high as 50% . . . The purpose of this paper is to provide an up-to-date review of this literature, and to report . . . the preliminary results of a meta-analysis of the available data.

Children with DMD have been reported to have Full-Scale intelligence quotients (FIQs) averaging around 80, or one standard deviation below the normal population IQ. However, other researchers have failed to replicate these findings, recording near to average IQs in children with DMD.

There were 1,146 individuals with DMD for whom the FIQ was available, and the distribution of their FIQ scores is shown in Figure 1. The mean FIQ of 80.2 . . . was statistically different from the [general] population average FIQ of 100 . . . The Kolmogorov–Smirnov test indicated that the FIQ frequency distribution did not differ significantly from a normal [distribution].

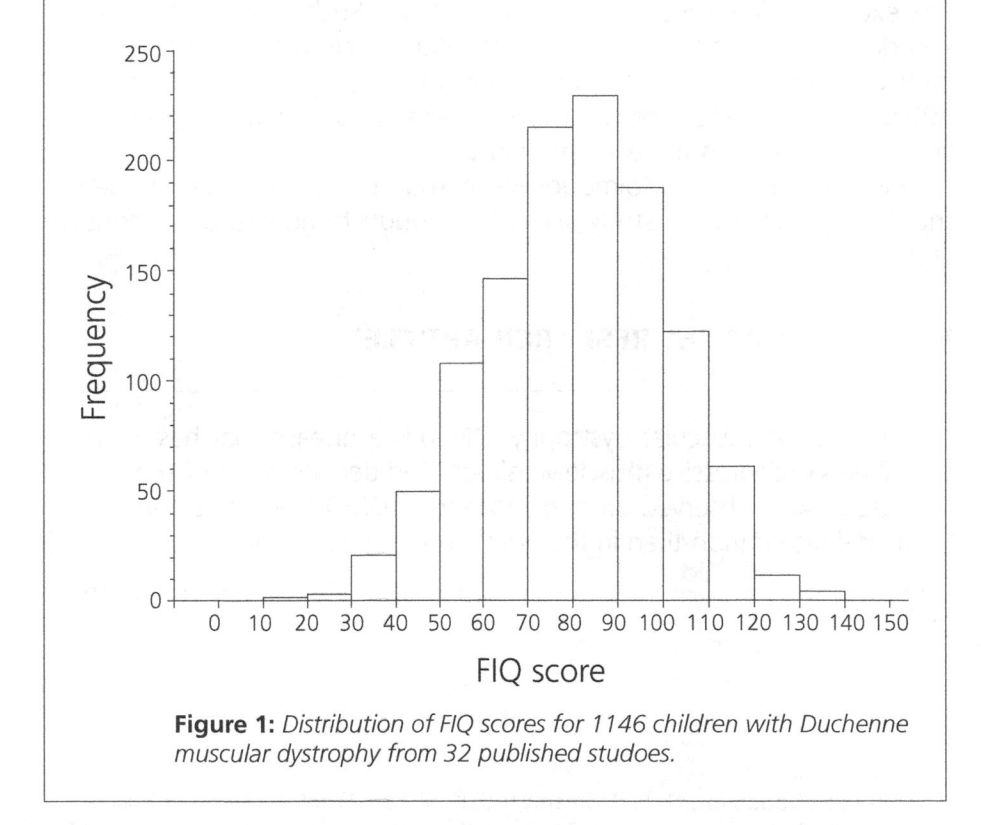

Figure 1: *Distribution of FIQ scores for 1146 children with Duchenne muscular dystrophy from 32 published studoes.*

STUDY QUESTIONS

Factual Questions

1. How many peaks does the data in Figure 1 have?
2. Is the distribution in Figure 1 generally symmetrical around the peak?
3. Do the tails of the distribution (the far left and right) in Figure 1 trail off to zero?
4. How does the distribution in Figure 1 appear to you?
   A. Very normal
   B. Somewhat normal
   C. Not at all normal.
5. Visually compare the histogram of made-up data in the Statistical Guide to Figure 1 in the study. Which one appears to be more normal in shape?
6. Do the authors report on a statistical test to show that the distribution in Figure 1 is sufficiently normal? If so, what does it indicate?
7. What is the sample size for the data in Figure 1?
8. Do you think sample size has anything to do with how normal a distribution is likely to be?
9. If the researchers had 30 participants in their sample, do you think that Figure 1 would have been normal, or nearly so?

Questions for Discussion

10. IQ scores in this sample are found to be (close enough to a) normal distribution. Is there another variable you think would be normally distributed, with these samples or others? If so, what is it? If not, why not?
11. What are examples of important variables that are *NOT* normally distributed in the population?

Excerpts on Sampling

Bias in Sampling

STATISTICAL GUIDE

In most research studies, a sample is investigated, and the researcher wants to apply the results from the sample to a broader population. For example, at election time, a pollster draws a sample of 958 likely voters. Based on what these 958 likely voters say, the pollster wants to make conclusions about all voters in a country, which might be millions and millions of people. In short, the pollster wants the sample to represent the population.

A sample will usually better represent a population if the method of selecting the sample is unbiased. In unbiased sampling, each member of a population has an equal chance of being included in a sample. Random sampling is the basic method used to obtain unbiased samples. There are lots of issues that can bias a sample: low response rates, undercoverage of particular groups, and any nonrandom method of selecting a study participant (e.g., choosing individuals who happen to be convenient to serve as participants in a study). Do not assume that a sample was drawn at random unless the researcher explicitly states this was done. Truly random samples can be expensive and take expertise to obtain, so if researchers have gone to the trouble of randomly selecting participants, they will likely tell you they have done so.

> Bias in sampling is not about visual displays of data. We chose to place this exercise here because sampling is an important issue in many of the subsequent exercises.

STUDY QUESTIONS

For each of the following excerpts from journal articles, indicate whether the sample is biased or unbiased and explain your choice. In some cases, you may answer "not sure" because there is insufficient information to make a judgment. If you answer "not sure" to an item, describe the additional information you would like to have before deciding if the sample is biased or unbiased.

1. Researchers state, "To help resolve the questions posed above [in this research report], a telephone survey of 1,000 California residents was conducted . . . using random digit dialing (RDD). Sampling by means of RDD avoids the threat of systematically excluding that portion of the population with unlisted telephone numbers."[1]

2. Researchers state, "For the analyses, we used a sample of Norwegian 13-year-old students ($N = 1,736$; 49% were girls) and 15-year-old students ($N = 1,622$; 51% were girls). The students were selected using a stratified, systematic sampling procedure, thus yielding a nationally representative sample. The sampling unit was the school class."[2]

3. Researchers state, "A total of 102 U.S. and 112 Japanese men participated in this study. The U.S. participants were recruited from an undergraduate student research pool in the psychology and educational psychology departments at a large public university in the Rocky Mountain region of the United States."[3]

4. Researchers state, "A sample of 60 was randomly selected from 125 people arrested on DWI offenses and referred by the county to a professional evaluator between May 2000 and December 2003."[4]

5. Researchers state, "Smokers (defined as individuals smoking 10 or more cigarettes per day) were approached at various locations on or near the University of Pittsburgh campus. The sample ($N = 102$) included 42 men and 60 women, with an average age of 27.78."[5]

(continued)

1 Greenwald, H. P., O'Keefe, S., & DiCamillo, M. (2005). Why employed Latinos lack health insurance: A study in California. *Hispanic Journal of Behavioral Sciences, 27,* 517–532. Reprinted under Fair Use.

2 Danielsen, A. G., Samdal, O., Hetland, J., & Wold, B. (2009). School-related social support and students' perceived life satisfaction. *Journal of Educational Research, 102,* 303–318. Reprinted under Fair Use.

3 Stillman, T. F., Yamawaki, N., Ridge, R. D., White, P. H., & Copley, K. J. (2009). Comparing predictors of sexual harassment proclivity between Japanese and U.S. men. *Psychology of Men & Masculinity, 10,* 30–43. Reprinted under Fair Use.

4 Nevitt, J. R., & Lundak, J. (2005). Accuracy of self-reports of alcohol offenders in a rural midwestern county. *Psychological Reports, 96,* 511–514. Reprinted under Fair Use.

5 Klein, W. M. P., & Monin, M. W. (2009). When focusing on negative and positive attributes of the self elicits more inductive self-judgment. *Personality and Social Psychology Bulletin, 35,* 376–384. Reprinted under Fair Use.

(continued)

6. Researchers state, "Participants were 307 students in a convenience sample of volunteers in 18 elementary and middle school classes. After we accounted for missing data, including student absences from school during 1 or more days of the intervention, the actual sample size for the statistical analysis was 268."[6]

7. Researchers state that "Briefly, a stratified random sample of 4,907 coronary artery disease patients undergoing an angiogram at one . . . New York State hospital . . . was selected for the medical records abstraction portion of the study."[7]

8. Researchers state, "We commissioned Survey Sampling Incorporated to provide a random sample of 1,000 Florida residents. Of the initial sample members, 198 had moved, had incorrect addresses, were deceased, or were otherwise unreachable. These individuals were replaced with additional randomly selected residents. Thirty-three of the replacements also could not be contacted but were not replaced. Thus, the total number . . . was reduced to 967."[8]

9. Researchers state that "a standardized questionnaire developed for use in this study was mailed to a stratified random sample of 750 hospitals drawn from the American Hospital Association membership list. Hospitals were stratified according to size, geographic location, and stage of managed care development . . ."[9]

10. Researchers state, "A randomized sample of 2,400 surveys was sent to clinical psychology ($n = 1,200$) and clinical social work

6   Andrade, H. L., Wang, X., Du, Y., & Akawi, R. L. (2009). Rubric-referenced self-assessment and self-efficacy for writing. *Journal of Educational Research*, *102*, 287–302. Reprinted under Fair Use.

7   van Ryn, M., Burgess, D., Malat, J., & Griffin, J. (2006). Physicians' perceptions of patients' social and behavioral characteristics and race disparities in treatment recommendations for men with coronary artery disease. *American Journal of Public Health*, *96*, 351–357. Reprinted under Fair Use.

8   Applegate, B. K., & Davis, R. K. (2006). Public views on sentencing juvenile murderers: The impact of offender, offense, and perceived maturity. *Youth Violence and Juvenile Justice*, *4*, 55–74. Reprinted by Permission of SAGE Publications, Inc.

9   Mizrahi, T., & Berger, C. S. (2005). A longitudinal look at social work leadership in hospitals: The impact of a changing health care system. *Health and Social Work*, *30*, 155–165. Reprinted under Fair Use.

(n = 1,200) clinicians from all 50 U.S. states. Of those 2,400 surveys, 711 were returned with usable data, for a response rate of 29.6%."[10]

11. Researchers state, "Participants were 230 first-year university students who responded to signs posted on campus or agreed to participate after being approached individually. Participation was anonymous and participants were paid $10."[11]

12. Researchers state, "Participants in Study 1 had been randomly selected from the membership lists of a large HMO. Because the focus of the research was on marital conflict, families were eligible only if they were intact (parents still living together)."[12]

13. Researchers state, "Participants were 3,446 Internet users . . . who had been involved in a close relationship. Each participant volunteered to complete an online questionnaire about their dating history at a Web site that features several psychological surveys . . ."[13]

14. Researchers state, "School guidance personnel selected a representative set of classrooms, taking into account grade level and academic difficulty."[14]

---

10 Craig, C. D., & Sprang, G. (2009). Exploratory and confirmatory analysis of the Trauma Practices Questionnaire. *Research on Social Work Practice*, *19*, 221–233. Reprinted under Fair Use.

11 Goldstein, A. L., & Flett, G. L. (2009). Personality, alcohol use, and drinking motives: A comparison of independent and combined internal drinking motive groups. *Behavior Modification*, *33*, 182–198. Reprinted under Fair Use.

12 Tschann, J. M., Pasch, L. A., Flores, E., Marin, B. V. O., Baisch, E. M., & Wibbelsman, C. J. (2009). Nonviolent aspects of interparental conflict and dating violence among adolescents. *Journal of Family Issues*, *30*, 295–319. Reprinted under Fair Use.

13 Swann, W. B., Jr., Sellers, J. G., & McClarty, K. L. (2006). Tempting today, troubling tomorrow: The roots of the precarious couple effect. *Personality and Social Psychology Bulletin*, *32*, 93–103. Reprinted under Fair Use.

14 Bogenschneider, K., & Pallock, L. (2008). Responsiveness in parent-adolescent relationships: Are influences conditional? Does the reporter matter? *Journal of Marriage and Family*, *70*, 1015–1029. Reprinted under Fair Use.

Finding Relationships:
Association and Prediction

CHAPTER INTRODUCTION

Does being bullied relate to academic performance? Are materialistic people less happy? Does depression affect a person's metabolism? These questions all share a basic form: does A relate to B? This is the next big question for us to consider in the progression of statistics. All the sections in Unit 4 are about this central question. The exercises show some of the many ways that researchers try to understand how two (or more) variables are associated with each other, how they relate to each other. The articles we will cover use two primary statistical methods to understand the relationship between variables: *correlation* and *regression*.

Throughout Unit 4, researchers will use fancy statistical terms like *amount of variance explained* or *multiple linear regression*. But, at the end of the day, all of these techniques are about how two (or more) variables are related, how A relates to B. If you keep that in mind, a lot of the fancy terminology will make more sense.

Unit 4 also introduces the idea of *meta-analysis*. This is a procedure for combining the results of multiple studies, possibly many studies. Meta-analysis is becoming a hallmark of the development of scientific knowledge. The idea goes like this: one study might have flaws or get bad data by a fluke of chance. Combining results across many studies helps to reduce these problems, and, hopefully, get at the truth of the matter. Research articles with a meta-analysis can be very complicated because they talk about tens if not hundreds of studies. But keep our one question in mind—is A related to B? This is still the fundamental question a meta-analysis is trying to answer.

DOI: 10.4324/9781003096764-4

Correlation I

Correlates of Depression

STATISTICAL GUIDE

A *correlation coefficient* indicates the strength and direction of a relationship between two variables. The most widely used correlation coefficient is Pearson *r*. When it is positive in value, the relationship is *direct*. In a direct relationship, those with high scores on one variable tend to have high scores on the other variable, and those with low scores on one variable tend to have low scores on the other variable. In a direct relationship, the closer *r* is to one, the stronger the relationship; the closer it is to zero, the weaker the relationship.

When the value of Pearson *r* is negative, the relationship is *inverse* (i.e., those with high scores on one variable tend to have low scores on the other variable). In an inverse relationship, the closer *r* is to −1.00, the stronger the relationship; the closer it is to.00, the weaker the relationship.

You might have caught this already, but 1.00 and −1.00 reflect the strongest possible correlations between two variables, 1.00 indicating a perfect direct relationship and −1.00 reflecting a perfect inverse relationship. The farther the value of *r* is from zero, i.e., as the absolute value of *r* gets bigger, the stronger the correlation is said to be. So negative correlations are not considered smaller than positive correlations. Distance from zero determines size.

The names of correlations can sometimes be confusing. Often when researchers are talking about a correlation coefficient, they simply use the word correlation and drop the word coefficient. In the table below, the researchers did the opposite and used the lengthiest name for the particular kind of correlation they used (i.e., "the Pearson product-moment correlation"). This longer name is the same thing as a Pearson *r* correlation—which is often referred to simply as a correlation. As we said, it can be confusing.

EXCERPT FROM THE RESEARCH ARTICLE[1]

Participants in this study were a volunteer sample of full-time undergraduate students at a small, private, liberal arts college in the South.

We measured depression symptomatology by using the CES–D. The CES–D is a 20-item, 4-point Likert scale commonly used to assess depressive symptomatology in the general population. Scores range from 0 to 60; a score of 16 or greater is considered positive for depression.

We assessed self-esteem by using the RSES, which is a 10-item, 4-point Likert scale considered to be a reliable and valid self-report scale commonly used to assess feelings of self-worth. The range of possible scores is 10–40; the higher the score, the higher the self-reported self-esteem.

The SCS-R is a 20-item, 6-point Likert scale used to "measure social connectedness as a psychological sense of belonging." Scores are summated and range from 20 to 120. Higher scores indicate greater levels of social connectedness and belongingness.

Table 1

Pearson's Product Moment Correlations Between the Dependent Measures (n = 227)

Measure	Depression	Social connectedness
Self-esteem	−.372	.414
Depression	—	−.619

STUDY QUESTIONS

Factual Questions

1. What is the value of the correlation coefficient for the relationship between Depression and Self-esteem?

2. How many of the relationships in the table are inverse?

3. What is the value of the correlation coefficient for the

---

1 Armstrong, S., & Oomen-Early, J. (2009). Social connectedness, self-esteem, and depression symptomatology among collegiate athletes versus nonathletes. *Journal of American College Health*, *57*, 521–526. Reprinted by permission of Taylor & Francis LLC.

strongest relationship in the table?

4. By visual inspection only, which one of the following pairs of variables has a stronger relationship between them?
   A. Depression and Social connectedness
   B. Depression and Self-esteem

5. By visual inspection alone, which one of the following pairs of variables has a weaker relationship between them?
   A. Self-esteem and Social connectedness
   B. Self-esteem and Depression

6. The correlation coefficient for the relationship between Depression and Self-esteem indicates which of the following?
   A. Those who experience more Depression tend to have higher Self-esteem.
   B. Those who experience more Depression tend to have lower Self-esteem.

7. By visual inspection only, what is the weakest relationship between two variables in Table 1?

Questions for Discussion

8. What are several possible explanations for why the relationship between Depression and Social connectedness is inverse?

9. Are you surprised that the relationship between Self-esteem and Social connectedness is direct? Explain.

10. In your opinion, does the Pearson r of $-.372$ prove that high depression *causes* lower self-esteem?

Correlation II

Community Violence and Achievement

STATISTICAL GUIDE

The title of Table 1 in the excerpt below refers to *bivariate* correlations—a term often used by researchers. The prefix bi- means two. Hence, bivariate refers to the fact that there are two variables involved in each correlation coefficient in the table. A large majority of correlations in the research literature are bivariate correlations; so researchers sometimes drop bivariate, and just use the word correlation alone. Still, using bivariate correlation is more precise than just using correlation.

To review inverse correlation, see Exercise 4.1.

Bivariate correlations are often presented in tables like the one below. To read the table, pay attention to the variable numbers, which are in bold. For example, 1 refers to "Community violence exposure," both in the column going down and the row going across, and 2 refers to "Bullying by peers," both in the column going down and the row going across.

BACKGROUND NOTE

Note that in Table 1 of the excerpt, SAT–9 stands for the Ninth Edition of the Stanford Achievement Test, a standardized test of academic learning. "SAT–9 Mathematics" measures math learning, while "SAT–9 Reading" measures learning in reading skills.

EXCERPT FROM THE RESEARCH ARTICLE[1]

Participants were recruited from an elementary school located in an urban section of Los Angeles County . . . The families living

---

1 Schwartz, D., & Gorman, A. H. (2003). "Community violence exposure and children's academic functioning." *Journal of Educational Psychology*, 95, 163–173. Copyright © 2003 by the American Psychological Association. Reproduced with permission.

in the surrounding neighborhoods have been conceptualized as "working poor" in recent demographic studies of the Los Angeles region . . . All children in 16 third-, fourth-, and fifth-grade classrooms from the participating school were invited to take part in the project. Of these children, 80% returned positive parental permission and assented to participate.

Community violence exposure. Children completed the Community Experiences Questionnaire . . . Items on this measure range in severity from threats to shootings; the 4-point scale ranges from 1 (*never*) to 4 (*a lot of times*).

Bullying by peers. [A second inventory] contained four items assessing bullying by peers ("kids who get hit or pushed by other kids," "kids who get bullied or picked on by other kids," "kids who have mean things said about them by other kids," and "kids who get left out of fun games or play when other kids are trying to hurt their feelings") . . .

Table 1
Bivariate Correlations Among All Variables

Variable	1	2	3	4	5
Violence exposure					
1. Community violence exposure	—	.20	−.24	−.14	−.26
2. Bullying by peers		—	−.19	−.07	−.25
Academic functioning					
3. SAT–9 Mathematics			—	.60	.64
4. SAT–9 Reading				—	.49
5. GPA					—

STUDY QUESTIONS

Factual Questions

1. What is the value of the correlation for the relationship between Variable 1 and Variable 2? (*Hint*: Find where the row for Variable 1 meets the column for Variable 2.)

2. What is the value of the correlation coefficient for the relationship between SAT–9 Mathematics and SAT–9 Reading?

3. How many of the ten relationships in the table are inverse?

4. What is the value of the correlation coefficient for the

strongest relationship in the table (by visual inspection alone)?

5. By visual inspection alone, which one of the following pairs of variables has a stronger relationship between them?
   A. Community violence exposure and Bullying by peers.
   B. Community violence exposure and SAT–9 Mathematics.

6. By visual inspection alone, which one of the following pairs of variables has a weaker relationship?
   A. SAT–9 Mathematics and SAT–9 Reading.
   B. SAT–9 Mathematics and GPA.

7. The correlation coefficient for the relationship between Bullying by peers and GPA indicates which of the following?
   A. Those who experience more Bullying by peers tend to have higher GPAs.
   B. Those who experience more Bullying by peers tend to have lower GPAs.

8. The correlation coefficient for the relationship between SAT–9 Mathematics and SAT–9 Reading indicates which of the following?
   A. Those who score higher in mathematics tend to score higher in reading.
   B. Those who score higher in mathematics tend to score lower in reading.

9. By visual inspection alone, the weakest relationship appears to be between which two variables?

Questions for Discussion

10. What kind of reasons can you give for the inverse relationship between Bullying by peers and GPA?

11. Are you surprised that the relationship between mathematics and reading is direct? Explain.

12. In your opinion, does the Pearson r of $-.26$ prove that being exposed to community violence *causes* lower GPAs?

Significance of a Correlation I

Correlates of School Attachment

STATISTICAL GUIDE

To review correlation, see Exercise 4.1.

Every correlation has a *p*-value, or probability value, associated with it. There is a complicated story for where *p*-values come from, but that story is for another time. Importantly for us, the *p*-value does an amazing thing—it tells us if a correlation is worth paying attention to. The technical name for correlations worth paying attention to is *statistically significant*. *p*-values range from 0 to 1, and really small *p*-values (typically less than .05) mean that the correlation is statistically significant. When *p*-values aren't really small (typically greater than .05), the correlation is considered to be statistically insignificant, or not worth paying attention to.

If there is absolutely no relationship between two variables, then the correlation between the two variables is *r* = .00. This *r* has a *p*-value of 1.00, the largest possible *p*-value. So the smallest possible *r* has the largest possible *p*-value. This is because the size of a correlation is inversely related to its *p*-value: bigger correlations have smaller *p*-values and smaller correlations have bigger *p*-values (holding everything else constant). The reason for this lies in what a *p*-value is. The *p*-value tells us the likelihood of a particular correlation occurring *purely by chance*. If a correlation has a high *p*-value, then it is *likely* to occur purely by chance. If a correlation has a small *p*-value, then it is *unlikely* to occur purely by chance. This helps explain why researchers use *p*-values to tell them if a correlation is worth paying attention to. If a *p*-value is high, then the correlation could easily have occurred by chance, and researchers conclude there is likely not a real relationship between the two variables, just a chance one. But if a *p*-value is low (like less than .05), then the correlation is unlikely due to chance, and researchers conclude there probably

is a real relationship between the two variables. So, a correlation with a *p*-value below .05 means a researcher might exclaim, "Eureka! I found a real relationship!"

One thing to keep in mind about *p* less than .05—it does not mean that the relationship between the two variables is definitely, for sure, without a doubt, 100% slam dunk, real. It means that a correlation of that size is *unlikely* due to pure chance. But unlikely things happen, including a correlation having a *p* less than .05 when only chance is operating. So researchers might *not* want to exclaim, "Eureka!" until they replicate their statistically significant findings. (Read up on Type I error if you want to know more about this.) You can see this if you think further about what a *p*-value specifically means. It is the probability (that's where the *p* comes from) of a result occurring purely by chance. So a *p*-value of .05 means that there is a 5% chance that chance alone, and not a real relationship, produced the correlation. 5% sounds unlikely, but if you run 20 correlations (or use *p*-hacking methods), you'll likely get at least one statistically significant correlation, even if there are no real relationships in the data.

In research studies, *p* less than .05 is written like this, $p < .05$. You can see it in Table 1 below. The table also includes $p < .01$, or *p* less than .01. Researchers like results with $p < .01$ more than $p < .05$, as it means the correlation is even less likely to be due to pure chance. In looking at Table 1, you'll notice that some correlations have a * by them, some have a ** by them, and some don't have anything by them. This is a standard way researchers communicate the *p*-value of a correlation. The correlations with a * by them have $p < .05$. The correlations with a ** by them have $p < .01$. And the correlations with nothing by them have $p > .05$, i.e., they are not statistically significant.

There are some general rules of thumb for interpreting the size of a statistically significant correlation. Most researchers describe correlations between .10 and .29 as "small," correlations between .30 to .49 as "medium," and correlations .50 and above as "large." (This rule applies to the absolute value of a correlation.) If a correlation is not statistically significant, researchers do not care about its size; its not significant.

BACKGROUND NOTE

In the study below, all variables were measured on a scale ranging from 1 to 10, with 1 representing the lowest level and 10 representing the highest level. This is true for all variables except for grade point average (GPA).

EXCERPT FROM THE RESEARCH ARTICLE[1]

The data on Latino youth in southwestern Minnesota were gathered through self-administered surveys . . . Fourteen junior and senior high schools of varying size in the region were selected randomly and agreed to participate in the study to help identify factors leading to greater attachment to the school . . .

The following question was used:

How much would you like to change to a different school?

In the correlations displayed in Table 1, we can see that there is an inverse, though relatively weak, relationship between how attached a rural Latino youth in the region feels to his or her school and several of the at-risk behaviors found in existing research.

Table 1
Measures of Correlation for the Desire to Change Schools

	Desire to change schools
Frequency of smoking cigarettes	.137**
Frequency of drinking alcohol	.173**
Number of fights or violent encounters in past two years	.191**
Number of times arrested by police in the past two years	.129
Length of time living in southwest Minnesota	−.019
Plans to attend college university immediately after high school	−.031
Serious thoughts about suicide since being at current school	.270**
Belief that white students have an easier time fitting in and succeeding at school	.181*
Belief that teachers try their best to make all students, regardless of race, feel welcome and appreciated	−.260**
How comfortable the student feels in raising hand in class to ask a question	−.235**
The student's grade point average	−.145*
Frequency of skipping school without the knowledge of parents	.195**

$* p < .05. ** p < .01.$

1 Diaz, J. D. (2005). School attachment among Latino youth in rural Minnesota. *Hispanic Journal of Behavioral Sciences, 27,* 300–318. Reprinted by Permission of SAGE Publications, Inc.

STUDY QUESTIONS

Factual Questions

1. In the excerpt, the researcher refers to inverse relationships. How many of the relationships in Table 1 are inverse?

2. The correlation between student GPA and Desire to change schools indicates that those with lower GPAs tend to have:
   A. lower desire to change schools.
   B. higher desire to change schools.

3. Is the relationship between Frequency of smoking cigarettes and Desire to change schools direct or inverse?

4. Is the relationship between the following variables direct or inverse: Desire to change school AND How comfortable the student feels in raising hand in class to ask a question?

5. Is the relationship between Plans to attend college/university immediately after high school and Desire to change schools statistically significant? Explain.

6. From a statistical perspective, is the correlation in Question 5 different from zero?

7. From a statistical perspective, is the correlation between Desire to change schools and Frequency of drinking alcohol different from zero?

8. Both Frequency of skipping school without the knowledge of parents and Belief that white students have an easier time fitting in and succeeding at school are significantly related to Desire to change schools. Which correlation is less likely to occur by chance? Explain.

9. Two of the variables are significantly related to Desire to change schools at the .05 probability level. How many of the other variables are statistically significant with smaller p-values? Explain.

10. The footnote to the table states that two asterisks (**) indicates $p < .01$. The probability of obtaining this result by chance alone is less than one in
    A. 10.
    B. 100.
    C. 1,000.

11. The footnote to the table states that one asterisk (*) indicates $p < .05$. The probability of obtaining this result by chance alone is less than five in
    A. 10.
    B. 50.
    C. 100.

12. Which of the following coefficients from Table 1 has the greatest distance from zero?
    A. .191.
    B. −.235.
    C. −.260.
    D. .195.

Questions for Discussion

13. In the excerpt, the researcher refers to the relationships between school attachment and at-risk behaviors as "relatively weak." Based on what you know about interpreting correlation coefficients, do you agree with this characterization? Explain.

14. Describe in words, without using numbers, the strength and direction of the relationship between Plans to attend college/university immediately after high school and Desire to change schools.

15. Describe in words, without using numbers, the strength and direction of the relationship between Belief that white students have an easier time fitting in and succeeding at school and Desire to change schools.

Significance of a Correlation II

Correlates of Alternative School Experience

STATISTICAL GUIDE

Throughout the rest of this book, we will consider p-values associated with many statistical tests, not just correlation. p-values work the same if you are considering a correlation, or an ANOVA, or multiple regression. So you can take the lessons learned here (and in the previous exercise) about p-values and apply them wherever a p-value is used.

> To review correlation, correlation tables, and p-values, see Exercises 4.1–4.3.

Keep in mind that the lower the p-value of a result, the less likely the result occurred solely by chance.

EXCERPT FROM THE RESEARCH ARTICLE[1]

Participants of this study were 102 secondary alternative school students in the 6th through 12th grades. Their ages ranged from 12 to 19 years (M = 15.19, SD = 2.13).

Results showed that students' sense of school membership correlated with their perception of teachers ($r = .52$, $p < .01$), perception of counselors ($r = .44$, $p < .01$), and perception of administrators ($r = .42$, $p < .01$). Students who had a more positive perception of their teachers, counselors, and administrators also reported a greater sense of school membership.

Academic achievement correlated with whether the student was employed ($r = -.24$, $p < .05$).

---

1 Poyrazli, S., Ferrer-Wreder, L., Meister, D. G., Forthun, L., Coatsworth, J. D., & Grahame, K. M. (2008). Academic achievement, employment, age, and gender and students' experience of alternative school. *Adolescence, 43*, 547–556. Reprinted under Fair Use.

Students who worked at a job reported higher grades than those who did not.

Results also revealed associations between perception of administrators and students' age and gender. Male students ($r = -.33$, $p < .01$) and older students ($r = -.21$, $p < .05$) tended to view administrators more negatively as compared to female or younger students.

Table 1
Bivariate Correlations Among Interval and Dummy-Coded Variables

		1	2	3	4	5	6	7	8
1.	Age	—							
2.	Gender	.11	—						
3.	Employment	−.14	.00	—					
4.	Academic achievement	.00	.03	−.24*	—				
5.	Sense of school membership	−.04	−.20	−.05	.18	—			
6.	Perception of teachers	−.19	−.10	−.01	.07	.52**	—		
7.	Perception of counselors	−.02	−.05	.03	.09	.44**	.41**	—	
8.	Perception of administrators	−.21*	−.33**	.03	.08	.43**	.71**	.40**	—

Note: Gender and Employment were dummy coded to be entered into the correlational analyses; 1 = Female, 2 = Male; 1 = Employed in a job, 2 = Not employed in a job.

* $p < .05$, ** $p < .01$

STUDY QUESTIONS

Factual Questions

1. What is the correlation between Perception of counselors and Perception of administrators?
2. By visual inspection alone, which two variables in Table 1 have the strongest correlation?
3. Is the correlation coefficient for the relationship between Age and Perception of administrators statistically significant? If yes, at what probability level is it significant?
4. The relationship between Sense of school membership and Perception of teachers is such that those who have a

high Sense of school membership tend to have:

A. a high Perception of teachers.

B. a low Perception of teachers.

5. Perception of administrators has non-significant relationships with which other variables?

6. There are how many statistically significant correlation coefficients in the table? Are they all significant at the same level of significance? Explain.

7. Statistically speaking, is the correlation between Age and Gender equivalent to zero? Explain.

8. What is the probability that the correlation between Academic achievement and Employment is due to chance alone?

9. In the footnote to the table, two values of p are given. Which one has less likelihood to occur purely by chance?

10. The correlation between Age and Perception of administrators is $-.21$, which in this study is statistically significant. Would you characterize this relationship as very strong? Explain.

Questions for Discussion

11. Does it surprise you that some of the negative correlation coefficients are statistically significant? Explain.

12. What do you make of the strong correlation between how students perceived counselors and administrators?

Meta-Analysis with Correlation Coefficients

Materialism and Personal Well-Being

STATISTICAL GUIDE

To review correlation, see Exercises 4.1–4.4.

In a *meta-analysis*, results from previous studies (usually conducted by a variety of researchers who have studied a single topic) are statistically combined to arrive at an overall result for all the studies. For instance, in the excerpt below, the mean correlation coefficient for 175 different studies was computed to get an overall estimate of the correlation between materialism and personal well-being. Typically, in the computation of the average correlation, researchers weight the studies according to sample size. That is, they give more weight to the results of studies with more participants than to the results of studies with fewer participants.

BACKGROUND NOTE

Meta-analysis articles always have a big table in the middle of the article that gives a list of all the studies included in the meta-analysis. The table will also report on a number of aspects of each study, like sample size, magnitude of the effect under consideration (correlation coefficient in this instance), or particular measures used in the study. For example, in Table 1 below, there are ten columns, each telling you something different about the studies included in the meta-analysis. Table 1 is only part of the summary table from the original article, as the full table is 16 pages long.

This meta-analysis reports on ρ (pronounced "row"). ρ is a slightly modified version of the correlation coefficient *r*—which is why the Greek letter for r is used as its symbol. ρ is the correlation if you try to correct for problems in the measurement of the variables in the correlation, specifically problems in reliability. Think of ρ as a slightly better version of *r*.

EXCERPT FROM THE RESEARCH ARTICLE[1]

Table 1
Studies Included in the Meta-Analysis: Effect Sizes and Study Characteristics

Study	N^a	r	ρ^b	Materialism measure	Outcome measure	Type of publication	Country	% female	Average age/ age group (years)	Population
Agarwal (2003)	240	−.14	−.18	Money	SWLS	Journal article	India	48	Over 18	Student
Auerbach, McWhinnie, Goldfinger, Abela, & Yao (2009)	406	−.30	−.34	AI-ext	RBQ-A	Journal article	China	50	16.2	School
Auerbach et al. (2011) Canada	255	−.04	−.04	AI	CES-D	Journal article	Canada	57	14.48	School
China	405	−.15	−.16	AI	CES-D	Journal article	China	50	16.18	School
Baller (2011)	487	−.22	−.28	AI	LS	Thesis	USA	74	Over 18	Student
Belk (1984)	338	−.18	−.31	BMS	LS	Journal article	USA	33	Over 18	General
Bertran, Casas & Gonzalez (2009)	*	−.23	−.39	BMS	Happy	Conference paper	Spain	50	Under 12	School
	5,140	.04	.06	Casas	PWB					
Bottomley, Nairn, Kasser, Ferguson, & Ormrod (2010)	142	.08	.10	CO	RSE	Journal article	USA	100	Under 12	School
Brdar (2006)	439	−.04	−.05	AI-FS	BPNS-competence	Journal article	Hungary	55	19.0	Student
	*	−.08	−.10	AI-FS	BPNS-autonomy					

(continued)

Study	N^a	r	ρ^b	Materialism measure	Outcome measure	Type of publication	Country	% female	Average age/ age group (years)	Population
Brown & Kasser (2005)										
Study 1	206	–.22	–.35	Mat	Happy	Journal article	USA	44	14.2	School
Study 2	400	–.31	–.41	AI	Affect Balance	Journal article	USA	66	43.7	General

Note: Variables have been scored so that materialism and positive well-being are high scores, and therefore, a negative correlation indicates that higher materialism is associated with poorer well-being. ρ = correlation coefficient corrected for reliability of the materialism measure and the outcome measure.

(continued)

In total, we used 151 reports that included 175 separate studies that, in turn, provided 258 samples . . . Median sample size is just over 200, with slightly more female than male participants (median proportion female = 57%) and predominantly participants of White ethnicity (85%). Median age is 24 years, and the large majority of reports (86%) use adult samples, with just over half of these being students in higher education . . .

From these 258 samples, we coded a total of 749 effects, that is, correlations between a measure of materialism and a measure of well-being. When graphed, the different sizes of the correlations across these 749 effects reveal an approximately normal distribution . . . The mean size of the correlation between materialism and well-being = −.15, the median = −.15, the 25th percentile = −.24, and the 75th percentile = −.05. When we correct the correlation for the reliability of the measures, the average effect is somewhat larger, $M = -.19$. Thus, taken over a wide range of different measures of well-being and of materialism, we found a modest but definite negative relationship between materialism and well-being.

STUDY QUESTIONS[2]

Factual Questions

1. How many separate studies are used in this meta-analysis? How many separate samples are used in this meta-analysis?

2. Provide the following demographic information about the participants in these studies:
   A. Median age
   B. Predominately identify as male or female
   C. Predominately identify with _____ as race/ethnicity

3. What is the mean size of the correlation between materialism and well-being (when not corrected for reliability)? Is this relationship direct or indirect?

4. Scanning the excerpt of Table 1, which column reports on the correlation in each sample? Which column reports on the correlation in each sample, corrected for reliability of the measures?

5. Scanning the values of r in the excerpt of Table 1, do these values fit with your answer

---

2 The researchers used a binary concept for gender/sex in this study. In addition, they did not highlight that female and male were self-identified by the participants.

in Question 3? (Recall the excerpt of the table includes only 13 of 258 samples in the meta-analysis.)

6. Is the same measure for materialism used in each study in this meta-analysis? Is the same measure for well-being used in each study in this meta-analysis?

7. What countries are the samples drawn from in the excerpt of Table 1?

8. What is the largest sample size listed in the excerpt of Table 1?

9. 749 correlations were included in this meta-analysis. Were most of them more negative than −.05?

10. How big is the effect between materialism and well-being?

Questions for Discussion

11. Can you infer from the result of this meta-analysis that materialism *causes* reduced well-being?

12. The entire meta-analysis includes samples drawn from 30 to 40 countries. Does this make you more confident in the generalizability of the findings?

Correlation and R^2 I

Alcohol Consumption, Depression, Fat Intake, and Exercise

STATISTICAL GUIDE

The *coefficient of determination* is an important concept that builds on correlation. It is symbolized by r^2 or R^2, which is pronounced "r squared." Calculating r^2 is straightforward. You simply square the value of the correlation. For instance, if $r = .50$, then, $r^2 = .50 \times .50 = .25$.

r^2 is a helpful statistic to know as it further explains the relationship between the two variables in the correlation. If you multiply r^2 by 100, you learn the percentage of variance that one variable explains in the variance of the other variable. This percentage is called the *explained variance* or *amount of variance accounted for*. So if $r^2 = .25$, then each of the variables in the correlation explains 25% of the variance in the other variable in the correlation. But remember to be careful and not fall into the trap of thinking that correlation implies causation. By saying that one variable explains 25% of the variance in the other variable, we are saying something like this: there is a 25% overlap between the two variables. We are not saying that one variable causes 25% of the other variable. Yikes! We are definitely not saying that.

The interpretation of r^2 for a negative value of r is the same as for a positive value of r. For instance, $r^2 = .16$ for an r of $-.40$. Multiplying by 100, we learn that the amount of variance explained is 16%. As you see here, r^2, unlike r, does not reveal if the relationship is direct or inverse, as a squared value will always be positive.

> To review correlation, see Exercise 4.1.

BACKGROUND NOTE

All the correlation coefficients in the excerpt are statistically significant at least at $p < .05$.

EXCERPT FROM THE RESEARCH ARTICLE[1]

Participants were 23 older adults (16 men and 7 women) . . . The majority of these individuals were in high-level corporate management positions.

The CES–D is a 20-item questionnaire designed to measure levels of depression . . . The Fat Intake Scale (FIS) is a brief dietary questionnaire . . .

Alcohol consumption. Alcohol consumption for each participant was computed by multiplying quantity (drinks per occasion) by frequency (drinking days per week). Self-reported levels of tension/anxiety were significantly negatively correlated with alcohol consumption ($r = -.45$), suggesting an inverse relationship between tension/anxiety and alcohol consumption. Neither depression nor any of the anger scores were correlated with alcohol consumption.

Saturated fat intake. Scores on the CES–D correlated with scores on the FIS ($r = .68$), suggesting a direct and positive relationship between the level of depression and saturated fat intake. Scores on the Trait-Anger scale and the Anger Expression scale were also correlated with the FIS ($r = .51$ and $.52$, respectively), also suggesting a direct and positive relationship between the level of trait anger and external anger expression with saturated fat intake.

Exercise: Aerobic and strength training. Scores on the Trait-Anger scale were significantly negatively correlated with the self-reported level of aerobic exercise ($r = -.44$), suggesting an inverse relationship between the level of trait anger and the level of aerobic exercise. Scores on Anger Expression were, however, positively correlated with the self-reported level of strength training ($r = .51$), suggesting a strong positive relationship between the level of internal anger expression and engagement in strength training.

STUDY QUESTIONS

Factual Questions

1. Is the relationship between levels of tension/anxiety and alcohol consumption direct or inverse?

---

1 Anton, S. D., & Miller, P. M. (2005). Do negative emotions predict alcohol consumption, saturated fat intake, and physical activity in older adults? *Behavior Modification*, *29*, 677–688. Reprinted by Permission of SAGE Publications, Inc.

2. The correlation for the relationship between CES–D depression scores and FIS fat intake scores indicates which of the following?
   A. Higher depression is associated with less fat intake.
   B. Higher depression is associated with more fat intake.
3. What is the value of r^2 for the relationship between tension/anxiety and alcohol consumption? Explain how you computed the answer.
4. What is the value of r^2 for the relationship between CES–D scores and FIS scores? Explain how you computed the answer.
5. What is the value of r^2 for the relationship between Anger Expression and level of strength training? Explain how you computed the answer.

6. The correlation between Anger Expression and FIS is .52. What percentage of the variance for Anger Expression is explained by the variance in FIS? Explain how you computed the answer.
7. What percentage of the variance for alcohol consumption is explained by the variance in tension/anxiety? Explain how you computed the answer.
8. In the excerpt, six correlations are reported. Which correlation has the largest value for r^2?
9. In the excerpt, six correlations are reported. Which correlation has the smallest value for r^2?
10. Consider the correlation coefficient of .68 for the relationship between CES–D and FIS. Would you characterize this relationship as *strong*? Explain.

Questions for Discussion

11. Consider the correlation coefficient of .68 for the relationship between CES–D and FIS. Then, consider the corresponding percentage of explained variance. Does consideration of the percentage of explained variance influence your impression of the strength of the relationship? Explain.

12. Does it surprise you that there is a direct relationship between depression and fat intake? Explain.
13. How many participants are in this study? Does this impact your assessment of the meaning of the results?

Correlation and R^2 II

Homeless Adolescents

STATISTICAL GUIDE

Remember that r^2 and R^2 are the same thing: both are symbols for an idea called the *coefficient of determination*.

EXCERPT FROM THE RESEARCH ARTICLE[1]

In the Midwest Longitudinal Study of Homeless Adolescents, homeless youth were interviewed directly on the streets and in shelters in eight Midwestern cities.

Physical abuse. Physical abuse was an indicator of parental/caretaker abuse. A mean of seven items (e.g., thrown something, hit with an object, pushed or shoved, slapped in the face, beaten up, threatened, and wounded with a weapon) was calculated.

Delinquent behavior. Youth reported on things such as lying, feeling guilty, setting fires, stealing at home or other places, using dirty language or swearing, and cutting classes.

Age on own. Age on own was a continuous measure, constructed from the age that adolescents reported they had first run away.

Deviant peers. Respondents were asked if any of their close friends had ever engaged in delinquent activities.

Substance use. Respondents reported how often they had used a list of substances in the past 12 months.

Postrunaway arrest and police harassment. Postrunaway arrest was a dichotomous construct that measured self-reported arrest

(continued)

1 Thrane, L., Chen, X., Johnson, K., & Whitbeck, L. B. (2008). Predictors of police contact among midwestern homeless and runaway youth. *Youth Violence and Juvenile Justice, 6*, 227–239. Reprinted by Permission of SAGE Publications, Inc.

(continued)

after running away from home the first time. Respondents were also asked if they had been hassled by the police in the past 12 months, but not arrested. Hassled by the police was dichotomized (0 = no; 1 = yes).

Age ranged from 16 to 19 years (mean = 17.4). Gender was coded 0 = males and 1 = females.

Table 1
Correlation Matrix (n = 354)

	1	2	3	4	5	6	7	8	9
1. Female	—								
2. Age	−.22**	—							
3. Physical abuse	.01	.13*	—						
4. Delinquent behavior	−.22**	.06	.15**	—					
5. Age on own	−.09	−.09	.24**	.13*	—				
6. Deviant peers	−.10	.16**	.21**	.33**	.22**	—			
7. Substance use	−.15**	.11*	.09	.38**	.07	.28**	—		
8. Hassled by police	−.24**	.13*	.16**	.23**	.13*	.26**	.27**	—	
9. Postrunaway arrest	−.20**	.14**	.11*	.31**	.25**	.22**	.18**	.12*	—

$* p < .05, ** p < .01$

STUDY QUESTIONS[2]

Factual Questions

1. Which *r* in the table has the largest value (just by visual inspection)?

2. What is the value of the correlation coefficient for the relationship between Hassled by police and Postrunaway arrest?

3. Those who are high on Delinquent behavior tend to have what type of score on Postrunaway arrest?
   A. Higher score.
   B. Lower score.

---

2 The researchers used a binary concept for gender/sex in this study. In addition, they did not highlight that female and male were self-identified by the participants.

4. Which correlation in the table has the largest r^2? (Try to answer this question without performing any computations.)
5. To two decimal places, what is the value of r^2 for the correlation you referred to in your answer to Question 4?
6. What is the percentage of explained variance (variance accounted for) that corresponds to your answer to Question 5?

7. To three decimal places, what is the value of r^2 for the relationship between gender and Delinquent behavior?
8. What is the percentage of explained variance (variance accounted for) that corresponds to your answer to Question 7?
9. What is the percentage of variance accounted for in the relationship between Postrunaway arrest and Substance use?

Questions for Discussion

10. Would you characterize any of the relationships in the excerpt as *strong*? Explain.
11. Before this study was conducted, would you have hypothesized that the relationship between Deviant peers and Hassled by police would be direct or inverse? Explain.

12. Consider your answer to Question 5. How much variance is not explained or accounted for? In your estimation is that a lot or a little left unexplained?
13. Would you be willing to generalize the results of this study to all homeless adolescents in the Midwest? Explain.

Simple Linear Regression

Dieting, Age, and Body Fat

STATISTICAL GUIDE

Regression builds upon correlation. Correlation shows how x and y are related. Regression shows how x predicts or explains y. Check out the scatterplots below. The regression line is the solid line running through the middle of the scattered points of data. The regression line is an attempt to summarize the scattered points with one line. Not many of the data points are on the line. So, the regression line does not necessarily do a great job of displaying actual, specific data points. Instead, it shows the general relationship between x and y.

> To review scatterplots, see Exercise 3.6.
> To review scatter plots and regression lines, see Exercise 3.7.

The regression line is generated by fancy math that attempts to make the line as close as possible to all the scattered data points. This is called the *best fit line*. The fancy math that generates the best fit regression line depends upon the correlation between the x and y. When the correlation between x and y is strong, the best fit line will do a good job of summarizing the scattered data points. When the correlation is weaker, the best fit line isn't able to do as good a job of summarizing the scattered data points.

Simple linear regression is one version of regression. The simple tag means that one x is predicting y, i.e., we have one predictor variable. (We'll do multiple regression next exercise.) The linear tag means we are using a straight line to summarize the data, instead of, say, a curved line. You might recall from high school geometry that the equation for any straight line is $y = a + bx$, where a is the y-intercept (i.e., where the line crosses the vertical axis) and b is the slope (i.e., the rate of change or the direction and angle of the line). The $y = a + bx$ formula is used for simple linear regression. For a direct relationship between x and y, the slope (b) will be positive in value (like the second scatterplot below); for an inverse relationship, it will be negative (like the first scatterplot below). We need the y-intercept (a) to make the equation work, but researchers often don't pay much attention to it. You can see the two

$y = a + bx$ equations for the regression lines in the scatterplots below. They are written as, $Y = 91.3 - .40x$ and $Y = 5.44 + .77x$. Notice they also give the correlations for the variables in each scatterplot, as regression depends on correlation.

A big advantage of regression over correlation is that the regression equation can be used to predict specific scores for the outcome variable y. Simply plug in a value for x into the $y = a + bx$ equation and see what y-value results. This brings up one last point. Researchers only use regression if they believe that x predicts or explains y. Since regression is built on correlation, it cannot show causation. The researcher needs to have a reason for why they think that x predicts or explains y (like maybe x happened before y). The math of regression can't figure this out for the researcher. The researcher needs to know it before using regression. Because y is thought to depend on x, y is called the *dependent variable*. Because x is thought to not depend on y, x is the *independent variable*.

BACKGROUND NOTE

In the study below, the subjects' body fat was pretested and posttested to assess the effects of a very low-calorie diet. Hydrodensitometry is a way to measure body fat in water. Bioelectrical impedance analysis (BIA) is an electrical measure of body fat.

EXCERPT FROM THE RESEARCH ARTICLE[1]

> Seventeen subjects (nine women and eight men) from an outpatient, hospital-based treatment program for obesity volunteered.
>
> Within ten days after the baseline measures (i.e., pretest measures) were obtained, the subjects began the 12-week VLCD [very low-calorie diet] portion of the . . . program . . . At the end of the 12 weeks, all measurements were repeated in the laboratory.
>
> *(continued)*

---

1 Burgess, N. S. (1991). Effect of a very-low-calorie diet on body composition and resting metabolic rate in obese men and women. *Journal of the American Dietetic Association*, 91(4), 430–434.

(continued)

Figure 1 demonstrates the relationship between age and percent of weight loss as fat. The correlation coefficient for this relationship was *r* = −.49.

Correlation between hydrostatic weighing and bioelectrical impedance was *r* = .63 for the 16 pretests and *r* = .84 for the 17 posttests. (Hydrostatic measurement of one male subject was not possible on the pretest because of discomfort in the water.) Correlation for the combined pretest and posttest trials (n = 33) was *r* = .837 (Figure 2).

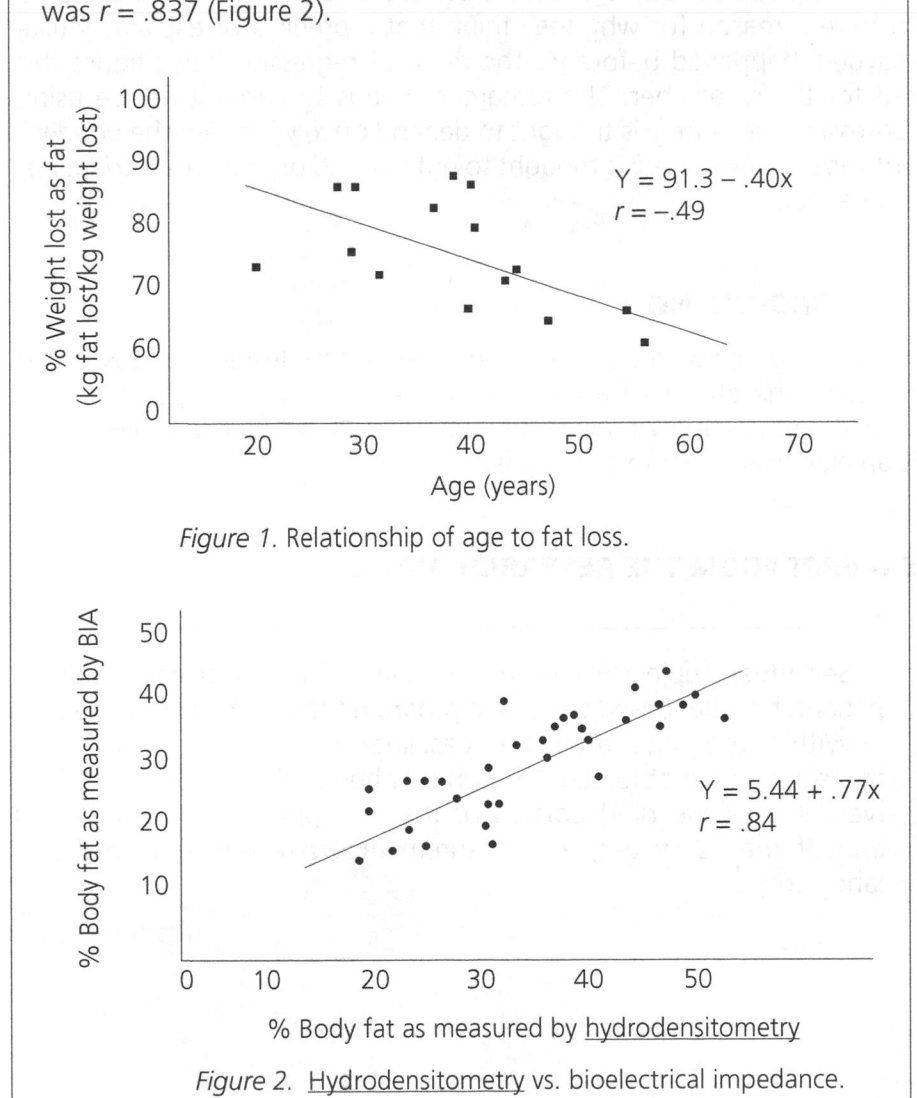

Figure 1. Relationship of age to fat loss.

Figure 2. Hydrodensitometry vs. bioelectrical impedance.

STUDY QUESTIONS

Factual Questions

1. Which figure illustrates a direct relationship? Explain.
2. Which figure has a negative slope? Is the corresponding correlation coefficient also negative?
3. If the line in Figure 1 was extended to the left, at what value would it meet the vertical axis (i.e., y-axis)? (Give an answer that is precise to one decimal place.)
4. What is the value of the y-intercept in Figure 2?
5. Is the relationship depicted in Figure 1 or in Figure 2 stronger? Explain.
6. Use the equation for the straight line shown in Figure 1 to predict the percentage of weight lost as fat for a person who is 60 years of age.
7. Use the equation for the straight line shown in Figure 1 to predict the percentage of weight lost as fat for a person who is 20 years of age.
8. Compare your answers to Questions 6 and 7. Do your answers make sense considering the inverse relationship? Explain.
9. Use the equation for the straight line shown in Figure 2 to predict the percentage of body fat as measured by BIA for a person who has 50% body fat as measured by hydrodensitometry.
10. The equation in which figure will yield more accurate predictions? Explain.

Questions for Discussion

11. Suppose the slope in Figure 2 had been 1.50 instead of 0.77. With a slope of 1.50, would the line rise (from left to right) more steeply or less steeply than the line in Figure 2?
12. The correlation between the two methods for measuring body fat is less than perfect (see Figure 2). What does this tell us about the two methods of measurement?
13. Speculate on why we use a line based on the entire group to make predictions instead of using the values of individuals to make predictions. (For instance, the person who is about 58 years of age in Figure 1 lost about 62% of weight as body fat. In the future, can we just predict that all individuals who are 58 years of age will lose 62% body fat?)

Multiple Linear Regression

Posttraumatic Stress Symptoms in an Intensive Care Unit

STATISTICAL GUIDE

Remember that simple linear regression uses this equation:

$$y = a + bx$$

where

y = dependent variable
a = y-intercept
x = independent variable
b = coefficient of the independent variable

To review the idea of regression, see Exercise 4.8. To review the idea of standard error, see Exercise 5.16. To review the idea of standardizing a variable, see Exercise 2.6 on z scores. To review the idea of confidence intervals, see Exercise 5.15.

Multiple linear regression uses the same logic. It just adds more variables to predict the outcome, i.e., more independent variables to predict the dependent variable. The multiple in the name comes from there being more than one predictor. Linear is in the name because we are still using a straight line to summarize the relationship between the predictors and the outcome. The equation looks a little more complicated than in simple linear regression but is essentially the same idea:

$$y = a + b^1x + b^2z + \ldots$$

where

y = dependent variable
a = y-intercept
x = first independent variable
b^1 = coefficient of the first independent variable
z = second independent variable
b^2 = coefficient of the second independent variable

One nice feature of multiple linear regression is that more variables can be added to the model to better predict the outcome. In the equation above, we have two predictor[1] variables, x and z, but the model can be expanded to include more predictors. In fact, it is common for multiple linear regression equations in the published literature to include six, eight, or ten predictor variables. For example, in the excerpt below, the multiple linear regression model includes nine independent variables. Notice that this means b variables will range from b^1 to b^9.

BACKGROUND NOTE

In this excerpt, Posttraumatic stress symptoms (PSS) are investigated with multiple linear regression. The excerpt refers to the multiple linear regression with the name *multivariate regression analyses*. This alternate name makes sense if you keep in mind that multiple linear regression is using multiple variables, i.e., so it's multivariate.[2]

In looking at Table 1 below, a few tips will be helpful. First, the researchers use B to refer to the b coefficient discussed above. Next to the B column, there is a column for $SE\ B$. This stands for the standard error of each B coefficient. Standard errors tell us how accurate an estimate is on average—in the standard case how wrong is the estimate. If the value of a standard error is large in comparison to the value of B, then the estimate for B has a wide range in which it might fall if the study were run again. Finally, there is β, which is pronounced "beta." If all the variables in the multiple regression are standardized (e.g., transformed into z scores), and then the multiple regression analysis is run, the coefficients are notated with β instead of B. The advantage of β is that it puts all the predictors on the same scale so you can readily compare their relative size. In contrast, the size of each B is dependent on the units of the specific measure, so B coefficients are difficult to compare (e.g., the units of the DASS are different than the units of the PSQI).

---

1   To be precise, a variable only predicts an outcome if the variable was measured before the outcome occurred.

2   If you talk to a statistician they will say that *multiple* refers to situations where there is one dependent variable and multiple independent ones, while *multivariate* is used when there are multiple dependent and multiple independent variables. Psychologists are not always this precise with their terminology, and the excerpted paper is an example of this. The authors use *multivariate* regression, when they might have more precisely used the term *multiple* regression—which is what they use in the title of Table 1.

EXCERPT FROM THE RESEARCH ARTICLE[3]

The study was conducted in an adult [intensive care unit] ICU at a university-affiliated hospital in New South Wales, Australia . . .

While in the ICU, participants completed self-report instruments . . . Two months after hospital discharge, participants reported on their quality of sleep over the last month and their experiences in ICU. Six months after hospital discharge, the participants again reported on their PTS symptoms, as well as depression, anxiety, stress levels, and quality of sleep over the last month . . .

Factors significantly associated with PTS symptoms . . . during bivariate comparisons . . . and factors known from published research to contribute to PTSD . . . were entered into a . . . multiple linear regression model. The PCL–S global score at six months was the dependent variable in the model. Independent variables were gender plus continuous scores for pain and anxiety at enrollment, stress, anxiety, depression, ICEQ . . . awareness of surroundings and frightening experiences at two months, and total PSQI score at six months . . .

Data from 160 patients were included in the multivariate regression analysis. The regression model explained 68.2% of the variability in the PTS symptoms according to PCL–S . . . scores. Higher PTS symptoms at six months were independently associated with, stress ($\beta = 0.31$, 95% CI [0.139, 0.490]) and depression ($\beta = 0.30$, 95% CI [0.139, 0.478]; DASS . . . subscale scores at six months after hospital discharge), global sleep quality (PSQI . . .) at six months ($\beta = 0.34$, 95% CI [0.081, 0.598]), and frightening experiences (ICEQ . . .; Component 2; $\beta = 0.31$, 95% CI [0.068, 0.551]) and higher pain intensity at enrollment ($\beta = 0.43$, 95% CI [0.081, 0.784]). The DASS Stress subscale contributed most to the variance regression model ($\beta = 0.29$, $p < .001$) (see Table 1).

3   Elliott, R., McKinley, S., Fien, M., & Elliott, D. (2016). Posttraumatic stress symptoms in intensive care patients: An exploration of associated factors. *Rehabilitation psychology*, *61*(2), 141. Copyright © 2016 by the American Psychological Association. Reproduced with permission.

Table 1

Multiple Linear Regression Analysis for Model of Variables Associated with Total PCL–S Score (n = 160)

Variable	B	SE B	β	p
Male gender	.873	1.055	.039	.409
Pain-intensity score in ICU	.433	.178	.119	.016
State-anxiety score in ICU	−.578	.487	−.062	.237
PSQI global score at six months	.340	.131	.152	.010
DASS stress subscale	.315	.089	.287	.001
DASS anxiety subscale	.214	.112	.130	.058
DASS depression subscale	.309	.086	.285	< .005
ICEQ Component 1 (Awareness)	−.144	.092	−.080	.120
ICEQ Component 2 (Frightening)	.310	.122	.140	.012

Note: R^2 = .682, p = < .005 (constant: 17.984 *SE*, 4.499). State-anxiety score = Faces Anxiety Scale score (FAS); PSQI = Pittsburgh Sleep Quality Index; DASS = Depression, Anxiety and Stress Scales; ICEQ = Intensive Care Experience Questionnaire.

STUDY QUESTIONS[4]

Factual Questions

1. What is the dependent variable in the multiple linear regression analysis? How many independent variables are there in the model?

2. How many variables in Table 1 are significant predictors of total PCL–S at a $p < .05$ level?

3. What is the total amount of PCL–S (6 months later) variance explained by all nine predictor variables combined?

4. How much of the variance of the PCL–S (6 months later) is *not* explained by the nine predictor variables?

5. There is a *B* and β coefficient for the Pain-intensity score in ICU. How many *p*-values are associated with Pain-intensity score in ICU? What do you think your previous answer means for the relationship between the *p*-value for *B* and β?

---

4   The researchers used a binary concept for gender/sex in this study. In addition, they did not highlight that female and male were self-identified by the participants.

6. Can you directly compare the size of the *B* coefficients for Male gender and DASS depression subscale? To help answer this question, consider the size of *B* and the *p*-values for each.

7. Can you directly compare the size of the β coefficients for Male gender and DASS depression subscale? If so, why?

8. Compare the *B* and β coefficients for the variables discussed in Questions 6 and 7. Which variable is a better predictor of PCL–S (at 6 months)?

9. By visual inspection alone, which variable appears to be the strongest predictor of PCL–S (6 months later)?

Questions for Discussion

10. Given the answers in Questions 3 and 4, how well do you think the nine predictors explain the amount of posttraumatic stress six months after a visit to the ICU?

11. The results indicate that depression and stress levels when in the ICU are strong predictors of posttraumatic stress symptoms 6 months later. Does this make sense given what you know about the relationship between stress, depression, and posttraumatic stress symptoms?

12. If you were designing this study, what variables would you add to the regression analyses to explain more of the variance in posttraumatic symptoms?

Group Differences with Normal Distributions

CHAPTER INTRODUCTION

Unit 5 includes more than 12 different statistical procedures, and each one has multiple variations. All that detail can be dizzying—especially if you are down in the weeds trying to follow every single aspect of a study and its statistical techniques. But look at Unit 5 with a big picture view. From 10,000 feet, all the statistical procedures in Unit 5 are basically about one idea—do two (or more) groups differ in a way that the researcher cares about?

Unit 5 will talk about different types of *t-tests*, and different types of *ANOVA*, and overlapping *confidence intervals*. The goal in each of these statistical procedures is to see if group A is different from group B (and maybe also group C). Again, there are very fancy statistical methods to ask this basic question, and we will cover a lot of them in Unit 5. But the heart of the matter is still the same: Is group A different from group B?

Once we know that group A *is* different from group B, the next logical question is, how big is that difference? *Effect size* is the statistical concept that captures this idea. Unit 5 has several exercises to familiarize you with effect sizes.

As we saw in Unit 4, meta-analysis is important. A meta-analysis gives researchers more confidence that group differences are real and not just the product of a single, poorly designed study or the happenstance of chance. Unit 5 covers meta-analysis in the context of group differences.

So in sum, is group A different from group B? If so, how big is the difference? That pretty much covers Unit 5. The rest is details. (Okay, those details are really important. And you should go and discover them for yourself in the following exercises. We just don't want you to lose the forest for the trees.)

DOI: 10.4324/9781003096764-5

Group Differences with Normal Disc Outcomes

CHAPTER INTRODUCTION

t-Test for Independent Groups I
Affection in Relationships

STATISTICAL GUIDE

To review normal curve, see Exercise 3.8. To review interval and ratio scale, see Exercise 1.7.

The *t*-test is used to see if the difference between *two* means is statistically significant. There are multiple kinds of *t*-tests. In this exercise, we will focus on the *t*-test for *independent groups*. This *t*-test is used if the two means you are comparing are drawn from unrelated groups, e.g., groups formed by randomization of participants. The *dependent* groups *t*-test, by contrast, compares means drawn from related groups, like having the same group take a test on two different occasions and comparing the mean score.

To use the *t*-test a number of assumptions need to be met. Two key assumptions are that (1) the data is normally distributed or nearly so, and (2) the data for the dependent variable is continuous, i.e., on an interval or ratio scale. If these two assumptions (as well as others) are not met, then different statistical tests should be used to compare the two group means (e.g., see Unit 6).

The *t*-test yields a *p*-value, which indicates the probability that chance or random sampling errors created the difference between the means. As with many statistical tests, most researchers consider a difference to be statistically significant when $p < .05$. If $p > .05$ for a *t*-test, then researchers typically assume that the group means being compared are statistically equivalent to each other.

As with correlation, when researchers present *t*-test results in a table (like Table 1 below), they often note statistically significant results with an asterisk or some kind of superscript. It is generally safe to assume that if a result has no asterisk or superscript then the result is non-significant. Still, reading table notes is necessary, so you can make sure you know what certain symbols in the table mean.

Like many things in statistics, the *t*-test for independent groups goes by multiple names. This can be confusing. The *t*-test for independent groups is also called: independent *t*-test for two samples, independent-samples *t*-test, and student's *t*-test.

EXCERPT FROM THE RESEARCH ARTICLE[1]

The married sample comprised members of 100 heterosexual couples (54% were women and 46% were men) from a Midwestern university. The dating sample also consisted of members of 100 heterosexual couples (59% were women and 41% were men) from the same Midwestern university. All the married and dating couples were Euro-American. A researcher selected subjects in a haphazard fashion and asked them to complete a short survey . . . The mean age of the sample was 26.7 years ($SD = 2.6$).

The Affectionate Communication Index is a 19-item index that . . . assesses the amount of verbal and nonverbal affectionate communication and support on a 7-point . . . scale, with anchors of 1 = partners *always* engage in this type of affectionate activity to 7 = partners *never* engage in this type of activity. [Thus, *lower* scores indicate *more* affectionate communication. Table 1 shows the results for the nonverbal activities.]

Table 1

Dating and Married Individuals' Reports of Nonverbal Affectionate Communication

Item		n	M	SD	t
Hold hands	Dating	100	3.7	1.9	3.3[†]
	Married	100	2.9	1.7	
Kiss on the lips	Dating	100	2.9	1.5	4.9[†]
	Married	100	2.0	1.1	
Kiss on the cheeks	Dating	100	3.6	1.6	4.5[†]
	Married	100	2.7	1.3	
Give massages to each other	Dating	100	4.2	1.8	5.0[†]
	Married	99	2.5	1.8	
Put arm around the shoulder	Dating	100	3.6	1.8	4.6[†]
	Married	92	2.5	1.5	
Hug each other	Dating	100	2.5	1.6	2.0*
	Married	100	2.1	1.2	
Sit close to each other	Dating	96	2.9	1.6	3.9[†]
	Married	100	2.0	1.6	

1 Punyanunt-Carter, N. M. (2004). Reported affectionate communication and satisfaction in marital and dating relationships. *Psychological Reports*, *95*, 1154–1160. Reprinted by Permission of SAGE Publications, Inc.

Item		n	M	SD	t
Look into each other's eyes	Dating	100	3.3	1.6	1.0
	Married	100	3.0	1.8	
Wink at each other	Dating	100	4.7	2.3	1.7
	Married	96	4.2	1.9	

*$p < .05$. † $p < .001$.

STUDY QUESTIONS

Factual Questions

1. If you visually inspect Table 1, which group had a higher mean score for kissing on the lips? (Pro tip: the text says that higher scores indicate less of a behavior.)
2. Is the difference between the two means for kissing on the lips statistically significant? If yes, at what probability level?
3. What do researchers conclude then about the two means for kissing on the lips?
4. Is the difference between the two means for hugging each other statistically significant? If yes, at what probability level?
5. What do researchers conclude then about the two means for hugging each other?
6. The differences are *not* statistically significant for which items?

7. Are the two means statistically equivalent for winking at each other?
8. How many of the differences in Table 1 are statistically significant at the .05 level but not significant at the .001 level?
9. The differences between the means for the items in A and B are statistically significant. For which one is the significance at a higher level? Explain your answer.

   A. The difference for hugging each other.
   B. The difference for sitting close to each other.

10. For which of the following might we be more confident that the means are different?

    A. The difference for hugging each other.
    B. The difference for holding hands.

Questions for Discussion

11. The group difference for kissing on the cheeks is statistically significant at the .001 level. Logically, is it also significant at the .05 level? (Note: If you have a statistics textbook,

examine the table of critical values of t to help you determine the answer to this question.)

12. The table contains five types of statistics (n, M, SD, t, and p). Which three are *descriptive statistics*? (Note: If you have a statistics textbook, you may want to consult it.)

13. The table contains five types of statistics (n, M, SD, t, and p). Which two are *inferential statistics*? (Note: If you have a statistics textbook, you may want to consult it.)

14. The researcher states that she selected the individuals for this study "in a haphazard fashion." What is your understanding of this term?

15. For all items for which there are statistically significant differences, the means for dating couples are higher than the means for married couples. If you had planned this study, would you have hypothesized this result? (Recall that higher scores mean lower frequencies of behavior.) Explain.

t-Test for Independent Groups II

Ethnic Identity of Korean Americans

STATISTICAL GUIDE

Every *t*-statistic has a probability associated with it. The larger the absolute value of the *t*-statistic, the lower the probability of obtaining that *t*-statistic by random sampling error or chance. So *t*-statistics with a larger absolute value will have lower *p*-values. As a general rule, *t*-statistics with an absolute value above 2.1 or 2.2 are likely to be statistically significant at $p < .05$.[1] You can see this idea in action with the *t*-values in Table 1 below. You can also see in Table 1 that the groups being compared are males vs. females[2] and 13–15-year-olds vs. 16–18-year-olds. These are considered independent groups because they are sets of different people, and the scores in one group are not systematically related to the scores in the other group. Check out Exercise 5.3 and 5.4 to see examples of groups that are systematically related.

EXCERPT FROM THE RESEARCH ARTICLE[3]

> The sample consisted of 217 Korean American students selected from ethnically diverse high schools in the Los Angeles area . . .
>
> Phinney's 14-item Level of Ethnic Identity subscale was designed to assess the degree of ethnic identity among adolescents . . . Items such as "I am happy that I am a member of the group I belong
>
> *(continued)*

---

1 This general rule has two caveats: (1) each group needs to have 20 or more participants, and (2) the initial hypothesis had to not state a prediction about which group mean would be larger, i.e., it had to be a two-tailed test.

2 The researchers used a binary concept for gender/sex in this study. In addition, they did not highlight that female and male were self-identified by the participants.

3 Shrake, E. K., & Rhee, S. (2004). Ethnic identity as a predictor of problem behaviors among Korean American adolescents. *Adolescence*, *39*, 601–622. Reprinted under Fair Use.

(continued)

Table 1

Means and Standard Deviations for Level of Ethnic Identity, Other-Group Attitudes, and Perceived Discrimination by Age and Gender

	Gender				Age				
	Male	Female			13–15	16–18			Total
	M (SD)	M (SD)	t		M (SD)	M (SD)	t		M (SD)
Level of ethnic identity	3.01 (.51)	2.99 (.56)	.18		2.91 (.49)	3.08 (.57)	−2.25*		3.00 (.54)
Other-group attitudes	2.83 (.60)	3.12 (.56)	−3.79***		2.98 (.55)	3.02 (.62)	−.41		2.99 (.59)
Perceived discrimination	1.90 (.75)	1.68 (.75)	2.09*		1.65 (.69)	1.89 (.80)	−2.36*		1.78 (.76)

Note: Scores for ethnic identity, attitudes, and discrimination range from 1 to 4.

* *p* < .05. *** *p* < .001.

to" . . . and "I have a clear sense of my own ethnic background and what it means to me" [were included in the scale].

Phinney's 6-item Attitudes Toward Other Groups subscale was designed to assess attitudes toward other groups . . . Respondents were asked to rate statements such as "I like meeting and getting to know people from ethnic groups other than my own."

A five-item checklist was developed to assess perceived discrimination. Items asked respondents' perception of society's unfair treatment of their ethnic group and also the personal experience of unfair treatment . . . Typical items stated "During your high school years, how often have you thought that your ethnic group is negatively stereotyped by mainstream people?"

STUDY QUESTIONS

Factual Questions

1. What is the mean level of ethnic identity for the total sample?
2. By visual inspection, do males or females have a higher mean on Perceived discrimination?
3. Is the difference between the two means in Question 2 statistically significant?
4. From a statistical perspective, are the two means in Question 2 different from each other?
5. For Other-group attitudes is the difference between 13–15-year-olds and 16–18-year-olds statistically significant?
6. From a statistical perspective, are the two means in Question 5 different from each other?

7. For Perceived discrimination is the difference between 13–15-year-olds and 16–18-year-olds statistically significant?
8. Four of the six values of t in Table 1 have an asterisk. Explain why two of the values do not have an asterisk.
9. Which of the two means in Table 1 appear to be most different?
10. Which of the following differences between males and females is more likely to occur by chance? Explain the basis for your answer.

    A. Other-group attitudes
    B. Perceived discrimination

Question for Discussion

11. This research was conducted with Korean adolescents in the Los Angeles area. Would you be willing to generalize the results of this study to Korean adolescents who live in other regions of the country? Why or why not?
12. Why might older participants in this sample perceive greater levels of discrimination?

t-Test for Dependent Groups I

Bilingual and Monolingual Friendship

STATISTICAL GUIDE

Just like other kinds of *t*-tests, the *t*-test for *dependent* groups is used to compare two group means. A statistically significant result shows that the group means are different, while a non-significant result indicates that the group means are statistically equivalent. Here, though, the two groups are dependent on each other, or are related to each other in some important way. Commonly, the two groups are related because it is the same people in each group. The people are just measured doing the same thing at two different times, or the same person is measured doing two slightly different tasks, like in the example below.

For a general introduction to *t*-tests, see Exercises 5.1 and 5.2.

Another name for this *t*-test is the matched-pairs *t*-test. If you can match each score in one group with a score in the other group, the data is made up of matched pairs. The pairs might be matched because it is the same people in each group, or maybe because the people in one group are the twins of the people in the other group. The key idea is that scores in one group are not independent of the scores in the other group; they are matched or related in some way. This is why this *t*-test is sometimes called the *t*-test for correlated data. The scores in the two groups are likely to be correlated because each score in one group is connected to a score in the other group. For example, in the study below bilingual participants make ratings of characteristics in their closest monolingual friendship and they also make ratings of characteristics in their closest bilingual friendship. Since the same person is making both ratings, the two ratings are likely related. For instance, people that tend to rate all their friendships as close will likely rate both their monolingual and bilingual friendships as close, while people who tend do the opposite, rate their friendships as less close, will rate both their monolingual and bilingual friendships as less close.

EXCERPT FROM THE RESEARCH ARTICLE[1]

A total of 46 bilingual (English- and Spanish-speaking) under-graduates (36 female, 10 male) participated. The average age was 20.6 years old, and the youngest student to participate was 18 years and the oldest 27 years.

Friendship Quality Scale (FQS). Participants answered 39 questions from the FQS (Bukowski et al., 1994) about their closest current bilingual and monolingual friendships. At the [beginning], they were asked to choose their closest current bilingual and monolingual friendships and place their names at the top [of the page] . . . The FQS measures five aspects of friendship quality: *closeness*, *security*, *help*, *companionship*, and *conflict*. Means were created for each of these variables for the closest bilingual friend and monolingual friend.

Table 1

Comparison between Closest Bilingual and Monolingual Friends: Means (Standard Deviations), Paired t-Tests, and Correlations for Friendship Qualities Scale

Features	Closest bilingual friend mean (SD)	Closest monolingual friend mean (SD)	Paired t-Test	Correlation between bilingual and monolingual
Closeness	4.48 (0.60)	4.08 (0.80)	3.63***	.47***
Companionship	4.11 (0.87)	3.46 (0.98)	3.68***	.17
Security	4.52 (0.58)	4.23 (0.71)	2.61*	.36*
Help	4.50 (0.60)	4.24 (0.73)	2.67*	.50***
Conflict	2.00 (1.01)	1.95 (0.93)	0.47	.64***

Note: n = 45.

* $p < .05$. ** $p < .01$. *** $p < .001$.

1 Sebanc, A. M., Hernandez, M. D., & Alvarado, M. (2009). Understanding, connection, and identification: Friendship features of bilingual Spanish-English speaking undergraduates. *Journal of Adolescent Research*, 24, 194–217. Reprinted by permission of SAGE Publications, Inc.

STUDY QUESTIONS

Factual Questions

1. What is the difference between the two means for Closeness?

2. From a statistical perspective, are the means in Question 1 different? Explain.

3. Can you say that the participants rated their bilingual friendships as closer than their monolingual friendships? Explain.

4. What is the difference between the two means for Companionship?

5. From a statistical perspective, are the two means for Companionship different? Explain.

6. Can you say that the participants rated their bilingual friendships as having greater companionship than their monolingual friendships? Explain.

7. How many of the means being compared in Table 1 are statistically equivalent?

8. Both Closeness and Security have statistically significant results. Which one has the t-value with a lower probability of occurring by chance? Explain.

Questions for Discussion

9. The value of t for Conflict is less than 1.00. If you have a statistics textbook, consult the table of critical values of t to determine whether a t-value between 1.00 and .4 is ever significant. What is your answer?

10. Describe the overall pattern of results in Table 1. Give an explanation for this pattern of results.

t-Test for Dependent Groups II

Characteristics of New Parents

STATISTICAL GUIDE

For a general introduction to *t*-tests, see Exercises 5.1–5.3.

In the example below, there are two groups, one composed of husbands and one composed of wives. The individuals in the groups are matched in an important way. Each husband in the husband group has a wife in the wife group (the converse is also true). Thus, the groups are matched pairs (literally!). In this case, then, the *t*-test for dependent groups is appropriate, as the answers that husbands give will likely relate to the answers their wives give, i.e., there will be a non-zero correlation between their responses. Take marital satisfaction, for example, which the sample was asked about. Husbands and wives won't necessarily give the exact same answer regarding how satisfied they are in their marriage, but their answers are likely to be related as they are participating in the same marriage.

EXCERPT FROM THE RESEARCH ARTICLE[1]

Couples were first contacted during an early meeting of a childbirth course. Approximately six weeks before their due date (at Time 1), both members of each couple completed several self-report scales after a class, privately and without consulting one another. Approximately six months after childbirth (at Time 2), both partners completed a second set of self-report measures . . . . Participants' desire to become a parent was assessed only during the prenatal

(continued)

---

1 Rholes, W. S., Simpson, J. A., & Friedman, M. (2006). Avoidant attachment and the experience of parenting. *Personality and Social Psychology Bulletin, 32*, 275–285. Reprinted by Permission of SAGE Publications, Inc.

(continued)

testing session. Parenting meaning/satisfaction and stress were assessed only postnatally.

The Desire to Become a Parent Scale . . . contains 12 items. Sample items include "I have a strong desire to have children."

Marital satisfaction was assessed by the Satisfaction subscale of the . . . Dyadic Adjustment Scale (DAS). Example items from this ten-item subscale are as follows: "Do you regret that you ever married?" . . .

Depressive symptoms were measured by the Center for Epidemiologic Studies–Depression Scale . . . Participants indicated the frequency of depressive symptoms *within the last week*. Sample items include "I was bothered by things that usually didn't bother me" . . .

Parenting stress was measured by the . . . Parenting Stress Index. Example items are as follows: "My baby is so demanding that it exhausts me" . . .

Table 1

Descriptive Statistics: Means, Standard Deviations, and Matched-Pair t-Tests

	Men		Women		
	M	*SD*	*M*	*SD*	*t*
Desire to become a parent (T1)	62.77	1.01	67.17	1.01	3.57**
Parent meaning/ satisfaction (T2)	46.12	8.28	50.25	7.11	4.17***
Marital satisfaction (T1)	41.83	4.15	41.93	4.70	0.29
Marital satisfaction (T2)	40.17	5.60	39.52	6.70	1.33
Depression (T1)	29.27	7.78	31.37	7.66	2.32*
Depression (T2)	29.11	8.31	30.42	8.47	1.38
Parenting stress (T2)	31.00	17.70	36.00	16.94	3.41**

Note: T1 = Time 1; T2 = Time 2.

* $p < .05$. ** $p < .01$. *** $p < .001$.

STUDY QUESTIONS[2]

Factual Questions

1. What are the largest and smallest *t*-values reported for the matched-pairs *t*-tests?

2. Given what you know about *t*-values, are either of the answers from Question 1

---

2 The researchers used a binary concept for gender/sex in this study. In addition, they did not highlight that female and male were self-identified by the participants.

likely to be statistically significant? (Consult the previous exercises or your statistics textbook if necessary.)

3. What is the mean difference for Marital satisfaction at Time 2 (i.e., the size of the difference between the means for men and women at Time 2)?

4. Is the *t*-value for Marital satisfaction at Time 2 statistically significant? Explain.

5. From a statistical perspective, is there a difference in how husbands and wives reported Marital satisfaction at Time 2?

6. By visual inspection alone, did men or women report greater Parenting stress?

7. Is the mean difference between men and women on Parenting stress statistically significant? Explain.

8. There are seven *t*-tests reported in the table. How many indicate the presence of a mean difference?

9. For Parenting stress, the *t* has $p < .01$. What does this mean?

   A. Odds are less than 1 in 10 that chance account for the difference.

   B. Odds are less than 1 in 100 that chance account for the difference.

   C. Odds are less than 1 in 1,000 that chance accounts for the difference.

Questions for Discussion

10. The difference for Desire to become a parent is significant at the .01 level. Is it also significant at the .05 level?

11. For Marital satisfaction at Time 1, the value of *t* is 0.29, which is less than 1.00. If you have a statistics textbook, consult the table of critical values for *t* to determine whether a value of less than 1.00 is ever significant at a $p < .05$ level. What is your answer?

12. The researchers had members of each couple complete the self-report scales privately and without consulting one another. In your opinion, was it important to have them complete the scales without consulting each other? Explain.

13. Matched-pairs *t*-tests are also called *t*-tests for correlated samples. Explain how the responses of the wives might be correlated with the responses of the husbands?

Effect Size (*d*-type) I

Summer Camp and Self-Esteem

STATISTICAL GUIDE

Effect sizes address a big problem in inferential statistics. A result in a study might be statistically significant, but that does not give any information on the size of the effect. A result with a *p*-value of .001 could be a very large effect, but it could also be a very small effect. The same could be said for a result with a *p*-value of .04. A low *p*-value tells you that an effect likely exists, but it doesn't tell you anything about how big or small that effect is. You need a separate calculation to determine that. You need an effect size calculation.

Effect sizes are calculated in different ways in different situations (e.g., correlation vs. a *t*-test). When two means are being compared, the *d*-type effect size is commonly used. While there are variations on how to calculate a *d*-type effect size, the basic idea is the difference between groups divided by the standard deviation. The result is *d*, sometimes called Cohen's *d*, which tells you how far apart in standard deviations the groups are from each other. It is common to interpret *d*-type effect sizes of 0.2 to. 49 as "small," .50 to .79 as "medium," and .80 and above as "large." So, if two means are .3 standard deviations away from each other, this is a small effect; if they are .6 standard deviations away from each other, it is medium effect; and if they are .9 standard deviations away from each other, it is a large effect.

Two final notes on *d*. First, researchers are most often interested in the absolute value of *d*, as the sign of it is arbitrary. Second, *d*, like all effect sizes, is only worth considering if the result is statistically significant, i.e., if we think the effect exists. We don't care about the size of effects we don't think exist.

EXCERPT FROM THE RESEARCH ARTICLE[1]

The present study was designed to test the hypothesis that a session of summer camp would increase the self-esteem of economically disadvantaged school-age children from New York's inner-city neighborhoods. The sample included 68 American children, ages 6–12 years . . .

As a measure of self-esteem, the Piers-Harris Children's Self-concept Scale . . . an 80-item self-report questionnaire, was administered as a pretest and posttest. Total scores for self-esteem range from 0 to 80, with higher scores reflecting more positive self-evaluations . . .

The scale taps six dimensions of self-esteem . . . popularity (12 items), physical appearance and attributes (13 items), intellectual and school status (17 items), happiness and satisfaction (10 items), behavior (admission of problem behaviors) (16 items), and anxiety (14 items). On behavior and anxiety scales, higher scores indicate the perception of fewer problems or less anxiety.

Size of treatment effect was based on Cohen's d for the overall score ($d = .15$) and for the popularity cluster scale ($d = .25$).

Table 1

t-Test Comparisons of Pre- and Posttest Performance on Piers-Harris Children's Self-Concept and Cluster Scales

Piers-Harris	Pretest		Posttest		t_{67}	p
	M	SD	M	SD		
Total	61.8	11.0	63.4	11.0	−2.29	.03
Popularity	8.3	2.3	8.9	2.4	−2.54	.01
Physical	10.5	2.5	10.7	2.5	−.88	*ns*
Intellectual	14.1	2.7	14.4	2.6	−1.30	*ns*
Happiness	8.4	1.9	8.7	1.7	−1.51	*ns*
Behavior	13.1	2.9	13.2	3.0	−.57	*ns*
Anxiety	10.3	2.9	10.6	2.9	−1.23	*ns*

1 Readdick, C. A., & Schaller, G. R. (2005). Summer camp and self-esteem of school-age inner-city children. *Perceptual and Motor Skills, 101*, 121–130. Copyright © 2005 by Perceptual and Motor Skills. Reprinted by permission of SAGE Publications, Inc.

STUDY QUESTIONS

Factual Questions

1. For Popularity, the mean on the pretest was 8.3. What was it on the posttest?
2. What is the value of p for the difference between the pretest and posttest means for Popularity?
3. From a statistical perspective, are the two means for Popularity different?
4. Just as a ballpark guess, for Popularity, what is the difference between the Pretest and Posttest divided by a standard deviation?
5. According to the information above, the effect size for the difference between the pre/post Popularity means should be labeled as . . .

   A. large.
   B. medium.
   C. small.
   D trivial.

6. Is the difference between the pre/post means for the Total scores statistically significant? Explain.
7. According to the information in Exercise 5.5, the effect size for the difference between the pre/post Total means should be labeled as . . .

   A. large.
   B. moderate.
   C. small.
   D. trivial.

8. From a statistical perspective, is there a difference in the scores for Happiness from Pretest to Posttest? Explain.
9. From a statistical perspective, is there a difference in the scores for Anxiety from Pretest to Posttest? Explain.

Questions for Discussion

10. Speculate on why the researchers reported effect sizes for only two of the seven differences.
11. The results of the study were in line with the hypothesis that self-esteem would improve through the course of summer camp. Can the researchers claim that the summer camp had a big impact on self-esteem?
12. Do the researchers have evidence to argue that summer camp had a big impact on the children's sense of their Popularity?

Effect Size (*d*-type) II

Foster Families and Technology

STATISTICAL GUIDE

In this example, we consider both *t*-tests and effect size together. Both the *t*-test and the *d*-type effect size are dependent on the differences between the two groups. The bigger the differences, the bigger the *t* and the *d*, and vice versa. So a *t*-value is conceptually related to a *d*-type effect size. Still, the two statistics are different in that the *t*-value has an associated probability (or *p*-value), while the *d*-type effect size conveys how far apart the groups are in standard deviation units.

In Table 1 below, the authors refer to the *d*-type effect with "ES," which stands for effect size. If the effect size is not given in a Table, you can often find it in the text of the Results section of a research article, like was done in the article in Exercise 5.5.

EXCERPT FROM THE RESEARCH ARTICLE[1]

As part of an intervention program, a sample of 34 foster families received computers, internet connections, and supportive services.

The Computer Confidence Scale (CCS) is a 13-item self-efficacy scale measuring self-reported confidence to perform computer tasks . . .

The Internet Confidence Scale (ICS) is a 16-item self-efficacy scale that measures self-reported confidence to use the internet to perform a specific task . . . or use internet-based communication.

(continued)

---

1 Finn, J., Kerman, B., & LeCornec, J. (2005). Reducing the digital divide for children in foster care: First-year evaluation of the Building Skills–Building Futures Program. *Research on Social Work Practice*, *15*, 470–480. Reprinted by permission of SAGE Publications, Inc.

(continued)

Table 1
Foster Child Outcomes

	BSBF Group (*n* = 40)				Significance of Difference/Effect Size
Dependent variable	Baseline		12 Months		
	M	*SD*	*M*	*SD*	
Computer Confidence Scale (CCS)	55.16	33.09	75.60	34.45	$t = -3.78$, $df = 39$, $p < .001$, ES = .61
Internet Confidence Scale (ICS)	55.26	44.21	94.27	42.72	$t = -7.39$, $df = 39$, $p < .001$, ES = .88
Self-rating of technology skills	2.48	1.02	3.23	.87	$t = -5.99$, $df = 39$, $p < .001$, ES = .93

Note: BSBF = Building Skills-Building Futures; ES = Effect Size.

Children rated their own skills from 1 (*no skills*) to 5 (*experienced user*).

STUDY QUESTIONS

Factual Questions

1. What was the mean score on the CCS at baseline?
2. For ICS, what is the difference between the mean at baseline and the mean 12 months later?
3. Using conventional levels for statistical significance, is Self-rating of technology skills different at Baseline and 12 Months later? Explain.
4. Using conventional levels for statistical significance, is CCS different at Baseline and 12 Months later? Explain.
5. All the *t*-tests in Table 1 have $p < .001$. This means the probability the results are driven by random chance are . . .

   A. less than 1 in 100.
   B. more than 1 in 100.
   C. less than 1 in 1,000.
   D. more than 1 in 1,000.

6. Each of the three comparisons in Table 1 are statistically significant at the .001 level. So is it appropriate to calculate an effect size for each of the three comparisons?
7. What size of effect is present for the three comparisons in Table 1?

8. The effect size is bigger than one-half of a standard deviation for how many of the three comparisons? Explain.

9. How is it that the effect size for Self-rating of technology skills is bigger than the effect size for CCS when the differences between the means for the former is so much smaller than the differences between the means for the latter?

Questions for Discussion

10. Just by looking at the *t*-values and the *d*-values in Table 1, what might you conclude about the relationship between *t*-values and *d*-values?

11. If someone criticized this study as inconsequential because the intervention was expensive and the effects were meager, how might you respond?

Meta-Analysis with *d*-Type Effect Size

Court-Mandated Domestic Violence Interventions

To review *d*-type effect size, see Exercise 5.5 and 5.6. To review 95% confidence interval, see Exercise 5.15.

STATISTICAL GUIDE

A meta-analysis is a study that pools data from many studies to see if an effect exists when all the data is combined. If results from a meta-analysis show an effect is present, researchers are more confident that the effect is real and not just based on a statistical fluke. If indeed the meta-analysis finds an effect, researchers are keen to know how big the effect is. This is where the *d*-type effect size comes in; *d*-type effect sizes can be combined across many studies to get an overall effect size for the intervention in the meta-analysis. The *d*-type effect size for all the studies in a meta-analysis is often referred to as the "Overall Mean *d*."

One note on terminology: in the excerpt below, the study refers to "standardized mean difference type effect sizes (*d*)." This is another way of saying *d*-type effect size. The *d*-type effect size is the mean difference which is standardized through dividing by the standard deviation.

BACKGROUND NOTE

The meta-analysis below considers programs aimed at reducing incidents of domestic violence after an offender has been to court for domestic violence charges. After their original court date, offenders were randomized to either receive special anti-domestic violence programming or to participate in a control condition. The studies then followed the participants and measured one of two outcomes, *official reports* of new domestic violence or *victim reports* of new domestic violence.

EXCERPT FROM THE RESEARCH ARTICLE[1]

The aim of this systematic review is to assess the effects of post-arrest court-mandated interventions . . . for domestic violence offenders . . . with the aim of reducing their future likelihood of re-assaulting above and beyond what would have been expected by routine legal procedures.

We searched numerous computerized databases and websites, bibliographies of published reviews of related literature and scrutiny of annotated bibliographies of related literature. Our goal was to identify all published and unpublished literature that met our selection criteria . . .

. . . For . . . experimental . . . designs, control conditions could be no-treatment or treatment as usual. That is, the no-treatment

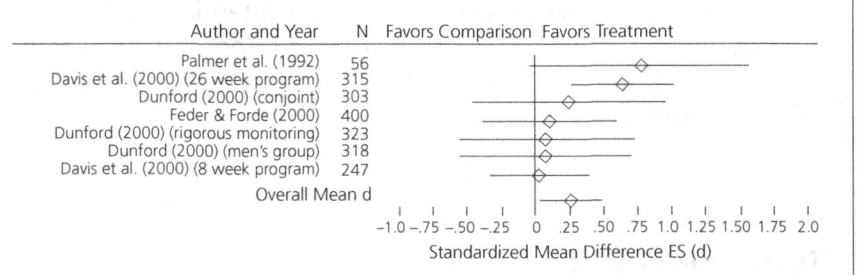

Figure 1: Effect Size (*d*) and 95% Confidence Interval for Official Measure from Experimental (Random) Studies

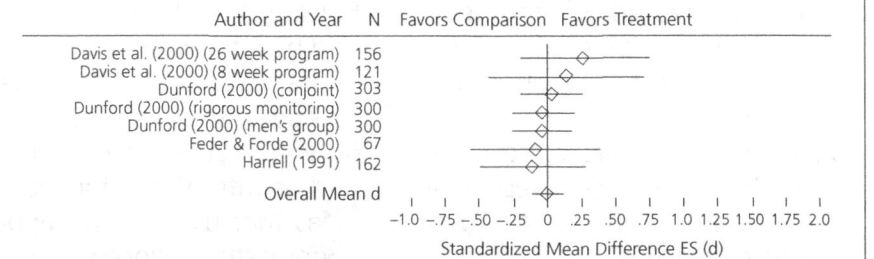

Figure 4: Effect Size (*d*) and 95% Confidence Interval for Victim Reported Measures from Experimental and Quasi-Experimental Studies with a No Treatment Comparison Group

Figures 1 and 2

(continued)

---

1 Feder, L., Austin, S., & Wilson, D. (2008). Court-mandated interventions for individuals convicted of domestic violence. *Campbell Systematic Reviews*, *4*(12). Reprinted under Fair Use.

(continued)

control condition could include routine legal interventions such as probation or a short jail stay . . .

This systematic review used standard meta-analytic methods . . . Effects measured on continuous type measures . . . were encoded as standardized mean difference type effect sizes (*d*) . . .

Official reports were either official complaints made to the police that may or may not have resulted in an arrest, or actual arrests for domestic violence . . . Figure 1 indicates a general pattern of positive effects on official reports of repeat victimization in these experimental studies . . .

Victim Reported Outcomes: A concern with official measures is that they may not accurately reflect the amount and severity of ongoing violence. Research consistently indicates that official reports capture only a small fraction of this abuse . . . As such, the victim is viewed as the best source for information on the offender's continued abuse. Given that, we turn our attention to the . . . estimates we have from these studies on the effect of these programs according to the victim's reports of abuse . . . The distribution of effects is shown in Figure 2.

STUDY QUESTIONS

Factual Questions

1. How many studies in the meta-analysis used official measures of repeat victimization as the outcome variable?

2. How many studies in the meta-analysis used victim report of domestic violence as the outcome measure?

3. What is the largest effect size for the studies using official measures of repeat victimization? What is the smallest? What is the Overall mean *d*?

4. What is the largest effect size for the studies using victim report of domestic violence? What is the smallest? What is the overall mean *d*?

5. How should the overall mean *d* be interpreted in the studies that used official measures of repeat victimization?

6. How should the overall mean *d* be interpreted for the studies that used victim report of domestic violence?

7. Does the 95% confidence interval for the overall mean *d* in Figure 1 include 0? Why does this matter? (*Note*: If you are unfamiliar with confidence intervals, please see Exercise 5.15.)

8. How many of the studies in Figure 2 have a *d* in the negative range?

Questions for Discussion

9. What do you make of the difference between the Overall Mean *d* in Figure 1 and Figure 2?

10. There are seven studies per outcome variable (official report and victim report). Does this seem like a small, medium, or large set of studies for a meta-analysis?

Statistical Power

Hypnosis and Sports Performance

STATISTICAL GUIDE

The statistical *power* of a study design is the capability of that study to correctly identify a real effect when it is present. Think of power as the amount of magnification a study has to see the effect under the microscope. If a researcher is looking for an effect that is really small, then the microscope needs a lot of magnification (a lot of power). If a researcher is looking for a big effect, then the microscope might not need much magnification.

To review the idea of effect size, see Exercises 5.5 and 5.6.

More precisely, power is the probability that a statistical test will find $p < .05$ when a real effect is present. Generally, researchers want the power of a study design to be at least 80%. This way, studies will have at least an 80% chance of correctly identifying real effects. (Missing a real effect is called Type II error, and something that necessarily happens some of the time when using p-values to decide if an effect is present.)

Researchers usually focus on two factors that influence power: (1) the size of the effect being studied, and (2) the size of the sample. If the effect is large (e.g., $d = 1.5$), then getting the power above 80% will be easier than if the effect being studied is small (e.g., $d = .15$). The larger the sample, the greater the power. The best way to increase power is to increase the sample size.

The power of a study should be calculated when the study is being designed. The power calculation guides researchers as they decide how many participants to include in their study, the one aspect of power that researchers can readily control. Since the study has not been run, the exact effect size is not known, but it can be estimated. Researchers typically consult published studies similar to the planned study to estimate an expected effect size.

Power is crucial to good study design. An underpowered study is likely to miss an effect that is really there (the magnification of the microscope

is too low). An overpowered study is a poor use of resources, e.g., running 200 participants when the study only needed 100 participants to find the effect.

Table 1 gives the number of participants needed per group for different levels of power and for different effect sizes (*d*-type), when comparing two group means. That's a bit of a mouthful, so let's walk through an example. If we want .8 or 80% power, and the expected effect is small, like *d* = .2, 393 participants per group, or 786 participants total, are needed. In that situation, running 193 participants in each group results in only 50% power, or a 50% chance of finding a true effect. The situation changes if the expected effect is large, like *d* = 1.00. In that case only 16 participants per group are needed for 80% power. Running 393 participants per group is really different than running 16 participants per group. A power calculation lets you know which you should do.

Table 1
Number of Participants Needed for Power Given a Specific Effect Size

	d										
Power	0.1	0.2	0.3	0.4	0.5	0.6	0.7	0.8	1	1.2	1.4
0.25	*	*	*	*	*	*	*	*	*	*	*
0.5	769	193	86	49	31	22	16	13	8	6	4
0.6	980	245	109	62	40	28	20	16	10	7	5
2/3	1,144	286	128	72	46	32	24	18	12	8	6
0.7	1,235	309	138	78	50	35	26	20	13	9	7
0.75	1,389	348	155	87	56	39	29	22	14	10	8
0.8	1,570	393	175	99	63	44	33	25	16	11	9
0.85	1,796	449	200	113	72	50	37	29	18	13	10
0.9	2,102	526	234	132	85	59	43	33	22	15	14
0.95	2,599	650	289	163	104	73	54	41	26	19	14
0.99	3,675	919	409	230	147	103	75	58	37	26	19

Source: Teixeira, A., Rosa, Á., & Calapez, T. (2009). Statistical power analysis with Microsoft Excel: normal tests for one or two means as a prelude to using non-central distributions to calculate power. *Journal of Statistics Education, 17*(1), n1. Reprinted under Fair Use.

BACKGROUND NOTE

Discussion of power calculations often occurs in the Method section of a paper. Authors typically only devote a few sentences to describe how they dealt with power in designing the study. Note that a "controlled study" is a study that includes a control group for comparison.

EXCERPTS FROM RESEARCH ARTICLES

> 1. Rumination-focused cognitive behavior therapy vs. cognitive behavior therapy for depression.[1]
>
> [W]e estimate a between-treatment effect size of Cohen's $d = 0.7$. To detect a difference in effect size of 0.7 between [Rumination-focused cognitive behavior therapy] and [Cognitive behavior therapy] at a . . . significance level of 5%, each treatment arm requires 44 patients to obtain 90% statistical power. Assuming a dropout rate of 20%, we will recruit 55 patients into each treatment arm.
>
> 2. Review of studies investigating the effects of hypnosis on sports performance.[2]
>
> [T]he majority of the controlled studies could be characterized as possessing limited statistical power, with four of the six studies incorporating 15 or fewer participants per experimental condition.

STUDY QUESTIONS

Factual Questions

1. According to Table 1, if a study wants 80% power, and past studies have found that d is around .5, how many participants are needed in each group?

2. According to Table 1, if the expected effect is small, like $d = .2$, and there are 200 participants in each group, about how much power will a study have?

3. In excerpt 1, the study aims for 90% power. What is the chance this study will not find an effect when the effect is really there?

4. According to Table 1, how many participants does the study in excerpt 1 need in

---

1 Hvenegaard, M., Watkins, E. R., Poulsen, S., Rosenberg, N. K., Gondan, M., Grafton, B., . . . & Moeller, S. B. (2015). Rumination-focused cognitive behaviour therapy vs. cognitive behaviour therapy for depression: study protocol for a randomised controlled superiority trial. *Trials*, *16*(1), 1. © Hvenegaard et al. 2015. Published by Biomed Central Ltd.

2 Milling, L. S., & Randazzo, E. S. (2016). Enhancing sports performance with hypnosis: An ode for Tiger Woods. *Psychology Of Consciousness: Theory, Research, And Practice*, *3*(1), 45–60. Reprinted under Fair Use.

each group to reach a power level of 90%?

5. Excerpt 2 mentions that many of the studies reviewed had 15 or fewer participants per group. If a study had two groups, how large would the effect have to be to have 80% power, with these group sizes, according to Table 1?

6. Is the answer to Question 5, a large, medium, or small d-type effect size?

7. Excerpt 2 states that many of the studies in the review had "limited statistical power." Explain what this means for the ability of these studies to find a real effect.

8. Suppose that the study in excerpt 1 decided to have 95% power, how many participants would they need in total, after dropout had already occurred, according to Table 1?

Questions for Discussion

9. Do you think it was wise for the study in excerpt 1 to consider dropout rates when calculating power and sample size?

10. Is it worth research dollars, researcher time, and participant time to run a study with 50% power?

One-Way ANOVA
Teletherapy with HIV Patients

STATISTICAL GUIDE

Like a *t*-test, *analysis of variance* (ANOVA) can be used to determine if two group means are significantly different. An ANOVA is an improvement over a *t*-test because you can also use it if you have more than two groups to compare.

Instead of yielding a *t-statistic*, an ANOVA yields an *F*-statistic. For a given set of data, with two groups, *t* and *F* will have the same *p*-value. Thus, the two tests are interchangeable when comparing two means. As with the *t*-test, when an ANOVA yields a value of $p < .05$, the means are considered different from a statistical perspective. The logic of the *F*-statistic parallels the logic of the *t*-statistic. Both are about the ratio of the differences between the groups over the variability within the groups. If the group differences are large, in relation to the variability, the *F*-value will be large and *p* will likely be less than .05. If the group differences are small, in relation to the variability, the *F*-value will be small and *p* will likely be greater than .05.

One drawback to ANOVA when comparing more than two groups, is that a significant result only tells you that one of the group means is different from at least one of the other group means. You have to run post hoc tests (see Exercise 5.10) to know which specific group means are statistically different from one another. So ANOVAs are typically used in conjunction with follow up statistical tests. Still, ANOVA by itself can be helpful whenever you want to see if a set of group means are all statistically equivalent, like at the outset of a clinical trial. For example, in the study below, the researchers wanted to know that the groups were similar before the treatment, so that any posttreatment differences could be attributed to the treatment.

One point on terminology—the more precise name for the ANOVA below is one-way ANOVA. The one refers to the fact that there is one independent variable, group membership. (We'll look at two-way ANOVA in Exercises 5.11 and 5.12.) And just because the statistics gods

can never give something only one name, its good to know that a one-way ANOVA is also known as a univariate ANOVA.

BACKGROUND NOTE

The excerpt below states, "one-way ANOVA compared demographic, clinical, and pre-intervention GDS values across study arms." We take this to mean that the study ran one-way ANOVAs on the following variables in Table 1: Age, Years of education, Years with HIV, and GDS score at pre-intervention.

EXCERPT FROM THE RESEARCH ARTICLE[1]

This clinical trial tested whether telephone-administered supportive-expressive group therapy or coping effectiveness training reduce depressive symptoms in HIV-infected older adults. Participants from 24 states ($N = 361$) completed the Geriatric Depression Scale at pre-intervention, post-intervention, and four- and eight-month follow-up and were randomized to one of three study arms: (1) 12 weekly sessions of telephone-administered, supportive-expressive group therapy (tele-SEGT . . .); (2) 12 weekly sessions of telephone-administered, coping effectiveness training (tele-CET . . .); or (3) a standard of care (SOC . . .) control group . . .

The primary instrument in the screening interview was the Geriatric Depression Scale (GDS) . . .

Chi squared tests of association[2] and one-way ANOVA compared demographic, clinical, and pre-intervention GDS values across study arms . . .

Participants were similar across study arms on pre-intervention demographic and clinical variables (see Table 1) . . . Tele-CET ($M = 6.4$, $SD = 4.6$) and tele-SEGT participants ($M = 7.4$, $SD = 4.4$) attended a similar number of teletherapy sessions, $F(1, 238) = 2.64$, $p = 0.11$.

(continued)

1 Heckman, T. G., Heckman, B. D., Anderson, T., Lovejoy, T. I., Mohr, D., Sutton, M., . . . & Gau, J. T. (2013). Supportive-expressive and coping group teletherapies for HIV-infected older adults: a randomized clinical trial. *AIDS and Behavior*, *17*(9), 3034–3044. With permission of Springer.
2 This test was used for the variables that were percentages, like "Psychological Treatment in the past 4 months." ANOVA is only used when the dependent variable is ratio or interval.

(continued)

Table 1 [a]

Demographic, clinical, and psychiatric characteristics at pre-intervention by treatment condition [mean ± SD or % (n)]

Variable	Overall (N = 361)	Tele-CET (n = 118)	Tele-SEGT (n = 122)	SOC control (n = 121)
Age	59.0 ± 5.1	58.8 ± 5.4	59.5 ± 4.9	58.7 ± 5.0
Years of education	12.7 ± 2.2	12.9 ± 2.4	12.7 ± 2.1	12.6 ± 2.2
Years with HIV	18.0 ± 5.8	17.7 ± 5.7	18.7 ± 6.0	17.5 ± 5.6
Progressed to AIDS	56% (201)	55 % (65)	59% (71)	54% (65)
Taking HAART	83% (299)	79 % (93)	84% (103)	86% (103)
Substance abuse Tx in the past 4 months	19% (69)	22 % (26)	18% (22)	17% (21)
Psychological Tx in the past 4 months	43% (155)	53 % (62)	40% (49)	36% (44)
GDS score at pre-intervention	15.0 ± 7.4	15.5 ± 7.4	15.7 ± 6.9	13.7 ± 7.9

[a] Only part of the original Table 1 is excerpted here.

STUDY QUESTIONS

Factual Questions

1. Are the three groups about equally sized?
2. What are the mean ages for the three groups at pre-intervention?
3. What are the standard deviations for the mean ages of the three groups?
4. Given your answers to Questions 2 and 3, does it make sense that the ANOVA found no differences between the ages of participants in the groups?
5. What is the F-value associated with the average number of teletherapy sessions attended? Is this F-value statistically significant?
6. The researchers did not report the F-values for any of the one-way ANOVAs in the Table 1. Why do you think that is?
7. Why are there not any superscripts or asterisks (*) in Table 1?
8. By visual scan, which group has the lowest pre-intervention GDS mean? Is this mean significantly lower than the GDS means for the other two groups?
9. If the mean discussed in the answer to Question 8 appears lower, why does the one-way ANOVA give a non-significant result?

Questions for Discussion

10. This is a study of telephone-administered psychotherapy. Why might researchers conduct a study on teletherapy instead of simply using in-person psychotherapy?
11. If the groups started with a difference in age, why might this matter to the interpretation of the results?

One-Way ANOVA with Post Hoc Tests

Race/Ethnicity and Self-Esteem

STATISTICAL GUIDE

A one-way ANOVA only tells you if the group means being compared are statistically *different*. It does not reveal which group means are larger or smaller. If you are comparing two group means, and the result is significant, this is not an issue. You can visually inspect the means and see which one is greater. But if three group means are compared, a one-way ANOVA, by itself, is less helpful. For example, say an ANOVA considering the means for Groups A, B, and C is significant. This result does not indicate which of the following differences are significant: (1) A vs. B, (2) A vs. C, or (3) B vs. C. The significant ANOVA only indicates that at least one of these pairs of means is significantly different. To pinpoint which pairs(s) are significant, a *post hoc test* (also known as multiple-comparisons test) is used. These tests are said to be post hoc because they are done after finding the ANOVA significant. If an ANOVA is not significant, then post hoc tests are not run because this result means all the pairs are statistically equivalent.

> To review one-way ANOVA, see Exercise 5.11.

There are several post hoc tests, each with a different name. One of them, known as *Duncan's test*, is reported below.

BACKGROUND NOTE

A one-way ANOVA was run for each row in the table in the excerpt. For each, a value of *F* is shown. If the *F*-value was significant, Duncan's post hoc test was run. In a given row, entries with superscript "a" have significantly different means from entries with superscript "b."

EXCERPT FROM THE RESEARCH ARTICLE[1]

As part of a larger study of family functioning, a total of 104 families (adolescents, mothers, and fathers) participated in this study. All participating families in the current study included an adolescent, the mother, and the father. Adolescents were required to have at least monthly face-to-face contact with their biological mother and their biological father for inclusion . . .

Participants completed the age-appropriate version of the Harter Self-Perception Profiles, which conceptualize self-esteem as perceived competence in multiple domains. The social acceptance domain assesses participants' perceptions of feeling accepted by peers, feeling popular, and feeling comfortable around others. The physical appearance domain assesses participants' self-perceptions of their attractiveness and their satisfaction with their appearance. The athletic competence domain assesses participants' feelings of their competence in sports and other physical activities. The global self-worth subscale assesses participants' feelings about themselves overall (i.e., not tied to any specific domain . . .).

Table 1
Means and Standard Deviations for Self-Esteem

Race/ethnicity

	Caucasian	African American	Hispanic/ Latino/ Latina	F-Value
Social acceptance				
Adolescents	3.15 (.76)	3.13 (.74)	3.38 (.51)	1.17
Mothers	3.23 (.67)	3.44 (.55)	3.25 (.60)	1.21
Fathers	2.98 (.71)	3.36 (.62)	3.20 (.66)	2.81
Physical appearance				
Adolescents	2.82 (.85)	3.06 (.77)	2.92 (.75)	0.81
Mothers	2.49 (.84)	2.82 (.84)	2.70 (.70)	1.56
Fathers	2.79 (.51)[a]	3.14 (.82)[b]	3.13 (.65)[b]	3.16*
Athletic competence				
Adolescents	2.79 (.87)	2.96 (.80)	3.18 (.66)	1.96

(continued)

1 Phares, V., Fields, S., Watkins-Clay, M. M., Kamboukos, D., & Han, S. (2005). Race/ethnicity and self-esteem in families of adolescents. *Child & Family Behavior Therapy*, *27*, 13–26. Reprinted by permission of Taylor & Francis LLC.

(continued)

Table 1
Continued

Race/ethnicity

	Caucasian	African American	Hispanic/ Latino/ Latina	F-Value
Mothers	2.04 (.79)[a]	2.49 (.78)[b]	2.07 (.64)[a]	3.95*
Fathers	2.79 (.58)	2.90 (.68)	2.88 (.75)	0.27
Global self-worth				
Adolescents	3.34 (.60)	3.35 (.66)	3.25 (.65)	0.23
Mothers	3.17 (.76)	3.32 (.67)	3.24 (.71)	0.39
Fathers	2.96 (.62)[a]	3.33 (.72)[b]	3.38 (.53)[b]	4.59*

Note: Standard deviations are in parentheses. Different superscripts signify significant mean differences.

* $p < .05$.

In order to test for the racial/ethnic group differences . . . a series of ANOVAs was completed for each informant (adolescents, mothers, and fathers). Significant ANOVAs were followed up by post hoc Duncan's tests.

STUDY QUESTIONS

Factual Questions

1. What is the mean score of adolescents on Physical appearance for African Americans?
2. According to the ANOVA result, are there statistically significant differences between the means for adolescents on Physical appearance? Explain.
3. According to the ANOVA result, are there statistically significant differences between the three means for fathers on Physical appearance? Explain.
4. Explain the differences between the three groups of fathers on Physical appearance.
5. According to the ANOVA result, are there differences in the set of three means for fathers on Global self-worth? Explain.
6. Explain the differences between the three groups of fathers on Global self-worth.
7. According to the post hoc tests, which of the following pairs of means for mothers

on Athletic competence are significantly different? (More than one answer is possible.)

A. Caucasian and African American
B. Caucasian and Hispanic/Latino/Latina
C. African American and Hispanic/Latino/Latina

8. According to the post hoc tests, which of the following pairs of means for adolescents on Athletic competence are significantly different?

A. Caucasian and African American
B. Caucasian and Hispanic/Latino/Latina

C. African American and Hispanic/Latino/Latino
D. None of the means are statistically different.

9. According to the post hoc tests, which of the following pairs of means for adolescents on Social acceptance are significantly different?

A. The difference between Caucasian and African American.
B. The difference between Caucasian and Hispanic/Latino/Latina.
C. The difference between African American and Hispanic/Latino/Latina.
D. None of the means are statistically different.

Questions for Discussion

10. Would you be interested in knowing whether the three racial/ethnic groups differed on demographics like age or class? Explain.

11. In light of the total sample size ($n = 104$ families), do you consider this study to be definitive?

Two-Way ANOVA I

Effectiveness of a Reading Program

STATISTICAL GUIDE

Two-way ANOVA is a powerful statistical tool for researchers. In a two-way ANOVA, there are two independent variables, which is where the two in two-way comes from. A two-way ANOVA allows researchers to investigate how two independent variables impact the dependent variable, the outcome of interest. The independent variables are usually nominal classifications, and the outcome variable is usually continuous. To get a sense of this, examine Figure 1 below, which is drawn from a study investigating a reading program. The first independent variable is Time (pretest and posttest). It is on the *x*-axis. The second independent variable is Condition (control and treatment), which is shown by circle vs. triangle. The outcome variable is GORT-4 fluency scores, a measure of reading ability, and it is on the *y*-axis of the figure.

To review nominal variables, see Exercise 1.6. To review ANOVA, see Exercise 5.9.

A two-way ANOVA allows researchers to examine the effects of each independent variable, which are called the *main effects*. It also examines the effect of the interaction between the independent variables, which is called the *interaction effect*. The results of a two-way ANOVA have a number of different wrinkles which are beyond the scope of this section. Check out a statistics text for more information on that topic. Here, we will highlight a few common interpretations of the results of a two-way ANOVA. First, researchers often portray the results of a two-way ANOVA with a figure like Figure 1, partly because if the lines cross, you can conclude that an interaction effect was present. Second, when time is one of the independent variables in a two-way ANOVA, researchers are often most interested in the interaction of time and the treatment, i.e., did the treatment improve the outcome over time? Two-way ANOVA allows researchers to answer this question.

EXCERPT FROM THE RESEARCH ARTICLE[1]

The major difference between the treatment and control groups was in how the basal reader was used. The control classes had minimal discussion or introduction prior to reading the story. They then did oral reading one at a time and some silent reading. In the treatment group, the basal readings included strong support and guidance from the teacher before and after reading and repeated readings of one selection in different formats on different days.

To examine the effects of the program, the Gray Oral Reading Test, Fourth Edition (GORT-4; Wiederholt & Bryant, 2001) was used as a standardized assessment of text reading fluency. The GORT-4 consists of a series of increasingly difficult passages that are read aloud. Scoring is based on the number of reading errors and the time it takes to read each passage.

To assess the effectiveness of the [treatment] . . . program for enhancing children's reading fluency, we carried out [a two-way] analysis of variance (ANOVA). We had one within-subjects factor, time (pretest vs. posttest), and one between-subjects factor, instructional condition ([treatment] . . . vs. control). This

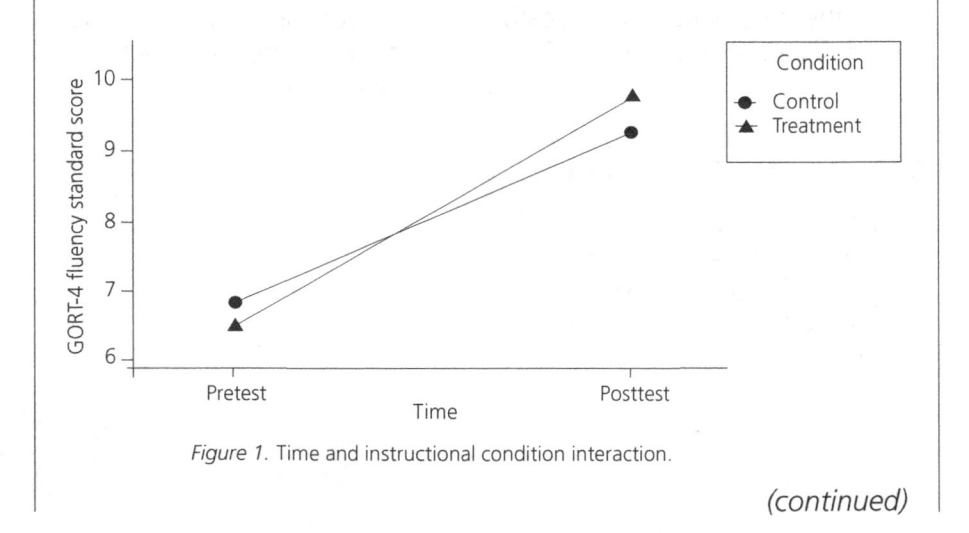

Figure 1. Time and instructional condition interaction.

(continued)

---

1 Morrow, L. M., Kuhn, M. R., & Schwanenflugel, P. J. (2006). The family fluency program. *Reading Teacher, 60,* 322–333. Reprinted with permission of John Wiley & Sons, Inc. © 2006 International Reading Association.

(continued)

analysis found a significant main effect of time, $F(1, 113) = 228.444$, $p < .001$, and a main effect of instructional condition that was not significant.

What is important, however, is the significant time and instructional condition interaction, $F(1, 113) = 4.96$, $p = .028$.

STUDY QUESTIONS

Factual Questions

1. Is there a main effect of time?
2. Is there a main effect of instructional condition (control vs. treatment)?
3. Does Figure 1 indicate that there is an interaction? Explain.
4. Is the interaction statistically significant at the .05 level?
5. Is the interaction statistically significant at the .01 level?
6. What is your interpretation of the significant interaction effect?
7. If the interaction effect had been non-significant, how should the effectiveness of the reading program be judged?
8. Suppose there had been no interaction. Briefly describe how Figure 1 would have been different.

Question for Discussion

9. Based on these results would you advocate for this reading program to be used in your local school system? Explain.

Two-Way ANOVA II

Vocabulary Improvement Program

STATISTICAL GUIDE

> To review
> ANOVA,
> review
> Exercise
> 5.9.

An experiment in which there is more than one independent variable is said to employ a factorial design. A two-way ANOVA is a common statistical procedure for factorial designs. As discussed in Exercise 5.11, a *main effect* is the impact of one independent variable by itself, and an *interaction effect* is the effect of two independent variables combined. The results of a two-way ANOVA can look a number of different ways, as each independent variable might (or might not) be significant, and the interaction might (or might not) be significant. In fact, there are at least eight different possibilities for the results of a two-way ANOVA. For example, in the previous exercise, the two-way ANOVA had one significant main effect and an interaction effect. Check out a statistics textbook if you want to see all the eight possibilities laid out. The study below shows two of the possible outcomes with a two-way ANOVA, as the procedure was run with data from two different sites.

BACKGROUND NOTE

The study below states that a *repeated measures* analyses was used with the data from each site. When researchers use the term repeated measures, they usually mean repeated measures ANOVA. The phrase "repeated measures" is used because the study repeats the same measure with the same participants, at different times. More precisely, this study uses a two-way, repeated measures ANOVA. This ANOVA is both two-way and repeated measures. It is two-way because there are two independent variables (Time and Condition). It is repeated measures because the outcome variable, oral vocabulary, is measured at two different times (Pretest and Posttest). Finally, in a study like this the researchers are most interested in the interaction effect, as they want to see if the treatment has an effect over time.

EXCERPT FROM THE RESEARCH ARTICLE[1]

Within each site, I performed repeated measures analyses on oral and sight vocabulary, with condition (treatment and control) as the between-subjects factor and time (pre- and posttest) as the within-subjects factor. Figure 1 shows graphic changes in oral vocabulary, with Site A pairs of pre- and posttest mean scores plotted in the lower half and Site B pairs of pre- and posttest mean scores plotted in the upper half. As suggested graphically in Figure 1, oral vocabulary gains appeared to be affected differentially by condition in Site A but not in Site B.

In Site A, results of the repeated measures ANOVA performed on oral vocabulary revealed a significant effect on time, $F(1, 114) = 12.95$, $p < .001$, a significant Time × Condition interaction effect, $F(1, 114) = 8.32$, $p < .01$, and a non-significant condition effect.

In Site B, results of the repeated measures ANOVA performed on oral vocabulary revealed a significant effect on time, $F(1, 148) =$

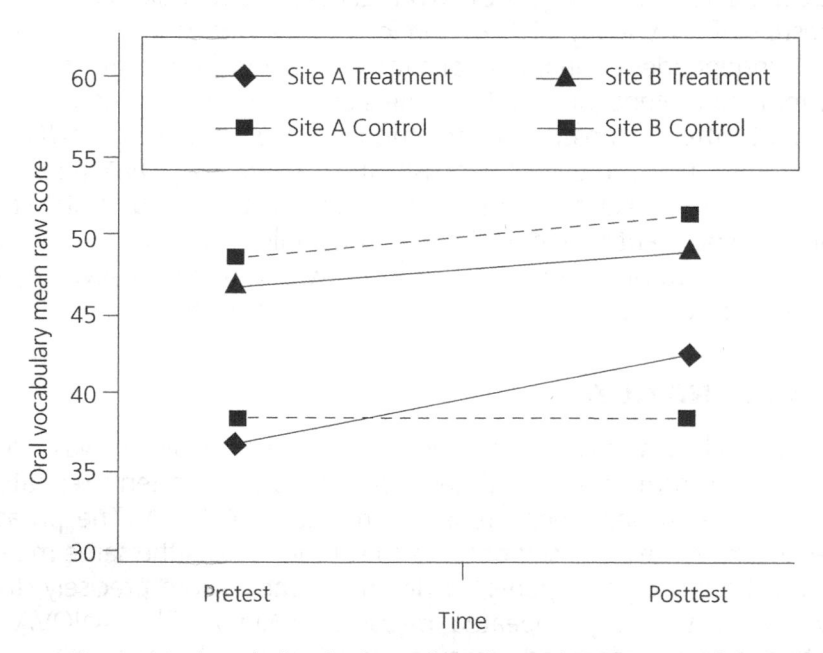

Figure 1. Oral vocabulary (Early Reading Diagnostic Assessment; full vocabulary composite) by time, site, and condition; highest possible raw score is 63.

---

1 Apthorp, H. S. (2006). Effects of a supplemental vocabulary program in third-grade reading/language arts. *Journal of Educational Research, 100,* 67–79. Reprinted by permission of Taylor & Francis LLC.

43.32, $p < .001$, but a non-significant Time × Condition interaction effect and a non-significant condition effect.

To summarize the effects on oral vocabulary as plotted in Figure 1, results indicate that teachers' use of Elements of Reading: Vocabulary had a significant and positive effect in Site A but not in Site B.

STUDY QUESTIONS

Factual Questions

1. By visual inspection alone, at which site did the average student have a higher score on the pretest?
2. For which site are the two lines more nearly parallel? (Note: Parallel lines indicate no interaction, as the lines don't cross.)
3. For Site A, is there a main effect of time? If yes, at what probability level?
4. For Site A, is there a main effect of condition? If yes, at what probability level?
5. For Site A, is there an interaction effect? If yes, at what probability level?
6. For Site B, is there a main effect of time? If yes, at what probability level?
7. For Site B, is there a main effect of condition (treatment vs. control)? If yes, at what probability level?
8. For Site B, is there an interaction effect? If yes, at what probability level?

Questions for Discussion

9. For Site B, why do you think the researcher did not give the p-value for the interaction?
10. Consider Site A. Would the results have been as informative if the researcher had not tested for an interaction? Explain.
11. Why might Site A find an interaction effect, i.e., that the treatment program improved scores over time, while Site B found no interaction?

Percentage, Standard Error, and 95% Confidence Interval

Attitudes and Beliefs About Cigars Among Adolescents

STATISTICAL GUIDE

Researchers collect information from samples and hope that it reveals realities about the population of interest. But sample statistics are not guaranteed to perfectly reflect what is true of the population. This is where *confidence intervals* are helpful. A confidence interval (CI) is a range of scores within which you are confident the true population value lies. Said another way, a confidence interval indicates how much sampling errors (i.e., errors created by random sampling from a population) might be impacting the results of a study. In polling, the margin of error is a kind of confidence interval.

To review percentages, see Exercises 1.1 and 1.2.

Confidence intervals are based on *standard errors*. There are several different kinds of standard errors in statistics, but the basic idea is that the standard error is an estimate for how off from the truth a particular study result might be. So, a standard error of a percentage is how off the percentage result might be. The standard error of a mean is how off the mean result might be. Whenever you see a confidence interval, you can know that it was built using a standard error. This and the following exercises in Unit 5 all use the idea of standard error.

The 95% confidence interval, or 95% CI, is one of the most commonly reported confidence intervals. Consider an example. Suppose a researcher found that 45% of respondents in a sample from a population believe that the economy is improving. The researcher computes the 95% confidence interval for this percentage and finds it is 42% to 48%. This means that if the study procedures were repeated exactly, then 95% of the time, the studies would find between 42% and 48% of participants believe the economy is improving. Researchers interpret the 95% CI to mean the range of values within which the true population value likely falls. The scores 42% and 48% (the end

points of the confidence interval) are referred to as the *limits* of the confidence interval.

Sometimes researchers use other confidence intervals, such as the 68% or 99% confidence interval. The basic idea is the same. The only difference is that the larger the percentage used (68% vs. 95% vs. 99%), the more confident one is that the true population value lies within that range. In addition, as the percentage goes up (from 68% to 95% to 99%), the size of the interval increases, e.g., a 99% CI will be larger than a 95% CI.

Because a confidence interval is an estimate of the true value in a population, when the intervals for two groups overlap, researchers usually conclude that they failed to establish a reliable difference between the groups. Conversely, if the two intervals do not overlap, researchers feel more confident that there is a reliable difference between the groups. This makes comparing confidence intervals a type of informal significance test. It is a way to see if there is a reliable difference without needing a *p*-value.[1] The Study Questions will give you a chance to apply the idea of overlapping vs. non-overlapping confidence intervals.

BACKGROUND NOTE

In Table 1, the term *lifetime use* refers to having ever smoked cigars, while *current use* refers to smoking cigars within the past month. Also, in Table 1, *all* refers to the total sample. Furthermore, the researchers use *N* as the symbol for the number of students in the total sample and *n* for the number of students in each subgroup.

EXCERPT FROM THE RESEARCH ARTICLE[2]

Schools were recruited by letters and phone calls to health coordinators in public middle and high schools across Massachusetts and were offered survey results in exchange for participation. Twelve

(continued)

---

1 There is currently a big debate among statisticians if comparing confidence intervals is superior to significance tests. Check back in about ten years. The debate might be settled by then.
2 Soldz, S., & Dorsey, E. (2005). Youth attitudes and beliefs toward alternative tobacco products: Cigars, bidis, and kreteks. *Health Education & Behavior*, *32*, 549–566. Reprinted by Permission of SAGE Publications, Inc.

(continued)

Table 1

Endorsement Rates for Attitudes and Beliefs About Cigars

Cigar attitudes	All (*N* = 5,016) % (95% CI)	Use			Gender		School Level	
		No use (*n* = 4,101) % (95% CI)	Lifetime use (*n* = 620) % (95% CI)	Current use (*n* = 295) % (95% CI)	Male (*n* = 2,451) % (95% CI)	Female (*n* = 2,565) % (95% CI)	Middle (*n* = 1,985) % (95% CI)	High (*n* = 3,031) % (95% CI)
Cigars taste good	11.4 (10.2–12.7)	1.6 (1.3–2.0)	44.9 (40.5–49.3)	74.0 (68.5–78.8)	18.9 (16.7–21.3)	4.3 (3.5–5.2)	5.5 (4.4–6.9)	15.2 (13.6–17.0)
Cigars smell good	23.1 (21.4–24.9)	15.3 (14.0–16.7)	52.1 (48.1–56.1)	69.1 (63.4–74.2)	30.1 (27.5–32.8)	16.4 (14.8–18.2)	14.5 (12.8–16.5)	28.7 (26.5–30.9)
Successful people smoke cigars	12.5 (11.6–13.4)	10.0 (9.1–11.0)	20.8 (17.8–24.1)	28.9 (23.8–34.5)	18.2 (16.6–20.0)	7.0 (6.0–8.1)	11.3 (10.0–12.9)	13.2 (12.1–14.4)
Cigars are not as bad for you as cigarettes	12.2 (11.2–13.2)	9.1 (8.2–10.0)	21.9 (18.6–25.7)	34.9 (30.0–40.2)	16.1 (14.6–17.7)	8.5 (7.3–9.8)	10.1 (8.8–11.5)	13.6 (12.3–14.9)
Cigars are cheaper than cigarettes	8.5 (7.6–9.5)	4.5 (3.8–5.3)	20.4 (17.1–24.0)	39.0 (33.3–45.0)	11.1 (9.7–12.6)	6.1 (5.1–7.2)	6.3 (5.0–8.0)	10.0 (8.8–11.2)
Cigars give you a good buzz	4.6 (4.0–5.3)	2.2 (1.8–2.7)	11.3 (9.2–13.8)	23.5 (18.7–29.1)	6.7 (5.7–7.8)	2.7 (2.1–3.4)	3.6 (2.8–4.6)	5.3 (4.5–6.2)
Cigars are something different to try	20.2 (18.6–21.8)	11.9 (10.7–13.2)	52.9 (48.9–56.9)	64.3 (58.5–69.6)	26.4 (24.0–28.8)	14.3 (12.7–16.0)	13.4 (11.6–15.4)	24.6 (22.6–26.7)

Note: CI = confidence interval.

schools responded. We strove to administer the survey to all students in a given school, but this proved impossible in many instances because of other demands [on students' time] . . . Participants are 5,016 7th through 12th graders from the 12 schools . . .

STUDY QUESTIONS[3]

Factual Questions

1. How many of the 5,016 students in this study were in middle school?
2. What percentage of the middle school students endorsed the statement that "Cigars smell good"?
3. What percentage of the high school students endorsed the statement that "Cigars are cheaper than cigarettes"?
4. What percentages of males and females endorsed the statement that "Cigars give you a good buzz"?
5. What are the limits of the 95% confidence interval for the No use group in response to the statement that "Cigars smell good"?
6. What are the limits of the 95% confidence interval for the Current use group in response to the statement that "Cigars smell good"?
7. The limits of the 95% confidence interval for males for the statement "Cigars taste good" are 16.7% to 21.3%. Does this interval overlap with the 95% confidence interval for females in response to the same statement (i.e., are any of the values in the interval for females included in the interval for males)?
8. Based on your response to Question 7, should a researcher conclude that there is a reliable difference between males and females in response to "Cigars taste good"? Explain the basis for your answer.
9. The limits of the 95% confidence interval for middle school students for the statement "Successful people smoke cigars" are 10.0% to 12.9%. Does this interval overlap with the 95% confidence interval for high school students in response to the same statement (i.e., are any of the values in the interval for middle school students included in the interval for high school students)?
10. Based on your response to Question 9, should a researcher

---

3 The researchers used a binary concept for gender/sex in this study. In addition, they did not highlight that female and male were self-identified by the participants.

conclude that there is a reliable difference between middle school students and high school students in response to "Successful people smoke cigars"? Explain the basis for your answer.

Questions for Discussion

11. Compare your answers to Questions 5 and 6. Does the difference between the two answers surprise you? Why or why not?

12. Based on an examination of the confidence intervals, all of the differences between males and females are reliable. Why might this be the case?

13. The second highest endorsement rate for the total sample was in response to the statement that "Cigars are something different to try" (20.2%). Does this surprise you? Why or why not?

Standard Error of a Percentage and Confidence Interval

Types of Child Abuse

To review percentages, see Exercises 1.1 and 1.2. To review confidence interval, see Exercise 5.13.

STATISTICAL GUIDE

The *standard error of a percentage* is a margin of error; it is an allowance for error in our study results. We use it when estimating the population percentage from what is found in a study sample. For instance, say 60% of a sample drawn from a population answers "yes" to a survey question. We don't believe so much in our sample results to think that 60% is the exact right percentage for the entire population. We suspect there is some error in our method of drawing a sample. So we calculate a *standard error of the percentage* for this sample statistic, and suppose it is 3 percentage points. This means we should allow 3 points on each side of 60% for sampling error. More specifically, we could say that there is a 68% chance that the true percentage in the population that answers "yes" to our question is between 57% and 63% (i.e., 60% − 3 = 57% and 60% + 3 = 63%). These values (57% and 63%) are what is known as the limits of the 68% confidence interval (CI).

If the standard error is multiplied by two, we can create a 95% confidence interval (CI).[1] So in our example above, if we multiply the standard error of 3 by 2, we get 6. Adding and subtracting the 6 from 60% (i.e., 60% − 6 = 54 % and 60% + 6 = 66%), we get the 95% CI. This means there is a 95% chance that the true percentage in the population is between 54% and 66%. These values (54% and 66%) are what is known as the *limits of the approximate 95% confidence interval.*[2]

BACKGROUND NOTE

The study below investigated child abuse among children in the welfare system. The researchers drew data for their article from a variety of

---

1 Technically one needs to multiply by 1.96, but using 2 makes the calculation a little faster and often provides a fine enough estimate.
2 It's approximate because we multiplied the standard error by 2 instead of 1.96.

sources. The statistics in Table 1 are from *Child Maltreatment 2001*,[3] a government publication. Take a minute to familiarize yourself with Table 1 before going to the Study Questions. Review the title, the column and row labels, and the notes at the bottom. Notice that there are five pairs of column labels which each have % and *SE*. The % gives the percentage for the sample for that category, and the *SE* is the standard error of that percentage.

EXCERPT FROM THE RESEARCH ARTICLE[4]

Table 1
Most Serious Type of Abuse of Children Involved with the Child Welfare System by Age

	Physical maltreatment		Sexual maltreatment		Neglect: Failure to provide		Neglect: Failure to supervise		Other		
	%*	SE	%*	SE	%*	SE	%*	SE	%*	SE	Total
Age											
0 to 2	22.6	2.2	6.1	1.7	29.9	2.5	36.6	3.0	4.8	1.7	100
3 to 5	23.6	2.9	12.8	2.8	23.8	3.8	30.3	2.6	9.5	2.3	100
6 to 10	31.2	2.6	11.1	2.4	18.9	2.4	26.1	2.4	12.7	2.1	100
11+	32.7	3.1	14.9	2.1	12.7	2.3	29.7	2.5	10.0	1.8	100
Total	28.4	1.5	11.5	1.2	20.4	1.5	29.8	1.5	9.9	1.2	100

Source: US DHHS, 2003.

* Percentages may not total to 100 because of rounding.

STUDY QUESTIONS

Factual Questions

1. Just looking at the % numbers, which age group had the lowest percentage for Physical maltreatment?

2. What percentage of the total sample had Physical maltreatment?

---

3 US Department of Health and Human Services Administration for Children and Families. (2003). *Child Maltreatment 2001*. Washington, DC: U.S. Government Printing Office.

4 Barth, R. P., Landsverk, J., Chamberlain, P., Reid, J. B., Rolls, J. A., Hurlburt, M. S., Farmer, E. M. Z., James, S., McCabe, K. M., & Kohl, P. L. (2005). Parent-training programs in child welfare services: Planning for a more evidence-based approach to serving biological parents. *Research on Social Work Practice*, *15*, 353–371. Reprinted by Permission of SAGE Publications, Inc.

3. For the total sample, the percentage for Neglect: Failure to provide is 20.4%. What are the limits of the 68% confidence interval for this percentage?

4. For the total sample, the percentage for Neglect: Failure to provide is 20.4%. What are the limits of the approximate 95% confidence interval for this percentage?

5. What are the limits of the 68% confidence interval for Physical maltreatment for ages 0 to 2?

6. What are the limits of the 68% confidence interval for Physical maltreatment for ages 11 and up?

7. Compare your answers to Questions 5 and 6. Do the two confidence intervals overlap (i.e., do any of the percentages in one interval include one or more percentages from the other interval)?

8. What are the limits of the approximate 95% confidence interval for Physical maltreatment for ages 11 and up?

9. Compare your answers to Questions 6 and 8. Which of the following confidence intervals is larger?

   A. The 68% confidence interval in Question 6.
   B. The 95% confidence interval in Question 8.

Questions for Discussion

10. In your opinion, how important is it for researchers to report standard errors when reporting percentages based on a sample from a population? In other words, how much less informative would Table 1 be if all the standard errors had been omitted?

11. Compare your answers to Questions 3 and 4. Note that the 95% confidence interval is larger than the 68% confidence interval. Does this make sense? Explain.

12. Note that in the table all the standard errors for the total sample are smaller than any of the standard errors for any of the age subgroups. Speculate on why this is so.

Standard Error of the Mean and 95% Confidence Interval

Gender Differences in Response to PTSD Treatment

STATISTICAL GUIDE

The *standard error of the mean* (SE_M) is a margin of error that is used when estimating the population mean from a sample drawn from a population. It is an allowance for chance errors created by sampling. The 95% confidence interval (95% CI) of a sample mean is based on the standard error of the mean. When a 95% confidence interval for a mean is reported, it means that if the study were repeated, 95% of the time the mean would fall within the 95% CI. Researchers tend to think of the 95% CI of the mean as very likely to contain the *true mean* (i.e., the mean we would get if we could eliminate sampling errors). For instance, if we tested a group of children with a mathematics test and got a mean of 55 and a 95% CI of 52–57, we could have some confidence that the true mean lies between 52 and 57.

Researchers often rely on the 95% CI to help see if two group means are reliably different. If the 95% CIs don't overlap, researchers are more confident there is a reliable difference between the two means. If the 95% CIs do overlap, researchers often conclude there is not a reliable difference between the two means. This is like a *t*-test or an ANOVA, but it does not involve using *p*-values.

When we report a single value such as a mean based on a sample, the value is sometimes called a *point estimate* (i.e., a single point estimated to be the mean for the population based on a sample). When we report a confidence interval, we are said to be reporting an *interval estimate* (i.e., a range of values that estimate the mean for a population).

The standard error of the mean is inversely related to the number of participants in a sample or group. So the larger the group, the smaller the standard error of the mean.

EXCERPT FROM THE RESEARCH ARTICLE[1]

The current study examines PTSD symptoms pre- and post-[treatment] for a large sample of male and female veterans treated in the same setting as part of routine [Veteran Administration] care, with appropriate power to find clinically relevant differences between [genders]. The investigation considers data from a PTSD Clinical Team (PCT) in an urban VA [Medical Center] located in the southeastern United States . . . The sample consisted of 292 (90%) male and 33 (10%) female veterans.

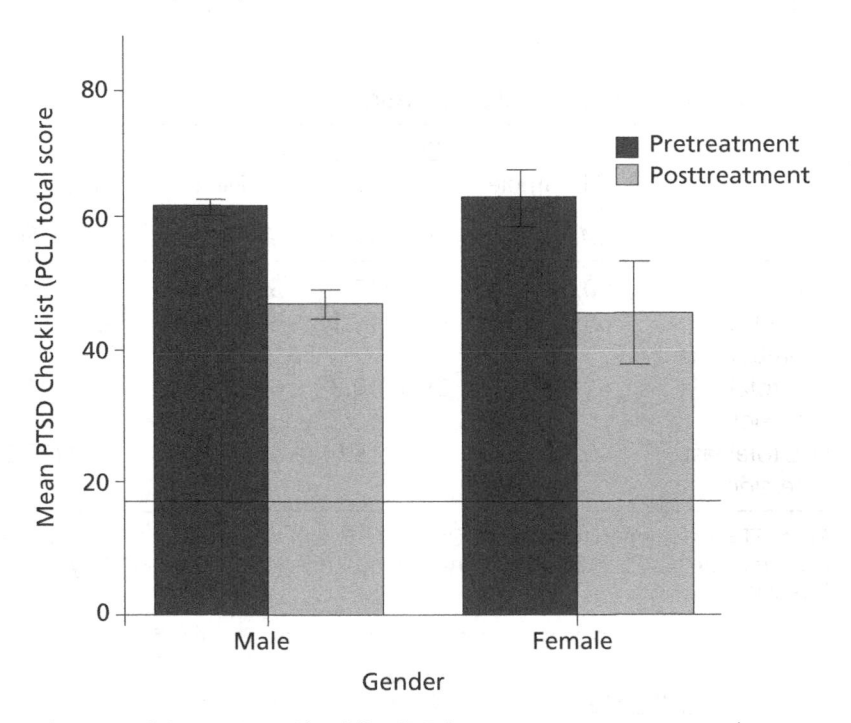

Figure 1. Mean PTSD Checklist (PCL) scores pretreatment and posttreatment with 95% confidence intervals for male and female participants. No gender difference was found in treatment effect for veterans treated with Prolonged Exposure for posttraumatic stress disorder. Confidence intervals are represented in the figure by bars attached to each column. The horizontal line represents the minimum score possible on the PCL.

(continued)

1 Mouilso, E. R., Tuerk, P. W., Schnurr, P. P., & Rauch, S. A. (2015). "Addressing the Gender Gap: Prolonged Exposure for PTSD in Veterans." *Psychological Services*, *13*, 308–316. Copyright © 2016 by the American Psychological Association. Reproduced with permission.

(continued)

Veterans in the sample were identified for treatment by . . . referrals to the PTSD clinical team (PCT) and assessed for PTSD diagnosis via the Clinical Administered PTSD Scale (CAPS . . .) as part of standard care. After a PTSD diagnosis was confirmed, clinicians contacted patients, discussed treatment options, and obtained informed consent for trauma focused treatment . . .

Prolonged Exposure therapy (PE . . .) is a manualized treatment for PTSD usually delivered in 8 to 15 weekly 90-min sessions . . .

The PTSD Checklist (PCL . . .) is a 17-item self-report measure of PTSD symptoms . . .

Table 1
Patient Demographics and Characteristics

	ITT Sample		Completer Sample		Men		Women	
	M	(SD)	M	(SD)	M	(SD)	M	(SD)
Age	50.7	(15.7)	49.6	(15.9)	51.8	(15.8)	40.2	(10.9)
CAPS total pretreatment	65.1	(19.0)	63.1	(18.1)	65.1	(18.8)	65.7	(21.2)
PCL total first session	61.8	(11.4)	59.1	(10.3)	61.5	(11.3)	63.8	(11.9)
PCL total last session	46.9	(17.1)	41.9	(15.5)	46.9	(16.9)	47.2	(19.2)

Note: ITT = Intention to treat; OEF = Operation Enduring Freedom; OIF = Operation Iraqi Freedom; CAPS = Clinician Administered PTSD Scale; PCL = PTSD Symptom Checklist.

STUDY QUESTIONS[2]

Factual Questions

1. Based on Table 1, what are the CAPS total pretreatment scores for the ITT sample? For men? For women?
2. Given your answer to Question 1, and given the size of the standard deviations, do there appear to be meaningful differences between the pretreatment CAPS scores by gender?
3. Based on Table 1, what are the point estimates for first

---

2 The researchers used a binary concept for gender/sex in this study. In addition, they did not highlight that female and male were self-identified by the participants.

session PCL total for men? For women?

4. What are the standard deviations for your answers in Question 3?

5. What is the difference between first session PCL total and last session PCL total for men? For women?

6. Visually inspecting Figure 1, do the 95% confidence intervals appear larger for the men or the women?

7. Consider your answer for Question 6. Given the differences in the group sizes, why might the answer to Question 6 be true?

8. If this study were repeated, is it likely that the posttreatment mean for the PCL total for women would equal 22?

9. If this study were repeated, is it likely that the pretreatment mean for the PCL total for men would equal 61.9?

10. Does the data in this study reveal the true population value for the pretreatment mean of the PCL total score for veterans seeking treatment for PTSD?

Questions for Discussion

11. Describe in words how much overlap there is between the pretreatment 95% CIs in Figure 1. Explain what this means.

12. Describe in words how much overlap there is between the posttreatment 95% CIs in Figure 1. Explain what this means.

13. Why might it be important to test to see if a treatment is as effective for women as it is for men?

Standard Error of the Mean and 68%, 95%, and 99% Confidence Intervals

Mindfulness and Adult ADHD

STATISTICAL GUIDE

The *standard error of the mean* (SE_M) is used to calculate the 95% confidence interval (95% CI) for the mean. It can also be used to calculate other confidence intervals around the mean. The two other most common are the 68% and the 99% CIs. The equation for SE_M is given in Question 1 below. You can readily calculate different CIs with this equation. To get the 68% CI, add the SE_M to the mean, and this is the upper bound of the interval. Subtract the SE_M from the mean, and this is the lower bound of the interval. For the 95% CI, use the same process but add and subtract 1.96 x SE_M.[1] For the 99% CI, use the same process but add and subtract 2.58 x SE_M. Why do 1.96 and 2.58 appear in these calculations? Because 1.96 is the *z* score that corresponds with the 95%, and 2.58 is the *z* score that corresponds with the 99%.

> To review standard error of the mean, see Exercise 5.15. To review *z* scores, see Exercises 2.6 and 2.7.

For the 68% CI, one would expect that if the study were run again the mean would fall within that interval 68% of the time. The same kind of reasoning is true for the 99% CI. If the study is run again, the mean should fall within that interval 99% of the time.

As mentioned last exercise, the SE_M is inversely related to the sample size. You can see this in the equation in Question 1. This means that as sample sizes go up, CIs get smaller.

BACKGROUND NOTE

The study below does not report CIs for means. You will be asked to calculate those yourself. It does report 95% CIs for the *difference* between

---

1   In an earlier exercise we used 2 instead of 1.96 to get an approximate 95% CI. Depending on how much precision you need, you can use 2 or 1.96.

two group means, a common practice in the literature. The logic behind confidence intervals for mean differences is similar to the logic for the confidence intervals around a mean. But note that it is a step up in complexity because you are making an interval estimate for the *difference* between two means, which is not the same thing as making an interval estimate for a single value, like the mean of one group. The interpretation of the 95% CI for group differences is the same, though. If the study were run again, the group differences should fall within the interval 95% of the time.

The study below states that $n = 55$ for the active group (MBCT) and n = 49 for the waitlist group (WL). Use these group numbers when asked in the questions to calculate the SE_M. Table 1 lists other numbers for group sizes but those can be ignored.

EXCERPT FROM THE RESEARCH ARTICLE[2]

> Patients were recruited at the specialist ADHD service of the Radboudumc outpatient department of psychiatry . . . [Participants had confirmed diagnoses of ADHD.]
>
> Participants were randomly allocated to mindfulness training (MBCT) ($n = 55$) or waitlist (WL) ($n = 49$) control condition by an independent researcher . . .
>
> The mindfulness training was adapted from the MBCT [Mindfulness-Based Cognitive Therapy] protocol developed for recurrent depression . . . The MBCT groups were instructed by two experienced mindfulness teachers: a psychiatrist specialized in ADHD with ten years of experience as a mindfulness teacher (S.H.) and a qualified nurse specialist meeting the advanced criteria of the Association of Mindfulness-Based Teachers in the Netherlands and Flanders (M.S.).
>
> ADHD symptoms were assessed by a clinician with the investigator rating version of the Conners' Adult ADHD Rating Scale . . .
>
> The self-report version of the Conners' Adult ADHD Rating Scale . . . consists of 30 items, which are rated on a 4-point Likert-type scale . . .
>
> *(continued)*

2 Hepark, S., Janssen, L., de Vries, A., Schoenberg, P. L., Donders, R., Kan, C. C., & Speckens, A. E. (2019). The efficacy of adapted MBCT on core symptoms and executive functioning in adults with ADHD: A preliminary randomized controlled trial. *Journal of Attention Disorders, 23*(4), 351–362. Reprinted by permission of SAGE Publications, Inc.

(continued)

Table 1

Differences Between Groups at the End of Treatment, Controlling for Baseline Levels

	Baseline		End of treatment		End of treatment Group difference [95% CI]a	Cohen's d-type
	MBCT	WL	MBCT	WL		
ADHD symptoms, CARRS						
Investigator (n = 68)						
Inattention	16.3 (4.7)	17.0 (4.5)	12.4 (4.6)	16.5 (4.2)	−3.6 [−5.5, −1.8]**	0.78
Hyperactive–impulsive	13.0 (5.6)	12.0 (4.8)	9.0 (4.6)	11.5 (5.3)	−3.2 [−5.0, −1.4]**	0.62
Total score	29.3 (8.7)	29.0 (7.1)	21.5 (7.7)	28.0 (7.5)	−6.7 [−9.8, −3.6]**	0.85
Self report (n = 74)						
Inattention	15.4 (3.9)	16.6 (4.5)	12.8 (4.2)	16.1 (3.8)	−2.7 [−4.3, −1.2]**	0.64
Hyperactive–impulsive	12.8 (4.8)	13.6 (4.5)	10.3 (4.2)	12.6 (5.0)	−1.8 [−3.4, −0.2]**	0.39
Total score	28.2 (7.0)	30.2 (6.5)	23.0 (7.3)	28.8 (6.9)	−4.5 [−7.3, −1.8]**	0.67
Depression, BDI (n = 74)	12.1 (8.7)	13.2 (8.3)	9.1 (7.8)	11.8 (9.8)	−1.9 [−4.8, 1.0]	0.22
Anxiety, STAI (n = 74)	89 (18.0)	97.2 (18.5)	78.5 (22.0)	90.8 (25.6)	−4.8 [−12.9, 3.3]	0.26

Note. MBCT = mindfulness-based cognitive therapy; WL = waiting list; CI = confidence interval; CAARS = Conner's Adult ADHD Rating Scale; EF = executive function; BRIEF-ASR = Behavior Rating Inventory of Executive Function-Adult Self-Report Version; BDI = Beck Depression Inventory; STAI = State-Trait Anxiety Inventory; OQ = Outcome Questionnaire; KIMS = Kentucky Inventory of Mindfulness Skills.

* Statistical significant difference for < .05. ** Statistical significant difference for < .01.

a Differences between conditions, corrected for baseline values.

> The Beck Depression Inventory . . . was used to assess the possible presence of depression symptoms. The BDI is self-administered and contains 21 items . . .
>
> To measure levels of state and trait anxiety, the Dutch version of the State-Trait Anxiety Inventory . . . was administered . . .

STUDY QUESTIONS

Factual Questions

1. What is the standard error of the mean for the depression score for the waitlist group (WL) at baseline? Use the equation below. Round your answer to two decimal places. (Note: *SD* stands for standard deviation, which can be found in the parentheses in Table 1.)

$$SE_M = \frac{SD}{\sqrt{n}}$$

2. What is the 68% confidence interval for the depression score for the waitlist group (WL) at baseline?
3. What is the 95% CI for the depression score for the waitlist group (WL) at baseline?
4. What is the 99% CI for the depression score for the waitlist group (WL) at baseline?

5. Which confidence interval (68%, 95%, or 99%), from Questions 2–4, includes the largest interval? Explain why this answer makes sense.
6. At the end of treatment, what is the 95% CI for the group differences on depression? Does this interval include the value 0? What do you think this means?
7. Are the end of treatment scores for depression different at a significant *p*-value? How do you think this relates to 0 being in the interval for 95% CI for group differences in depression?
8. Do any of the group differences with significant *p*-values have a 95% CI that contains zero? Do all of the non-significant group differences contain zero in their 95% CI?

Questions for Discussion

9. Do the results of this study support the claim that mindfulness training helps reduce depression and anxiety for individuals with ADHD? What is the evidence for your answer?
10. Do the 95% CIs for group differences give you confidence that mindfulness training reduces inattention in individuals with ADHD?
11. Can the results of this study be generalized to the general public? Explain why or why not.

p-Hacking

Progesterone and Birth Outcomes

STATISTICAL GUIDE

In the 2010s researchers in the social and health sciences experienced a number of earthquakes, as supposedly established findings kept failing to replicate. This means that one researcher wasn't able to reproduce an effect that another researcher had reported finding. Failures to replicate kept popping up in this and that field, and researchers started to worry that something was wrong with the standard methods researchers were using to establish that an effect or a finding is real. Some started to say that science was broken. And, in fact, it was (and still is) in some important ways. There were a number of biased researcher practices that were part of this, i.e., ways of doing things that made it more likely for a researcher to find the effect in their study they wanted to find, even when the effect wasn't real. One of the practices that we now know is biased is *p-hacking*.

To review meta-analysis, see Exercise 5.7. To review 95% confidence interval, see Exercise 5.15–16.

Since finding an effect in a study is usually based on finding a statistically significant *p*-value, researchers have been, often without realizing it, manipulating their statistical analyses to make it more likely to get a significant *p*-value. That is what *p*-hacking is. There are a lot of ways to *p*-hack, but one common way is to run the analyses a number of different ways (e.g., with just the men or just the women) until you get a result with $p < .05$. Then the researchers conveniently forget about all the analyses with $p > .05$ and only report the one that was statistically significant. We hate it, but, if we are being honest, we (the authors of this book) must admit that we have *p*-hacked in our own research. The researchers in the excerpt below also admit they've done something like this. In recent years, we've heard many prominent researchers admit to *p*-hacking. Are we all maniacal scientists bent on proving our hypotheses, truth be damned? No, we just didn't realize that *p*-values were so easily manipulated. Now we know, so we have to 1) stop *p*-hacking and 2) comb through past findings to uncover where results might be false because they were based on *p*-hacking. The study in the excerpt below does this second thing with respect to research on the effect of giving

pregnant women progesterone to improve birth outcomes, a practice that was supported by a number of studies and even meta-analyses. They find that when *p*-hacking is eliminated that progestogen does not improve birth outcomes.

BACKGROUND NOTE

The meta-analysis below takes all the studies on progesterone and birth outcomes and separates them into two piles, prospectively registered (or pre-registered) studies and those that weren't prospectively registered. In a pre-registered study, before collecting the data, researchers announce exactly how they will run the analyses, thereby making it very difficult (maybe impossible) to *p*-hack. The authors report that a number of meta-analyses (19, in fact!) had found that progesterone had a positive effect on birth outcomes, but the researchers argued that if those (19) meta-analyses were full of non-pre-registered studies, they could be based on *p*-hacked results. So, the authors planned to only look at progesterone results when the study was pre-registered. There were 22 of those studies and the figure below reports on 3 of those 22.

Recall that researchers think that any value in a 95% CI for a result could easily occur if the study were repeated. Below researchers apply this logic to the mean difference between study groups (progesterone vs. placebo). If the 95% CI for the mean difference of the groups includes zero, there is a reasonable chance that if the study were repeated the difference between the groups would be zero. This means there would be zero difference between the progesterone and placebo groups on the outcome of interest, which is pre-term birth in Figure 3 below. Researchers typically interpret a 95% CI that includes zero to mean that the result is not statistically different than zero.

EXCERPT FROM THE RESEARCH ARTICLE[1]

Progestogens have been evaluated in numerous trials and meta-analyses, many of which concluded they were effective. However, two large trials PROMISE and OPPTIMUM have recently

(continued)

---

1 Prior, M., Hibberd, R., Asemota, N., & Thornton, J. G. (2017). Inadvertent P-hacking among trials and systematic reviews of the effect of progestogens in pregnancy? A systematic review and meta-analysis. *BJOG: An International Journal of Obstetrics & Gynaecology*, *124*(7), 1008–1015.

(continued)

Study or Subgroup	Progesterone			Placebo			Weight	Mean Difference IV, Random, 95% CI	Mean Difference IV, Random, 95% CI
	Mean	SD	Total	Mean	SD	Total			
1.2.1 Preterm Birth									
Senat 2013	45	27.1	82	52	27.3	83	36.0%	-7.00 [-15.30, 1.30]	
Winer 2015	76	35.7	51	72	36.7	54	16.4%	4.00 [-9.85, 17.85]	
Wood 2012	255	15	42	254	16	42	47.6%	1.00 [-5.63, 7.63]	
Subtotal (95% CI)			175			179	100.0%	-1.39 [-7.47, 4.69]	

Heterogeneity: Tau^2 = 8.81; Chi^2 = 2.84, df = 2 (P = 0.24); I^2 = 29%
Test for overall effect: Z = 0.45 (P = 0.65)

Total (95% CI)			175			179	100.0%	-1.39 [-7.47, 4.69]	

Heterogeneity: Tau^2 = 8.81; Chi^2 = 2.84, df = 2 (P = 0.24); I^2 = 29%
Test for overall effect: Z = 0.45 (P = 0.65)
Test for subgroup differences: Not applicable

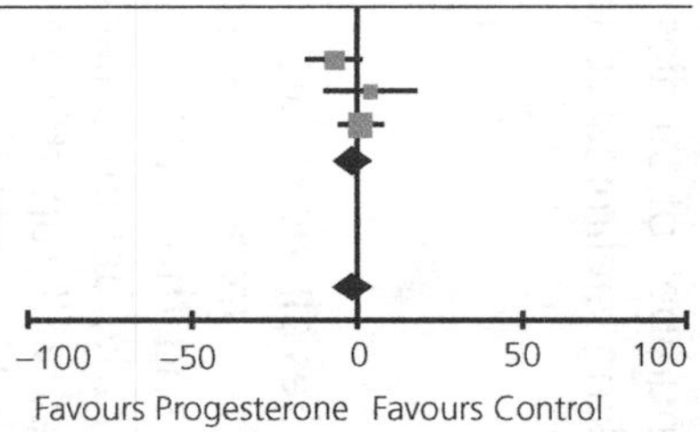

-100   -50   0   50   100
Favours Progesterone   Favours Control

Figure 3. Progesterone versus placebo: primary registered continuous outcome.

concluded that progesterone was ineffective. This raises the possibility that earlier studies and reviews had been biased by either selective publication or selective choice of outcomes, so called "P-hacking."

[Our objective] was to compare the findings of all progestogen trials and systematic reviews with those of trials with pre-registered primary outcomes which avoided selective outcome reporting . . .

We identified 29 systematic reviews [on progesterone]. These reported results of 93 [randomized controlled] trials . . .

Nineteen of twenty-nine meta-analyses concluded that progestogens were effective. Twenty-two trials reported their pre-registered primary outcomes. There was no effect of progesterone on primary registered dichotomous outcome RR 1.00 (95% CI 0.94–1.07). Only one of the 22 showed a nominally statistically significant benefit.

Discussion

When evaluated in registered double-blind trials with analysis restricted to predefined primary outcomes, progestational agents in pregnancy are ineffective for all indications they have been tested for. One trial appeared to show a marginally significant result according to conventional tests of significance. This could well be a chance effect, on average one out of 20 perfectly conducted randomized trials will show an effect at the conventional $P = 0.05$ level of statistical significance. We also found the two well-known trials by Meis et al. and Fonseca et al. were unregistered and registered late respectively.

It was disappointing that we identified more systematic reviews of this drug in pregnancy ($n = 29$) than prospectively registered trials ($n = 22$). We hope readers will forgive us adding to the former number and that in future more research effort will be spent on well conducted primary research.

STUDY QUESTIONS

Factual Questions

1. How many meta-analyses had previously investigated the effect of progesterone on birth outcomes?

2. How many found a positive effect?

3. What might explain the difference in the answers to

Question 1 and 2? (*Hint*: Part of the answer is in this exercise and part of the answer is in Exercise 5.8.)

4. Of the three studies in the figure, how many have a mean difference 95% CI that includes zero?

5. What does the 95% CI for the total (or subtotal) mean difference in the figure tell you? (*Note*: the middle of the diamond shape on the total and subtotal lines is the point estimate for the average result and the left and right edges are the 95% CI for the average.)

6. In total, how many studies were pre-registered?

7. What percentage of studies on progesterone were pre-registered and what percentage were not pre-registered?

8. The authors note that one of the pre-registered studies had a marginally significant result. How do they explain this?

9. The authors note that studies well known in their field (Meis et al. and Fonseca et al.) were not pre-registered. Does a study being well known mean it used the best methods?

Questions for Discussion

10. What do you think about the percentage of pre-registered vs. not pre-registered studies when it comes to progesterone and birth outcomes?

11. Why is it such a big deal that progesterone might not have any effect at all?

New Methods to Prevent *p*-Hacking

Limiting *p*-Hacking in Clinical Trials

STATISTICAL GUIDE

p-hacking can take many forms, but the heart of it involves running statistical analyses multiple ways until getting a result with $p < .05$; then reporting that one result and not reporting the other analyses. For example, a (well-meaning) researcher might be looking to see if a treatment for Obsessive Compulsive Disorder (OCD) works. Maybe they originally thought that after the intervention they would compare everyone in the treatment group with everyone in the control group, but then the comparison (say a *t*-test) turned out to have $p > .05$. The researcher really believes in the treatment and so thinks the original result must be a fluke and the truth is hiding in the data somewhere. So, they run the analyses with only participants over age 50, then only those under age 50, then only men, and then only women. Each time getting a *t*-test result with $p > .05$. Still believing in the treatment, they continue. They think, "Ah, maybe the treatment works best with those who start with moderate OCD symptoms instead of severe symptoms," which is a reasonable enough idea. So, they run the analyses excluding participants who started the trial with severe OCD symptoms, and . . . presto, they get a *t* test result with $p < .05$. Eureka! they think, believing this result reveals the truth. They write it up and submit it. Journals have not been watching out for *p*-hacking until recently, so the article passes peer review. Now it is out in the world and researchers, clinicians, and policy makers think the treatment works

effectively for moderate OCD, when in fact the result is most likely just a product of p-hacking.

What most researchers did not realize until recently is that obtaining a result with $p < .05$ is not that unlikely when researchers run analyses multiple different ways searching for a statistically significant result. We used to think that results with $p < .05$ were *always* incredibly rare, like a double rainbow after the rain. Turns out, they aren't rare at all when you p-hack. Ultimately, a p-hacked result with $p < .05$ is pretty poor evidence that an effect is real. So, the solution is eliminating p-hacking.

BACKGROUND NOTE

The article excerpt gives guidelines in Table 2 below for how to avoid p-hacking in clinical trials. The main strategy the authors propose is *pre-specifying* the statistical analyses. This means researchers publish specific and detailed plans for how they will analyze the data before collecting any data. Take our example above. Prior to recruiting participants, the researcher could have published that they were going to use an independent groups t-test (intervention vs. control), with the entire sample, and with a specific measure of OCD symptoms as the dependent variable. Then when the researcher submitted the manuscript for peer review, the reviewers could say, "Hey, wait a minute. The pre-specified analyses said you were going to use the entire sample, but you only used participants who started with moderate OCD. What gives?"

Table 1 below reviews common gaps in pre-specifying analyses that the authors found when they reviewed published results from 170 clinical trials.

1 Kahan, B. C., Forbes, G., & Cro, S. (2020). How to design a pre-specified statistical analysis approach to limit p-hacking in clinical trials: the Pre-SPEC framework. *BMC medicine, 18*(1), 1–7.

(continued)

Table 1

Common issues in pre-specifying statistical analysis approaches in clinical trial protocols

Issue	Problems associated with issue	Aspect	Prevalence[a]
		Estimated prevalence	
Omitting an aspect of the analysis approach	Investigators could run multiple analyses, and selectively report the most favourable	Analysis population:	27-47%
		Analysis model:	11 -20%
		Covariates:	27%
		Missing data:	66-77%
Insufficient detail around an aspect of the analysis approach	Investigators could run multiple analyses, and selectively report the most favourable	Analysis population:	64%
		Analysis model:	42%
		Covariates:	23%
		Missing data:	17%[b]
Analysis approach allows some aspects of the final analysis to be subjectively chosen based on trial data	Investigators could run multiple analyses, and selectively report the most favourable	Analysis model:	19%
		Covariates:	8%
Multiple analysis approaches specified, without one being identified as the primary	Investigators could selectively report the most favourable result, or to elevate its importance compared to less favourable results.	Analysis population:	11%
		Analysis model:	11%
		Covariates:	9%
		Missing data:	2%

[a] Based on references [5] and [2]; one study evaluated protocols and published results for 70 randomised trials approved by the ethics committees for Copenhagen and Frederiksberg, Denmark in 1994-5; the other study evaluated 100 protocols of randomised trials indexed in PubMed November 2016.

[b] 15/99 protocols gave insufficient detail around how they planned to implement multiple imputation, 2/99 protocols but gave insufficient detail around their planned inverse probability weighting procedure

(continued)

Table 2
Framework for pre-specifying a statistical analysis strategy (Pre-SPEC)

Pre-specify before recruitment	Pre-specify the analysis strategy before recruitment to the trial begins.
Single analysis strategy	Specify a single primary analysis strategy.
Plan each aspect	Each aspect of the planned analysis should be covered, including analysis population, statistical model, covariates, and handling of missing data.
Enough detail	Provide sufficient detail to allow a third party to independently perform the analysis (ideally through statistical code).
Choices made deterministically	For adaptive analysis strategies which use the trial data to inform some aspect of the analysis, use deterministic decision rules that prevent analysis choices being driven by results.

STUDY QUESTIONS

Factual Questions

1. According to Table 1, what was the second most common issue in pre-specifying statistical analyses in the reviewed trials?

2. Is the issue identified in Question 1 like the OCD example in the Statistical Guide above? If so, how?

3. According to Table 1, what was the most common issue in pre-specifying statistical analyses in the reviewed trials?

4. What was the problem associated with the issue in Question 3 according to Table 1?

5. According to Table 1, what is the issue with researchers reporting multiple analysis plans without identifying the primary analysis?

6. How often did the issue in Question 5 occur in the reviewed trials? (Answer is a range.)

7. What does the *Pre* in Pre-SPEC stand for?

8. Does the answer to Question 7 seem like a reasonable expectation for researchers to meet?

9. What part of the Pre-SPEC approach did the hypothetical OCD researcher in the Statistical Guide violate?

Questions for Discussion

10. What do you think about the percentages of trials in Table 1 that did not have pre-specified analyses that meet today's best standards for research?

11. Why is it a big deal if large percentages of published trials do not meet the highest standards for pre-specifying statistical analyses?

Nonparametric Tests for Group Differences

CHAPTER INTRODUCTION

Unit 4 asked, "How is A related to B?" Unit 5 asked, "Is group A different from group B?" But we glossed over something important about the statistical techniques in Unit 4 and 5. There are big *assumptions* to these statistical techniques. Unit 6 addresses many of those assumptions.

For most of the statistical tests discussed thus far, we have assumed (1) that variables were normally distributed (see Exercise 3.8) and (2) that groups had similar amounts of dispersion in their variables. (The second assumption is a little technical, but do not get hung up on it.) When you assume (1) and (2), you are in a branch of statistics called *parametric* statistics. But that is just one branch. There is also *nonparametric* statistics. (I know, what a creative name.) As you might guess, in nonparametric statistics, you do not assume (1) and (2). Basically, you can think of parametric statistics as when the data is behaving the way we want it to. Nonparametric statistics is the back-up plan when the data are messier than we would hope.

There is one other scenario when nonparametric statistics is needed. Remember that in Exercises 1.6 and 1.7, we talked about scale of measurement and nominal vs. ordinal vs. interval vs. ratio? No? Go and check that out for a second if you want to.

Nonparametric statistics, like the *chi-square test* discussed in Exercise 6.1 and forward, are used when all the variables are nominal. We will talk through a number of examples of this, so you will get the hang of it.

Even though we are now in the new territory of nonparametric statistics, the driving questions are the same—Is A related to B? Is group A different from group B? Unit 6 just asks these questions in slightly different situations.

DOI: 10.4324/9781003096764-6

Chi-Square I

Money Management After Acquired Brain Dysfunction

STATISTICAL GUIDE

The *chi-square test* looks to see if there are differences between groups, just as many other statistical tests do (e.g., *t*-test or ANOVA). What is unique about the chi-square test is that it is designed to study group differences when the outcomes of interest are *frequencies*. Previously, we looked at group differences when the outcomes of interest were means, and we used a *t*-test or ANOVA for that.

Percentages are a form of frequency, and so the chi-square test is often used to look at differences in percentages between two groups. For example, say you are interested to see if different percentages of men and women endorse a certain political belief. Say 52% of men in a sample endorse the belief, while 73% of women endorse it. You would use the chi-square test to see if this difference was statistically significant.

Just like the *t*-test and ANOVA, chi-square test results have a *p*-value associated with them. The *p*-values are interpreted in the same way as with other tests—if $p < .05$, the result is statistically significant; if $p > .05$, the result is not statistically significant.

The symbol for the *chi-square* test is χ^2.

BACKGROUND NOTE

It is traditional to report values of chi-square with the associated probabilities. In the excerpt below, though, we have only included the *p*-values for the chi-square tests. Because decisions are based on the probability levels, the results of the chi-square test can be interpreted without the chi-square values.

The study below investigated money management among individuals who acquired a brain dysfunction at some point in life (as opposed to individuals who are born with a brain dysfunction.) Table 1 shows

comparisons between those with acquired brain dysfunction and a control sample. In particular, it is looking at the frequency of money management problems between the two groups. Finally, the text below states that 35 people with acquired brain dysfunction were recruited for the study, but Table 1 says $n = 32$ for this group. This means the study didn't get responses for the variables in Table 1 from three people.

EXCERPT FROM THE RESEARCH ARTICLE[1]

Thirty-five people were recruited through ABD (acquired brain dysfunction) case management and accommodation services [primarily those with alcohol-related brain injury].

In addition, 15 healthy community volunteers were recruited through advertisements . . . This control group was matched with the clinical sample on a number of relevant demographic variables, including age, gender, and main source of income . . . The control group was also matched as closely as possible to the clinical sample on years of education and National Adult Reading Test . . .

Table 1

Percentage of Participants with Money Management Problems in the ABD and Control Groups

Money management problem	ABD ($n = 32$)	Control ($n = 15$)	p
Problems with ATM	37	0	.001
Don't often check change	42	18	.064
Pay bills or rent late	66	47	.219
Thrown out of accommodation	3.2	0	.371
Owe money for debts	22	6.7	.166
Spend all money within the first few days	59	20	.010
Go without essentials	25	0	.009
Very problematic impulse buying	56	6.7	.000
Spend all money on things they like	47	6.7	.003
Need to borrow money	52	20	.036

Note: ABD = acquired brain dysfunction; ATM = automatic teller machine.

---

1   Hoskin, K. M., Jackson, M., & Crowe, S. F. (2005). Money management after acquired brain dysfunction: The validity of neuropsychological assessment. *Rehabilitation Psychology*, *50*, 355–365. Copyright © 2005 by the American Psychological Association. Reproduced with permission.

STUDY QUESTIONS

Factual Questions

1. What percentage of the control group Pay bills or rent late?

2. The table shows that 20% of the 15 members of the control group Need to borrow money. How many of the 15 need to borrow money?

3. The table shows that 56% of the 32 members of the ABD group have Very problematic impulse buying. How many of the 32 have this problem?

4. From a standard statistical perspective, are the groups different on the rates of Don't often check change? Explain your reasoning.

5. From a standard statistical perspective, are the groups different on the rates of Need to borrow money? Explain your reasoning.

6. Are the groups different on the rates for Go without essentials at the .001 level? Explain your reasoning.

7. For which money management problem are the rates between the groups closest if you just go by the basic difference between the percentages, i.e., compare the numbers in the two columns in Table 1? What is the *p*-value that goes along with this difference?

8. The differences for Problems with ATM and Spend all money within the first few days are both statistically significant. Which difference is less likely due to chance?

9. Using .05 as the minimum level for significance, how many of the ten differences in the table are statistically significant?

Question for Discussion

10. The control group was matched with the ABD sample on demographic characteristics and reading ability. In your opinion, is matching an important element in this study? Explain.

Chi-Square II

Self-Employed Hispanic
Persons by Gender

STATISTICAL GUIDE

This exercise will give you another chance to familiarize yourself with the chi-square test, one of the most common statistical tests in the psychological and health sciences. One thing to know is how the chi in chi-square is typically pronounced. The ch is pronounced with a k-sound, like in kick. It is *not* pronounced with a soft ch, like in chicken. So the chi-square test is *not* said like chai tea. This is because the test uses this symbol, χ^2, which is one of those ancient Greek letters. So, it has a unique pronunciation.

> To review chi-square, see Exercise 6.1.

BACKGROUND NOTE

The table below presents the percentages for men and women[1] in various self-employed occupations and related chi-square test results. The chi-square result on a row pertains to the percentage of men vs. women for that particular row. For example, in the first row $\chi^2 = 22.27$, and this result addresses if the 19.0% for men is different (or the same), from a statistical perspective, than the 14.7% for women.

In the table below, $p < .10$ is reported in addition to the more traditional .05 and .01 levels. This is somewhat unusual, especially given the large size of the sample. So be cautious about the results with $p < .10$. Also, note that chi-square values are only given for comparisons that are statistically significant.

The statistics in the excerpt are from a sample of Hispanics in California. The data was originally collected by the United States Census Bureau, which used a sample of California residents.

---

1 The researchers used a binary concept for gender/sex in this study. In addition, they did not highlight that female and male were self-identified by the participants.

EXCERPT FROM THE RESEARCH ARTICLE[2]

The sampling frame included the following: only heads of households, persons 16 years of age and older who self-identified as Hispanic regardless of race, householders who worked at some point [during the year], and householders who were employed in their own unincorporated business and professional practice . . . The final sample consisted of 7,760 Hispanic self-employed persons, 64% (n = 4,931) who were self-employed men and 36% (n = 2,829) who were self-employed women.

Table 1

Percentages of Variables for Self-Employed Hispanic Persons by Gender

Variable	Self-employed men	Self-employed women	Test statistic for difference between samples
Occupation			
Managerial and professional	19.0%	14.7%	χ^2 = 22.27***
Technical, sales, or administrative	16.9%	20.9%	χ^2 = 18.77***
Service	8.9%	55.1%	χ^2 = 2012.26***
Farm, forestry, and fishing	14.8%	1.4%	χ^2 = 359.65***
Craft, precision production, and repair	29.4%	3.1%	χ^2 = 785.47***
Operators, fabricators, and laborers	11.0%	4.7%	χ^2 = 87.99***
Education			
Less than high school	48.7%	48.3%	
High school graduate	18.9%	20.5%	χ^2 = 3.07*
Some college	22.1%	22.5%	
Bachelor's degree or more	10.4%	8.7%	χ^2 = 5.81**
Immigrated to the United States	62.2%	62.5%	

* p < .10, ** p < .05, *** p < .01.

2 Zuiker, V. S., Katras, M. J., Montalto, C. P., & Olson, P. D. (2003). Hispanic self-employment: Does gender matter? *Hispanic Journal of Behavioral Sciences, 25,* 73–94. Reprinted by Permission of SAGE Publications, Inc.

STUDY QUESTIONS

Factual Questions

1. How many more men than women in the sample were self-employed?
2. For which occupation is there the largest percentage difference between men and women?
3. What is the value of chi-square for the occupation of Operators, fabricators, and laborers?
4. What is the p-value that goes along with the chi-square value in Question 3?
5. Based on your answer to Question 4, should the percentages of men and women who are Operators, fabricators, and laborers be considered different from a statistical perspective?
6. Are all the differences in percentages between occupations statistically significant at the same probability level? If yes, at what level?
7. For which levels of education do the men and women have similar percentages? Explain how you know this.
8. Just by looking at the percentages in Table 1, for which result do the women and men have the closest percentage? Is the chi-square significant for this comparison?
9. For which comparison do the women and men appear most different? Explain.

Questions for Discussion

10. If you have a statistics textbook, determine if the textbook discusses the use of the $p < .10$ level in significance testing. Write your findings here.
11. Compare the differences in the results for Occupation vs. Education. Do you see any patterns? If so, what do you make of these patterns?

Chi-Square and Crosstabs
Predicting Child Behavior Problems

STATISTICAL GUIDE

To review chi-square, see Exercise 6.1.

Recall that a chi-square test is the way to see if there are statistically significant differences in the *frequency* of a variable across different categories, like gender or political affiliation or age group. A *cross-tabulation*, or *crosstabs*, is a helpful way to look at the same kind of data, as it presents information on the relationship between nominal variables. For example, consider Table 1 below. In the first section, the two variables being "crossed" are age range and yes vs. no (meaning the presence or absence of child behavioral problems). The "tabulation" part is the frequencies, or percentages, in each cell—like 36.5% Yes and 63.5% No for 18–34. So the "cross" and the "tab" gives you "crosstabs." The chi-square result tells you if a statistically significant difference in a set of frequencies is present.

Recall how in ANOVA, when you have three or more groups, a significant result tells you that the group means are different, but it does not tell you exactly how the means are different. The same kind of idea is true with chi-square when more than two independent cells are being compared. A significant result on a chi-square test simply tells you that a difference exists in the frequencies across the groups, but this result, by itself, does not tell you which group is bigger/biggest, or smaller/smallest. *Post hoc tests*, or follow-up tests, must be run to determine the ordering of the frequencies in the groups. Exercise 6.6 will cover post hoc tests with chi-square. So in this exercise, if a chi-square is significant, we know that there is a relationship between the two variables in the chi-square, but we won't necessarily know which levels are different in a statistically significant way. So we'll know some things but not everything.

EXCERPT FROM THE RESEARCH ARTICLE[1]

This study used the 1995 Detroit Area Study (DAS) data, a . . . survey conducted . . . to assess . . . social influences and . . . personal life. Respondents 18 years of age or older who lived in [the Detroit Metro Area] were randomly selected . . .

Age, household size, and education were included as the sociodemographic measures . . .

Work hassles were assessed by asking respondents to respond "yes" or "no" to whether they experienced "hassles at work" in the past month. To assess trouble balancing work and family demands, respondents provided a "yes" or "no" response to the question: "in the last month have you experienced trouble balancing work and family demands?" We assessed spousal problems by asking if, in the past month, respondents had experienced any problems with their spouse/partner. Response categories were "yes," "no," or "inapplicable" . . .

Table 1

Prevalence of Child Behavior Problems Across Categorical Predictor Variables

Child Behavior Problems

	χ^2(df)	Yes	No
Age (*n* = 827)	32.39(3)***		
18–34		36.5%	63.5%
35–54		40.0%	60.0%
55–64		23.7%	76.3%
65+		17.3%	82.7%
Education (*n* = 827)	14.33(3)***		
< High School		41.7%	58.3%
High School		26.7%	73.3%
Some College		28.6%	71.4%
College Degree		36.8%	63.2%
Household Size (*n* = 827)	32.57(4)***		
1 person		17.4%	82.6%
2 person		24.8%	75.2%

1 Watkins, D. C., Pittman, C. T., & Walsh, M. J. (2013). The effects of psychological distress, work, and family stressors on child behavior problems. *Journal of Comparative Family Studies*, 1–16. Reprinted under Fair Use.

Child Behavior Problems

	χ^2(df)	Yes	No
3 person		32.8%	67.2%
4 person		36.5%	63.5%
5 or more persons		48.2%	51.8%
Work/family balance problems (*n* = 806)	77.17(1)***		
Yes		55.5%	44.5%
No		23.3%	76.7%
Hassles at work (*n* = 809)	26.73(1)***		
Yes		47.2%	52.8%
No		27.5%	72.5%
Marital status, Spousal problems (*n* = 686)	20.11(2)***		
Divorced		43.0%	57.0%
Married, No		26.7%	73.3%
Married, Yes		44.5%	55.5%

The dependent variable of interest for this study was child behavior problems. This variable comprised one item that asked the respondents if they had experienced any problems with their child/children in the past month. The response categories for the dependent variable were "yes," or "no." This dichotomous dependent variable poses a limitation, as the binomial nature of this variable may not capture the complexity of behavioral difficulties among children . . .

STUDY QUESTIONS

Factual Questions

1. How many age range categories are there in Table 1? By visual inspection alone, which one appears to have the lowest rate of child behavior problems?

2. Is the chi-square result for child behavior problems and age range statistically significant? From the results in Table 1 alone, can you determine which age range had the highest rate of child behavior problems?

3. How many categories are there for education level? By visual inspection alone, which category appears to have the highest rate of child behavior problems?

4. Is the chi-square result for child behavior problems and educational level statistically significant? From the results in Table 1 alone, can you determine which educational level had the highest rate of child behavioral problems?

5. In Table 1, how many categories are there for Hassles at work? By visual inspection, which one appears to have the lowest rate of child behavioral problems?

6. Is the chi-square result for child behavior problems and Hassles at work statistically significant? From the results in Table 1 alone, can you determine which category of Hassles at work had the highest rate of child behavior problems?

7. Table 1 does not specify what *** means for the level of statistical significance. Given your past experience, what do you think it means? (*Note*: the authors state the meaning of *** in an earlier table in the paper; a table not reproduced here.)

8. According to Table 1, how many different variables affect the rate of child behavior problems?

Questions for Discussion

9. The child behavior problems measure was one item that had dichotomous answer choices (i.e., yes or no) as opposed to answers on a scale (e.g., not at all, a little, somewhat, a great deal). How do you think this impacted the results?

10. Table 1 says that multiple variables impact the rate of child behavioral problems (see Question 8). Does this seem plausible to you?

11. This study questioned parents of a broad range of ages. How do you think that impacted the outcome with regard to the rates of reported child behavioral problems?

Chi-Square and Cramer's *V*

Gender Differences in Drinking Problems

STATISTICAL GUIDE

To review chi-square, see Exercise 6.1.

In most researcher situations, we want to know if an effect exists, and, if so, how big it is. A statistically significant chi-square test gives evidence that an effect exists, but it does not give a ready way to understand how big the effect is. This is where Cramer's *V* helps out. Cramer's *V* is a measure of the strength of association between nominal variables, the kinds of variables in a chi-square test. You can think of Cramer's *V* as an effect size for the chi-square test.

Cramer's *V* ranges from 0 to 1. A value of zero means the variables are unrelated, and a value of 1 means they are perfectly related. As a rule of thumb, Cramer's *V* values .1 to .29 are *small*, .3 to .49 are *medium*, and .5 or bigger are *large*.

Recall that an effect size is only calculated if the effect exists. So Cramer's *V* should only be calculated if the chi-square is significant.

Note that *f* is a symbol for *frequency*.

EXCERPT FROM THE RESEARCH ARTICLE[1]

College freshmen (age *M* = 18.24) . . . responded to an anonymous questionnaire . . . as part of an adjudication process for having been cited by campus authorities . . . for violating rules concerning under-aged drinking or the use of illicit drugs.

The Alcohol Change Index (ACI) . . . is a single-item question: "In the past three months, how would you describe your pattern of

(continued)

1 O'Hare, T. (2005). Comparing the AUDIT and 3 drinking indices as predictors of personal and social drinking problems in freshman first offenders. *Journal of Alcohol and Drug Education*, *49*, 37–61. Reprinted under Fair Use.

(continued)

alcohol use?" Responses were classified as "increased drinking" or "not increased drinking."

Binge drinking measures whether or not participants consumed five or more drinks at one sitting within the past two weeks (four or more for women).

Heavy drinking was indicated by usually drinking five or more drinks per week.

The ten-question AUDIT includes three questions on alcohol consumption, four questions on dependence, and three on consequences. A respondent who obtains a cut-off score of greater than or equal to eight is considered a problem drinker in this analysis.

The College Alcohol Problem Scale asks "How often have you had any of the following problems over the past year as a result of drinking too much alcohol?" Because the subscale for distributions are very positively skewed, both the personal and social problem subscales were recoded into dichotomous measures (experienced one or more incidents of a problem or did not) . . .

Table 1

Univariate Data for Major Factors for Total Sample (n = 389) and by Women (n = 143) and Men (n = 246)

	Total		Female		Male			
	f	%	f	%	f	%	Chi-square	Cramer's V
ACI	73	18.8	23	16.1	50	20.3	.99	
Binge drinking	241	62.0	66	46.2	175	71.1	23.98**	.25**
Heavy drinking	142	36.5	31	21.7	111	45.1	21.44**	.24**
AUDIT (≥ 8)	257	66.1	73	51.0	184	74.8	22.75**	.24**
Personal problems	145	37.3	47	32.9	98	39.8	1.88	
Social problems	191	49.1	55	38.5	136	55.3	10.24**	.16**

** $p < .01$

STUDY QUESTIONS[2]

Factual Questions

1. What percentage of the females reported Binge drinking?

2. What percentage of the males reported Binge drinking?

---

2 The researchers used a binary concept for gender/sex in this study. In addition, they did not highlight that female and male were self-identified by the participants.

3. Are there gender differences in the endorsement rate of Binge drinking in this sample? If yes, at what probability level?

4. What was the value for chi-square and Cramer's *V* for Binge Drinking?

5. Consider the value of Cramer's *V* for Binge drinking. Does Cramer's *V* indicate that there is a strong relationship between gender and binge drinking? Explain.

6. Binge drinking, Heavy drinking, and AUDIT (≥ 8) all have similar chi-square values and Cramer's *V* values. Why do you think this is?

7. Social problems, by visual inspection, has a smaller Cramer's *V* than the three variables discussed in Question 6. Why do you think that is?

8. Which two variables have similar rates across gender in Table 1?

Questions for Discussion

9. Notice that the researcher reported values of Cramer's *V* for only four of the six variables. Why did they not report the values for all six?

10. Four of the six percentages in Table 1 are lower, at a statistically significant level, for females than for males. Why do you think this pattern of results is present?

Chi-Square and Odds Ratios

Mental Health and
Chronic Medical Diseases

STATISTICAL GUIDE

When an *odds ratio* (*OR*) equals 1.00, it means the odds that something will happen in one group are equal to the odds it will happen in another group. For instance, if we compare the lung cancer rates for a group that regularly drinks bottled water with another group that regularly drinks filtered water, we might expect to get an odds ratio of about 1.00. This would mean the odds that bottled water drinkers get cancer are the same as the odds that filtered water drinkers get cancer. On the other hand, if we compared lung cancer rates for groups that smoke versus those that don't, we would expect there to be a difference. Let's suppose that the odds ratio in one study of this issue is 3.50. This means that the odds of getting lung cancer if an individual smokes are 3.50 times greater than the odds of getting lung cancer if an individual does not smoke.

Because of random errors, an *odds ratio* (*OR*) will sometimes be greater than (or less than) 1.00 even if there is no true difference between the groups. Suppose in our study of the effects of bottled versus filtered water on lung cancer rates, we get an *OR* of 1.32, with the bottled water drinkers having a higher rate of cancer. Whether this *OR* is meaningful or not can be determined by a statistical test, like the *chi-square test*. If a chi-square test with this data is not statistically significant, the *OR* of 1.32 can be interpreted as not being meaningfully different from 1.00.

Confidence intervals (CIs) can be calculated for an *OR*. Like other confidence intervals, this tells us the likely range within which the *OR* value would fall if the study were run again. Researchers like to look at the 95% CI of an *OR* to see if 1 is included in it. If it is, researchers reason that if the study is run again, the group differences might not be present, i.e., that an *OR* of 1.00 might be found. If the 95% CI of the *OR* does not include 1.00, researchers feel more confident there is a real finding present.

> To review chi-square test, see Exercise 6.1.

EXCERPT FROM THE RESEARCH ARTICLE[1]

Routinely collected primary care, psychological therapy clinic and hospital data were extracted for the registered population of 20 practices ($N = 121,199$) . . .

Table 1
Recorded Prevalence of Long-Term Conditions for Population Age 16 and Over

Common mental health problem (CMHP)

Population >16yr		Present		Absent		All	Odds ratio (OR)	Chi-square
		N	%	n	%	n	(95% CI)	P
Population		**12,210**	**10.1%**	**108,989**	**89.9%**	121,199		
Any LTC	Y	2,665	21.8%	20,466	18.8%	23,131	1.21 (1.15–1.26)	$p < 0.001$
	N	9,545	78.2%	88,523	81.2%	98,068		
Diabetes	Y	775	6.3%	6,081	5.6%	6,856	1.15 (1.01–1.24)	$p < 0.001$
	N	11,435	93.7%	102,908	94.4%	114,343		
CKD	Y	644	5.3%	4,974	4.6%	5,618	1 16 (1.07–1.27)	$p < 0.001$
	N	11,566	94.7%	104,015	95.4%	115,581		
CHF	Y	105	0.9%	860	0.8%	965	1.09 (0.89–1.34)	$p = 0.403$
	N	12,105	99.1%	108,129	99.2%	120,234		
IHD	Y	574	4.7%	4,012	3.7%	4586	1.29 (1.18–1.41)	$p < 0.001$
	N	11,636	95.3%	104,977	96.3%	116,613		
HT	Y	1,901	15.6%	15,631	14.3%	17,532	1.10 (1.05–1.56)	$p < 0.001$
	N	10,309	84.4%	93,358	85.7%	103,667		
COPD	Y	133	1.1%	680	0.6%	813	1.75 (1.46–2.11)	$p < 0.001$
	N	12,077	98.9%	108,309	99.4%	120,386		

Key: LTC = Long-term conditions, CKD = Chronic Kidney disease, CHF = Chronic Heart Failure, IHD = Ischemic Heart Disease, HT = Hypertension, COPD = Chronic Obstructive Pulmonary Disease, 95%, CI = 95%Confidence Intervals. Bold represents total population.

(continued)

1   de Lusignan, S., Chan, T., Arreal, M. C. T., Parry, G., Dent-Brown, K., & Kendrick, T. (2013). Referral for psychological therapy of people with long term conditions improves adherence to antidepressants and reduces emergency department attendance: controlled before and after study. *Behaviour Research and Therapy*, 51(7), 377–385. © Elsevier.

(continued)

This analysis focuses . . . on people with long term conditions (LTC). This study collected information on the following long-term conditions: Diabetes mellitus, Chronic Kidney Diseases (CKD), Heart failure, Ischemic Heart Diseases, Hypertensive disease and Chronic Obstructive Pulmonary Diseases (COPD). A derived variable called "LTC" was defined as a diagnosis of at least one of these conditions.

[Common Mental Health Problems (CMHP) was most commonly depression and anxiety.]

STUDY QUESTIONS

Factual Questions

1. What percentage of those with any long-term condition (LTC) also had a common mental health problem (CMHP)? What percentage of those with any long-term condition (LTC) did *NOT* have a common mental health problem (CMHP)?

2. What is the odds ratio for having any long-term condition (LTC) and also having a common mental health problem? What is the *p*-value for the chi-square test of this relationship?

3 What is the 95% CI for the odds ratio in Question 2? Does this range include 1.00? What does this mean?

4. What percentage of those with COPD also had a common mental health problem (CMHP)? What percentage of those with COPD did *not* have a CMHP?

5. What is the odds ratio for having COPD and also having a CMHP? What is the *p*-value for the chi-square test of this relationship?

6. What is the 95% CI for the odds ratio in Question 5? Does this range include 1.00? What does this mean?

7. Which long-term condition has the greatest odds ratio in its association with CMHPs? Which long-term condition has the lowest odds ratio in its association with CMHPs?

8. Do any of the 95% CIs of the odds ratios include 1.00? Which one(s)? What is the associated *p*-value(s)?

9. If you have hypertension (HT), how much greater risk do you have for CMHP when compared to someone who does not have hypertension?

Questions for Discussion

10. From the evidence in this excerpt, can you say that mental health problems caused long-term conditions or vice versa?

11. Does the evidence in this article show that you have no risk for developing a common mental health problem if you do *not* have any long-term condition?

Chi-Square with Post Hoc Tests

Experiences of OCD and Tourette Syndrome

STATISTICAL GUIDE

Recall that a *chi-square test* reveals if there is a statistically significant difference between the frequencies of a variable across different groups. But if you have more than two groups in the comparison, the chi-square test only signals that there is at least one difference between all the frequencies. It does not tell you which groups have smaller or larger frequencies. Like with ANOVA, *post hoc tests* must be run to determine the relative rankings of the group frequencies. The chi-square test is run first, and if the result is significant, then post hoc tests are run as a follow up to determine which group differences are significant and the relative ranking of the group frequencies.

> To review chi-square tests, see Exercise 6.1.

EXCERPT FROM THE RESEARCH ARTICLE[1]

> The sample comprised 1,001 patients. Half were in treatment at the [Brazilian Research Consortium on Obsessive–Compulsive Spectrum Disorders] at the time they participated. The rest came from the community or other mental health services.
>
> The SCID-I [a clinician-administered diagnostic interview] was used to determine the presence of . . . OCD. Tic disorders were

---

1 Shavitt, R. G., de Mathis, M. A., Oki, F., Ferrao, Y. A., Fontenelle, L. F., Torres, A. R., . . . & Miguel, E. C. (2014). Phenomenology of OCD: Lessons from a large multicenter study and implications for ICD-11. *Journal of Psychiatric Research*, 57, 141–148. © Elsevier.

also diagnosed according to DSM-IV criteria. [Chronic Tic Disorder] (CTD) was diagnosed when a patient had . . . either vocal or motor tics . . . [Tourette Syndrome] (TS) was diagnosed when a patient had . . . both motor and vocal tics at some point . . .

The OCD + TS, OCD + CTD and OCD without tics groups were compared using . . . the Chi-square test for categorical variables . . . Post hoc analyses were performed with . . . the Chi-square tests for the categorical variables with the Bonferroni correction.

Types of sensory phenomena [related to OCD] include: (1) Physical sensations (tactile and/or muscle-joint), defined as uncomfortable sensations localized in a specific region of the body (skin, muscles, or joints), which precede or occur along with repetitive behaviors; (2) "Just right" perceptions, triggered by tactile, visual, or auditory sensations, including the need for things to feel, look or sound "just right"; (3) Feelings of incompleteness (i.e., inner feeling or perception of discomfort that makes the patient do things indefinitely, or until feeling "complete"); (4) Energy release (i.e., generalized inner tension or energy that builds up and needs to be released by an action) and (5) Urge only (i.e., "have to do it" perception related to the repetitive behavior).

Table 1

Types of Sensory Phenomena in OCD Patients with Tourette's Syndrome, OCD Patients with Chronic Tic Disorder and OCD Patients Without Tics

Sensory phenomena	OCD + TS	OCD + CTD	OCD	p-Value*
	N = 90	N = 154	N = 757	
Any Sensory Phenomena, N (%)	76 (84.4)[A]	117 (76.0)[A]	457 (60.4)[B]	**<0.001**
Physical sensations, N (%)	58 (64.4)[A]	78 (50.6)[A]	232 (30.6)[B]	**<0.001**
Just-right sensations, N (%)	63 (70.0)	94 (61.0)	362 (47.8)	0.654
Feelings of incompleteness, N (%)	19 (21.1)	36 (23.4)	117 (15.5)	0.504
Energy release, N (%)	23 (25.6)	31 (20.1)	84 (11.1)	0.133
Urge only, N (%)	38 (42.2)[A]	48 (31.2)[A]	154 (20.3)[B]	**0.021**

Abbreviations: OCD = obsessive–compulsive disorder; TS = Tourette's Syndrome; CTD = chronic tic disorder.
* Chi-square test; [A, B] Post hoc tests with Bonferroni correction (A different from B in post hoc tests).

(continued)

(continued)

Author note: Table 1 uses the notation N (%). The N refers to the raw number count in that category. For example, 76 participants of the 90 who were OCD+ TS experienced Any Sensory Phenomena. If you divide 76 by 90, you get 84.4%, which is the percentage in the parentheses next to the 76 above.

STUDY QUESTIONS

Factual Questions

1. For each group in Table 1, what number of participants had any sensory phenomena? What percentage?
2. What is the *p*-value for the chi-square comparison for Any Sensory Phenomena?
3. Which group had the lowest rate of Any Sensory Phenomena?
4. Which group had the lowest rate of Physical sensations?
5. For which chi-square comparisons in Table 1 is it not necessary to run post hoc tests?
6. In Table 1, for which kind of experience are the group percentages the most similar to each other? (Only use visual inspection.)
7. In Table 1, the energy release percentages *look* different across the groups (11.1% vs. 20.1% vs. 25.6%). Why is it wrong to say that the OCD group has fewer energy release experiences than the OCD + TS group?
8. In Table 1, when there are statistically significant group differences, is there a pattern to these differences?

Questions for Discussion

9. Do you think the study supports the conclusion that sensory phenomena are substantially different for individuals with OCD + TS vs. individuals with OCD only?
10. Which of the five different types of sensory phenomena discussed in the excerpt do you think would be most impairing for daily functioning?

Wilcoxon-Mann-Whitney Test

Fathers' Values for Their Newborns

STATISTICAL GUIDE

To review median, see Exercise 2.1. To review ordinal measurement, see Exercise 1.6. To review interval and ratio measurement, see Exercise 1.7.

The *Wilcoxon-Mann-Whitney test* is a test for comparing two independent groups, like the *t*-test for independent groups or ANOVA. The question at hand for all these tests is the same—is group A different than group B when it comes to the outcome of interest, the dependent variable. But unlike *t*-test and ANOVA, the Wilcoxon-Mann-Whitney test is used when the dependent variable is either (1) in the form of ranks (i.e., ordinal data) or (2) not normally distributed.

Like other inferential statistics, the Wilcoxon-Mann-Whitney produces a test statistic. It is called *U*. When a *U* has a $p < .05$, researchers consider the result statistically significant. This means that the two groups being compared are different in how they ranked the ordinal dependent variable. If $p > .05$ for *U*, then the two groups are judged to have ranked the dependent variable in a similar manner.

So coming back to the *t*-test, we can better see how it is parallel to the Wilcoxon-Mann-Whitney. Both are asking, is this group different from that group? The only difference is that the *t*-test is asking with an interval or ratio dependent variable, and the Wilcoxon-Mann-Whitney is asking with a dependent variable that is ordinal.

As we have seen with other tests, the Wilcoxon-Mann-Whitney test has multiple names. (Argh! Are the statistics gods trying to make things difficult?) It also goes by the *Mann-Whitney U test* or the *Wilcoxon rank sum test*.

BACKGROUND NOTE

In the study below fathers ranked the 18 values in Table 1, giving a rank of 1 to the value that they most wanted for their newborns, a rank of 2 for the value they wanted second most for their newborns, and so on. For

each value, Table 1 gives the median rank (*Mdn*), i.e., the middle ranking given for that value in that group. Table 1 also lists the "Composite Rank" for each value. The authors do not specify exactly how they calculated the composite rank, but it can be interpreted to mean the overall rank for that value in that group. In addition, the researchers use the term alpha level, which refers to the probability level at which they call a result statistically significant.

EXCERPT FROM THE RESEARCH ARTICLE[1]

Men in the waiting room of a maternity ward in a large public hospital, which serves primarily the inner-city, and men in the waiting room of a maternity ward in a nearby private hospital, which serves primarily the middle-class, participated [in the study] . . .

Inner-city fathers were younger, less educated, and less likely to be employed than the middle-class fathers. Inner-city fathers were more likely to be Hispanic and Catholic.

The Wilcoxon-Mann-Whitney test with an alpha level of .05 was used for value comparisons . . . of fathers.

Inner-city fathers emphasized instrumental values connected to conformity and self-control in children, while middle-class fathers emphasized personal qualities involving resources of the mind, such as "imaginative" and "intellectual." Middle-class fathers also emphasized values connected to benevolence, such as "loving" and "honest."

Table 1

Rokeach Instrumental Scale: Median Ranks and Composite Rank Order of Fathers' Instrumental Values for Child

	Rank				
	Inner-city fathers (*n* = 95)		Middle-class fathers (*n* = 28)		
Value	*Mdn*	Composite	*Mdn*	Composite	Wilcoxon-Mann-Whitney *U*
Ambitious	6.50	2	8.00	6	.72
Broadminded	10.30	13	9.25	10	.50

---

1   Minton, J., Shell, J., & Solomon, L. Z. (2005). Values of fathers for themselves and their newborns. *Psychological Reports*, 96, 323–333. Copyright © 2005 by Psychological Reports. Reprinted by permission of SAGE Publications, Inc.

	Rank				
	Inner-city fathers ($n = 95$)		Middle-class fathers ($n = 28$)		
Value	Mdn	Composite	Mdn	Composite	Wilcoxon-Mann-Whitney U
Capable	8.70	5	11.50	13	2.00[‡]
Cheerful	10.75	14	7.42	5	.88
Clean	10.77	15	16.67	18	4.20*
Courageous	9.17	6	8.40	8	.07
Forgiving	10.00	12	9.50	11	.13
Helpful	10.81	16	11.33	12	.87
Honest	6.21	1	2.50	1	3.04[‡]
Imaginative	13.93	18	8.50	9	3.60*
Independent	9.94	11	8.33	7	1.68
Intellectual	9.79	9	7.25	4	2.02*
Logical	13.61	17	14.20	16	.61
Loving	7.00	4	3.25	2	3.81*
Obedient	9.88	10	15.20	17	3.31*
Polite	9.75	8	12.25	15	1.99[‡]
Responsible	6.80	3	6.50	3	.49
Self-controlled	9.28	7	12.20	14	2.27[‡]

* $p < .001$. [†] $p < .01$. [‡] $p < .05$.

STUDY QUESTIONS

Factual Questions

1. What is the median rank for Loving for inner-city fathers?
2. What percentage of the inner-city fathers gave Loving a rank of more than 7?
3. Which values were the least desired by the inner-city fathers and the middle-class fathers, respectively?
4. Which group had a lower median rank for Intellectual? What are the composite ranks for Intellectual?
5. From a statistical perspective, did the groups give different rankings for the value of Intellectual?
6. Honest is the number one composite rank for both groups. How then can the result of the Wilcoxon-Mann-Whitney U test still be significant?
7. Which group had a lower median rank for Obedient? What are the composite ranks for Obedient?

8. From a statistical perspective, did the groups give different rankings for the value of Obedient? If yes, at what probability level?

9. How many of the 18 values did the two groups of fathers give similar rankings, from a statistical perspective?

10. What are the largest and smallest medians for the inner-city fathers?

11. What are the largest and smallest medians for the middle-class fathers?

Questions for Discussion

12. Compare the median values for the number one composite rank value for the two groups. Explain what the difference in these median values might mean for the two groups.

13. The researchers state that "middle-class fathers emphasized personal qualities involving resources of the mind, such as 'imaginative' . . ." Do the results in the table support this statement? Explain.

14. In addition to differing in terms of being inner-city versus middle-class, the two groups of fathers also differed, to some extent, regarding religion and ethnicity. In your opinion, is it important to consider these additional differences when interpreting the results of this study? Explain.

Wilcoxon Matched-Pairs Test

Neural Correlates of Infant Detection of Pro- and Antisocial Agents

STATISTICAL GUIDE

To review
the normal
distribution, see
Exercise 3.8.
To review *t*-test
for dependent
groups, see
Exercise 5.3.

The *Wilcoxon matched-pairs test* investigates if two sets of scores, obtained from matched pairs, are statistically different from each other. You might ask, "Isn't that the purpose of the *t*-test for dependent groups?" If so, you'd be right. Both tests essentially ask if the scores from group A are different from the scores from group B. In fact, the Wilcoxon matched-pairs test is basically equivalent to the *t*-test for dependent groups, except for one big difference. The Wilcoxon matched-pairs test does not assume that the scores on the dependent variable are normally distributed. This is why it is called a *nonparametric* test and is covered in this unit. Lots of outcome variables are often non-normal, such as reaction time measures, or neuroscience measures like in the study below. The Wilcoxon matched-pairs test helps out in such situations.

For Wilcoxon matched-pairs tests, *W* is the test statistic. *W* is like the *t* for a *t*-test. Every *W* has an associated probability value, which is interpreted in the same way that all probability values are typically interpreted, i.e., $p < .05$ is considered statistically significant. But there is one wrinkle. Unlike with *t*-values, smaller *W* values are less probable. So, a smaller number for *W* will have a smaller *p*-value associated with it.

Just like lots of things in statistics, this test has more than one common name. It is also called the *Wilcoxon signed-rank test*.

BACKGROUND INFORMATION

The excerpt below reports on infant perception of pro and antisocial agents. Infants watched short videos of moving geometric shapes that

either had eyes or did not have eyes. The eyes were meant to suggest to the infants that the geometric shapes were agents trying to accomplish a task, while the lack of eyes was meant to suggest that the video was simply geometric shapes moving around on a screen. The infants wore a cap on their scalps that measured electrical activity in the brain (known as an EEG measure). P400 is a brain wave that can be measured by EEG. Other research has connected P400 to the processing of social interactions.

The researchers used a Wilcoxon matched-pairs approach because the dependent variable, P400 data, was non-normal. The study is matched pairs because the researchers compared P400 activity within each infant. For example, in Experiment 1, P400 activity was compared between two situations, one when an infant watched the helping agent videos and one when they watched the hindering agent videos.

The authors conclude that the results show that P400 is a part of the infant brain's processing of pro and antisocial interactions. This is why there was different activity in P400 in Experiment 1 and no differences in P400 in Experiment 2.

EXCERPT FROM THE RESEARCH ARTICLE[1]

The current study is the first to investigate neural correlates of infants' detection of pro- and antisocial agents. Differences in ERP component P400 over posterior temporal areas were found during 6-month-olds' observation of helping and hindering agents (Experiment 1), but not during observation of identically moving agents that did not help or hinder (Experiment 2).

Experiment 1

Fourteen 6-month-old infants . . . were included in the final analysis . . .

The training set included six movies (three helper and three hinderer) in which a protagonist (a red ball with eyes) attempted and failed to climb a hill. In each movie the protagonist made three failed attempts to climb the hill, after which the protagonist was either helped or hindered by another geometric shape (a blue square or a yellow triangle with eyes).

1 Gredebäck, G., Kaduk, K., Bakker, M., Gottwald, J., Ekberg, T., Elsner, C., . . . & Kenward, B. (2015). The neuropsychology of infants' pro-social preferences. *Developmental Cognitive Neuroscience, 12*, 106–113. © Elsevier.

The study was a within-subject design, as such each infant was presented with both helper and the hinderer trials . . .

EEG recording and analysis

Age appropriate [sensors] were used to record EEG signals . . .

Amplitude data for P400 was aggregated over electrodes and . . . [tested] . . . with non-parametric Wilcoxon Matched-Pairs Test . . .

A Wilcoxon Matched-Pairs Test demonstrated a significant effect of trial type, $W(14) = 20$, $p = .04$ for the P400 . . .

Experiment 2

Fourteen 6-month-old infants . . . were included in the final analysis.

The general properties of the stimuli remained the same as described in Experiment 1 above. The test stimuli and procedure were identical. The main difference between the two training stimuli sets was the ball's absence of eyes and self-propulsion. Thus the ball was inanimate and moved only when being pushed up . . . or down . . . the hill. The movements of the two agents as they pushed the ball up and down the hill were identical to in Experiment 1 . . .

A Wilcoxon Matched-Pairs Test demonstrated no significant effect of trial type, $W(14) = 31$, $p = .18$ for the P400.

STUDY QUESTIONS

Factual Questions

1. How many participants are in Experiment 1? How many participants are in Experiment 2?
2. What statistical test was used in each experiment to detect differences in P400 activity?
3. Consider the answer to Question 2. Why do you think the authors used this statistical test in this situation?
4. In Experiment 1, what is the W value for trial type? What is the p-value associated with this test statistic?
5. In Experiment 2, what is the W value for trial type? What is the p-value associated with this test statistic?
6. Which experiment had statistically significant results? What does this mean for the paired ranks that were compared?
7. Since the study design is within-subjects, would it have been appropriate to use a t-test for dependent groups to test for group differences?

Questions for Discussion

8. Do you think it is important to know how brain processes are connected to prosocial and antisocial behavior?
9. Do you think the study results should be generalized to 2-year-olds?
10. Do you think this study is adequately powered to find statistically significant results? (See Exercise 5.10 to see a discussion of statistical power.)

11. Do you think the infants interpreted the videos when both geometric objects had eyes (Experiment 1) as social interactions? Do you think the infants interpreted the videos when only one of the geometric shapes (Experiment 2) had eyes as non-social events?

Unit 7

Test Construction

CHAPTER INTRODUCTION

Throughout this book, we have used lots of different test and measurement instruments: Intelligence tests, the Posttraumatic Stress Disorder (PTSD) Checklist, the Asian Values Scale, or the Semi-Structured Clinical Interview for Diagnosis (SCID). These instruments do not fall from heaven with an instruction manual. All tests must be created and developed through the painstaking work of researchers. During the process of developing a new test, but especially toward the end, a number of statistical procedures are run to investigate how the instrument functions. The new instrument goes through a series of test runs, with test samples, to see if it works as it was designed to work. Unit 7 covers some of the most important statistical procedures that are part of this process.

By working through Unit 7, you should get a sense of how researchers try to show that a new instrument really is a reliable and valid tool for measuring what it is supposed to measure. So, for example, a PTSD instrument should accurately measure PTSD and not Obsessive Compulsive Disorder (OCD). You want an OCD measure for that.

Standard methods of test construction are not foolproof, so some of the measures researchers use today are more error-prone than we'd like. (Ack! Including some of the measures used in this workbook.) Still, the science of test construction is improving, and the exercises in Unit 7 will give you a sense of the many strengths of the test construction process.

DOI: 10.4324/9781003096764-7

Item-Total Correlations

Behavioral Inhibition in Infants

STATISTICAL GUIDE

To review correlation, see Exercises 4.1 and 4.2.

Suppose you are developing a new self-report scale for the personality trait of extraversion. Your scale is intended to measure extraversion and nothing else. If that is the case, then it makes sense that each item on your scale should correlate with other items on the scale, as each item is trying to measure the same thing, extraversion. If your scale had ten items, you would hope that item 1 would relate to all the other items. You would hope the same thing for item 2, etc. This is the logic of *item-total correlations*, where each item in a scale is correlated with the total score minus that one item. So, on your extraversion measure, scores on item 1 are correlated with the total of the scores for items 2 thru 10. If this correlation is significant, then it suggests that item 1 measures something that goes along with items 2–10. This process is repeated for each item in the scale. If an item has a non-significant item-total correlation, it suggests the item does not measure what the rest of the scale measures. In that case, you would likely drop that item from your scale.

Keep in mind that the most item-total correlations can tell you is if individual items go along with the rest of the other items. These correlations cannot tell if you are *validly* measuring what you want to measure, which is extraversion in our example. There are other ways to establish the validity of your scale.

Sometimes scales are broken into sub-scales. If so, the *item subscale correlation* is also considered, which is the correlation between an item and the subscale total (minus that item). In general, but not always, item subscale correlations should be higher than item-total correlations. If you think about it, that is what a subscale means. The scale can be broken down into subcategories that are more tightly linked together.

As a general rule, researchers often believe that item-total correlations (or item subscale correlations) should be larger than .3, though in some instances .2 is used as the boundary. If the correlation is smaller than that, the item will often be deleted from the scale as it is too weakly related to the rest of the items.

EXCERPT FROM THE RESEARCH ARTICLE[1]

[T]his study aims at the development of the parent-reported "Retrospective Infant Behavioral Inhibition" (RIBI) questionnaire covering *behavioral inhibition* (BI) in the first and second year of life . . .

[P]roperties of the RIBI were studied in two samples . . . Participants included a child and his or her primary caregiver, mostly a parent . . . 119 caretakers of 126 children . . . completed the initial 26-item pilot version of the RIBI . . .

The basic theoretical orientation for the test construction of the RIBI was based on the three behavioral features of BI in children according to Kagan and colleagues: Distress to Novelty, Fear, and Shyness . . .

Item analysis and item selection . . . resulted in a questionnaire with a reduced number of 20 items. Each item showed an item-total correlation of > .30 concerning the hypothesized subscale and the complete behavioral inhibition scale. One item of the initial scales "Distress to Novelty" and "Fear" had to be excluded, respectively (item-total correlation .26 and .27). Four of the initial thirteen items referring to "Shyness" were excluded for redundancy . . . Table 1 gives a summary of all items in the final order with the respective percentage of symptomatic answers (p_{it}), item subscale correlation ($r_{it\text{-}sub}$), and item-total correlation ($r_{it\text{-}com}$).

Table 1

Item Analysis, Items per Subscales, Sample 1

Item		p_{it}	$r_{it\text{-}sub}$	$r_{it\text{-}com}$
Factor	"Distress to Novelty"			
1	She/He was ill at ease (cried, wanted to retreat) when confronted with loud noise (aspirator, radio, etc.)	.33	.53	.33
2	She/He got easily frightened at sudden loud noise (siren, door banging)	.45	.56	.40
3	She/He got easily frightened, when suddenly manipulated or taken up	.28	.69	.60

1 Gensthaler, A., Möhler, E., Resch, F., Paulus, F., Schwenck, C., Freitag, C. M., & Goth, K. (2013). Retrospective assessment of behavioral inhibition in infants and toddlers: development of a parent report questionnaire. *Child Psychiatry & Human Development, 44*(1), 152–165. With permission of Springer.

Item		p_{it}	$r_{it\text{-}sub}$	$r_{it\text{-}com}$
4	When supposed to have a bath, she/he was easily frightened (stiffened itself, wanted to retreat) at contact with water	.19	.50	.46
5	She/He approached new objects (e.g. in an apartment) only slowly	.22	.65	.59
6	In a new surrounding she/he felt quite uncomfortable before starting to explore	.39	.51	.69
7	She/He reacted with crying and distress to a change of appearance of a parent (new color of hair, cutting of the beard, wearing glasses etc.)	.19	.45	.49

Factor "Fear"

8	While going for a walk, she/he approached new objects promptly and was unafraid. (–)	.32	.49	.68
9	As soon as to he was able to climb, she/he was faster up than one could watch. (–)	.37	.51	.37
10	She/He usually kept close to a caregiver when outside, for not getting lost	.54	.45	.35
11	She/He usually acted cautiously not to harm her/himself	.53	.64	.35

Factor "Shyness"

12	She/He did not want to contact (eye contact, handshake, etc.) unfamiliar adults initially	.41	.73	.63
13	She/He cried or turned away when new adults wanted to take her/him in their arms	.44	.72	.67
14	She/He clutched the parents or hid behind their legs when unfamiliar adults addressed her/him directly	.38	.76	.69
15	When someone unfamiliar came for a visit, she/he promptly approached the person curiously. (–)	.54	.79	.68
16	She/He involved unfamiliar adults, who came for a visit, directly into her/his play or current activity. (–)	.59	.71	.61

(continued)

(continued)

Table 1
Continued

Item		p_{it}	$r_{it\text{-}sub}$	$r_{it\text{-}com}$
17	When meeting unfamiliar children, she/he approached them by her-/himself and wanted to play with them. (–)	.46	.60	.54
18	She/He needed quite a long "warm up", when meeting unfamiliar children	.38	.67	.62
19	In a new surrounding she/he got quite clutching (wanted to sit permanently in the arms or on the lap etc.)	.39	.79	.79
20	When unfamiliar people present, she/he was reticent (withdrew, stopped talking)	.41	.78	.74

(–) = inversely coded r_{it} = item-total correlation, p_{it} = percentage of symptomatic answers.

STUDY QUESTIONS

Factual Questions

1. For item 2, what is the item subscale correlation and what is the item-total correlation? Which one appears to be larger?

2. For item 11, what is the item subscale correlation and what is the item-total correlation? Which one appears to be larger?

3. Which item(s) appears to have the largest item subscale correlation?

4. Which item appears to have the largest item-total correlation?

5. Does the factor or subscale for "Shyness" appear to have items that go along with each other; are they measuring the same kind of thing?

6. Does the factor or subscale for "Fear" appear to have items that go along with each other; are they measuring the same kind of thing?

7. Below what item-total correlation did the authors decide to delete an item from the scale entirely?

8. Consider the answer to Question 7. Why do you think the authors chose this level of item-total correlations for deleting an item from the scale?

Questions for Discussion

9. Do you think fear and shyness in 1-year-olds are two different things? If so, do you think it makes sense to divide them into subscales on this measure?

10. Do you think that parents are accurate reporters on their young children's distress with novelty, fear, and shyness? Can you think of anyone who would be a better reporter on these tendencies in a young child?

Test-Retest Reliability and R^2

Emotions and Behaviors in School-Age Children

STATISTICAL GUIDE

To determine *test-retest reliability*, a test is administered to one group of examinees twice (often with a week or two intervening between the two administrations of the test). This yields two scores for each examinee. Computing a correlation for the relationship between the two sets of scores reveals the stability of the scores over time. A high test-retest correlation indicates that those who scored highly on the first administration tended to score highly on the second administration and vice versa. Typically, if a researcher is interested in test-retest reliability, it is because they expect it to be high, like a correlation of .75 or higher. Correlations of .85 or higher indicate especially strong test-retest reliability.

> To review correlation, see Exercises 4.1 and 4.2. To review R^2 and percentage of explained variance, see Exercises 4.6 and 4.7.

When a correlation is used to express the stability of test scores over time, the correlation is commonly referred to as a *test-retest correlation* or *test-retest reliability* or even as a *reliability coefficient*. Despite the different names, test-retest reliability is mathematically the same as a standard correlation. And just to make things a little more confusing, researchers sometimes simply use *reliability* when they mean *test-retest reliability*. In such instances, the reader must read the Method section carefully to confirm what the researcher means by reliability.

EXCERPT FROM THE RESEARCH ARTICLE[1]

> We assessed the reliability of the Behavioral and Emotional Rating Scale–Second Edition: Parent Rating Scale (BERS–2; PRS).

---

1   Mooney, P., Epstein, M. H., Ryser, G., & Pierce, C. D. (2005). Reliability and validity of the Behavioral and Emotional Rating Scale–Second Edition: Parent Rating Scale. *Children & Schools*, *27*, 147–155. Reprinted by permission of Oxford University Press.

Table 1
Means, Standard Deviations, and Test-Retest Correlations for the BERS-2 Parent Rating Scale

| Subscales | Elementary school sample (N = 33) | | | | | Middle school sample (N = 45) | | | | | Total sample | | | | |
| | First testing | | Second testing | | | First testing | | Second testing | | | First testing | | Second testing | | |
	M	SD	M	SD	r[a]	M	SD	M	SD	r[a]	M	SD	M	SD	r[a]
Interpersonal	9.64	3.31	9.18	2.93	.91	10.96	2.82	10.96	2.67	.89	10.40	3.08	10.21	2.90	.89
Family involvement	9.91	2.73	10.06	2.68	.94	10.91	2.83	10.91	2.76	.92	10.49	2.81	10.55	2.74	.93
Intrapersonal	10.39	3.11	10.27	2.93	.93	10.04	3.16	11.11	2.90	.88	10.77	3.14	10.76	2.92	.90
School functioning	9.76	3.12	9.30	3.12	.86	11.33	2.74	11.49	2.49	.88	10.67	2.99	10.56	2.96	.86
Affective	11.09	2.65	10.76	2.70	.90	10.96	2.92	10.98	2.77	.82	11.01	2.79	10.88	2.73	.86
Career	8.69	3.42	8.19	3.67	.80	10.71	2.43	10.55	2.24	.90	9.92	3.01	9.57	3.12	.85
Strength index	100.88	18.31	99.16	17.37	.90	106.80	17.52	107.20	16.30	.87	104.29	19.99	103.79	17.13	.88

Note: Means are reported as standard scores.

[a] p < .001.

(continued)

(continued)

All parents of kindergarteners through to second graders at the elementary school (N = 122) and sixth graders at the middle school (N = 169) received by mail a . . . copy of the PRS . . . Parents were informed that on receipt of the first protocol, a second PRS would be sent to them that was also to be filled out and returned . . . A return rate of 26.8% was achieved.

Assessments like the PRS, which may be used for screening, planning, and evaluation purposes and for which data are reported individually, should have reliability coefficients of at least .80.

STUDY QUESTIONS

Factual Questions

1. For the elementary school sample, which subscale appears to have the lowest test-retest reliability coefficient?

2. For the middle school sample, which subscale appears to have the highest test-retest reliability coefficient?

3. For the total sample, what is the value of the test-retest reliability coefficient for School functioning?

4. The researchers state that measures used to assess individuals should have test-retest reliability coefficients of at least .80. Do all the subscales meet this criterion?

5. For the total sample, what is the value of the test-retest reliability coefficient for Family involvement?

6. What is the value of R^2 for your answer to Question 5?

7. Based on your answer to Question 6, what percentage of the variance on one administration of the Family involvement subscale is explained by the variance on the other administration of that subscale?

8. The researchers state that measures used to assess individuals should have test-retest reliability coefficients of at least .80. For a coefficient of .80, what percentage of the variance on one administration of the scale is explained by the variance on the other administration of the same scale?

Questions for Discussion

9. The measure in this study, the BERS–2, parent report, intends to measure the strengths and capabilities of elementary and middle school-age children. Do you think that children in that age range have stable traits when it comes

to interpersonal skills, family involvement, and the other subscales of this measure? How does your answer relate to the test-retest reliability coefficients in Table 1?

10. The return rate, or completion rate, for this study was 26.8%. Does this surprise you?

11. Does the fact that the response rate was considerably less than 100% affect your evaluation of this study? Explain.

Internal Consistency and Cronbach's Alpha

A Measure of Prosocial Tendencies

STATISTICAL GUIDE

Internal consistency refers to the extent to which all the items in a measure hang together or are consistent with each other. (Sorry to use the word in defining the phrase!) If a measure is intended to measure one thing, e.g., extraversion, the items should agree with each other as each item is measuring one thing, extraversion. So, when an investigator is developing a new measure (of one thing), they typically try to establish that their measure is internally consistent.

Item-total correlations are one way to show internal consistency. High item-total correlations reveal that each item is consistent with the total score. But there is another way to measure internal consistency that researchers like even more. Take a measure, split it in half, total the items in each half, and then correlate the two halves. This is called a *split half reliability*. It tells you how similar the halves are to each other. If the correlation is high, like .8, then the halves are pretty similar. This means the halves are consistent with each other, which they should be if the measure is measuring one thing. Say it's a measure of extraversion that is being developed, then a split half reliability should be high because the investigator wants both halves to measure one thing, extraversion. If the correlation is lower, like .3, then the halves are somewhat dissimilar. This makes it seem more likely that the halves are measuring more than one thing, maybe extraversion and conscientiousness.

Suppose we have an extraversion measure with 20 items, and the first split half reliability we calculate is split according to odd items and even items. Say that a second split half reliability we calculate is split according to the first ten items and the second ten items. Suppose further that we figure out every possible way to split the scale in half (there are a lot of ways), and we calculate all the split half reliabilities for each case. The

> To review correlation, see Exercise 4.1. To review item-total correlation, see Exercise 7.1. To review test-retest reliability, see Exercise 7.2.

average of all those correlations has a special name, *Cronbach's alpha* (α). This is the most commonly used measure of internal consistency.

Technically, Cronbach's alpha (α) can range from 0 (total absence of internal consistency) to 1.00 (perfect internal consistency). Typically, alphas greater than .7 are seen as acceptable, with even higher values indicating strong or excellent internal consistency. If alpha is lower than .7, researchers become concerned that a measure that is supposed to be measuring one thing is really measuring more than one thing, i.e., is not internally consistent.

A goofy analogy might help. Say you have a big bowl of mashed potatoes. From the outside, it might look like you only have one thing in the bowl—mashed potatoes! But as you put your fork into the mashed potatoes you realize the consistency changes. Low and behold, there are several large carrots in the mashed potatoes. In this case, your alpha for mashed potato-ness will be lowered because your bowl of mashed potatoes is not internally consistent; it is not just one thing. Basically, most researchers don't want carrots in their mashed potatoes. (By the way, in this goofy analogy extraversion is the mashed potatoes and conscientiousness is the carrots.)

EXCERPT FROM THE RESEARCH ARTICLE[1]

> The six types of prosocial behaviors in the PTM–R [Prosocial Tendencies Measure–Revised] include public, anonymous, dire, emotional, compliant, and altruism . . . Public prosocial behaviors were defined as behaviors intended to benefit others enacted in the presence of others (four items; sample item, "I can help others best when people are watching me"). Anonymous prosocial behaviors were defined as the tendency to help others without other people's knowledge (five items; "I think that helping others without them knowing is the best type of situation"). Dire prosocial behaviors refer to helping others under emergency or crisis situations (three items; "I tend to help people who are in real crisis or need"). Emotional prosocial behaviors are behaviors intended to benefit others enacted under emotionally evocative situations (five items; "I respond to helping others best when the situation is highly
>
> *(continued)*

1   Carlo, G., Hausmann, A., Christiansen, S., & Randall, B. A. (2003). Sociocognitive and behavioral correlates of a measure of prosocial tendencies for adolescents. *Journal of Early Adolescence, 23*, 107–134. Reprinted by permission of SAGE Publications, Inc.

(continued)

emotional"). Compliant prosocial behaviors refer to helping others when asked to (two items; "When people ask me to help them, I don't hesitate"). Altruism refers to helping others when there is little or no perceived potential for a direct, explicit reward to the self (six items; "I often help even if I don't think I will get anything out of helping"). Data were coded such that high scores on each of these scales reflect a stronger endorsement.

Table 1
Cronbach's Alphas and Test-Retest Reliabilities for the PTM–R Scales by Age Group

Variable	# of items	Cronbach's Alpha		Test-Retest Reliabilities	
		Early adolescents	Middle adolescents	Early adolescents	Middle adolescents
Compliant	2	.80	.75	.64	.73
Public	4	.76	.86	.54	.56
Anonymous	5	.76	.84	.66	.78
Dire	3	.71	.75	.72	.63
Emotional	5	.86	.82	.72	.82
Altruism	6	.59	.80	.76	.73

STUDY QUESTIONS

Factual Questions

1. Which variable had the largest number of items?
2. Which variable had the smallest number of items?
3. Researchers typically think a measure should have a test-retest reliability of .70 to be considered sufficiently reliable to use for the assessment of individuals. Which variables are sufficiently reliable for Middle adolescents according to this rule?
4. For early adolescents, which variable appears to have the greatest test-retest reliability?
5. For early adolescents, which variable appears to have the lowest test-retest reliability?
6. For early adolescents, which variable exhibited the most internal consistency?
7. For middle adolescents, which variable exhibited the most internal consistency?
8. What is the value of Cronbach's alpha for the variable Dire for early adolescents?
9. Describe in your own words the internal consistency for the variable Altruism for the two groups of adolescents.

Questions for Discussion

10. Looking at the sample items for each variable, which one, to your mind, best illustrates the variable it is intended to capture, e.g., is "I can help others best when people are watching me" a good item for public prosocial behaviors?

11. The researchers calculated the values of Cronbach's alpha separately for each of the six variables. Speculate on why they did this instead of calculating a single value of alpha for all items on the PTM–R.

12. Participants in this study might give socially desirable responses to the items on the PTM–R even if those responses were not fully true. If this occurred, do you think it would lower or increase the calculated value for the measure's internal consistency?

Validity Coefficients and Test-Retest Reliability
Mathematics Anxiety Rating Scale

STATISTICAL GUIDE

The *validity* of a test is a big deal. Validity refers to the extent to which a test measures the thing it is supposed to measure. For example, a *valid* extraversion test will measure how extroverted someone is, and a *valid* math achievement test will measure how much math someone has learned.

To review correlation, see Exercise 4.1. To review test-retest reliability, see Exercise 7.2.

If a test isn't valid, i.e., if it doesn't measure the thing we think it measures, that's a big problem. So, establishing the validity of a test is a big deal. One method for estimating validity is to administer the test (e.g., a reading ability test) to a group of examinees and to obtain another set of scores on a variable that should be related to reading ability (e.g., teacher ratings of student reading ability). To the extent that the two variables are related in the expected direction (i.e., reading test scores are positively correlated with teacher ratings of student reading ability), the test is said to have shown a degree of validity. When correlation coefficients are used in this way, they are usually called *validity coefficients* because they are helping establish the validity of a test or measure.

Note that when a *correlation* (like Pearson's *r*) is used to describe reliability or validity, it is calculated using the same formula as always. So, it really is just a plain old correlation being put to use in a specific situation. It's also interpreted in a similar manner, e.g., positive means direct relationship and negative means inverse relationship and zero means no relationship. Still, researchers often give it a different name than correlation; they might use *reliability coefficient* or *validity coefficient* to indicate the specific purpose for which the correlation is being used.

Excerpt From the Research Article[1]

As a measure of mathematics anxiety, the Mathematics Anxiety Rating Scale (MARS) has been a major scale used for research and clinical studies since 1972 . . . Despite the usefulness of the original scale, researchers have sought a shorter version of the scale to reduce the administration time of the original 98-item inventory . . .

The purpose of this study was to develop systematically a shorter version of the Mathematics Anxiety Rating Scale . . . The study also aimed to provide information on validity and test-retest reliability for the brief [30-item] version.

The 98-item MARS (MARS 98-item) and a shorter 30-item version (MARS 30-item) were [each administered twice to] 124 female and male volunteers (63 women and 61 men), introductory psychology students . . . in a state university in two sessions one week apart. Introductory psychology is a broad survey course involving students in a broad range of majors. . . .

The one-week test-retest reliability for the MARS 30-item version was .90 ($p < .001$), which is equivalent to the test-retest reliability of .91 ($p < .001$) of the longer MARS 98-item obtained during this study.

Validity for the MARS 30-item version was first measured by calculating Pearson correlations with the MARS 98-item scale. Tests from both Weeks 1 and 2 correlated significantly. At Week 1, $r = .92$ ($p < .001$) between the two scales, and at Week 2, $r = .94$ ($p < .001$).

As further validation, it was predicted that high scores on mathematics anxiety would be negatively correlated with grade point average (GPA) in mathematics courses since mathematics anxiety is presumed to interfere with mathematics performance. Results were as predicted. Correlations between each of the measures of mathematics anxiety (MARS 30-item first testing, MARS 30-item second testing, MARS 98-item first testing, MARS 98-item second testing) and grades in high school mathematics courses were, respectively, $-.41$ ($p < .001$), $-.31$ ($p < .007$), $-.46$ ($p < .001$), and $-.34$ ($p < .003$). Thus, high scores on mathematics anxiety were significantly negatively correlated with mathematics performance in high school; the shorter and the longer scales actually showing similar magnitudes.

1   Suinn, R. M., & Winston, E. H. (2003). The Mathematics Anxiety Rating Scale, a brief version: Psychometric data. *Psychological Reports*, 92, 167–173. Reprinted by permission of SAGE Publications, Inc.

STUDY QUESTIONS

Factual Questions

1. In order to estimate test-retest reliability, each version of the MARS (i.e., 30-item and 98-item) was administered twice. How many weeks separated the two administrations?

2. What is the value of the test-retest reliability coefficient for the MARS 98-item version?

3. Were the test-retest reliability coefficients for the two versions of the scale comparable? Explain.

4. What was done to first measure validity for the MARS 30-item?

5. At Week 1, the students took both the long and the short versions of MARS. Were the two sets of scores obtained at that time highly correlated? Explain.

6. At Week 2, the students took both the long and the short versions of MARS for a second time. Is the correlation coefficient for this administration of the two tests statistically significant? If yes, at what probability level?

7. The correlation between the two scales at Week 2 is .94. How strong is this association in terms of common magnitudes for correlation coefficients?

8. What is the reason the researchers gave for predicting a negative correlation between scores on mathematics anxiety and grade point average in mathematics courses?

9. What was the value of the validity coefficient between MARS 30-item first testing and grades in high school mathematics courses?

10. What was the value of the validity coefficient between MARS 98-item first testing and grades in high school mathematics courses?

Questions for Discussion

11. Consider your answers to Question 10 and 11. Do they suggest that MARS 30-item and MARS 98-item have similar validity?

12. For test-retest reliability, the researchers waited one week between the two administrations. If you have a statistics textbook that discusses test-retest reliability, what interval does the textbook author recommend?

13. In the first study, the MARS 30-item scores were correlated with the MARS 98-item scores. Does it surprise you that the correlations were so large (i.e., .92 on the first administration of the two scales and .94 on the second administration)?

14. MARS scores correlated −.31 to −.41 with high school math grades. While substantial, why do you think these correlations are not higher?

Index

Contents

First published 2022
by Routledge
605 Third Avenue, New York, NY 10158

and by Routledge
2 Park Square, Milton Park, Abingdon, Oxon, OX14 4RN

Routledge is an imprint of the Taylor & Francis Group, an informa business

Library of Congress Cataloging-in-Publication Data
Names: Cox, Keith S., author. | Holcomb, Zealure C., author.
Title: Interpreting basic statistics : a workbook based on excerpts from
    journal articles / Keith S. Cox and Zealure C. Holcomb.
Identifiers: LCCN 2021008399 (print) | LCCN 2021008400 (ebook) |
    ISBN 9780367560515 (hardback) | ISBN 9780367561970 (paperback) |
    ISBN 9781003096764 (ebook)
Subjects: LCSH: Statistics—Problems, exercises, etc. | Sampling
    (Statistics) | Social sciences—Statistical methods—Problems,
    exercises, etc.
Classification: LCC HA35.15 .H65 2022 (print) | LCC HA35.15 (ebook) |
    DDC 519.5076—dc23
LC record available at https://lccn.loc.gov/2021008399
LC ebook record available at https://lccn.loc.gov/2021008400

ISBN: 978-0-367-56051-5 (hbk)
ISBN: 978-0-367-56197-0 (pbk)
ISBN: 978-1-003-09676-4 (ebk)

DOI: 10.4324/9781003096764

Typeset in Frutiger Light
by Apex CoVantage, LLC

Access the companion website: routledge.com/9780367561970

Interpreting Basic Statistics

A Workbook Based on Excerpts
from Journal Articles

Ninth Edition

Keith S. Cox and Zealure C. Holcomb

Routledge
Taylor & Francis Group

NEW YORK AND LONDON

The questions in each exercise are divided into two parts: (1) Factual Questions and (2) Questions for Discussion. The Factual Questions require careful reading for details, while the discussion questions show that interpreting statistics is more than a mathematical exercise. These questions require students to apply good judgment as well as statistical reasoning in arriving at appropriate interpretations.

Each exercise covers a limited number of topics, making it easy to coordinate the exercises with lectures or a traditional statistics textbook.

Keith S. Cox is a Clinical and Personality Psychologist. He teaches research methods and statistics at the University of North Carolina Asheville, where he holds the rank of assistant professor. He uses the research methods and statistics covered in this book as he investigates Posttraumatic Stress Disorder (PTSD) and personality.

Interpreting Basic Statistics

Interpreting Basic Statistics gives students valuable practice in interpreting statistical reporting as it actually appears in peer-reviewed journals.

Features of the ninth edition:

- Covers a broad array of basic statistical concepts, including topics drawn from the New Statistics
- Up-to-date journal excerpts reflecting contemporary styles in statistical reporting
- Strong emphasis on data visualization
- Ancillary materials include data sets with almost two hours of accompanying tutorial videos, which will help students and instructors apply lessons from the book to real-life scenarios

About this book

Each of the 63 exercises in the book contain three central components: 1) an introduction to a statistical concept, 2) a brief excerpt from a published research article that uses the statistical concept, and 3) a set of questions (with answers) that guides students into deeper learning about the concept.

The questions on the journal excerpts promote learning by helping students

- interpret information in tables and figures,
- perform simple calculations to further their interpretations,
- critique data-reporting techniques, and
- evaluate procedures used to collect data.

"The ninth edition of this workbook is an engaging and invaluable tool for teaching students how to interpret statistics as they encounter them in articles written within the psychological, social, and health sciences. By choosing article excerpts that are sure to interest undergraduate readers, the authors may entice those many students who say they fear numbers into taking their first halting steps toward understanding. By providing clear and concise descriptions of key concepts and posing astute questions, the workbook demystifies the scientific enterprise and explains its importance for comprehending the social world. And by starting with the simplest ideas and gradually, step by step, moving toward a more complex understanding, the authors gently lead students on a learning journey that is sure to be deeply informative – and maybe even fun!"
—Dan P. McAdams, the Henry Wade Rogers Professor of Psychology, Northwestern University, USA

"This introduction to reading and understanding statistics is very basic and easy to understand, but at the same time it is scientifically oriented, contemporary in outlook and forward looking in methodology. It points students in exactly the right direction, emphasizing meaningful interpretation of scientific results over recitation of cookbook formulas. Students will come away with the tools they need for comprehending graphical analysis, effect size, and statistical power."
—Eric Turkheimer, PhD, Hugh Scott Hamilton Professor, Department of Psychology, University of Virginia, USA

Foreword

So Here's My Problem...

S o HERE's MY problem: when it comes to generating writing material, teenagers are gold. Their world is a narcissistic, anarchic, paranoid hell of anxieties and stresses about how they look; how popular they are or aren't; and how fast or slowly, big or small their private parts are growing. As an observer, it's fantastic. Hilarious, at times. Poignant and heartbreaking. It is all the stuff of great human drama because, before your eyes, you get to witness character transformation. Boy grows into man. Girl grows into woman. Writers strain to make this shit up.

But – and here's the catch – we dare not discuss any of this if we want our kids to trust us or ever talk to us again. And that's because, lifts and pocket money aside, teenagers crave *privacy* – the need for which hatches both swiftly and silently while we're sorting out the laundry. It's as if they suddenly wake up one day creeped out by the thought of all those years we wiped their butts and helped them put on their undies and they go into lock-down. They smoke us out, put up walls, close their doors, shut down their stories, and waft, earphoned, through our homes in a shroud of hormones and appetite. Their lives – in which, until recently, we participated with Too Much Information and gross oversharing – suddenly become 'none of our business'.

So you'll appreciate it was something of a start-up challenge to try to write about things I'm not even supposed to *talk* about. On top of that, I've no desire to add to the oversaturated, over-analysed market of parenting books on how to tell if our kids are gifted, depressed, indigo, suicidal, special, different, dyslexic or catatonic, or have ADHD, ADD, Asperger's or anxiety. (Read enough of these books and you are sure to feel depressed, anxious, suicidal and catatonic yourself.) I'm ambivalent about the theoretical inclination when it comes to parenting after having spent most of my first pregnancy studying the books as if I were expected to complete a dissertation between contractions. Before childbirth, I fancied myself as something of an expert on the baby-to-be. I can now confirm that there is no text that can prepare one for thirty-six hours of labour followed by a Caesarean. Or mastitis. Or colic. The books help pass the time in the ob-gyn's waiting rooms but they're useless at 3 am when you have a screaming baby and a dried-up bosom.

Likewise, what can anyone say to prepare us for parenting teenagers? All the psychology books insinuate that if we don't get it right in the first two years of our kids' lives, with the right amount of bonding and breastfeeding, we've buggered up the source code. By the time our kids are telling us to *get a life*, it may be too late. Continuing to self-flagellate with the whip of being a 'better parent' long into the teenage years may amount to a personal neurosis for self-improvement, rather than offer any benefit to the offspring.

So you'll probably be relieved to hear that this is not another how-to book. It is my ethical obligation to inform you right here on page xi that I do not have a single qualification for writing a book about parenting teenagers. Other than a few legal ones, I have no university degrees that might give you a modicum of confidence that your money has been well spent. I am confident that by the end of this book you will not know whether your teenager is secretly smoking, doing drugs or giving blow jobs behind the canteen at recess.

I made the decision a while back to stop reading books about parenting and take up the guitar instead. At this point, my parenting aim is to simply get my kids through school and into their own lives so I can get back to mine. I'd prefer for them to be reasonably resilient, responsible and not idiotic with money. If my wishes have any bearing on who they turn out to be, I hope they believe in something, anything god- or spirit-like; that they take enough care of their bodies; and that they use protection when they start shagging (eventually, way into the future).

But what I know for sure is that who they will become has very little to do with my desires. There's as much chance my kids will turn out to be atheist capitalists as they will vegan animal-rights activists. In fact, the teenage manoeuvre is precisely to position oneself in opposition to anything that whiffs of authority, rationality or reasonableness. So, as reverse psychology might have it, it may yield a better procreative result if one were to live one's life as a philandering, profligate rogue rather than a principled, respectable Samaritan.

This raises the dangerous question of whether attempts to be a good, solid parent to a teenager are a waste of time and effort. We're still unable to extract a perfect mathematical formula to determine to what extent we can apportion blame to nature or nurture for our children's imperfections and failures. It seems safest to assume that each influence is equally guilty, and therefore aim to offset any dodgy biological kinks by creating a civilising environment around our children as they clink and bubble into adolescence.

Love in the Time of Contempt addresses some of the thorny questions that have arisen for me in the years of shepherding adolescents to what I can only hope will be the safe harbour of adulthood (though maturity can feel more like being in the trenches than reaching an oasis, but our job is to withhold this knowledge from our kids lest, as Cormac McCarthy writes in *All the Pretty Horses*, 'they'd have no heart to start at all').

This book is about the unfamiliar territory we must inhabit as we scramble to find ways of staying in their worlds while they keep trying to nudge us out.

When I was a kid, my mother gave me the book *What's Happening to Me?* by Peter Mayle; it was filled with caricatures of erections, wet dreams, periods, breasts, pimples and all the afflictions of the adolescent body. I guess the aim was to lull one, through humour, into a sense of 'this is manageable' – though, frankly, some of those cartoons made me wish I could frog-leap over the whole disfiguring transition into adulthood. The point is that change is scary, especially when you have no control. Especially when that change involves parts of your body you are still not quite sure how to use. I don't wish to detract from the horrors for the victims of these adjustments; however, there are few books that tackle how it feels to be *the parent* of someone sprouting hair, tits and attitude all over the place. It is a tussled, frazzled and complex business to remain mature while supporting someone to become an adult. At the very least, it raises the question of whether we have, in fact, done enough growing up ourselves.

In a book about teenagers, there are certain topics that cannot be avoided. There is no getting away from periods, pimples and pubic hair. I'm reminded at this point of the valiant Mr Davenport, the hapless phys. ed. teacher who was allocated to teach us sex education in Year 5 – I'm guessing he picked the short straw at some staff party. A big, burly fellow, he walked into class and said, 'Okay, let's get all the giggling done upfront: penis penis penis vagina vagina vagina testicles testicles testicles clitoris clitoris clitoris,' as we all erupted like fizz balls into puerile cackling. In this spirit, I invite my teenagers not to take the mention of any unmentionable body parts personally.

This book does not, and is not meant to, cover the entire spectrum of experiences parents of teens confront. There are many books out there that do that. I can only speak from my own limited experience. This book is therefore a collection of snapshots of some of the issues that have loomed large for me in the past few years, as I've tried to make sense of what is happening to me as my kids try to figure out what's happening to them. To protect the privacy of my kids, I've 'fictionalised' some of the interactions and drawn from conversations I've had with parents of other teenagers. But I assure you, I have not made any of this up. When it comes to teenagers, truth is way scarier than fiction.

—JOANNE FEDLER

If there is anything that we wish to change in the child,
we should first examine it and see whether it is not
something that could better be changed in ourselves.

CARL JUNG

Chapter 1

Get a Life

THERE WILL COME a time when a person you most likely pushed out through your vagina and nursed from your nipples, whose bottom you wiped, and whose snot and spit you cleaned up over several sleep-starved years will apprehend you with a mixture of boredom and irritation and say, 'Get a life, Mum.'

This would be a good time to remember that a) violence never solved anything; b) teenagers don't have a full brain yet – the prefrontal cortex that controls the ability to make important distinctions, like who controls the pocket money, only kicks in around the age of twenty-four; and c) you are, in fact, the adult.

Also, it would be a mistake to take this personally. Firstly, our kids never knew us when we had a life. You remember? The dope-smoking, hitching rides with strangers, sex on car bonnets,

1

all-nighters, skinny-dipping, dancing on tables … Trust me, these stories are best kept to ourselves. For one thing, we don't want to model bad behaviour and, for another, it will only gross them out.

Speaking for myself, it's been a cold, hard slap to the ego to accept that aspects of my hard-won identity – my creative, extrovert self, for example – are, in fact, nothing but embarrassments to my teenagers, Shannon (sixteen) and Jordan (fourteen). I don't even try to predict what will embarrass them anymore. It's not like I've taken up pole dancing or have become the face of a new brand of extra-absorbent panty liner. We're talking about a teensy nose stud. Making casual chitchat while driving them and their mates between parties, prompting Jordan to huff, 'Mum, do you *have* to talk to my friends?'

These days I find myself second-guessing my impulse to sing along to pop songs, or even wear clothes I bought long before they had opinions about fashion or were even *born*. Behaviours that used to be *mine* have somehow, by procreative osmosis, become *theirs* (just like my make-up collection and jewellery have become Shannon's). If I choose the red Vans, they're 'daggy'. If I recommend a book or movie, 'It's not my kind of thing'. My approval is a death sentence. My enthusiasm a fatal contaminant. It is hard to know what to do with all the opinions and wisdom I have gathered over my forty-seven years, which I was hoping to hand down. It seems they're only good for a St Vinnies chute or a willing orphan.

Shannon and Jordan would likely find it less traumatic if I were to throw up over them than to contemplate the idea that I ever had sex in the past, was considered sexy by someone or (God forbid) could be regarded as sexy by someone now. I've had to pull the plug on finding other people sexy because, apparently, it's just grotesque. Shannon actually moved three seats away from me during *Snow White and the Huntsman* because I mentioned that Chris Hemsworth 'did it for me'. 'That's just gross, Mum,' she grimaced. Truth was, I'd toned it down for her sake.

'Just face it, Mum,' Jordan said recently, 'men don't look at you anymore. Get over it.' Which is untrue, by the way. Just the other day during my hamstring curls, a guy at the gym suggested we 'go for a drink'. So what if George has a pacemaker and bowel 'issues' (he offered this by way of banter), still ... he works out, okay?

There's My Version of Me. It includes my history pre-kids – the times I've been called fun. Sexy. Smart. Other cool things. And then there's My Kids' Version. Reconciling the two is like trying to get your eyes to focus on different images as the brain tries to fertilise them into 3D. It can make you giddy. It's easier just to close one eye and accept Their Version.

Sometimes the dissonance between how they see me and how I remember myself is too much of a strain, so I just forget who I was and collapse into being their middle-aged mum without a life. It's a role I've been playing since they kicked and cried their way into the world courtesy of my girl parts. It wasn't just a newborn the obstetrician handed me after the summer picnic of labour, but a new identity.

I remember clutching a tiny infant's head to my bosom, trying to work out how the nipple goes in the mouth, and having a vague sense that the life I had Before Children (BC) was over – a life that involved French lace bras *just in case*, a promising career, rapacious libido and hectic social life. Once you're wearing slippers to the supermarket and have become oblivious to the week-old reflux on your t-shirt, you think, 'Fuck it, I might as well go for seconds.' Which I did. Some go back for thirds. And ... seriously? (You've lost me at four kids.) So one gives up keynote-speaker opportunities to hang out in playgroups and sing 'Little Peter Rabbit Has a Fly upon His Nose'. One passes on tickets to Leonard Cohen concerts because someone came down with a sudden fever. One cancels a weekend away because it's the basketball final. But what sort of a parent keeps a ledger on the sacrifices? Instead, we tell ourselves, 'It's not forever', and get on with it.

As the years pass, we get better at Being Their Mother. We don't have to think about the role consciously – our kids are woven into the fabric of our everyday shopping lists, worries, hopes and dreams. We don't even call it 'sacrifice' anymore. It's just what parents do.

Then one day we turn around and realise they can tie their own shoelaces, make their own toast, tell us about the habitat of the wombat or explain how the digestive system works – and we take a step back and begin to exhale. That moment of recession, as the ratio between their cuteness and their emerging selves shifts, is a revelation. Though we've been marvelling at their hatching personalities since their first smile, we begin to notice that no matter how smart, funny, clever or gifted they must surely be, cuteness is *not* the overriding personality trait of a particular child, but rather aggression, introversion, whimsy, flamboyance, melancholy, anxiety, wussiness – traits we may neither recognise nor find particularly appealing. Consequently, a sort of parental dysphoria can set in as they peel themselves from our expectations like a banana skin from the flesh. It's a shock, it always is, when we really 'get' it – that they're Someone Else. And how we're connected to them becomes mysterious all over again.

Depending on our level of narcissism, this will either be a great relief or a great disappointment to us. Regardless of whether we respond to their individuality with smug self-satisfaction or crushing disenchantment, we're all in for the same course ahead. The Kilimanjaro of raising little kids will be followed by the Everest of Teenagehood for which there is no training, but for which, I am warning you, you will need to muscle up, especially if you, like me, are sentimental about the role you think you play in your children's lives.

You will need to stay calm as you witness the candy floss in your daughter's smile harden into brittle bitchiness. You will need to muster a new resolve as your son's fascination with Pokémon shifts to porn. You will have to recalibrate your mothering instinct to accommodate the notion that not only do your children poop and burp, they also masturbate, drink and smoke. As their bodies, brains and worlds rearrange themselves, you will need to do your own reshuffling. You will come to see that, though you gave them life, they're the ones who've got a life. They've got 1700 friends on Facebook. They've got YouTube accounts (with hundreds of sub-scribers), endless social arrangements, concerts, Valentine's Day dances and Halloween parties. What we have – if we're lucky – is a 'Thanks for the ride, Mum, don't call me, I'll call you,' as they slam the car door and indicate we can run along now.

Do not be so easily dismissed.

You're needed now. More than ever. Just not the way you're used to.

Chapter 2

How the Game Has Changed

THE OTHER NIGHT, in an attempt to 'engage' with them, I called Shannon and Jordan to my study to watch a YouTube video of a father in the US end his rant against his teenage daughter's 'I-hate-my-parents' Facebook post by emptying the barrel of a gun into her laptop.

I suppose I hoped it would dawn on them that I'm not such a terrible parent for insisting that electronics be shut down at 9 pm and they each do one chore a week. Instead, they looked at each other and rolled their eyes. 'Just proves what a dickhead of a father he is,' Jordan grunted in disgust. 'Tragic,' Shannon sighed and sauntered off to continue the intricate artwork of stitches, hearts and diamonds she'd been drawing on her left arm with a Sharpie over the past week. (It's only a matter of time before it becomes a permanent tattoo.)

Now that they're teenagers, the years of claustrophobic motherhood that left me feeling exhausted have been replaced with this: me feeling a bit silly. It's not like I want to be worshipped or anything. Just respected. I'd even settle for not being dissed. Problem is, I'm not impressive anymore. They used to ask me things and take my word as gospel. Nowadays they know more than I do about too many things. I need their help with my iPhone and Foxtel. They snicker, as if I'm some nerd who's been under a rock and only just emerged into the daylight of popular culture. It's not easy to retain an air of authority about appropriate bedtimes when I can't download songs on iTunes.

When I bought myself a guitar a few years ago, conscious of not cramping her style, I approached Shannon, an accomplished guitarist and singer, and told her I planned to learn how to play it. She raised her teenage eyebrows, her face a mixture of genuine scepticism and pity.

'Don't worry,' I assured her. 'It will take me a very long time to get as good as you.'

'I'm not worried, Mum, you'll never be as good as me.' She shrugged.

Which is probably true but, like, why say it?

By the time she was sixteen, Shannon was my height. We could share clothes. Since then, Zed (my husband, their dad) has refused to fold the laundry after he once held up a pair of undies and said, 'Yours or hers?' and then, 'I can't do this anymore.'

Their comebacks are witty and withering. The other day when a TV ban was issued for rude behaviour, which got ramped up for answering back, Shannon icily left us with a 'We're not Nazis, you know.'

'Don't come in, I'm filming,' Jordan intermittently calls down the passage, as if he's Spielberg or something. I have no idea what's actually going on in his room, except that later there'll be YouTube downloads of his 'gameplay' which he then insists I watch – it gives him 'views' which is currently how he measures his self-worth. We nearly came to blows over Call of Duty, which I refused to allow in our home, even though I was ruining his social life in the process. I held out, through the crippling pressure. Now he's mining and dodging zombies. For all I know Minecraft is frying his brain, not creating new neural pathways. And he's got friends in his room 24/7 on Skype. I miss the good old play date, when kids went home eventually.

Parenting teenagers came upon me suddenly. One day I was in parks, eating icy-poles and pushing little bodies on swings, and the next Shannon was saying, 'Give me a break, I have PMS,' and Jordan was insisting that 'Roll-on works better, but aerosol is more manly.'

Overnight, Time Out and Naughty Corners became obsolete and ridiculous. 'Eat your kale' is now met with a '*You* eat my kale,' or 'I've decided to give up green vegetables.' I try insisting, but a teenager will quote the Convention on the Rights of the Child and claim that his right to eat what he wants has been recognised by the UN. I'm usually too tired to argue and since no-one is scared of me anymore, raising my voice just makes it seem like *I'm* the one having the tantrum.

I have to constantly update my parenting techniques, like a daily Facebook status. Our kids are changing, nightly, by the glow of their computer screens, the click of a mouse, the tweet in the night, and we have to keep up if we want to stay in the game. There's a Buddhist lesson about impermanence in there somewhere.

Sometimes when I see a mum cuddling her toddler in the park, I get that twisted-pretzel feeling under my ribs. I can't remember when last I got some of that action. When Jordan was little, he'd catapult himself into the bath with me and natter about dinosaurs and Yu-Gi-Oh! until his jaw cramped or the water got cold. Sometimes we'd have bubble-bath fights. But sometime in his ninth year, he stopped. A year later, after a horrible day at school, I offered, 'Bubble-bath fight?' He paused, frowning; I could almost see him weighing his thoughts. 'Yes …' he finally said, 'but make the most of it, Mum.'

That was the last time.

Since then, I've had to steel myself against an avalanche of tiny rejections. The other day I asked him if he wanted to go to the beach for a swim.

'No, thanks.'

'It's so hot, let's just go for a quick dip.'

'I hate my boardies, they're too tight.'

'C'mon, it's such a beautiful day. We should swim.'

He paused, I swear he paused, but then he let it out: 'I don't want to go to the beach … with you.'

I could see how bad he felt about being this scalding – even in the name of honesty. I pinched a smile together – 'I get it, no problem' – and slunk off in search of the cat. Don't judge me – a few pats and purrs can get a person through the day when that's all the love on offer.

This is a time of plummeting, as we drop in our kids' affection like the mercury during an icy spell. All I seem to be doing is getting in the way of their big venture, which is to be as different from me and as similar to everyone else in their peer group as possible. Andrew Solomon, in his astonishing book *Far from the Tree*, calls this a 'horizontal identity'. The snug, old, hand-me-down identity they share with me and Zed (religion, class, gene pool and so on) isn't doing it for them anymore. In fact, they're combing out all the bits of our influence like hair knots.

Shannon used to love it when people said she looked like me. Now she scowls as if she's been told she resembles Barney the Dinosaur. When Jordan sinks a three-pointer, my whoops just embarrass him. 'Be cool, Mum,' he grimaces, shaking his head.

It's my dignity I miss.

Recently, at a bar mitzvah, I found myself chatting to an acquaintance. We did the 'How's Noah? How's Lucy? How's Camilla?' dance of inquiring after one another's kids. 'Is Lucy doing her HSC *already*?' and 'I can't believe Jordan has grown so tall. Is that facial hair?'

'It's a horrible time,' she offered, unsolicited.

'What's happening in your household?'

'Well, it's just like I feel battered by it. They're so … abusive. Especially my youngest. He's a feral, foul-mouthed little bugger.' As she said this, I remembered that not so long ago she was still breastfeeding her youngest at the age of three. She loved it so much she couldn't bear to give it up.

'I told him the other day that it's like he's got Tourette's, he has a swearing tic,' she continued, 'and his response was, "What the fuck's a tic?"'

You've got to laugh. A robust sense of humour is the only way to ride the level of low-grade abuse, which one ought never to take personally. When my kids were small, I used to reassure them that being called a 'dag' or 'fat' by the playground bully didn't make them fat or daggy. It's time to take my own advice and remember that teenage mutterings about my 'idiocy' and 'wussiness' need not stick. These are the thunderbolts and hailstones we must dodge through the storms of adolescence, knowing that our kids do not entirely control their internal weather. And that the contempt will pass.

As I search for new meaning in my role as their mum, their need for independence stretches me to breaking point. I have to trust them in the world, and the world with them, or risk crippling them with my neurosis. They may be growing up, but I'm having to toughen up, to withstand the shame of asking someone a quarter my age what LMFAO means, or to explain the word 'meme'. When they say, 'You remember that thing Kanye West did to Taylor Swift?' I nod. Sometimes you just have to wing it. Their snappy, cool comebacks make me say puerile things like, 'I carried you for nine months of my life, is it such a big deal to carry two shopping bags to the kitchen?'

Be prepared for the fogginess, the blurring of boundaries. It's sometimes hard to tell who's the adult and who's the child. Just the other day, after I had a freak-out at Jordan for not taking out the garbage as he'd promised, he said, with chastening authority, 'Settle down, will you?' And you know what? I did.

They're preparing me for a shattering ego-shift ahead. Possibly for a midlife crisis. With closed doors, private conversations and peer secrets, they're letting me go. They're shrugging me off like old skin. *Get a life, Mum.* A life that doesn't include lunchboxes, school drop-offs, netball games and basketball practice. I don't know if I'm ready for it to be all about me … and Zed, of course (that's if we've still got anything in common). Their lives seem so much more interesting. Right now I'll settle for a role in their support team, and not being de-friended by them on Facebook.

It's not that I resent that for sixteen years I've put them first and demoted my own preferences, choices, desires, wishes and career options (I wanted kids, I'd do it all again). My gripe is that, to my kids, my sacrifices are invisible, unacknowledged. But I'm warning you: don't even try to point this out to your teenager. It just comes across as whingeing white noise.

What comes as a shock is the loss. It happens incrementally – the falling away of that world of unparalleled intimacy, of covering a little face with kisses. Of bedtime stories and 'don't-let-the-bugs-bite'. Of 'The World's Best Mum' Mother's Day cards when those words aren't meant ironically. No-one ever told me to prepare for a certain kind of grief as my kids outgrow outfits, Play-Doh, fluffy toys, The Wiggles and idiosyncratic obsessions with dinosaurs and Bratz dolls.

But this anguish is just the start. There's more. There's also the crippling envy. Because whatever it is they are reaching for – life itself, a sense of possibility, a deep engagement with an emerging self – we're desperately trying to hold on to.

Mums score extra depression points if our kids' teenage years coincide with the squall of menopause. Just as we're drying out and drying up – sagging and creasing and wondering, 'Is this it?' and 'Did I really follow my dream?' – our teens are plump with collagen and adrenalin, surging and gusting with youthful glamour and dreams. It's a very in-your-face business, because whatever it is they're approaching head-on, we're leaving behind. As their teenage sons pop with testosterone and preposterous biceps, it's no wonder dads droop into their midlife crises, contemplating during their morning shave if they've squandered their best years and why young women in elevators are entirely at ease doing their make-up in their presence. Just when did they become so invisible?

So we turn away and something sharp gets us under the sternum. We examine the face in the mirror and suddenly we don't quite know how to do the job we've been doing all this time – being their parents. The game has changed, the rules are unwritten. And we realise, in a crushing moment of insight, that despite the complaining we've done over the years about how consuming, exhausting and thankless the whole hands-on parenting job is, we never really wanted it to end.

Not like this.

Not on their terms.

When *we* were ready, Goddammit.

Chapter 3

Never Speak of These Things

Now, I'M NOT saying I'm a better parent than Zed. He, for example, is much calmer than I am in most situations (unless it involves mess). He does not panic. He is excruciatingly neat. He doesn't jump to conclusions, or assume a cough is lung cancer or a headache is a brain tumour. He is happy to drive out at midnight to pick up a child at a concert whereas I will try to talk the kid out of going in the first place.

But when Shannon was nine months old, I had to travel for a few days for work. I left Zed with an encyclopaedia of instructions for Caring for Our Infant. I called a few times a day to check on what she'd eaten for lunch, how long she'd napped and how many times he'd changed her nappy. 'Everything's fine, stop worrying,' Zed chided.

The day I returned, we arranged to meet at a cafe for breakfast. I saw Zed approaching from the opposite direction, pushing Shannon in her pram, and from two hundred metres away, I knew something was wrong. My baby was bright red. She was floppy. When I finally reached them, I could see she was feverish and sweaty.

'She's sick!' I yelled.

'She's fine.' He shrugged.

'Look at her! She's burning up. Look at her head lolling.'

'She's a bit sleepy but overall she's been behaving well.'

It's not a competition about who was right or wrong, but it turned out she had roseola virus.

In another example of Zed's dodgy judgement: last year, I went to Bali for five days and returned to find the cat had a lopsided meow. Zed hadn't noticed, despite the fact that Tanaka sleeps on our bed. The vet confirmed she had Bell's palsy and couldn't blink or flick her ear. I had to give her eye drops for six weeks twice a day to prevent her getting an acute dried-out eyeball. Thank God for me, then.

I notice *everything*.

I know when my kids have had a crappy day, when they don't finish their breakfast, when they watch too much reality TV or don't want to swim. I notice what time they made their last Facebook entry and who's commenting on their pages.

This stems from my long history of TMI about my kids which began in those newborn days when I observed with studious precision everything about them: the particular anti-clockwise whorl in which Jordan's hair grows, the widow's peak of Shannon's forehead, the tiny birthmark on Shannon's right heel, and how Jordan's baby toe lies at right angles like his dad's.

Just as a scientist studies the habits, life cycle and habitat of field mice or a particular breed of turtle, I have watched my babies. I have spent years noting the colour and frequency of their poop and their liquid intake and output. I have become a specialist in detecting the textures of their heartbreak and fascinations. I pride myself in knowing the bullies in their dreams and on the playground. I am viscerally invested in the shape of their toe-nails, the curl of their eyelashes and how they lost each of their milk teeth.

Not only do I observe, I cheerlead. Every inch of height has been marked on their doorposts; each tooth lost sealed in marked envelopes; every graze brought home from the playground, plastered, kissed better. Love is a kind of witnessing that acts as a bulwark against invisibility, lest my kids ever imagined they weren't noticed in this vast, indifferent world.

But some years ago, things started shifting. They stopped running naked through the house and jumping in and out of my bath. I no longer found myself wrapping towels around shivering limbs and helping them in and out of bathing costumes. The fila-ments of my familiarity with their bodies began to fray. I'd find myself asking, 'What happened to your leg?', 'Where did you get that bruise?', 'When did you outgrow those shoes?' The textbooks said that my kids were 'differentiating' themselves from me and Zed. Turns out 'differentiate' is just a fancy psychological term for telling us to fuck off.

This is how it went: they stopped telling me things. They stopped showing me things. They never let me see them unclothed. Of course, there was great relief in having only one butt to wipe, and to actually have time to apply make-up in the morning instead of helping someone with their socks. But there was a cost. My witnesshood was revoked. Years went by and I only saw what they wanted me to see.

So imagine the shock if one were to, say, barge into the bathroom thinking one's husband was in the shower, only to discover – amidst shrieks of 'Get out!' – that it was, in fact, one's teenager.

I admit: I was not ready.

The hair *down there* will shock you. You will be certain that it does not belong on your child, even though you understand the rudiments of human biology and the inevitable march of maturation which none of us is spared. It's hardly a surprise to learn that the word 'puberty' derives from the Latin *pubescere*, which means to be 'covered with hair'. No kidding.

Of course, one will be overjoyed that things are progressing normally in the onset-of-puberty department. One might even be flushed with a sort of pride that the biological system we grew inside our own bodies works. We'll be thankful for all the folate tablets we swallowed and the glasses of shiraz we declined during our pregnancies. That's the mature part. The rest of us will be giddy with 'How the hell did we get here so soon?' and 'That's my baby, there.'

I am not squeamish when it comes to my kids. I've dealt with all manner of body functions in various times of ill-health so nothing about them grosses me out. I'm always up for a decent conversation about constipation, flatulence, burning wees, strange rashes and itchy bums; I'd imagined this would extend naturally in adolescence to discussions about changing bodies, tampon insertion, menstruation cramps and pimple management. I have never wanted my kids to think there are no-go topics or subjects that make me queasy.

But the arrival of the hair down there coincided with a new censorship law that outlawed a) noticing; and b) drawing attention to any new developments in the underarm, leg and facial hair department; the promotion from a 34B to a 36DD cup; or the breaking of voices.

Other forbidden topics included weight, height, the shortness of skirts, the unkemptness of hair, the weather in reference to clothing (*Take a jumper; You'll be cold in shorts; Is the hoodie necessary?*) for the following reasons:

- If they wanted our opinion they'd have asked for it.
- Actually, no-one cares what we think.
- Were we looking at them? Did they ask us to look at them?

Any commentary is felt as harassment and intrusion. These bodily transformations, as much as they may spin a parent into a state of shock, are actually the private business of the person to whom they are happening. As with the walls of a cheap motel room, we must pretend that we've seen nothing.

I speak from experience. When I was growing breasts, my father drew me a card for my twelfth birthday showing two little bumps on a girl's chest captioned with, 'Why are you hiding apples under your shirt?' I hated that birthday card.

Your best bet is to discreetly share these confidences with the spouse or the cat, both of whom will likely pretend you have said nothing since neither has any coping mechanism to assimilate such information. (Zed recently walked into our bedroom, eyes blinking wildly, and gasped, 'My God,' doing that thing men do with their hands to illustrate a massive set of breasts. He didn't want to talk about it.)

In the aftermath of such encounters, pour a stiff Scotch and try to forget what you have seen. Like the first sign of spring, the hair down there is an augur of what's to come – and we all know there's no turning back. A new season is on its way.

Ready or not, here it comes.

Chapter 4

Stranger-zoned

THE HAPPINESS OF a household surely depends on the number of available bathrooms at any given time. What begins as two adults and two children sharing one bathroom becomes four adults sharing one bathroom. Adult ablutions are far more serious and time-consuming than the pee-pee, poo-poo and *don't forget to flush and wash* of former eras.

The other morning I found myself outside the closed door of our bathroom having forgotten to put on my deodorant. But Shannon was in the shower. 'Can I just come in and get my deodorant? I won't look at you,' I called through the door.

'No!' she shrieked.

'Oh, come on, I've seen it all. I have the same as you. We're both women.'

'Stay out!' she yelled.

I thought about barging in, hands over my eyes, grabbing the Rexona and bolting. Instead, I waited, exasperated, outside. And Shannon took her sweet time. As I rested my head against the door, I experienced that odd chest spasm that seems to be a symptom of these teenage years. My daughter doesn't want me to see her naked. I mean, really. I *made* all those bits she doesn't want me to see.

But the thing is, she doesn't have any conscious memories of my pregnancy or her birth, or that first year of almost-attachment parenting. Those are *my* memories. Hers begin around the age of four. She'd be as affronted if I walked in on her in the shower as if that old curmudgeon Tom from next door barged in. It is an act of great maturity on my part to come to terms with being stranger-zoned in this way, and not take it personally.

Zed has been feeling cut out for ages now. When Shannon was little, he used to take her fishing. They would spend hours silently casting off. He lay on her floor at night for two years and read every single one of the Harry Potter books to her. They built Lego together.

'It all changed when I couldn't tickle her anymore,' he once confessed. 'I sort of lost my footing with her.'

The Tickle – one of the parent's magic manoeuvres for bringing a child close, to diffuse tension and break the circuit on a fight. In our home, the chant was, 'Tickle you 'til you wee, Tickle you 'til you wee,' and the tickle would always end with someone having to change undies. But when Shannon was twelve and Zed tried the tickle on her one night, it all went wrong. 'Get off me!' she yelled. 'Just get off me,' and she shoved him away, furious.

Zed was shattered. The time for the father–daughter tickle was well and truly past. This withdrawal of physical affection is as brutal as any break-up I've ever experienced.

Now Zed bonds by watching TV shows he would never otherwise endure: *Glee* and *Supernatural*. The two of them sit and watch together, talking about Kurt and Rachel and the Winchester brothers. He also asks her for help when he's struggling with his ukulele chords.

For Zed the roughest it gets as the father of a daughter is driving her and her friends around. 'I feel completely awkward and have no idea what to talk about so we just put on the music and I drive in silence.' He shrugs as pathetically as I've ever seen a can-do marathon runner like him concede.

While Zed used the tickle, I favour the hug. But Shannon isn't into hugging me anymore either. It's sometimes as much as I'm allowed to just stroke her hair, or squeeze her shoulder as she clambers out of the car in the morning during school drop-off. To say that I miss the hugging would be a lax confession. I feel the withdrawal as a drunk feels involuntary sobriety.

As tickles and hugs slip away, we have to become satisfied with comfortable silences and the occasional shared joke. Essentially, it's an intimacy diet. To survive, we need to figure out how to live comfortably in the hunger.

For now, Shannon's body is entirely her own. She controls its revelations. It is her right to decide who sees and touches it. But I want it to go on record that she has not learned to be self-conscious about her body from me. I still have the same open-door bathroom policy I had when my kids were little and freely roamed in and out, often both climbing into the bath with me. At home, I wander around in various states of undress, especially on Sydney summer days when the air clings to you like wet oatmeal, and certain body parts require ventilation or they will suffocate.

But to Shannon, nude is 'rude'. She's between intimacies – past ours and pre-romance. She has yet to learn the comfort of sisterly nudity: skinny-dipping with girlfriends in a crowd of non-judgemental eyes. I only learned this in my twenties when the self-consciousness of adolescence ultimately gave way to self-acceptance as I pushed my body and experimented with aerobics, dancing, hiking and the Kama Sutra.

Growing up is a process of learning how to hide ourselves, to disguise what we feel and fear. Our toddlers exhaust us because they do not pretend to be what they are not: when they are tired, hungry, angry or afraid they let us know so in unambiguous terms. But, as we learn from the creation story of Adam and Eve, as soon as self-consciousness kicks in (others are watching, judging), our children fig-leaf their naked needs and feelings. They hide the soft tissue of their beings under the chitin of self-protection. They withdraw from us, conceal and bury who they truly are. It starts with their bodies, but it creeps into their beings. As our teens slowly accrue the rewards (and burdens) of personhood – opinions, personalities, preferences, hopes and fears – they make us redundant: *I'm sorry but we're going to have to let you go.* We are asked to turn away. To not see what is in front of us.

Still standing at the closed bathroom door, I mused that there's got to be a sweet spot between the full-body burqa and Annie Sprinkle's tricks (she invites audience members on stage to look at her cervix through a speculum) and each of us has to find that place on our own. Shannon is perfectly comfortable displaying her ample cleavage and astonishing long legs; we have regular fights because her school skirts aren't long enough to hide a tampon string. But what gets me is that the gaze of peers and boys – which can be harsh and judgemental – is infinitely more tolerable to her than the intense loving gaze of her own mother. Not that I'm trying to be intense; love just works that way. I want her to strut her beauty and find a sensual peace in her wild nakedness. I just have to accept that I will never be there to witness it.

I made a mental note to buy an extra roll-on to keep in my bag (so many household annoyances can be noiselessly solved), and sighed loudly, reminding Shannon I was still waiting.

'Give me a minute!' she barked.

It was going to be a long wait.

Of course, I understand the need for long spells in the bathroom. I have spent many hours there myself, often in the presence of hot wax or foul-smelling unctions that relieve one of natural body hair because, unlike European women, I've bought into the idea that beauty entails less hair than God intended.

I've ensured that Shannon has never caught me in these shameful acts because … well, I don't want to pass this neurotic vanity on to her. But she's imbibed it anyway. Whether this is my doing or the claws of mainstream culture, I'll never know. Our kids pick up what's 'normal' by what is treated as such within the closed circuit of their family.

This puts me in something of a quandary regarding my own bikini line. Because for the past couple of years, while I've been quietly celebrating the arrival of the hair down there on my kids, I have been in the clandestine process of getting rid of my own.

It all began on a whim – inspired by a binge of self-help books – to do something I'd never done before on each of my birthdays. One year, it struck me that I'd never had a Brazilian wax. It sounded so … exotically South American. Turns out it was more like voluntary root canal than a romantic encounter with Latin culture.

As a chatty woman in her sixties with bright pink hair yanked at my bits, she revealed that the 'effect' only lasts for four weeks before the entire vulvular torture needs to be re-enacted.

Despite my aversion to the adult prepubescent labia popularised by mainstream porn, I confess that the neatness and smoothness appealed to me. Then – and goodness knows how they got my email address – I began to receive monthly emails from Shine-On Laser Beam enticing me with specials on Brazilians and underarms. I began to fantasise about never having to grab a rusty razor on a hot day to get rid of underarm hair, or dashing down to the beach for a swim that was not carefully scheduled a week prior to the event. I was sold.

Of course, the whole business sits uncomfortably with my feminist leanings, not to mention my terror of excruciating physical pain, for which I was unprepared when I pitched up for my first laser treatment. (What was I expecting? Reiki?)

It is far simpler for me if my kids don't notice I have very little pubic hair when theirs is in full bloom, lest I have to account for my own hypocrisies (and teenagers love nothing more than to catch you out in a double standard). While I consider it my parental duty to offer my kids rational explanations for most phenomena, perhaps this does not extend to an explanation of why my vajayjay looks like it didn't make it through puberty. But just in case, here are some responses I've conjured if my kids ever question me:

- 'I've done it for you, to avoid embarrassing you when I raise my arms cheering in a basketball match or go to the beach with pubes halfway down my thighs.' (The Selfless Mother)

- 'I've done the pubic hard yards. When you've done yours, you can elect to get rid of it, too.' (The Long-Suffering Mother)
- 'At my age, pubic hair is very unattractive.' (The Vain Mother)

There is, of course, a fourth option which I've learned from my kids: 'It's none of your business.' (The Bitchy Mother)

Now that we've entered the age of secrets and exclusions, I'm no longer the person in whom they will automatically confide. Shannon will never reveal who she's got a crush on and Jordan will never, ever dob on which of his friends watch porn or hook up at parties. If I ask too many questions they'll tell me to stop. Of course, I care about what is happening to them, but at a certain point inquisitiveness and prying become creepy. My curiosity or need to know just doesn't swing it. I have to be content with knowing just enough. Enough to help. Enough to understand. Enough to reach out. But most of the time, their business will be none of mine.

While it hurts to be cut out of the loop, I have to remain mature about this. I cannot keep making what's happening to them about me. Besides, their newly claimed privacy has a kickback. It gives me the space to claim more of my own. And I'm certainly not about to tell them the real reason I have no hair down there.

That's Zed's and my little secret.

Chapter 5

Been There

BESIDES, I REMEMBER my whole life being a secret from my parents when I was a teenager.

Not that my kids believe I ever was one.

Apparently I don't understand anything, and couldn't possibly know how they're feeling. It's obviously lost on them that I have 'been there and done that' when it comes to all things adolescent, give or take a bit of technology. To them I am, and have always been, forty-something with a bit of a belly and a Caesarean scar. But I still clearly remember the angst and drama of getting boobs and pubes and tracing the pale striations of stretch marks on my thighs – praying they would fade in time – as my body grew too fast for my skin. I can't forget the hours I spent in front of mirrors dabbing cover-up on spots, or on my bed, sobbing because the guy I 'loved with all my heart' had a blind spot when it came to me.

In my teens:

- I spent hours sprawled on my folks' bed talking on the landline (remember those?).
- My father developed a verbal tic that went like this: 'The telephone is a line of communication. Say what you have to say and get off.'
- I was impatient for boobs but when they came, I felt cheated – they looked nothing like the ones in my friend Shawn's *Hustler* magazine (one was bigger than the other – I mean, really! Couldn't I even get a set of matching ones?).
- I believed there was a direct correlation between my pants size and my happiness.
- I *wanted* to give blow jobs.
- I thought 'old' was anyone over the age of forty.
- I cried listening to pop songs, especially 'Living Next Door to Alice'.
- I wrote long, rambling (and rhyming) love poems to different boys every week as my 'soulmate' kept changing.
- Once, in the middle of summer, I ran up and down a hill outside the house of my crush, hoping he'd catch a glimpse of me and … I guess I never thought further than that. I nearly got heatstroke.

It's just as well I kept a journal from the age of fourteen lest these priceless insights get lost:

'I'm sixteen today. The best present was that Max came on the bus too – all the girls wanted him to know that I'm LEGAL. Then Max came to sit near me at the back and I really do adore him a very lot.'

'This year is a year for a new me (Diet that means) and a new boyfriend ... watch out boys ...'

'Last night Ian came over. He kept on wanting to kiss me and hug me and hold my hand – sometimes I honestly wonder if we are just friends.'

'I hope the holidays aren't too boring, and if they are then I hope at least that it is very hot so I can catch a tan ...'

'On Friday Jane came over to my place and we talked and talked the whole day about how we are both dying for a boyfriend and how we really MUST do something about it.'

'Dave and I went out for coffee ... and then he drove me home. He Frenched me at the front door and it wasn't bad, better than the ones before.'

'Liquids today!'

'Cathy came over today so I could help her with maths. She is a great friend and I do love her but boy do I envy her stunning blue eyes and her gorgeous figure.'

Reading over my teenage diaries is a kind of personal torture. I cannot tell you what a relief it is that I survived the idiocy of being a vacuous, insecure, boy-hungry, exclamation-mark-overusing teenage girl. What I needed back then, it seems, was a life. Thankfully I wasn't a lone freak. When I asked a bunch of adults what they remember about their teenage years, here's what they said:

- 'Being in love with several boys (at different times) who didn't know I existed. So sad; today most of them are losers.' (Sharise)
- 'Depression and loneliness – and the comfort of reading.' (Crystal)

- 'My music, my books and playing music made it tolerable.' (Kevin)
- 'Friends, friends and friends. And now they're FB friends. And, of course, many an unrequited crush.' (Jackie)
- 'Not being part of the in-crowd, or any crowd really, and hating school.' (Alex)
- 'Not fitting in, always wearing the wrong clothes, living in the wrong neighbourhood and being misunderstood. And being called a lesbian for having a motorcross bike and riding it better than the boys.' (Suzette)
- 'Lingering in the change rooms at the squash centre to satisfy my emerging (gay) sexuality – and having one of the guys approach me with his police badge, suspecting me of thieving.' (Tim)
- 'The intensity of feelings: love, loneliness, injustice. And of finding my own space. My memory of being with my friend Kate after a school play, sitting alone crying at the injustice of that play and the moon was so intensely beautiful and feeling so intensely hopeless and aware of how helpless and insignificant we were in the world – and we knew we could change the world as soon as we got out of school.' (Ingrid)
- 'I hated school. Every single thing about it. Every day, every aspect. HATED it.' (Gloria)
- 'Always wondering who my first proper kiss would be from.' (Michelle)
- 'My life was BOYS + DIETING … and friends. My family really didn't feature. They were loving and wonderful but I felt that only my friends could possibly understand me and what I was going through. I remember my brother saying,

"Stephanie went into her room at thirteen and came out at eighteen."' (Stephanie)

- 'Meeting a boy at a *Grease* party and dancing and dancing and dancing and feeling for the first time when one is in absolute sync with another.' (Helen)
- 'Lots of kissing. Parties, slow dancing and kissing. Being in love ALL the time.' (Stephanie)
- 'I remember getting drunk and fighting.' (Warren)
- 'My most enduring crush fell in love with someone else (a sweet girl whom I couldn't hate) but mostly I spent my teenage years as a lonely freak looking for a place to belong.' (Lauren-Joy)
- 'Never quite fitting in any group, wanting boobs and an hourglass figure, fighting constantly with Mum and Dad, switching rapidly amongst three simultaneous emotions.' (Ali)
- 'I had very small boobs at fourteen. I was so envious of my friends with big breasts. I was convinced no boy would love a girl who wore a size 32AA bra. I remember stuffing my bra with tissues and cottonwool and one night my date put his hand into my bra and came up with a handful of padding. So embarrassing!' (Cyndi)

This imbecility, it seems, is a rite of passage and we should leave our teenagers to it. In their world, it all seems to make a certain kind of mad sense – the dieting, the obsession with sexual relationships and peers and parties. It's impossible to explain it to adults who throw around big words like 'consequences', 'self-esteem' and 'responsibility'. It's simple: if the person we like likes us, we have self-esteem. If he or she doesn't, we don't. And no amount of parental input about how smart, special and talented we are makes us feel any better about ourselves. Teenagers live on a highway of peer traffic, in the superlative lane. Every friend, encounter, song and glance is 'the best' or 'the worst'. Being a teenager is an extreme sport of its own kind.

Likewise, every adult is a survivor of those catastrophic years of being flung between rocketing euphoria and sky-falling desperation. We all remember being that half-kid, half-adult creature – desperate for sex but not getting it, obsessed with how we look and what others think, hungering for independence but clueless about how to make it work.

But what I also clearly recall is freaking out when adults said, 'I know how you're feeling.' The active listening, the 'I also had a crush on someone who didn't like me back ...' and 'They're not really your friends if they didn't invite you ...' gave me the creeps and made me feel even lonelier.

Back then, I didn't want grown-ups to 'get it'. Their 'getting it' meant they understood me and what adults don't seem to 'get' is that the crux of teenage identity is to *not* be understood. Teens rely on their disaffection from parents so they can figure out who they are. They don't want to hear that someone else has walked their path. The narcissistic fantasy of being a teenager is the belief that you are perfectly unique and no-one could possibly ever understand you. Then you grow up and realise that most people felt just the same, and there's nothing very special about you and your experience at all.

Part of understanding teenagers is allowing them their fantasy.

And, to be fair, being a teen today is heaps harsher than it was back in the dark ages. For one thing, we got to do all our stupid things before social media. We didn't have to endure, during the most vulnerable time of our lives, the relentless social blitz of Facebook, Twitter, Tumblr, Instagram, Ask.Fm – never being able to escape knowing where everyone else was on Saturday night, who was at the party and who hooked up with whom. Our kids are ruthlessly accosted with updates on other peoples' lives when being part of the crowd is all that counts. They live without any social protection, no interactive condom to prevent rejection infection. Theirs is a crueller world and they need serious muscle to survive it.

So maybe we're dumber than they are in some respects – their brains have been wired for the internet; their technological intelligence is intuitive (evolutionary, even) and they're connected to the events of the world in ways we weren't at their age. But to parent confidently and unflinchingly, we must remember that we're still smarter than they are simply because we've been around for longer. Perspective is a form of wisdom no Google-search can match.

What I know that Shannon and Jordan don't is that as much as we remember the teen years, we also forget them. We forget all but a pocketful of details – the name of our favourite teacher, the night we first smoked dope or that time our best friend taught us how to give a blow job on a Coke bottle. Just the other day I got a Facebook message from a guy called Wes: 'I am SO happy I found you at last! You have been on my mind so much, and I just wanted to touch base and find out how life is treating you.' I recognised the name, but was he the boyfriend of a school friend, or a guy I dated briefly in my twenties? I had to click on all his Facebook pictures to work it out. That friendship had slipped clear through the cracks of the years.

Most of it will wash away: the good with the bad, the ugly with the sublime. When I read back on my diary entries, more often than not, I have no idea who I am bitching about or 'loving until I take my final breath'. What we remember won't matter anyway. Life will take care of it all. Which is not to say that it didn't matter at the time. But, in the end, nothing will shatter us or save us. None of it. Being the popular girl at school will not guarantee us happiness in life, much as being the bullied nerd will not doom us to a life of shrinking victimhood. In fact, there is a strange boomerang effect to the imperatives of high school – what made us popular at school will be irrelevant in the real world and what sidelined us will become our magnetic charisma.

We can try to share this profound wisdom with our teens, but they'll ignore it. That's okay. Sympathy for what they're going through might mean we go light on teen veteran stories – just enough to remind them that we survived and they probably will too. I sometimes have a crack at: 'I don't really know how you feel, so why don't you tell me? Help me to understand.' Mostly, I score the old eye-roll and a 'Why would I want to talk to *you*?'

As I nurse that ache of rejection, I get a little reflux of my own teenage memories of being on the outside. Maybe this is a valuable dynamic: our teenagers mirror what is most wretched about being transitionally powerless, and witnessing their struggles can prompt us to stay in conversation with those parts of ourselves that also feel lonely, displaced and misunderstood. We may have been teens before selfies, planking and YouTube downloads. But our adolescent madness and stupidity still belong to us. They're still a source of been-there experience and wisdom we can draw on to soften our judgements of our teenagers and create bridges between our worlds.

So it turns out we have more in common with our teens than we believe – given that we're also freaking out behind closed doors, wondering, 'Who the fuck am I?'(Except they've got youth and time on their side.)

If we've never contemplated an identity beyond parenthood, their identity search can spark a renewed hunt for our own, if we let it.

Chapter 6

The Big Why

MY LATE GRANNY Bee got married when she was still a teenager. She was only nineteen. Then again, she belonged to an age when it was an extravagance for girls to finish school or have a career. When one just 'got on with it' after one's mother died suddenly at the age of thirty-six of tuberculosis and one's father married one's aunty in quick succession. There was no therapy, no grief counselling ('Goodness me, not at all.'). She struggled for many years to conceive. After several miscarriages, she finally fell pregnant with my mother in 1939, just as the world had gone to war.

I once asked her how she felt about this. 'Felt?' she asked, as if feelings were some high-tech gadget she hadn't come across. 'Oh, my darling, I just sobbed and sobbed. I kept wondering what sort of a world I was bringing my child into. I thought I'd made a terrible mistake.'

Now, my granny was no philosopher, but she understood that having a child is contextual. It is a historical act. At the very least, it is a statement (whether conscious or unconscious) about our optimism that the sun will probably come up tomorrow (which is not to say that depressives shouldn't procreate, even though in my darker moments I've wondered whether this isn't a weirdly split-off impulse or, at the very least, a mindless experiment with someone else's soul).

The world today is arguably a better place than it was in 1939, but somehow that doesn't matter at 3 am. I can work myself up into as much of a lather as my poor granny must have done in the wee hours, except I angst about global warming, tsunamis, bush-fires and madmen in movie theatres who open fire while people are getting stuck into their popcorn and choc-tops. I think of that poor woman who was raped and killed in Melbourne on her way home from a party, and boys who spike girls' drinks.

I make my way to the bathroom for a wee, but back in bed lesser agonies gnaw at me: I worry about whether all that computer time is frying Jordan's neural pathways and what Shannon's Vitamin D levels are. I can jolly well keep myself up 'til 4 am trying to remember when Shannon last invited a friend over or Jordan ate anything with Omega 3s; or wondering what it means that Shannon would rather watch *Australia's Next Top Model* or *Project Runway* than go for a swim or a bike ride. By 4.30 am I'm obsessing over the effects of Ask.Fm on Shannon's self-worth, especially those anonymous questions about her 'tits' and whether she 'takes it up the arse' (I know, I know, I shouldn't have pried).

By the time I hear the first birds cheeping outside, I have lost hours of sleep to my fear that I have delivered my kids into a world I do not trust. And what good has it done me? I will be cranky and awful to be around today. And the world didn't get any safer because of my sleepless night.

At least my insomnia is offset by my sense that I am a caring mother. No-one can say I don't grapple with the big questions of how I can prepare my kids for this world. I do not assume they will automatically be empathic to real suffering. I am doing my best to make them into good people (which is more than I can say for the parents of that foul little bitch Ashleigh, who handed out invitations to her sixteenth birthday party in front of Shannon to everyone but Shannon).

I am not romanticising neurosis: too many of us over-think parenting. But, then again, some of us don't think about it enough. What becomes clear as our kids slide into teenagehood is that it's just not good enough to live the unexamined life.

If we've never asked ourselves why we had kids (beyond the societal expectation of heterosexual procreation) then now is the time. If we had our kids while on a life trajectory autopilot, once we hit the teen turbulence we can't escape the inquiry.

We might have screamed, 'Why? Oh, why?' as a person in a white coat sporting a head torch suggested we 'push'. But that doesn't really count. Early parenthood is a street party of 'What was I thinking?' moments, but sleep deprivation is a corrupting force even to the most stable of minds. The toddler years deliver their own brand of 'God help me' moments as shrieking kids take to flopping facedown in the aisle when urgent items such as chocolate and toilet paper haven't yet made it into the trolley. As our kids stretch, the lulls between these WTF??s grow;

they may only come knocking again at a particularly gruelling parent–teacher interview or when cleaning out our teenage son's wastepaper bin (which we should never do).

Like resetting a watch or rebooting a computer, intermittently reconsidering why we had kids is good internal housekeeping. Self-examination, like the pelvic floor, is a radically underworked muscle. Having kids is the master class that forces us to do this internal work.

Discounting the contraceptively disadvantaged Third World and unwanted pregnancies, if we're fortunate to procreate voluntarily, our answers to this question may help us navigate the sometimes bewildering terrain of parenting teenagers. Knowing why we are doing something helps us get clear about our expectations and locates the airbag of self-insight we might need to inflate when parenting hits the rough spots. *Why* is a homing question. It loops us back to the start, to when things began. *Why* also becomes a stopover in times of stress or crisis.

The question *why* is not just practical but philosophical. It is also a core question at the heart of our identities, which, whether we're aware of it or not, we've been in the process of creating since we ourselves were teenagers. At some point we all ask the big questions like: Are you there, God? Yarmulke or keffiyeh? Jesus or Buddha? Boys or girls or both or neither? Chase the money or the music? City or suburbs? Who is my tribe? What's the purpose of my life? What gives my life meaning?

Some of us try to meet these questions by having children. Through them, we form our sense of belonging and identity. Our kids, then, inadvertently and quite without their knowledge or consent, sometimes become the answer to our own big *Who am I in this world?* questions.

That's a lot of pressure to put on a kid.

So why did I have kids?

While some girls go soggy thinking about their dream man, I used to fantasise about my dream babies. From the age of five I planned my offspring, including the sex and names of the four children I would someday have. On our second date I announced to Zed that I wanted a baby the following year. Motherhood, you could say, has been on my agenda from the start. While I've always believed I'm just one of those 'love kids' people (unlike those 'can't-stand-kids' people), there is more to it than that. Through-out my childhood my folks were naturally distracted by the demands of a child with special needs (my older sister, Carolyn, was born hard-of-hearing). Despite how much my parents loved me and my two fabulous sisters, I kind of always felt alone in the world. So, if I'm honest about my motivations for having kids, it was to give them all the love and attention I felt I was short-changed on as a child. Do you see what I'm saying here? I had them for *me*. To fix my problems.

Perhaps there's nothing inherently pathological about having kids to satisfy a sense of personal fulfilment, especially if we bring self-awareness to our parenting. At least I didn't have kids to expand my personal labour force or to score a baby bonus from the government.

Still, I wish I could say that becoming a mother was some grand, selfless submission to the Spirit in the Sky or Fate or Destiny. Or because Shannon's and Jordan's souls chose me as a vessel and I volunteered to offer up my body, life and energy for the sake of their human incarnation. Frankly, I didn't really think much about who my kids would be once they were all grown up and I was finished playing mummy-mummy with them.

When they were babies, I dressed them up like dolls and paraded them for the specific purpose of being admired by others. When Shannon had her six-week vaccinations and cried, I cried. When Jordan broke his leg last year and was writhing in agony, I needed painkillers. Sometimes it's hard for me to tell the difference between their pain and mine. Let's not even talk about that swelling feeling I get in my chest when they sing or exhibit kindness, or when people tell me how gorgeous, clever and special they are. The boundaries between us are that fuzzy. When I talk of *my* children, that's as possessive a pronoun as you can get.

But here's where I have to be careful. Firstly, they are not *mine*. In a world post-slavery, we don't own people (we know this, right?). Secondly, pride is not blacklisted as one of the seven deadly sins for no reason. It languishes in the thesaurus as a synonym for hubris. A little too close to arrogance and self-conceit, even sometimes confused with haughtiness, it seems to be socially acceptable as soon as we feel it on behalf of our kids. The Jews have fused pride with parental love and given us the word *nachas*, which applies to just about any situation involving one's offspring; for example, 'My darling, you've given me such *nachas* by winning that Most Improved Behaviour Award' or 'What *nachas* you must have from Indiana playing the flugel horn at the Sydney Opera House last month' or 'Selwyn, when you recite *A Midsummer Night's Dream* in Japanese, I get such *nachas*.' *Nachas* is to the Jewish mother what oxygen is to other life forms. This accounts for the joke: what's the difference between a Rottweiler and a Jewish mother? A Rottweiler eventually lets go. The stereotype of the Jewish, Italian, Greek, Lebanese and other Mediterranean mother is one who 'lives for her children' – as if that weren't an emotional noose that tightens with every utterance.

Kahlil Gibran was probably specifically addressing these mothers when he wrote:

Your children are not your children
They are the sons and the daughters of life's longing for itself
They come through you, but they are not from you
And though they are with you, they belong not to you.
You can give them your love but not your thoughts
They have their own thoughts
You can house their bodies but not their souls
For their souls dwell in the place of tomorrow
Which you cannot visit, not even in your dreams
You can try to be like them but you cannot make them just
    like you
You can strive to be like them but seek not to make them like you

Whatever our reasons for having kids, it seems a big ask that they live out their lives as extensions of our CVs for the sole purpose of being our boast material. Yet we treat their achievements as proof of our success as parents and their failures and imperfections as personally crucifying. We act as if parenting ought to be a feel-good business built on the sweat of self-sacrifice.

However we make meaning of this strange, bewildering relationship with our kids, we have to watch out for that virus of living vicariously through them. Carl Jung warned that 'the greatest burden a child must bear is the unlived life of the parents'.

Whether we had them by default or design, they do not belong to us. If we do not know this inherently, they will teach this to us as they become teenagers. No matter how close we are to our kids when they are little, they will shift into the shadows of their teenage selves; and whatever hold we believed we had, whatever pull, influence or magic we once cast over them, will loosen.

We are scripted into their procreation – their lives flow from us but manifest as something separate. They come through us and they leave us, too. The parenting earth on which we stand has a deep, natural fault that breaks so that their continent can disconnect from ours, and they can float away. They do not belong to us like an heirloom or a family farm. We can't tag them, brand them, have them valued and expect them to increase our status or earn interest on our behalf. They belong to us in the mercurial way that our history belongs to us, like memory belongs to us.

Our work is to accept the inevitability and rightness of that separation. Childbirth is never over. We're always birthing them, letting go of them, giving them to the world.

Our kids will not – and should not – tolerate being lived through.

They know this.

Which is why they tell us to *get a life*. To make room in their own for themselves.

Chapter 7
Get Your Story Straight

I AM GRATEFUL TO law school for two things: for Zed, and for my ability to make fine distinctions.

Zed and I met as first-year law lecturers and, with offices next door to each other, it was only two years before the friendship took a Harry-met-Sally turn. In law school, I also learned the value of subtle distinction. For example, there is a big difference between a moral obligation and a legal obligation. If you walk past a drowning person, legally you can keep walking – unless you owe a duty of care to that person. The law won't hold you responsible if that person drowns (though good luck trying to live with yourself after that). Also, when someone is charged with a crime, they're not guilty until a court of law finds they are. So when talking about the 'Boston bombers' it's correct to say 'alleged Boston bombers' unless there is a legal confession or a court has convicted them.

My legal training has been excellent preparation for parenting teenagers, particularly during interrogation. Every couple of months Jordan tries to guilt me into letting him get some violent video game with an MA15+ rating. He explains that he knows it's 'just a game'. He tells me he has no intention of killing anyone, hijacking cars, hiring prostitutes or robbing banks 'in real life'.

Like a rational parent, I go onto YouTube to watch the gameplay so that when I refuse I actually know why I'm refusing. Then I tell him, 'Nice try.' And I brace myself for the avalanche of invective.

Apparently everyone else's parents allow their kids to have these games.

Apparently I am stunting his growth and ruining his social life.

Apparently all his friends think I'm a bitch.

He tells me I'm a hypocrite because I let him watch movies that are MA15+ but I won't let him play video games. 'How can you justify this?' he says, and, 'I just don't get your logic.'

I calmly explain that video games have an addictive quality that movies don't. That in most cases when he's watching an MA15+ movie, it's with adult supervision.

'So what? What difference does adult supervision make?'

I know this is a good question and I have absolutely no idea what the answer is. But do you see how they will grill you?

In answering Jordan, I make up some waffle that 'having an adult presence there breaks the circuit of the impact ...' and I mumble a few other things about brain chemicals and dopamine and hope he'll just let it go.

I think guiltily of the author Jonathan Safran Foer, who, when his wife was pregnant with their first child, spent a year investigating factory farming so as not to inflict his vegetarianism on his forthcoming kid without being able to rationally and scientifically justify it. He subsequently wrote *Eating Animals*, a deeply considered treatise on human cruelty to innocent creatures.

Not all of us can be so scrupulous with our life choices, so mindful of the totalitarian regime that is the parenting experience on the life of a child – nor so lucky as to spend a year doing research while living off an advance from a publisher. But Safran Foer certainly raises the bar on the old parental 'because I said so'.

Jordan rolls his eyes at me. He mutters some obscenities under his breath. He tells me that in a court of law, no-one would support my argument because it sucks and is full of holes and when he goes to his friends' he's going to play these games anyway, so what's the difference, because I can't stop him.

Which is true. I have to recognise the limits of my ability to control him.

But this is not where the conversation ends because there are two things I do control: I control my value system and the home environment in which my teens are growing up.

When our kids become teenagers they force us to up our consciousness game. So I have a responsibility to make sure my kids know who I am, what I stand for and what I expect of them. Just because I can't control what they do doesn't mean that my home becomes a free-for-all. Our kids generously give us about ten to twelve years to get our story straight. Until then, we can lie, make things up, dodge and weave without any danger of being found out. Little kids will innocently accept our pronouncements either out of fear (if we're a scary parent) or because we said so and we know everything. It's a decent window of time for us to work out who we are and what we stand for. If we don't, our teenagers will expose our every emotional and psychological weakness – even stowaways we had no idea we were hiding on board. They will insult us, reject us and make us minuscule while they're experimenting with their own identities. If we are insecure, we may find ourselves smashing the kitchen counter with a soup ladle or screeching mean things at people who cross the road too slowly when we're in a hurry. It's not a dignified space to occupy.

Few provocations will set off a hormonally ravaged teenager as much as a juvenile adult who hasn't got his shit together. Teenagers will cross-examine us until they find the cracks because they can only start to figure out who they are by testing us on who we are. They need to know that we know who we are. We must have confidence the way men who wear budgie-smugglers have confidence; in other words, we cannot worry what others think of us. Except that we should care what our teens think of us because we need them to respect us. This is a conundrum, but it's not unworkable.

'Because I say so' may need to be a last-resort option because it's harder for them to respect an unjustified decision. But saying 'Because this doesn't fit with my value system' is a handy alternative. And, having said that, we had better be clear just what our value system is.

Parenting, therefore, needs a framework, a vision of life that it is in service to. Otherwise it is just an accrual of impulsive, reactionary blunders, impelled by anxiety and ego. So we must begin with understanding what that vision is: who we are, what we are about. What are the things we believe make for a meaningful life? These are some of mine:

- kindness
- service – to others, to humanity
- generosity, sharing

- creativity
- travel
- conversation
- books and movies
- sex and intimacy (all in the right time and place)
- ritual, spirituality and prayer
- exercise, movement
- healthy eating – as much fruit, vegetables and organic, non-processed foods as possible
- touch
- friendship
- music
- charity, giving
- taking (calculated) risks
- being vulnerable
- solitude and down time.

The only way for me to pass on these values is to live them because, frankly, nobody wants a lecture.

Teenagers need to feel the tent-pegs of our choices around them, holding them in place. If they sense we are lazy or that decisions haven't been made about whether pornography, smoking, drinking, lying or taking things that don't belong to you are acceptable, they play silly buggers with our slackness. Our values set the bar on what we expect of them and kickstart their own internal conversations about what their values might be.

My friend Mimi grew up without any parental expectations, which left her feeling unmoored and unsure. Her beautiful green eyes flash brightly as she insists, 'Our kids need to know where we stand and that we have expectations of them. This "whatever you do is cool" attitude doesn't cut it. We must stand firm so they can fight hard to work out who they are in relation to us.'

These are her expectations of her children:

- I expect you to respect me and yourself.
- I expect you to respect the natural world.
- I expect you to try hard in school – and do your best, not in every subject, but in the subjects you enjoy.
- I expect you to follow your passions.

The follow-through – where it all really sinks in – happens when the talk becomes our walk.

In my early twenties I went on a self-defence course after a spate of attacks on women in my social circle. There I learned how to say 'No!' and mean it, as well as how to puncture someone's Adam's apple with a pen or a forefinger should such an undiplomatic gesture ever be necessary. Trust me, I had to be *taught* how to do this. Nothing in my training as a human being made this seem natural – to bare one's teeth, shove back, kick, elbow or poke someone with the intention of getting them to back off.

As parents, we must be able to bare our teeth – metaphorically and verbally – so our kids know when the lines have been crossed. There's a subtle distinction between exerting power over our teenagers and setting the limits on obnoxious behaviour.

A while back I was chatting to a woman who confided that her teenage sons always make sexist and misogynist comments. She was confounded and deeply upset by this. 'They just don't respect me,' she said miserably.

I made suggestions about 'laying down rules' and 'invoking consequences for rude behaviour' but she shrugged: 'They'll just laugh at me.'

'What does your husband say about this? Why doesn't he step in and let them know that it's not okay to disrespect women?' I asked.

'Where do you think they learn it from?' she asked helplessly.

I learned an important lesson from my conversation with this tormented mother: that we cannot lose control of the reins of our parenting, otherwise our teenagers, sensing weakness, will take over and start to bully us. I've seen too many parents who are afraid of their own kids.

This begs the question: where do teenagers learn their bullying? From us, of course.

C'mon, we all know that parenting young children is just a sanctioned form of bullying. We make the rules and we enforce them. Sometimes we even hurt our kids physically to make them comply. We embarrass and shame them to keep them doing what we want them to do. We shout at them, make them eat their broccoli, deny them dessert and make them stand in the naughty corner. We remove privileges and treats. All this is done without us ever having to account for our decisions and actions. No-one monitors whether our actions were justified. We get free bullying rights.

We also chart the course of our kids' lives: where they are born, where they live, what religion they're exposed to (if any), what school they go to, and the food they eat. If you are reading this book, you probably don't live in a country where your kids are regarded as part of your labour force or personal wealth. But there are still too many societies today in which parents decide whether and to what extent their kids will be educated (the girls usually draw the short straw) and when and who they will marry. For daring to disobey, kids can be banished from the family home, disowned and cut out of the will, or even killed for insubordination or bringing 'shame' on a family.

In a moderated version of this tyranny, even the most liberal of us, to a greater or lesser extent, lay down rules around smoking, drinking, drugs and who our kids can hang out with. We lock doors, we impose curfews, we punish rebelliousness, sometimes even with physical assault. Some parents 'forbid' their kids to be gay, transsexual or transgendered and force them to study law, accounting, dentistry or animal husbandry even when the kid has a particular aptitude for building sand sculptures or playing the drums.

We parents can all too easily slide into a form of boundless megalomania around our children because of this mistaken belief that they belong to us. We exert power over them for so long that we begin to imagine we *have* power over them.

So, during the teenage years when they realise that we are not all-powerful, they bully back. It's payback time. It's only fair. But see, we are the adults and we know how to deal with bullies. We cannot give in to them. We have to stand our ground while keeping our reactivity in check – which comes from having our shit in order and remembering that we are their parents. It is our job to *parent* them.

There is a line between normal teenage rudeness and downright shitty, unacceptable behaviour. Our job is to build a Great Wall of China between the two so that no-one is in any doubt about where that line is and who's actually still the boss (we are, remember?). Without that barrier, they'll just slide from being teenage bullies into being adult bullies.

So when I finally run out of answers for Jordan and I am, obviously, 'illogical', 'ridiculous', 'inconsistent', 'pathetic' and 'irrational' I simply agree. Okay, I am illogical. But I'm the grown-up and I still make the rules in this house. I know who I am and I will not allow those games into our home. He, in turn, is free to hate my guts.

I'm not here to be a 'cool parent' or my kids' friends. I won't smile benignly and turn the other cheek at foul-mouthed, prick-like disrespect. I will not become a parenting wuss, a spineless, wheedling, mollycoddling softie.

No way will I fold and become my teenagers' *beyatch*.

Chapter 8

The Brain behind the Mouth

'**Y**OU DON'T MIND if I sidle up next to you?' a man holding a beer drawled at me.

I was at a friend's barbecue and he was clearly a couple of beers ahead, which is probably why he didn't notice my wedding ring. I graciously indulged him by laughing at his terrible jokes and feigning flattery at his fumbling flirtatiousness despite the beer breath and badmouthing of his ex. But when he took out a cigarette and prepared to light it, I asked him sweetly if he would mind not smoking right next to me. To which he replied, 'Who the fuck do you think you are, telling me what to do? Do you think you're better than me?'

Startling avalanches such as this response are what we come to expect from the most innocuous of interactions with a teenager. It is too easy to get into an argument with them, by which I mean you will not see it coming and will stumble into it like you would into a pothole on the sidewalk. For example:

'Did you eat your lunch, Jordan?'

'Why are you hassling me? You never stop hassling me.'

'I'm just asking if you ate your lunch.'

'Will you just get off my back? I'm sick of being cross-examined.'

'I'll take that as a no.'

'I don't have to answer any questions! Just leave me alone, Goddammit!'

Or: 'Whose party are you going to?'

'A friend's.'

'Does your friend have a name?'

'What difference does it make? It's a friend of mine, okay? You don't know them.'

'I want to know who the adult in charge is.'

'Their parents, okay? Do you want their driver's licence and their passports? Don't you trust me? You're such a neurotic mother.'

To work one's way out of these exchanges without becoming ridiculous is an art. No-one strives to straggle out of an argument with a teenager clutching the shreds of one's temper and dignity. A modicum of adult poise, combined with rudimentary knowledge of the system one is navigating, is vital. Just as it is prudent to glance through the instruction manual before operating a piece of equipment, we may need some understanding of the brain behind the mouth to help regulate our reactions.

First up, we are navigating two systems of transition that can roughly be broken down into the bio-neurological and the emotional (adolescence or puberty refers to changes to the body and its chemistry – the humps and bumps, the influx of hormones and the brain changes) and the social (being a teenager is an identity). They overlap but are by no means the same. Combined, they present a daunting force to be reckoned with.

Like antibiotics, the radio and TV, the 'teenager' is a twentieth-century invention. Not so long ago, in the early twentieth century, humans were children and then at some undefined point they became adults. There was no identity associated with puberty. A child was a child until s/he was old enough to work or get married (which could have been as young as thirteen). Kids were celebrated largely because they were cheap labour and could be sent down mines, up chimneys and into fields and factories. It was only post World War I, when a modern, humane sensibility kicked in, that children began to be seen as people with special needs – primarily that of needing a childhood. Enlightened nations woke up to the fact that forcing children to work was, in fact, exploitation (a form of sanctioned slavery) and that kids needed a longer and more comprehensive education to help them succeed in a fast-changing world. Today the term 'child labour' is a dirty phrase and not one you want to bandy around (as in 'Let's bring it back') in civilised company – though, of course, it's still prolific all over the Third World.

Sociologists and psychologists began to use the term 'teenager' in the US around 1920 to describe this interim phase between childhood and adulthood. This coincided with a couple of significant historical and social changes: the proliferation of high schools and the invention of motor cars. Until this era, kids were stuck at home indefinitely, scraping by with what little home-schooled education was on offer, helping out with the family farm or business, and sneaking behind sheds to experiment sexually with neighbours and family friends.

With cars came freedom and independence. Teens could escape parental scrutiny, go out on dates and experiment with different relationships. Four wheels and an engine took the 'courtship game' out of the hands of parents who, until then, orchestrated and controlled it from introduction to marriage, and put it in the hands of young people themselves, who redefined it as the 'dating game', which they could now control themselves. Cars offered privacy. Snatched kisses under the watchful gaze of fretful parents quickly evolved into heavy petting and 'all-the-way' fumblings on back seats.

But that's not all. Cars and buses shifted horizons: adolescents were no longer stuck at the family home and could be schooled far away and for longer periods. Young people began to leave home to go to high school. This escape from grown-ups and the opportunity to gather in large groups of others of the same age created the perfect conditions for the emergence of a teenage culture. And with youth on their side, they embraced it like a new religion.

So the term 'teenager' is not a biological description but a cultural or social one. Like all identities, it becomes heavily politicised, in the sense that it is larger than the individual. Because it is a horizontal identity, in Andrew Solomon's terms, teens do not share it with their parents and this helps them differentiate from us. It is this identity that accounts for peer pressure, popularity and other group-driven dynamics. Trying to stop a teenager from following the crowd is like trying to hold back the pull of a tide. But tides aside, there's a shitload going on biologically, too – and we're not just talking boobs and pubes and hormones. We're talking brains here.

I am, generally speaking, a great admirer of nature and the mysterious functioning of the human body, which seems to have been designed with sacred perfection. The adolescent brain, however, is a flagrant exception, largely because of the bizarre timing of these changes.

The human brain goes through two major growth spikes – the first is in utero, the second in adolescence. Then in the first twelve years of life, the brain grows like weeds, in every direction, which explains why small kids pick up new languages, musical abilities, swimming and sports so easily. The thickening of grey matter in the brain peaks when girls are eleven and boys twelve and a half. Then, come adolescence, there is a massive thinning out or pruning as the old structures of the brain get discarded and new connections are forged to make the brain function more specialised and sophisticated. The white matter becomes denser, which makes nerve transmissions faster and more efficient. The purpose of brain development in adolescence is to increase integration, which allows different areas of the brain to connect. It's a neuron get-together, a synapse conference that allows more complex functions to emerge.

So how does the brain know which neurons to thin out?

Okay, this is scary news for parents. The pruning process is driven by activity. Busy neurons will be retained and promoted, lazy ones hanging around doing nothing will be cut. The activities that our teens spend most of their time on (Xbox, video games, watching porn, Facebooking, texting, watching TV, playing guitar, taking photographs, writing poetry, playing sports) determine the connections that will be strengthened and reinforced. Our kids' brains become stronger at whatever they're engaged with. This is one hell of a powerful reason for us to limit the number of hours they spend in mindless, addictive, brain-squelching passivity.

In the disco of their craniums, the party moves to the limbic area of the brain, which regulates emotion, motivation, evaluation and attachment. Teenagers are flooded with emotions: passion, excitement and a kind of intensity that can be frightening to onlookers. Let's not forget the hormonal influx – including adrenal sex hormones in the limbic system, which affects serotonin and other neurochemicals that regulate mood and excitability. A teenager is a tinderbox of feelings. Their brains are circuits of extremes. Not only do they experience explosive emotions but, like ants to the picnic, they are also drawn to actively seek out experiences that will give them these mad rushes of emotion. They have a hunger for thrills, intense sensations and experiences, and are magnetically drawn to risky experiences. Telling them to 'be careful' and 'not do anything stupid' is like trying to negotiate with a bull terrier to 'play nicely' as he spots an Alsatian in heat.

If their incessant whines about how 'bored' they are drive us batty, dopamine could be to blame. Dopamine is the neuro-transmitter that helps control the brain's reward and pleasure centres. During adolescence, baseline levels of dopamine are lower – which means teenagers find most things boring. It is a neurochemical challenge for teens to feel motivated unless it's by something immediate that affects their day-to-day lives. But when dopamine is released, for example during gaming or any activity that inspires reward, the levels are much higher, which is why teens are so compelled to do new and risky things, why their impulsivity is enhanced and why their susceptibility to addictions is increased. What we think of as perverse, thrill-seeking teenage madness is just a powerful cocktail of brain chemicals.

The pineal gland starts to secrete melatonin, but in teens it takes longer for these levels to rise. So their brains are programmed to go to sleep later – which is why it's so hard to wake a sleeping teenager.

Now, this is where the biology really seems perverse: the last part of our teenager's brain to be chiselled and shaped is the prefrontal cortex. This lobe helps to plan, prioritise and measure the consequences of our actions and suppress our impulses. It is the centre for decision-making and inhibiting antisocial behaviour. It actually only fully develops at the age of twenty-four. Do we wonder why teenagers have poor impulse control and are excruciatingly self-conscious? When we rail against reckless risk-taking, rule-breaking, emotional outbursts and the impassioned pursuit of sex, drugs and rock 'n' roll, we're decrying a *biological* function. So, just to spell it out: the final part of the brain to grow up is the part able to decide, 'I think I'll study for my maths test first, feed the dog and then I'll Facebook my friends or play FIFA for four hours.' Adolescents struggle to be more responsible because the part of their brain that regulates responsibility hasn't grown yet.

Brain changes during adolescence mean that teenagers are chemically driven to take mad risks and seek emotionally frenetic experiences at a time when their ability to control their impulses is at its lowest – and not necessarily due to any lack of will on their part. If you weren't shitting yourself before, I'll bet you are now.

All this brain-changing can be destabilising. The onset of mental illnesses such as schizophrenia and bipolar disorder typically occurs in adolescence and contributes to high rates of teenage suicide. As parents, we need to be vigilant and monitor our teens' behaviours so we can intervene if it seems called for.

But getting their attention is a real challenge. For the first twelve years, our kids develop attachment to us, their primary caregivers, for a sense of safety and belonging. In adolescence they slough us off and look for attachment from their friends and peers. They no longer want what we offer because they're getting it elsewhere. This rejection coincides with their infuriating insistence that we get them the right 'stuff' (the coloured Nikes, the beats, the latest iPhone). To us they seem spoilt and selfish (because the demands usually come with a sense of entitlement) but all this stems from their overwhelming compulsion to fit in and belong. They need to wear boardies halfway down their butts with Hugo Boss or Bonds undies sticking out, or copy whatever is trending. These totems are their entry passes, their passports into the group. Without these 'things' they feel tribe-less, lost, alone. (Not that we should keel over each time they demand the latest thing so they can keep up with the Kardashians, but it helps to understand their desperation.)

So what are we to do? Stand by helplessly as our teenagers move in packs, spurred on by other teens to do reckless things like planking in dangerous places, swinging off ropes, driving drunk, or having unprotected sex at parties? Firstly, we need to remember that what we call 'irresponsible behaviour' is often just a brain operating without a prefrontal cortex. All the laws that allow teens to drive, drink and vote are arbitrary rather than based on scientific evidence. (This research certainly raises interesting questions about the extent to which teenagers are responsible for their criminal actions before twenty-five.) When they are oppositional and defiant of our authority, we can temper our reactions by reminding ourselves that their brains are still under manufacture and, to the extent that we can, we have to be their prefrontal cortex.

Secondly, it is vital that we keep this information to ourselves. There's no benefit in our kids knowing any of this so they can justify their laziness, carelessness and recklessness by blaming it on their half-arsed brain. We can't allow neuroscience to become an abuse-excuse. What's going on biologically may be the fault of nature, but it interacts with nurture, and that's the part we control. So while it's only fair for us to modify our expectations of our teens, knowing they're operating on a dodgy system, we can simultaneously encourage them to practise behaviours that don't necessarily come naturally to them, in the hope of forging new neural pathways in the process.

Finally, our cat has been a wonderful teacher in the lead-up to managing teen behaviour. See, Tanaka has a puking problem. She guzzles her food as if she's not sure where or when her next meal is coming from, and then she throws it all up. I resign myself good-naturedly to the mess when it's on the kitchen tiles, but am far more irritable when chunky, pre-digested Whiskas ends up on my desk, my unpaid bills or the freshly laundered bed linen. I have been known to get furiously cross, shout, banish her outside as punishment and lock the cat flap for an hour so she can't get back inside. My rage, however, is ridiculous. She hasn't figured out the pattern – guzzling causes vomiting. She can't help it. She is just a cat of little brain.

Sometimes when I feel my ire rising at the freakishly stupid behaviour of my teens, I just imagine they're a puking cat who doesn't know any better.

Chapter 9

Watch Them Break

WHEN THEY WERE little, I fielded my kids' questions with ease. Even when they'd ask impossible ones like 'How many penguins are there in the Antarctic?' or 'Does it rain on the moon?' I'd still offer an answer. If I was a little fuzzy on the precise facts, I'd rustle something up. It's imperative that your children believe – even for a time – that you are the oracle of wisdom and possess the answers to all of life's questions. Only irresponsible parents allow small kids to think the world is a chaotic place with insoluble problems.

But there was a definite turning point sometime in the tween years when their emotional and spiritual software kicked in and their interrogations of life became more self-conscious. Suddenly their questions became trickier to deflect deftly. They transitioned from needing information and solutions to craving meaning.

Instead of wondering where homeless people sleep when it rains, they started to wonder how people become homeless. Instead of wanting to know how far away the planets are, they questioned whether there might be life on other planets and, if so, what that means. According to Rudolph Steiner, the cognitive awakens between the ages of twelve and fourteen, when 'true thinking' emerges. Thinking is 'unconscious antipathy' – which basically means our kids start to give us a hard time.

Shannon was thirteen when I got a call from her geography teacher, who was 'concerned' because my conscientious, rule-abiding bookworm of a daughter hadn't handed in her assignment on time. I was confused. Shannon? Was the geography teacher sure we were talking about the same kid? She was sure.

I found Shannon sprawled across her bed amongst her 632 plushy toys and asked her what the deal was with the geography assignment.

'What's the point?' she sighed.

'It counts for fifty per cent of your year mark,' I pointed out.

'So?'

'If you get zero for the assignment, it will bring down your mark for geography and that will drag down your whole year mark.' This was not stuff she needed me to explain.

'So what?' she said. 'What's the point of studying geography? So what if I fail the year? I don't see the point of assignments, I don't see the point in school, or in doing well … the ozone is dying, there's war and violence and poverty, animals are becoming extinct … what difference does it make if I hand in my geography assignment or not?'

I blinked. Up 'til then, we were having a light but stern-ish conversation about high school reports and academic awards.

We were roughly in the vicinity of personal responsibility and time management to meet one's deadlines. Now where were we? Philosophy? Theology? Psychology? I scrambled while trying not to panic, which I tend to do when something doesn't feel right with my kids. Right then I was convinced she was depressed. That she needed a psychologist. Maybe even pills.

'I guess when you put it like that …' I offered lamely. 'I mean, it's not the end of the world if you don't hand it in …'

'Yes, the end of the world will happen either way,' she exhaled sadly as if she were the Lorax and had just watched the last Truffula tree fall.

Her shoulders sank dejectedly into her pillows and she cuddled a fluffy kiwi bird to her bosom. 'Please close the door on your way out,' she said before turning away from me to face the wall.

I spoke to Zed, who said, 'She'll be okay. It's just a phase. It's normal.' (This is Zed's response to all matters relating to our kids.)

I asked Shannon if she'd like to speak to me about how she was feeling.

'No, thanks.'

I asked her if she'd like to speak to someone else.

'Like a stranger?' she apprehended me, mortified.

'Yes, like a … qualified …'

'Psychologist?' she spat out.

'A counsellor,' I offered. 'Someone who knows all about how you're feeling.'

'No-one knows how I'm feeling. No-one will ever know.'

'Perhaps someone who has a lot of experience dealing with teenagers …'

'I am not going to see a shrink,' she said. 'What if someone saw me in the waiting room?'

I conceded that I hadn't thought through all the ins and outs.

I called a few psychologist friends. Eventually I found a lovely adolescent therapist who makes house calls. Clearly she understands the teenage psyche.

Shannon was furious that I'd arranged for the therapist to come to the house.

'You don't have to talk to her,' I said. 'Let's just hear what she has to say ... maybe she'll have something useful to offer.'

Shannon seethed at me for days. 'I'm not coming out of my room,' she threatened. 'It will be embarrassing for you. You'll have brought her here for nothing and you'll have to pay her, too.'

The therapist came. She sat in our lounge room. Shannon – perhaps out of begrudging politeness – joined us, and after ten minutes she started talking.

What I can say about that conversation is that leaving childhood is a wrench of the soul from the plastic wrapping of those early magical years. It brings up all the other losses our kids have borne silently on their hearts and can make them feel bleak and indifferent to handing in geography assignments, even if they do count for 50 per cent of the year mark. And sometimes, as much as we love our children, they need a third person to speak to. As much as we want to be the ones to help them through their hard times, we may not be the right ones. Sometimes our stories are too entwined in theirs for us to help them untangle and make sense of their own.

There was a lot of talking and crying that afternoon. Followed by some hugging, the boiling of kettles and the making of tea.

After the therapist left, Shannon asked if I wanted to watch *Teen Wolf* with her.

Which, of course, I was dying to do because there's nothing like watching other teenagers turn into bloodthirsty werewolves and maul each other to make one feel better about one's own kid.

As we shared a tub of macadamia and salted caramel ice-cream and debated whether Tyler Posey is more or less adorable than Taylor Lautner, I felt as if we'd got off lightly. I wondered anxiously if anxiety and depression would turn up for Shannon often in her life and, if so, how she'd figure her way through it. Watching her suffer is the hardest place for me as a mother. I'm a fixer, not a spectator. But watching our kids suffer is built into the nurturing package and we've got to become braver witnesses.

One day, your teenage son might break a leg. It will be your fault. Even if it's not your fault it will feel like your fault. Why weren't you there when it happened? Why didn't your maternal instinct kick in when he casually said, 'Just going across the road to kick a ball'?

It might happen on a perfectly pleasant Sunday afternoon, just as you were contemplating what's on TV and whether you might get Indian or Thai takeaway for dinner. Your phone will ring and you will not recognise the number. You will think, 'It's a Sunday afternoon, I'm not picking up calls from people I don't know. It can wait 'til Monday.' Your husband's mobile will ring and it will be the same number. You will think, 'Someone is really trying to get hold of me,' and you'll answer. And it will be the strangled voice of your son, who is lying across the road on the field, 'Please come now.' You will panic. You will never ever have heard that urgency in his voice. You will shriek to your husband and the two of you will rush to find him crumpled in a heap, a strange man sitting beside him – a kind, strange man who lent him his mobile phone (that unrecognisable number) – and between 3 pm and 8 pm, there will be a 000 call, an ambulance, paramedics, a lot of powerful drugs, nurses, the setting of a leg in plaster and, all through this, the deep howls of your son that blast the membranes of your DNA because you know that he has never in his life touched this pain.

You will need to sit. You will need to be strong. You will need Rescue Remedy (bugger that, you will need a Valium and a stiff whisky). You will need to not let him see that watching him suffer is worse, far, far worse, than your own suffering. You will need to be brave. And not allow him to know what you know – that basketball, sport, running, everything he lives for – is gone for the next three or four months. You will comfort him with all the silences, non-disclosures and platitudes that this calls for.

Over the next few weeks he will need help showering, getting dressed, getting in and out of bed, and this is how you will come to learn that in the years since he ran naked as a toddler through the house or jumped into the bath with you, much has changed. It will make you feel strangely pleased and weirded out, all at the same time. It will be imperative for you to keep all this to yourself and proceed as normal, even as you feel like Rip Van Winkle, who awoke to find a child in a man's body. For it is an unspoken law of parenting to spare our teenagers our reactions to what's happening to them while we OMG in the privacy of our own thoughts.

For the foreseeable future, you will empty his urinal bottle, change his sheets, help him wash, feed him painkillers, tell him, 'This will be over soon.' You will suggest that he will be a better person for this challenge. Some day. You will tell him to be grateful it's just a broken bone. You will suggest that he think about children who are really sick and don't have a chance at getting better; or remind him about children in the Third World who have no medical care, whose broken bones heal crooked, without painkillers. He will tell you that you are a terrible mother. Like maybe the worst that's ever lived.

You will want to throttle him, but only in those moments when your heart is not bursting with wretchedness for what he's experiencing. Quietly you will know that this time is a gift. That once he has his body back to himself, he will disappear into the vortex of adolescence. You will not be allowed to do anything for him. You may never again be allowed to hand him a towel, help him with his bags or rub Arnica into his leg. For these precious weeks, he is yours to take care of again, like when he was little. You must never ever let him know that, secretly, you are making the most of the access you have to him. That, for now, he needs you. You know, like a beggar counting coins, that your time with him is running low and that you will never regret the times when he called, 'Mum, I need your help,' and you were there.

You will know that the gifts are yours and yours only, and that for a thirteen-year-old boy barred from sport for four months and two seasons of basketball there can be no gifts – only a FOMO (fear of missing out), MO (missing out), banishment, isolation and misery and that it is his right to wallow in self-pity. Perspective is not a lobe yet developed in his testosterone-marinated brain. Nonetheless, it will be your job to keep throwing the fruit of perspective at him while he's in the stocks, hoping something will stick in the long term.

When our children suffer, this is our job – to be as ridiculously hopeful, as unbreakable, as a prayer flag battered by the wind.

Enduring suffering builds resilience. That's their lesson.

Watching them suffer builds resilience. That's ours.

Chapter 10

Dangerous Parents

I GET OFF THE phone to my friend Susan. She's been in tears for the past half an hour. Her daughter Brianne has been having a rough time this year.

Susan is a single mother who works long hours as an estate agent to cover their living expenses. Her only daughter, Brianne has always battled with authority and often gets in trouble at school. She's become a highly anxious teenager who picks the skin around her nails until her fingers bleed. She has some OCD traits, and insists on vacuuming her room in the morning and night, obsessed with making sure no bugs get in.

Suddenly, soon after she turned fourteen, Brianne started having panic attacks 'out of nowhere' and suffering from insomnia. Susan tried talking to her, but Brianne just shut her out. But after a terrible day at school, Brianne broke down and cried, saying, 'I don't want to be here. Why do I have to be here? Life is just too hard. I hate the system, why does nothing ever work out for me?' Susan confessed to me that Brianne has talked about suicide in the past but said 'she's too scared to actually go through with it'. My friend has been out of her mind worrying about her daughter, especially after doing some internet research about adolescent depression. In fact, she's terrified Brianne might have adolescent bipolar disorder and sought the advice of an adolescent psychologist.

The psychologist's advice was that as long as Brianne was having good days and bad days, this kind of 'bipolar' behaviour is normal in a teenager. 'Let her have her black days – as long as she's having her bright yellow days, her grey days and her pink days. It's all part of the intensity of adolescence.'

'But I want to understand what's going on for my daughter, she seems to be suffering so much,' Susan pressed.

The psychologist told her, 'Don't try to make too much sense of it. You don't need to understand it. You can't merge with the madness in adolescence.' Parents, she suggested, must be 'dull, clear and hopeful'. Our kids are the ones who get to be hopeless and morose – it is their developmental right. But 'there can only be one fourteen-year-old in the family'.

One evening Susan dragged me along to a talk on adolescent depression. Admittedly, we were out of our depth – the room was full of shrinks. We were the only two without psychology degrees and the lingo. The speaker, a professor, talked about a 'developmental depression' in teenagers who are unable to achieve a 'real self'. It seems as if a real self exists when we 'know our thoughts and feelings and can reflect on our inner world'. She talked generally about teens who can't self-soothe, commit or follow through (which sounds like every teenager I know). She said that many teens these days feel worthless and, as a result, cannot 'self-activate'. She went on to say that if a teenager cannot 'act out' they get depressed. Depression in teens is due to their early developmental needs not being met. The whole evening was filled with all kinds of psychological terminology like 'maternal availability' and 'early unconscious adaptation'. Apparently, when mothers are available to their kids early on, it sets off a cascade of chemicals that prune the synapses in a good way. Maternal warmth seemingly helps the brain grow in the early years.

In the car on the way home, Susan was silent for a while before she turned to me and said, 'It sounds like she was blaming the mother for a teenager's depression.'

I confessed that, indeed, that is what it sounded like.

'Well, how the bloody hell am I supposed to go back and fix the past?'

Ah, I knew where Susan was going with this. These teenage years are so confronting because we can't help but reflect on our early parenting decisions and wonder, 'Did I get it right?' Back then, our mistakes didn't seem irreversible: yelling when you'd had a bad day; getting caught out in a lie; insisting they eat the pumpkin or there'll be no dessert. When they were little we always imagined we could change course. Now it's too late. The fruits of our fuck-ups have fermented and have been bottled and corked.

'You can't,' I said, putting my arm around her. 'You're here now with her, and you're busting your seams to help her.'

And then I told her what Zed always says to me when I self-flagellate and feel guilty: 'Don't beat yourself up just because it's your fault.' Which is a joke, of course.

Thankfully, she found this hysterically funny.

We can never know to what extent our behaviour, genetics and mistakes impact on our kids. All our goodness as well as our messiness will mesh with their growth. It's how the system works. We can only control what we model for them – and we can choose not to model guilt and self-pity. We can *listen*, and then *act* with the best interests of our kids at heart.

Beyond that, it's a faith game.

I've been reflecting on what gets triggered in me when my kids suffer. See, I'm a bit of a wuss, really. I will happily give sky-diving, scuba diving – any kind of diving, to be honest – a big miss. I vomit at speed, which kind of put an end to rollercoasters and amusement parks early on in my life. Even the word 'adventure' gives me mild palpitations, implying, as it does, that there may very well not be a warm shower or a cosy bed waiting for me at the end of a long day. I favour 'luxurious' as an adjective to describe one's holiday destination, conjuring up fluffy pillows and the like. Getting caught in a thunderstorm, or in a rip, or fronting up with wildlife of any sort, is not my idea of fun. I do not court danger, nor seek out its adrenalin shots. Ungenerous onlookers might demote my risk-averse nature to 'boring'.

So, let me be clear: when it comes to my children, this is precisely what I hope for them, a boring and uneventful life. I pray that they never have to flee in the dead of night, watch their homes burn, run for their lives or hide for cover. I would be perfectly happy if they never encountered a snake or a deadly spider. I want them to have the fewest available opportunities to hurt themselves.

Of course, this is a delusion. I have banned my kids from engaging in inherently dangerous activities. Jordan wanted to play rugby when he was ten and I said, 'No son of mine ...' Finally, after weeks of nagging, I relented, and a week afterwards he broke his wrist playing tips at a friend's house. A year later he broke a toe at school sport while mucking around with a friend on the beach. The following year he broke his tibia and fibula one pleasant Sunday afternoon while kicking a soccer ball around on the field across the road by himself. It is obvious that all the inherently dangerous activities I am keeping him from are far less dangerous than life itself.

A friend of mine lost his wife from breast cancer when their son was three years old. He allowed his son to ride a bike to school along the busiest streets and even to ride a motorbike. I guess tragedy taught him that 'protecting our loved ones' is a fallacy.

Parents like me inch from protecting our kids from 'the dangers out there' to an eternal hover. We steer them away from bad crowds and friends with creepy tattoos and eyebrow studs. We encourage them to only date nice boys and girls. We want them never to be stood up, rejected, or have their hearts broken – never to experience loss or pain. We want them to always be happy. We want them to not be human.

The reason is that we have to watch. If there's one thing worse than suffering, it is watching our children suffer. I would exchange places with a child who is being bullied, who is afraid, anxious, needs an operation or is in physical pain. I would take double to shield them.

But it's this squeamishness at witnessing our children suffer that deeply harms them. The Buddha said: life is suffering. So what is it we want for our kids? A different brand? The doesn't-cause-cancer label? The never-cries-itself-to-sleep kind? The always-gets-what-it-wants sort?

It's really *our* problem not theirs that we don't want to watch them suffer or make terrible errors of judgement. From where they are, they're just hungry for life – and as Rilke said, 'Experience it all, the terror and the beauty.' Life is full of grace and horror. We deny our kids the full experience of their humanity when we try to pick out the best bits, like the red and black gums from the lolly pack. We can't stop them from suffering but we can be there for them when they suffer. That's all, really.

We spend so much of our time excising the pain from life so our kids don't have their feelings hurt. We julienne moments into little slivers of perfection, we shave off the bitter spikes of truth and leave them with the soft, little artichoke heart of experience. We may even lie outright to 'protect' them. It is a mistake. We churn out kittens instead of tigers if we treat them this way. Tiger mothers believe our kids are much more resilient than we give them credit for, that kids can take hard stuff and work through it. They can handle difficult situations and information. They learn that life is problematic at times and that they will need to be good problem-solvers.

I remember once parking my ute, leaving Jordan in the passenger seat, and in a moment of distraction, forgetting to put on the handbrake. I was halfway out when the ute started to roll back. 'Pull up the …!' but my vocabulary failed me. In my panic, I couldn't find the word for 'handbrake'. But, at ten, Jordan calmly reached out and pulled it up. Just in time to prevent the car from rolling into a BMW parked behind us. Nothing I had done had prepared him for this moment. He had prepared himself. He had it in him to respond in a crisis with calm and intelligence. That moment gave me immense faith.

When he broke his leg, I knew that some day he'd look back and see that he'd survived an unimaginable setback. As it turns out, he made it through the physical and mental anguish of it. With each day he struggled, silently a muscle inside him was being built, one that he couldn't see or feel at the time, but that some day would be iron-hard. That terrible experience has given him a quiet architecture of spirit, a scaffolding of character that will hold him together when the real shit hits the fan – as it does in every life – and he has to front up to a lost job, a failed relationship or plans in life that crash and burn. Allowing our kids to survive intolerable hardship shows them that they can survive.

Whatever our kids are going through, we can help them lift their gaze from the mess in front of them to the possibilities beyond: to something that hovers on 'meaning'. Meaning is a function of perspective. To struggle with all the catastrophes of life is to be human. We are here to help our kids practise being people.

When our kids are little, we have to find a balance between always picking them up when they cry and leaving them so they can learn to soothe themselves. As parents we're always assessing: pick up or let them learn? When our kids' distress is beyond their control, we have to come in and help. But many times, they're able to get over it themselves and our jumping in pre-emptively doesn't give them the chance to learn those skills.

Psychologist Jerome Kagan encourages parents not to give in to all our kids' wants and needs. He says this leads to 'oversatiation of desire', which is a condition created by having too many of our needs met. Psychologically, this over-pampering disempowers our kids and makes them feel as if they cannot create their own satisfaction but must rely on others for everything.

Another adolescent psychologist I spoke to said teenagers need two kinds of support: self-support (internal resilience) *and* environmental support (parents, mentors or teachers). They develop internal resilience by being given the opportunity to problem-solve on their own instead of having the hovercraft of Mum or Dad swooping in to solve every problem or crisis that arises (sometimes even pre-emptively). They also learn it by having it modelled in their environment (they're surrounded with adults who are resilient) and by making mistakes and learning through them. But they also need adults who recognise when to jump in and help them out of the forest when it gets too dark and they are truly lost. Our job is to manage our discomfort when they're struggling, and to become masters of discernment to decide: do I stand back and let them work it out by themselves or do I throw them a lifeline?

Ultimately, what I want for my kids is for them to know that life will not break them. So, sometimes the best I can do is to get out of the way and let them face whatever is hurtling towards them, to let them bear the impact rather than shield them from the truth or the hurt or the broken bones.

As my friend Gary says, 'I wait and catch them if they fall. I don't stop them from climbing.'

Chapter 11

Pick Your Fights

I DON'T QUITE UNDERSTAND the parental hysteria around piercings. In fact, I like a few well-placed studs and rings – on others and myself – and don't have any problems with a twinkle in just about any part of the human body.

When I turned forty, I had my nose pierced. Why? Because I wasn't allowed to when I was eighteen. And I was self-conscious about my nose at eighteen in a way I am proud of it now. If a teenager wants to put a stud through their eyebrow/ear/lip/nose/nipple or bellybutton, I say, 'Pierce the hell out of it – it's your body.' Aside from my personal predilection for piercings, the point is: am I going to wage a war over a stud? I do not have the energy to expend on such battles. Furthermore, this is one easy way to be on our kids' side. They need to be reminded of our support now and then.

I feel pretty much the same about hair. Colour it, shave it, do what you want to it – but do not ask me to pay hundreds of dollars for it. I am generous in helping out with bargain-bin make-up and will spend money on good hair and skin products. But hair colour, highlights, streaks and other fancy flourishes in a salon are simply out of my budget (and for my hair, too).

But if a teenager has a job and saved up $400 which he or she then wants to blow on a single hairdo – be my guest. There's nothing like pissing away hard-earned cash in three hours to learn the value of money.

I do, however, have a slightly different take on tattoos, only because what you think is clever and pretty at eighteen is certainly not what you think is clever and pretty at forty. My kids just need to trust me on this one. I am saving them from regret, from having to look at two bluebirds and a rose stem and *Life is Beautiful* on their wrist every time they brush their teeth, especially on days when life sucks and the last thing you need is a pep talk from your forearm. You have to be married for a good ten years to fully appreciate just how annoying looking at the same thing every day can be. Not that looking at Zed is annoying, but I'm just saying.

Sometimes, though, I'm not entirely clear whether my objections are principle- or budget-based. If I object to a kid shaving half her head and dyeing the other half green, is it because:

- I don't think it looks classy?
- I'm concerned what others will say and think about me as a parent?
- I wasn't allowed to do that as a kid?
- I know my teen is just trying to piss me off and look as weird and unloveable as is humanly possible?

- It costs a small fortune and is a waste of money?

Clue: if I have a strong negative reaction, it's probably not about my kid, it's about me. While it's handy and much less hard work, I can't just shove all my unresolved stuff onto my kids as if they were a cupboard under the stairs. I have to work through it all first, separate what is mine from what is theirs, and then be a parent, which involves 1) listening to what they have to say; 2) taking into account how they feel; and 3) making an independent decision even if it's going to make them temporarily despise me.

———

We're looking at old photos. 'Oh my God,' Shannon guffaws. 'What are you wearing?'

It's my formal photo. And there I am in that dove-blue chiffon dress, all lace and puffy shoulders. My hair permed. The cream cummerbund. The matching cream shoes which, I have to say, were very 'in' in the eighties.

I had wanted to look my most beautiful on that night – just like any teenage girl does. I couldn't think beyond the blue chiffon and whether my date would thrust his hand down my cleavage or his tongue down my throat before the night was out, though I do remember both wanting and dreading these outcomes. I don't recall what the dress cost, but I know my father blanched when I picked it out – yet seeing my delight, he dug deep and bought it for me. On the night, I blow-dried my own hair and my mum allowed me to use her make-up. My parents dropped me and my date at the before-party and picked us up from the after-party. It was a sane venture from start to finish.

But something sinister has happened since I stood in Shannon's shoes. See, conversations that begin with, 'Mum, how much are you willing to spend on my formal dress?' don't end well in our household. I will sell the clothes off my back to make sure my kids have whatever they need – and largely whatever they want – as long as these non-essential purchases take place alongside conversations about poverty in Third World countries and the importance of donating to charities. I happily dished out the dosh for Katy Perry *and* One Direction tickets, and even slip Shannon extra pocket money when she *needs* the latest magazine with Zayn or Niall on the cover. I want my kids to be happy and to fit in. But does that mean always giving them what they think they want? At what point does saying 'No' become an ethical imperative to bring them back into the real world?

Discussions went way beyond the dress for her Year 10 formal (Year 10? Is this like a practice formal?). They became about the hair and make-up ($150–$220). The shoes. The Hummer to get them there (WTF?!). The tickets at $150 per person (and we had to pay for her date's); $40 per person for the after-party venue. When I have to get out my calculator, it's not looking good.

I explained to Shannon that these are celebrity expectations and we are not celebrities. I told her that everything about this formal conflicted with our value system. She rolled her eyes and told me I just don't get it. She wondered aloud why I had to give her such a hard time when her friends' parents weren't fussed by any of this. Apparently, some girls in her class were spending up to $500 on their dresses – as if that was going to convince me to chill out and lighten up. She showed me a Facebook page that had been set up so the girls could post photos of their dresses to prevent anyone turning up on the night wearing the same dress.

I pointed out that her formal was costing more than my wedding. She sighed and plugged in her earphones.

I understand adolescent vanity and its entanglement with peer pressure. I know the shame of not being able to keep up with your peers – even if they are a bunch of spoilt brats. I appreciate how crippling it is to feel like you don't fit in. But I'm a veteran, having navigated the Call of Duty onslaught with Jordan. I didn't care if all his friends were playing violent video games and that their parents were too weary, worn down or bullied to say 'No'. That madness in the guise of a game did not come into our home. So I was reviled for a few months. But, soon enough, the crowd turned and it became about Minecraft, which I was happy for him to have. And then I was despised a little less.

Parenting teens is about enduring intermittent bouts of contempt and not taking it personally. It's about picking the fights that are worth having because through them your kids get to know who you are, what you stand for and what you will not tolerate. I've come to believe that *this* is where parenting counts – when we don't just take the path of least resistance and give in. Our challenge is to raise socially conscious children who are caught up in a materialistic world that is neither their fault nor of their making. Though we can't control them or force them to agree with the way we see the world, we can help them engage critically with 'what everyone else is doing' by not always making things easy for them.

And by letting them win some, every now and again.

I said yes to the dress. No to the shoes. Yes to the make-up and hair. No to the Hummer and the after-party.

And she still had the best night ever.

Chapter 12

Who's Surviving Who?

I GET PARTICULARLY IRRITABLE with arguments that blame mothers for everything that goes wrong with their kids. I get equally annoyed when these accusations come from conservative (often male) politicians as I do when they emanate from stay-home mums who have sacrificed their lives for their children. The notion that we are culpable for everything our kids do, fail to do or become is an error of over-identification and a mismanagement of boundaries. It also arises from not understanding Gibranese.

Blame is a legal concept, and when it comes to parenting we need to access a particular kind of nuance the law can't achieve. Of course we are not to blame. But we are most certainly *responsible* for our children. This is a corollary to the notion that we don't control them but we do control the values with which we raise them.

We all want our kids to be smart, emotionally well adjusted, healthy, socially adaptable, resilient, happy ... (add your own preferences). Actually, we *expect* them to be all these things – with a few bonus features to make them stand out in a crowd. We act as if it's our birthright to have teenagers who are not depressed/anorexic/pregnant at fourteen/addicted/violent/at risk and so on, without ever imagining we may actually have to *do something* to prevent these potential outcomes. Of course, there are a gazillion factors out there over which we have zero power. No matter what we do right, there is no guaranteed immunity from some of the serious problems teenagers can present us with. But it's a cop-out to imagine we can't have a positive and powerful impact on our kids' lives if we're willing to do some hard work.

Smokers are often bewildered when they're told they have to change their lifestyles – as if it's such a surprise that inhaling toxic smoke for twenty years has clogged up their airways, given them a nasty cough and terrible morning breath. Likewise, insomniacs are almost offended when you suggest limiting the caffeine and winding down before bed with reading, low lights and a glass of warm milk.

When our kids present us with problems, we're similarly bewildered, and swear we will do *anything it takes* to sort the issue out, as long as we don't have to change anything *we* are doing. We'll find the best therapists and treatment programs; we'll throw as much money as we can at the problem. Humans want change without having to change anything. We want problems to get fixed without our having to take responsibility for them. I know this because I suffer from this indolence. We are, at core, a deeply lazy lot.

Maybe that's harsh – perhaps we're not lazy as much as we are busy. Busy with work, housework, tax returns, social arrangements, early-morning gym classes, buying groceries and picking up dry-cleaning. Modernity has engulfed our lives, crammed us with options (soy, almond, lactose-free – and that's just the milk in your coffee), sold us on to-do lists and speed. Thanks to feminism, women who would have had no choice but to be stay-home mums now have access to the public sphere, the ability to earn our own money, run our own companies and challenge gender stereotypes. But these pressures have a cost – high divorce rates result in many single-parent homes. The load is heavier – on everyone. After a long day in court, at the desk, behind the wheel, we all just want to come home to relax.

In this modern era, if we can outsource a problem, we will. To many of us, the gift of extra time often outweighs the dubious benefits of self-improvement. We'd much rather kick back and watch mindless TV than engage with a contemptuous, difficult, irrational teenager who is clearly attention-seeking.

Dani Klein, a clinical psychologist who has worked with adolescents for twenty years, describes parenting today as 'a paradox of absence and presence'. She says parents are physically and emotionally more absent but, ironically, overly intrusive, tending to bubble-wrap and hover over their kids at all times. So when a teenager starts to act out – by skipping school, taking drugs, binge-drinking, staying out all night, getting into fights or sleeping around – we naturally locate the problem in them and focus all our attention on getting them sorted out. But here's a thought: a teenager doesn't just arrive one day in our home like an unwanted visitor. A teenager is like rising damp: he or she has grown out of the environment in the home. Teens are not alien but organic, not separate from the family in which he or she has been raised, but part of it – just as a pimple or ulcer is not imported from outside the body that produced it.

Systems thinking (developed by organismic biologists in the first half of the century) recognises that properties of an organism are not separate entities but arise from the interactions and relationships between the parts. Properties of the parts can only be understood by considering the organisation of the whole in context. If we want to get all scientific about it, quantum physics has shown that what we call a part is merely a pattern in an inseparable web of relationships. What really turns me on about this idea is that it's *empowering*. Each family member has a role to help change the dynamics that are contributing to someone in the family going through a hard time. It gives us the chance to take responsibility for what's happening in our families rather than keep outsourcing the problem to highly paid specialists. A family is a network of relationships, based on conversations and interactions. We can all learn how to master those.

Murray Bowen founded a school of thought, called Bowen Family Systems Therapy, that does not pathologise the person who is acting out, but treats the whole family unit when someone is experiencing difficulties. It's the domestic relationships, the interconnectedness of everyone's issues, the tangle of stories that cause problems. A wayward teenager, for example, would not be singled out for treatment, but would be seen as the symptom-bearer expressing whatever is going on in the home. The aim is to help the family change and function better, which in turn helps the individuals within that family to change and function better.

A theory is only interesting if it's useful. So how useful is it to think about our kids in terms of systems theory? Our kids' lives are affected not only by physical geography, climate, social setting, and political and economic environment but also by the emotional topography and microclimate of the home environment. We are the world into which our kids are born.

When our kids are little we forget that they are watching and absorbing all our behaviour. When they're teens we realise that all their watching and absorption has coloured their personalities. We may recognise how our irritations have shaped their tolerances. How our sarcasm has become their sharp tongue. How our pettiness has become their selfishness. It's not easy to see. And what's worse, we don't often make the connection. We blame them. We locate the problem in them. We indulge in the fantasy that individuals manifest spontaneously instead of arise from the system of the family we have helped create.

What if we accepted that a system is responsible for how each of its members turns out? What if we removed the sting of blame and approached this conversation without self-flagellating whips or reactionary denial? The human psyche is complex. There is no single reason why our kids turn out in any particular way. But there are patterns, and there are dominant cultures in families. And if we have the emotional resilience to examine our own behaviour, we may just get an insight not only into our kids, but into ourselves, too.

Now, this is not an easy topic to write about because people will hear me saying that parents are to blame for how their kids turn out. I'm the first to say, 'Give parents a break, we're just doing our best.' But then again – are we really doing our best? Are we willing to look critically at ourselves and make changes that could help alter the dynamics in our families?

The thing is, we just have to get over ourselves and not take it personally. If we've done the work to get our own story straight, our sense of self should be robust enough to take a critical look at how our behaviour – invariably motivated by the best intentions – may be (unintentionally) contributing to the issues our teenagers are facing. We may have to leach the emotion out of it and think of our family as an organism, like a body, in which all the parts are interrelated.

There is a price tag no matter what sort of parents (and people) we turn out to be – whether we're the helicopter type who don't let our kids breathe without supervision; whether we stay with the other parent for the sake of the kids or we leave for our own sanity; whether we had postnatal depression, lost a parent, were retrenched or stifled in a job that mangled our self-esteem; whether we're racist, sexist, homophobic – all these textures will declare themselves in our kids in strange and unexpected ways. Our choices ripple into our kids' lives. Nor can we predict the social pressures that will find their way into the soft tissue of our kids' beings once they hit the streets and are subject to the blowtorch of peer impact.

But one thing seems pretty straightforward. If we, as parents, crumple under stress, failure, disappointment – *this behaviour* is what we're modelling for our kids. How we react to what's going on for our kids – indeed, to anything – is our choice. We teach them how to handle stress, success, grief and loss, heartache, failure, anger, frustration, joy, peer pressure and money by the way we handle it.

We are meant to parent imperfectly. Our mistakes mark the start of the important conversations we must have with our kids. They need to learn to discern, to forgive, to work things out for themselves. If we always got it right, we'd starve them of the ingredients they need to grow into rounded, thinking, self-reflective human beings.

There is some element to this parenting business that is not calculable or measurable. It does not work according to the laws of causality the way science or logic does. It is partly mystical and it relies on trust. So we have to model the behaviour we'd like to see in our kids, and to keep modelling it, even as they reject and scorn our way of doing things. We must quietly get on with the work of loving them, supporting them, speaking calmly, taking time out, doing work we love, being responsible and kind, not abusing others, paying our debts ... and hope that somehow, through projective identification, they start to copy us. Just the same way we might pick up a new language after hearing it spoken year after year.

There are, of course, no assurances. We may have to wait a long time to see evidence of any copying. Furthermore, we can't make our kids care about the things we care about. We can only get on with caring about those things – without moralising or making them feel guilty about not caring.

As parents we can learn from the principle of obliquity in business theory, which holds that some values cannot be pursued directly, only indirectly. There is no straight line between who we are and how our kids turn out. But there is a squiggly line. Whatever we rant about will squiggle into them. What we deem sacred will equally squiggle. But we don't control the outcome.

The way to pass on the good stuff is not to cram our values down our kids' throats. Our kids are not our personal foie gras. They imbibe our values by immersion. Our deepest embodied and practised values seep into them. Not what we say, but what we do and who we are. We have to trust that our deepest lived values create the environment in which they live.

But if it turns out that they stray from our values, all we can do is acknowledge their individuality. The measure of our own adulthood lies in our ability to tolerate and respect difference – to accept that our kids might turn out fundamentally different to who we are.

Our kids might very well turn away from who we are – unless they're seeking our approval subconsciously. They may form themselves in contrast. So there comes a moment when we realise our teens are surviving us, and not the other way around. They have to make it through our backstory in order to find their own story.

When we realise this, then we know we've grown up.

We are finally mature enough to help our teenagers become adults.

Chapter 13

Always Be Connecting

S HANNON DOESN'T TALK much in the mornings. While driving her to school, I focus on the road and not on the lethal cocktail of not-enough-sleep, interrupted teenage bio-rhythms and unbecoming snarkiness in the passenger seat next to me. She likes the radio on in a way that I find maddening at times. Music is her white noise. Quiet is mine.

A song comes on the radio, a sort of rap song. I quite like it. I tap my fingers to the beat on my steering wheel and ignore her bristles of irritation as I do. As if music were meant only for her.

'That song is my jam,' she says. It is almost an offering.

I consider this statement. I am perfectly sure that I do not understand it. Does she mean she likes to jam on her guitar to that song? Or has 'jam' somehow come to mean something new and unpredictable, like 'sick' (which, when I was growing up meant 'ill' not 'cool'). To me, 'jam' (when we're not talking about the stuff you put on toast) means when musicians improvise together.

'What do you mean?' I ask.

'It's my JAM,' she says, as if saying it in capital letters will yield its meaning.

'Do you like to jam to it?'

She sighs. 'No …'

'So what does that mean?'

'I can't explain it. If you don't understand it, you're not meant to.'

I drive for a bit. 'Imagine if that was my attitude every time you asked me a question,' I say. I hope I am not sounding hurt.

She turns and looks out the window as if I haven't spoken.

We arrive at her school.

'So you aren't going to tell me?' I ask.

'Just forget it, Mum.' She shuts the door.

I have work to do – you must believe me. But when I get home, I take to the internet.

First, I find a site that tells me JAM is an acronym for Just A Minute. But I am pretty sure that wasn't what Shannon meant. I then get caught in a web of slang acronyms and I learn that DYJHIW means Don't You Just Hate It When …, GJWHF = Girls Just Wanna Have Fun, HJNTIY = He's Just Not That Into You, IJAF = It's Just A Fact. I become slightly mesmerised, the way we do when we encounter an entirely new world about which we know nothing. So I feel the need to share with you the wealth of information I gathered, should you ever need to decode some teenage-ese:

IJK	I'm Just Kidding
IJS	I'm Just Saying
IJWTS	I Just Want To Say
IJWTK	I Just Want To Know
J2LUK	Just To Let You Know
J4F	Just For Fun
J4L	Just For Laughs
JAF	Just A Friend
JAS	Just A Second
JATQ	Just Answer The Question
JBH	Just Being Honest
JGI	Just Google It
JGL	Just Get Lost
JICYDK	Just In Case You Didn't Know
JJ	Just Joking
JK	Just Kidding
JKL	Just Kidding, Loser
JBY	Just Be Yourself
JMHO	Just My Humble Opinion
JSMN	Just Shoot Me Now

I have edited this for your convenience. Trust me, it ran to *pages*. I mean, this is practically a new language. But by now I'd wasted an hour on this internet site and I was no closer to working out what 'It's my jam' means. Another hour and I found out that there is actually a song called 'It's My Jam'. I figured that must be the name of the song we'd heard. I felt like Nancy Drew after nailing a case.

When Shannon got home, I told her, 'I know what "It's my jam" means.'

She shrugged. 'Good for you, Mum,' and walked down the corridor.

'Hang on, don't you want me to tell you?'

'I already know what it means,' she said, closing her bedroom door on me.

———

One of the features of Shannon's teenage-ness is how little she confides in me. I must guess at her inner world, a practice that is not a perfect science even if you are someone's mother. Mostly, this will deteriorate into some form of projection. Much as she is flesh of my flesh, she is not held together emotionally or spiritually by the filaments of my psyche. She is her own interior creation. This is both a redemptive and estranging thought. How well can I know her? How well do I know myself?

To make matters worse, she certainly does not want my curiosity or guessing to intrude on her life. She would prefer it if I were less curious about everything when it comes to her. My questions must be careful, unobtrusive, open-ended, caring but not prying. Teenagers are disdainful and mistrustful of anything resembling the pry. So I must develop a certain nascent form of honouring that is almost at odds with the natural instinct to protect. To honour is to step away from something out of respect. To bow one's head, not make eye contact or God forbid scrutinise in a way that might invite judgement or criticism. I must close my eyes and learn to listen better. To the silences. To the patterns of her personality. Almost the way a dentist will tap on a tooth and be able to tell by the sound whether the tooth is healthy or not. As my vigilance recedes, my intuition must grow. If she is ever in trouble, she may or may not come and tell me. Either way, I will have to learn to 'know' it by the disquiet in my gut. Somewhere far from my own anxieties and thoughts, which only clutter our interaction.

I have to accept that I won't always know or understand the dialect she's using and maybe that's how she wants it. I have to keep reminding myself of that criss-cross manoeuvre she's doing in forming her identity – the horizontal line running right across the vertical one I keep trying to reinforce. She's immersed in an emerging culture with her peeps and homies, and language is a key part of keeping me out. The way I show respect for her privacy is by not being a try-hard or forcing interactions. Being an adult is knowing when you're not welcome and not taking it like a personal slap in the face, even when it feels that way.

After being her first port of call for so many years, it's time for me to stand back and take my place in the wings. But I can never lose sight of what I'm doing here. I have to keep my eye on the goal.

I've had some practice with this kind of focus. Many years ago in my radical feminist past, it was my job to help abused women get AVOs against their husbands and boyfriends. Mr Newnham, the magistrate, was a skinny, grey-moustached man who wore some of the most awful corduroy trousers I've ever seen anyone with a wardrobe choice don. He genuinely did not understand how a man could hurt a woman he purported to love. So he was generous with issuing AVOs and, for this reason, I overlooked the fact that he called women 'girls' and tended to be more responsive if I came in person to see him, wearing a low-cut blouse.

Now, if you think I was behaving unethically that's because I was. I would even go so far as to say that in my presence Mr Newnham forgot that he was a fifty-something-year-old man with ear hair and a terrible moustache, and I did as much as I could to encourage his amnesia. When it came to Mr Newnham, my goal was not to educate him that his belief in women's essential powerlessness was a manifestation of his unconscious sexism. My goal was to get my client an AVO while navigating a flawed and objectionable system, and if Mr Newnham got a hard-on in the process, well, that was just a perk of his job.

Likewise, when it comes to my teenagers I must keep my eye on the goal, not on the objectionable behaviour I may have to navigate in order to achieve the goal.

So what is my goal? What is the single, overall parenting objective I am pursuing? I try to keep it simple, like Alec Baldwin in the movie *Glengarry Glen Ross*, who tells the team of real-estate salesmen that the ABC of selling is: Always Be Closing. My ABC for raising teenagers is: Always Be Connecting.

My aim is to engage with my kids. The arteries of my connection with them must be unclogged and clear. My gestures should draw them in, not push them away. I need to remain interested but not curious. Involved but not interfering. They must sense my presence at all times, like someone who's got their back, not hovering overhead.

So I do what I can to create conversation opportunities – I chat, ask them questions and inquire about their opinions. When they were little and tantrumming, I'd chant, 'Use your words.' It's even more important now that their thoughts are sharper, and their deliberations with the world more interesting and complex.

Of course, it is a strain on one's patience to engage with someone who is endlessly being a pain in the arse. They will, in fact, make it hard – sometimes impossibly hard for me. But I won't allow them to freewheel into silence. I'm the adult. I'm the one with a fully functioning brain, and I understand the rudiments of psychology enough to know that often a mood or a particular skirmish is a front for an underlying malaise. I have to become a parental detective and Sherlock Holmes the truth out of them. Carefully and not by entrapment. Mostly by listening.

My first serious boyfriend and I struggled to communicate. When I was upset, he'd stare at me dumbly while I recoiled. 'Tell me what to do, tell me what to say ...' he'd beg. 'If I have to tell you, then what's the point?' I'd sniff. I naively expected him to read my mind and know exactly how to comfort me.

That relationship crashed quickly. The mark of maturity is the ability to be in conversation – not only with ourselves, but with others. The idea that others should know what we think is a narcissistic fantasy. We do this a lot with our lovers and partners. We become defensive and proud. We may assume far too much, when a small and gentle conversation can clear up everything.

We may assume that our kids ought to know what we think and what we expect of them. But we should assume nothing. Everything important deserves a conversation. We must teach them how to ask for things and to argue for what they believe in. We must show them by example how to object to injustice, how to negotiate, how to disagree, how to fight fairly and kindly, how to express gratitude and love.

Which is not to say that we should overtalk everything. Silence and knowing when to allow quiet are also part of understanding the dynamics of conversation. Connecting doesn't necessarily involve jibber-jabber. It's the state of our hearts and minds that matters.

So while talking is crucial, it's a lot like make-up – we shouldn't overdo it. Talking keeps relationships oiled. Too much talking makes the wheels spin. It makes people feel stuck. Talking needs the companion of silence. I'm still learning when to talk and when to shut up. Sometimes I find just letting things go is the best way to move on. I have to learn to state my case: 'That was unacceptable behaviour, I expect you to know better ...' and then let it pass. Equally, not speaking up when it's required is weak, and doesn't count as parenting.

The only way for me to keep track of our connection is to be in touch with my own emotions during all my interactions with them.

Like the other day I walked past Shannon's room and was genuinely assaulted by the mess. 'Can you maybe think about tidying up here a little?' I ventured.

'Why? It's my room. You don't have to come in here.'

Which is perfectly true. My indignation at the chaos was mine to navigate. What purpose was served by escalating the issue into 'Tidy your room right now'? Only my own sense of control. Over Shannon? Ha! We've already covered that – I can't control her. Over my environment (as in 'While you live under my roof, you'll abide by my rules')? I could get really cranked up over this but, then again, surely this is one I can let go? Unless I am OCD or have PMS. If I do choose to push it, it will end in ugliness, door-slamming, spikes in cortisol. And really, who needs that?

To Always Be Connecting, I need to remember that teenagers are experiments. They're just trying out their personalities, play-ing with boundaries and investigating who they are. They don't know what is going to happen if they say 'No' when told, 'Please take out the garbage.' So sometimes I make allowances for a bit of experimentation, while trying not to get triggered into losing it – at least not verbally. For example:

'I've already asked you twice to take out the garbage.'

Jordan: 'In your dreams.'

'I'm not your friend. That's not how you talk to me. Try that again.' (While thinking, 'You snarky little bugger.')

'I don't think so.'

'I'm not asking again. And if it's not done I'm not taking you to basketball later.' ('You infuriating little shit.')

'Can't you see I'm busy in the middle of a FIFA game?'

'I understand this isn't the best time for you. Please do it when you're finished.' ('Goddammit, you little bastard.')

They're mad scientists, trying out new minerals, curious about what the impact will be if they mix refusal, disdain, contempt or any other unused reaction with parental authority. To remain in control, we have to refuse to react to their outlandish experimentation. One father of three teenage girls I interviewed put it like this: 'Don't trust your first reaction.'

To master the ABC of parenting these people, we have to get really slick at managing conflict.

Which begs the question: how *do* we manage conflict?

Not all of us are good at it. We may hate any kind of drama, outdoor voices inside and temper flares, and will do anything to avoid them. If we come from families of origin where fighting was common, violent and never properly resolved, we're really gonna hate these teenage years. Likewise, if we come from families that never fought but bottled everything up, we're going to have to acquire some moves. Learning how to fight – robustly, fairly and constructively – is an important life skill. So how we fight with our teenagers will model how to fight later on in life when they form their own relationships. By knowing who we are, taking a stand, refusing to be bullied, not stonewalling, speaking calmly (or raising our voices when it's appropriate), being able to listen to an opinion that we don't like, disagreeing respectfully and not holding grudges, we show our teens: this is how to manage conflict.

Our relationship with our teenager is not a Ming vase – it can withstand a few rounds of combat. But we need to know how to have vigorous interactions from which we can all bounce back rather than shatter. As the adult we have to model fair play – to understand the power dynamic between us and them: when it shifts, and how not to manipulate or exaggerate our own power; to allow them also to have power; not to back them into a corner or to use the unfair advantage we have over them.

I want my kids to be able to say 'I'm sorry' and 'I love you'. The best way I know to teach them is to say these things often, to make them the easy currency of our interactions so that we don't have to ever strain for them and my kids learn that apologising and telling people how you feel is no big deal. That fights can be easily overcome.

My rules are: never linger. Move on. Don't stay to enter the madness. Just state what must be stated and leave it alone. My job is to prod them back over the line whenever they step beyond, keeping in mind that my job is to Always Be Connecting.

But how do we do this when they won't even talk to us? How do we show them we are still holding them in our regard, we are still watching out for them, when they don't want us to observe them?

Here's my trick: by acts of kindness.

What teenagers need from us in this socially brutal, gotta-be-cool, be-popular-or-die world is a fierce kindness. Especially when they least deserve it. When they feel alone, they need to feel that we are on their side. Not that we necessarily agree with them, but that we will back them, that we've got their backs.

Always Be Connecting also means that I must be the bigger person. I am the adult, after all.

I must be steady when they are rocky. I must be calm when they feel panicky. I must murmur, 'It's going to be okay, it's going to work out.' I must speak with kindness and not overreact, to invite a calm inevitability to the way things pan out. This is just a more advanced form of potty-training. Back in the days of diapers, we kept putting them on the potty and explaining how to do it. We did this over and over again, until one day they got it. These days we're training them to handle stress, failure, disappointment, heartache and the rest of it.

Someone has to be there, saying, 'There's the potty, that's where you sit, this is how you push …' in all life situations.

In the timeless words of Dr Seuss: 'Someone, someone has to, you see.'

And tag, we're it.

Chapter 14

The Know-It-Alls

B<small>UT SOMETIMES, AS</small> hard as I try, my ABC goes to hell. Here's how.

Jordan tells Shannon she is a nerd. A 'creepy-arsed nerd', to be precise. It's an ordinary drive home after school pick-up and I've no clue what has inspired this invective. I try not to get involved too early, to give them the opportunity to practise resolving conflict on their own, like two adults.

'Just be respectful,' I mumble.

'Well, you're a geek,' she throws back.

'What's the difference between a nerd and a geek?' I ask, nerdily.

'Nerds study, they read books,' he says. 'It's way worse than being a geek.'

'I am not a nerd,' Shannon says haughtily, taking umbrage at the classification.

'Well, I'm only a semi-geek. A sports geek,' Jordan says. 'A geek is not as bad as a nerd.'

'I still don't understand the difference between a nerd and a geek,' I say.

'Don't try to make me into a normal nerd. I'm so not like anyone else, okay?' Shannon huffs.

'She's trying to be indie,' he mocks.

'I'm not trying to be anything,' Shannon preens.

'I'd rather be a sports geek than a nerd like you.'

'You seem pretty nerdy, given all the basketball statistics you know,' I say to Jordan.

He rolls his eyes. 'I play the sport, so I'm not a nerd. A nerd is someone like Joel, who plays FIFA but doesn't play the sport in real life. It's way worse to be a nerd than a geek.'

'I consider myself a weirdo.' Shannon pronounces it like a title.

'In your dreams you're a weirdo; you're just a nerd,' Jordan says.

'Am not. No-one's as weird as me.'

'You're not weird, you're normal.'

Shannon takes mighty offence at this.

'Can you be weird to yourself?' I ask innocently.

'Do you think suicidal thoughts? No. Do you stab yourself? No,' Jordan huffs.

'That's emo,' Shannon says. 'What do you know?'

'I can't keep up,' I sigh. 'What is Savanna?' I ask. Savanna is a girl in Shannon's year who shaves half her head and wears the other side long.

'She's a try-hard,' Shannon says. 'Totally uncool.'

'Does she stab herself with a compass?' Jordan asks.

'I wouldn't be surprised if she did,' Shannon offers.

'What's the difference between being weird and being strange?' I ask. No-one bothers with my questions.

'Actually, I am more quirky than weird,' Shannon revises, almost talking to herself.

'What makes you quirky?' I ask.

'My interests. Like my obsession with *Supernatural* and my taste in music.'

'A TV show doesn't qualify as an interest,' Jordan weighs in.

'Then my fandoms – like Harry Potter. I'm also creative in quirky ways. I do things others don't do.'

'She thinks cos she's an artist …' Jordan says. 'That makes you arty not quirky.'

'I have a quirky sense of humour. I have a quirky sense of fashion …'

'Remember how you used to ask me if what you were wearing was okay?' I ask wistfully.

'What was I thinking?' Shannon sighs.

'Bitchy,' I say.

'You are a bitch,' Jordan agrees. And, as if he's waited his entire life to empty out the basement of his grievances, out it pours. 'You treat me like a three-year-old. I have a consciousness now. You can't beat me up anymore.'

'You used to be besties,' I say. I mournfully recall them sharing a room until Jordan was six and Shannon was nine, when she announced that she 'needed her own space'. Shannon used to make up stories for him, and do hand-puppets on the wall.

'I can't think of a single positive of having her around,' Jordan says bitterly. 'She's like the most useless family member.'

'Take that back,' I say to Jordan. 'That's hurtful. That's too far.'

Shannon is clearly unruffled. 'Well, if I wasn't around, who would point out your many faults?'

Jordan sulks out the window. 'She doesn't do anything. What does she do that benefits the family?'

'I contribute knowledge, conversation, music, *Glee* ...' Shannon rattles off.

'Bitchiness, mood swings ...' Jordan adds.

'Mood swings are nothing. Wait 'til you get acne like me. Welcome to your future.'

'Gross.'

'The Roaccutane seems to be working,' I try, grabbing an off-ramp from this volatile interaction. 'You may not get acne as badly as Shannon did,' I tell Jordan. 'She seems to have inherited Dad's genes – remember she had boils when she was a little girl.'

'She's like the walking plagues. Frogs' legs, boils, blood every month ...'

'You so don't want to go there, little boy,' Shannon says. 'Do not speak about my periods. You know nothing about them.'

'It's just so freaky. That you bleed,' he mumbles.

'I read a three-page description on Tumblr about periods,' Shannon says. 'It was pretty accurate.'

'You read three whole pages about periods?' Jordan asks. 'Get a life.'

'Oh yes, there's me wasting my life by *reading*!' Shannon spits.

'Yes, when you could be outside *exercising*!' Jordan shoots back.

'Excuse me for being smart rather than sweaty.'

'Well, excuse me for being fast instead of being a nerd.'

'There's more to life than chasing a stupid ball.'

'Says who?'

'Says smart intelligent women, who will one day be your boss.'

'Don't get all feminist on me. Feminists are so annoying.'

'Excuse me,' I say, 'I am a feminist.' But really, I am not in this conversation at all. I'm just the driver.

'Do you believe men and women are equal?' Shannon asks him.

'Duh!'

'Then you're a feminist,' she says.

'I'm not a feminist. I just believe in equality,' he says. 'Don't call me a feminist.'

'Just do me a favour: please don't rape anyone,' Shannon says to him, at which point I yell out, 'Enough, enough of this conversation. As if, Shannon – as if your brother would do such a thing. Both of you, just think before you speak! Now shut the hell up.'

I turn up the volume on my Buddhist chanting music as high as it will go and screech along to the soothing sounds of *om mani padme hum*. So much for letting them sort it out like adults.

I don't pull rank often. For example, I would never mention in conversation that (a long time ago) I went on a Fulbright scholarship to Yale where I did a Masters in Law. Not only are there exceedingly few opportunities to chuck this into daily chitchat but, seriously, who gives a damn? The only achievement I do sometimes boast about is that I was awarded Asshole of the Month by *Hustler* magazine in 1994 for the work I was doing on violent pornography and its impact on women's rights. To my teenagers, the fact that I went to Yale is no more interesting than that I once went to the Grand Canyon or Madame Tussauds. It's something they know about my past without any sense of the effort it took to get there or the stress I endured trying to keep up with so many astonishingly brilliant minds. Besides, what I remember most fondly about Yale is a hunger strike I participated in to free the Haitians from Guantanamo Bay and, in a rare moment of abandon, posing nude for a photographer.

When it comes to my kids, it's not like I want to be considered an oracle of wisdom or anything. On many issues, such as Middle Eastern politics and astrophysics, I am, I assure you, 'a dumb-arse', to quote Jordan. I am increasingly astonished at bloggers and columnists who seem to have the answers to all of life's difficult questions because I am finding that, as I age, I'm shedding opinions like dead skin cells and am less certain about most things. But if I pass an occasional view, say, on literature or grammar or anything to do with writing stories, chances are it's the distillation of years of reading and thinking, and that I've spent a long time mulling over it. It's likely not the first lazy thought that's occurred to me, unlike a Facebook status update.

While driving Shannon and Jordan home from school one afternoon, I make the mistake of passing an opinion about a literary reference in an advertisement on the back of a bus. I suggest it is a King Midas meme. My kids disagree. They tell me that 'I just don't really understand it.' Now, for some reason, this really pisses me off. Usually, I would refrain from arguing with someone who has less experience than I do about a subject. I would simply agree to disagree and think to myself, 'You poor idiot.' I explain to my kids that perhaps I know a little more about these things than they do, but on this they disagree, too. They clearly know far more about current cultural references than I do. I find myself degenerating into juvenile fury and – God help me – I mention that I went to Yale. I mean, really.

'So what?' Jordan says. 'You studied law there, not cultural references.'

'Do you even understand what a meme is?' Shannon pipes in. 'Because you kind of use it in the wrong way all the time.'

I inhale deeply. I muster compassion for their lack of humility and their big-mouthed know-it-all-ness. I even have deep respect for the many ways in which they are smarter and better at things than I am.

'Is it possible that I know more about anything than you?' I ask my kids from the pulpit of the driver's seat.

There is silence.

'About some things,' Jordan muses. 'Like how to cook lamb.'

'Anything else?'

They cannot come up with any specific examples. I try to find this funny. But at the core of this they really, truly think they're smarter than I am. Which, in many ways, they are – technologically and musically, for starters. But as I silently fume, I remember arguing with my dad as a teenager and him saying to me, 'I'm still older than you are and have more experience than you,' and me thinking, 'You are so out of your depth, old man.'

I, too, was un-humble, up myself to my eyeballs. I, too, argued with him about things he knew more about. I realise that what irked me wasn't so much what we argued about as it was his need to let me know he knew more. I had no idea what it meant to 'have experience' and how maturity is a form of wisdom and knowledge. It's like sex or childbirth or parenthood – you know nothing about them until you're living them. It's like trying to have a discussion about Nietzsche with a toddler. Or contraception with a five-year-old. They have no frame of reference.

Teenagers are like optical illusions – they look like adults and they even speak like adults at times, but they are not adults. We need to remember this. And since I am the only real adult in the car who knows this, it's up to me to behave like one. I exhale and keep driving.

'It's okay,' Jordan consoles, placing a hand on my shoulder. 'We don't expect you to know it all.'

Chapter 15

Unbribable

I HAVE TAUGHT THE cat to use a cat flap despite her initial reluctance. I have taught two toddlers to do their business on the toilet rather than in their Huggies. I have convinced Zed to dance with me even when he hasn't had enough to drink. But I cannot think of a way to make a teenager do something he or she doesn't want to do. They are as unbribable as goldfish.

We're not talking about chores. There are two chores that are assigned in our household: Jordan takes out the garbage on Tuesdays and Shannon feeds the cat every day at 4 pm. These are non-negotiable. If they are not done, I will not serve dinner. I will repeat, quietly but with cumulative menacing reiteration, that the garbage needs taking out or Tanaka is starting to nibble on the carpet. My kids have understood that these chores will get done and there is no wheedling out of them.

So I am thinking now of non-chores, like getting Shannon to play her new electric acoustic guitar for me. Or getting Jordan to sing the latest song he's learned in a band. Or getting my kids to come with me to visit someone in hospital who is sick and in need of visitors.

With teenagers, 'I don't feel like it' seems, in the lexicon of their moral vocabulary, to be a free pass into doing whatever the hell they like. Apparently, feeling like doing something is the motivation required to take action. On this premise, it seems to me, very little would get done in my household because I do not – despite my actions to the contrary – feel like getting up at 6 am every day to make Jordan his special banana protein shake or travelling a forty-kilometre round trip every day to take my kids to school and then to their drama rehearsals, self-defence classes and basketball practice. Come to think of it, most of my life is about doing things I don't feel like doing. I wonder if this is healthy.

The other day Jordan walked into my study, soft and ruffled with sleep. 'I just had the weirdest dream …' he said, yawning widely.

I turned to face him and removed my reading glasses. I know all the active listening tricks. I looked him in the eyes. He had my full attention.

'Me, you and Dad were in a car …' he began. Then he stopped. 'Actually … forget it.'

'Go on, tell me,' I said. I have spent many years grasping for ways to understand how my boy ticks. Here he was about to offer something from the depths of his inner world only to snatch it away.

'I don't want to anymore.' And just like that he ambled out of my study, leaving me in my active listening pose wondering why he'd changed his mind. Was his dream too disturbing? Doesn't he trust me? Did I not listen actively enough?

Here's what you learn with teenagers: your curiosity can burn you like battery acid, but you can't let it show. You cannot get a teenager to confide in you, in much the same way that you cannot get someone to love you. Trust is a negotiation over which we only have 50 per cent control. The rest is up to the other. Can we bear to be so helpless?

I want to know what is going on with my kids. I want to know if they are being bullied and the names of the people bullying them. I want to know if there are horrible teachers making their lives a nightmare. I want to know if they're smoking, doing drugs or anything illegal. I need to know if they are lying to me. I want this information so I can parent them through these rapids. But I do not need to know certain things – like whether they are masturbating and how often. Truly, that is none of my business. I hope – in a sort of generic way – that they are. I think it's important to be someone who can, you know, pleasure themselves. I would like them to point out the people they have crushes on, but I realise that this is pushing things. I need to be satisfied, and respect, that they have their secrets.

I can't chase their stories, only receive what is offered when it's offered. I can't be too keen, just make a space that determines how I listen, how I regulate my curiosity and nosiness about their lives. I can turn to face them when they come to me. It's what practitioners of Chinese philosophy would call being in a Yin space. I can't always be in pursuit, or dogged. Just open.

The following day I tried again. 'I'm really interested to hear about your dream …'

'Just forget about it, okay?' he huffed furiously.

I gathered myself. The trick here was not to sulk. Not to wheedle or cajole or harass. Not to manipulate or punish with silence or iciness. Not to feel catastrophically rejected. This was a stretch for me.

I smiled and kissed him on the head. I started to tidy up the breakfast things, trying not to clank the dishes with unnecessary, rebuffed clatter.

'Maybe later, okay?' he said.

That was my cue to drop it. To never mention it again. To respect his privacy and trust him. That if he wanted me to know, he'd tell me. But that he might decide not to. I had to be okay either way.

One afternoon, I asked Shannon to accompany me to the hospital to visit a friend's child, who was ill. 'I've got period pains and I think I'm getting a cold,' she said, bundled up in her onesie in front of the TV with her week's worth of recorded programs lined up. Riiiight.

Now, I pick very carefully the battles that end in me saying, 'As long as you live under my roof, you will do as I say.' I do so for two reasons: my father used this line on me rather generously while I was growing up and I have a distaste for this kind of power play by parents. I also know that it only breeds resentment in the long run. Or kids mumbling under their breath (or at the very least thinking), 'You are a psychotic bitch.' And as long as my kids think I am a psychotic bitch, they couldn't care less what I think is the right thing to do. Whereas if I manage to retain their respect, however tenuous, by a) not losing my temper; b) not manipulating them; c) not threatening them or shaming them; and d) modelling by my own behaviour what I would like them to do, there is some small possibility that they will feel bad about how they've behaved and maybe do the right thing next time around.

See, sometimes you have to sacrifice the present imperfect moment for a possible perfect later moment. So in this regard, parenting teenagers is the art of unguaranteed delayed gratification.

I ask Zed whether we have failed as parents. 'Does she know what the right thing is to do?' Yes, he assures me, she does know. She will feel bad.

'What's wrong with her moral compass?'

He says, 'The moral compass is there, but the laziness is stronger.'

'How do we know the moral compass is there?'

He says, 'You have to trust.'

I suppose I should feel encouraged that my Shannon is not intimidated by me. That she isn't a people-pleaser and doesn't try too hard to do the right thing. I should be proud that she is prepared to say, 'This doesn't suit me.' She's not going to be one of those people who acts one way and feels resentful later. Maybe I have something to learn from her. And maybe she has something to learn from me – that even when I don't feel like doing things, I still do them because sometimes it's 'the right thing' to do.

But perhaps you have to be a parent first to learn about sacrifice. I can't really blame her for not having walked that long path. She's still only clocked up sixteen years, and maybe when I was that age I would have liked to say to my parents, 'I don't feel like it' now and then. But as the 'good daughter' in my household, I didn't try that option.

Later I ask Shannon if she knows that her choice was a selfish one. 'Yes, of course I know,' she says, as if I'm the stupid one.

And since she knows, all I can do is sniff in a righteous sort of way and leave her to her TV viewing.

As far as I can see, my job is done. The rest is up to her.

———

Later, when I put my head around Jordan's door to say goodnight, he says, 'Come give me a hug.'

As I bend down to kiss him on the top of his head he asks, 'Do you want to hear my dream?'

I stay super cool. 'Only if you want to tell me.'

And he did.

Curiosity is my weakness, a dead giveaway that I'm over-invested. How precariously we are poised to win our kids' confidence or lose it. How robustly we must stay receptive: ears attuned, hearts flung open to catch their stories. Love, like trust and respect, doesn't respond to commands or bullying, but grows through patience and open-hearted detachment.

Just so happens that those are my weakest personality muscles.

Chapter 16

Eve Who?

I DON'T GET TO talk very much about vaginas in my home. Only Zed is interested in hearing anything I have to say on the topic, and there's one direction that conversation's heading. Teenagers don't want to hear their mums talking about their intimate parts and would prefer to forget that we even have them. Still, I try to normalise things and throw the odd 'vagina' into everyday chitchat so that Shannon might grow up feeling comfortable around the word, and Jordan won't call it by its many other names so popular amongst his peers. However, both my kids flinch when I say 'vagina'.

So a while back, when Eve Ensler came to Sydney, I excitedly booked tickets for both Shannon and me to go see her talk.

'Who is she, again?' Shannon asked.

'Eve Ensler. You know, the one who wrote *The Vagina Monologues*?'

'Never heard of her,' Shannon yawned. 'And why would anyone write about vaginas? Gross.'

'You should read it sometime,' I said. 'You might not think it's so gross afterwards.'

She reluctantly let me drag her along to the Sydney Theatre and sat through the hour of Eve's talk. I was in tears listening to her talk about her human rights work all over the world, including the safe villages she's created for women fleeing gender violence. Afterwards I ran to stand in the long line to finally meet her and have her sign my book.

Shannon surveyed the long queue. 'I'll wait outside.'

'Don't you want to meet her?' I asked. 'It's a once-in-a-lifetime opportunity.'

'Nah. I'm not into all this men-are-the-enemy stuff, anyway.'

And with that, she turned and left me standing alone in line, with my dog-eared copy of *The Vagina Monologues* in my hands.

Okay, so maybe Eve Ensler wasn't Shannon's thing. But as she's artistic, I figured she'd be fascinated by Casey Jenkins, a Melburnian artist I came across on YouTube who has taken up vaginal knitting.

I assumed from the title that Jenkins is one of those talented people born without hands who taught herself to knit by holding the needles in her vagina (don't laugh, I have seen a man play the guitar with his toes on YouTube). And really, how inspiring would that be? But it transpires she uses her hands, it's just wool she's knitting with – silly me. She uses her vagina as the wool-holder: inserts balls of wool and then gently pulls it out and knits over a period of twenty-eight days. The artwork is called *Casting Off My Womb*. Given that the vagina is a temperamental creature, with its happy days and grumpy days, the knitting is textured and coloured by its different moods, including, very dramatically, the menstrual week.

I couldn't help wondering what my beloved granny might have made of this new form of the ancient craft which she so carefully taught me with bright pink wool on large plastic needles that went clickety-clack. I don't believe my granny ever uttered the word 'vagina' as long as I knew her. She was, however, a fabulous knitter.

Reactions to Jenkins's performance on social media ranged from 'Eeeuww' to 'I just vomited in my mouth' to 'Gross. I don't get it' to 'I just saw the video and wish I could unsee it'. The intensity of the abhorrence intrigued me. Is it disgusting for an artist to explore her body? Is the female body disgusting? Is the root of all this revulsion the very eurotophobia (vagina phobia) Jenkins is drawing our attention to, especially regarding menstruation?

What I find gross is female circumcision. Women being raped. Women dying after childbirth from terrible tears and no access to doctors or hospitals. Women who hate their bodies, who starve themselves into androgyny precisely because they cannot handle the (presumably 'gross') thought of menstruation. But a female artist gently pulling wool from her fanny and knitting to experience the colours and textures of her body does not sicken me.

In fact, I found Jenkins's vaginal knitting *interesting*. Maybe even brave. It's not like she's the first artist to push a taboo. There is a rich history of artists using their bodies as a canvas in these confronting ways. In the early 1970s, Vito Acconci, in his performance piece *Seedbed*, masturbated under a gallery floor as his audience walked above him. Oddly, there was nothing seedy about it. In 1975, Carolee Schneemann pulled a paper scroll out of her vagina at a performance entitled *Interior Scroll*.

Artist Hannah Wilke covered her torso with vulvas made out of hardened chewing gum to disrupt the viewer's erotic gaze and to draw attention to the way women's bodies are objectified. In her performances, artist Karen Finley coats herself with chocolate and, in a 1986 performance piece called *Yams up my Granny's Ass*, she poured a can of sugared yams on her bottom. Recently, artist Andrea Fraser recorded herself having sex with a collector who paid her $20,000 to be part of her artwork. In this company, vaginal knitting seems a little tame. A visit to the Museum of Old and New Art (MONA) in Hobart offers viewers both disturbing and confronting moments – plenty of opportunities to go 'eeuw'.

Art is often about transgression and confrontation, forcing us to examine our squeamishness. Where does it come from? What does it say about our culture? What does it say about us? Art isn't meant to be neat, 'nice' or 'well behaved'. Its power lies in how it can change the way we think and feel. Vaginal knitting may not make us feel 'comfortable' but it's a fabulous conversation-starter – or so I thought.

Of course, when I told Shannon about it, she put her hands over her ears and said, 'That's just gross. Can we just not talk about vaginas, please?'

On the first day I got my period, my father made a tearful announcement at the dinner table that 'his little girl had grown up'. I curdled inside. Surely, whatever was going on between me and my sanitary pad had bugger-all to do with my father, and how dare he even mention that I was menstruating, let alone cry about it? But according to the narrative in my family, we 'shared' everything and 'expressed our emotions', so I assumed my unwillingness to have my news announced over Monday night spaghetti and meatballs meant I was just immature. (As an adult, I realise I had an inkling of what constitutes a boundary.)

Managing blood flow from a body part you can't see is a private business and does not require a support group or any form of congregational activity. Trying to remain upbeat about periods when – let's face it – they curtail physical and sexual adventures, ruin expensive Egyptian cotton sheets and cramp you up seems insincerely cheery.

But then in my twenties I fell into a crowd of feminists, women who had special 'circle ceremonies' and treated 'menses' as sacred (who calls a period 'menses', for God's sake?). I learned that when women bleed we are 'releasing attachment energy', and that we need to have 'sacred connection and prayer practices so the womb doesn't fill with negativity'. Despite this, I have never quite been able to translate these ideas into my own menstrual cycle; but, never mind, I decided I'd make up for these deficiencies with my own daughter. I fantasised that on that special day, there'd be some deep unspoken bond between us. I'd cover her with rose petals and pass on pieces of jewellery handed down in my family.

But let me tell you now that our plans for what will happen when our teenage daughter gets her period may not materialise. There may very well be no 'bleeders uniting', no comparing of notes or chatting about which tampons are better and which pads more absorbent. For instance, our daughter may not let us know that her period has arrived. Or she may not want to talk about it. She may prefer to confer with her peers about how to insert a tampon and leave us out of it altogether. One must be prepared for such eventualities.

When I mentioned my plans for a special ceremony, with candles and incense and other women bearing gifts to welcome her into the fold, Shannon's face crinkled in a mixture of mortification and horror. 'Don't you dare,' she said. I was crushed. I thought perhaps having a feminist as a mother might have infiltrated her psyche the way my genes have taken up occupancy in her DNA.

But on reflection, I realised that at thirteen, feminism is as incomprehensible as childbirth. You don't get politicised by osmosis. Also, bleeding isn't a political act. It's a biological one. And despite what your mother thinks – or even what you think – about how biologically discriminatory it is; despite Gloria Steinem's essay, 'If Men Could Menstruate'; despite all the earth mothers who have bled into the earth and the African tribes that celebrate the onset of menstruation, the truth is that a period is no fun. Especially for the person bleeding.

Turns out Shannon is a private person. She is all over differentiation without even knowing it, drawing those boundaries clearly and sternly. She made me see that I can't keep making what happens to her about me.

She went on to point out that by writing a chapter in which her name appears in the same sentence as the word 'menstruation' I'm doing exactly what my father did to me. Only, like, a gazillion times worse.

Which is harsh. But probably true.

All I can say to that is, 'I forgive you, Dad,' and hope she'll do the same some day to me.*

---

* Shannon read this entire manuscript and gave me the all clear before I sent it off to my publisher. Just so you know.

Chapter 17

The Right to Be Rude

I AM TAKING LOTS of deep breaths. It's supposed to calm the parasympathetic nervous system and I need a lot of calming. On the other end of the phone Jordan's French teacher is describing the various and novel ways he has found to be rude to her.

'He told me that I had just wasted the class's time during the lesson.'

I apologise profusely. I tell her that 'his dad and I will talk to him'. I think I even promise that we will punish him. I thank her for her patience.

When Jordan comes home, I sigh and say, 'I am sick of getting emails and calls from your teachers. Don't be rude.'

'Can I just tell you my side of the story?'

'I don't care what your side of the story is, JUST STAY OUT OF TROUBLE.'

'This is only, like, the third time this year!' he shouts. 'What do you expect?'

'I expect none,' I counter. 'You're old enough to stay out of trouble.'

'I'm not perfect, you know,' he spits. 'I'm sorry, but I'm just human. We can't all be perfect like you.'

'I'm not perfect,' I say, scrounging for the ways in which I am very fallible.

'Of course you are, name one way in which you're not perfect.'

My hesitation infuriates him and he slams his bedroom door shut.

I fume around the kitchen because, the truth is, I am still vulnerable to embarrassment. Somewhere inside me I want other people to use words like 'well-behaved' and 'polite' when they refer to my kids. Why? Because people assume that your kids' rudeness is, in some fundamental way, the direct result of your abject failure as a parent. It is the direct consequence of your inability to say 'No' or instil good values and good manners. Folks assume that if your child has no respect, you have not taught them to be respectful. I hate thinking about what that French teacher might be saying behind my back, and in French too.

I take the schnitzels out of the fridge and pound them flat. *Goddammit*, I seethe.

As I fry the schnitzels, I remember travelling in Malawi with a boyfriend many years ago. We met a young man called Binos whom we paid to take us out to Lake Malawi in a dugout, which is a hollowed-out tree trunk. On the side of the dugout were carved the words 'Let Them Say'. We asked Binos what it meant. He explained that people in Malawi subsist by fishing. To be a successful fisherman, one needs a dugout. To buy a tree from the

Malawian government costs a lot of money. Those Malawians rich enough to buy a tree know that people will say behind their backs, 'That man is rich.' *Let them say.*

I smile into this memory.

As I lift the schnitzels onto paper towel, I wonder how important it is, really, what Jordan's French teacher thinks of me. Do I really give a rat's arse if she assumes I'm the worst parent ever to have lived?

Peeling the potatoes, I think of Keith, a man I knew in my twenties. Keith was a seriously perfect gentleman. He arrived at my door on time, well dressed and recently showered. He paid for my dinner and had impeccable manners. In fact, I felt completely self-conscious about my table manners and found it hard to have a real conversation with him – he was so delightful, inoffensive and PC. I dated Keith. Once. My God, it would've been more fun spending the evening peeling potatoes.

Then I think to myself that Jordan is not boring. That it takes a certain ballsiness to tell a teacher, 'You just wasted our time in this lesson.'

As I chop the carrots I imagine Jordan getting worked up and telling it like it is. I know how rude he can be. And that's unacceptable. But there is something … brave about it. He'll never be Keith.

I start to wonder whether, in fact, I want a kid who just 'does what he's told'. What sort of a person would I be raising if he never spoke his mind? If he just slunk into obedience whenever someone with authority threatened him? He'd end up like Keith. I have not sweated my ovaries out to raise Keiths.

Though it would be easier, less of a stretch for me, I don't actually want my kids to adopt my view of the world without doing the hard work of figuring it out for themselves. Yes, I could ram my beliefs down their throats and force them to do things my way, but how would that help them become who they want to be? I bucked my parents' systems. I rejected their ways. I dated non-Jewish guys when my dad was going through a particularly Orthodox stage. I brought shame on my family and apparently embarrassed my father in front of his friends. Why? Because I was living my life, not his. I want my kids to think their own way into the world.

As I rinse the lettuce leaves, I realise that compliance is not one of my values. I want my kids to have the backbone to confront authority, not to be intimidated; to speak up and to defend themselves. Being defiant is how they develop those personality muscles. And we are their laboratory.

The more I ponder this and think of the pettiness and latent bullying inherent in so many teachers with unresolved power issues, the more I soften. By the time dinner is ready I have done a complete 360 on the French teacher.

I knock on Jordan's bedroom door.

I tell him that I think it's brave of him to speak his mind when a teacher is frustrating. I offer that it's a good idea to sometimes write down what you're thinking before you say it and ask yourself whether saying it might get you in trouble. I tell him that I don't mind if he gets in trouble, but that his life will be more miserable because he'll have to stay for after-school detention and miss basketball. I suggest that sometimes it's not what we say but how we say things that gets us into trouble. I also remind him that his ability to speak the truth is one of his greatest strengths, but that being strategic is an important life skill. Teachers who like us are on our side. Those who don't are not. Surviving school is about making sure you have as many people on your side as possible. Some day, I tell him, it may be a police officer or a bouncer giving him a hard time, and the consequences of shooting your mouth off will be far more inconvenient than an after-school detention.

He nods. I can see this makes a sort of sense to him.

'See, I'm not perfect,' I say. 'I got cross with you and I was wrong and I'm sorry.'

'I forgive you,' he says, billowing a little.

'That's generous,' I say. 'And by the way, you still have to write an apology note to your French teacher.'

Chapter 18

Skinny Love

I WASN'T ALWAYS PERFECT, you know.
As a teenager, I was neither pretty nor skinny.

Not for want of trying or wishing. But there it was. I had 'big bones' and a big nose, but my father assured me that even though I'd never be a model, I'd be 'other things'. At fourteen, I privately wondered whether, with a bit of plastic surgery, those offending bits could be tamed into submission. Certainly, if I was pretty and skinny, James Kringle would want to French-kiss me, which was, for a large part of my teenage life, as high as my personal aspirations reached.

I kept a secret scrapbook in which I stuck pictures of models I had cut out from fashion magazines. I had a page for legs, for breasts, for thighs, for faces. Miraculously, I survived my teenage years without ever voluntarily throwing up in the toilet as a form of weight control. Nor did I ever seriously consider swallowing a tapeworm. My mother's approach was sensible: 'Eat everything in moderation.' My dad reminded me that I was 'striking' and 'intelligent' and 'special', which is what parents say to their over-weight teenage daughters, and only served to further convince me that he just didn't understand. James Kringle liked pretty and skinny.

I was never the object of school boys' furtive obsessions. I did not, like Leonie Wells, receive seven Valentine's Day cards from a rugby team of covert admirers. I watched from the side-lines and wondered whether a rhinoplasty might make me more Valentine's Day material (back in the eighties, a nose job was a coveted pre-formal gift parents gave their teenage daughters). With skinny and pretty out of reach, all that was left for girls like me was 'smart'. So I went for it full tilt and, as my father promised, I became other things: a Fulbright scholar. A lawyer. An activist.

I learned to hate how women become desperate to fulfil the cultural stereotype of beauty through anorexia, boob jobs and labiaplasties. Nonetheless, I think it's true that though women say we'd rather be thought of as intelligent than beautiful, most of us mean we'd like to be thought of as both. I include myself in this sad generalisation, though ageing and maturity have certainly diluted the madness.

Just to prove how far I've come, I went out to buy groceries in my slippers the other day. As I stood paying at the counter, a man standing next to me said, 'Nice slippers.'

'I don't care what people think of me, I'm married,' I said, holding up my wedding ring.

'That's just as well.' He nodded.

See, it is much easier to be an overweight and unattractive middle-aged person than it is to be an overweight and unattractive teenager. This is because teenagers haven't given up yet. They also have to contend with the jackhammer of peer popularity.

One of the great liberations of middle age is the realisation that popularity is a high-school illusion. It is a force field that pops the day you graduate. Popularity is the dome of oppression high school generates in which the opinions of our (generally more idiotic, bitchy, bullying) peers become the measure of our self-esteem.

When Shannon was being bullied in primary school, she asked me one morning over porridge, 'Mum, what makes people popular?'

I had no idea. I thought back to my school days and who the popular kids were. Good looks didn't seem to be the qualifying factor. Not even sporting prowess. Intelligence even less so. One of the popular girls had the fattest ankles in the school. Another had freckles and red hair and smoked a lot of weed. Nastiness and bitchiness weighed in with some of them. Some of the popular kids were also decent – in a kind of unreliable way. They were nice kids, but not always inclusive. They were sometimes inclusive but then not very nice. Some were funny. Some were always getting into trouble for the wrong uniform or talking back to a teacher.

I googled 'What is popularity?' and found these answers by teenagers:

'If you're hot.'
'If you're a virgin.'

'What sports you play.'
'Who you sit with at lunch.'
'How much you put out.'
'How good-looking you are.'
'Being awesome at everything.'
'At my school, it's if you sell drugs.'
'Being cool.'

I am so glad I got that all cleared up.

What you'll notice is that popularity is a self-referential system with no rules and a circular, often contradictory, logic: being a virgin *and* putting out? 'Cool' and 'awesome' have no discernible coordinates. They mean what a particular group deem them to mean at any given time, in any given place. The mafia of popularity is a closed system. It just isn't true that all we need is to be Greased up like Sandy in a pair of tight leather pants and a cigarette to make Danny Zuko want to date us.

What makes popularity – determined and dictated by peers – so pernicious is that it kicks in just when the adolescent brain is wired to seek out and fit into the pack by any means necessary. And it works – but for only a small in-group. For the rest, popularity is an oppressive, bullying, classist system of unmeasurable privileges – some flow from being 'cool', some from being beautiful.

On Tumblr, I found teens expressing their pain at how beauty privilege works:

'Beauty privilege is being able to imagine yourself in a Bruno Mars video.'

'I can't even post selfies – pretty people suck.'

'Beauty privilege is buying a vibrator without people thinking it's gross.'

'Sometimes I wonder what life would be like if I were one of the pretty people. I really do, and it breaks my fucking heart to know that no amount of surgery will make me look like a model, or help me make more money as a server in a restaurant or get all the perks that come with being attractive in this world that just hates ugly people so fucking much. I can't have anything easy. I have to work hard for every fucking thing I have and you people are just disgusting, posting your selfies. I can't POST any selfies because I won't get noticed. Or if I do, people will just be cruel. I'm sick of being oppressed.'

Mandy Goldstein, a petite and warm-eyed woman, meets me for a coffee outside her offices. I've come to chat to her about anorexia. As a psychologist, it's her speciality. I admit, I'm still a little freaked-out by my research, having spent the last few days combing through Pro-Ana (anorexia) and Pro-Mia (bulimia) websites. I ask Mandy how she reacts to patients who believe that 'anorexia is a lifestyle, not a disease' or who tell her, 'I just wanted to hear those words, "Have you lost weight?"' How does she help someone whose life is dictated by the pyramid of thinspiration? It's an infographic of a triangle, with water at the bottom (8–10 servings), then a tier of diet pills (3–5 servings) and diet soda (2–4 servings); then cigarettes (2–3 servings) and coffee (2–3 servings) and finally, a pointy end where food should be 'used sparingly'.

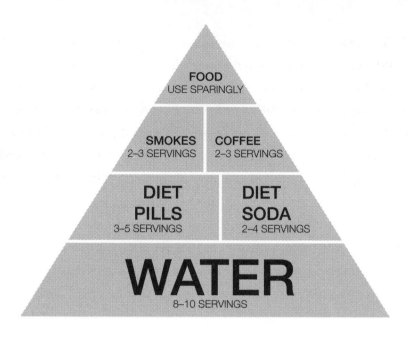

I mean this is sick, right?

'It's so disturbing that I don't even look at those websites,' she confesses.

She doesn't need to. She sees young people every day who do not eat so that they don't 'feel so gross all the time' and 'boys can pick me up, wrap their arms around a tiny waist or I can sit in their lap'. They're obsessed with not having a roll of fat when they sit, or a 'fat face' or a 'stomach that droops' over their pants. They will starve themselves for a thigh gap. I don't mean this hyperbolically. It's impossible to isolate the origins of this insanity, though we know that skinny celebrities, the media and the fashion industry keep it very simple for us: thin equals beautiful. But still. Starvation?

'Why do some people become anorexic or bulimic and others not?' I ask Mandy. 'And can it be traced to parental behaviour – like overly critical fathers or mothers obsessed with their own weight?'

'In treating eating disorders, I take an agnostic approach,' Mandy says. 'No-one is to blame, which is not to say that there aren't often behaviours and dynamics in the family that might have contributed – like a mother always on a diet, obsessions with food or health, fanatical exercisers or an overweight parent, and so on.

'But if parents feel they are to blame, they become paralysed. They might get clouded up in their own feelings of guilt or remorse and may not be able to act. We need active, energised, robust parents who can go the distance in standing up to the eating disorder, enforce the regime of treatment and get their child to recovery. Though we don't blame parents, we insist that they are responsible for helping their child get well.'

I love how this approach lets parents off the hook of blame but forces us to lift our own game.

The treatment program Mandy uses is Family-based Treatment for Adolescent Anorexia, known as the Maudsley Approach developed by James Lock, Daniel le Grange, Ivan Eisler and Christopher Dare. This approach treats the eating disorder not as an expression of family dysfunction, but rather as an *illness*, like diabetes, schizophrenia or cancer. The family, then, is the *solution* to the problem of getting rid of the eating disorder.

After my meeting with Mandy, I research the Maudsley Approach. The more I read, the more I understand how profoundly helpful it is – and not only in treating eating disorders. Philosophically, it's all about engaging parents in their kids' problems and empowering us to stop self-flagellating and just do the work that's needed to keep our kids connected, loved and humanised. Many of us give up when we feel as if our kids have locked us out. We feel redundant so we act redundant. We don't pitch up for work. We don't investigate what's going on behind closed doors. When we get told, 'It's none of your business,' we buckle, we back off.

We let our kids loose and, in doing so, we let them down.

Dani Klein, the clinical psychologist, believes that our kids are a generation of anxious, sad and lonely teenagers.

'More so than in previous generations?' I ask.

She thinks so.

We discuss how their screen-dominated existence contributes to their isolation. The irony is that while they're hyper-connected (scrolling, texting, fishing for 'likes', which is the only way to know if your peers notice you), they're stunted in their ability to emotionally engage. Our kids have few opportunities to learn how to read body language or social cues. Even picking up a phone and talking to a person in real time can feel like too much of an ask – much easier to text or Snapchat.

A life lived through social media flattens the complexity of interaction, promotes anxiety and shreds self-esteem. Girls spend hours looking for the perfect photo to post, and then poll their popularity by the number of likes they get. Our teenagers are forever comparing themselves to others and attempting to construct the perfect imposter identity that can compete on the catwalk of online profiles.

I ask Dani why girls cut themselves. (It seems to be more prevalent amongst girls.)

'To numb the internal pain. It's an acting-out behaviour. It happens in private and it is a physical, graphic representation of deep internal distress,' she says. 'They feel adrift, not attached, and need to experiment with extremes.'

Dani tells me that cutting and eating disorders largely manifest in higher economic groups, and that kids who are materially spoiled often feel empty and emotionally deprived. They come from families of high-powered, successful parents – in which it's common for both parents to work – who take their kids on expensive, fabulous overseas holidays once a year to make up for their absence the rest of the time.

Boys who feel like this, she says, often withdraw and internalise rather than externalise their pain. They may resort to drugs and alcohol.

Both cutting and eating disorders are self-harming behaviours. Sometimes they represent a fear of growing up. Eating disorders are often about preventing oneself from becoming a woman and remaining androgynous because thinness stops normal maturation. Girls cut themselves to release internal distress, and disfigure their bodies when they feel apprehensive about becoming a woman. But once the eating disorder and cutting take hold in the adolescent psyche, they can become habitual.

I leave Dani's office, saddened. As I mull over the socially and emotionally distorted universe our kids inhabit, I think about what parental responsibility requires of us in these changed times. We need to be more mindful. We can't just flop into parenthood. It's not like a decision to buy a plant, for example, because one day it seems like a good idea to bring a bit of green into the room even though we're not really plant people. We can opt for a house plant that we can forget about for weeks on end, one that can last while we're on holiday without being watered, one that will do its photosynthesising quietly and just get on with the job of being a plant.

But we can't opt for this sort of kid.

A child is not a cactus. Kids need the sunlight and water of our attention. Even teenagers do. Ignoring us is their right.

But we cannot reciprocate. We need to recognise just how much they suffer when we ignore or neglect them.

I am not in any way suggesting a slide back into a pre-feminist era when mothers were expected to give up their lives to be stay-home mums (some of us survive parenthood only because we have lives outside the home). And parenthood is way tougher on the inside than it looks from the outside. But once we have them, kids are not a mistake we can rectify, or a job we can quit, or even a marriage we've outgrown. As soon as we become parents we have no option but to pull up our Big Momma panties or zip up our Dad suits and bloody well be there for them: to hang out with them, as annoying as they find it; to talk to them, even if they don't respond. It is our duty to be there at least sometimes when they wake up and go to sleep. Our physical and emotional presence is needed to break the circuit of their distorted engagement with the online world and to soften the anxiety, sadness and loneliness that makes them reach for a razorblade before reaching out for a hug.

—

Some days later Shannon and I are lying on the beach. We talk about some of the girls in her year who are in trouble with their eating habits and body image. She tells me there are even some who are cutting themselves.

'I think I'm going to start wearing bikinis,' I say, lazily looking around at the shapes and sizes of all those wearing them.

'Yeah, why not?'

'Well, it's the belly, the thighs ... you know,' I say, knowing that this is the worst form of parenting on the planet. Probably scarring her with every word. I know that if I want her to love her body I have to love my own, and I do, I do, just you know … I could love it more.

'You know what the requirement is for wearing a bikini?' Shannon asks.

'Flat stomach? Killer abs? No cellulite?'

'Having a body. Everyone is entitled to wear a bikini without being judged.'

In that moment, hearing those words from my sixteen-year-old daughter, I have something resembling hope.

I feel myself succumbing, and I don't resist. I let myself really soak it in, warming me to my marrow: *nachas* that this girl, *this* girl is *my* daughter.

Chapter 19

Driving Me Crazy

'JUST LET THE handbrake down slowly,' I say.
Shannon reaches out with her left hand, wrist encircled by the bracelet of coloured skulls that gives me the heebie-jeebies but which she loves, and releases it.

'Sloooowwwlly …' I don't like how squeaky my voice sounds.

'Are you okay?' she asks.

'Perfectly fine,' I chirp. 'Just keep your eyes on the road.'

'Mum, we're in a parking lot!'

'There could be cars about. Never be complacent.'

'You are freaking me out,' she says. 'I'm never gonna learn to drive.'

I hold back my instinctive reaction, which is, 'I'd prefer it that way.'

She is only sixteen. There is no part of my training as her mother that has prepared me for this. In all the years I have attended to her, watched her, loved her silently and fervently, in admiration and in frustration, I have not allowed myself to think of her behind the wheel of a car. If I allowed myself, I could almost mouth the words, 'I will drive you anywhere, at any time, always.' I could psychotically commit to this, I know I could. I have to muster all my self-resilience and my knowledge about the importance of allowing children to become independent and force my face into a smile so she can see just how happy I am for her that she will soon be free of me in ways I have come to rely on for my identity.

I have moaned plenty over the years about the schlepping. This way and that way. To this rehearsal and that museum. To concerts and shopping malls and to that friend who lives over the bridge and *why can't you find friends who live closer?* And then she discovered public transport. During the first year she caught buses, I made her text me when she got on the bus and when she got off. In between the texts, I worried about the length of her skirt and the innocence of her grace, the glossy splendour of her hair and the many ways in which she does not see her own beauty. Even today, I'd much rather drive her there and back so I don't have to worry about lurid men looking at her *in that way* when she is only sixteen. Never mind that *there and back* works out to be four trips for me (there and back, there and back). I'd do it a thousand times if only it would guarantee her safety.

I shuffle in the passenger seat beside her, aware that my presence is as calming to her as a bee trapped in the car.

'Don't you trust me?' she huffs.

'O-of course I trust *you.*'

It's Them I don't trust. All the nameless, drunken, idiotic, testosterone-pickled Thems out there, hooning it up when that prefrontal cortex hasn't yet kicked in. Show-offs, know-it-alls, macho boys and silly girls who have never contemplated their own mortality and how a couple of tonnes of metal can put an end to it all. I know mothers who have lost their teenagers in just this outrageously needless way.

Shannon has never experienced this sense of power. There is something primal, perhaps even sexual, about being in control of such a potent piece of machinery. I've heard girls talk about horseriding in these terms. The first time I ever drove a car on my own, I cranked up my Leonard Cohen tapes until the tape-deck rattled. I sang at the top of my lungs. I took wrong turns. I found my way back on my own. I swore I'd never ask anyone to take me anywhere. I'd do it myself because I was finally in the driver seat of my own life.

To Shannon, all my protective gestures feel like a roadblock to her independence and self-expression. But when I ask, for instance, 'Isn't that a little low cut?' as she steps out the door, I'm not criticising her fashion sense or denying her right to wear whatever the hell she wants. I'm indicating that guys can get creepy and we cannot control other people's behaviour, whether they're pressing up against us on public transport or distractedly changing the radio station while driving.

'Now, just get into first gear and release the clutch slowly ...' I try to sound calm and helpful.

She engages the gear shaft and we shudder into motion.

'Th-that's it ...' I manage.

I watch her frown and focus and I try to unclench my hands. There is not much I can teach her in this savvier-than-thou world she inhabits. I am always a few steps behind, playing catch-up to the latest social media craze. This is perhaps the last chance I get to show Shannon that my experience can help her.

I remember watching her take her first steps, Zed and I applauding as she stumbled and fell to her knees, but then stood up and tried again. Now I am teaching her to operate heavy machinery. It is her right to be filled with excitement and adrenalin. It is my responsibility to contain my anxiety.

'Dad is so much more relaxed about this than you are,' she mumbles as she pulls us into second gear.

'Yes, just as well your father has a couple of things he does better than I do,' I sniff. 'It's important for his self-esteem.'

'Just chill,' Shannon says. 'You are making me nervous.'

She's driving my car and I'm making *her* nervous. 'I'll try be more … turn the wheel, turn it, more, more … Now straighten out …'

'Don't shout,' she says. 'I've only done this twice before.'

'Sorry, sorry,' I mutter.

Parenting is a 'ready or not' business. Ready or not, the time has come for me to surrender her to the roads. To traffic. To other people's bad driving habits, road rage, texting while driving, drink-driving and lack of attention. Right now, in the passenger seat of my own car, it feels too much to ask of a mother. She is only sixteen. No-one on the road loves her like I do.

'It gets easier and easier with practice,' I say.

It's as much for me that I articulate this as it is for her. Because right now, while she's practising her indicating and clutch release, I need to practise having faith that this almost-woman will find her way – through life and on the roads – without me driving her.

Chapter 20

Zipping Up

I<small>T'S NOT ALL</small> a clench-and-dread business. With teenagers, you can relax somewhat – especially when it comes to supervising their TV-watching. For a while now I've assumed that anything on prime-time TV won't scar my fourteen- and sixteen-year-old any more than they've already been scarred. However, a few weeks ago, I wandered into the lounge room early one evening and glanced at the TV, only to see a man shagging a woman doggy-style. It was not some kind of spoof. This was genuine fucking. Jordan eyed me guiltily.

'They're brother and sister,' he offered chattily.

'What the hell is this?' I demanded.

'*Game of Thrones*,' Shannon hissed. 'Shhhh, we're watching.'

'I don't think this is appro—'

'Muuumm, I'm old enough,' Jordan said indignantly, anxiously anticipating an upcoming ban on 'incest-porn'.

I watched, transfixed, as a young boy climbed a tower, investigating the sounds of sex. Nothing prepared me for what happened next. 'Oh, the things I do for love,' the brother said as he casually pushed the kid out the window, who in turn fell to what must have been inevitable death. Sex is one thing, but sex and violence against children? This was too much.

'Okay,' I announced, 'this requires supervision.' I planted myself in front of the TV.

'We don't need supervision. Jaime's evil, he's the Kingslayer,' Jordan said, explaining to me that he understands the difference between right and wrong and he knows that this is clearly all wrong.

'Why are they having sex?' I asked.

'They love each other,' Shannon said with exasperation. 'They feel like they're one person.' Was she explaining incest to me?

'I'm not happy about this. I don't know what this is.'

'God, where have you been? Under a rock?' she exhaled. 'It's *Game of Thrones.*'

'I don't care what it is, but what I do know is that it's not appropriate.'

My rough guidelines for what is appropriate follow no set of rules. It's more of a gut feel and is often determined by whether I can chill and watch the same things as my children without wanting to switch off the TV or leave the room.

'You let us watch *Breaking Bad,*' Shannon said, raising her eyebrows as if she'd nailed me with my own hypocrisy.

'Well, I'm not happy about that either.'

'I'm not gonna cook crystal meth,' Jordan said. I hated that he even knows that crystal meth has to be cooked.

'You took me to see *Django Unchained*,' Shannon said.

'Yes, but I was there to supervise.' Guiltily, I remember that I was the one desperate to see the latest Tarantino movie, glossing over the knowledge that Tarantino's movies invariably devolve into human abattoirs, but Shannon had assured me that after *Supernatural* nothing could be bloodier. Should I be comforted by the fact that she's inured to the violence? That it has no effect on her? Surely this is a huge parenting failure on my part?

Of course, I couldn't leave them to watch this gore alone, so I stayed to oversee the rest of the program. My supervision consisted entirely of intermittent squeals of, 'OMG, I can't believe this; Jordan, close your eyes' and 'I feel sick – are those his bowels?' The more freaked-out I got, the calmer they became. In the end, I decided I would have to be present for all subsequent episodes, just to make sure that … well, someone is there to provide commentary on the bloodshed, the gratuitous sex and the medieval ghastliness; though frankly, I could have done with some supervision myself.

———

Jordan told me the other day that the two most common Google searches are 'How to get a six-pack' and 'free porn'. How does he know this?

In my day, porn magazines were coveted treasures traded between guys during lunch breaks at school. Good wanking material was hard to come by. These days it's all too easy. Jordan can access just about anything in his room with his Mac.

My friend Linda told me that she found her son Tamon (not yet fourteen) watching porn. 'I went to the loo late one night and saw the flickering of his computer screen through the crack of his door so I went in, thinking he was on Facebook. He shut down the computer and I confiscated it. But when I got back to my room and opened the computer, I saw he'd been watching full-on, hard-core porn,' she told me, laughing. 'All boys do it. It's normal. There's nothing wrong with it, unless his younger sister comes across it and then God help him.'

Linda has also told Tamon that for his sixteenth birthday, she's hiring a prostitute to teach him how to please a woman. Tamon recently asked his mum if he has to wait until he's sixteen.

I have no intention of getting involved in Jordan's sex life the way Linda plans to intervene in Tamon's. He's just going to have to muddle his way through it on his own.

A while ago, when I was reading the trilogy of *Fifty Shades of Grey,* Shannon announced that she would like to read it too.

'No, you can't,' I said.

'Why not?'

'Because I want you to have a healthy sexual relationship first. This is about being tied up and even hurt, and I don't want this to be your first impression of sex.'

'As if it would be my first impression ...'

'I don't want you to read them.'

'You can't stop me. I'll just get them from a friend.'

'I'm asking you not to. I want you to have the best sex life ever ... please trust me, I know things you don't ...'

'You don't know anything ...'

My kids think I'm neurotic. I'm glad they don't know what I know.

In my twenties, while working as a women's rights advocate, I researched the porn and prostitute industries – and let's just say they're not career moves for women with choices. Ask these women how they ended up there, and you'll hear too many histories of sexual abuse. The porn business exploits young girls (what would *you* charge for twenty blow jobs?). Sometimes these girls are physically hurt, especially when they're made to perform all kinds of things that (barring what passes for 'consent' in those power relationships) are strikingly similar in nature to physical and sexual assault. I would never condemn anyone for their choices, but I'd love a world in which women had the option of making a buck as easily and quickly without having to spread their legs for strangers. One young prostitute I interviewed will remain forever in my heart. When I asked her, 'Why do you do this?' she answered, 'You either have to be stupid or hate yourself.'

'And which are you?'

'Well, I'm not stupid.' She shrugged.

I'm not anti-porn per se. I am certainly not anti-erotica. Let's be frank – there's some really hot porn out there. Porn made by women for women. The next best thing to having sex is watching others having sex, right? My ambivalence stems from knowing too much about what goes on off-camera.

But even assuming we could justify the exploitation in the industry – that most porn is made by men for men, and it's the producers who make the real money not the poor sods shagging themselves to a pulp – I still have two unresolved niggles about porn when it comes to our kids. Firstly, the research suggests that excessive exposure to online porn affects the wiring in our boys' brains. This is not a political argument, it's a biological one. If you spend your teens jacking off to porn, you will find it more difficult to have healthy sexual encounters with real people because your brain won't know how to.

Secondly, there are research-based claims that porn desensitises men to women and that there may be a link between porn and sexual violence. But even if this can't be proven, what we *do* know is that porn divides the world into 'sluts' and 'goddesses' and nothing good can come from this kind of dualistic thinking. A woman can – and probably should – be a little bit of both and a lot more in between.

So what can we do? Our kids will see porn, they're going to masturbate to it, and we can't stop it. So, we need to zip up our adult suits and talk about it with our kids. This isn't easy or cosy because what fifteen-year-old boy wants to talk about his masturbation habits with his parents? But somehow we have to get the words in there – in between the porn and the wanking – that the sex in porn is not real sex. How will our boys know if we don't tell them?

Porn doesn't teach our boys to come like gentlemen, and to take the hit themselves rather than targeting the other person. Very few young girls would choose to have a guy come all over her face – sorry to break it to you, chaps. From what I've heard, it stings when it gets in the eyes and it's a bugger to wash out of the hair. A sperm shower may be the money shot in porn, but in real life it's kind of a shock. Yet our porn-saturated boys believe that this is what girls want and expect. One seventeen-year-old girl I chatted to confirmed that in her experience, boys are 'just trying to relive a porn scene'.

As for the orgies: if boys took a moment to think about it, who would want to be simultaneously rammed up the front and the rear while two other men masturbate all over you? This is a *sexual fantasy* – a penis tea party where there are too many phalluses for any one person to enjoy.

In an intimate relationship between two people, of course, everything is up for negotiation. But teenage sexual contact is often opportunistic, experimental and not within the safe confines of an intimate, respectful relationship. Indeed, it leaves many girls feeling empty and used.

Sex therapist Dr Marty Klein is not panicking about porn. There are some troubling things on the internet and some not-so-troubling things, he says, and we must be careful not to confuse them. He diffuses the hysteria about porn by debunking some of the common concerns:

- It encourages sexual curiosity (what's wrong with that?).
- It leads to early sexual activity (not necessarily the case).
- It leads to perversion or porn addiction (again, this ain't necessarily so).
- It creates antisocial behaviour (may be true in some cases, but not all).
- It leads to unhealthy relationships (sometimes but not necessarily).
- It encourages masturbation (of course porn encourages masturbation – that's what it's *for*. If we're uncomfortable with that, it's a great opportunity to ask why).

The problem, Dr Klein says, is that the laptop provides an endless source of undemanding stimulation, and the human brain was not adapted to deal with infinite hunting opportunities. Porn addicts feel isolated, lonely and bored when they're not watching it. Just as a nutritionist might suggest cutting down on chocolate to a food addict, Dr Klein suggests being more 'disciplined' with porn. 'If porn is swamping your life, there is a problem and you may need to look at what's really going on. The only way to find out what to do about it is to stop using it,' he says.

He brings us to an important inquiry. 'Why do people turn to porn in the first place?' he asks. The reason is that many of us don't have decent sexual or emotional relationships. 'For many people, the alternatives to porn are boring sex, sex that induces guilt, or lack of sex.' The answer, he suggests, is for us to be honest about the sex that turns us on, which is also a developmental task of becoming an adult.

'There are people attached to the end of the plumbing and that's what sex is about. They still don't make porn that kisses and hugs and cuddles,' he says.

I feel somewhat reassured after hearing Dr Klein's take on things. He's not hysterical about pornography, and I don't want to be either.

I recently connected with Karen B. Chan, a fabulous sex educator in Canada whose divinely named website is Fluid Exchange. She doesn't think it's helpful to talk about sexuality as good and bad. 'Sexuality is changing, and what things mean is constantly changing – nudity, body parts, genitals, dirty dancing. Look at the outrage at Miley Cyrus's "Wrecking Ball" music video: decades ago, people had the same reaction to Elvis,' she says. She's adamant that seeing images of erotic desire is important, human and inspirational. For her, the focus should be on how we use porn as a tool to inspire ourselves (and young people) to become the people they want to be instead of debating the good and bad. She'd like to encourage more people to make their own porn and create images in their own likeness, to add to the collective imagination. In her opinion, mainstream porn creates laziness because it saturates us with repetitive images. Most people stop there, get their fix and move on. The problem, she says, is that our age suffers from a 'crisis of imagination'. The illusion of endless choice often leads to apathy, indifference and gestures of convenience. Porn is not the problem; the problem is that the large mainstream industry is a symptom of capitalist, consumerist saturation of sexual stimuli.

I find Chan's approach both radical and sensible. Imagine if we could support our kids to become sexually intelligent. Nothing would kill mainstream porn more quickly than if it became a big ho-hum.

As parents, we're going to have to hack our way through the quagmire of porn-hysteria and fear-mongering. Surely our hopes for our kids include that they will become sexually active, sexually functioning human beings, not people addicted to watching other people have sex on a screen?

Of course, if we haven't got our own sexual story straight – if we're repressing, suppressing and tangled up in a good and bad sexual debate with ourselves – this is going to be a bumpy ride. Though it's the last topic in the world our teens want to talk with us about, we have to muscle up, do the research and tackle the difficult conversations.

Then we have to send them into the world, armed with condoms and an imagination, and let them learn on the job.

Chapter 21

Behind Closed Doors

I WANT SHANNON TO have a boyfriend. I want it because when I was her age, I wanted a boyfriend. She wants to finish her HSC and to 'focus on her music'. I want someone to love her, hold her hand, touch her hair and make her feel cherished, because I'm not allowed to do that anymore.

'One day, a penis is going to pitch up on our doorstep, and then you're going to be sorry,' Zed warns me. But I don't mind. See, I am not afraid of penises in precisely the way Zed is.

Growing up in a family of girls, somewhere in the drama between fourteen and fifteen, I became fascinated with boy parts – like, how do they work? That erection thing? Boys were only too happy to demonstrate and I took my learning seriously and strictly unilaterally (my body was off limits). I was in the market for an education not an STD, an unwanted pregnancy or (shudder) a Reputation.

When I was fifteen, my boyfriend and I commuted between our home towns, sleeping over at each other's houses – always in different rooms. But see, parents fall asleep, eventually. At eighteen, when I started dating Norman (who was twenty-four), my mother, who is a doctor and fearlessly practical, promptly put me on the pill. Though Norman wasn't allowed to sleep over at our house, I lied and simply slept over at his.

So, now that Shannon is sixteen, the question is: can boys sleep over? Zed's take on this is primal. It goes something like 'Over my dead body.' But okay. He's still coming to terms with the fact that she menstruates and wears bras. Somewhere inside every father is a land of denial in which it is an offence, punishable by imaginary castration, for boys to look at his daughter the way he once looked at young women. Ask him about Jordan, and you get the old nudge nudge, wink wink; that it would be perfectly okay (read manly, virile) for him to have girls in his bed.

'Double standard,' I point out. 'Not to mention sexist.'

He shrugs. 'I know.'

'Wouldn't you rather she was experimenting in the safety of our home than in bushes or cars or clubs?' I ask.

'I'd rather she wasn't experimenting at all.'

I remind him that he's reaped the benefit of all *my* experimentation. At which point he puts his fingers in his ears, and sings 'La la la', as if by doing so Shannon will magically transform back into his little girl, where the only thing getting laid is the table for her teddy bear's tea party.

For most of us, the thought of our kids' sexuality is as squirm-inducing as that of our parents'. But when parenting teens, this is an inevitable confrontation. Teenagers are bristling with hormones, sexually curious and understandably reaching for the cherry that's dangled in front of them in music videos, MA-rated movies, fashion magazines and effortlessly accessed online porn.

But should we make it easy for them to experiment? Should we be facilitators or bouncers? The parents I chatted to had different takes.

Sarah, who is now eighteen, is Angela's only child. When Sarah was fifteen, her boyfriend was allowed to sleep over. He didn't have a car and lived far away, so it was about convenience. 'He was religious and didn't believe in sex before marriage.' Sarah smiles. 'But Mum allowed him to sleep over before she knew this.'

A girl in Sarah's class lost her virginity while blind drunk in a bathroom at a party. 'I walked in on them by accident,' Sarah says. 'It was terrible. Within five minutes, everyone at the party knew. That poor girl didn't go out for weeks afterwards and has been badly scarred by the experience.'

Angela is adamant that if she's somehow involved in the arrangements, Sarah will be less susceptible to things getting out of control like that. 'I always offer her and her friends rides to and from parties and clubs,' she says. 'I want her to have independence with a back-up, knowing she can call on us any time if she needs us.'

Recently, Sarah lost her virginity to a new boyfriend (who was also a virgin). Angela is grateful that Sarah's first experience of sex took place in a loving relationship, and in the safety of her home. Angela's only reservation is that perhaps Sarah is a bit naive about the real world. Angela is convinced that there are some things kids can't do with the knowledge, or in the presence, of their parents. 'You only get street-smart by being rebellious, and I haven't given Sarah many opportunities to rebel.'

Dr Michael Carr-Gregg, an adolescent psychologist, is clear that teen sleepovers require careful monitoring and supervision because the adolescent brain is unable to predict the consequences of its actions. 'Add to the mix an 800 per cent increase in testosterone (in boys), poor impulse control, peer pressure on steroids, and a desire to rebel – it's a volatile cocktail,' he says.

Still, he doesn't believe in 'one size fits all' parenting. 'There are some young people who, through personality and temperament, have a track record of making good decisions and keeping themselves safe. The litmus test is that the greatest predictor of future behaviour is past behaviour. So there are some kids who have always hung out with sensible peers, never made poor choices and don't have a sensation-seeking temperament; I'd be more inclined to trust those ones.'

But what are the assumptions that underpin our parenting decisions? Is it true that teens will jump at sex if they have the opportunity? (Not in Sarah's case.) Don't maturity and the personality of a kid play a part? And family values that have trickled into them? We know they won't abstain just because they don't have easy access to each other. Teenagers who want it will find a way and a place, even if they end up being intoxicated in the bathroom at a party.

Laura, a paralegal and mother of three, only allowed her eighteen-year-old son Daniel's girlfriend to sleep over after she'd spoken to the girl's mother, who gave the all clear. 'As soon as I endorsed his status as a grown-up like this, our relationship became stronger,' Laura says.

Laura also didn't mind when her fourteen-year-old son, Harry, spent time alone in his room with a girlfriend, though she'd knock intermittently and announce, 'Parent approaching,' and give them a few moments before entering. She's comfortable with her children exploring their sexuality, but doesn't want them to be precocious with it. 'You can be sexual without having sex,' Laura says. 'Everything in its right time. There's no rush.'

Laura's only reservation is that her six-year-old daughter Tessa is getting the message that it's cool to have boyfriends and girlfriends doing 'stuff' alone in the bedroom. When it came to Daniel, Laura believes it was the girlfriend's mother's call. Laura is aware of the gender contradiction, and admits she's limited by her own stuck thinking. 'I don't want my daughter to feel I can't embrace her sexuality. I'd rather if she had sex it was in a safe and contained place, but I'll have to wait and see how I feel when she's older.'

Do these parents resemble those who do drugs with their kids at home to ensure a controlled environment? In which case, should parents provide condoms? The pill? The Kama Sutra? Sex toys? Sex isn't just about safety, it's about pleasure, too. Just how involved should we be?

It's not only religious and sexually conservative parents who are against sleepovers. Eve, a finance manager with two boys (eighteen and twenty), has never allowed her boys' girlfriends to sleep over. 'It's the ultimate voyeurism,' she claims. 'I don't want to know my children's sexual business. That is their private life.' She believes that either you're an adult or a child. 'If I still have to tell them to clean their rooms and I'm still supporting them, they're too young to be having sex under my roof. No-one's having sex in my house except me.'

As a feminist, Eve wants to raise men who respect women. She believes too many women sell themselves short. 'If a girl wanted to sleep over at my house, I'd take her aside and give her a talking-to about self-respect and self-esteem. Girls need to treasure themselves and not give themselves away cheaply.' Eve believes teenagers don't 'get' intimacy. 'If a teenager needs sexual release, there's always masturbation. Knock yourself out, I say – but I don't want to know about that either.'

Eve is proud that she didn't raise her boys to be 'cool'. She thinks cool kids set the pace of sexual experimentation, and want to be seen to be the first having sex or taking drugs. She wants her boys to value women and any sexual connection they have. Making it hard for them to have sex on her watch is her way of letting them know that there's a time and place for everything.

A mother of four, Helen has only one girl, fifteen-year-old Jade. Helen thinks sleepovers encourage teens to experiment sexually and fast-track an experience that she believes should be delayed until at least eighteen (Helen lost her virginity at eighteen). Jade disagrees. 'If you're at home, you're more in control of the situation. There's less of a chance of being pressured. If a boy is in your zone, it's easier to back out and say no. You can just kick him out.' She also disagrees that sleepovers lead to sex. 'All that might be happening behind the closed door is talking and cuddling. Besides, at sixteen you're legal, so why shouldn't we be allowed sleepovers?'

'Maybe I'm just a prude,' Helen counters, 'but I can't stand the thought that there are kids in a room in my house having sex.' She'd only change her views if Jade were in a long-term relationship (at least fourteen months). Helen admits that she'll probably feel differently about her boys. She's confident two of her three boys will be respectful of girls – but she's not so sure about the eleven-year-old. 'He's wilder. If any of my kids will have one-night stands and use girls, it'll probably be him. But I'll sort him out before then.'

By the time teenagers are exploring their sexuality, much of our work in that department is done. If we're sex-squeamish, they pick it up. If we haven't modelled healthy sexuality in our own lives, if sex is a taboo topic and our kids don't feel they can comfortably bring their uncomfortable questions to us, and there are quiet shadows of shame looming in our sexual histories, our kids will get tangled up in that mess. It is largely in the unspoken that our kids learn from us.

If they're going to take risks and do stupid things, that's already locked in temperamentally, just as they've shaped themselves around the yes or no to drugs by then. The best we can do is set boundaries, keep conversations going and empower our kids with information and a strong self-image – and hope like hell that we've prepared them to make good decisions when confronted by them.

If we want to raise kids with robust self-esteem and a healthy differentiation of self, we may have to accept that a 'good choice' may not necessarily be the same one we'd make. As Jade says, 'Parents can try and control their kids as much as they like, but they'll still do what they want. You have to have faith in your child. Parents can't prevent their children from going through heartbreak. There comes a time when a parent can't protect you and you have to make your own mistakes and learn from them.' True, except no parent wants to see their kid learn the hard way that an unplanned pregnancy or STD was 'a mistake'.

Like most parenting issues, the answers to whether it's appropriate for our kids to have sleepovers with girlfriends or boyfriends are personal and reside in our own value systems, which we may be called on to defend in the face of judgement and condemnation. While our kids are under our roof it's our job to draw the battlelines, knowing that if boundaries are reasonable, they're more likely to be respected, whereas if they're dictatorial, our kids will likely rebel and do things behind our backs.

I wonder if, as parents, we don't get overly hung up on what's being touched and who's touching whom. I want my kids to know they can come to me in a crisis and ask for my help if and when they need it, the way I always knew I could go to my mum. She saw me as a whole (sexual) person, not just her good little girl.

And secretly, I think she was happy for me. That Norman was a real spunk.

Chapter 22

The 'No' I Need My Daughter to Know

SOMETIMES I THINK I'd be completely satisfied if I raised a son who is not an arsehole and a daughter who is not a bitch.

I once told Shannon that 'bitchy girls have bitchy mothers' – for where else would these girls learn such cruelty? But I wonder whether I wasn't wrong about this. Because I have noticed the creep of bitchiness into my own daughter's behaviour and, let me tell you right now, she hasn't learned that from me.

Firstly, my own mum is not a bitch so I wasn't raised by one. Secondly, I've always preferred to stand up for people rather than put them down – even when people are bitchy to me. I'm not making a case for my own faultlessness; I admit I can be irritable, rude and aggressive in the right circumstances. But not bitchy.

I hope I have taught my kids that kindness is a virtue to be prized above all others. However, when it comes to Shannon, she needs to know that gestures of kindness do not extend to boosting others' self-esteem by letting them put their hands down her pants. Girls are expected to be kinder than boys. But the lines get blurred when it comes to these sorts of sexual transactions. A sexual overture must be distinguished from a friendly gesture in much the same way that it must be differentiated from the offer of a chocolate bar. It's okay, for example, to say yes to a chocolate bar to avoid someone feeling rebuffed by the refusal of their offerings, yet saying no to a hand on the nipple or a tongue down the gullet is perfectly acceptable, even if makes the donor feel shit and damages his self-esteem. Kindness ought not to be a consideration if the overture is unwanted. So, learning kindness and learning to say no must be taught simultaneously just as the adductor and abductor muscles must be equally exercised, lest the one out-strengthen the other. (I speak from experience here – I once pulled my left hip out when one set of muscles got a little up themselves and started bullying the slacker ones.)

When it comes to teenage girls, kindness must weigh in to counteract the bitchy gene, but the ability to say no must similarly – and maybe even more robustly – be taught to protect them from indiscriminate groping.

What I remember most about being a teenager is how undiscerning boys were about who touched their genitals. I had a couple of male friends who talked endlessly about masturbation and who they fantasised about (mostly our middle-aged maths teacher). With all due respect to the burgeoning of male sexuality, one only has to read Philip Roth's *Portnoy's Complaint* or watch the movie *American Pie* to grasp that a teenage boy really doesn't care where he puts his penis as long as the place is soft and wet. This is something teenage girls need to grasp lest they mistake attention for affection. Boys' need for sexual gratification is urgent, removed from scruples or even consequence. Teenage boys are hard-ons looking for a place to land. Girls shouldn't take their interest personally. This isn't depressing; it's an opportunity for our daughters to practise saying no and get some experience – but on their own terms. It's based on a simple economic principle: where there is a glut of demand, whoever controls the supply has the power. I'm reminded of a cartoon where a boy, bragging to a girl, points to his penis and says, 'I bet you wish you had one of these.' To which the girl replies, pointing to her privates, 'With one of these, I can have as many of those as I want.'

I know Shannon has an inkling of this power as I watch her bundle away her girlishness. I notice how she hikes up her skirt, just as all her friends do, their hemlines as high as their panty lines, their stockinged or bare legs on display for all eyes. I know what they think – that it's sexy, cute, boys'll like this – because I was once there, too. I was sixteen and overly eager for boys to see me, want me, touch me, tell me they loved me. And, Goddammit, girls should have the right to wear (or not wear) whatever the hell they like.

But as the mother of a teenage girl, I cannot ignore what is real about the differences between men and women. Too many years spent counselling raped and battered women taught me that no matter how 'powerful' we are as women, most men have a physical advantage over most of us. There are a million reasons to celebrate this – they're the ones expected to carry heavy luggage and do the objectionable menial tasks while we can sit back and file our nails. They must hunt while we gather.

But this is a serious disadvantage when it comes to unwanted sex. Girls are rightly frightened of male aggression coupled with strength. So we have to teach our daughters to avoid situations that could potentially lead to a physical-strength showdown. In encouraging our girls to develop strong intuitive muscles, we must teach them about intelligent anticipation of potentially risky situations. Not to be afraid, but to be smart.

The number of girls who are abused by family members will shock you – if you yourself escaped your childhood unscathed. This means that there are heaps of mums of teenagers who were abused in the past. How, in the squiggly hand-me-down of our stories, might this affect how they parent their teenagers?

One of my closest friends, Fiona, was sexually abused by her older brother from the age of nine. When she finally told her, her mother refused to believe that her 'golden boy' would do such a thing. So, when Fiona's first child was born – a son – she knew she would only ever have one child. 'I would never take the chance of having a girl after having a boy,' she told me.

Janine was sexually abused from the age of seven by a distant family relative. She never told her parents – out of shame and to protect them. 'Ours was a loving, stable family so this would have shattered them,' she says. She told me that she forgave her abuser long ago 'so I could move on and no longer be a victim [even though the abuse] probably shaped a large part of who I [am] and my future sexual behaviour'.

Growing up, Janine was aggressive towards boys and would get into fistfights if they tried to touch her. She couldn't watch any kind of physical intimacy on TV or in movies. She hated her developing breasts and wanted to be a boy so she played soccer, rode dirt bikes and did everything her brother did. Losing her virginity at twenty-one was an ordeal. She felt as though a part of her had been ripped out forever and that she was no longer in charge of her body. She had to work really hard to accept that sex does not have to involve control or manipulation.

In mothering her two teenage girls, Janine admits that her experience of abuse has affected her parenting and made her paranoid about her girls being abused. When they were very young she started teaching them about stranger danger, reminding them never to allow anyone to touch their private parts without their consent. She was obsessively careful about where they were allowed to sleep over. When they reached their teenage years, she explained the rudiments of sex, saying that it's 'something special between two people' and that they should never feel forced or obligated to do it.

'Boys will tell you, "I love you, you have beautiful eyes, we were meant for each other ..." but will then say, "Take off your clothes" and walk away afterwards, to boast to their friends about how they "got some action", leaving you feeling used and abused,' she'd tell them.

If they ever found themselves pushed for sex, she told her daughters, they should call their dad and say, 'Dad, there's someone here who wants to ask you something,' then hand the phone to the guy and say, 'You'd better ask my dad if it's okay if you have sex with his daughter.' She asked her girls to remain virgins until they finished school, and to wait three months into a relationship before having sex. At twenty, her youngest daughter is still a virgin and is happy to wait for the right guy. The message she gave her daughters is that their virginity is 'a precious, one-of-a-kind gem which, once given away, you can never, ever get back', and to 'save it for someone really special who'll treat it with the respect and care it deserves'.

As a teen, Janine's sister was wildly sexually promiscuous. They fought regularly and Janine called her horrible names. She only found out recently that her sister was also abused by the same person. Now she's ashamed for never understanding that her sister's behaviour was linked to the abuse. As an adult, her sister went into deep denial about her history. She put her kids into small schools and forbade them from watching or reading anything deemed 'unfit', including many Disney movies. When they became teenagers, they were not allowed relationships with the opposite sex and were only permitted to socialise with others at church functions. The eldest complied but the younger one rebelled, wanting to go to a 'normal' school and be able to watch 'normal' movies like everyone else. It was only after her younger one attempted suicide that Janine's sister and her husband loosened the reins and allowed their kids some freedom.

Janine and her sister are survivors of their childhood. All of us carry wounds – sexual, emotional, physical or psychological – from our histories. Repercussions of past abuse ripple into our parenting, shaping all that we become and, in turn, all that our children are steered to become. The most we can do is try our best to heal so as not to pass on our suffering to our kids.

———

But not all sexual encounters are this devastating. As parents, we have to learn to distinguish between abuse and good old curious experimentation.

At fourteen, I towered above the boys in my year by a whole head or more. I was way too big to be considered girlfriend material by any boy of my own age. Female enormity, I learned early on, is only considered a turn-on when it comes to bra size. So I set my sights on older boys. Unfortunately, height and maturity have a disobliging habit of being mismatched. As tall as I was, I didn't understand that older boys have different expectations.

I was at a friend's family function when Stuart, the cousin of a friend of mine, asked me out on a date. I let my parents know that I'd be going out with him that Saturday night.

'That's not going to happen,' my father said.

'What do you mean?'

'How old is Stuart?'

'Twenty-seven,' I said, quietly thrilled.

My father laughed. 'What do you think a twenty-seven-year-old wants with a fourteen-year-old? You think he's going to hold your hand all night?'

These questions had slunk around the edges of the dance floor of my mind, but I was fourteen, all right? I could handle a man. I knew all about French-kissing and blow jobs. But no, my father made me call it off.

And that – my mortification at having to cancel Stuart aside – was that. I hated my father. But honestly, I couldn't have been more relieved.

It's astonishing how the years can reload a memory and replay 'Hot Stuart asks me on a date' as 'Creepy Stuart stalks minor'. As the mother of a sixteen-year-old, if I ever saw Stuart again, I'd punch him in the nuts. Thankfully, my folks knew better and they steered me out of his sweaty palms and into my own body.

Then, when I was sixteen, my friend Tyrone and I went out for dinner with his uncle while his aunt and cousins were away. After dinner, his uncle dropped Tyrone at home first before driving me home. But then he pulled into a side road, stopped the car and confessed that he found me 'very attractive'. The next thing I knew, his hands were up my skirt and in my bra. He then proceeded to remove his trousers and showed me what a married man's erection looked like. I do not recall what I thought of all this, except that I was intrigued and vaguely aware that it was 'wrong' but I was equally fascinated. I asked him why he was doing this given that he was married. Apparently, his wife just didn't turn him on anymore. In the vacuum bag of my adolescent self-image, I was exhilarated by the thought that my taut sixteen-year-old body was a bigger turn-on than that of a thirty-something woman. He made me promise not to tell Tyrone. I could see why Tyrone's knowledge of our encounter could complicate things. I could feel myself falling in love.

So I was somewhat crushed when the uncle did not call me or attempt to make contact with me again.

Looking back on these experiences, I am not sorry for any of them. I was a sexually curious teenager and I engaged in my own gauche adolescent flirtations with older men. I was looking for something I didn't yet understand or have language for, but I wanted sexual attention. To be noticed, admired, desired. From where I was, it seemed perfectly okay that men in their late twenties and thirties were interested in me. I looked like a woman. But I was far from a woman. I was a girl in a woman's body, playing a big girl. I was flirtatious without really understanding what I was flaunting or offering men. I know this because of the way my body shook after the experiences – a mixture of adrenalin, excitement and fear.

But Tyrone's uncle awoke something in me I am very grateful for – how it felt to be used. I didn't much care for it. After that, I decided to take control and to use boys for my own experience.

I was very clear that no-one would get to touch my body unless I knew they really liked me.

When it comes to my own kids, I need to remember all this, and remember it in the right way. Of course these men were creeps, and there will always be Rolf Harris types trying to touch my children in their sacred places before they might be fully ready for it. But I don't want to pole-vault from the legitimate curiosity and agency I felt as a sexually awakening teenager into the hysterical, restrictive moralising of adulthood. Our kids need to experiment to learn whatever it is that exploratory sexuality teaches us. My father was right to say no to my date with Stuart, but I am not sorry for my experience with Tyrone's uncle. It gave me a weird sense of power and self-confidence, even though it was misplaced.

Our mistake is to tip feminist discourse into Victorian puritanism, and deny the agency that young girls have, and need to have, in sexual situations. I did not feel abused or violated. I felt desired. Even though Tyrone's uncle was adulterous and vile, the encounter taught me that married men are not to be trusted and that I didn't ever want to be married to a man who needs a sixteen-year-old girl to give him a blow job. It awoke me to the fact that sexuality is complicated.

Of course, he could have turned out to be a psychopath and he could have raped me. But he didn't. And because I cannot protect my kids from men like him, or situations that could potentially spiral out of control, I'd like to think that if my kids ever got themselves into such a situation, they'd find a way through it using their wits, intelligence and intuition.

While doing research for this book, I came across rainbow parties. Innocuously named though they are, the phenomenon (if indeed it is not entirely a fiction) is enough to induce parental hyperventilation and moral panic. Apparently, the girls line up, each sporting lipsticks of different colours, and perform communal fellatio on the boys, leaving rings of rainbow shades up the length of their penises. The 'winner' is the guy with the most colourful cock.

How degrading, how shocking, how unhygienic … The parent in me shudders.

But somewhere else in me, the wild teenage girl is going, 'Rainbow parties? All we ever got was spin-the-bottle.' These parties may be nothing more than urban myth. But the truth is, if I'd ever been at a rainbow party as a teenager, I might very well have lined up with my fire engine–red lipstick. Why? Because teenagers will do ridiculous things. They're catastrophically curious. Frankly, once you're all grown up and in an intimate relationship, the opportunities for idiotic behaviour involving one's genitals are ruthlessly curtailed, unless one goes for the whole orgy or swinging thing, which I personally don't.

We are also not meant to be witnesses to everything our kids get up to, in the same way that certain sexts are not meant for the public eye. (I always feel a little sorry for high-profile people whose sexual texts end up in the newspaper for everyone to read. I'm guessing none of us would like our iPhones monitored. I once got stung after Jordan came across some silly sexts I sent to Zed which I forgot to delete. The recovery was excruciating.)

We have to be grown up about what teenage sexuality really is. It's transgressive. Experimental. Driven by an I-wonder-what-will-happen-if-I … impulse. We can ooh and aah, clutch our breasts and shake our heads in terror about it all – or we can engage in some intelligent, non-judgemental conversations with our kids. Some teens will want to join in with whatever's going on around them and others will have none of it. Some will take part because of peer pressure and some will want to but won't because they're too sensible or afraid of getting a reputation.

My job is to help my kids make good choices in situations as bizarre as a rainbow party. My advice: take smart risks, ones whose consequences you can live with. STDs are real. How safe is this risk (physically, emotionally, socially)? And remember: *everyone* has an iPhone. Do you really want one stupid night of your life to be captured on candid camera forever? Can you live with a seemed-like-a-good-idea-at-the-time moment ending up on someone's Facebook update or Twitter feed? Nothing is sacred anymore; nothing is secret. Everything we do follows us.

As we navigate this tricky terrain, we must be careful to distinguish our understanding of how social media invites the exposure of everything we do from our moral take on teenage sexuality. We're not going to approve of everything our kids do. Our mistake is in becoming too knotted up over sexuality – we're not meant to know everything our kids get up to or fantasise about, just as we don't need them to know these things about us. They may engage in sexually risky behaviours – but didn't we?

When it comes to sex, we need our kids to be smart and to be able to make empowered choices. We have to give them guidelines and yardsticks, information about STDs and teenage pregnancy.

But mostly, we need to model healthy sexuality in our own lives so that they grow up looking forward to, not being terrified of, the delicious fluid exchanges that await them.

Chapter 23

Coming out into the Light

I FIND MYSELF SINGING along to Katy Perry, who kissed a girl and liked it. Especially the taste of her cherry chapstick – and who doesn't love a cherry chapstick?

Shannon remarks that Katy Perry did no favours to the gay community by singing, 'It's not what good girls do'. 'She's implying that being gay is bad,' she huffs. She is very principled in this way.

A while back she asked me to proofread a short story she wrote for English. Halfway through I realised her main character was gay, so I asked her about it.

'Oh yeah,' she said casually, 'I guess I've been influenced by Tumblr.'

'What do you mean?' I still don't know how Tumblr works, but it irks me that Tumblr is missing a vowel. It literally makes me feel like I'm missing something.

She tells me the Tumblr community is an inclusive, accepting one full of gay, bisexual, transsexual, pan-sexual and any-other-kind-of-sexual people. On Tumblr, sexuality is 'no big deal'. It made me feel a whole lot better about the amount of time she spends in that online world.

Secretly, I wondered whether I could take any credit for this. Zed and I have always given our kids the message that they can love and marry whomever they want – gender is irrelevant.

When Shannon was little and had four Barbies and only one Ken – like some macabre toy version of *The Bachelor* – I suggested that the Barbies could marry each other, even as she shook her head, 'Noooooo.' You get kids early enough and you can imprint them with just about anything: racism, sexism, anti-Semitism, vegetarianism, just by normalising it. I've also spent many years of my life telling Jordan that calling someone 'gay' because they don't play basketball is not only an incorrect use of the term, but is homophobic – which is as bad as being racist. I'd always imagined that homophobia is a function of immaturity that most people eventually grow out of through intelligent debate, open-mindedness and growing the hell up. Yet Shannon has bypassed it entirely. This must be some massive feat – either of Zed's and my parenting, or of modern society. It gives me confidence in her generation that they're a more advanced, evolved species than ours.

By contrast, when I was Shannon's age, my friends and I giggled at the word 'homo'. We'd use the words 'faggot' and 'queer' and shriek when we discussed what gay people do to each other. One of my closest friends at school was obviously gay but pretended otherwise. We colluded and helped set him up on dates with the most beautiful girls. Thankfully, as soon as he left school, he embraced his identity and is now a hot-shot designer in a long-term relationship with a gorgeous Swedish guy.

Steven, who is now in his forties, was ten when his mum died. He was sent to live with his aunt. Though he didn't officially come out until he was eighteen, everyone knew he was gay. While at school, he was repeatedly sent to psychologists to 'fix him'. His childhood was a litany of social exclusion, rejection, shame, guilt and, with the rise of the AIDS epidemic, disease and death. He was continually warned not to bring shame and disgrace to the family name and to keep his dirty secret hidden. Coming from a Jewish family, he was not allowed to drink from the same *Kiddush* cup (Sabbath wine cup) as everyone else on Friday nights. His family insisted he use a scrubbing brush and detergent to clean the toilet after he had finished. He was reminded over and over that had his mum lived, she would have rejected him.

When he lived in the UK, Steven met young guys from working-class backgrounds whose mothers pimped them out to older men to supplement the family income. His Saudi friend, now in his late twenties, underwent forced electro-shock therapy for two years and the local imam still comes to his parents' house to force-feed him holy olive oil.

Steven's reflections about growing up gay are heartbreaking: 'Most of us felt isolated, guilty and ashamed. We knew we were different and that we harboured a secret. Like the Lady of Shalott, we were stuck in a tower, segregated from society, watching reflections of the world pass us by that for the most part did not include us.'

But, Steven says, 'It's a very different world for young gay people today.' Much has changed. Big-name celebrities like Ellen Degeneres, Elton John and Adam Lambert have transformed how gay people feel about themselves. Gay pride parades, TV shows like *Modern Family* and *Queer as Folk*, and movies with out and proud gay characters are part of the mainstream. Gay helplines and support groups for parents and teenagers are easy to access. Human rights laws and gay marriage are recognised in about seventeen different countries.

'Had I grown up twenty years later in a freer society with conscious parenting magazines on the coffee table, who knows how my story may have turned out?' Steven reflects. 'And for gay teenagers today, the narratives seem vastly different. For many of them, whilst individual battles and skirmishes still need to be fought, the war is mostly won.'

As much as things have changed, there are still many parents who will not accept a gay son or daughter. They'd rather lose the relationship and never see their child again. It makes my head spin.

I remember receiving a phone call from my friend Neil's mum when I was in my twenties and Neil had just come out. She was in tears and begged me to 'reason with him and talk him out of it'. She was convinced he just hadn't met the right girl. I asked her why she was so upset; he hadn't changed except in his dating habits – but how did that affect her?

'Just you wait until you're a mother,' she sobbed. 'Then you'll understand. What about AIDS? Discrimination? No wedding, no grandchildren ... nothing ...'

Then I got it. It wasn't only about Neil, or his happiness. It was also about her and her expectations of what he, in an implied parent–child contract, was supposed to give her.

'Maybe it's just a phase and he'll grow out of it,' she reasoned. She was clearly at the bargaining stage.

'Nothing's changed,' I repeated. 'He's still your same amazing son.'

'Many years later she became pretty cool about it all and was even ashamed of how she'd initially responded,' Neil says.

Today she'd probably be the kind of mum who'd join him in a gay pride parade.

My friend Shane is the fifth child, with four older sisters. When he came out to his mother, she said, 'If I'd known how things were going to turn out, I'd have tried to have another son.' It took Shane many years to understand that she wanted someone to carry on the family name; her words weren't meant to be unkind. 'But it still took me a long time to reach that realisation and get over it. Parental words can hurt with long-lasting effect when they're thrown around glibly,' he says.

My friend Gaby's fifteen-year-old daughter, Rebecca, came out some years ago to her parents. Gaby always suspected her daughter was gay, and first said as much to her dad when she was as young as four. At thirteen Rebecca confessed that she thought she might be bisexual. A week later, and in tears, she said, 'Actually, I think I may be gay.'

Gaby told Rebecca that it made no difference to how she feels about her, and that 'it doesn't matter'. Thinking back now, Gaby revises, 'Of course it matters! It was silly of me to respond like that.' Later she told Rebecca that she loves her – all of her, which includes her sexual identity. Gaby is sick and tired of Rebecca's grandmother assuming that Rebecca is desperate for a boyfriend. She has encouraged Rebecca to tell her, 'Gran, I like girls' to shut her up. But Rebecca doesn't want to. Gaby hates secrets, but is loath to push her daughter. 'It's her choice when and whom to tell,' she says.

But having a gay kid brings its own brand of anxieties.

'I know it's a cliché, but I do worry about how hard it might be for Rebecca to have a relationship that isn't yet fully accepted by society,' she says.

She agonises that Rebecca isn't having the same crushes and dating experiences as straight kids. Even though there are gay kids and a transgendered kid at Rebecca's school, it's a small school, and gay girls are an even smaller subset. Gaby is concerned that until she reaches university, Rebecca may not have social interactions with kids with whom she can identify.

Gaby is also anxious about the dangers associated with being a gay person, even as a middle-class kid. 'You just never know when some homophobic arsehole might get pissed off and do something terrible.'

Gaby lives in South Africa where lesbians can be targets for 'corrective rape' to punish them and show them their place. The term was coined after Eudy Simelane, a football star and lesbian activist who was training to be the first female referee at the 2010 World Cup, was raped, beaten and stabbed to death in the outskirts of Johannesburg. These stories, as well as the homophobic backlash in Russia and Nigeria, must strike a particular kind of terror in a mother's heart, despite South Africa being a democracy that recognises gay marriage.

Even with such supportive parents, Rebecca suffers from depression and anxiety. 'It's hard to accept that while I seriously couldn't give a flying fuck whom she is attracted to, it still hurts her to be different,' Gaby confesses. She'd be completely comfortable for Rebecca to have a girlfriend sleep over in the same room. 'I hate to think of kids in unsafe places because home is not welcoming to them.'

When I ask Gaby what she's learned from Rebecca, her answer is heartrending: 'That it's not enough that I love her as she is; she has to love herself, too.'

All Gaby wants is for her daughter to 'meet a wonderful woman who will love her as much as I do, with some fun before that ;-),' she writes.

Shannon overhears me talking on the phone to someone I'm interviewing for this book. After I'm done, she tells me that my question – 'When did you come out to your parents?' – is 'so last century'. 'Coming out,' she tells me, 'is so heteronormative. Why should gay people have to come out when straight people don't?' This, I concede, is an excellent question.

As much as the world has changed and Shannon and Rebecca represent a new era of coming out into the light, there are still too many teens who are bullied, abused and rejected by their families, their churches or communities for being gay. Their parents deny the reality of their kids' sexuality and refuse to talk about it. These young people can easily spiral into depression or develop eating disorders, like my friend Matthew, who still battles bulimia and anorexia, a physical expression of his self-hatred. The shame they feel about who they are is so powerful that they often contemplate or resort to suicide.

How can we understand a parent's rejection of a child because of their sexuality? Is it a deep narcissism or a repressed shadow? If our kids' sexuality makes us uncomfortable, shouldn't we be curious about why? Either we cannot tolerate difference or we're denying similarity. Could it be that homophobic reactions are a denial of our own latent homo- or bisexuality? Maybe this is another opportunity not to trust our first reaction but to dig a little deeper and learn something about ourselves.

As parents, we all battle at some point with the dissonance of looking at a child and thinking, 'You came through me but I don't know you,' and having to love a child through the difference. Our narcissism is not a reliable parenting rudder; our need for replication of a mini-me cannot be our guide. We forget: our kids are not here to be our Promised Land. They are here for themselves.

This is part of our challenge as adults. This is how we grow up: by holding paradox – the familiar and the strange, the known and the unknown – and honouring the mystery of our children's unique soul-prints so we can become full human beings ourselves.

Chapter 24

Choosing the Beautiful Risk

S HANNON IS GOING off to a concert on her own. She is all dressed up and twittering with anticipation about being able to enjoy the music without worrying about whether her friends are having a good time. It's the middle of exams and none of her friends want to risk a late night, but it's Bastille and Shannon is an obsessive fan.

'Do not accept any drinks from anyone,' I advise her at the front door.

She rolls her eyes. 'As if, Mum.'

'And be careful in the moshpit, people get crushed …'

'It's not that kind of concert,' she sighs.

'Girls get groped by strangers …'

'Will you just chill out?' she says as she leaves.

'Have a grea—' But the door slams before I finish trying to be cool about it all.

Chill out? I will chill out when I hear her key in the door after midnight.

I send her a text: 'Please text when the concert is over and you're on the bus home.'

I wait a minute. 'K,' she texts back. Then another text: a smiley face.

'She'll be fine,' Zed says. 'We're doing the right thing by letting her go. It's a safe risk.'

I sigh. I know it's the right thing, so why do I feel like I need a tranquilliser?

When I think back on my teen years, I shudder at the memories of driving home blind drunk then emptying my guts into the toilet, having unprotected sex with people whose sexual histories were a blank to me, smoking 'til my lungs ached and hitching rides from strangers in the days before mobile phones, when I had no way of letting my folks know where I was. The mother in me would like to go back and tell my smart-arsed self, 'You're grounded, young lady!'

Outwardly sensible, focused on my school work and deeply engaged with social issues, I was still capable of inexplicable idiocy when it came to taking risks and assessing danger. And I wasn't even a particularly risk-driven teenager. Of course, I could argue in defence of my adolescent self that I made it into adulthood so all those risks paid off.

Yes, well, some of my friends weren't so lucky. A girl I grew up with contracted herpes from unprotected sex (and committed suicide in her early twenties; I've no idea if the two are causally related). Another developed anorexia and died in her early thirties, never having married or found any joy beyond her high school years. Another friend became a drug addict and watched friend after friend die off – some alone in public toilet cubicles with needles in their groins, others choking on their own vomit.

Sometimes I think it's by grace alone that teenagers make it to the Happy Valley of adulthood.

Because we've been there and done that, we're excruciatingly aware of what awaits our teenagers. It's not as much fun being on the other side of the party fence. There's enough ugliness out there to sink our hearts and every chance our kids will encounter any number of trolls (cigarettes, drugs, alcohol, bullying, depression, violence or unplanned pregnancy) as they trit-trot across the bridge to the lush valleys of the futures we've planned for them.

Since we were teens, a whole new species of dangers has spawned to haunt our parenting nightmares, including cyberbullying, school shootings, online gaming, internet porn addiction, planking, butt-chugging (inserting alcohol rectally), eyeballing (taking a shot of vodka to the eyeball), Chatroulette (talking randomly to strangers on webcam), the condom challenge (snorting a condom through the nose and pulling it out the mouth), the choking game (tightening a noose around the neck until you pass out) … anyone would think our kids are bored. What trippy lunatic comes up with these ideas?

As parents we have no choice but to adopt double standards: 'Do not do as I did, do as I say.' It would be kind of a dereliction of our guardian duties to high-five driving intoxicated and popping ecstasy, even though parental approval would ironically render the fun dead on arrival. Likewise, evidence of our own involvement in similar behaviour in the past automatically disqualifies it as 'cool'. Still, I don't know a parent brave enough to experiment with parenting Bizarro-style to try to get the nerdy stuff trending and the hazards lame-zoned.

So we dutifully teach our kids to recognise and stay away from perverts, drugged drinks, chat rooms, impulse sex, bad boys, bad girls, needles and stuff that happens in dark corners in clubs. God knows we've drummed it into their heads to 'just say no' and walk away. To never get behind the wheel blotto or look for a fight. To never walk home alone after dark or accept lifts from strangers. But we also know that they're not thinking (did we, back then?). They're riding a wave of prefrontal cortex deficiency which makes playing cards on the median strip on a highway at night seem like a good idea at the time. One stupid misjudgement of a situation and they can be hurt – devastatingly or (heaven forbid) fatally. All it takes is being in the wrong place at the wrong time, like Sydney teens Thomas Kelly and Daniel Christie (both eighteen) who died on a night out in Kings Cross when they were king-hit without provocation.

But we know we have no control over what happens online, gets shoved in their drinks, slashed against their faces or rubbed up against them on the dance floor.

So how do we play this? How do we stay sane while reconciling the double standards of our own history and watching our kids dance on the precipice of jeopardy?

For starters, we cannot get frantic every time our kids go out. Sobbing at the front door or banning them from having a good time may keep them safe the way a maximum security prison keeps its inmates safe, but it will Chinese foot-bind their spirits and cause emotional and psychological collateral damage. We have to find a path between our anxiety and letting our kids have a life, knowing that they will probably experiment with at least everything we experimented with – and then some stuff that hasn't even been invented yet. That's how they get from kid to adult.

We can't protect our kids or strip the world of menace. But we can prepare them by having the right kinds of conversations. As psychologist Jerome Kagan says, 'Parents are the first source of a child's conscience.' We must tell our kids what we think is right and wrong, and then follow up with positive reinforcement when they copy our values, and 'punish through criticism' when they don't.

Our job is to give our kids a strong armoury in the form of self-esteem, sound judgement and self-knowledge to navigate the perils.

So while they're making their choices, our choice is to worry ourselves sick over the possibilities or … worry a little less. Recently, I've reduced what I'm prepared to worry about after my yoga teacher said one morning, 'Worrying is praying for things we do not want.'

———

If we can boil parenting down to a single goal, it's probably the art of training others how to solve problems. When our kids are small, we tell them what to do: 'flush and wash', 'brush your teeth', 'say thank you'. We teach them about stranger danger and swimming between the flags. When someone is being mean, we coach them to use their words. We expect that practising good problem-solving will shape our kids to make decisions that steer them away from STDs, drugs, jail, terminations, destitution, addictions and suicide. We hope that by the time someone offers them heroin instead of lollies or a drunken ride home, they'll make intelligent choices.

But here's the problem: making sound choices involves risk. Our kids are not training to be monks. They're in training to be ordinary people – who've made (and hopefully learned from) mistakes. Who've sometimes chosen well and sometimes chosen appallingly. All we can do is be there when their terrible choices lead to consequences that are difficult for them to face alone.

So if we're funnelling our kids towards constructive decisions, we probably need to understand the neuropsychology of choice a little better. How do teenagers make decisions?

Usually in one of three ways: reacting against us, imitating their role models or following their intuition.

In his book *Brainstorm*, Dr Daniel Siegel writes, 'Teens won't do as we say – their brains are programmed to reject what we tell them to do.' Teens might do a backflip, using us as the measure of all they don't want to be, like the character Saffy (Saffron), daughter of Edina in *Absolutely Fabulous*. Far from taking WWMD (What Would Mum Do?) as their guide, they'll opt for WWFMO (What Would Freak Mum Out?). Just to be themselves.

We help our kids become effective problem-solvers by modelling sound decisions in our own lives, by staying calm in unexpected and difficult situations. To pull this off with conviction we've got to be grounded in our own beings and trust our intuition. How have we acquired those skills? Through failure and experience. In other words, we can only practise trusting ourselves by facing risks and experimenting with problem-solving.

Most decisions, by the way, don't pass through our logical brains. It's our intuitive minds – the fast, Gladwellian 'blink' of the hidden 'gut' that is turbo-powered and responsible for most of what we say, do, think and believe. Professor Daniel Kahneman from Princeton University showed how the intuitive mind is riddled with cognitive biases (including confirmation bias, hindsight bias, the halo effect, loss aversion, the negativity bias) that influence our decisions. The present bias – the tendency to focus on now rather than later – which causes overeating, smoking, texting and driving, and having unprotected sex – accounts for many a stupid choice (and not only in teenagers).

Given that we can never predict how our teens will react in any situation, how can we help them navigate dangers and assess risk? Siegel suggests that we teach them to trust their gut, not their thoughts. He calls this *introception*, a form of self-awareness to access the internal compass. His techniques (similar to meditation) can help adolescents develop the capacity to reflect on themselves and their inner processes (though I have no idea how one gets a teen to sit still and concentrate long enough to do this).

'We can help them access their intuition. We can teach them to pause and ask, "Does this feel right?"' he says. 'Their emotions may be egging them on, but there are neural networks around the heart and intestines that can act as a counter-pull when risky behaviours are luring them.'

As we can't always be around to act as their prefrontal cortex, self-insight is the greatest gift and safety catch we can encourage our teens to develop. Of course, the more self-insight *we* have, the better our chances of passing on these skills.

———

A few years ago, my friend Emma's daughter Megan 'went off the rails' after Emma's husband left. Megan would leave home without telling her mum, and stay out all night. She had a gazillion piercings, was binge-drinking and smoking. Emma was out of her mind with anxiety over Megan's behaviour, until a counsellor told her, 'She's your only normal child.' Though Emma went through hell for a year or so as a single parent without any support, she says, 'I knew she'd come out the other side.' When her daughter asked for her help in cutting out her nose-ring with pliers, Emma didn't say, 'I told you so.' She just helped and gave her a huge hug.

Emma believes that if we limit our kids from doing every single thing they want to do – 'no piercings, no concerts, no boyfriends, no sleepovers' – we waste good parenting capital and thereby the power to say no to the stuff that really matters. The main message she gives her teens is: 'Don't do it (drugs, smoking, drinking, sex). But if you do and you get into trouble as a result, come to me. No-one else is going to look out for you.'

Laurie Matthews runs The Caretakers Cottage, a refuge for teens in Sydney who are homeless or at risk of becoming homeless. He believes that teenagers have a tougher lot these days. 'They're all trying to put their own stamp on their lives, and find their way through Mum's apron strings and Dad's thumb. Some can do this skilfully and others can't.' Laurie's take is that our kids' generation lacks social skills and a sense of community. 'They live in an estranged world. Many teenagers feel so very alone.'

His words echo those of psychologist Jerome Kagan, who says kids these days are 'tense and worried'. His concern is that this is a generation overly driven towards success in a crowded, competitive market. This leaves them poised to take risks they may not otherwise chance.

At the Caretakers Cottage, the social workers help teens to take control of their lives, and support them to achieve goals that boost self-confidence. Risk diminishes in the presence of 'stabilising behaviours' – getting back to school, becoming resocialised so they don't keep getting into fights, stopping alcohol and drug abuse, and having routines to follow. The team works with the teenager to implement a plan of action to generate income, find work or sort out health issues. Here teens are equipped with the skills to successfully navigate the hurdles of an ordinary life. It's a place where chaos is calmed and kids are taught to value themselves.

Laurie is emphatic that parents are crucial at this time in a kid's life, especially in instilling in them optimism for the future. 'Kids learn a lot from their own parents' happiness and wellbeing.'

The extended family is vital too. In bonded communities (such as Pacific Islander, Muslim, Jewish, Greek and Italian) Laurie sees more family participation, where aunts, uncles and cousins are willing to get involved and help out when there's a problem with teenagers – even 'rehoming' them. In today's world, he stresses, there is even more of a need for elders in the community to provide this kind of support to teenagers and their families.

Isolation and boredom are fuel for risk-taking.

Though there is no way to danger-proof our teenagers, we can work harder to help our kids feel connected to a parent, family member, community and sense of purpose; and to develop self-esteem, sound judgement and self-knowledge until dopamine levels even out and the prefrontal cortex develops with the passage of time.

As a single mother, Rochelle raised both her kids on her own. When her son was sixteen, she heard rumours via his friends that he was 'doing drugs'. A schoolteacher then called her and told her he'd disappeared from school one day. When he came back, his eyes were red and he was 'out of it'.

Rochelle responded by getting help, not only for her son, but by going into therapy herself so she could support him. She and her ex-husband banded together in this crisis and agreed to send him to an overseas wilderness therapy program in the USA, where he spent eighty-one days in the bush. The program is designed to build character and self-esteem by teaching seven values derived from Native American culture: courage, self-discipline, respect, honesty, developing a work ethic, trust (in themselves and others) and compassion (for themselves and others). The focus is on reverence for the environment, positive peer culture and rites of passage that recognise personal growth.

The program gives these kids the opportunity to engage in real but beautiful risks, and therefore develop the parts of their personalities that are desperate to grow. Jennifer Senior writes in *All Joy and No Fun: The paradox of modern parenthood*: 'It's possible that adolescents would be less inclined to throw eggs at houses, drive at 113 miles an hour … if they had more positive and interesting ways to express their risk-taking selves.' She quotes Berkeley psychologist Alison Gopnik, who argues that adolescents these days take mad and dangerous risks because 'our culture gives teenagers too few chances to take constructive, tangible and relevant risks'.

On this wilderness program, the kids have to read and complete introspective writing exercises as well as learn challenging survival skills, such as fire-making and trapping, to help them internalise the cognitive and behavioural aspects of each value.

Rochelle and her ex-husband were simultaneously put through a range of confronting exercises in which they were asked to examine their role as parents, and how they had communicated with their son around issues of boundaries and trust. They had to write 'parent narratives' for their son to read.

The parents' stories are integral to the teenager's treatment. For the first time in their lives, kids hear their parents' histories and hopes and dreams for them. They're in a space to actually listen instead of muting their parents' voices. The philosophy is that 'it becomes more difficult for the teenager to find excuses for his behaviour, or ignore or hide the facts of his or her life. Importantly, he or she cannot minimise or trivialise his parents' love and support.'

The teenagers also write autobiographies for the parents to read during the healing process. The sharing of these stories starts to build bridges between estranged parents and their teenagers.

Rochelle says her son came back a changed kid, but after eight months he relapsed. I asked her if this felt like a failure, to which she said, 'Definitely not – it was part of the process. There are no miracle cures.'

When he was eighteen, she told him he had to leave home and go live with his dad. Today he is twenty-two, studying full-time and living with two friends. 'He's okay for now, but when he's stressed, I do worry about him relapsing,' Rochelle muses.

Rochelle is committed to setting up a similar wilderness program to help kids in Australia. 'One thing I am sure of is that kids need to be out in nature. They learn things in the bush that they cannot learn in their peer group.' This echoes author Jay Griffiths, who writes in her book *Wild: An Elemental Journey*, 'From indigenous people all over the world, I learned that going out into the wilds is a necessary initiation, and that for young people, lost in the wastelands of the psyche, the only medicine is the land.'

What advice would Rochelle offer parents of teenagers doing drugs?

'Parents should seek help in understanding their teen's behaviour when in a crisis. They need to think broader than the issues they are facing because these are only symptoms. Parents need to dig deep and make changes in how they parent their kids. Treatment is only effective when it is done with kids and their families. Parents must realise that it could be a long journey of recovery and that the process takes time. It requires a huge commitment to the recovery process, and lots of patience.'

Long after my conversation with Rochelle, I find I'm musing over the lessons in the wilderness-as-therapy philosophy that we can all adopt in our day-to-day parenting of our kids, who will all be 'troubled' at some point. I keep seeing fractals of systems theory wherever I go.

These phrases shimmer in the dark shadows that are closing in on our teenagers: 'sharing narratives', 'building bridges' and 'listening to each other's stories', which echo my own ABC of parenting, Always Be Connecting.

We need more language like this. Language that replaces the hype with hope.

———

Way past midnight, I hear Shannon's key opening the front door. She pops her head around our bedroom door and whispers quietly, 'I'm home.'

'How was it?' I ask.

'Oh, Mum, it was the best night – they were amazing.'

'I'm so glad,' I say, feeling tears prick my eyes, not really understanding why.

I reach for Zed's hand in the dark.

'See?' he says. 'Tonight you both grew up a little.'

Chapter 25

'A Permanent Solution to a Temporary Problem'

I'VE ALWAYS THOUGHT teenage depression is 'normal' – an appropriate response to the changes and challenges of transitioning from child to adult. As their brains grow, teenagers become rightly switched on to the injustices not only of peer popularity but of the wider world; the cruelty not only of playground hierarchies but of social and financial ones; the random brutality of inclusion and exclusion; the unattainable standards of beauty and of unrequited love. In an age of vanity and popularity, it can't get more devastating than having a face full of pustules or being the only one without a date for the formal. Add to that real problems – bullying, mental illness, disability, addiction to alcohol or drugs, failing at school, not feeling wanted at home, confusion (and guilt) about sexuality, falling pregnant, exclusion from social groups, moving cities and schools – and their souls can crumple like a Coke can under a garbage truck.

At the same time, we know that teenagers are prone to histrionics. They will say things like, 'I want to die', 'I hate this world', 'I don't want to be here', 'I wish I could kill myself', 'I hate you,' and 'I wish you were dead.' Some of this is just 'typical teenage behaviour'. Teens don't want to be where they are. They want their freedom, they want things they can't yet have. In the heat of emotional intensity, they can feel and express sentiments that chill us to our core when, most of the time, they're just letting off steam.

As parents, we have to find a way to distinguish the ordinary madness from the dangerous madness and not to confuse the two. This requires us to be mighty vigilant.

Because teenagers do commit suicide. They're ripe for it. Firstly, their brains are not fully grown yet. Secondly, they are deeply, biologically wired to take risks. They lack perspective that this terrible time of their lives will a) be over soon enough; and b) not determine the course of the rest of their lives. They live in a frozen magnification of a tiny close-up, unable to zoom out and get a wide-angle and long-distance shot of their lives. In Phil Donahue's words, they sometimes resort to a 'permanent solution to a temporary problem'.

So how do we tell when there is a real threat that our kids might take their own lives? How do we determine when they're in trouble, especially at a time when they keep so much from us?

———

Shannon was bullied in primary school. I still see the scars it left on her. Those emotional welts hardened – she once stood up to a girl who was tormenting one of her friends, daring her to try her best shot. The bully threw the rude finger before skulking off, and Shannon was a hero that day. But there are moments when I catch a glimpse of the pain it caused her. A shrinking hesitation in certain social situations. Spikes when softness is the better choice. The 'I don't really care's she casually tosses around to throw me off the scent of her disappointment. She's tough, but what if that toughness calcifies, becomes her default?

These days bullying is muscled by the surging Hulk of social media. It's now anonymous, easier to inflict and more devastating. No case captures the horror of these combined forces as poignantly as that of Amanda Todd, a Canadian teenager who posted a video on YouTube on 7 September 2012, telling her story to the world. One teen commentator describes it as 'The most saddest video I have ever seen.' By holding up handwritten flashcards to a webcam, Amanda shares how she was bullied, assaulted and finally broken.

It all began with her wanting to connect with people online, and buying a webcam. She met men who told her she was 'stunning, beautiful, perfect, etc ...' Then one of these men asked her to flash her breasts for him. So she did.

A year later, she got a message on Facebook from a man who knew all her personal details. He told her that if she didn't 'put on a show for him' he'd post her boobs all over the internet, which he did, setting off a cascade of terrible events. She started having panic attacks. She became depressed, began taking drugs and drinking alcohol. A while later, the same man tracked her down and set up a Facebook page with her breasts as his profile picture. School became a nightmare. She tried changing schools, but 'nobody liked me'. She was called names.

'*I can never get that photo back, it's out there forever,*' one of her flashcards read.

She sat alone at school every day because no-one wanted to be her friend. This led to cutting, to further destructive behaviour. She was beaten up, bullied, left in a ditch. Some kids filmed this on their phones.

'*I felt like a joke in this world … I thought, nobody deserves this. I was all alone … I wanted to die so bad.*'

She drank bleach in a suicide attempt, but when she was discharged from hospital, kids had posted messages all over the internet like 'She deserved it, I hope she's dead.'

She then moved to another city and another school. But six months later, people started posting images of bleach and tagging her, saying, 'She should try a different bleach. I hope she dies this time and isn't so stupid' and 'I hope she sees this and kills herself.'

Her notes then read: '*I messed up, but why follow me?*' and '*Every day I think, "Why am I still here?"*' and '*life's never getting better … I can't go to school, meet or be with people, I'm constantly cutting, I'm really depressed … I'm stuck … what's left of me now? Nothing stops. I have nobody. I need someone.* ☹'

Finally, on 10 October 2012, this lovely imp of a girl, with her whole life ahead of her, hanged herself.

She was just a vulnerable teenage girl like any other. She just wanted to be liked and included. It wouldn't have taken much for her to have found enough hope to live through this awful time in her life. Just a friend or two. Someone to stand between her and the terrible onslaught that slowly crushed her.

What turns kids so *Lord of the Flies*? Who are their parents? How does something like this happen? And why did nobody reach out to help her?

And where were Amanda's parents? we might wonder.

The terrible truth is that they were there. They tried to help her. They moved schools, cities. They did what any one of us would do.

Yet still, Amanda felt alone in the world.

———

While Shannon was being bullied, on those days when boys bruised her heart and girls pushed her up against the school fence, I was oblivious. When I finally found out, I felt like a shipwreck of a mother for not having sleuthed it out sooner. Why didn't Shannon just come out and tell me? I guess she was embarrassed. She was trying to protect me. And she knew there was very little I could do to stop it.

Teens are as vulnerable as freshly hatched turtles crossing a beach for the safety of the water. They tussle and turn and fret within the confines of their strange and newly forming bodies and psyches. We're clueless because they hide their torment from us – out of shame, a desire to protect us and fear of our reactions. So they suffer in silence and we keep the silence up from our side because they don't want to talk to us and, anyway, we don't quite know what to say.

We know they change when they hit the pre-teens. They get quieter, more aloof. Less chatty. And sometimes it's that withdrawal from us that protects the bullies, and endangers our kids. As parents we often have to work out what's going on with our kids from observing their bizarre and difficult behaviour, which all along we've assumed was 'normal teenage' acting out.

Without any prior experience or training as parents, we have to move largely on instinct. But if we've outsourced all our power to parenting books and experts, and are out of touch with our teens because staying connected to them has just been too hard, our instinct is rusty. We don't trust our teenagers and we don't trust ourselves.

But here's exactly where we're needed. Because of their limited life experience, teens don't yet understand how pain and trauma wire us for resilience; how insult can be chiselled into insight; how early hardships are the foundations of our strengths (as well as our wounds). Their pain is unfiltered and seems interminable.

'Life's never getting better …'

'I'm stuck …'

'What's left of me now?'

'Nothing stops.'

In their world, it feels as though there will be no end to their suffering. Parents really need to 'get' this. Not to undermine or undervalue the weight of their pain, but to hold it with them. We've had longer life experience than they've had. This counts for something. We know that unendurable situations end, and that solutions we can't 'work out' sometimes reveal themselves when we least expect it. We need to find a way to let them know this.

———

In early 2013, one of my publishers sent me a manuscript and asked me to write a shout for *Boy: The story of my teenage son's suicide* by Kate Shand. Weak with sorrow after having just lost my beautiful friend Emma to a tragic death, I wasn't sure I could look at this kind of pain straight on, but I agreed to read the manuscript.

'I have a son my son is dead I had a son ... I had a son he was fourteen years old he hanged himself.'

The opening lines tore into me like a hook in the throat. I couldn't stop until I'd read the last word. I had wanted to find that there was something 'wrong' with Kate's son, JP: that he had a mental problem or that Kate was a dreadful mother. I read, looking for an explanation that differentiated JP from my son. But all I found was the gruelling self-scrutiny of a mother who had loved her son (and her three daughters) deeply, who was herself desperate to understand why. It was the account of an ordinary mother, with a seemingly ordinary fourteen-year-old boy – one who'd been bullied (who hasn't been?), who was quiet and withdrawn (what teenager isn't?), who was experimenting with marijuana (most do), who hated school (don't they all?), who one day decided that it was all too much.

Earlier that day, Kate had planned to take JP for a burger and 'have a chat' when she got home from work, the kind of thing I might do with Jordan when he's having a rough time. But she never got to sit with him and find out what was weighing on his heart with such force that he couldn't imagine living through it.

Kate writes that being the mother of a child who commits suicide comes with the torment of both knowing how much pain your child was suffering and the guilt of not being able to prevent it. Her son's suicide made her question everything about her abilities as a mother. Throughout the book she ruthlessly examines the way she mothered him, her history as well as her ex-husband's, desperately looking for answers. It is a book of savage courage and honesty; Kate strips herself down to the bone, taking us with her to the edge of what is bearable.

Kate and I became friends through her book. In one of our conversations she said one of the bravest things I've ever heard a mother utter: 'My son didn't shout out to be listened to – he was so very quiet with his call for help that I didn't hear. If I was quieter, calmer and more peaceful in my parenting, perhaps I would have heard – and this isn't guilt, it comes from deep introspection and a commitment to transform from this tragedy and *not* to stay the same or parent the same. It's about taking responsibility, not for his death, but for my life going forward and my parenting going forward.'

I've chatted to Kate about my friend Susan's daughter, who sometimes expresses suicidal thoughts. Kate's belief is that there's safety in words. She wishes that JP had spoken to her and had the language to express what he was going through. The fact that he didn't speak much and was a quiet and withdrawn child is what pains her so deeply. If only we knew how to open the conversations about life and suicide and the meaning of it all, and let our kids vent their worst frustrations, without scuttling away in fear of the storms in their hearts.

While writing this chapter, I read *Stay* by Jennifer Michael Hecht, in which she argues that suicide 'unfairly pre-empts your future self'. She says 'suffering and surviving are ways of serving humanity, and that, in and of itself, can bring some happiness'. Teenagers are good at suffering. They inhabit it passionately. As a teenager, my favourite quote was by Ralph Waldo Emerson: 'The purpose of life is not to be happy. It is to be useful, to be honourable, to be compassionate, to have it make some difference that you have lived and lived well.'

These days I think what the hell was Emerson trying to say, differentiating happiness from compassion and living well? In his book *Man's Search for Meaning*, Viktor Frankl got it right when he forged the connection between making meaning in our lives and happiness as a by-product of that meaning.

Our teenagers need to understand that when life doesn't feel like a party, it doesn't become meaningless. That being able to survive the horror of bad days and grief and thwarted expectations and not making the team or getting the lead role is, in itself, meaningful.

One of the worst parenting mistakes I ever made was listening to the advice in parenting books that insist on Time Outs for bad behaviour. When he was little, Jordan suffered the fallout of my idiocy in believing everything I read in the parenting books. Time and time again I banished him to naughty corners and to the aloneness of his room for 'unacceptable behaviour'. His tantrums got worse. I read more books. I followed through more vigorously. He got more out of control.

Finally, a friend who is a psychologist suggested I 'be with Jordan' when he got worked up. She explained that when a child suffers from overwhelming emotions, they need someone to contain those emotions. By sending a child to a room all on his own, we're implicitly telling him: 'Your overwhelming feelings are too overwhelming for me. Go off and deal with them on your own.' A tantrum is a child's way of letting us know that they *can't* do exactly that. Banishment only aggravates the problem.

I cannot describe the self-loathing and sorrow I felt when I realised what I had been doing all those years. The next time Jordan had a tantrum, I tried the new approach. I looked in his eyes and I saw his pain. I saw his anger. I told him, 'I am here for you. I know you feel overwhelmed, but it's okay. I am here. And I won't leave you.'

He continued to thrash about and shout verbal abuse.

'Are you okay?' I asked him.

'Of course I'm not okay!' he screamed.

'What do you need?'

'Nothing, I hate you, I hate my life, I hate everything,' he yelled.

'I'm still here,' I told him. 'Let me know if you need something … maybe a hug?'

I don't know how long it took of this soft cooing, this gentle repetition of my presence, but eventually his rage left him. He nodded. He let me hug him.

And, as I held his body and felt his sobs, I realised that when people rage, they feel so alone. They need to know they are still loved, that they are still precious, even when they feel worthless.

I have never forgotten this lesson. I have never blindly followed the advice in any subsequent parenting book.

Examining philosophies and reactions to suicide, Jennifer Michael Hecht suggests that when people feel needed and valued, even in their anguish, they might choose to 'stay'. As she writes:

> One needs to practise believing in the power of small actions to change the way one feels. In an acute state of misery, it may be impossible to initiate this kind of belief: one tries to imagine connecting with others, and gets nowhere. Just as we cannot get drunk by thinking about vodka, we cannot feel the good feelings that come with being connected with people by thinking about connecting. We have to act and then be aware of how acting changes our outlook and vigilantly remember the

experience. If we have done the work of thinking about these things in advance of our dark times, they may become accessible to us when we need them to help carry us through to better days.

With our kids, we need to do the work of bringing the shadow into the light, of equipping them with verbal and emotional resources to give shape and language to their thoughts and feelings. We cannot shy away from hard conversations – life isn't all picnics and ponies. Life gets real very suddenly in the teen years. Instead of shutting our teens up when they raise difficult topics with, 'Don't upset your mother/father by talking about depressing things,' or whispering behind their backs about cancer, terrorism and suicide, we should welcome these conversations as gateways to a robust consciousness that can hold paradox, work through difficulties and seek creative solutions to emotional problems.

On a practical level, there are other jobs for us to do. If we're concerned about our kids' safety (not in a reactionary, panic-induced way) we must find professional help, like my friend Holly did. When her daughter Jacqui was fifteen she was diagnosed with depression and prescribed antidepressants, which have helped her get through her teens.

We can do the research so we understand teenage depression – what it looks and feels like. We can banish platitudes and admonitions of 'You should be grateful for what you have, instead of dwelling on what you don't.' We want our kids to trust us with their sadness. The act of making ourselves available to them, without judgement or criticism, and simply sitting with them in their pain can often relieve their feelings of unbearable loneliness. Research shows that teenagers with strong support networks – family, peer or through sport, social, cultural, musical or religious organisations – and who feel part of something bigger than their suffering selves have outlets to help them manage their overwhelming feelings.

Kate's book on her son's suicide has been one of the most powerful teaching tools in my parenting journey. Her honesty and willingness to look at herself have raised the bar for me in my will to search within as a way of understanding my kids.

Life is full of all kinds of anguish and we must teach – and model for our kids – how to experience it well. To be broken by pain, and recover from it, just in time to be broken again. Being a teenager is a time of terrible loneliness: *'I have nobody. I need someone. ☹'*

We must listen to our teenagers – to their rants and their silences. We must see and acknowledge the agonies they are grappling with. We can help them find the humour and silliness in the everyday. We can encourage them to exercise; ensure they're eating as much fresh fruit and vegetables as we can sneak into the meals we prepare; and perhaps we can suggest they read books in which others have grappled with depression.

Most of all, we can remind them how much we love them and how valuable and important they are to us. As Jennifer Michael Hecht writes:

> We are all in this together. The twin insight is that, first, you have a responsibility not to kill yourself; and second, the rest of us – and you yourself – owe you our thanks and respect. We are indebted to one another and the debt is a kind of faith – a beautiful, difficult, strange faith. We believe each other into being.

We are the invokers of their futures-to-be; we are there to remind them that 'this too shall pass' and that for now, they are not alone.

Chapter 26

The Dangerous System

THE MOTHERS ARE dressed up in high heels and lipstick, the dads in their business suits and ties. I am still in my yoga clothes from my morning series of salutes to the sun. I look for seats near the back so that Shannon and I can slip out when we've got the gist of this parent-information evening about subject choices and academic expectations, and to reassure us that we made the right decision in sending our kids to private schools.

When I look around I see Shannon sitting with a group of friends a few rows ahead of me. I try not to feel self-conscious sitting all by myself. I smile briefly at the unfamiliar parents who pass me to find seats upfront. I don't know many of them by name, and I certainly don't socialise with any of them the way I did when Shannon was at primary school. Most are in teams – mothers and fathers. Zed and I always do the 'I'll go this time, you go next time' shuffle. We clearly don't take our school responsibilities seriously enough anymore. Twelve years of these annual, obligatory taking-up-of-a-parent's-free-time evenings has wearied me. I am, in reality, a silent heckler.

I take out my iPhone and check Facebook to avoid engaging in phatic chitchat. I listen to a podcast of Dan Savage talking about what gay people can teach straight people about sex. When he came to Sydney a few months ago to speak at the Festival of Dangerous Ideas, I took Shannon with me and managed to get whatever sex education was still outstanding wrapped up in an hour. It was the first time she'd heard the word 'pussy' spoken in public, and I want her to feel at ease with some kind of terminology (since 'vagina' clearly isn't doing it for her).

I glance up as the principal clears his throat, welcomes us warmly to the school and reminds us how well the school ranked in the last national examinations. 'None of our students ranked below seventy per cent.' He beams. The parents nod smugly, gratified that our money is being well spent.

'And this is by far the smartest year we have ever had,' the principal continues. 'We are expecting wonderful things from them.'

The hall swells with anticipatory pride.

The principal reminds us how important it is that our children 'choose their subjects carefully'. So much hangs on subject choice. Their HSC results. How they will be weighted. Their university prospects. Their futures.

I sigh audibly. On the way here Shannon was fretting in just this way about her subject choice. I had told her, 'It really doesn't matter all that much.' But before I could finish and tell her that the subjects she chooses to study at sixteen will not lock her onto tracks from which she will never be able to escape, that she has the rest of her life to figure out who she wants to be and how she wants to express her talents in the world, she had cut me off. She told me that I don't really know what I am talking about and that 'Things have changed since you were at school'.

I had kept quiet. I have zero credibility and so cannot convince her that it's simply not true that if she takes chemistry instead of drama, she will have 'better prospects', that her life will not implode if she does art instead of maths, that no-one lies on their deathbed and churns over their subject choice in the last year of high school.

I am not attached to what my children decide to do with their lives once they leave home. I have no investment in their being doctors, accountants, entrepreneurs or teachers. As long as it's not illegal or immoral, and gives them sufficient income to pay their debts and enjoy their lives, they can make their living shovelling dirt, packing shelves, delivering goods or writing memos. However, if either of them tells me they want to become a lawyer, I'll try to talk them out of it. Why? Because there is no happiness in law and if there's one thing I do want for my kids, it's for them to be happy. Why doesn't school steer them in that direction?

When Jordan was nine he told me that 'school had crushed his soul'. I watched in quiet despair as he thrashed about in his little public school, unable to accept the rules he perceived as arbitrary, skipping classes he didn't like because 'they just give us the same worksheets over and over', and generally hating every teacher who was 'annoying and stupid'. He never gave me the weekly notes he brought home to get signed for 'unacceptable behaviour'.

I recently asked him why he always used to run out of class in the middle of a lesson.

He thought carefully before answering me. 'Sometimes when there was too much going on – it was noisy or the teacher wasn't controlling the class – I'd feel crowded inside my head. I needed to escape.'

I think now of the countless times he was called 'naughty' for making a dash out the classroom into the playground and sometimes even out the school gates. How many teachers berated him for not behaving. How much punishment he was subjected to in place of understanding. How wrong adults can get things.

School is not for everyone, and yet everyone has to go to school by law. Some kids see right through it. They don't want to be stuck in a system that is designed to produce sameness. For years I wondered whether I should have had the conviction to send him to a Rudolph Steiner school, where they recognise the emotional, physical and spiritual changes in adolescents that make sitting for long hours in class an agony. When I once raised this with Jordan he scowled at me. 'They don't learn to read or write until they're, like, in puberty. That's, like, so … dumb.'

So we've battled it out in 'the system'. The system he hates as he navigates the pettiness of teachers and institutionalised enforcement of uniform rules (black socks only, with a detention for white socks), sponge balls in place of real balls (in case, God forbid, anyone 'gets hurt') and teachers who 'treat the girls differently from the boys' and 'have favourites'. I am all too aware that, for him, school is a kind of torture, one Zed and I believe we have to inflict on him, if only to give him practice accepting things he doesn't like and finds annoying.

Some years after her son, JP, committed suicide, Kate and I were hiking up a mountain. I followed her sure footsteps, listening as she spoke. She told me about a Canadian man she'd met, whose youngest son, at fourteen, after many years of unhappiness at school and moving schools, told his parents that he didn't want to go back to school. The man had a Masters degree, so education was an important value in his family. But his son wanted to go on walkabout. After much deliberation, he and his wife allowed him to leave school, earn money to travel and then take off. The only condition they imposed was that he had to phone home whenever he arrived at his next destination so that his folks could always keep track of him. He travelled all over Canada and the US for years.

Kate turned to me, cheeks flushed and eyes bright with the cold and said, 'I remember so clearly how I felt when he told me the story – and he was also reserved and circumspect; I think all parents are when their children's lives don't pan out quite as the mainstream expects – and I felt WOW: I didn't have the courage to do that. It was the bravery of this family to make a decision that was contrary to society and its expectations. They listened to their child and did right by him. The family allowed their instinct – no, their intuition – to guide them ... I felt sad that I hadn't been able to do the same for my son. I had too many doubts and *what if*s beating at my head. My heart said JP could do anything – even go live in the bush – and my head said, *No, what will become of him?* At least at school he is being socialised and, if not, at least he is being babysat – and he needs to finish his education and then do what he wants. How ridiculous. When a child is so unhappy in the world – and mostly at school – why continue the pain and trauma of it? We continue with it because we are scared that they won't receive an education, won't be socialised, won't be normal, won't be able to get a job and support themselves – when the world is such a big, beautiful place, providing many opportunities and options that don't require formal education. School is there so that we all conform and support the status quo. It's not there to meet the needs of our children. We are scared to listen to our hearts because of where it may lead us … as parents we know when our children are being damaged by the system – but we don't act and we don't trust our intuition because we can't imagine the alternatives.'

Is it ultimately a failure of imagination that blocks our sense of possibility, or lethargy at the thought of having to come up with something new that isn't already packaged for our convenience? Why is it so hard for us to connect with who our children are as individuals so we can work out what they need?

Kate's words make me think of Dr Benjamin Spock, whose book *Baby and Childcare*, first published in 1945, marked a break from the strict routines and discipline advocated by behaviourists who tended to enfeeble parents by labelling them 'ignorant'. The opening lines of his book were simply, 'Trust yourself. You know more than you think you do.'

If Dr Spock had written a book about teenagers, he'd probably have begun with those same sentences.

Self-help guru Dr John Demartini was diagnosed with dyslexia and a speech impediment and told by his first-grade teacher that he'd never read or write, and certainly wouldn't go very far in life. He hated school, and at fourteen dropped out. He lived on the streets, and at seventeen moved to Hawaii to surf. His life changed after he did a yoga course. He is now one of the most successful motivational speakers in the world.

In a later email to me, Kate wrote:

… what has changed [since JP died] is that I no longer care about [my kids'] lives running in a linear fashion – no more expectations. I want their lives to have their own rhythm – there is no urgency to [finish school] with A's and go to university and qualify and get a job – I want gentleness and happiness and no stress – I don't care if the [Maths] teacher is actually one of the mums, and who knows what my daughter is learning, if any [Maths]! If my eighteen-year-old needs another year to three or four or the rest of her life to study further it doesn't make me anxious – like it used to. I was the sort of mum who would get stressed if one of my children missed a day of school or an extramural dance class – there was an urgency – as if somehow they would be doomed to a life of mediocrity and a poor salary – as if they would miss some vital building block and fail because of it!! Now I just don't mind – like I've finally got a beautiful wide perspective, and staying at home for a week while an ear infection heals gently on its own isn't going to define the rest of my six-year-old's life – well, it might but in a positive way – in a way that says to her she's important – not what she does or achieves. But her wellbeing is what I value.

Back in the hall, I put in my earphones to shut out the droning of Shannon's principal and go back to Dan Savage's podcast. As I watch the mute gesticulations of the man in the suit and tie standing in front of us, I remember a post I saw on Facebook a while back: 'About all some parents accomplish is sending their child to Harvard.'

Sometimes, as parents, we get so caught up in the system that we lose sight of what we really want for our kids.

Chapter 27

All That Spiritual Shit

WHILE HARVARD OR Yale might be some parents' dream for their kids, mine is getting Shannon and Jordan to believe in something transcendent. Call it God, divine energy, spirit … I'm not fussy about titles. Some teenagers fall fervently into religion in their early teens – praying every night; conscientiously attending synagogue, mosque or church; refraining from masturbation or any contact with the opposite sex. Some dream of becoming nuns or rabbis. But see, my teenagers don't believe in God. To them, God is for old people. Like me. I guess it's easier to believe in God after you've had babies. You can't expect someone who doesn't understand the divine connection between PMS and a baby to believe. 'Believe' is a word teens use about One Direction. Teenagers tend to reject the irrational and the non-material. They know who Taylor Swift is pashing and that Lindsay Lohan lost a $75,000 fur coat in a club. If you don't read it in a gossip magazine or see it in a YouTube clip, how can you believe it?

When I was a teenager my father embraced an orthodox form of our religion which required he wear a black hat, grow a beard and pray several times a day. As a girl I was excluded from meaningful participation in the exciting holy rituals, forbidden from shaking the rabbi's hand or sitting in the synagogue alongside my father. It was not hard to feel like a huge walking herpes virus. All that was expected of me was to marry a nice Jewish man, have a heap of babies and learn how to make kosher chicken soup.

It wasn't for me (though I did end up marrying a Jewish guy, having babies and I can make a mean chicken soup).

I've fashioned my own concoction of spirituality over the years: a tapestry of Buddhist meditation, yoga and silent, internal conversations some people call praying. I regularly go on meditation retreats to sit in silence and psychically post some lovingkindness and forgive all those I'm silently churning my insides over. Each night, before I turn out my light, I pray for things like the health of my friend Lisa's daughter and for a good man to show up in Danielle's life.

My kids have grown up with Moments of Silence. The Lighting of Candles. Offerings. Gratitude Rituals. Zed and I have also put on a good show of Jewish tradition, to make them comfortable with the holy customs should they ever choose to take our religion seriously. My kids understand that in our family, we 'tithe'. It doesn't matter how much: whatever money comes in, some must go out. That's how we remember we're all connected on this planet and that there are others worse off than us.

As the matriarch of my clan, I have unilaterally inflicted my spiritual idiosyncrasies on my family. When they were little, the kids participated enthusiastically in my New Year's Eve celebrations by writing their wishes on coloured cloth that we turned into prayer flags and strung up on our fire-escape. On the first day of spring, we'd 'wash away our sadness' with an ocean swim. We once even 'hosted' angels in our home for a week, with an altar in our lounge room. Until recently, my kids tolerated all these practices with good humour and a spirit of 'why not?'

But as the teenage years have crept in, their involvement has petered out, along with their awe, and been replaced with cynicism and slight impatience. Until recently, I only had to fight Zed for the lounge-room space where my meditation cushions sit neatly stacked, waiting for the television to be switched off and meditation music to start up. It was a fair fight – one against one. These days my fight is three against one.

My kids now treat me as they might an eccentric aunt – the one who wears frangipanis in her dreadlocks, drinks her coconut water from real coconuts and talks about 'releasing attachment energy during menses'. Now when I suggest a quick meditation or ritual instead of watching *Modern Family*, there's a collective sigh and exasperated huffing.

'Mum, we're just not into all that spiritual shit,' Shannon mumbles.

I try, I really try, not to let it sting. Of course, she doesn't remember her 'welcome to the world' ritual under the tree in our garden when she was a few months old, where my Buddhist teachers passed a saffron thread from hand to hand as a symbol of our connection to each other. Everyone brought her a gift that cost no money, and we murmured blessings and prayers for her life.

She doesn't know how many times I have cast white light over her, or whispered her name in my prayers, or beseeched the universe to take the most extra-special care of her. I think she'd find all that 'kinda creepy' and totally unnecessary anyway because there's no proof that God exists and praying is just, like, 'weird, okay?'

A year ago, Jordan stood in a synagogue, wearing a crisp white shirt and a yarmulke. He read in Hebrew from the ancient scrolls without making a single mistake, despite having a meltdown a week before because there was no way he'd be ready and this bar mitzvah was 'really stressing [him] out'.

'It's such bullshit,' he said.

'What is?'

'This whole "now you are a man" thing. We all know I'm not a man. I'm still a kid.'

Of course he's right, but this was a rite of passage. Rituals are transforming because they mark transition, even unseen, unfelt ones. As we pass through these spiritual gateways, we embrace future projections of who we want to be, even if we spend the rest of our lives playing catch-up.

Now that they're teenagers, I can escape on the occasional weekend to sit for days in noble silence and listen to the sounds of my own breathing. When I explain to my kids that I will be spending the week with a group of people I have never met, that there will be hours of cross-legged, closed-eye sitting, interspersed with very slow walking, no talking, no TV, no internet, no texting, tweeting or even reading, they shudder. 'It sounds worse than jail,' Jordan says.

'You're paying to do this?' Shannon asks incredulously.

'It's very relaxing,' I affirm.

'I just don't get it,' Jordan says.

This is an age-appropriate response. Except that Zed responds in the same way. 'Whatever rocks your boat,' he says, relieved I am not dragging him along with me. How do I explain how much I love to be in the company of strangers, where no-one wants anything from me, and wouldn't even know my name to ask for a tissue? These meditation retreats are as far from the chaos of my daily life as I can get – and they recharge me for my work as a mother.

On my last retreat, my Buddhist teacher taught us about the *bramaviharas*, the noble attributes of all human beings, as defined by the Buddha.

The first is lovingkindness, which is an attitude of gentleness towards all beings. It's unlike our usual take on parental love because it is both impersonal and generous. Sentimentality or manipulative gentleness is not the same as lovingkindness. I can see how this might be a useful tool in my parenting kit.

When lovingkindness meets suffering, it becomes com-passion. It is not compassionate to say to someone who is in pain, 'Just get over it.' The trick is to stay present with someone in their suffering. As a mother, if I can feel compassion for my kids when they're suffering, this can grow into the next attribute of sympathetic joy.

Sympathetic joy arises when we are happy for someone else's happiness, even if it is not what we want for ourselves. It never asks, 'What's in it for me?' When Shannon talks about going to live in Europe as soon as she finishes school, it's this impossible emotion – sympathetic joy – that I need to access, without feel-ing abandoned, unappreciated or bypassed. The only questions I need to ask are: is she following her dreams? Is she living her best life?

Finally, if we get all these right, we can attain a state of equanimity. This is the first prize – to be peaceful in all situations, not only when thing are going well, but also, especially, when things get out of whack.

I mull over these *bramaviharas*, filtering the wise words through the prism of my deepest longings to be the best parent I can be.

I'm grateful for all this spiritual shit. It's helping me hang on through this time and into the unknown future.

I still have fantasies of taking my kids walkabout some-day. Going on meditation retreats together. Taking them to the great spiritual sites of the world. I want to share with them what gives my life most meaning. But here is where my influence ends. Spirituality is a private business, much like a love affair between two people. Love cannot be inflicted or inherited. It must be sought. Faith is a secret pact, a personal commitment. I am not in charge of their spiritual lives. If they have them, that will be their personal doing. I am not an evangelist, nor do I want to exact compliance or participation through force or manipulation.

All I can do is stitch my words into their lives, just keep fixing the world the only way I know how, and hope that witnessing works like a neural pathway: that over time, witnessed enough, a story of faith is planted, fixed into the grooves of the soul-lines that are yet to appear. I can only do my quiet work with them and myself. I can only care about the world. I can't force them to care. But maybe some day, when choices have to be made, the memories of what we made possible here will return as a kind of inner power. A way of reaching for faith. A way of knowing that there is more to life than this body.

Right now, for Jordan, God is in the hoop. I can help keep him focused on getting his ball in there with a swoosh. For Shannon, the Mystery is in the strings of her guitar, and as long as she keeps picking and strumming at them, she's on track. God is where they find their passion, their strength, their joy.

Chapter 28

The Last Holiday

As our family headed off to New Zealand for ten days in a campervan last December, I lurched between cold fear and nauseating sentimentality about what a precious time this was going to be. Who knew how many more family holidays there would be before our kids cast us aside completely? Zed and I are bench players. A social last-resort. The slow premonitory ache of regret at not carpe diem-ing was gnawing at me.

Ten days on top of each other in a space the size of a large bathroom was a risk. In a campervan, you hum a tune while your earphones are in and you've sucked the silence. You turn around and you elbow someone in the back. You can't pass wind without it being a family affair. It's an emotional tinderbox even without the mood swings and testosterone surges. There are also endless chores, including emptying the sewage. Learning this, Jordan informed us, 'I'll just hold it in for ten days.'

We'd been threatening to take the kids camping since they were little. But we couldn't face the endless repeat of 'Are we there yet?' and having to entertain small people on long stretches of road for ten hours at a time. Campsites where kids can wander off into the dark and other people's tents made me anxious. So we kept on putting it off … and off … But we were running out of time. So I finally booked the holiday and informed the kids they were coming with us, fobbing off their 'Do I have to?'s and reassuring them how much fun it was going to be.

But I was nervous. It was going to be ten days without wifi or internet access. Ten Facebook-less days. There didn't seem much in it for them. We got them each a Kindle and loaded them up with books. Given their ages, it didn't seem right that they share a double bunk, so I shared with Shannon, Zed with Jordan.

After twenty-four hours, Jordan was bored, homesick and wanted his friends. 'There's nothing to do,' he noted, time and time again. He sank dejectedly into his iPhone and his eighty basketball podcasts. For two days he refused to help with chores. Between bouts of wanting to throttle him, I remembered being his age and feeling that same longing tinged with embarrassment at being seen hanging out with my parents. As if I had nowhere more exciting to be.

Shannon stayed blissfully in her pyjamas, wrote her novel, played her guitar and sang, while we listened quietly.

A trampoline was a campsite highlight. I managed to convince Jordan to jump with me for a bit while I held on to my waistband, explaining that all the bouncing around was making me wee unexpectedly, which happens at my age.

'TMI,' he gagged, jumping off, bored or disgusted (sometimes I can't tell them apart). These unilateral terminations of interaction come upon you unexpectedly, just when you were thinking, 'Gee, this is going well …'

Watching parents chasing toddlers around swimming pools, Zed sighed. 'They look like toys. Don't you love how big ours are?' I do. But it's a punitive irony that just as we can relax on a family holiday while our kids go off to the communal bathrooms and games room by themselves, they'd rather be somewhere else – anywhere else – but with us.

In public, apparently I talked too loudly so Shannon shushed me because 'people are looking'. I looked around for these people, but no-one was looking.

At a water park near Hamilton, we met Mike, with no front teeth, and his sixteen-year-old daughter Sade, tattooed with her current boyfriend's name on her left breast. She rolled her own cigarettes. I watched from the corner of my eye as Shannon took in the differences between her life and Sade's, and saw how she loved this tough, smoking girl who'd just dropped out of school to become a hairdresser. Mike played Adele's 'Someone Like You' on his battered and graffitied guitar while Shannon sang, above the splashing of the rain on the plastic awning. Sade ran in the rain to the car to get her video camera to film the singing and told us she'd put it up on Facebook. Mike's parting words to Shannon were that she will 'go far with her singing' and Shannon genuinely smiled.

'Let's swim,' I encouraged on a sunny day in the Bay of Islands.

'Nah, I've just washed my hair, Mum,' Shannon said.

'You used to be a gypsy. Doesn't gypsy beat teenager?' I asked.

'Teenager *always* wins over gypsy.'

I swam alone.

I was chuffed when I found the exact goth earring she'd been searching for in a gift shop. Still, she refused to wear my spare hat in the blistering sun. 'It's daggy,' she shuddered. I resisted sermonising about the dangers of melanoma. Teenagers hate a lecture. In this regard they are just like ordinary people. They also believe they're immune to the laws of nature. In this regard they're very much like celebrities, but without the fame.

Ignoring their protests, we dragged our kids to see the thermal geysers, down the Waikato river on a kayak, to Cathedral Cove over 7 kilometres in a sea kayak and across 1700 kilometres of New Zealand's beauty. Over those ten days we made hot chocolate and pancakes, microwave popcorn and Nutella sandwiches amidst endless stops and singing and a game of cards. We let them sip our champagne on New Year's Eve and we spoke philosophy and politics after watching *Thelma and Louise* one night on the tiny DVD player. They spoke to us about school and friends, we made family jokes, we told them stories from our childhoods.

Despite the fighting, whingeing and truly disgusting teenage behaviour at times, I loved every moment of it. Not only because it was very likely our last family holiday, but because for those ten days my kids were mine again. I slept next to my big girl for the first time since she was a toddler. I got to really look at her, without her feeling scrutinised. As much as teenagers would rather die than be noticed, they still crave our attention – as long as it's not critical or judgemental. We got them away from their peers and sank our love into them.

Our role now is to be speed bumps – not roadblocks – on the highway of their adolescence, where everything is done at breakneck speed. We can help slow and calm everything down long enough for them to breathe and think, and maybe even to be mindful. We can remind them that we want to spend time with them, even if the feeling is not reciprocated. We can take them to our 'peaceful' even if it feels like their 'boring'. While they're still halfway in our lives, we can take them to those quieter places, and be there with them. We can show them that *this* (with all its disasters) is what it means to be a family.

When we returned home everyone scuttled into their rooms, shutting the doors. Next year, they will probably choose to be with friends, or to stay home, rather than be with us. It's a special kind of pain, to know when you have crossed a threshold. The 'last one' of anything is so bittersweet.

Some months later I was on a meditation retreat. Zed was running a marathon in the Blue Mountains, Jordan was at a friend's and Shannon was home alone. I felt a moment's grief, thinking how my family was scattered. But no, I reasoned: each of us is doing exactly what we want to do.

Being together is one kind of love. And being gladly apart another.

Chapter 29

No Need to Panic

I LOOKED FORWARD TO the teen years like one might a root canal. The language alone – 'princess bitchface', 'binge-drinking', 'king-hit', 'choking game', 'cyber-bullying' – had me holding my breath and praying for a miracle.

I braced myself for it to get grisly. We all know how rough it can get; let's not be silly about it. And, yes, it's got its tortures.

But what's taken me by surprise is how much I love teenagers. The dissing and contempt aside, I love their willingness to experiment, take risks, push boundaries, constantly update themselves and not take other people's word for it. I have found it exhilarating to meet my kids as young adults, to hear their answers to life's questions even as I've had to adjust in all kinds of ways. It has been chastening to recognise that I am responsible for only a small part of who they are – and that they are making themselves.

My dented self-esteem looks like it's been in a six-ego pile-up. It's not quite a write-off, but I'm going to have to trade it in for a different model.

Of course there are days when the impudence infuriates me, the lack of appreciation for all I do fries my nerves and I churn myself into a froth about the 'dangers that lurk' (aware that my anxiety and worrying jeopardise my kids as much as any threat 'out there'). I am sometimes flabbergasted at the narcissism they so effortlessly exhibit. But then I remember: I was also once as clueless.

I was eighteen when my father's father died. He was a refugee from Lithuania and lived in an old house with stale smells. He came from a world I could not imagine. He'd had a tough life and had written a book about it, but I couldn't have been less interested in knowing about it then. Twenty years later, I picked up my grandfather's book and savoured each word, limp with regret that I'd never taken the time to ask him about his astonishing life when he was alive.

I do not hold this narcissism against myself – for now I see that appreciation is the afterbirth of insight, and insight is the slow accretion of maturity steeped in loss and all its attendant stripping-away.

I've come to think that my need for appreciation from my teenagers is premature. To appreciate something, it must first be noticed. Our kids do not notice what we do because they do not see the world the way we do. They haven't had our experience. Their memories begin way after ours. They're oblivious to how long and hard we may have tried to conceive them. They can't possibly know how we felt during pregnancy, childbirth and the early years of their lives. I recently told Shannon that I remember her lying in my arms and playing with my hair while I breastfed her. That memory is, in the words of my favourite poet Mary Oliver, one of the 'bright hawks of my life'. Shannon looked at me blankly. That intimacy is concealed from her, at least consciously. My view of our relationship is a long shot, dense with eras obscured to her. Hers is a close-up. We don't see each other in the same way. I cannot hold her short-sightedness against her.

Right now, our visions are as disparate as our needs. The best part of being a teenager is getting to explore that window of freedom between childhood and adulthood. While I have to learn to stay with the discomfort of her independence as she pulls away from me, she gets to explore and experiment with who she is, free of the burdens of commitment and adult responsibility. It would be sheer spitefulness to get all huffy about this and stifle the joy from her freedom.

So when a teenager tells us to 'Get a life', they're reminding us to get out of the way, and to let them have space. There comes a time when our attention, like clothes they've outgrown, becomes tight-fitting and uncomfortable. Like salmon swimming upstream, our kids have to battle against the sheer vehemence of our backstories and the current of our love mixed with all our fears for their future, just to make it through. We don't make it easy for them.

Our mistake is in thinking it's all over for us. But there's no need to panic. When they start catching buses, earning money at McDonald's, babysitting other people's kids, going to concerts in packs, buying their own clothes and making out with each other, teenagers cast the illusion that they don't need us anymore. But they do. All that changes is *how* they need us.

We forfeit our position in their lives like someone who leaves a coat on a front-row seat to dash out for a wee, and returns only to find the seat has been occupied. But we mustn't leave. We just need to shift a few rows back. Move from their foreground to their background. Instead of being protagonists in their lives, we become the support cast. Instead of directing them, we guide them. Instead of shouting, we whisper. Instead of standing in front of them, we take our place quietly behind them. Parenting teenagers requires us to become subtle. To take our cues from them.

They need us in more ways than they know.

While they skid through their lives with their moods, rejections, hurts and self-loathing, we are there to squelch the drama out of their histrionic universe, to bring them back. We are their harbour. A safe place of still waters, where overwhelming emotions can be tethered (*you will not die of heartache, even though it feels that way/by next week no-one will remember that humiliating Facebook pic of you that was posted*). Who else will tell them about the stupidity of experimenting with suffocation to enhance orgasm, warn them to stay away from psychopaths and narcissists, sneak goji berries into their morning smoothies, say 'hmmm' a lot and nod sympathetically when they rage about their 'worst day ever'?

In these years we become their mentors, the silent pillars that hold up their world. Of course, they are not to know of this, or even fully register the immensity of our presence. We must do all this by stealth of love, by sleight of conversation.

The teens are a messy time for those going through it and what they need is cleanliness and order. As the adults, we have to do our internal laundry, a proper spring clean to make ourselves a haven for them. This is not entirely a selfless act of parenting.

In doing so, we both learn and teach them how to manage conflict, hang on through the bumpy rides of change, and hold on to a part of themselves immune to the vicissitudes of popularity, peer pressure and heartbreak.

While they are fire, we must be earth.

If we have never asked ourselves the big Why? now is the time. If we haven't had a midlife crisis yet, having teenagers might be just the catalyst we need. We live most of our lives in the literal lane – there is no avoiding the drudge of laundry, lifts, groceries, stubborn stains, bath rings, emptying out the vacuum cleaner and the rubbish. But we can expand our experience by living metaphorically too, by serenading the questions: what am I doing? and why I am I doing this? to help us make meaning or, in the words of the poet Jim Harrison, 'to make music of this puzzle'.

To raise a child is a catalogue of tasks, but it is also something else – it has its poetry. Children are lifted from us, like those temporary tattoos from their paper. They stick to the skin of their own lives and we are left, discarded, just the adhesion they rode in on. The gift they give us is the chance to turn inwards and ask: where do I end and my children begin? They give us a chance to make sense of ourselves unbranded by our role as parents.

I sometimes suspect that the hype and paranoia about the teen years give us an excuse to turn away from self-scrutiny. Our teenagers challenge us in all kinds of ways, but mostly in how deeply we're willing to look at ourselves.

To raise a teenager into adulthood is about making sure we've got there first.

Chapter 30

The Kids Will Be Okay. What about Us?

I AM NOT GOOD with goodbyes. I think I am not alone in this. If I feared the teenage years, I am dreading the empty nest. I cannot imagine that our busy, messy home will at some point have two empty bedrooms, no noise and no bickering over whose turn it is to stack the dishwasher. But what was I expecting? Kids who never want to leave home? That's a mothering fail of epic dimensions.

Just as we left them at day care all those years ago, screaming for us to 'Come back', so they will soon do the leaving. The babies we loved and toddlers we adored have disappeared into the arc of our children's self-acquisition. The ghosts of their many smaller incarnations haunt our hearts. Their leaving brings up a sense of impending loneliness. Who will we be when they leave us?

I am trying hard not to be tragic about this. But, Goddammit, why didn't anyone let me know that this would hurt like hell?

It's easy to develop a disorder of the heart if we have not done the internal housekeeping of the spirit. If only we would read the small print of this existence and accept the terms: shift happens. The suppleness of youth will pucker into the creakiness of old age, our pert good looks will exhale into a countenance of wrinkles, the chores we complain about when we are exhausted with early motherhood will become redundant. This is the good news – nothing lasts forever. We get a time limit on all suffering. It will end. But there is also a time limit on the happinesses that are bundled into those moments. So, we can choose to mourn them, or to be fully in them while they're here. The only way to honour them is with our deepest presence in each moment.

But instead we pretend we can manipulate these terms. We try to disturb the natural order of things by confusing and muddling the issues with our own fears and neuroses. We become grief-struck.

But not my friend Angela, who says, 'There must be something wrong with me. Georgie was ready to leave home at eleven. Frankie says she's never leaving and I feel devastated. There is nothing more inspiring and affirming than watching your child get a life and want one without you. Especially in girl children. They must go. As soon as they can.'

Intellectually, I know that Angela is right. But my heart is trying to rewrite the future.

Angela goes on to say:

Georgie is my home. Everything about her is my haven. She is my history and my present. But she is not my future. She is her future. And I am one of the many villagers in her world. She's my mobile home. When I see her, I am in our home again whether for an hour or a day. And it is utterly safe and delicious … I love watching her influence her world. And I love being part of her broad audience. When she speaks now, I feel less of a mother. I feel like I had my chance. It is over. In a good way. Because when I was her real mother, I celebrated that every day and knew with each year she knew more about who she was and what she wanted. She is the love of my life and always will be.

Another friend, Helen, who has boys in their late teens writes:

I can't wait … already I can feel the endless expanse of time where there is freedom of movement and choice for me as a woman. Finally, at last, I can make choices that do not need to factor in who needs lifting when, is the fridge full and how come at 3 am I have not yet heard the key in the door? I adore my boys and their girlfriends but it's my time now.

The kickback of this deal, of course, is that as our kids gain more freedom, so do we. As they become their own people, and shrug us off, they give us back to ourselves. As they start to grapple with the questions, 'Who am I?' and 'Who do I want to be?' we get to ask these questions all over again, too. But this time with greater freedom because we've had our kids. Our biological clocks are packed away. We don't have to choose between career and family anymore. The guilt of 'not being there for the kids' evaporates. The season of sacrifice is over. With every step forward they take, we retrieve aspects of our shelved identities.

If we get lost, we just need to look to our teens for inspiration. In all they do and are becoming, they remind us to rethink our own values, to keep up, to keep being new. As we learn to let them go, we learn to surrender into a deeper letting go – the letting go of our need to control them (and our future) and the need for guarantees of certain outcomes (there are none) – and to live in faith that what we have birthed, grown and shared with the world will find its place – with or without us.

Getting a life is about holding steady – for them and, by generous serendipity, for ourselves, too. We learn to receive who we are in a new way when our kids are no longer attached to us like leeches.

I've nowhere near mastered this, but I am slowly expanding my horizons and dreaming up the life they keep telling me to get. Who knew of the secret deal between us – that as they grow into themselves, they give me back to myself, while I get to watch from the sidelines as they unfurl into funny, opinionated, interesting people I like?

But hang on, I'm getting ahead of myself.

They haven't left yet. For now, while they're still teenagers, it's a rich environment. My children are enigmas-in-motion. Here I get to watch the breaking and unbreaking of self, the horror of self-consciousness, the fragility of the ego, the gravity of an unknown future bearing down into the stiletto of the present, the quickening of personality threaded with fresh intelligence. And watch is what I must do. Shannon and Jordan are whirling into the shape they will inhabit, and I am air-traffic control, a speck far away, a lighthouse in the dark, willing them to land safely on the airstrip of their invented futures. They are a landscape of human unfolding in which I, too, am invested.

I stand at their closed bedroom doors and know it is an act of cherishing to let their doors be closed. On my side of the door, I feel shut out. On their side, they get to inhabit their own space. I try not to take their need for secrecy personally and to manage my need for intimacy graciously. I am grateful just knowing that they are in their rooms. Safely there. Under my roof. For now.

The clock of our hours with them is ticking and I feel the solvent of time, which erases all things – even us. But I cling to the solvent of humour, the solvent of conversations that corrodes the worst of our moments with them. I look to fill the cracks with the resin of attention – of my genuine fascination with who my teenagers are and what they are becoming. Through all the mistakes they're making, I can be generous with my praise of what they are doing right and tap into my own sense of pleasure in them. I can be kind, honest and present.

My friend Kate's words are wise and comforting:

I am trying not to respond to the 'catastrophes' that get sent to me daily by the children: messages such as 'Phone me now, it's an emergency' or 'Mum, I'm so depressed.' My six-year-old telling me she wants to die, she doesn't want to live (often when she's not getting her own way); the feeling that if I don't dive in and solve it or smother it, somebody else will die. [I am working at reconnecting] to that place well hidden inside of me that is peaceful and calm and can surrender and understands that we can't control the outcome. Now I just want to be calm, and I am learning very, very slowly that I don't have to react, I don't have to solve it or fix it, that I have no control over the outcome, just my response. So I try to be more measured and softer and gentler and slower. I try just to be present to them and the crisis – it's very difficult for me, I either want to shut it out, make it go away or solve it. So (now) I try to sit and listen and respond in a way that they feel heard – and that's all I can do.

Through the grumbling and grunting, the catastrophes and the contempt, I try to remember that I've been given precious time with small people, who are becoming bigger people, whom I am raising to leave me.

It is a strange, sweet, searing sensation – to love this much, and to have to let go so completely.

While I was finishing this final chapter, I found an old diary I took on a Buddhist retreat in my twenties, in which I found this quote: 'Unhappiness arises when we try to change things that are not ready to change or when we try to resist things that are ready to change.'

I am working hard at being happy.

Afterword

S HE NAMES HIM Archie. He has white paws and a white nose and bib. The rest of him is marked in tiger stripes. He has a perfect bullseye shape on his left side.

The first time Shannon holds him, he reaches out his paw to gently touch her cheek. He had her right then. She doesn't even want to look at another one.

The Cat Protection Society had labelled him a cruiser. We explained we needed a calm but confident kitten because Tanaka is a sour old bitch of a cat who hates newcomers.

After two days at home, he has a complete personality change and turns into a dynamo. He takes over the entire apartment with his new-found freedom. After a week he works out how to lift the lid of the bin and there he scavenges for leftovers. Every time I open the fridge, he jumps in. He even tries to jump into the dishwasher and oven.

'This kitten is mad,' I mutter. 'We got him under false pretences.'

He struts about, climbs onto everything that can be stood on, he bats the hanging light switch, shreds the toilet paper and climbs on the table while we're eating. We spray him with water, smack his nose and shout, 'No, Archie!' Archie pretends he cannot hear us. If there's the chance of food anywhere, he'll go for it, even if he knows he's going to get into trouble.

He has the confidence of the clueless and the remorseless optimism of the naive. Time and time again he approaches Tanaka, despite her death stares at him. He jumps on her tail as if it's a toy and inches up to her while she's eating, hoping she might spare him a pellet or two. Each time she hisses at him like some feline Voldemort. She growls an evil, high-pitched snarl and whacks him with a left-right-left-right. She sulks and refuses to come indoors between meals. He preens around like he owns the place. In truth, he does. We are all totally in love with him.

I come back from gym one day to find him in the kitchen, surrounded by broken glass, with a guilty 'I've-really-fucked-up-this-time' look on his face. He's managed to knock over a glass bowl of tuna fish, which was sealed with a Tupperware lid. Amongst the shards of glass he stands on his white paws, picking out the tuna mayonnaise.

I call the vet in a panic. The vet tells me not to panic. That he doesn't need to have X-rays or have his stomach pumped.

'You are driving me crazy!' I shout at Archie while he licks his paws and I clean up the mess.

There are times when his wildness is too much for me. I am middle-aged and I am not up for newborn antics. I am terrified of the day we let him outdoors and the trouble he will find himself in. I am trying not to think about the birds and the rats he will bring inside. Or the busy road that runs outside our apartment.

Shannon calls him a 'dweeb' and posts videos of him doing cute kitten things on Facebook. She adores him.

Jordan, too, until he stops wanting to be held and cuddled.

Then Jordan tells me, 'Archie is an arsehole. He doesn't come when I call him, and he scratched my arm – look at this.' He shows me his wound.

'He'll grow out of it,' I say, hopefully. 'And you can't hate him, he's just a kitten.'

'He doesn't like me. He won't sit on my lap. I hate him.'

'You love him,' I say.

'I don't love him if he doesn't love me.'

'Yeah, you do. You love him no matter what he does. You'll keep hoping he'll come sit with you, and one day when you least expect it, he will. And then all your love will be worth it, just for that moment.'

Jordan huffs. 'We should have got a puppy.'

Love is a funny thing.

We're able to wring it out even in the midst of frustration, despair and antipathy. Once something has claimed our hearts, that's it.

In Lorraine Hansberry's play, *A Raisin in the Sun*, Walter has lost all his family's money and they're about to lose their house. Walter's sister Beneatha screams at their mother: 'Love him? There is nothing left to love!'

And the mother says:

There is always something left to love. And if you ain't learned that, you ain't learned nothing. Have you cried for that boy today? I don't mean for yourself and for the family cause we lost the money. I mean for him: what he been through and what it done to him. Child, when do you think is the time to love somebody the most? When they done good and made things easy for everybody? Well then you ain't through learning – because that ain't the time at all. It's when he's at his lowest and can't believe in hisself cause the world done whipped him so. When you starts measuring somebody, measure him right, child, measure him right. Make sure you done taken into account what hills and valleys he come through before he got to wherever he is.

These are the years when we measure our children. Teenagers stress-test our love. They make our love true.

A week after my conversation with Jordan, I'm walking through the apartment, switching off the lights, and I find him curled up in front of the TV, his long lanky body a gangly sculpture of limbs, his face soft in sleep, his huge feet sticking out from under the zebra-striped TV blanket. I wonder whether I should wake him and send him to bed, but then I notice the white nose and single stretched-out paw peeking out from under the blanket.

I turn and let him be.

You thought the book was over, but it's not quite over yet (a bit like parenting). I wrote an extra chapter and some other useful material just for you, which you can download here: www.joannefedler.com/love-contempt/. Or join my Facebook group, Love in the Time of Contempt, *to connect with other parents, share your wisdom and stories, and get support. Let's keep the conversation going.*

Bibliography

Viktor Frankl, *Man's Search for Meaning*, Pocket Books, Simon and Schuster, 1946, New York.

Jay Griffiths, *Wild: An Elemental Journey*, Penguin, 2006, USA.

Lorraine Hansberry, *A Raisin in the Sun*, Random House, 1959, USA.

Jim Harrison, *Saving Daylight*, Copper Canyon Press, 2006, USA.

Jennifer Michael Hecht, *Stay*, Yale University Press, 2013, New Haven & London.

Peter Mayle, *What's Happening to Me?*, Lyle Stuart Inc., 1975.

Cormac McCarthy, *All the Pretty Horses*, Picador, 1992, New Jersey.

Mary Oliver, *Evidence*, Beacon Press, 2009, Boston.

Jennifer Senior, *All Joy and No Fun: The paradox of modern parenthood*, Virago, 2014, UK/Great Britain.

Kate Shand, *Boy: The story of my teenage son's suicide*, MF Books, 2013, South Africa.

Dr Daniel Siegel, *Brainstorm*, Tarcher Penguin, 2013, New York.

Andrew Solomon, *Far from the Tree*, Scribner, 2012, New York.

Dr Benjamin Spock, *The Common Sense Book of Baby and Childcare*, Duell, Sloan and Pearce, 1946, New York.

Acknowledgements

IN DECEMBER 2012 I received an email from Fran Berry, the publishing director at Hardie Grant, asking me if I'd be interested in writing a book about parenting teenagers. She was 'mulling over a very different sort of parenting book', prompted by my (apparently) 'excellent, wise articles in Fairfax's *Sunday Age* on various aspects of parenting teenagers'.

It had been a long time since anyone had called me 'wise'. And indeed, the first time I had been approached by a publisher. Fran wasn't after another book by a parenting expert, but rather 'dispatches from the trenches' to offer comfort and solidarity to parents, not advice. It all seemed terribly enticing.

This book, then, is entirely Fran's brainchild. Without her scouting eye, and generous championing of this work, *Love in the Time of Contempt* would never have made it into my head, never mind the world.

Before the book, there were the articles. My thanks go to *Sunday Life* editor Danielle Teusch for her continued support of my writing about parenting teenagers over the years.

A book owes its life to the characters who inhabit it – and in this case, there is a massive cast. The words that finally made it onto the page travelled a long path through countless conversations with different parents, professionals and teenagers.

These people generously shared their stories and insights with me: Terri Soller, Angela Tuck, Mimi Nettle, Gary Aaron, Lisa Schroder, Graham Meyerowitz, Suzette Kaulfield, Helen During, Gloria Castrillon, Deb Zerbst, Tracy Segel, Katrina Reisel, Mary Barker, Michelle Favero, Martin Kahn, Scott Whitmont, and Rochelle Bennett. My dear friend Kate Shand and her book *Boy* have deepened my thinking about all I do in the name of parenting. I hope the spirit of her son JP lives on in these pages.

I am thankful to these people for sharing their professional insights with me: Dani Klein, Justin Denes, Belinda Blecher, Dr Michael Carr-Gregg, Karen B. Chan, Mandy Goldstein, and Laurie Matthews from the Caretakers Cottage. Karen B. Chan's wonderful video about safe sex can be found here: http://youtu.be/bgd3m-x46JU.

Thanks to my friend Hadass Segel who fed me interesting links and articles about adolescents during the writing of this book.

I'm grateful to my Facebook community for responding to my posts about what they remembered most about their teenage years: Sharise, Crystal, Kevin, Jackie, Alex, Ingrid, Helen, Stephanie, Lauren-Joy, Warren and Ali.

Thanks to Rose Michael for being such a staunch supporter of this book from the start and for her wonderful insights while she worked on it, as well as the team at Hardie Grant for all their hard work, energy and efforts, especially Meelee Soorkia.

The manuscript found its way into the hands of Nadine Davidoff, who edited it with insight and sensitivity, allowing the text to expand and billow in all the right ways. I am indebted to her for her contribution to the final text.

Just as a child needs parents to love her first, to whisper 'You can do anything' and 'I believe in you', so does a book. Three months before this book even came out, 212 of my Facebook friends offered to become 'early adopters' and help me get this book into the hands of a million stressed-out parents. If this book soars, they will have been its wings. To my co-parent and best friend, Zed – the yang to my yin, the 'no' to my 'yes', the rock to my hard place – I have loved raising our rascals together and look forward to spending more time with you in our empty nest someday.

Finally, to the subject matter of this book, my two teenagers, Jesse and Aidan: being your mother has been a rollicking journey both inwards and outwards, giving me endless opportunities to grow. Just last week, Aidan confessed that being the bad guy in Grand Theft Auto is much more fun and provides a more satisfying gaming experience. As I was about to launch into the usual diatribe about how terrible this is, and what on earth is the world coming to, he said, 'Mum, isn't it better to choose to be a bad guy in a game and a good guy in real life?'

Which highlights a profound truth Jesse penned in my birthday card: 'You have taught me so much already and I think the best of that is that I now sometimes have to teach you.'

Thank you both for helping me become a proper grown-up.

Thanks, too, to my feline companions Tanaka and Archie – especially Archie, who often enhanced the text by walking over my keyboa^%$FhudweualjO9EUR1-(*wq*y#@HOI